DICTIONARY OF BUSINESS

OTHER ECONOMIST BOOKS

The
Economist

Dictionary of
Business

Graham Bannock
Evan Davis
Paul Trott
Mark Uncles

THE ECONOMIST IN ASSOCIATION WITH
PROFILE BOOKS LTD

Published by Profile Books Ltd
58A Hatton Garden, London EC1N 8LX

This edition published by Profile Books
by arrangement with Penguin Books, 2003

The greatest care has been taken in compiling this book.
However, no responsibility can be accepted by the publishers or compilers
for the accuracy of the information presented.

Where opinion is expressed it is that of the author and does not
necessarily coincide with the editorial views of The Economist Newspaper.

Typeset by Rowland Phototypesetting Ltd, Bury St Edmunds
Printed by St Edmundsbury Press, Bury St Edmunds

A CIP catalogue record for this book is available
from the British Library

ISBN 1 86197 178 8

PREFACE

In this completely new *Dictionary of Business*, we have attempted to produce a volume of use both to those pursuing business studies or MBA courses, and also to those in business who need a guide to the increasingly jargon-ridden and academic field that business studies and management has now become.

In this book you will find entries on the main areas of business: economics, finance and accounting; marketing, communications and consumer analysis; business strategy, production and operations management; organisational behaviour, human resource management and industrial relations. You will also find potted guides to a large number of business thinkers, and a selection of terms relevant to the institutions of modern business life. Terms from psychology, sociology, statistics, mathematics, computer science, information systems, operations, research etc have been included where they are commonly used in business. In general, this book is something of a cross between a dictionary, outlining simple definitions, and a brief encyclopaedia, with interesting reflections on key terms. We have attempted to exclude terms of obvious general meaning, such as *public utility* or *table* ('a means of presenting statistical data in the form of columns and rows' according to one of our competitors) unless we have felt we have some particular value to add in our describing it (as we do with *economic growth* and *absenteeism*).

The decision to cover all major areas of business means the coverage of any one area cannot be as thorough as a discipline-specific dictionary, such as those on accounting, banking and finance, business law and taxation, economics, marketing and international business, operations management, organisational behaviour and strategy.

A dictionary of this sort is a wonderfully democratic and egalitarian work: it can be a useful study aid for the most advanced scholar, simply because the brevity of the dictionary form forces the writer and the reader to think about a topic in its essence, stripped of unnecessary detail; in short it sorts the wood from the trees. Yet at the same time, it is a useful aid to those relatively uninitiated in the field of business studies and management, because it is (usually) written in terms that allow any motivated and intelligent lay-person to understand.

The entries vary in length enormously, but we do strive to offer detailed cross-referencing to assist those using the dictionary merely to obtain definitions, as well as those wanting to obtain explanation. There are single and double arrows to indicate two types of cross-referencing:

> ➤ **elasticity** Means 'see elasticity for a fuller account', or for everything you need to know.

> ➤➤ **elasticity** Means 'see also elasticity, for an entry that raises interesting parallel issues'.

The first means you probably need to see this other entry. The second means 'someone interested in this entry, might also be interested in this other one'.

Most terms are defined with an international readership in mind. Therefore the vast majority of entries are applicable to a business audience in any developed modern economy. However, there is a Western bias, and, in particular, institutional entries have an Anglo-American focus. In many instances local examples can be substituted to illustrate equivalent principles (e.g. the principles governing trading on the New York stock exchange are broadly similar to those governing trading on the Paris Bourse).

'He' and 'she' are used randomly. In all instances this should be read as 'he or she'.

Subject areas were broadly divided between us, with Graham Bannock on banking, finance and the City, accounting, company law and the business gurus; Evan Davis on economics and economic policy; Paul Trott on strategy, and operations management; and Mark Uncles on marketing, consumer analysis, organisational behaviour, and human resource management.

The assistance of Alex Allan, Margot Decelis and Panna Kothari is acknowledged with gratitude and thanks. We welcome comments and criticisms from readers, particularly any omissions that you stumble across.

December 2002

A

abbreviated accounts (UK) Under ➤directives of the EU incorporated in UK company law (➤incorporation), small and medium companies are permitted to disclose less information for public inspection than larger firms. The shorter accounts they file are known as 'abbreviated accounts'. Small and medium companies are defined in terms of ➤turnover, ➤assets and employment (small: 50 or fewer employees, and medium: 250 or fewer employees).

ABC classification of entry A system for classifying and prioritizing different items of stock by ranking them in terms of their *value* to the organization. Some items will have a high monetary value so these need to be closely monitored to avoid high levels of inventory. Other items of stock will have a very high value in terms of their usage rate; hence, these are of particular importance to the organization. A common approach is to classify different items of stock by using the two variables individual value multiplied by usage rate. It is generally accepted that a relatively small proportion of the total items of stock will account for a large proportion of its total value. This phenomenon is known as the ➤80 : 20 rule or Pareto principle. ➤Pareto analysis. It is used to classify stock and to allow managers to concentrate their efforts on the more significant items. For example, a firm may use the following system:

(1) Class A items represent those 20 per cent of high-value items, which account for around 80 per cent of the total stock value.

(2) Class B items represent the next 30 per cent of medium-value items, which account for around 10 per cent of the total stock value.

(3) Class C items represent 50 per cent of items stocked, but are low-value items that account for only 10 per cent of the total stock value.

Abilene paradox In management decision-making, the situation where managers drift along with their colleagues with everyone assuming this is the course of action each other wishes to follow. Then, when things go wrong, everyone blames everyone else, because in effect everyone disagreed with the selected course of action but did not want to be seen to object. This reveals that there was only ever the appearance or pretence of agreement.

above-the-line communications The conventional term for marketing communications involving the purchase of media, notably mainstream media advertising on commercial television and radio, and in magazines, newspapers, cinemas and outdoor, e.g. bus shelters, tube stations, etc. In the past, a sharp contrast was drawn with ➤below-the-line communications. With recent changes in the

1

media industry, traditional distinctions have become blurred and the term is less useful. Direct response television, for instance, combines elements of mass-media communication and direct communication between the buyer and seller.

absenteeism The failure of employees to report for work. It is important for management to know why an employee is absent. Sickness, unrelated to work, is only one possible reason. More common, perhaps, is work-related sickness, arising from high levels of employee ➤**stress**. Absenteeism is also a sign of low morale, disillusionment, and a lax view of work. The co-ordinated failure to report for work by many employees is a form of ➤**collective action**, e.g. 'sick-ins'. Various models have been suggested to account for these different forms of absenteeism: (a) the 'medical model' is associated with absence through sickness and stress; (b) the 'withdrawal model' with low morale and job dissatisfaction; (c) the 'deviance model' with a disposition on the part of some individuals to truant; (d) the 'economic model' with attempts to use absenteeism as a bargaining lever, and (e) the 'cultural model' that suggests absence is related to group norms, e.g. the practice within some groups to see 'sickies' as entitlements. These models imply very different management strategies; the medical model argues for stress management programmes, whereas the cultural model calls for a change in employee ➤**attitudes**.

absorption costing ➤management accounting.

accelerated depreciation ➤depreciation.

acceptable quality level (AQL) The level or percentage of defects in a batch which an organization decides is acceptable. The term is associated with quality control systems in production processes. In particular, it concerns the inspection of batches of products after they have been manufactured and deciding whether the goods are acceptable or not. In certain industries, such as aircraft manufacture, several levels of quality assurance are necessary. A criticism of acceptance sampling is that it assumes that some amount of defect is acceptable to the organization. More recent approaches such as ➤**total quality management** argue that organizations should be attempting to eliminate defective items rather than accommodate defects.

acceptance The act of accepting (i.e. agreeing to honour) a ➤**bill of exchange**. By extension, the document itself.

accepting house An institution specializing in accepting or guaranteeing ➤**bills of exchange**. All accepting houses have taken on other functions as the use of bills of exchange has declined, returning to their original, wider, function of merchant banking. ➤**merchant bank**.

account day (UK) The day on which all transactions made during the previous account at the ➤**stock exchange** must be settled (hence ➤**settlement** day). On the ➤**London Stock Exchange**, as in the US and much of Europe, the markets use rolling accounts (➤**settlement**) which are settled after a fixed number of days after the transaction – at present three days, or 'T + 3' (eventually T + 1).

accounting equation, basic ➤balance sheet.

accounting principles Policies used in drawing up the ➤**annual accounts** or other financial statements and covering such matters as the valuation of ➤**assets**, accruals (➤accrual accounting) and the treatment of research and development expenditure. ➤accounting standards; generally accepted accounting principles.

accounting standards Rules to be followed in the preparation of company accounts. The Accounting Standards Board (ASB) sets accounting standards for the UK and issues Financial Reporting Standards (FRS). For the US ➤Financial Accounting Standards Board. The European Commission (➤European Union (EU)) has proposed that all EU-registered companies should adopt ➤international accounting standards which are set by the ➤International Accounting Standards Committee. ➤➤generally accepted accounting principles.

accounts payable Amounts owed to trade creditors and included as current ➤liabilities in the ➤balance sheet.

accounts receivable Invoiced or billed amounts owing to a business which are outstanding from ➤debtors and included under current ➤assets in the ➤balance sheet.

accrual accounting Where expenses have been incurred, or income is due, but not paid or even invoiced at the time accounts are drawn up but are nevertheless included in the accounts. For example, accountancy fees or the cost of electricity consumed in an accounting period can be included in the accounts as liabilities even though these costs have not been paid and invoices have not yet been received.

achievement motivation model ➤attribution theory.

acid ratio The ratio of current ➤assets minus ➤stock to current ➤liabilities. Used as a crude test of ➤solvency. Also referred to as the ➤liquidity ratio or the ➤quick ratio.

A C Nielsen Corporation The world's largest market research company. It is based in the US but operates in over eighty countries. It was founded in 1923 and established a reputation for retail auditing. Retail measurement remains a mainstay of the company, taking the form of continuous tracking of consumer purchases at the point-of-sale through scanning and in-store audits. It also conducts large-scale ➤consumer panel research, mainly through the use of in-home scanners. A C Nielsen undertakes ➤audience measurement in many countries – this enables media managers from television stations and affiliates, commercial radio stations, newspapers and magazines, web sites, etc., to determine the size, demographics and viewing/listening/reading habits of their audiences. ➤audience rating. This information serves as the 'currency' for negotiating advertising placements and rates, in a process that sees competing advertisers bidding for the most attractive audiences. The A C Nielsen Corporation also conducts other forms of market research, including ➤BASES in the new product development area. The two largest direct competitors are both European owned: the ➤Kantar Group which includes Millward Brown and Research International, and ➤Taylor Nelson Sofres. There are many smaller competitors.

ACORN ➤geodemographic segmentation.

acquisition A term used to refer to a firm that has been purchased usually by another firm. This is also referred to as a ➤take-over, especially if there has been resistance to the purchase by the directors and managers of the newly acquired firm. ➤➤hostile take-over.

acquisition accounting ➤consolidated account.

activity-based costing (ABC) ➤Kaplan.

activity sampling A technique in which a large number of on-the-spot observations are made over a period of time of a group of machines or workers. It is used to try to build a picture of what is happening over time, with each observation contributing to this picture. The percentage of observations recorded for a particular activity is a measure of the amount of time over which that activity occurs.

actuary A senior ➤insurance company official, expert in statistics and particularly in those of mortality and loss incidence, responsible for estimating future claims and disbursement requirements and for calculating necessary fund and ➤premium levels. Actuaries may not call themselves such unless they have passed the examinations of the Institute of Actuaries (UK) or the equivalent elsewhere. Actuaries are also employed not only in pensions and insurance institutions but also elsewhere, particularly in the financial services industry.

Adair, John Original, pioneering British thinker on leadership. Adair is training-oriented, perhaps from his personal observation of the value of military training. He believes that leadership can be taught (like ➤Bennis, Warren). Adair's Action Centred Learning model is based on the idea that: (a) leaders have to get the task done but, (b) at the same time ensure cohesion of the working group, and (c) the individual satisfaction of the members of that group. Single actions affect all three of these needs: this is the essential unity of the leadership challenge. Adair is now an independent consultant but has held academic posts at Oxford and Surrey universities. Among his many books are: *Effective Leadership* (1983), *Not Bosses but Leaders* (1988) and *Understanding Motivation* (1990).

addictive consumption A physiological and/or psychological dependence on certain products and services. This is most often associated with products such as cigarettes, alcohol, drugs, betting and gambling. However, consumers have been known to become addicted to almost any type of product. High-levels of addiction are regarded as pathological and often result in maladaptive behaviour, e.g. credit-card fraud, robbery, violent attacks, etc. Clinical treatment and psychological therapies may be required. Most consumption, however, is not addictive, it is merely habitual. ➤buyer behaviour; endogenous preferences.

ad hoc **research** A market research study that is undertaken for a single client and for a specific purpose. Typically, this is a one-shot consumer survey, in contrast to ongoing studies such as sales monitoring, tracking studies and longitudinal studies of consumers (using, for example, ➤consumer panels). These one-shot surveys are a very common form of ➤marketing research.

adoption The decision by a consumer to buy a product, use a service, or take on board an innovation. It is the outcome of a considered decision by the adopter, based on available information, and it implies the product will be bought and used regularly. This differs from low-level trial, which might not result in regular purchase or use. Adoption is of practical significance in understanding the ➤**diffusion of**

innovations and ➤new product development, and underpins the concept of the ➤product life cycle.

ADR ➤American depository receipt.

ad valorem 'By value'. An *ad valorem* tax is a tax (➤taxation) on the price of a good or service. The *ad valorem* principle is used, for example, in import ➤tariffs and ➤value added tax.

adverse selection An undesirable feature of a market in which those who are most likely to participate in a transaction are the least attractive with whom to do business. The bad customers are the ones who self-select themselves into the market. Adverse selection has sometimes been labelled the 'lemon problem'. It is particularly seen as an impediment to the smooth running of insurance markets: the people who have the biggest incentive to insure against a hazard are the ones who are the worst risks. It has also been used to explain large differences between new and secondhand car prices: the people who are selling their cars are disproportionately likely to be the ones who know their car is a 'lemon', with all sorts of nasty problems; buyers thus treat secondhand cars with disproportionate suspicion, making it hard for anyone with a good secondhand car to sell it at a fair price. Adverse selection derives from the fact that there is asymmetry of information between buyers and sellers: the bad risk knows his bad risk; the insurer or the car buyer cannot easily tell a bad risk from a good risk. ⏵⏵moral hazard.

advertising Any paid-for publicity concerning a product, service, or idea. It is a form of external communication, between an organization (the advertiser) and its ➤target audience, using paid-for media (television, radio, magazines, newspapers, web sites, etc.) and employing the services of various agencies, e.g. full-service advertising agencies, creative hot-houses, design agencies, media buying agencies, market research agencies, etc.

There is contention about the main purpose of advertising. Some see it as informative, others as persuasive and manipulative. At a minimum, the purpose of advertising is to publicize a product, service, or idea. This means informing consumers in the target audience that a product (specifically, a ➤brand) is available for purchase and use. For established products, the process is one of reminding consumers that the brand continues to be available and perhaps reinforcing past purchasing habits. For new products, the process is to build awareness and stimulate trial purchase – in combination with other marketing activities that can bring about these outcomes, e.g. in combination with distribution policies. Whether the product continues to be used will depend on in-use experience, although further advertising may help to reassure consumers of the wisdom of their choice (this is an example of post-purchase ➤cognitive dissonance reduction). The ➤ATR + N theory describes this view of advertising.

A very different view of advertising is to see it as persuasive. That is, the job of advertising is to persuade people in the target audience to buy products they would not otherwise buy. This is the popular conception of advertising and also the view held by critics who see advertising as manipulative, e.g. Vance Packard's highly influential attack in *The Hidden Persuaders* (1960) and the more recent bestseller by Naomi Klein, *No Logo* (2000). It is embodied in the ➤AIDA model. In practice, most advertising expenditure is for brands, where the aim is not to get the target audience to buy something it would not otherwise buy, but to have them buy a particular brand. The question is not 'Shall I fly?', but 'Shall I fly with BA or Air France?'

Advertising is sometimes described as 'promotion', although this tends to cover a broader range of communication activities – not only media advertising, but also customer and trade promotions. These are, in fact, quite distinct activities. Promotions are usually designed to boost sales in the short term ('getting the sale today – at a cost'), whereas the goals for advertising are longer term (to inform and remind consumers, reinforce past purchasing habits and steadily nudge sales upwards).

External communication also can be achieved through ➤direct marketing, ➤public relations and the salesforce; however, these are more personal and direct forms of communication. Historically at least, advertising has been associated very closely with mass media advertising (making use of media that have mass audiences, such as television) and therefore very different from personal and direct forms of communication. However, over the past two decades greater use has been made of direct-response advertising (e.g. free-call numbers, e-mail addresses, etc.), often in conjunction with other forms of external communication. This has necessitated a more integrated approach. ➤integrated marketing communication. Many advertising agencies have redefined themselves as broadly based 'communication agencies', recognizing the fact that typically advertisers have a set of communication goals to achieve, for which a mix of communications methods are needed.

advertising clutter The situation where many advertisements, and associated messages, compete for the (limited) attention of consumers in the same medium or place.

advertising cycle ➤media planning.

advertorial An advertisement in the guise of an editorial. Typically, these are found in consumer publications, magazines or newspapers, where the reader is used to seeing editorial material in a particular format that then can be replicated in the advertisement.

Advisory Conciliation and Arbitration Service (ACAS) (UK) A body set up in the UK in 1974 to act as a mediator in industrial disputes and to arbitrate in cases of individual conflict. ➤arbitration; mediation. It set down general guidelines on ➤collective bargaining and ➤negotiation through a variety of codes of practice, as well as becoming engaged in specific cases. In the 1970s this had considerable impact on the thinking of successive British governments, the Trades Union Congress (TUC) and the Confederation of British Industry (CBI). With changes to the industrial landscape, mediation and arbitration services of this type do not carry so much influence and weight today.

affect A person's emotions and feelings about an object of interest, including liking of, and preferences for, the object. Affect is one of the three components of an ➤attitude, and therefore is the focus of much study in management. Brand managers are interested in consumers' likes and dislikes. Some products are designed to arouse people (a gaming machine) or offer pleasure (a bunch of flowers). Service providers want to know how customers evaluate their services – what do customers feel about the behaviour of staff, the ambience, the delivery process, and so forth? Human resource managers want to know an employee's feelings towards her job, her ➤role, her colleagues, her supervisors and subordinates. In sales, the sales person has to gauge the emotional reaction of prospective customers to a presentation or pitch.

Two key elements of affect are 'emotion' and 'mood'. Emotions are strong and intense feelings in response to a specific event, person or incident. It may be an encounter in-store or even a film of an encounter (as in a television commercial). ➤**advertising**. There are accompanying physiological changes, including increased heart rate and perspiration, higher blood sugar levels and changes in eye pupil dilation. There are many different types of emotion and there is no agreement about how to categorize them. Many psychologists identify eight basic emotions: fear, anger, joy, sadness, acceptance, disgust, expectancy and surprise. But others envisage a much longer list of basic emotions coming under the umbrella of three dimensions known as PAD: *p*leasure (e.g. joy, pride, affection, etc.), *a*rousal (e.g. surprise, activation, interest, etc.) and *d*ominance, e.g. anger, fear, guilt, etc. The mix and intensity of emotions will vary over time and across people. Thus, on hearing that your baggage has been lost, you may initially feel intense anger and then become resigned to the fact, whereas another traveller may merely feel a sense of irritation, having had many similar experiences in the past.

Moods, by contrast, are temporary states of mind that are largely independent of specific events, people or incidents. This may be a general positive feeling or a general downbeat feeling. It is evident that emotions and moods will influence a customer's assessment of a ➤**service encounter**, and influence an employee's evaluation of an organization, but they are not easily controlled (or responded to) by management. For practical purposes, management has to concern itself with reasonably common affective responses to standard situations, i.e. feelings and emotions that generally occur. It is too costly and time-consuming to respond to all the ephemeral and idiosyncratic feelings of people. However, general questions can be asked. Do most employees, most of the time, feel positive towards the organization? How do most people feel when their baggage is lost? Can we provide more information to customers so that, in general, they feel less angry when there is a service failure? In attempting to manage affect, there may be an impact on people's behaviour as well as their feelings. Thus, those who feel less angry about a service failure are not only less likely to attribute blame to front-line staff, but also less likely to abuse or assault them. ➤**attribution theory**. This is important in commercial contexts, but perhaps even more so in public service contexts where the person is often a reluctant customer, e.g. at job centres, social welfare offices, tax offices and immigration services.

affinity programme A form of ➤**customer relationship management** programme that is designed to enhance the emotional bond between an individual and a brand. Usually mechanisms are set up to enhance two-way communication in order for the individual to get to know the brand (or organization that stands behind it), and for the organization to learn more about the individual. Examples include telephone helplines, club memberships, newsletters, web site chat groups, etc. These mechanisms enable individuals to identify with certain brands more than others. No direct economic benefit is offered to the individual, in contrast to incentive-based ➤**loyalty programmes**. However, a third party may derive economic benefit, e.g. by using a branded credit card, the graduate may be able to reward her university or the member may be able to reward his favourite charity. In these circumstances, the brand owner is hoping to benefit from some of the emotional bonding that occurs between the individual and the third party.

affirmative action programme Workplace programmes that are designed to advance the interests of particular groups of people with regard to recruitment and selection, employment terms and conditions, and promotion and status. ➤**equal opportunity.**

aftermarket Dealing in ➤securities immediately after a ➤new issue.

agency cost The inefficiencies associated with employing a representative to carry out a task for you, rather than carrying it out yourself. In any situation where people are employed to perform a task, those employees – or ➤agents – may well have their own interests, quite separate from those of the employer (often referred to as the 'principal'). Agency costs refer to the loss of efficiency in the conduct of a task from the fact that agents may let their own interests temper their behaviour. ➤agency theory. For example, a travel agent may sell a more expensive ticket than necessary to obtain a bigger commission. In the modern corporation, company executives are agents of the shareholders, and their stewardship of the firm may be designed to suit their own interests (e.g. prestige and self-aggrandizement) as much as creating shareholder value. Agency costs are ubiquitous in economic relationships, but only prevail where the behaviour of the agent is hard to monitor directly. ➤➤**separation of ownership from control.**

agency theory A theory of principal–agency relationships. Consider the separation of ownership and control in most organizations: a board of directors (the principal) will usually delegate decision-making and implementation to managers (➤agents) who are paid for their services. These managers are likely to have their own goals and objectives that do not directly accord with those of the directors, e.g. for reasons of self-interest a manager may not take enough risks. This is termed 'goal incongruence'. A second problem is 'information asymmetry', i.e. that the principal has less information than the agent about the characteristics of the agent (➤**adverse selection**) and the decisions made by the agent. ➤**moral hazard.**

E J Zajac spelt out these concepts for organizational research ('CEO Selection, Succession, Compensation and Firm Performance: a theoretical integration and empirical analysis', *Strategic Management Journal*, 1990). Agency theory has been used to explore principal-agency relationships in a couple of different ways, either by describing how things are in an organization or by showing how they might be improved. Practical implications follow, e.g. whether to make more of a manager's pay dependent on overall firm performance, how to share risk-taking among directors and managers, and how directors can best monitor the decisions of managers.

Beyond the confines of a single organization, the theory has application in many other contexts where there are principals and agents. For example, in the advertiser–agency relationship, advertisers (principals) will emphasize sales goals and the cost-effectiveness of marketing communications, whereas agencies may be more inclined to think of creative goals and image-enhancing media placement, e.g. attention-getting commercials that will be noticed by peers. There will also be asymmetries with respect to information about consumers, media users, media rates, etc. Retail franchising affords another example, where the interests of franchisors (principals) are known to differ from franchisees (agents) over such issues as the size and exclusivity of trade areas, or spending on co-operative advertising versus outlet-specific advertising. ➤➤**separation of ownership from control.**

agent An intermediary who represents buyers or sellers on a relatively permanent basis, who performs only a few functions, and who handles goods rather than taking title to them, e.g. wholesalers, brokers, travel agents and real-estate agents. A broader definition would also include marketing specialists (e.g. advertising agencies, market research agencies, media buyers, creative 'hot-houses' and call-centres); in these instances, agents do not take title to the goods (the producer's ➤**brand**), but create a good or service of their own. In exchange for services rendered, the agent receives a fixed fee or ➤**commission** or a combination of the two. ➤**Decision-support systems** are available to try to optimize the balance of fees versus commission, so as to give incentives for the agent to work in the best interests of the party being represented. ➤**Agency theory** provides a theoretical understanding of the relationship between agents and buyers and sellers.

agglomeration economies ➤clustering.

AGM ➤annual general meeting.

AIDA model A theory of how some forms of marketing communications work, e.g. ➤advertising. The acronym stands for: *a*wareness–*i*nterest–*d*esire–*a*ction. As a result of being exposed to a print advertisement, for example, a person becomes acutely aware of the ➤**brand**, develops an interest in it, comes to consciously desire it and therefore takes action to buy it. According to this theory, there is a direct and measurable sales response arising from specific marketing communications. This 'strong theory' implies that specific marketing communications can be powerful determinants of a person's ➤**attitudes** and ➤**buyer behaviour**, and therefore these communications can be construed as persuasive and manipulative. AIDA is similar to other ➤**hierarchy-of-effects models**, and contrasts with the ➤➤**ATR + N theory**.

aided recall A line of questioning in ➤**marketing research** where respondents are given prompts and asked if they recall the prompt and what (if anything) they can say about it. Respondents might be asked to recall whether they saw a BT or AT & T television commercial the previous night, with the company name serving as a prompt. This contrasts with ➤**unaided recall**, where respondents are asked to list the commercials they saw the previous night – without there being any prompt.

AIM ➤Alternative Investment Market.

AIOs Three psychographic variables – '*a*ctivities, *i*nterests and *o*pinions' – used by consumer researchers to group individuals in ➤**segmentation** studies.

Aktiengesellschaft (*AG*) (Ger.) Public limited company. ➤incorporation.

allotment letter A letter addressed to a subscriber to an issue of shares informing him of the number of shares that has been allotted, accompanied by a cheque for the balance of subscription monies if the issue has been ➤**oversubscribed** or a request for payment of the amount due as appropriate.

alpha coefficient In finance theory, a statistical measure of the price volatility of a share against the volatility of all shares or selected risk-free assets. It identifies the price fluctuations inherent in the ➤**security** as distinct from those in the market as a whole (➤systematic risk), which are measured by the ➤beta coefficient. These terms are used in ➤portfolio theory and the ➤capital asset pricing model.

alternative investment market (AIM) (UK) A market for small and young companies introduced in 1995 by the ➤London Stock Exchange. The AIM enables companies to raise ➤capital, secure a listing and offer shares for trading, without the full listing requirements required by the main exchange. AIM companies must appoint a nominated adviser or sponsor and a nominated broker; the first of these advises and informs the directors of their responsibilities under AIM rules; the second makes a market in the shares of the firm. ➤market maker. Similar markets have been introduced by other stock exchanges around the world.

AMA ➤American Marketing Association.

American depository receipt (ADR) (US) A certificate registered in the holder's name or as a ➤bearer security giving title to a number of shares in a non-US-based company deposited in a bank outside the US. These certificates are traded on US stock exchanges.

American Marketing Association (AMA) The largest and most comprehensive society for professional marketers in the world. It publishes two of the leading marketing journals – the *Journal of Marketing* and the *Journal of Marketing Research* – as well as professional magazines and specialist books. It also publishes directories, ➤codes of practice and hosts conferences for academics and practitioners in marketing.

American Stock Exchange (AMEX) (US) The smaller of New York's two stock exchanges, listing mainly smaller and younger companies than those listed on the ➤New York Stock Exchange. Also referred to as the Little Board and the Curb Exchange.

AMEX ➤American Stock Exchange.

amortization, amortize To pay off ➤debt over time or to provide for the replacement of an ➤asset by building up a ➤sinking fund. Compare ➤➤depreciation.

anchor store Major retail outlet that serves as a magnet for shoppers. These stores help attract custom to a centre/mall as a whole, in line with the ➤retail gravitation principle. In addition, they are instrumental in directing pedestrian traffic within a centre/mall, e.g. by being placed at the far ends of a central court, anchor stores encourage shoppers to flow between the two, passing all other shops. In the 1930s and 1940s Woolworth's stores anchored many shopping strips. Department stores such as Marks & Spencer took on this role in the second half of the twentieth century. More recently, retail outlets like Toys 'Я' Us and IKEA have had the same role in large out-of-town planned shopping centres/malls.

annual accounts A yearly statement of a company's ➤profit, loss, ➤balance sheet and ➤cash flows. All limited liability companies (➤incorporation) must file accounts or financial statements for public inspection each year. For larger companies, and especially quoted companies which need to distribute accounts to shareholders, the annual accounts (or report and accounts) are elaborate documents including reports of the directors and auditors as well as balance sheets, ➤profit and loss account and ➤sources and uses of funds statements. Smaller companies file

➤**abbreviated accounts.** As comprehensive sources of information, these documents are of potential use for internal communications with employees and external communications with a variety of stakeholders and commentators. ➤**public relations.**

annual general meeting (AGM) A yearly meeting for the shareholders of a public limited company. ➤**incorporation.** All such companies in the UK are required by law to invite all shareholders to a general meeting with directors each year. (US = *annual meeting, annual stockholders' meeting*). Among other things, the meeting elects directors, appoints ➤**auditors** and fixes their remuneration.

annual percentage rate (APR) The true statement of the annual cost of financial charges levied on ➤**consumer credit**, as required by the ➤**Consumer Credit Act 1974** in the UK and the Truth in Lending Act 1969 in the US. The lender's administrative costs, profit margin and interest charges on the loan are normally incorporated in an added charge payable throughout the term of the contract and expressed as a percentage of the value of the transaction. Until legislation was adopted, the percentage was often shown as a rate per month, a figure clearly smaller than the rate per year. The legislation made annual quotation compulsory.

annuity 1. A regular annual payment of money. **2.** A future stream of guaranteed annual income purchased by an immediate lump-sum payment. The lump sum is calculated by ➤**discounted cash flow** and varies according to the ➤**rate of interest**. Some annuities offer protection against the erosion of the real value of income at higher cost, e.g. by a guaranteed increase of 5 per cent or some other percentage each year, or the income may be tied to the profits of a life fund. Annuities may be guaranteed for a certain period even in the event of death, or may be joint annuities on the lives of partners.

Ansoff, Igor Ansoff's *Corporate Strategy: an analytical approach to business policy for growth and expansion* (1987) sets out, it says in the preface, 'a practical method for strategic decision-taking within a business firm'. It distinguishes three classes of decision: (a) strategic (the selection of the product/market mix); (b) administrative (structure), and (c) operating (process). Strategy to meet objectives is developed by adaptive search within the constraints of the business environment and the resources available. ➤**Synergy** is an important component of strategy and is defined as the '2 + 2 = 5 effect to denote the fact that the firm seeks a product–market posture with a combined performance that is greater than the sum of the parts'. Ansoff's analytical tools such as 'competence grids', flow matrices charts and diagrams, are common currency in contemporary management literature and his use of the term ➤**competitive advantage** anticipated Michael ➤**Porter**. Though intricate in its analysis, *Corporate Strategy* is clearly written and based on practical management experience rather than theoretical deduction.

Igor Ansoff was born in Russia, the son of a US diplomat. After a doctorate in mathematics he worked for the Rand Foundation and Lockheed before pursuing an academic career.

Ansoff product/market expansion matrix A conceptual framework for helping managers consider the opportunities for growth that may exist for their business ('Strategies for Diversification', *Harvard Business Review*, 1957). It considers market

11

and product growth opportunities. ➤**Ansoff**, the father of strategic management, developed his simple matrix that has been popularized over the past 30 years in textbooks on the subject of business and marketing strategy. Much of its popularity was due to its relative simplicity. According to Ansoff, firms should focus their strategic thinking on three fundamental issues:

(1) Definition of the firm's core objectives.

(2) Whether the firm should ➤**diversify** and, if so, into what areas.

(3) How the business should exploit and develop its current product–market position.

However, like all frameworks and models it has its limitations, most notably that the framework assumes that opportunities for growth exist in the market; this may, of course, not be the case.

anti-trust legislation ➤competition policy.

applied research A particular activity within a ➤**research and development** department that focuses on the use of existing scientific principles for the solution of a particular problem. It is sometimes referred to as the 'application of science'. It may lead to new technologies and include the development of patents. It is from this activity that many new products emerge. ➤**new product development**. This form of research is typically conducted by large companies and university departments. For example, the development of the Dyson vacuum cleaner involved applying the science of centrifugal forces first explained by Newton. Centrifugal forces spin dirt out of the airstream in two stages (or cyclones), with airspeeds of up to 924 miles an hour. This technology led to the development of several patents.

appreciate To rise in value, as of a ➤**security** on the stock exchange or a currency against other currencies in the ➤**foreign exchange market**.

appropriations ➤below the line.

APR ➤annual percentage rate.

AQL ➤acceptable quality level.

arbitrage The exploitation of differences between the prices of financial assets, currencies or commodities within or between markets by buying where prices are low and selling where they are higher. If wheat is cheaper in Chicago than in London, after allowing for transport and dealing costs, it will pay to buy in Chicago for sale in London. Unlike speculation, arbitrage does not normally involve significant risks because the transactions take place almost simultaneously. Arbitrageurs, sometimes termed 'arbs', perform a useful economic function because they help to eliminate price differences between markets.

arbitration The process of resolving conflicts where a third party ('the arbitrator') has authority to dictate agreement. The parties may come to arbitration voluntarily or through compulsion. Within an organization, arbitration will tend to occur at the cross-over point immediately above the conflicting parties. For instance, in a dispute between two salespersons, the most likely and immediate point of arbitration would be the sales manager. Ideally, resolution should occur at this point; however, arbitration often moves up the hierarchy as intermediate managers pass on the problem to senior managers. Where conflict extends beyond the organization – as in an industrial dispute between representatives of employees and management – it may be necessary to seek independent arbitration and prior agreement that both parties will be bound by the final judgement. ≫collective action; conflict; negotiation; trade union.

architecture The network of relationships, alliances and contracts both within and around an organization. The concept was popularized by John ➤Kay in his book *Foundations of Corporate Success* (1993). He argued that a firm is defined by the contracts and relationships that it is able to develop with customers, suppliers, competitors and potential competitors. These relationships are designed to secure outcomes in which all parties gain. Architecture is more than ➤organizational structure as it concerns the relationships developed over time. It is a combination of structure, culture and heritage of the organization. He cited a number of firms that have achieved ➤competitive advantage based upon the unique architecture that they had developed over time. Benetton, Kay argued, had developed an effective subcontracting and franchise arrangement using its ➤brand. Marks & Spencer had developed a competitive advantage through developing an architecture based on efficient supplier relationships and excellent customer relations. These firms were able to establish effective information exchanges throughout their operations and to create ➤organizational knowledge. For Kay, successful strategy is about doing things well that other firms are unable to do or cannot do readily. ≫resource-based theories of strategy.

articles of association (UK) The internal regulations on the running of a company. They are registered when the company is formed. The articles are subject to the ➤memorandum of association (US = *articles of incorporation*) and must not contain anything illegal or *ultra vires*. They can be altered by the company by special resolution at an ➤annual general meeting.

articles of incorporation (US) ➤articles of association.

artificial intelligence (AI) Computer software that accesses a large knowledge base of facts and rules, usually in the form of a database. The purpose of such systems is to make available to average practitioners or generalists the skills and know-how of experts in certain fields. ➤Expert systems and the entire field of artificial intelligence are rapidly being developed particularly in engineering and science.

'A' shares A class of shares that carries different rights from ordinary shares, e.g. they are usually non-voting shares.

assembly line A group of activities linked together often in a line to assemble a product. The assembly line is associated closely with the concept of the ➤division of labour, where the complete assembly operation is divided into a series of simpler tasks. The use of the assembly line approach to production was developed and popularized by Henry Ford in the 1920s. It was the use of the assembly line principle that enabled him to produce large volumes of vehicles at relatively low cost. The large volume automobile manufacturers continue to use assembly lines to produce their vehicles today. These assembly lines are extremely complex operations with the line operating continuously for days and even months.

assessment The evaluation of a person as part of a process of job selection or staff appraisal. Assessment may be based on specific criteria, 'criteria-referenced'

13

(how does a person compare against pre-defined factors?) or on certain norms, 'norm-referenced' (how does a person compare with others?). Evaluation can be based on written evidence (such as the person's c.v. and performance reviews, or the reports of referees, subordinates and superiors), ➤psychological testing and exercises (possibly through an assessment centre), and interviews (involving meetings with the person being assessed, but also with those who know or work with the person). It is usually assumed that fairness and equity underlie the assessment process, leading to merit-based outcomes. However, other factors often intervene, including: (a) the influence of stereotyping and various forms of bias (gender bias, racial bias, etc.); (b) using norm-referencing when criterion-referencing is appropriate (and vice versa); (c) selectively reading the evidence, and (d) being inconsistent when making assessments (by giving different weights to the criteria when assessing different people). In making assessments there is a tendency to give too much weight to internal factors (such as personality), and too little weight to the external context in which a person's behaviour is enacted. For example, the 'super-salesperson' may simply have the easiest territory in which to work, rather than be exceptionally good at her job. This is a form of attribution error. ➤attribution theory. Also, while assessment can draw on lots of information about a person, many assessments are based on very limited information and considered in haste. ➤➤personality trait; role.

asset Something that has value or earning power. On the ➤balance sheet of a company the following categories of assets are distinguished: (a) current assets (cash, bank deposits and bills receivable); ➤trade investments; (b) fixed assets (land, buildings, plant and machinery, vehicles and furniture); (c) intangible assets (➤goodwill, patents, etc.). Financial assets are titles to cash such as, for example, a bank deposit or ➤securities such as ➤ordinary shares.

asset-backed security An ➤issue in which ➤security or ➤collateral is the return on a financial ➤instrument, e.g. a ➤mortgage, ➤credit card receivables or a currency ➤hedge. The process of turning loans into securities is termed ➤securitization.

asset stripping A term for describing the process whereby a firm with hidden value is purchased and the hidden assets revalued and sold, thereby creating substantial cash for the owner. In essence, the firm is acquired at a price less than its ➤break-up value. This practice is particularly common with firms with substantial physical assets such as property. An under-performing company with a large property portfolio may have a low market value yet have substantial assets.

asset value The value of the ➤assets of a company, sometimes termed ➤break-up value. When calculated from the ➤balance sheet, asset value is defined as ➤net assets.

assignment The transfer of rights and obligations in property to a third party, as in the assignment of a lease or an insurance policy.

associate company (UK) A company over which another company has some influence, normally through a minority shareholding of less than 50 per cent but more than 20 per cent. ➤➤consolidated account.

ASX All Ordinaries Index An index designed to reflect share price movements in approximately 500 companies traded on the Australian Stock Exchange. It was given a base value of 500 in January 1980.

atmospherics The management of space and ambience in the design of service outlets to create more positive feelings in consumers towards the service itself, or service staff, or the organization. ➤**servicescape**. This is largely achieved by influencing people's emotions through the ➤**affect** component of consumer ➤**attitude**. For example, by dimming the lights in a restaurant, customers feel a sense of intimacy which may be pleasurable or arousing. However, atmospherics may also encourage customers to think about the service, staff or the organization in more positive ways – thereby influencing the cognitive component of attitude. Grocery retailers who arrange merchandise with customers' shopping lists in mind will help customers think through the process of shopping and this might result in greater liking for the store or even increased patronage.

ATR + N theory A theory of how some forms of marketing communications work, e.g. ➤**advertising**. The acronym stands for: '*a*wareness–*t*rial–*r*einforcement + *n*udging'. As a result of being exposed to a print advertisement, for example, a person becomes vaguely aware of the ➤**brand**; this may give rise to a tentative trial purchase of a new brand or reinforce purchase of an existing brand. If the brand is satisfactory, sales might nudge forward a little. According to this theory it should be possible to measure an individual's response to marketing communications, but the sales impact may be hard to discern. This 'weak theory' implies specific forms of marketing communication are not strong determinants of a person's ➤**attitudes** and ➤**buyer behaviour** – other factors are at work (notably in-use experience with the brand; also, the accessibility and availability of the brand, ➤**brand salience**, and the impact of ➤**integrated marketing communications** as a whole). It also means these communications should not be construed as highly persuasive and manipulative, which contrasts with the ➤**AIDA model** and ➤**hierarchy-of-effects model**. The main advocate of the ATR + N model has been A S C Ehrenberg, initially in 'Repetitive Advertising and the Consumer', *Journal of Advertising Research*, 1974, and then refined in subsequent papers.

attack strategy A range of aggressive approaches to competing with rivals. As with much of the strategy literature, the roots of attack strategy can be traced to military origins. In any analysis of competitors, it is important to recognize approaches they may use against each other or against a ➤**new entrant**. Such an approach usually involves one of the following strategies:
(1) Head-on attack against the market leader.
(2) Flanking or targeting a particular market segment.
(3) Occupying a new territory through ➤**innovation** or by finding a new market niche.
(4) Grasping a short-term opportunity.

attitude A lasting general evaluation of an object of interest. Individuals are viewed as having attitudes to many different objects ('attitude objects'): ➤**brands**, products, services, organizations, advertisements, issues, ideas, activities, conditions and individuals. For instance, in marketing, the objects might be brands, but also particular ➤**advertising** stimuli during an exposure occasion ('attitude towards the advertisement') or even the buying process ('attitude towards the act of buying'). ➤➤**brand communication effects**.

These lasting general evaluations are perceptual, knowledge-based, learned, evaluative, predispositional and action-oriented. This is formally expressed in the standard three-component model of attitude (the tri-component attitude model):

(1) Cognitive component. This component is concerned with a person's beliefs about an object of interest. In a branding context, is a person aware of the brand and what knowledge does the person have of the brand and its attributes? A number of beliefs may be held about the object. A brand of jeans may be seen as hard-wearing, of good quality and low price. These beliefs are based on perceptions. The jeans are perceived to be of low price, whether or not they really are low in price.

(2) Affective component. This is concerned with a person's emotions and feelings about the object of interest. This includes a person's liking of, and preferences for, the object of interest. Does a person like and feel positive towards the brand of jeans?

(3) Behavioural component (also called the 'conative component'). This is concerned with a person's predisposition and preparedness to take action. A typical measure would be a person's intention-to-buy – does the person intend to buy the brand of jeans? The behavioural component is only a preparedness to take action, and should not be confused with the actual taking of action. ➤buyer behaviour.

Attitude theory holds that these three components should be consistent, adding up to a general evaluation. A key issue in attitude research is measurement. Attitudes are not directly observable, therefore they have to be measured indirectly using ➤attitude scales. The simplest and most commonly used scale in business is nominal, where attitudes are classified into two or more categories ('yes', 'no', 'don't know'). Nominal scales are easily employed to study any component of attitude, e.g. 'Are you aware of a brand – yes or no?', 'Do you like the brand – yes or no?', 'Do you intend to buy it – yes or no?' In more formal research a variety of ➤rating scales are used, particularly in the context of studying the cognitive and affective components of attitude, e.g. 'The brand's design is eye-catching – strongly agree, agree, neither agree nor disagree, disagree, strongly disagree?'. The prompts can be graphic (e.g. a smiling face to indicate strong agreement) or verbal (e.g. the words 'strongly agree'), and numbers can be assigned to these ordered categories for purposes of data analysis. Although very commonly used, there are problems associated with these scales, e.g. responses can be influenced by the number of points on a scale (1–5, 1–7 or 1–9), whether there is a midpoint or not (7-point scale versus a 6-point scale), and the choice of prompt (graphic images or words). ➤Likert scale; semantic differential scale.

To obtain a measure of attitude – a general evaluation – the results from individual rating scales must be combined. For this purpose use is made of a 'multi-attribute attitude model'. In its simplest form this is the sum of a person's beliefs about all attributes of an object of interest, the sum, for example, of beliefs about a brand of jeans being hard-wearing, of good quality and low price. An extension of the model is to weight each attribute by its importance to the person – low price may be twice as important as the other attributes, and therefore the rating on this attribute is given twice as much weight in the summation. In multi-attribute attitude models weights are usually based on 100-point constant-sum scales, e.g. low price may be given a weight of 50, and hard-wearing and good quality are each given weights of

25, adding to 100 in total. A further extension is to relate the rating to an 'ideal' – in general, a person may rate low-price jeans as better than high-price ones, but too low a price may signal very poor quality, therefore the assessment is best made by reference to the ideal level of low price. The seminal work on attitudes and attitude measurement was published by Martin Fishbein and Icek Ajzen (*Belief, Attitude, Intention and Behavior: an introduction to theory and research*, 1975).

Attitudes are very widely studied in management because they are seen as predictors of behaviour and/or explanations of behaviour. ➤➤**buyer behaviour**. Hence, their investigation in everything from surveys of people's attitudes to brands, through to surveys of employees' attitudes to their jobs. There is also considerable interest in attitude formation and attitude change, normally as an indirect route to influencing behaviour. Thus, the aim of many ➤**advertising**, ➤**promotions** and ➤**sales** programmes is to try to influence attitude formation or change attitudes, which – if successful – will have an impact on behaviour and the 'bottom line'. Attempts can be made to influence each of the three components. Cognition can be influenced by trying to change beliefs (getting people to see Levi's jeans as harder-wearing than competing offerings), changing the importance of a belief (increasing the importance of the hard-wearing attribute), changing the ideal (making it easier for Levi's to be seen as hard-wearing), and/or introducing new beliefs (by emphasizing the rugged look of jeans this raises the overall evaluation of Levi's). With affect, the goal is to increase liking. This can be achieved through classical conditioning (e.g. by continually linking Levi's with something people like, such as a popular band, so that some of the liking for the popular band transfers to Levi's), affect towards the advertisement (whereby liking for an advertisement carries over to liking for the brand), and mere exposure, i.e. simply by presenting Levi's to people many times through advertisements, publicity, wide distribution, etc., they come to like it. In these instances it is not necessary for beliefs to change or for people to be persuaded by factual information. ➤➤**learning**. Intentions are increased directly through product trials and promotions; these strongly suggest to consumers that they should buy the brand, even though they may not have any clear beliefs or emotions about it.

In 1980, Icek Ajzen and Martin Fishbein wrote another influential book (*Understanding Attitudes and Predicting Social Behavior*). In this they integrated all the components of attitude, and the associated measures, to derive a model that would offer better explanation and better predictions of consumer behaviour, recognizing the uses to which attitude theory was being put. This resulted in the 'theory of reasoned action'. This theory states that the best predictor of behaviour is purchase intention. This, in turn, depends on the consumer's 'attitude towards the behaviour' (i.e. overall, how favourable is the person to the purchase?) and the 'subjective norm', i.e. overall, how would others view this purchase? For example, a child might believe a Häagen-Dazs variant of ice-cream is low in fat and evaluate it as tasting nice, which together encourages the child to look favourably on purchasing the brand (attitude towards the behaviour). The child might also seek to gain the approval of peers, so he will try to gauge whether his peers approve of the brand or not (social norm). A positive assessment overall will lead to the intention to buy, and therefore actual behaviour (purchase).

However, people do not necessarily act on their attitudes – nor even their behavioural intentions. There are good reasons for this: (a) respondents may be unable to act on their intentions, e.g. their funds are insufficient to make the purchase; (b) situational factors may intervene, e.g. price promotions at the point of sale may encourage consumers to buy a brand other than their intended purchase; and (c) behavioural action may depend on others, e.g. the purchase is made jointly by a couple. Also, the attitude–behaviour link may be weak because of the problematic nature of attitudes themselves. The assumption that the three components of attitude are consistent may be invalid – a person can feel positive towards a brand without intending to buy it. Moreover, attitudes may not be well formulated, e.g. prior to purchasing and consuming a brand, knowledge of the brand and feelings towards it may be ill-defined, and intentions only weakly formed so that these weak attitudes may explain and predict little. Nor may attitudes be as general and enduring as the theory implies; situation dependence often comes into play – an intention to buy a particular brand of jeans could differ depending on whether they were for smart-casual use or very casual use. In fact, much communication and distribution activity is designed to make attitudes *less* attitude-like; the aim is to selectively *change* beliefs, emotions and intentions. Added to which are the problems of measurement, notably the problem of deciding which attributes to measure and how to weight them.

attitude scale ➤attitude; ➤➤Likert scale; rating scale; semantic differential scale.

attitude survey The administration of questionnaires to people to find out their overall evaluation of, or ➤attitudes to, something. In organizations, questionnaire-based surveys are used to find out the attitudes, thoughts and beliefs of employees to their work, jobs, ➤work groups, subordinates, supervisors, and the organization for which they work. ➤employee attitude survey. In service situations, questionnaires are used to gauge levels of customer satisfaction with staff, facilities and operations. Market research organizations administer surveys to see how ➤target audience individuals evaluate existing products and services, and how they might evaluate new products and innovations. Attitude surveys have traditionally been *ad hoc*, i.e. one-off special-purpose surveys; however, there is a trend to more continuous monitoring of employee and customer evaluations. There is also more interest in the temporal pattern of attitudes among target audience individuals. ➤audience measurement. This provides reference points and benchmarks ('are evaluations improving or declining?') which in most cases prove to be of greater use to management than having isolated evaluations.

attribution theory A theory of how people ascribe behaviour to internal or external causes. For example, is the success of a particular salesperson because of his own personal characteristics (drive, ambition, skill, etc.) or because he has been given easier territories in which to work (reflecting external salesforce management decisions)? The question can be looked at either from the viewpoint of the salesperson himself (why have I succeeded?), from that of an independent observer (why has he succeeded?), or from that of an interested observer (why has he succeeded and I have not?). A further aspect is whether the cause of behaviour has remained stable or not – if the salesperson attributes his success to ability, is this something fairly stable or is it strengthening?

Depending upon the way attribution unfolds, it may lead to quite different outcomes – a person who attributes success to his own ability (even if this is not the real reason for his success) may be motivated to achieve more (the ➤**achievement motivation model**), whereas someone who ascribes failure to himself (even if this is in error) may become very passive (the ➤**learned helplessness model**). However, there is a general tendency to take credit for successes (a self-enhancing bias), and deny responsibility for failure (a self-protecting bias). Failure, then, is blamed on external causes.

Attribution theory was developed in social psychology, but has been widely applied in management. In ➤**organizational behaviour**, it has been used in studies of ➤**assessment**, ➤**leadership**, ➤**performance evaluation**, and ➤**impression management**. There are also applications in areas such as ➤**services marketing**. For example, if baggage fails to arrive off the conveyor at the airport, does the flier ascribe blame to a specific person (the baggage handler), the system (logistics at the airport), a situation (bad weather has caused disruption), or himself (because he failed to pack his baggage properly)?

According to F Heider (*The Psychology of Interpersonal Relations*, 1958) people faced with these kinds of situations are trying to find underlying causal mechanisms in order to control their environment. It is argued that behaviour, such as whether to complain or not, will be governed by the attribution that an individual makes. If blame lies with a baggage handler, a complaint can be made to him or his supervisor. If it was not known who to blame, the appropriate course of action would be unclear. However, the problem is more complex than this because the employee may not accept blame and instead point the finger at the system (or even to some failing on the part of fliers). Because of these biases, employees and customers may have quite different assessments of service levels, service quality, and satisfaction/dissatisfaction. ➤**customer satisfaction/dissatisfaction; perceived service quality**.

audience measurement The process of surveying people's media habits (viewing, reading, listening, and usage). Usually this is undertaken continuously over time or at set intervals, so that trends and patterns can be discerned. One method is to employ a ➤**consumer panel**. In the past, respondents on a consumer panel had to complete diary sheets, e.g. in television monitoring, respondents would indicate whether, and what, they were watching in each 15-minute period. The process is now automated using monitors attached to television sets. Aggregated data are used to calculate ➤**audience ratings** for each station, programme and time slot, and it is on the basis of these figures that media rates are set. Similar procedures are used to gather information about people's readership of newspapers and magazines, their radio-listening habits, and their use of the internet. In the latter case, automation has been relatively simple because the medium is digital and permits routine collection of hits, page views, visits and unique visitors. Global leaders in the area of audience measurement are ➤**A C Nielsen Corporation** and ➤**Taylor Nelson Sofres**.

While the emphasis of audience measurement is on behaviour, systems are in place to monitor people's liking of what they view, read, hear, etc. In general, there is a strong correlation between the number of viewers and liking, although other factors come into play, e.g. more people are able to view prime-time television, regardless of programme quality. For advertisers, the question is not so much whether people like the programmes and editorial material, but what ➤**attitudes** people have to the advertisements and advertised brands. For this reason, audience measurement has been extended to include continuous tracking studies. Over time, a succession of respondents is interviewed to assess how many are aware of the advertised brand, how many are aware of the advertising, and how many are aware of the specific messages being conveyed by the advertising. If an advertiser such as Orange spends heavily on television commercials it would hope to see a rise in awareness of the Orange brand, an awareness of the commercials, and that people are able to play-back key messages from the advertising ('Orange leads the way in new technology'). The dominant force in tracking research is Millward Brown, a subsidiary of the ➤Kantar Group.

audience rating A measure of the proportion of people tuned-in to a specific channel/station at a particular time. The denominator is the percentage of households in a market that have at least one television/radio switched on at a particular time, i.e. 'households using television' (HUTs). The numerator is the percentage of households in the market who are tuned-in to the specific channel/station at the particular time (during which an advertisement might be broadcast). Ratings are an important 'currency' in setting media rates. Broadly, the greater the proportion of households that are tuned-in to the specific channel/station, the higher the rate that can be charged to advertisers. This needs to be qualified somewhat because advertisers are primarily interested in specific ➤target audiences, not simply the overall proportion of households tuned-in. Therefore, it is more appropriate to measure 'target audience rating points' (TARPs), where a 'rating point' is the percentage of the target audience that is tuned-in to a particular television/radio station at a particular time. ➤➤advertising.

audit The verification of accounts by an external qualified accountant or auditor. Larger limited companies (➤incorporation) are required under the Companies Acts (UK) to have their accounts audited by a member of a recognized accountancy body. In the US, those registered with the ➤Securities and Exchange Commission must be audited. The auditor's report is intended to give an opinion on whether or not the accounts give a 'true and fair view' of the affairs of the business and also that the accounts comply with the requirements of the Companies Acts.

An accountant or firm of accountants is appointed by the directors on behalf of the shareholders of a company, and this is approved at an ➤annual general meeting. Smaller companies and individuals also may use auditors to help them in the preparation of tax returns.

auditor ➤audit.

audit trail An investigation of a sequence of related transactions, to establish the propriety of all those involved in them. An important advantage of the ➤market maker or ➤quote driven system of ➤securities dealing is that computer files can be maintained of price quotations and transactions so that irregularities may be investigated along the audit trail. Checks may be made, e.g. to ensure that when dealers buy or sell from their own account from or to a client they have done so at a price that is fair in relation to the prices being made by other market makers at the time.

authorized capital (UK) The amount of share ➤capital fixed in the ➤memorandum of association and the ➤articles of association of a company as required by the Companies Acts (UK). ➤incorporation. US = *authorized capital stock*.

automated stock ordering system A system for re-ordering stock to help avoid stock-outs occurring. In manufacturing plants, some firms may use a safety stock to help avoid the production having to be halted. The introduction of ➤just-in-time systems has placed greater emphasis on automated ordering systems. Retail stores rely on effective automated stock ordering systems to ensure they do not continually run out of lines of stock. Such systems are linked to the tills in the shops through the ➤electronic point-of-sale system and automatically generate an order to replenish that item. The system is also able to anticipate orders for each item based on the previous week's sales and is able to send orders to suppliers. The current day's sales are continually reviewed and any additional items required are ordered.

autonomy The degree to which an employee has freedom and discretion in planning his work and in determining the procedures used to carry it out. Autonomy is a factor in the investigation of employee ➤stress. In general, it is argued that greater autonomy helps employees cope with stress (because they will have some discretion over how to manage the sources of stress). Also, it is known that some employees value autonomy, e.g. research scientists. However, others might find it unsettling not to have clearly defined plans and procedures, giving rise to anxiety about what is expected and who is accountable for outcomes. ➤➤role.

average A single number calculated to summarize a group of numbers. An *arithmetic mean* is the sum of the values of the items in the group divided by the number of items. The *median* is the middle value in a group of items ranged in order of size. The *mode* is the most frequently occurring value in such a group. A *geometric mean* is the root of the *n*th product of a series of numbers multiplied together, where *n* is the number of values in the series.

average cost The average cost that a company incurs to produce each unit of output. It is sometimes referred to as unit cost. ➤➤cost.

average purchase frequency ➤buyer behaviour.

Averch–Johnson effect The tendency for a company whose ➤rate of return is capped by ➤regulation, to engage in excessive accumulation of capital in order to expand the volume of allowed profit. If a firm is told it can earn a maximum 10 per cent return on capital, the more capital employed, the bigger the absolute volume of profit a 10 per cent return implies. Such a firm may choose to 'gold-plate' its offices if it can get away with it, knowing that it will earn 10 per cent on the gold employed.

B

back-to-back loan Borrowings in one ➤**currency** that are matched by borrowings in another currency to overcome ➤**exchange control** in aid of investment.

backwardation (UK) **1.** On the stock exchange a sum of money paid by a ➤**bear** to a ➤**bull** for the right to delay delivery of ➤**securities** sold forward at a fixed price. **2.** The situation in a ➤**commodity** market where ➤**spot prices** are higher than prices quoted for future delivery. **3.** ➤**crossed**.

BACS ➤clearing house.

balance In financial accounting, the balance is the amount required to be inserted in one of two columns of ➤**debits** and ➤**credits** to make the totals equal. ➤**double-entry bookkeeping**. A bank balance is the amount standing to the credit or debit (➤**overdraft**) of a customer.

balanced scorecard A form of accounting that not only considers financial data and ratios, but also focuses on the market/customer perspective (e.g. market shares), internal processes (e.g. percentage of sales from new products) and organizational learning and growth, e.g. employee turnover and percentage of customer-facing employees with on-line access to customer information. In many respects, this merely represents the discovery by accountants (notably ➤**Kaplan**) of what marketers and human resource managers have known for decades, although they have all expressed their ideas in somewhat different ways. In bringing these disciplines together there is increasing attention on measuring, and accounting for, non-financial factors in management. Signs of this are to be seen in the focus on ➤**key performance measures**, ➤**marketing metrics** and ➤**marketing performance measures**.

balance of payments A measure of the income of a nation, with respect to its transactions, with other nations. The balance of payments consists of credits and debits: there are three main credit items: (a) the income derived from sales of goods and services abroad (exports); (b) investment income earned abroad, and (c) any gifts or transfers made to the nation. The debits consist of purchases of goods and services from abroad (imports), investment income made at home, but despatched to foreigners, and transfers abroad (like overseas aid, or duties payable to the European Union, for example). The balance between these items represents what is typically referred to as the 'balance of payments', or more strictly should be referred to as 'the current account of the balance of payments'. A surplus on the current account implies income exceeds outgoings (exports exceed imports). A deficit implies the reverse.

However, the current account does not represent the whole story. A deficit on the current account has to be paid for, and implies a net outflow of assets. A surplus implies the reverse. For example, if a nation imports more than it exports (i.e. runs up a balance of payments deficit) it still has to pay for those imports with some kind of cash. Either that involves borrowing the money from foreigners, or it involves selling domestic assets to foreigners. There is no other way that the imports could be paid for. The payments that offset the current account are referred to as the capital account. For example, in simplistic terms, if the UK runs a deficit on the current account with, say, imports exceeding exports by £10 billion in a year, there must be flows of capital account payments of £10 billion. The net foreign assets of the UK must have declined by £10 billion, with foreigners now having £10 billion of extra claims on the UK.

The concept is not that different to the income and outgoings of an individual: if someone spends more than their monthly income within a single month, it is as though they are running up a personal balance of payments deficit. It has to be financed by borrowing, or a run-down of savings.

The performance of the balance of payments is strongly influenced by the performance of national savings. If individuals, government and companies in an economy are all spending less than they are earning, then the economy will tend to export capital, and run a balance of payments surplus.

The balance of payments is often confused with the ➤**balance of trade**. The latter only includes the balance between exports and imports of goods and services traded. Hence, it is possible to run a trade deficit with imports exceeding exports, while running an overall balance of payments surplus on account of investment income or transfers.

balance of trade ➤➤balance of payments.

balance sheet A statement of the wealth of a business or organization at a particular date (usually the end of the ➤**financial year**) as distinct from a ➤**profit and loss account** (which records changes over a period). The balance sheet is in two parts: ➤**assets** on the left-hand side or at the top, and ➤**liabilities** on the right-hand side or at the bottom. The assets of the company (➤**debtors**, cash investments and property) are equal to the claims or liabilities of the persons or organizations owning them (the ➤**creditors**, lenders and shareholders). This is the principle of ➤**double-entry bookkeeping**.

According to the basic accounting equation, assets equal liabilities plus equity; therefore, assets minus liabilities equal ➤**equity**. Equity, shareholders' interest or *net worth* (which are all the same thing) may not reflect true market value, since assets are normally written into the balance sheet at historical cost (➤**cost, historical**) without any adjustment for *appreciation*. ➤**appreciate**; **inflation accounting**. ➤➤**Fourth Directive**.

balloon payment The final payment on a loan that is substantially larger than earlier payments. Designed to defer the burden of debt repayment.

bank ➤banking.

bank deposit The amount of money standing to the ➤credit of a customer of a bank. Bank deposits are simply IOUs written in the books of a bank and do not necessarily represent holdings of cash by the bank. ➤banking. A deposit may be on ➤current account or ➤deposit account (US = *demand deposits* and *time deposits* respectively). ➤➤deposit; sight deposit.

bank draft A ➤cheque issued by a bank, in effect a certified cheque in which the recipient may have confidence. Banks will issue drafts for customers for a fee where a ➤creditor will not accept an ordinary cheque.

bank giro ➤giro.

banking The business of taking ➤deposits and making ➤loans. As ➤financial intermediaries, banks may also offer a whole range of other financial services, such as ➤insurance, ➤credit cards and foreign exchange, but their distinguishing characteristic is their role in the money supply through the creation of deposits. When a bank makes a loan it incurs a book debt to a customer in return for a promise to repay it. The ability of a bank to create money in this way is limited in many countries by government controls on lending (➤credit control) as well as by its obligation to pay out ➤current account deposits in cash on demand. Since the bank's customers meet most of their needs for money by writing ➤cheques on their deposits, the cash holdings the banks need are only a small fraction of their total deposits. ➤liquidity ratio. The settlement of debts arising between banks through cheques drawn on one bank and deposited in another is made through a ➤clearing house. Banks are supervised and regulated in most countries by the ➤central bank, which acts as ➤lender of last resort. In the UK banks are now regulated by the Financial Services Authority (➤Financial Services Act). Banks provide a range of services to business including transfers and accounts in foreign currencies (➤hedge), bank loans and ➤overdrafts. Through subsidiaries they provide ➤factoring, ➤hire purchase, ➤leasing and ➤venture capital.

The traditional distinctions between banks and other financial intermediaries are breaking down, e.g. in the UK, ➤building societies now offer cheque accounts. In some countries banks are not allowed to hold ➤equity stakes in their client companies or to act as ➤investment banks (➤Glass–Steagall Act), and some US states have *unit banking* laws that require each bank to be a single enterprise without branches. Germany, The Netherlands and Switzerland have *universal banking* systems that allow banks to act as investment banks and to provide a very wide range of other financial services. ➤➤commercial bank; electronic banking; wholesale banking.

banking directive One of several ➤directives of the European Union (EU) intended to remove impediments to the provision of banking services across borders in Europe. The *Second Banking Directive* (1989) allows banks to offer services anywhere in the EU provided they are authorized in their home state (the principle of mutual recognition). The Second Directive has provisions for minimum capital for credit institutions and gives the EU the right to suspend licences for banks headquartered in countries outside the EU where those countries do not give equal treatment to EU banks. Other banking directives include Own Funds, Solvency Ratio, Large Exposures, Money Laundering, Deposit Insurance, Capital Adequacy. The *Investment Services Directive* (1993) has similar objectives to the Second Directive for firms providing investment products such as ➤**unit trusts** and allows, for example, cross-border access to stock exchanges.

bank loan A ➤**loan** by a bank, normally for a fixed period and for a specific purpose. The term *bank loan* is also loosely used to include ➤**overdrafts**, bank ➤**mortgage** loans and personal loans, as well as ➤**term loans**, though it is more common to use the generic term *bank advances*. Bank loans are normally secured (➤**collateral** security) and repaid in regular instalments, with interest charged at rates that vary with the bank's ➤**base rate**.

bank mandate ➤mandate.

Bank of England The ➤**central bank** of the UK. In mid 1997 the UK government announced that the bank's responsibility for supervision of the banking system would pass to the Financial Services Authority. ➤**Financial Services Act**. At the same time, the bank was made solely responsible for determining UK interest rates, a function until then exercised by the Treasury. The bank thus became independently responsible for ➤**monetary policy**. ➤➤**Monetary Policy Committee**.

bankrupt A private person or sole trader declared insolvent by a county court (UK) or equivalent elsewhere. The financial affairs of such a person/sole trader are then placed in the hands of a trustee who sells off the bankrupt's assets to raise money to pay the latter's debts.

bankruptcy A declaration by a court of law that an individual or company is insolvent, i.e. cannot meet ➤**debts** on the due dates. A bankruptcy petition may be filed either by the debtor or by their creditors requesting a receiving order. An inquiry into the debtor's affairs is then conducted by, in the UK, the official receiver; the business has then passed into receivership. If the receiver thinks fit, he may call a meeting of the debtor's creditors and, if the creditors wish it, declare the debtor bankrupt. The debtor's assets are then realized and distributed among the creditors either by the receiver or by a trustee appointed by the creditors. In the case of a company it goes into ➤**liquidation**.

US procedures are similar to those of the UK, but under Chapter 11 of the Bankruptcy Reform Act 1978 a firm may apply to the court for protection from its creditors while it carries out a reorganization of its affairs so as to be able to pay off its debts. In a similar way companies in the UK may be placed under administration rather than go into liquidation. The Insolvency Acts 1985 and 1986 codified existing law and made the handling of the affairs of insolvent debtors the responsibility of a registered insolvency practitioner. The Acts introduced a wide range of sanctions against directors who act negligently, as did the Company Directors Disqualification Act 1986.

banner advertisement An advertisement that stretches across the top of the printed page or across a web-page. ➤➤**advertising**.

bar code The recording of data in a form that can be read instantly, usually by a laser. Most commonly used on food products in stores where they appear as a series of black lines like a bar, hence the name. It is a coding system that is much in use in the retailing and manufacturing industries as it allows the automatic reading of items. Scanning devices are connected to computers and they can rapidly read the information contained in a bar code. The system is now spreading into other uses which require high speed or that deal with large ➤inventories.

bargain (UK) A purchase or sale on the ➤London Stock Exchange.

bargaining In business, employers and employees will bargain over various aspects of employment, principally ➤pay, hours of work and working conditions, but in some cases also recruitment and hiring policy, equity and diversity policies, decision-making processes, etc. Bargaining takes a variety of forms. 'Individual bargaining' occurs between an employer and individual employee. This contrasts with ➤➤collective bargaining, where negotiation takes place between an employer and organized employee representatives. ➤➤trade unions. A further distinction is between 'distributive bargaining' – negotiation that seeks to divide up a fixed amount of resource (where there will be winners and losers) – and 'integrative bargaining' – where an attempt is made to agree one or more satisfactory settlements (thereby creating a win-win solution). ➤negotiation.

Barnard, Chester One of the first management thinkers to break out of the rationalist frameworks of Frederick ➤Taylor and Max ➤Weber, by emphasizing the importance of communication and shared values in organizations. ➤organizational behaviour. Barnard saw the co-operative nature of business organizations and their need for morale and morality. An important role of the chief executive was to inculcate and safeguard corporate culture. ➤culture. Barnard made a distinction between an organization's effectiveness (the extent to which it achieves its objectives, including its values) and its efficiency in the technical sense of outputs versus inputs. While both had to be aimed for, it was the first – effectiveness – which determined long-term survival. The distinctions Barnard drew appear to be of enduring importance. Surveys of institutional investors reported upon in an article by Paul Coombes and Mark Watson in *The McKinsey Quarterly* (4, 2000) found that these investors would pay more for shares in a well-governed company than for those in a poorly governed one with a comparable financial performance. The premium varied from 18 per cent in the UK and US to 27 per cent in Indonesia and 28 per cent in Venezuela, reflecting the extent to which investors believe there is scope for improvement in the quality of financial reporting and other aspects of governance.

Barnard spent the whole of his career as a business executive with the Bell Telephone Company but found time to write two influential books, *The Functions of the Executive* (1938) and *Organization and Management* (1948).

barometric forecasting A method of predicting the course of one variable, by looking at the behaviour of another variable – a barometer – which experience suggests tends to move in advance of the first. For example, if one found a consistent historical relationship between machine tool orders in one period, and the growth of industrial production in the next period, one could use machine tool orders as a forecasting barometer of industrial production.

barrier to entry Any factor which creates an impediment to new competition in a market or industry. Such barriers come in a variety of forms. For example, they may be legal (a government prohibiting competitive entry against a national lottery, perhaps, or banning new planning consents for out-of-town shopping centres). Or barriers may be natural (➤**natural monopoly**), in which case the cost structure of an industry makes it unlikely the market could sustain an extra producer, and where the incumbent has already incurred ➤**sunk costs** and is thus unlikely to withdraw from the market. In this case a new entrant would be saddled with costs that incumbents no longer have to bear. Barriers also may be tactical (companies can use more or less aggressive techniques to deter new entrants). Very high levels of expenditure on marketing may be seen as a barrier to entry, e.g. if the 'weight' of advertising expenditure is far more than is needed to build brand recall and brand awareness. Or a barrier to new competition may simply reflect the ➤**competitive advantage** of an incumbent, e.g. a good brand name, established contracts with suppliers, or an unbeatable product or technology. ➤➤**contestability**.

barrier to exit   Restriction on the ability of a producer to withdraw from an activity, or to redeploy its resources to an alternative activity. Such restrictions may be legal, designed to protect communities from the discomfort of factory closure. In this case, they often, in fact, act as deterrents to new entry into a sector (which becomes more risky if exit is not an option), and as an impediment to economic transformation. However, in ➤**game theory**, barriers to exit have been seen as tactical business weapons. Companies may paradoxically want to restrict *their own* ability to withdraw from an industry as a means of dissuading a potential competitor not to enter the industry on the ground that the incumbent is committed to remaining inside it. ➤➤**barrier to entry**.

barrier to trade   Generally, any feature of a nation's economy which impedes international trade and, thus, has the effect of fostering a more national-oriented economy. Most often, discussion of such barriers is preoccupied with government-imposed barriers to trade. Such barriers most often used to take the form of tariffs, which are explicit taxes on imports, designed to promote the interests of domestic producers. Quotas on imports have also been a much-used weapon. These can be compulsory, or take the form of voluntary export restraints, in which foreign companies are persuaded or cajoled to limit their sales. Administrative barriers (bureaucratic licensing and certification requirements, for example) have sometimes been deployed. Sometimes, seemingly innocent regulations can be motivated by a desire to limit trade, e.g. an attempt to regulate the type of hops used in beer was seen as an attempt by Germany to block imports, as foreign producers did not use the specified hops. In all these cases, attempts have been made through the ➤**World Trade Organization** and its forebears, and through regional trade regulators such as the ➤**European Union** and Mercosur, to limit government-imposed barriers. For trade in goods, such attempts have been very successful; for trade in services, and in the regulation of investment flows, success has been slower. However, not all barriers are the responsibility of the authorities: trade is impeded by transport costs and cultural factors, too. Finally, there have been many practices that do have the effect of impeding trade, but arguably may not constitute a barrier in the usual sense of the term. For example, Japanese support for small shops was long held by foreign companies to be an impediment to their ability to launch products in the Japanese market with ease. Whether one describes such support as a barrier to trade, or as a natural feature of the market-place into which those companies wished to do business, has been a controversial issue.

Bartlett, Christopher A Business school academic specializing in the structure and functioning of international companies. Joint author with Sumantra Ghoshal of the influential book *Managing Across Borders: the transnational solution* (1989), who identified three types of cross-national firms: (a) *multinational companies*, such as Unilever, that are conglomerates; (b) *global companies* with centralized decision-making and largely standardized products (e.g. Ford), and (c) *international companies* focusing upon joint development and world-wide sharing of knowledge, e.g. IBM. None of these three types was suitable for the turbulent global environment of the late 1970s and 1980s which was leading to the emergence of the *transnational company*. This evolving organization is able to combine simultaneously the key capabilities of the previous three forms: responsiveness and flexibility, efficiency, and transfer of learning, respectively. The transnational has a strong shared vision and culture but subsidiaries collaborate in specialized and complementary ways, e.g. in the manufacture of components or taking the lead in rolling out new technologies. There are echoes here of Tom ➤**Peters** and Waterman's simultaneous loose-tight properties and of their, and other writers', emphasis on the need for flatter, more flexible organizational structures to encourage creativity and customer responsiveness. The changes that Bartlett and Ghoshal perceived were needed have continued with growing pace and are observable in all cross-border companies. ➤**organizational behaviour.**

Christopher Bartlett has been Professor of Business Administration at Harvard Business School since 1979 and was previously with ➤**McKinsey** in London and Baxter Laboratory in France. He is Professor of Strategic Leadership at London Business School and was at the European Institute of Business Administration (INSEAD), Fontainebleau, France. He is also founding dean of the new Indian School of Business in Hyderabad.

base period The reference date for which an ➤**index number** of a time series is calculated.

base rate (UK) The rate of ➤**interest** that forms the basis for the charges for ➤**bank** loans and ➤**overdrafts** and the deposit rates of the ➤**commercial banks**. Actual rates are set at up to about 5 percentage points above base rate according to the creditworthiness of the borrower. In the US, the *prime rate* is the rate at which a bank will lend to its most creditworthy customers. Though to some extent now superseded by ➤**cost of funds** rates, the prime rate is still an important indicator of ➤**money market** trends.

BASES A test marketing service used to help companies launch new products. Owned by ➤**A C Nielsen Corporation** and particularly heavily used in the US. ➤**new product development.**

basic research A particular activity within a ➤**research and development** department that focuses on work of a general nature intended to apply to a broad range of uses or to new knowledge about a scientific area. This activity is also referred to as 'fundamental science' and is usually only conducted in the laboratories of universities and large organizations. Outputs from this activity will result in scientific papers for journals. Some findings will be developed further to produce new technologies for the business. New scientific discoveries such as antibiotics in the 1940s belong to this research category. ➤➤**applied research.**

basing-point pricing A form of pricing strategy where the seller designates a particular city as the 'basing point' and charges all customers the freight cost from that city to the customer's location, regardless of the city from which the goods are shipped.

basis point 0.01 of 1 per cent. A measure normally used in the statement of interest rates, e.g. a change from 5.75 to 5.81 per cent is a change of six basis points. First used in the US, now common everywhere.

batch production The manufacture of a set number of identical products. For each stage of the production process work will be completed for the whole batch before the next stage commences. This provides ➤**economies of scale**. This type of production differs from one-off ➤➤**job production** and large-scale ➤➤**flow production**.

BATNA The best alternative to a negotiated agreement ➤**negotiation**.

battle of the sexes A situation – popularly characterized in the economics of ➤**game theory** – in which people or institutions have a strong interest in co-ordinating their behaviour, but disagree over quite how to behave. An example would be the setting of an industry standard for a pipe fitting. Everybody may agree that it is overwhelmingly important that some standard fitting is agreed, but each firm may have its own view as to what that standard should be. The characterization of such situations as a 'battle of the sexes' derives from a simple parable used in game theory to model them: a husband and wife want to spend the evening together, but disagree over the precise activity to engage in. She wants to watch some boxing; he wants to go to the ballet. A table of their preferences between different activities for the evening is shown below.

Game theory

	His ranking preference	Her ranking preference
Go to ballet together	First	Second
Go to boxing together	Second	First
He goes to ballet, she goes to boxing	Third	Fourth
He goes to boxing, she goes to ballet	Fourth	Third

It should, of course, be possible to agree on an evening together at the ballet, or the boxing, but the crucial feature of these situations is the possibility that a struggle by husband and wife to get their first-best option may result in them each getting their third-best option. For example, if he insists on going to the ballet, and she insists on going to the boxing, they may end up going their own way, even though both would prefer to be together. A business example of such a situation may arise in the creation of a ➤**joint venture**. Resolving the battle of the sexes peacefully is possible, either if the situation is frequently repeated (➤**repeated games**), in which case the partners can lose some battles and win others, or if the partners can agree some process to resolve the battle, without conceding a specific outcome to the game (agreeing to toss a coin for example). The game is not as commonly discussed as the ubiquitous ➤**prisoners' dilemma**.

Baumol effect   The idea that certain services become relatively more expensive as economies develop, and that some manufactured goods become relatively less expensive. It was outlined by W J Baumol in 1967, and was based on the following reasoning: it is increases in ➤**productivity** in a sector which allow prices of a product to fall; it is new technology which drives increases in productivity, and new technology emerges most quickly in capital-intensive sectors – those sectors employing machines, for example, rather than just people. As manufacturing industries tend to be more capital-intensive than services, they would enjoy relatively falling prices.

It is true that in less developed countries, the price of manufactured goods tends to be very high compared to the price of services; whereas in rich countries, services tend to be very expensive. But the Baumol effect should not be overstated: many non-manufacturing sectors (such as telecommunications) have enjoyed spectacular increases in productivity based on new technology. Moreover, it is argued that it is hard to measure productivity in service industries, where outputs are often hard to define precisely. (It is difficult to tell just how the productivity of a lawyer or teacher should be defined.) ➤**credence qualities**.

The Baumol effect is partly used to explain the growth of government spending, as government primarily provides services rather than goods to the public. ➤**deindustrialization**.

Bayes' theorem   A formula in probability theory that allows us to calculate the chance of an unknown prior event having occurred, given the observation that a known subsequent event did occur. For example, imagine trying to work out whether the failure of a construction company to complete a new building on time is the result of poor management. While the fact the building project was late tells us it was *probably* bad management, it cannot tell us that with certainty, because even good builders have bad luck sometimes. Bayes' theorem allows us to apply precise magnitudes to the chance we had a bad builder, given some precise magnitudes about the market generally. If we know the proportion of good builders who deliver late buildings, the proportion of bad builders who deliver buildings on time, and the number of good and bad builders out there, we use Bayes' theorem to calculate the probability that our particular builder was a bad one. It is best understood by further example: suppose 60 per cent of builders are bad and that 40 per cent are good; suppose that bad builders deliver late 80 per cent of the time and good ones deliver late 20 per cent of the time. That means of 100 buildings delivered,

60 have bad builders, of whom 48 will deliver late, and 12 on time, and

40 have good builders, of whom 8 will deliver late, and 32 on time.

We can see that out of every 56 late completions (8 + 48), 48 are from bad builders; or 86 per cent of them. Bayes' theorem says that having observed a late completion, we have an 86 per cent chance of having had a bad builder.

The precise equation is: the probability of a prior event E having occurred given that a subsequent event S did occur, is equal to: The prior probability of E with or without S having occurred, times the probability S occurred given that E had occurred, all divided by the probability of S having occurred one way or the other:

$$\text{probability our builder was bad} = (0.6 \times 0.8)/0.56.$$

BCG matrix   Boston Consulting Group matrix. ➤**Henderson, Bruce D; portfolio planning**.

BDT ➤behavioural decision theory.

bear A speculator who sells ➤securities because he expects a fall in prices; the antonym of ➤bull. A bear who sells securities that he does not possess is described as having *sold short* (➤position). If he did possess the securities that he sold, he is described as a *covered* or *protected* bear. A *bear raid* is an attempt by a number of investors acting in collusion to drive down the price of a share by selling stock. This has been done to defeat a ➤take-over by depressing the shares of the predator. A *bear market* is one in which prices are falling. ➤➤bear squeeze.

bearer security A share or ➤bond that is not registered in the name of the holder, who can sell it or claim a ➤dividend on simple presentation to a bank or ➤broker. Once common on certain continental European stock exchanges, bearer securities have the attraction that the tax authorities cannot identify the owners. For this reason dividends and interest on bearer securities are usually subject to a ➤withholding tax. In most countries owners of securities are registered. ➤registrar.

bear hug ➤bear squeeze.

bear market ➤bear.

bear squeeze The purchase of ➤securities, currency or commodities in the markets by the authorities, thus raising prices and squeezing the ➤liquidity of speculators who have been selling short (➤short selling) in the expectation of falling prices. Also termed *bear hug*.

bed and breakfast (UK) The sale of a ➤security on one day and its repurchase the following day in a previously agreed transaction for the purpose of establishing a ➤capital gain or loss. A transaction of this kind does not establish a loss or gain for tax purposes in the US but until recently did so in the UK.

behaviour ➤buyer behaviour.

behavioural decision theory (BDT) A body of theory about how people make decisions, especially how they make seemingly irrational decisions. The concern is with finding holes in rational decision theory (specifically, in showing the failings of some kinds of economic theory as a means to describe decision-making under risk). ➤prospect theory; risk aversion.

behavioural equation An equation describing the precise relationship between different variables which are hypothesized to interact in the real world. So-called, because if the hypothesized relationship is correct, the equation says how the world behaves. For example, a behavioural equation might be of the form:

$$D_t = \alpha + \beta P_t + \delta Y_t$$

where D_t represents the demand for a commodity in period t, P is the price of the commodity, and Y is the level of national income. The equation hypothesizes that P and Y determine D. If that hypothesis is correct, we can use the statistical techniques of ➤econometrics to make the best estimate possible of the precise relationship between D, P and Y, putting magnitudes to the Greek ➤parameters, α, β and δ. ➤beta coefficient. Thus, given knowledge of P and Y in future, we can make sensible estimates of D in that period. ➤➤choice modelling; model; regression analysis.

behavioural intentions theory ➤attitude.

behavioural learning ➤learning.

behavioural theory of the firm An attempt to elucidate corporate decision-making in terms of the particular motivations of the different players within the organization. The behavioural theory – developed by R Cyert, J G March and H A Simon – dispensed with the simplifying assumption of most economists (i.e. that firms purely strive to maximize profits) and instead sought to view the firm as a collection of sometimes competing interests and interest groups. A key text was R M Cyert and J G March (*A Behavioral Theory of the Firm*, 1963). Economists have not been persuaded to abandon their old models, but ➤**organizational behaviour** has emerged as a respectable discipline outside economics departments.

belief A descriptive thought that a person holds about something, such as a product, service, organization, person, employee or idea. This contrasts with an ➤attitude, which is evaluative in character. As an example, consider the difference between the belief statement 'Microsoft is a computer software company' and the attitude statement 'Microsoft is a very good computer software company'. Beliefs are often quite widely held, even by people who do not buy or use a product, or do not engage with an organization or employee. This is because descriptive thoughts can exist as a matter of common knowledge. Thus, most people would know that Microsoft is a computer software company, whether or not they had ever purchased its products. Evaluations, by contrast, require the person to have additional, specialist information – possibly gained through in-use experience. In order to say with any conviction that Microsoft is a very good computer software company it is necessary to have direct experience of using its software or something akin to this, e.g. discussions with users about the relative merits of alternative computer software suppliers. Despite the conceptual distinction, the terms 'belief' and 'attitude' are sometimes used loosely and interchangeably. ➤consumer behaviour; marketing research.

below the line Items in the ➤profit and loss account which are underneath the line at which the total trading profit for the period is struck. In reported results for a ➤quoted company, extraordinary items that arise from transactions which are outside the ordinary trading activities of the company (e.g. the sale of an office building) may be taken below the line for the purposes of calculating ➤earnings per share, whereas exceptional items that do derive from the ordinary activities may be taken above the line for that purpose. Appropriations such as ➤dividends, transfers to ➤reserves or taxation are below the line.

below-the-line communications The conventional term for marketing communications that do not involve the purchase of media. This includes ➤direct marketing, ➤promotions, and 'free media' that come as a result of media relations management and ➤public relations activities. It contrasts with paid-for ➤above-the-line communications. The term is somewhat vague, and has become of even less use with recent changes in the media industry. Media relations, for instance, may involve a paid-for element, as in the case of programme magazine sponsorship deals and ➤infomercials.

benchmarking A technique for comparing performance against that of others, typically competitors in the same industry. The technique was first used extensively in manufacturing environments where producers could compare their performance with that of others. This is usually achieved by looking at the most efficient firms within an industry or in similar industries. The technique has since been used in many other environments to see how a business's activities compare with its competitors'.

beneficial interest Ultimate ownership of property. For example, UK directors of companies are required to declare beneficial interests in their companies even where these shares are held by ➤nominees or in ➤trust.

benefit in kind ➤fringe benefit.

benefit segmentation ➤segmentation.

Benelux The group of countries comprising Belgium, The Netherlands and Luxembourg, which as long ago as 1932 agreed to band together for trading purposes in the manner that the ➤European Union has adopted.

Bennis, Warren Acknowledged guru on ➤leadership issues. In his second major book, *On Becoming a Leader* (1989), Bennis lists five basic ingredients of leadership: guiding vision, passion, integrity, curiosity and daring (a willingness to take risks). Bennis' some twenty-six books and numerous articles are very readable and he has coined many aphorisms, e.g. 'The manager is a copy; the leader is an original', and 'The manager does things right; the leader does the right thing'.

Bennis is founding chairman of the Leadership Institute at the University of Southern California and Professor of Finance and Business Economics.

beta coefficient 1. In finance theory, the degree to which the returns on an asset track those of the market generally. A beta of 1 means that, on average, returns on the particular asset track those of the market. A higher beta implies that returns tend to move in the same direction, but with a more extreme amplitude. A beta of zero means the asset has no correlation with the market. A negative beta implies that the asset's returns tend to rise when market returns tend to fall. ➤alpha coefficient; capital asset pricing model; portfolio theory. **2.** In ➤econometrics, the Greek letter usually used to denote the relationship between two variables under scrutiny.

bid price The price at which a ➤market maker will buy shares or a ➤commodity.

Big Bang (UK) The term used to encapsulate the changes culminating on 27 October 1986 with the abandonment of the ➤commission agreement between members of the ➤London Stock Exchange and of strict segregation of ➤jobbers and ➤brokers. In July 1983 the government agreed to exempt the London Stock Exchange from the provisions of the Restrictive Practices Act in return for lifting a number of restrictions. In 1982 the Stock Exchange Council had raised the limit placed on any one outside shareholder from 10 to 29.9 per cent and in 1985 decided that this limit would also be abandoned. Many banks and other financial institutions have acquired interests in, or control of, stock exchange companies since March 1986. Other changes associated with the Big Bang have been the closure of the trading floor of the stock exchange in favour of electronic off-the-floor telephone and electronic dealing, and a major expansion in dealings in international ➤securities. Fixed commissions were abandoned on the ➤New York Stock Exchange in 1975.

Big Board ➤New York Stock Exchange.

bilateral monopoly A situation in which a single buyer confronts a single seller. ➤monopoly; monopsony. An example might be a large employer facing a strongly unionized workforce. When monopoly only exists on one side of a market, relatively simple economic models can make intelligent predictions as to prevailing prices or output. Bilateral monopoly turns out to be more challenging; the outcome requires an understanding of bargaining processes. ➤➤collective bargaining.

bill broker A firm or individual that deals in ➤Treasury bills and ➤bills of exchange on the London ➤money market.

billion Originally a term meaning 1 million million, now conventionally used to mean 1,000 million.

bill of exchange An order in writing addressed by one person to another and signed by the person giving it, requiring the person to whom it is addressed to pay, on demand or at a fixed date, a specified sum of money. The bill is made out by the signatory (the *drawer*) always with the consent of the person to whom it is addressed, who signs or *accepts* it (➤acceptance), and mainly in relation to the sale of goods or produce. Bills are ➤negotiable in the ➤money market, so enabling drawers to obtain their money at once.

bill of materials A list of the materials and component parts required to manufacture a product. This is an essential input into a ➤material requirements planning system. It shows which parts and how many of them are required to go into other parts. Bills of materials are often illustrated as a product structure diagram showing all the component parts and how they fit together to eventually make the final product. Usually this is represented as different levels of assembly, with the highest level being the finished product.

BIMBO Buy-in ➤management buy-out.

Black–Scholes formula A complex equation used to establish a fair price for ➤options in financial markets. The formula, which is used to solve what had previously been considered a difficult problem, was published in 1973 by Fischer Black and Myron Scholes and at about the same time by Robert Merton. It was based on looking at the price of a basket of financial assets which carried the same risk and return as an option. ➤replicating portfolio.

blue chip issue Shares in leading ➤quoted companies that can be easily bought and sold without influencing their price. ➤liquidity. The term derives from poker chips, but it is less frequently used nowadays because several blue chip companies have got into difficulties and the risk-free connotations of 'blue chip' have been impaired.

blueprinting The activity for documenting how the processes involved in an operation combine to create the final product or service. ➤Flow charts are a common technique for presenting such processes. They should identify all inputs into a process and all outputs and should identify all the different activities necessary to deliver the finished product or service. ➤flow-charting the customer experience.

blue sky law (US) State law in the US that requires a ➤security to be registered with a state before it can be traded there. ➤**National Market System** stocks traded on the ➤**National Association of Securities Dealers Automated Quotation system** (NASDAQ) are now exempt from these laws.

boiler room ➤bucket shop.

bona fide 'In good faith.' The phrase is used frequently in the law of contract, and therefore in business.

bond A form of interest-bearing ➤**security** issued by central or local governments, companies, banks and other institutions. Bonds are usually a form of long-term security, but they do not always carry fixed interest (➤**variable rate security**), they may be irredeemable (➤**redemption date**) and they may be secured or unsecured. In the US the term *bond* includes ➤**debentures**. ➤**bearer security; Eurobond;** ➤➤**term structure of interest rates.**

bonus 1. A free share or *scrip* issue. ➤**bonus issue. 2.** A distribution of life assurance company investment profits. ➤**insurance. 3.** Payments to employees, usually based on results. ➤**pay.**

bonus issue A term virtually synonymous with *scrip issue* and *capitalization issue* (US = *stock dividend* and *stock split*), describing shares given without charge to existing shareholders in proportion to the shares already held. A scrip issue does not add to the ➤**capital employed** by the firm but is made where the capital employed has been increased by retaining profits and is therefore out of line with the ➤**issued capital**. Consequently, it is a pure book-keeping transaction. For example, ➤**dividends** will, after a scrip issue, be divided among a larger number of shares, so that the dividend per share will fall in proportion to the number of bonus shares issued. The motive for splitting shares in this way may be to capitalize retained profits or it may simply be to reduce the unit price of the shares (without altering the ➤**yield**) and so improve their marketability. ➤➤**drip; heavy share.**

book value The value of an asset as it is written in the accounts of a company, as opposed to the real market value of the asset. Many assets are valued in company books at the amount they cost at the time of purchase, and those values are not always updated as the true asset value changes. ➤**net asset.**

Boston Consulting Group ➤Henderson, Bruce D.

Boston Consulting Group matrix ➤portfolio planning.

bottleneck A term used to describe delays in a production process. The rate of throughput for any production system is dependent on all stages of the system being able to operate with the same capacity. The production stage with the least capacity is referred to as the 'bottleneck stage'. The term is sometimes used to describe shortages of products and services in a whole economy.

bottom-up investment ➤investment approaches.

bottom-up planning Plans generated by individuals and departments and passed to senior management which are then synthesized into corporate plans and functional plans, e.g. ➤**marketing planning**. This is in contrast to top-down planning that involves senior management handing down specific objectives to subordinates without the latter's participation in the planning process. Bottom-up planning uses the skills and experiences of the staff who will be responsible for implementing the plans. The involvement of staff in the planning process usually motivates individuals in the achievement of the targets that emerge from the process. ➤**business strategy**.

bought deal A term used in ➤**venture capital** where the financing company acquires a subsidiary from a large firm with a view to syndicating the acquisition later through a ➤**management buy-out** or other means. ➤**syndicate**.

bought ledger The accounting record of purchases by an organization from its suppliers.

bourse (Fr.) French term for ➤**stock exchange**, also used in Belgium, Switzerland and other European countries. ➤**Paris** *Bourse*.

brand The name, logo, symbol, slogan, jingle, character, packaging or design that is intended to identify a product or service and differentiate it from competitors. This can be achieved at a corporate or product level. ➤**brand hierarchy**. In principle, brands provide value to consumers in a number of ways: (a) they simplify decision-making; (b) provide a guarantee of product safety and quality, and (c) offer predictability and consistency over time and space. These factors may justify a price premium, i.e. consumers may accept that it is worth paying a little more for something they can trust and that will be of a certain quality. More subjective factors may be at work as well: consumers may use brands to signify their membership of a peer group or indicate their status, and at an emotional level they may relate to the symbolism that is associated with a brand (or its publicity), e.g. any symbolism that implies the product is genuine, authentic, exciting and fun.

For organizations that have, and support, brands there are direct financial benefits – notably the ability to charge a price premium and the possibility of securing higher-volume sales (thereby gaining production and marketing economies of scale and keeping unit costs low). ➤**brand equity**. These financial benefits arise as a consequence of consumers trusting branded more than unbranded items. Other benefits include the maintenance of customer loyalty/retention, the scope for developing distinctive products (which may form the basis of a competitive advantage), the possibility of leveraging the brand when extending into new markets (➤**brand extension**), and bargaining strength with intermediaries, e.g. distributors, retailers, brokers, ➤**agents**, etc. Legal protection is a further benefit for organizations – brand names, trademarks, and highly distinctive colours and shapes (➤**visual equity**) can be registered and granted legal protection in many jurisdictions. This protects any investment the organization has made in supporting its brands, helps brands to remain distinctive and reduces the chances of consumer confusion.

Within an organization, a branding strategy serves as something of a catalyst for thinking about the product and its customers. This may be of value in its own right, e.g. it may help to ensure consistency between advertising messages and a consumer's direct experience of a product, salesperson or customer service representative. It also helps the organization to portray a consistent 'look and feel' through job and recruitment advertisements, internal newsletters, intranets and web sites. The term 'employer/employee branding' has been used in this context.

Despite all these benefits, branding strategies are continually struggling against ➤**competitive parity** and ➤**commodification**. Consumers may come to believe there are few significant differences between competing branded products, or even between branded products and ➤**generics**, ➤**private labels**, and ➤**look alikes**. Then choice is most likely to be governed by price alone, rather than other attributes for which a price premium is justified. For this reason, branding strategies must be actively managed and there must be individuals within the organization who are designated champions of specific brands. Recognition of this led to the emergence of ➤**brand management** and ➤**category management** systems.

brand attitude ➤brand communication effects.

brand awareness ➤brand communication effects.

brand communication effects The way aspects of marketing communication are linked to a specific brand. If these effects are not linked, expenditure on communication (e.g. ➤**advertising**) will be wasted. There are several different ways to make the link, depending on whether the goal is to create or maintain 'brand awareness' and/or 'brand attitude'.

Brand awareness refers to a person's ability to identify the brand, within a product category, in sufficient detail to make a purchase. It has two components: 'brand recognition' and 'brand recall'. Brand recognition is achieved at the point of sale through the design elements of a brand, i.e. shape, colour, illustration and graphics. ➤**visual equity**. Individuals need to be able to read (decode) the visual cues. Brand recall occurs prior to purchase, when there is a need for the product category. Individuals must be able to remember a brand or respond to prompts, e.g. verbal cues.

Brand attitude refers to a person's assessment of the brand with respect to its ability to offer certain benefits. These benefits are seen as satisfying particular purchase motives, e.g. removal of a problem, restocking after supplies have been depleted, offering sensory gratification, providing intellectual stimulation, etc.

An understanding of brand communication effects is crucial for any assessment of consumer-based ➤**brand equity**. Also, depending on which effect is deemed to be working, different creative communications strategies are implied, e.g. if the benefit offered by a brand is 'problem-removal', the creative work must illustrate this benefit or demonstrate how the brand does, in fact, remove the problem. ➤➤**involvement theory**.

brand equity The value of a ➤**brand**. One view of brand equity is to see it largely as a financial valuation ('financial-based brand equity'). An important reason for taking this view has been the move to list brands on company balance sheets (along with other ➤**intangible assets**), or to agree a value when brands are being bought, sold or licensed, or when corporate mergers and acquisitions are in train and brands have to be accounted for or disposed of. This viewpoint came to prominence in 1988 when almost $50 billion was paid for a number of brands in just four mega-deals (acquisitions by R J R Nabisco, Philip Morris, Grand Metropolitan and Nestlé).

However, there are problems associated with the financial-based view of brand equity – notably, the issue of separability (the value of a successful brand is impossible to separate from the rest of the business), the premise of value (the value of a brand as a going concern will differ from its value to third parties, but without an active market in brands this is hard to establish), and the treatment of depreciation (the value of tangible fixed assets is depreciated in traditional (➤**cost, historical**) accounting, whereas marketers would see successful brands appreciating and contributing to future profits in a ➤**current cost accounting** framework). Ways can be devised to cope with these problems. Thus, the issue of separability has been handled in three main ways: (a) the price premium approach; (b) the royalty payments, or royalty relief, method, and (c) the brand earnings/alternative return on assets approach. All three approaches give a base year cash flow or earnings figure for a brand. Future profitability (value) can be estimated using a ➤**discounted cash-flow** approach or an earnings multiplier approach, using the base year figure as the starting-point. While these approaches have some appeal, the validity of the methods has been called into question: reliance is placed on (very uncertain) forecasts, a large amount of subjectivity is involved, valuations are likely to be imprecise and inconsistent across valuers, and all this raises concerns about the ability to audit brand valuations.

In contrast, marketers – particularly in North America – have tended to describe brand equity as the value of a brand that arises from high levels of brand loyalty, name awareness, perceived quality, strong brand associations (➤**brand image**), and other proprietary brand assets such as ➤**patents** and trademarks (collectively called 'consumer-based brand equity'). An important synthesis of this perspective was provided by David Aaker (*Managing Brand Equity*, 1991). Ideally, this definition requires the creation of a brand equity measurement system, in which the components of equity are measured and tracked over time, e.g. where levels of name awareness among consumers are monitored over time. As a practical matter, these components need to be correlated with one another, e.g. there is little point in consumers having high awareness of a brand name if the brand does not have legal protection. Because of this, some experts have argued that consumer-based brand equity can be approximated by simple measures that encapsulate all the correlates, e.g. ➤**market share** – brands with high market share tend to have higher levels of loyalty, name awareness, etc., and therefore they are expected to have high equity. ➤**brand salience**.

The failure to agree on a single definition has meant there are now several proprietary brand equity measures. These include: Image Power (Landor Associates) based on brand familiarity and esteem, the Conversion Model (Market Facts Inc) which measures willingness to continue purchasing a brand, the Brand Asset Valuator (Young & Rubicam) that has measures of differentiation, relevance, esteem and familiarity. Most of these are consumer-based approaches; however, the leading brand valuation company Interbrand has taken a broader view (even its early evaluations were based on a combination of factors, including market leadership, the market context, long-term trends, the level and consistency of marketing/financial support, the length of time a brand has been on the market ('brand longevity'), success in extending the brand and legal protection).

brand extension The use of an established brand name to launch a product into a new category. The category will be new in the sense of being new for that organization. Thus, the product being launched may be new-to-the-world or simply a modification of an existing product, but either way it would not previously have been associated with the established brand. Brand extensions are designed to lever off the value of the established ➤**brand** – carrying across strong brand associations, positive quality associations, and high levels of awareness and presence. These factors should give rise to trial purchase and even enhance the value of the established brand. However, there are considerable risks. In particular, the name may fail to help the extension because the fit is seen as poor or confusing. ➤**congruency theory**. Even worse, the good name of the established brand could be tarnished. ➤➤**line extensions**.

brand hierarchy The levels at which brands are found in an organization. 'Corporate brands' are the most general, e.g. Sony, Shell, IBM, Ford, and Accenture. At this level, ➤**corporate image** is of particular significance, i.e. the overall set of associations that consumers have of a company based not only on the image of specific products, but also pricing policies, service levels, support and assistance, salesforce conduct, communications, social responsibility, employee management, business performance and conduct. Chief executive officers will take a direct interest in this level of the hierarchy. Next come 'family brands', also called 'range' and 'umbrella' brands. These describe a range of related products, but do not embrace all the activities and products of an organization, e.g. Healthy Choice covers a diverse range of food products; however, the parent company – ConAgra – is also involved in other areas of activity. Further down the hierarchy are individual 'product brands' (Procter & Gamble's Ariel, Tide and Dash laundry detergents). Here ➤**brand image** is of concern. It is at this level that traditional systems of ➤**brand management** have been employed. At the lowest level of the hierarchy are 'models' – these are highly specific identifiers. In ➤**packaged goods**, models are specific product lines (➤**line extensions**) and individual ➤**stock-keeping units**, and these are not necessarily publicized to consumers. However, in fashion and technology markets, innovative new models may be heavily publicized in conjunction with higher-level branding, e.g. Microsoft Office 2000, Volvo sedan S60.

Elements of the hierarchy can be used and combined in various ways. Product brands can dominate (Marlboro dominates the name of its corporate owner Philip Morris), corporate brands can dominate (Xerox), names can be given equal prominence, or some mixture (Sony Trinitron screens). Also, there has been a growth in 'dual branding', 'co-branding' and 'partner-branding', where a single product is marked with the brand names of two or more companies (Nike and Du Pont) or where complementary branded products are promoted jointly (Sony computer monitors and Hewlett Packard printers). The goal is to bundle together the product benefits of each brand in its own specialist area, so as to enhance the consumer's evaluation of the overall offering (saying, in effect, 2 + 2 = 5).

brand image The holistic impression that people have of a brand, often expressed in relative terms ('brand A has a better image than brand B'). This overall impression will reflect the way people perceive the brand, their attitudes to it, and any behaviour they exhibit towards it, e.g. purchase, usage, stock-holding, shareholding, etc. Brand image can be seen as equivalent to ➤**corporate image**, but at the level of an individual product or service ➤**brand**. In principle, it should be much easier to manage brand image because it is a singular thing, in contrast to an organization-wide image that may embrace very different brands and activities.

brand management A system of management whereby each brand in the organization is controlled by a brand manager who is instructed to behave like an independent entrepreneur, even where the organization has other brands in the same or a related product category. Thus, brands from the same organization compete head-on. The manager is expected to make all the marketing and sales decisions for the brand. As a formal system of management, Procter & Gamble is credited with 'inventing' brand management with the introduction of Camay soap in the US in the 1930s. It was then widely adopted by ➤**packaged goods** and consumer goods companies.

The principal argument in favour of brand management is that new and risky brands need an entrepreneurial advocate who will secure resources for the brand and do everything required to maximize market opportunities. Also, the notion that, through competition, the strongest and fittest will survive. Another way of seeing this is that managers of established brands are kept on their toes – they cannot afford to become complacent or lazy; instead, they must continue to innovate, push the brand through retail channels and pull custom to it using marketing communications. A by-product of this system is that junior managers gain valuable experience which helps them as they move up through the organization.

There are, however, several major disadvantages. ➤**Cannibalization** is a problem if the established and new brands directly compete for the same group of customers. ➤**Product proliferation** is another very common problem if nobody takes responsibility for evaluating the independent decisions of brand managers. In combination, these two outcomes result in too many small lines that return low levels of profit. The system also creates a culture that is opposed to the sharing of resources and information, leading to wasteful duplication of research and development investments and associated ➤**marketing research**. A failure to secure bulk-purchase economies when negotiating with suppliers and agencies is another difficulty, e.g. the bulk purchase of media space for ➤**advertising**.

From the late 1980s, this system of management was questioned by leading multinationals and there was a general shift to ➤**category management**. A factor that brought this to a head was the increasing power of retailers. Market-dominant grocery retailers could exploit the fragmented nature of the producers with whom they dealt; therefore, the onus was on producers to shift to a less fragmented system of management.

brand recall ➤brand communication effects.

brand recognition ➤brand communication effects.

brand salience 1. 'Top-of-mind' awareness of a ➤**brand**. A salient brand is said to 'stand out' in the mind of consumers. This is a narrow definition of brand salience. **2.** An alternative definition is to see salience as the *overall* prominence of a brand, which includes, but goes beyond, top-of-mind awareness. According to this view, salience depends on different measures of brand performance correlating. Thus, all of the following tend to be true for the salient brand: the consumer is more aware of the brand, is more likely to have it in the ➤**consideration set** (of brands that might be bought), will have it in the purchase repertoire (where there is a repertoire), be familiar with the brand and say she likes it ('familiarity leads to liking'), believe that it's more likely to be available, regard it as value for money, feel that it has other positive attributes (e.g. that she intends to buy it in the future), talk more about it in ➤**focus groups**, recognize and recall its ➤**advertising** and generally show signs of greater ➤**consumer loyalty** (by any measure of loyalty). Across consumers, the salient brand is one where these measures start to add up, e.g. where most consumers think a particular brand is more likely to be available, be value for money, have prominent advertising, etc. This will reflect market realities (i.e. the salient brand actually will be more available, be value for money, have prominent advertising, etc.); this degree of support can be afforded and justified because the brand is salient to so many people. The logic is circular because all the different elements are correlated.

Brand salience offers an explanation for why the functional differences between directly competing and substitutable brands are usually quite minor and yet the leading brand may be ten times as big as the tenth biggest brand. The product features of the leading brand are unlikely to be ten times better, or its advertising is unlikely to be ten times better. Rather, there are that many more people for whom the brand is salient. This is of importance in thinking about the success of brands such as Sony, Ford, Coca-Cola and McDonald's, all of which are highly salient. This line of argument calls into question traditional notions of ➤product differentiation (which suggests the successful brand must have one or two very distinct – if not unique – attributes) and also casts doubt on attempts to find one-way causal relationships between components of marketing and brand success, e.g. it is not that advertising recall helps to cause brand sales, but that the two are correlated.

breakeven analysis The point at which the total costs of an undertaking are equal to the total revenue. This is usually presented in the form of a graph to show total revenue and costs at a variety of levels of output (a *breakeven chart*). The aim is to show the profit to be achieved at different levels of sales. The actual point at which total revenue and total costs meet is referred to as the 'breakeven point'. Breakeven analysis is undertaken prior to the launch of a new project or new venture in order to assess the projected financial viability of the activity. For undertakings that are up and running, breakeven analysis helps managers assess whether financial targets are likely to be met.

breaking bulk The process of buying large or bulk quantities of a product from a supplier and breaking this into smaller quantities for resale to, for example, a retailer. This process is traditionally known as wholesaling.

break-up value ➤asset value.

bridging finance A short-term loan provided by a ➤venture capital provider while a company is seeking alternative finance, e.g. by ➤flotation.

broker An intermediary between a buyer and a seller in a highly organized market (e.g. a ➤stockbroker, a commodity broker or a market operator) working on his own account, e.g. as a pawnbroker or bill broker.

brokerage The commission charged by a ➤broker.

broker–dealer A person or organization buying and selling ➤securities, ➤commodities and ➤contracts, both on his own account (i.e. as ➤principal) and as agent for clients. Prior to the ➤Big Bang in the UK, ➤brokers on the ➤London Stock Exchange were not permitted to act in this dual capacity because of the possibility of conflicts of interest. ➤➤market maker.

B2B marketing ➤business-to-business marketing.

B2C marketing ➤business-to-consumer marketing.

BTG A British public limited company (plc) operating in the field of ➤**technology transfer,** ➤**licensing** and intellectual property. This was formerly a government body established after the Second World War to try to capture economic wealth from research being undertaken in public laboratories and universities. It was previously known as the National Enterprise Board and then the National Research Development Corporation. It became a public authority in 1981 and a plc in 1993.

bubble ➤speculative bubble.

bucket shop A term of US origin meaning an unregistered and illegal firm of ➤stockbrokers, but now used to refer to any low-price sales operation, e.g. bucket-shop travel agencies that sell discounted air tickets. A 'boiler room' is a share-pushing operation selling dubious ➤stock by telephone.

buffer stock A quantity of resources either at the input or output side of an operation to minimize disruptions of the complete system. Sometimes referred to as a 'safety stock'. All operations are subject to environmental changes and sometimes this can disrupt supplies within an operation system. To prevent this, buffer stocks are used to enable operations to continue. Any interruptions or shortages in the system will initially be absorbed by the buffer stock.

building society (UK) A financial institution engaged in the provision of ➤mortgages and other financial products, deriving its funds from ➤deposits by the general public. Building societies are non-profit-making bodies (➤mutual). Interest is paid on deposits at rates varying with amount and term of retention. Under the UK Building Societies Act 1986 wider consumer services were permitted for building societies, including the provision of unsecured personal loans, the management of ➤unit trusts, the operation of estate agencies, activity in insurance broking and the sale of ➤personal pensions. These changes enabled the societies to compete on more equal terms with ➤commercial banks and other ➤financial institutions. The Building Societies Act 1997 *inter alia* reaffirmed the principle that the major business of building societies was the provision of mortgages on residential property. Equal voting rights were accorded to borrowers and lenders (depositors). The range of activities of building societies was widened in that any business, except certain forms of financial trading, was permissible provided it was set out in a society's memorandum. Recently a number of building societies have given up mutual status and become listed companies, such as Alliance and Leicester, Halifax and Northern Rock. In mid 1997 the UK government announced that the building societies industry was to be placed under the supervision of the Financial Services Authority, rather than the Building Societies Commission. ➤**Financial Services Act;** ➤➤**savings and loan associations.**

bull A speculator who buys ➤**securities** in the belief that prices will rise and that they will be able to sell them again later at a profit. The antonym of ➤**bear**. The market is said to be 'bullish' when it is generally anticipated that prices will rise.

bull market A period of time during which ➤**stock market** prices are rising. Antonym of ➤**bear market.**

bundling The provision of more than one product or service to a customer at an inclusive price, e.g. 'free' life insurance with a loan. ➤**pricing policy.**

burn rate The rate at which a company consumes its capital in order to stay in business. The phrase came to be commonly used at the time of the dot com bubble in 1999, when start-up loss-making companies simply burned up their initial capital before having to close down.

business angel A person who provides advice and equity to new and start-up firms. Usually these people have made their own money as entrepreneurs. Such individuals are able to assess the potential of new business ventures and offer much needed expertise and hands-on support and advice. Business angels bridge the gap between the personal savings of entrepreneurs and the 'second round' of financing which venture capitalists are able to offer. In the US, they have helped to fuel the self-sustaining innovation and economic growth of the past decade – especially for Internet and dot com start-ups. Traditionally, banks have been the source of finance for new business ventures; however, many banks are unwilling to lend against intangible assets, and many of the Internet firms have few tangible assets; hence, recourse to business angels.

business cycle The name given to the pattern of short-term fluctuations in national income. In the medium to long term, an economy can grow at a ➤trend growth rate. But no economy has avoided following cyclical ups and downs around that trend level. The business cycle is typically seen as a result of fluctuations in the overall amount of spending in the economy – or the quantity of demand. There are numerous theories as to why spending may fluctuate: perhaps most ubiquitous have been accounts of the business cycle as an investment phenomenon. Companies may have a desired stock of capital, and their investment spending may move up or down very considerably, depending on whether they are above or below that desired stock. Confidence and the performance of financial markets can swing from the exuberant to the depressed, causing savings and consumer spending to fluctuate. Also, economic policy can create swings in spending. Some economists have suggested the business cycle is simply a result of more-or-less random shocks to the real economy – in the form of unpredictable technological developments or other surprises. Particular business or industry sectors tend to be affected in different ways and at different stages of the cycle, e.g. building industries are often affected quickly and dramatically by an economic downturn. ➤➤output gap.

business development function ➤sales.

business ethic The moral value which governs business behaviour, and restrains companies from pursuing the interests of shareholders at the expense of all other interests. Economists tend to think of firms as nakedly pursuing the maximization of profits, but in practice one observes that there are other values which appear to matter to companies; not all decisions can actively be seen as profit-maximizing, such as donating to charity, for example. It is also obvious that cultural pressures – often from within companies – shape the limits of acceptable behaviour. And what is reasonable behaviour in one country may not be required of a firm in another.

Some people attempt to rescue the idea of profit-maximization by saying that in the long term, firms do maximize profit by behaving as good citizens; but this is such a broad notion of profit-maximization that it is rather vacuous. There is every reason to believe that firms, which are run by human beings after all, are subject to conflicting pressures of selfishness and social behaviour. ➤➤organizational culture.

Towards the end of the 1990s, when protests against multinational companies became popular, a fashion towards *corporate social responsibility* emerged, with companies falling over themselves to demonstrate their ethical credentials. This partly appeared to be a response to protestors, partly a genuine attempt by companies to use their influence for the social good, and partly as a trendy means of attaching attractive values and positive attributes to brands. ➤➤**corporate image**.

business finance The provision of money for commercial use. When relating specifically to companies it may also be referred to as 'corporate finance'. The short-term ➤**capital** of a business may come from ➤**retained earnings** or from ➤**factoring**, bank borrowings (➤**banking**), other borrowings, ➤**bills of exchange**, trade creditors (➤**trade credit**) and expense creditors. These are all sources of short-term capital that in theory should be used only for investment in relatively liquid ➤**assets** (➤➤**liquidity**), so that it is readily available to discharge the liability if necessary. Sources of long-term capital include ➤**reserves** and ➤**depreciation provisions**, ➤**equity** share capital and long-term loans such as ➤**debentures** and ➤**term loans**.

business judgement The act of evaluation and decision-making by managers, undertaken either collectively or individually. In most decision-making it is unlikely that all the necessary information will be available, and therefore there will inevitably be an element of judgement. This will usually be based upon a combination of experience, logic, theory and expertise. ➤➤**business stimulation; decision rule**.

business performance indicator ➤**key performance measure**.

business plan A formal document used by third parties to help them systematically examine the merits of a business proposal. Usually such business plans are presented to banks or other financial institutions for ➤**venture capital** to secure investment for the proposal. The plan would normally be organized as a report with the following headings: introduction, the product/service offered, objectives, marketing research, competition, distribution, personnel, organization, premises, legal formalities and financial matters.

business process redesign (BPR) A term used to describe the fundamental rethinking and reorganization of the business's processes to improve the overall effectiveness of the business. The underlying principle of the BPR approach to organizing a business's operations is that they should be organized around the process(es) that add value. BPR has its critics who argue there is nothing new in it and it is just another management fad. Supporters of the technique argue that it is based upon a few simple principles that take advantage of information technologies and in so doing help businesses to improve performance. ➤**re-engineering**.

business process re-engineering ➤re-engineering.

business simulation A tool used in management education, training and development to help students and managers 'learn by doing' – to learn through simulated experiences. An example is MARKSTRAT, a very popular marketing simulation in which teams compete, make investment decisions, consider how to position and support a portfolio of products, and have the opportunity to launch new products. This simulation was devised by Jean-Claude Larreche and Hubert Gatignon (*MARK-*

STRAT: a marketing strategy game, 1977). Business simulations are used in many other contexts, including mergers and acquisitions, strategic investment decisions, project management, and commercial negotiations.

Learning by the participants comes from their direct experiences as players in the game. Typically, the simulation is interactive and dynamic, with firms competing and making decisions in pursuit of a goal. Participants must think about the consequences of their actions and the responses of their competitors. They must cope with unexpected outcomes and a degree of ambiguity. They may have different starting positions, to reflect the fact that there are no level playing fields in business. Apart from the substantive learning that occurs (about marketing, mergers, etc.), participants also learn about management processes. Through having to bond together to make successive decisions and achieve a goal, they have a chance to reflect on group decision-making processes. ➤**decision rule; group development; group-think.**

Given the difficulty of studying management processes (e.g. problems of gaining access to organizations, the time horizons over which decisions are made, concerns about commercial confidentiality, etc.), business simulations also have been used as laboratories for management research. Studies have been conducted to see how managers make decisions, bond together, negotiate, take on roles, sense competitive threats, assess market risk, make use of information, etc. Increasingly, real business organizations are self-consciously reflecting on these issues, as a way to improve their own learning and understanding. ➤**organizational learning.**

The precedents for this form of learning go back to childhood. When children play (whether it is with building bricks, cardboard boxes or computer games) they are experimenting, acquiring information, and testing out ideas. These can be seen as small-scale 'what if' experiments, e.g. 'What if I stack ten bricks on top of one another – do they rise, shift, fall, or stay there?' Moreover, because this is playful, the learning can be internalized reasonably painlessly (and it is memorable). Another source of precedents is to be found in military training, where peacetime exercises help personnel to get into the mindset of opponents, gain on-the-job practice by concentrating experience into a short timeframe, and test out alternative strategies without causing undue harm.

Despite their popularity, there are perils in using business simulations. Good simulations create a convincing reality of their own, but this is only ever going to be an imperfect representation of external reality. Participants can spend time trying to decode the simulation (especially if it is a computer-based one), rather than simply playing the game. The desire to win can become overwhelming, whereas the learning is in the quality of decision-making rather than in the winning. ➤**simulation.**

business strategy The plans and actions necessary for a business to achieve a particular aim. This will involve the development and use of resources to deliver services and products in a way which users find valuable. In addition, the firm must meet the financial and other constraints imposed on it by key stakeholders such as shareholders, governments, suppliers and customers. There are many different schools of thought on this vast subject of strategy. Prior to the 1960s the subject was known as business policy. It was in business schools in the US during the 1960s that strategic management emerged as a distinct subject. ➤**strategic management; strategic planning.**

business-to-business (B2B) **marketing** Marketing activity where the focus is interbusiness buying and selling, e.g. the case of a management consultancy providing services to a bank. The tendency in B2B marketing is to stress the importance of relationship-building, key account management, face-to-face meetings, commercial negotiation and the establishment of business networks and alliances. ➤**customer relationship management; relationship marketing**. The implication is that B2B transactions are larger-scale than consumer transactions, and therefore they demand a more involved approach. While this is often the case, not all B2B transactions are complex. Many are straight rebuys, e.g. the re-ordering of photocopy paper or a replacement printer cartridge.

business-to-consumer (B2C) **marketing** Marketing activity where the focus is final consumers, e.g. purchasing of laundry detergent and confectionery by a household. Typically, there are a large number of consumers and mass marketing techniques have to be employed (notably, the ➤**advertising** and ➤**promotion** of ➤**brands**). This, however, is beginning to change, and many organizations involved in B2C marketing are embracing principles from ➤**customer relationship management**. This has been facilitated by advances in technology.

buy-back 1. An agreement to repurchase something on certain conditions, e.g. an entrepreneur may agree to sell ➤**shares** in his business to a ➤**venture capital** company on the understanding that they may be bought back at a certain price if financial performance targets are achieved. **2.** A company may buy back its own shares and cancel them so as to reduce the number of shares at issue and improve. ➤**earnings per share**.

buyer behaviour The revealed actions of consumers, including purchase (exchange), repeat-purchase and purchase-related actions (such as making word-of-mouth recommendations). An understanding of these actions is of central importance in business because for trading organizations they are the main source of sales, revenue and profits (though there also may be some non-consumer-based sources of financial return such as property sales or treasury trading).

The basic unit of analysis is the 'purchase occasion' – an event where exchange occurs between the buyer and seller. Individual buyers (or households) have the opportunity to buy a ➤**brand** on one or more purchase occasions, over some prespecified time period such as a week or a year. There are two components: 'purchase incidence' (the number of purchase occasions or events) and 'brand choice' (the choice of brand on each purchase occasion). While analysis might start with data about the buying behaviour of individual buyers, for most practical purposes data must be aggregated for a population of interest – this may be the total national population or a more narrowly defined population or segment. ➤**segmentation; target audience**.

In ➤**marketing research**, considerable use is made of a number of aggregated buyer behaviour measures, notably:

(1) Penetration. The number of buyers buying the brand at least once in the period, divided by the total number of buyers in the population of interest.
(2) Average purchase frequency. The average number of purchases per buyer during a given period of time.
(3) Sales (per hundred buyers). Penetration multiplied by the average purchase

frequency. Sales could alternatively be grossed-up for the whole population, rather than per hundred buyers. Moreover, instead of referring to purchase occasions, sales could be expressed in weight units (i.e. taking pack sizes into account), or in monetary terms, i.e. by taking price into account. Across buyers, there will be variation in average purchase frequencies – from light buyers (those buying only once or twice during a given period) to heavy buyers (those buying more often than the average). Typically, there are many light buyers and few heavy buyers (the ➤**80 : 20 rule**).

(4) Share of category requirements. The share over a period of the average buyer's total requirements that are accounted for by the specific brand, measured as the average purchase frequency divided by the total amount of the product category bought in the period by buyers of the brand.

(5) Duplicate buying. The proportion of buyers buying one brand and who also buy specified other brands. Typically, for any lengthy period, buyers of one brand will buy other brands at least some of the time. This has implications for how ➤**consumer loyalty** is conceived.

(6) Repeat buyers. The percentage of buyers who buy in one period and who also buy in another equal-length period. If a hundred consumers bought a particular brand in a 4-week period, and fifty of them also bought in the next 4-week period, there would be fifty repeat-buyers (a 50 per cent repeat-buying rate). The second equal-length period is typically an adjacent period, but it need not be, e.g. the buying by consumers might be assessed in a 4-week pre-advertising period and a 4-week post-advertising period, but not during the 6-week campaign itself.

(7) New buyers. The percentage of buyers in a second equal-length period who did not buy in the first equal-length period. Note that 'new buyers' may not be new in a strict sense – buyers may have had previous experience with the product category, and even the brand, but just not in the study period.

(8) Lapsed buyers. The percentage of buyers from the first period who do not buy in a second equal-length period. Again, lapsed buyers are not necessarily lapsed in a strict sense, but they are for the period of study.

The choice of period length is an important consideration for all these measures. As a rule of thumb, it should be at least the length of the average interpurchase cycle, i.e. at least as long as the time for people, on average, to make another purchase from the product category. Thus, for breakfast cereals, 2-week periods might be studied, whereas for car purchases the relevant period might be 3 years. This form of analysis is most appropriate for ➤**packaged goods** and other repeat-purchase markets, e.g. consumer services, transportation, etc.

For consumer durables, where interest is in the uptake of brands, possibly for the first and only time, key measures are:

(1) Trial purchase. The proportion of people in the population who have bought the brand at least once thus far (6 months since launch, say).

(2) Adoption. Also defined as the proportion of people in the population who have bought the brand at least once thus far; however, implicit in the word 'adoption' is the idea that people have consciously chosen the brand, not simply tried it.

By examining trial purchase or adoption each month from launch, the growth of penetration can be plotted. Usually this describes an S-shaped growth curve. ➤**diffusion of innovations**.

These measures are routinely collected by market research agencies using ➤**consumer panels** and automated data-capture systems at the point of sale. ➤➤**A C Nielsen Corporation**. It is possible to describe and model patterns of buyer behaviour with them, either to understand a market ('How do people repeat-buy in the underwear market?'), or to provide benchmarks ('Are rates of repeat-buying for our brand lower than expected, higher, or about right?'). A classic synthesis of thinking in this area was written by A S C Ehrenberg (*Repeat-Buying*, 1972), in which he showed that many aspects of purchase incidence are predictable (using the Negative Binomial Distribution model). This work was subsequently extended to show that purchase incidence and brand choice are predictable (using the NBD–Dirichlet model). Because of the wide availability of consumer panel data, both models have been extensively tested and verified.

In the field of ➤**consumer behaviour** an attempt is made to describe and explain why certain behaviours are observed. The focus is on individual decision-making, starting with need/problem recognition, moving on to consider ➤**information search**, alternative evaluation and selection, purchase, post-purchase and, finally, satisfaction/dissatisfaction. Within this framework, it is possible to see how one person's behaviour may have an impact on others. For example, word-of-mouth recommendation for a consumer durable may become an important element in another person's information search process (especially if the source of the recommendation is seen as credible). This may outweigh the impact of formal marketing communications like ➤**advertising** and ➤**direct marketing**.

Armed with an understanding of these antecedents of buyer behaviour, it is possible to model the decisions of individuals (both their purchase incidence and their brand choices). This is the goal in ➤**choice modelling**.

buyers' bargaining power The extent of power and influence of buyers in an industry. In ➤**Porter**'s model for analysing competitors and industries – the so-called five forces model – he uses the term 'bargaining power of buyers'. This power is said to increase if:

(1) There are few of them.
(2) The products available in an industry are similar (such as commodities).
(3) The buyer is able to integrate backwards and take over the role of the seller.
(4) The firm's selling price is of negligible importance compared to the total costs faced by the buyer.

buying-in share ➤incorporation.

buy-out Purchase by the management of the shares of its company, so making it the owner; or purchase by a company of its shares held by the public, so making the company a private company. ➤**management buy-out**.

bylaw ➤memorandum of association.

by-product A product that is produced via a production process for which it is not the main purpose. For example, sawmills produce timber for use in building, but sawdust and woodchip are by-products that are now sold as products in their own right.

C

CAC 40 (*Compagnie des Agents de Change 40 Index*) An index designed to reflect movements in the share prices of 40 companies traded on the ➤**Paris** *Bourse*. It was given a base level of 1,000 in December 1987.

CAD ➤computer aided design.

call option ➤option.

call plan The sequence of sales visits that a salesperson makes. Because sales calls are so costly, a key issue in salesforce management is the optimization of call plans so as to minimize costs and maximize sales revenue. Marketing ➤**decision-support systems** exist to assist in this process. A further issue is to ensure the salesperson concentrates effort on the most important prospects, even though they may not be the easiest of calls. In ➤**business-to-consumer marketing** sales calls often have been replaced by telemarketing, but face-to-face sales calls remain important in ➤**business-to-business marketing.** ➤➤**sales**.

CAM ➤computer aided manufacturing.

cannibalization The phenomenon where a new brand extension or line extension takes sales away from established brands that are owned by the same organization. This will occur when both brands are bought by the same group of consumers. This is a severe problem if it's unintended and if the shift is from high-margin brands to lower-margin ones. For example, it might have been hoped that a new cheaper brand would appeal to a more down-market segment of consumers, but if the traditional buyers of the established brand are price-sensitive and trade down to the new cheaper brand, there will be a squeeze on margins. Cannibalization is hard to avoid completely because, to a degree, consumer segments within a product category are often overlapping. The issue, therefore, is whether the gains from launching new brand extensions and line extensions outweigh the cannibalization effects. Systems for ➤**category management** address this issue directly, whereas traditional ➤**brand management** practices encourage managers to pursue independent goals rather than make allowance for cannibalization.

cap 1. An abbreviation for ➤**capitalization**, as in ➤**small cap stocks. 2.** A limit or ceiling, usually setting the maximum ➤**interest** that may be charged on a loan. Where there is also a 'floor' or lower limit to protect the lender, the arrangement may be described as a 'collar'.

capacity planning The process of planning the use of a firm's operational resources. Every firm will have facilities that have a maximum processing capability. For example, a restaurant may have ten tables and thirty seats. But its capacity in any one evening will be far higher than thirty. The restaurant manager will have a capacity plan linked to the opening times of the restaurant. It is a major objective for operations managers to try to balance the capacity of the firm's combined resources with that of demand for its products and services. This activity is known as 'capacity planning and control'. Achieving the appropriate balance between capacity and demand can generate optimum profits for the firm. Similarly, the wrong balance can lead to wastage and missed opportunities (if there is under-use of capacity) or dissatisfied customers (if there is over-use of capacity).

capacity requirements plan (CRP) A plan to project the production volumes necessary from individual work stations, machines or employees in a given period. Such a plan is usually generated from a ➤**manufacturing resource planning** (MRP II) system. Indeed, the CRP is an integral part of the MRP II system.

CAPI ➤computer-assisted personal interviewing.

capital In general, the accumulated (i.e. unspent) wealth of a business or individual that is capable of generating income, but the term has no precise meaning out of context. Nominal share capital, for example, is the ➤**par value** of funds subscribed by shareholders. ➤➤**capital employed; paid-up capital; shareholders' equity; undercapitalized**. Capital may be in the form of money or of physical assets.

capital adequacy A measure of the value of the capital owned by the shareholders of a financial institution, relative to the total amount the institution has lent out. An institution with lots of its own capital is generally regarded as safer than one with little capital, because if loans are not paid back, there is more of a cushion for the institution to fall back on.

Various regulatory bodies set minimum capital requirements for ➤**financial institutions** such as ➤**unit trust** managers. Until recently, capital adequacy requirements were set only at a national level, e.g. ➤**Federal Reserve System; liquidity ratio**. The increasing globalization of the world financial system now requires international agreement on capital adequacy standards. In December 1987, 11 countries and the then European Community signed an international agreement for capital adequacy for ➤**commercial banks** under the auspices of the Bank for International Settlements (BIS) (the Basle Agreement). The agreement provided for common prudential ratios and a common definition of risk-adjusted assets. Banks operating in signatory countries now need to have capital (➤**equity** and long-term ➤**debt**) equal to 8 per cent of risk-adjusted assets. The percentage adequacy requirement can vary with an individual bank's exposure to foreign exchange risks and ➤**derivatives**.

Experience of the application of the agreement and changes in capital markets have led the BIS to propose new standards for introduction by 2005. The changes include the addition of a minimum capital requirement, more categories of defined risk, regulatory supervision and more disclosure by banks. ➤➤**banking directives**.

capital asset pricing model (CAPM) A model of the market in financial ➤**assets** which assumes that, in equilibrium, asset prices will adjust to ensure that the return on an asset compensates investors for *systematic risk*, i.e. risk that cannot be eliminated by portfolio diversification. ➤➤**portfolio theory**. The model has dominated economists' understanding of the pricing of shares. Under simplifying assumptions, the following propositions hold: (a) everybody will hold a portfolio of assets which is as diversified as possible, as this minimizes risk; (b) this means the risk of each individual asset will be unimportant because the ups and downs of assets' performances will cancel out; (c) there will, nevertheless, be some remaining market risk – the risk of factors that affect all the assets together; (d) this risk depends on how closely the assets' performances coincide; (e) the risk any particular asset adds to a portfolio will thus depend only on how closely its performance tracks that of the rest of the portfolio; (f) the price of assets which closely track other assets will be low because they are unattractive – when other assets do well, they do well and vice versa (➤**beta**), and (g) the price of assets which hardly move at all with the market will be high, because they pay out good returns when they are needed most.

The CAPM is a development of this chain of reasoning. It can be used to calculate an expected return on any particular asset, as a function of the rate of return on riskless assets, plus a risk premium based on the degree to which the asset tracks the market. It thus provides one basis for assessing a cost of capital.

capital budgeting The process by which companies appraise investment decisions, in particular by which capital resources are allocated to specific projects. Capital budgeting requires firms to account for the time value of money, and project risk, using a variety of more-or-less formal techniques. ➤**cost of capital; internal rate of return; net present value; payback.**

capital, cost of The ➤**rate of interest** paid on the ➤**capital employed** in a business. Since capital will be drawn from a variety of sources, it will be an average cost derived from a weighted average of the costs of each source, including ➤**equity**. The average cost of existing sources of capital may be higher or lower than the marginal cost, i.e. the cost of additional capital. ➤➤**weighted average cost of capital.**

capital employed The ➤**capital** in use in a business. There is no universally agreed definition of the term. It is sometimes taken to mean ➤**net assets** (i.e. fixed plus current assets minus current ➤**liabilities**), but more usually ➤**bank loans** and ➤**overdrafts** are included and other adjustments made for the purposes of calculating the return on net capital employed (➤**rate of return**), such as the exclusion of intangible assets and the revaluation of ➤**trade investments** at market prices. ➤➤**investment appraisal.**

capital expenditure The purchase of fixed ➤**assets** (e.g. plant and equipment), expenditure on ➤**trade investments** or acquisitions of other businesses and expenditure on current assets, e.g. ➤**stocks.**

capital gain A realized increase in the value of a capital ➤**asset**, as when a ➤**share** is sold for more than the price at which it was purchased. Strictly speaking, the term refers to capital appreciation outside the normal course of business. In the UK and many other countries, capital gains are subject to capital gains tax (CGT).

capital gearing (UK) Bank borrowings and other ➤**debt** as a percentage of ➤**net tangible assets.** ➤**gearing.**

capitalization ➤**market capitalization.**

capitalization issue ➤**bonus issue.**

capital market The market for longer-term loanable funds as distinct from the ➤**money market**, which deals in short-term funds. There is no clearcut distinction between the two markets, although in principle capital market loans are used by industry and commerce for fixed ➤**investment** and acquisitions. The capital market is an increasingly international one and in each country consists of all those institutions that canalize the supply of and demand for capital, including the ➤**banking** system, the ➤**stock exchange**, companies providing ➤**insurance** and other ➤**financial intermediaries**.

capital reserves Undistributable ➤**reserves**. Some items in the reserves of a company cannot be distributed because they are part of the equity capital of the business, e.g. sums received from the issue of new shares at a price in excess of the ➤**nominal value**.

capital structure The make-up of the ➤**capital employed** in a business or other organization. The most prominent characteristic of capital structure will be the relationship of ➤**debt** to ➤**equity** (➤**gearing**), the use of short- and long-term borrowing, ➤**retained earnings** and ➤**off-balance-sheet finance**.

CAPM ➤**capital asset pricing model**.

captive A company providing ➤**investment** or other services that is owned by an institution offering related services, e.g. an ➤**insurance company** or ➤**venture capital** company owned by a ➤**bank**, or a ➤**hire-purchase** firm owned by a car manufacturer.

capture theory ➤**regulatory capture**.

carried interest A share in, or ➤**option** on ➤**equity** in, or the value of, a ➤**venture capital** investment fund granted to the managers of that fund.

cartel An arrangement between otherwise competing producers to act in collusion with the goal of raising prices and collective profits. A cartel attempts to create ➤**monopoly**-type conditions in what should be a competitive industry – with participants restraining the amount they produce in order to keep supply down and thus prices high at the expense of consumers. The classic explicit cartel is the Organization of Petroleum Exporting Countries (OPEC), which sets production quotas in order to keep oil prices high.

In most developed countries, cartels are outlawed, and agreements between companies that could have cartel-type effects are banned, or at least have to be registered and sanctioned by the authorities. ➤**competition policy; Office of Fair Trading**.

Cartels do not have to be explicit, based upon written agreements; sometimes nods and winks, based on limited social contact is sufficient to get them going. The determination of the authorities, particularly in the US, to outlaw the threat of such behaviour has scared some competitors in high-profile industries from seeing each other lest any contact should arouse suspicion.

But while it seems that cartels can be created easily, and while it is usually in the interest of producers to arrange a cartel, in practice it turns out to be hard to maintain cartel discipline. The essential reason for this is that if one firm, Bloggs Widgets, can persuade its rivals to restrain output and keep market prices high, it then pays Bloggs Widgets to 'cheat' on the agreement and produce a lot, which it can sell at the higher market price. In other words, it pays the members to join a cartel, but it also pays them to break its rules. The tendency has been obvious in OPEC, which sporadically finds itself having to reset its quotas as discipline breaks down. The economics of ➤game theory, and the simple caricature of the ➤prisoners' dilemma have been used to model the incentives of cartels.

cash flow The movement of money into (cash inflow) and out of (cash outflow) a business. It is generally defined as net ➤profit plus ➤depreciation (net cash flow) but may be used more loosely to include all cash movements. ➤discounted cash flow.

category management A system of management whereby each product category within the organization is controlled by a particular category manager. This manager makes decisions about, and has direct profit responsibility for, all brands and lines within the category. Thus, for a producer of white goods, all brands and lines of refrigerator made by that company would be the responsibility of one category manager. Procter & Gamble is credited with introducing the system in the late 1980s as an improvement over ➤brand management (where managers for each brand act as independent entrepreneurs, without regard to the viability of other brands owned by the company in the same or related product categories). From the producer's viewpoint, a benefit of category management is that it puts them on an equal footing with retail buyers (who, typically, make listing decisions for a product category and are much less concerned about whether to stock a particular brand).

CATI ➤computer-assisted telephone interviewing.

cause-related marketing The case where a business organization links itself with a cause, in the hope that benefits will flow both to the business and the cause. A 'cause' in this instance is any not-for-profit organization, e.g. a charity, arts body or sports association. The cause must be seen as consistent with: (a) the image of the business; (b) with characteristics of the ➤brand, and (c) the audience demographics of both the business and the cause. ➤➤congruency theory. Thus, a Johnson & Johnson line of first-aid products has been linked with support for the American Red Cross. American Express has supported artistic events where it knows card-holders have an interest. These forms of sponsorship are distinct from selfless philanthropy, in that there is a clear business goal associated with cause-related marketing (an improved ➤corporate image, changed ➤attitudes to the organization and greater ➤consumer loyalty). Although widely practised, there are dangers for all parties in cause-related marketing. A portion of consumers may question, or even disapprove of, the link. In subtle ways the link may change the mission and conduct of the not-for-profit cause, it may change the attitude of people to the cause and alter their pattern of charitable giving.

caveat emptor Legal expression meaning 'let the buyer beware'. Generally speaking, the law presumes that a person uses common sense when buying goods, and if that person suffers loss through his own fault he will not find the law sympathetic.

CEDEL ➤*Centrale de Livraison de Valeurs Mobilières.*

cellular manufacturing A type of layout for an operation, where all the resources for each distinct part of the operation are placed together. After being processed in a particular such cell, the transformed resources may go on to another cell. The type of layout selected for an operation will largely depend on the volume and variety required. For example, an aircraft manufacturer may use a cellular layout to process the servicing of gearboxes for helicopters. This enables a cell to receive the worn gearbox, repair or replace the worn parts and reassemble, rather than passing each activity on to another station as would occur in a ➤**production line** layout.

The principle of cellular layout is also applied beyond manufacturing operations. Many supermarkets now have 'lunch' areas for those customers who enter the store only to purchase lunch. An area or cell is set aside in the store to provide all the products that customers may wish to purchase for lunch such as sandwiches, yoghurts, crisps and drinks. ➤➤**process layout**.

central bank   A bankers' bank at the centre of a country's monetary system. ➤**monetary policy**. Central banks act as ➤**lenders of last resort**, lead the interest rate structure, accept ➤**deposits**, make ➤**loans** to the ➤**commercial banks** and in many countries supervise the ➤**banking** system. The central bank also acts as the government's own bank, sometimes manages the national debt and controls the note issue. Central banks deal with each other in conducting transfers of currency and bullion between countries and are heavily involved, with finance ministers, in international economic relations. ➤**Bank of England; European Central Bank; Federal Reserve System**.

central bank discount rate   The interest rate at which a ➤**central bank** will ➤**discount** eligible bills and ➤**Treasury bills**.

Centrale de Livraison de Valeurs Mobilières (*CEDEL*)   One of the two settlement systems for ➤**Eurobond** trading established in the late 1960s, CEDEL is a clearing house, an agency for dividend collection and a provider of capital to market dealers. It collaborates with ➤**SWIFT** in organizing settlements. Its owners are a number of international banks. ➤➤**Euroclear**.

certainty equivalent   A sum of money that, if received with total certainty, would have the exact same value as a risky proposition. For example, imagine a risky investment that offers the prospect of £20 million of profit, or £10 million of loss with about equal proportions. The ➤**expected value** of the project is the average return (£5 million). However, most people would rather have a certain return of £5 million, than a risky return with an expected value of £5 million. The certainty equivalent is the precise amount that would have the equivalent utility to the risky £5 million. It may be, say, £4 million.

In ➤**capital budgeting**, the certainty equivalent can be an important concept in accounting for the cost of risk across time. Risk is a cost that has to be accounted for. In assessing the value of a potential investment, for example, which generates uncertain cash flows over time, the correct procedure is to estimate the certainty equivalents of those cash flows, and then to discount them using a risk-free rate of return to arrive at a ➤**net present value**. This is not the procedure that is always used, however. Sometimes, financial analysts use the expected values of the cash flows, and discount them at a high rate of interest that reflects the cost of risk. This latter method yields a poor assessment of a project whose risk profile changes over time. For example, a project which involves risky product testing early on, but which is then relatively safe, should not be appraised using a high rate of interest for all yearly cash flows.

certificate of deposit (CD) A ➤negotiable claim issued by a bank in return for a term ➤deposit. The document is normally a ➤bearer security. The advantage of the CD to depositors is that the latter can place their money in a fixed-term or long-maturity deposit, so obtaining a higher rate of interest while knowing that they can sell the CD in the ➤secondary market whenever they may need to recover the money. The advantage to purchasers in the secondary market is that they can invest in and divest the instrument at will. The advantage to the bank is that it can acquire deposits perhaps not otherwise forthcoming and can hold them. CDs can be sold and resold at a ➤discount, so varying the ➤yield.

CDs were first issued in the US in 1961 and gained immediate favour. After the partial suspension in 1970, and final suspension in 1973, of the application to CDs of ➤Regulation Q, the market grew rapidly. CDs were issued in ➤Eurodollar form in London in 1966. Sterling CDs were issued in 1968. The market in CDs is made up by the ➤discount houses and the ➤interbank market in London and by the banks in the US. ➤Special drawing right CDs have been issued in London, and a substantial yen CD market has developed in Japan, after introduction in 1979. In 1983 the US Tax Act required all dollar CDs to be registered, i.e. not in bearer form. ➤Futures contracts in CDs are traded in the US and on the ➤London International Financial Futures Exchange (LIFFE).

Chandler, Alfred D A distinguished economic historian who, in a series of major books, has charted the development of the large enterprise and the evolution of management structures from the second half of the nineteenth century. *Strategy and Structure* (1962) came first, followed by *The Invisible Hand* (1977). This second book dealt with the evolution of modern business in the US (the visible hand of management replacing Adam Smith's invisible hand of the market). *Scale and Scope* (1990), appropriately a 900-page book, compared the evolution of business in the US, Germany and the UK. Chandler has been criticized for applying to Europe an ethnocentric model based on the multidivisional corporation of the US (e.g. Du Pont and General Motors) and of neglecting the roles of alternative structures and smaller firms. However, in his more recent book written with Franco Amatori and Takashi Hikino, *Big Business and the Wealth of Nations* (1997) which covers many more countries, there is more recognition of the scope for organizational diversity. Alfred D Chandler Jr, who is a Pulitzer prizewinner, is a professor at the Graduate School of Business at Harvard University.

change agents ➤change-management programme.

change management A particular aspect of management that focuses on ensuring a firm responds to changes in the environment in which it operates. The need for change arises from the development of new products, the entry of new competitors, shifts in consumer tastes, and from alterations in the cultural, political, economic and legal frameworks within which a firm operates. There are two basic approaches to the management of change. One is to forecast all environmental changes relevant to the firm that might occur and then predict how the organization will be affected by them. The other is to list all the firm's major functions and follow this with an analysis of all the environmental factors that might affect these functions. Formal ➤change-management programmes are now widely used by organizations.

change-management programme A plan and process to implement and manage change within an organization. Change results in new roles for individuals and new business practices for groups within the organization, e.g. project-based cross-functional teams might replace functional units. It is recognized that this can be stressful, may cause anxiety and lower employee morale. Therefore, organizations will try to plan and manage change through the use of special programmes and change agents, i.e. people who can serve as catalysts for change and take on responsibility for managing it.

The pressure to change comes from many factors external to the organization, e.g. technology, competition, economic shocks and social trends. It also comes from the business sector itself, e.g. from investor demands and the desire to make managers more accountable, both of which tend to focus attention on changes to secure performance improvements. Organizations respond with initiatives to change people (e.g. reshaping employees' ➤attitudes to work), structures (e.g. flatter organizational hierarchies), systems (e.g. the use of new technologies) or environments, e.g. going to 'hot-seating' in an open-plan office. These initiatives may form part of a broader process, as with ➤total quality management, business process ➤re-engineering, and ➤downsizing.

A degree of resistance to change is normal, because some people will see change as damaging, disruptive, stressful, and anxiety-producing. Mostly this is described in a negative way (people are seen as having unreasonable fears of the unknown or groups are criticized for protecting their 'turf' at the expense of wider organizational goals), but a degree of scepticism may be healthy because not all changes are necessary ('Why break what isn't broken?') or productive ('The chairs have been rearranged, but nothing has really changed'). In particular, the downside of continual change needs to be faced. Continual change means that there is the danger that nobody is ever clear of their ➤role in the organization, there is never any prospect of consolidation, nor of 'refreezing' to ensure changes are fully accepted.

Various techniques are used to help implement change-management programmes, including consultative and participatory processes, team building within and across units, ➤t-groups, internal communications, and ➤negotiation. However, a certain amount of change is likely to be introduced through compulsion, manipulation or coercion. A degree of ➤politicking by change agents and those who resist change is always to be expected.

channel of distribution The way goods and services are brought to market. In developed societies it is usual for ➤intermediaries to be used, notably importers/exporters, wholesalers and retailers. However, direct purchasing by sellers from producers has experienced a revival with the growth of on-line shopping. ➤interactive electronic marketing. A process of ➤disintermediation has been observed, although there are also signs of new intermediaries emerging. The number of channels used, and the seamlessness of exchanges between these channels, are two key issues that impact on the efficiency of a channel of distribution. Efficiency has also been related to the way one channel member exercises ➤power over another, something that varies from one business format to another, e.g. the way a retail franchise chain operates differs from a solely owned retail chain.

chaos theory A concept concerned with the highly complicated and unpredictable outcomes that can be generated by relatively simple systems. The central feature of chaotic systems is the 'butterfly effect'; the idea that a small impact event (such as the flapping of a butterfly's wings) can have effects that ripple out (air movements from the wings) which themselves have effects which ripple out, and which can ultimately have a big impact (causing a hurricane many steps down the chain). Systems such as the weather, and often the behaviour of financial markets, which appear to be chaotic are not random – they can conform to quite ordered rules (and may even be written down in the form of a few simple non-linear equations) – but they are hard to forecast.

In business, the concept has been used to propose that since disorder and confusion are endemic to business situations, management should accept that anything can happen and, hence, not attempt to plan and control long-term future activities. Rather, organizations need to be able to learn from past and current events and develop rapid and flexible responses to fast-changing environments. The concept suggests that in the future control and order will be difficult to maintain in continuously innovating systems.

CHAPS ➤clearing house.

Chapter 11 ➤bankruptcy.

charge 1. To ➤debit to, or impose a price for a good or service, as in bank charges. **2.** To take a pledge, ➤mortgage or ➤collateral against a loan.

charge card ➤credit card.

chartist A stock market analyst who predicts ➤share price movements solely from the study of graphs of share prices and sometimes trading volumes. Chartism – which often involves more-or-less sophisticated extrapolation of patterns of lines on pieces of paper – is derided by economists, who use the ➤efficient markets hypothesis to suggest that no such technique can perform better than the market on average. ➤➤technical analysis.

checking account (US) ➤current account.

cheque (UK) An order written by the drawer to a ➤commercial bank or ➤central bank to pay on demand a specified sum to a bearer or a named person or ➤company (US = *check*). A cheque may be open or crossed. Crossed, the cheque is payable only into the bank account of the payee. A cheque becomes ➤negotiable when endorsed by the payee.

chicken An interaction between different players – notable from popular culture and in the economics of ➤game theory – in which big rewards accrue to the player who is most willing to take big risks for the longest. Drawn from the familiar cult 'teen game, in which players drive towards each other at high speed to see who swerves first, the winner of a game of chicken is he who carries on risking danger the longest. The game has been used as a parable to describe certain recurring business dilemmas, e.g. companies operating in a market of excess capacity, where all participants are losing money, but where large returns will accrue to the company that sticks around longest after others have been forced out; or in a price war.

There is no obviously winning strategy in a straightforward game of chicken, as the benefit of holding out until last may be offset by the risk that all players end up dead. The best strategy is either to avoid entering a game of chicken, or to adopt the so-called 'commitment' strategy, i.e. to commit yourself to winning the game, thus scaring rivals out of the way early on. For example, in the original game, commitment might imply breaking the steering wheel off the steering column, and being seen to throw it out of the car window. In business strategy, a commitment of this kind can be made by, for example, pre-publicizing a commitment to always beat rivals' prices.

chill-chain   In the distribution of frozen and cold products, the chain from the producer's factory to the final consumer's refrigerator.

chinese wall   A communications barrier between members or departments of a financial institution intended to prevent the transfer of price-sensitive information. Chinese walls are imaginary but are taken seriously in an attempt to minimize conflicts of interest, e.g. between clients of a broking department of a ➤**merchant bank** advised to buy ➤**shares** that an investment department might wish to dispose of.

choice modelling   The formal description and analysis of individual consumer choice, where there are discrete alternatives. Many choices are of this nature – brands X, Y and Z, or cars that are blue, red and yellow – and questions arise as to whether an individual would prefer one alternative over another. The choice is likely to be influenced by decisions made by management (product design, pricing, distribution) and/or policy-makers (availability, equity, public welfare considerations). Choice modelling has been widely applied to problems in marketing (➤**brand management**), transportation management, healthcare and economics.

Formal choice modelling has its primary roots in the work of R D Luce (*Individual Choice Behavior: a theoretical analysis*, 1959), K Lancaster (*Consumer Demand: a new approach*, 1971) and S Rosen ('Hedonic Prices and Implicit Markets: product differentiation in pure competition', *Journal of Political Economy*, 1974). A key proposition is that consumers choose the characteristics that goods possess, not the goods *per se*. Over the past quarter-century this proposition has been viewed within the framework of random utility theory (RUT) (although measurement theory offers another way of viewing choice modelling). RUT provides a theoretical context for the models that are now used, notably the set of discrete-choice models (including multinomial logits). Work in the 1970s by economist Daniel McFadden was particularly influential in this regard.

A generic framework for choice modelling is as follows: management makes available products (including, perhaps, a new product or a new attribute), consumers perceive these alternatives with their varying attributes, they evaluate the attributes of each alternative (utility formation) and make an holistic evaluation (utility function), there then follows a choice process (the consumer decides whether to choose, wait or never choose) and, if there is a choice, a specific alternative is selected. When looked at across consumers, these individual choices sum to determine product demand, brand shares, etc. (*see* Jordan Louviere, David Hensher and Joffre Swait, *Stated Choice Methods: analysis and application*, 2000).

Embedded within this generic framework are two alternative approaches: (a) 'revealed preference methods', and (b) 'stated preference methods'. Revealed preference methods examine actual choices made by customers. The data for this may come from direct observation, an automated procedure of data capture (e.g. electronic scanning at the point of sale) or ➤**marketing research**, e.g. diaries from a ➤**consumer panel**. With stated preference methods, respondents are placed in experimental conditions to understand the hypothetical choices consumers might make. This allows key factors of managerial interest to be manipulated, while controlling for extraneous factors. ➤**experiment**. Each approach has its merits, and there is considerable advantage in combining the two approaches to tackle specific problems.

churn rate ➤employee retention.

CIM Computer integrated manufacture, ➤**computer aided manufacturing**.

CIT Critical incident technique ➤**critical incidents**.

classical conditioning A form of behavioural learning. ➤**learning**.

classical system ➤corporation tax.

clearing The offsetting of ➤**liabilities** or purchases and sales between two parties. ➤clearing house.

clearing bank (UK) A member of the London Bankers' Clearing House. ➤**clearing house**. Now used synonymously with ➤**commercial bank**.

clearing house Any institution that settles mutual indebtedness between a number of organizations. The UK banks, through the *Association of Payment Clearing Services* (APACS), have: the *Bankers Automated Clearing System* (BACS), which provides interbank clearing; the *Clearing House Automated Payments System* (CHAPS), which now provides instant clearing for electronic transfers through the *Real Time Gross Settlement System* (RTGSS); and ➤**electronic funds transfer at point of sale** (EFTPOS). There are similar institutions in other countries, e.g. the *Clearing House Interbank Payment System* (CHIPS) in New York. There is also a global system for settling payments that flow through the foreign exchange markets, e.g. the *CLS services* set up by the large banks. There are similar arrangements on the stock exchanges and other markets. The clearing house is normally financed by membership subscriptions and other dues of the market.

client relationship management ➤customer relationship management.

close company (UK) A ➤**company** effectively controlled by not more than five shareholders (US = *closed company*).

closed-end fund An investment company with a fixed capitalization. ➤**investment trust**.

closed-loop system A control mechanism in which data on current performance automatically adjust operations in order to rectify divergences between planned and actual output or activity.

closing price The price as it stands at the end of each day's trading session in the ➤security and ➤commodity markets.

cluster analysis A statistical technique used for the classification of consumers into a small number of mutually exclusive groups, based on similarities among the consumers. The groups are not predefined, so the technique first has to determine how many groups there should be, and then determine group membership. Cluster analysis is widely used in ➤**quantitative market research**, especially for ➤**segmentation** studies.

clustering The observed phenomenon that, within many successful industries, firms operate within a relatively confined geographical area. The City of London, Silicon Valley and Hollywood all exemplify the tendency. Economic geographers and regional scientists have described and modelled this phenomenon, based on an understanding of agglomeration economies. The principles and virtues of such an arrangement were restated in *The Competitive Advantage of Nations* by Michael ➤**Porter** (1990). Clustering can promote a more efficiently functioning market in key inputs, such as skilled labour; it can promote a faster flow of best practice; it fosters a more competitive dynamic. And in the case of Hollywood, where the product is a complicated arrangement involving many different participants, clustering can make it far easier for informal networks to develop.

CNC ➤computer numerical control.

Cobb–Douglas production function ➤production function.

co-branding ➤brand hierarchy.

cobweb model A depiction of the path of output and prices in a market where there is a lag between production decisions and production itself. It is a model that was most aptly applied to agriculture, where lags between planting and harvesting arise. The key feature of the model is that producers (perhaps stupidly) look at prices this season, in deciding how much to produce for the next season. But actual prices next season will, of course, reflect the outcome of all producers' decisions in this. A high asparagus price in 2003 may induce many planters to convert fields to asparagus only for them to find that in 2004 the price has plummeted. While considered as something of an archaic relic, the model reasonably captures the working of the investment cycle in many industries – which do exhibit a pattern of over-investment followed by under-investment as businesses fail to anticipate the decisions of rivals – and in doing that, can be seen as a crude underpinning to the economics of the ➤**business cycle**. Economists prefer to make the simplifying assumption that business people do anticipate the decisions of others, and avoid systematic mistakes of the kind assumed here. ➤**rational expectation**.

code of practice Self-regulatory control. Created, maintained and policed by professional and industrial bodies, these codes of practice set out rules governing the conduct of members, establish procedures for compliance with the rules, ensure there is adherence to the rules, establish grievance and appeals procedures, and impose penalties where rules have been violated. Examples are codes of practice in ➤**advertising**, ➤**marketing research**, ➤**direct marketing**, sales promotion, and telemarketing, building and construction and insurance. For example, the Market Research Society Code of Conduct has rules about a researcher's responsibilities to informants, to the public and business community, the mutual responsibilities of clients and agencies, and conditions of membership. Specific rules relate to the relationship between marketing research and issues concerning data protection and privacy. Also, it prohibits selling in the guise of conducting marketing research ('sugging'). Although many codes of practice are thorough and well-intentioned, the extent to which they have an impact is open to debate. Complaints may rarely result in penalties and, even where penalties are imposed, they may not be severe or are easily circumvented, e.g. an errant firm may continue to work in inappropriate ways by withdrawing from the professional body.

coercive power ➤power.

cognition ➤attitude.

cognitive dissonance The theory that after having done something people think about what they have done, prompting doubts, questions and reservations. Is the job I have just accepted the right one? I am now not so sure about the terms and conditions. Or, is the two-bedroom house I have bought appropriate? Should I have held out for a three-bedroom house? The theory was articulated by L Festinger (*A Theory of Cognitive Dissonance*, 1957).

Post-purchase cognitive dissonance is studied in ➤consumer behaviour, in an attempt to manage actively any lingering doubts which might otherwise give rise to negative evaluations of the purchase or result in customer complaints. Cognitive dissonance can be reduced by a salesperson talking-through concerns with a customer after purchase, or by the use of advertisements and brochures that reassure consumers a wise choice has been made. Also, following purchase, consumers tend to notice other people using the product and have greater awareness of marketing communications publicizing the product – these, too, can offer reassurance.

In ➤personnel management lingering doubts about a new job can be addressed at an initial appointment meeting and through the use of staff induction programmes, probationary employment arrangements and performance reviews.

cognitive learning ➤learning.

collaboration ➤strategic alliance.

collar An ➤instrument, on which interest is contained within a maximum and minimum bracket. ⟫cap.

collateral Originally the US term for ➤security, now used more widely. The official US definition (under the US Commercial Code) includes goods, intangibles, paper (➤negotiable ➤instruments and documents of titles) and proceeds.

collective action Action by an organized group of employees to express their viewpoint in a dispute with their employers. As with ➤industrial relations, the underlying assumption is that ➤conflict between employees and employers is endemic. Collective action by employees takes many forms: strikes, picketing, secondary picketing, overtime bans, working-to-rule, and sick-ins (also called co-ordinated ➤absenteeism). Particularly disruptive are abrupt unofficial and unanticipated strikes ('wildcat strikes'). Action by employers can be equally confronting, e.g. 'lay-offs' (where employees are temporarily or permanently laid off) and 'lock-outs' (where employers insist on certain terms being met before employees are allowed back into the workplace). Collective action by employees is associated with ➤trade unions, in that these provide the means by which employees can organize collectively. Over the past 100 years the intensity of collective action has waxed and waned, and also varied between countries. For example, the incidence of strikes has fallen dramatically in the UK and the US over the past 20 years – reflecting legislative changes (e.g. restrictions on secondary ➤**picketing** in the UK as a result of the Employment Act 1980), declining trade union membership, a shift away from mass-employment manufacturing, and new work practices, e.g. ➤**human resource management**. In more individualistic work environments, employees will express their viewpoint through direct communication with employers, and if a dispute is not resolved they may change employer. ➤**employee retention**.

collective bargaining Employee representatives acting on behalf of employees taken as a group, to put forward a view on matters that affect their interests. The right of employees to organize in this manner is explicitly accepted by employers. Typically, the collective group is a formally constituted ➤**trade union**. Sidney and Beatrice Webb coined the term 'collective bargaining' in 1897 in *Industrial Democracy*, and for 80 years the proportion of employees covered by collective bargaining grew in most industrialized Western countries; however, over the past 20 years the proportion has declined. This shift reflects the decline of mass-employment manufacturing, political and policy changes, increased competition for skilled employees, and changing employment practices, e.g. outsourcing. Historically, in Europe collective bargaining has been at an industry level (i.e. employee representatives have negotiated an agreement covering all employees in an industry, e.g. all miners, all transport workers, all teachers. By contrast, in the US and Japan there has been a tradition of 'enterprise bargaining', with separately negotiated agreements for each organization or ➤**work group**. Over the past two decades Europe, too, has moved towards increased use of enterprise bargaining. ➤**arbitration**; **bargaining**; **negotiation**.

collectivism An attribute of ➤**national culture** that describes a social framework in which people work closely together for mutual support and protection, in contrast to 'individualism'. An appreciation of collectivism is important in ➤**international business**, particularly in the context of understanding non-Western business.

commerce A general term used to describe processes of exchange in a trading context. Now largely superseded by the more specific terms, such as ➤**international business** and ➤**e-commerce** (also e-business).

commercial bank Privately owned bank (➤**banking**) whose primary function is to accept deposits, make loans and offer payment services such as cheque accounts to business or individual customers. Otherwise referred to as ➤**clearing banks** (UK), national banks and state banks (US), joint stock banks and, in Western Europe, credit banks, to distinguish them from ➤**investment banks**.

commercial paper (CP) An ➤**unsecured** ➤**note** issued by companies for short-term borrowing purposes. It differs from a ➤**bill of exchange** in that it is *one-name* paper; a bill of exchange contains the names of the drawer and the drawee, both of whom are liable, whereas commercial paper has only the name of the issuer. Commercial paper has been in use in the US for many years but was for long frowned on in the UK. In April 1986 sterling commercial paper was authorized by the ➤**Bank of England**, subject to a number of conditions, in particular that maturities should not be less than 7 days and not more than 1 year and that the right to issue should be restricted to companies having net assets of not less than £50 million and that are listed on the stock exchange. Issues began in May 1986. CP is frequently sold by the issuer direct to the investor, the latter normally being institutions, namely ➤**money-market** funds, ➤**insurance companies**, corporations, bank trust departments and ➤**pension** funds. CP is also placed by intermediary banks or securities dealers. Unlike ➤**acceptances**, CP is not tied to a particular trade transaction.

commission Payments made to ➤**agents** for services rendered. The size of commission often varies with the value of the goods or services handled, e.g. a broker may receive a greater percentage on a larger contract than a smaller one.

commodity **1.** In economic theory, all subjects of production and exchange, i.e. all goods and services. **2.** Raw materials, or primary products, used in manufacturing and industrial processing, consumed in their natural form. **3.** Those commodities traded in commodity markets. **4.** A competitively produced item of a homogenous kind, sold at a low mark-up.

Companies Act ➤incorporation.

Companies House ➤company secretary.

company **1.** An incorporated business. ➤**incorporation**. **2.** More loosely, any business organization, which may be a ➤**sole proprietorship**, a ➤**partnership** or another form.

company limited by guarantee A company (➤incorporation) in which the ➤**liability** of the shareholders is limited to the amount they guarantee to pay in the event of ➤**liquidation**, rather than by the amount of the ➤**equity**.

company secretary A statutory position, usually a member of senior management in a limited company (➤incorporation), who maintains the share register and the company's statutory books and records. All limited companies are required to have a company secretary, but practice varies. Many smaller firms appoint their accountant or one of his staff, or one of the directors may perform the role. Maintaining the share register may be put out to a ➤**registrar**. Among other things, the company secretary will probably arrange the ➤**annual general meeting** and file the annual report and accounts at Companies House, which also keeps records of directors and share capital. ➤**annual accounts**.

comparative advantage The activity that a person, a company or a nation can specialize in, at least cost in terms of having to forego other activities. Comparative advantage is as fundamental to economists as ➤**competitive advantage** is to business strategists. But having a comparative advantage in something need not imply you are very good at it. It simply implies you are less bad at it than you are at other things. Thus, imagine that the US has twice the productivity in apple-growing than the UK, and three times the productivity in butter production. Clearly, the US is 'better' at both apple and butter production, but because it is 'more better' at butter, it has a comparative advantage in butter production, and the UK has a comparative advantage in apple production. The ➤**opportunity cost** of devoting resources to apple production rather than butter production is lower in the UK than in the US and in this crucial sense, the cost of apple production is lower, even though the person-hours required to produce apples is higher than in the US.

Comparative advantage is used to explain the benefits of free trade between nations, who can efficiently specialize, even where one nation will inevitably be far less productive and poorer than another.

The notion of comparative advantage can be applied to companies as well as countries, but only with care. A country must always have some comparative advantage however dismal its performance at everything, as long as it is relatively less bad at something. The same is not true of companies, which could be closed down with the resources deployed elsewhere. However, companies which have incurred large ➤sunk costs in the production of an item may have a comparative advantage in producing it, even though their total costs are high.

compensation The forms of financial reward that are given to employees. Direct compensation includes salary and wages (➤pay), performance bonuses, overtime payments, profit-sharing schemes and stock/share options. Indirect compensation relates to private health insurance, pension and superannuation contributions, employee privileges and ➤fringe benefits. In compensating employees for their labour, management must consider whether the reward will be motivating and whether non-financial rewards should be offered as well as financial ones. ➤➤efficiency wage hypothesis; motivation; reward.

compensatory consumption The consumption of a good or service that compensates for a deficiency elsewhere in a person's life. A person may have low self-esteem, but feel better about himself as a result of consuming something. Usually this is fairly innocuous – we treat ourselves to a restaurant meal or we buy an extra pair of shoes. However, it can lead to addictive and maladaptive behaviour, such as problem gambling. In this case, gambling is not undertaken for its inherent attractions (fun, excitement, etc.), but as a response to other problems in a person's life. ➤➤consumer behaviour.

compensatory decision rule ➤decision rule.

competency The knowledge and skill that resides in an organization. Competencies include technical know-how, technical skills, business process know-how and business skills. Distinct competencies are those things that the organization is better at doing than its competitors. ➤➤knowledge management system.

Competition Commission The UK tribunal responsible for making detailed investigations and recommendations into mergers and anticompetitive behaviour. The Commission is an independent public body established by the Competition Act 1998 and replaced the Monopolies and Mergers Commission on 1 April 1999. The Commission is best known for its detailed inquiries into matters referred to it by the ➤Office of Fair Trading, concerning monopolies, mergers and the economic regulation of utility companies. But it also hears appeals against decisions of the Director General of Fair Trading and the regulators of utilities. ➤➤competition policy. The Commission has no power to initiate inquiries.

competition policy Government intervention into the workings of the business sector, designed: (a) to prevent the abuse of ➤monopoly power and to restrict or punish anticompetitive behaviour (such as ➤predatory pricing); (b) to control business agreements that might be anticompetitive in effect, or which might have the effect of creating ➤cartels; (c) to regulate ➤mergers, and (d) to promote competition generally. In the UK, policy is upheld by the ➤Office of Fair Trading and the

➤Competition Commission, and much important competition work is pursued by national authorities in most countries, often at a local level.

However, the important development of the last decade has been the increasingly international character of competition policy, with the authorities of the ➤European Union (EU) and US dominating the arena, even to the extent of investigating mergers between companies of other jurisdictions (the EU investigated the merger of the American giants Time Warner and AOL in 2000, for example). At the level of the EU, the European Commission is responsible for competition policy, acting most importantly under the broad terms of Articles 85 and 86 of the Treaty of Rome (now renumbered 81 and 82) supplemented by subsequent regulation and interpretation. It is worth reprinting the actual text as EU law applies throughout the EU, and is the basis of much domestic law as well. Article 81 outlaws cartels, and says:

The following shall be prohibited as incompatible with the common market: all agreements between undertakings, decisions by associations of undertakings and concerted practices which may affect trade between Member States and which have as their object or effect the prevention, restriction or distortion of competition within the common market, and in particular those which:
1. (a) directly or indirectly fix purchase or selling prices or any other trading conditions;
   (b) limit or control production, markets, technical development, or investment;
   (c) share markets or sources of supply;
   (d) apply dissimilar conditions to equivalent transactions with other trading parties, thereby placing them at a competitive disadvantage;
   (e) make the conclusion of contracts subject to acceptance by the other parties of supplementary obligations which, by their nature or according to commercial usage, have no connection with the subject of such contracts.
2. Any agreements or decisions prohibited pursuant to this Article shall be automatically void.
3. The provisions of paragraph 1 may, however, be declared inapplicable in the case of:
   – any agreement or category of agreements between undertakings;
   – any decision or category of decisions by associations of undertakings;
   – any concerted practice or category of concerted practices,
   which contributes to improving the production or distribution of goods or to promoting technical or economic progress, while allowing consumers a fair share of the resulting benefit, and which does not:
   (a) impose on the undertakings concerned restrictions which are not indispensable to the attainment of these objectives;
   (b) afford such undertakings the possibility of eliminating competition in respect of a substantial part of the products in question.

Paragraph 3 is important, in offering wide scope for individual or block exemptions from the tight control against so many business agreements inherent in paragraph 1. Article 82 outlaws the abuse of monopoly power, and says:

Any abuse by one or more undertakings of a dominant position within the common market or in a substantial part of it shall be prohibited as incompatible with the common market in so far as it may affect trade between Member States.

Such abuse may, in particular, consist in:

(a) directly or indirectly imposing unfair purchase or selling prices or other unfair trading conditions;

(b) limiting production, markets or technical development to the prejudice of consumers;

(c) applying dissimilar conditions to equivalent transactions with other trading parties, thereby placing them at a competitive disadvantage;

(d) making the conclusion of contracts subject to acceptance by the other parties of supplementary obligations which, by their nature or according to commercial usage, have no connection with the subject of such contracts.

In addition to these provisions, there is a Merger Regulation which allows the Commission to regulate mergers which have a 'Community dimension'.

In the US, competition policy is upheld by the Federal Trade Commission and the Anti-Trust Division of the Department of Justice.

Experts differ in their view of how competition policy should be handled. On one side are those who believe in activist competition policy, exemplified in the US Department of Justice case against anticompetitive behaviour by Microsoft in the late 1990s. On the other side is the more *laissez-faire* school (associated with economists at the University of Chicago) which believes unfettered markets tend to have benign effects, and that even if monopolies emerge, they will tend to do so where they offer real consumer benefits, and will usually be transient. On no issue do the two schools clash more than that of ➤**vertical restraints** – agreements between firms and their suppliers or their customers. In the 1960s in the US, and in the 1990s in the European Union, these kinds of arrangements were treated with great suspicion. But the non-interventionists argued these were typically legitimate business arrangements, with a number of benefits to firms and consumers alike, and that only where firms with large market shares attempted to restrict trade should the authorities intervene.

Recently, a synthesis of the different attitudes seems to have emerged in the main jurisdictions: (a) tough penalties for anticompetitive behaviour; (b) a discretionary case-by-case approach to the sanctioning of mergers, and (c) a midpoint between intervention and non-intervention in the case of vertical restraints.

competitive advantage A term used to describe the above-average performance of a firm in an industrial sector, which then enables that firm to invest its additional profits into the business to ensure it maintains its advantage over its competitors. The advantage may be due to lower costs, better-quality products, unique technologies, or exceptional customer service, e.g. BMW's reputation for technical excellence, or the commitment of American Express to service quality. Whatever the difference, it is the ability to differentiate the product or service and charge a higher price that delivers a competitive advantage. ➤**differentiation**. However, some of these factors can easily be copied or imitated by competitors; hence, the advantage is invariably short-lived.

The exception to this is where differentiating factors are not easily imitated. Then substantial benefits can accrue over time. This is described as 'sustainable competitive advantage'. Frequently, these advantages are in the form of skills and know-how that have been acquired over time and become embedded in the organization's routines. For instance, intellectual property that is protected and ➤**brands** are forms of competitive advantage that are difficult to imitate. ➤**brand management**. Sustainable competitive advantage involves every aspect of the way the organization competes in the market-place: prices, product range, manufacturing quality, service levels and so on. However, these competitive advantages need to be deeply embedded in the organization – in its resources, skills, culture and investments over time. Thus, a firm such as Kellogg's might be able to offer a price advantage, but this could easily be copied, whereas the advantages that stem from its brand investment and its sheer size in the cereals market are not easily imitated.

For many commentators on strategy the development of sustainable competitive advantage lies at the heart of ➤**strategic management**. The writings of Harvard professor Michael ➤**Porter** were particularly influential in the 1980s: *Competitive Strategy: techniques for analyzing industries and competitors* (1980) and *Competitive Advantage: creating and sustaining superior performance* (1985).

competitive mapping ➤competitor analysis.

competitiveness A loose term, popularly used to reflect the ability of a nation to grow successfully, and to maintain its share of world trade. While there have been several government White Papers on the subject in the UK, a wide-ranging debate about it in Europe and the US, and while league tables of national competitiveness are regularly produced by reputable business authorities, the term has never impressed academic economists. It is used as though it refers to the state of the productive base of the economy, yet attempts to apply a precise definition have foundered. It either reduces to a measure of how rich a country is, measured by its ➤**gross domestic product** per head of population or to a measure of the price of tradable goods expressed in foreign currency (primarily a reflection of the ➤**exchange rate**). Yet those who use the term appear to believe they are talking of a broader concept than either of these. Those who have criticized the growth in usage of the term argue that basic economic theory of international trade and ➤**comparative advantage** makes clear that we should not view the world as a group of nations competing in a ➤**zero-sum game**.

competitive parity A situation where competing brands match each other in important respects. This is typically discussed in terms of pricing, where competitors match each other's retail prices. But it is common to many other aspects of marketing and ➤**brand management**, e.g. competitive parity in the setting of advertising budgets, in the development of particular creative ideas, in the launch of ➤**line extensions**, in the addition of product features, etc. It has the effect of eroding a brand's ➤**competitive advantage** and diluting any distinctive qualities it might have. It is particularly evident in mature markets where ➤**zero-sum games** are being played, i.e. where the size of the pie is fixed and one brand gains only at the expense of others. This can degenerate into a 'negative-sum game', where the process of intense competition imposes costs on all brands (as in price wars). While this may benefit consumers in the short run, quality is likely to suffer longer term. In practice, with publicly available information (regarding retail prices, advertising expenditures, etc.) and free markets it is hard to prevent competitors from matching one another if they so choose and negative-sum games are common.

While typically seen as a problem by management, there are circumstances when competitive parity among incumbents may serve as a ➤**barrier to entry**, thereby keeping newcomers from entering a market. For example, a high level of advertising spend throughout a market may not give any single incumbent a differential advantage, but it could disadvantage (and discourage) a potential new entrant. In the longer term, however, those who raise the cost of doing business are always in danger of creating a gap for lower-cost operators to fill (as has been seen with no-frills grocery retailing, no-extras airlines and non-advertised generics).

In emerging markets the process is somewhat different. It is frustrating for pacesetting and innovative brands to find their ideas being matched and imitated, but all players may be able to reap benefits if there is a significant growth in primary demand. The rise of ➤co-option, alliances, networks and co-operative exchange relationships illustrate how organizations have attempted to come to terms with competitive parity in both mature and emergent markets.

competitive rivalry A form of prolonged and intense competition between firms operating in very competitive markets. This rivalry is most intense when competitors are of similar size, e.g. Unilever versus Procter & Gamble versus Kao. In such instances rivalry may take the form of examining price changes and matching any move immediately and ensuring any product and service changes are also immediately matched (➤competitive parity).

competitive strategy A theory of strategic management that focuses on relating a firm to the competitive environment within which it operates. According to Michael ➤Porter five major factors determine this environment and he brings these together in the form shown opposite (the five forces framework):
(1) Ease with which competitors can enter the industry.
(2) Bargaining power of customers.
(3) Bargaining power of suppliers.
(4) Ease with which substitute products can be introduced.
(5) Extent of competition between existing firms.
➤competitive advantage; generic strategy.

competitor analysis The study of a firm's major competitors. While a firm may have many competitors – especially if it is operating in several different markets – it is extremely useful to analyse in detail a few close competitors. This will provide insight into those resources that set a firm apart from others and make it a formidable opponent. Some rival firms may have strong ➤brand names or unique technology protected by ➤patents or cost advantages that enable them to achieve superior profits. Large firms have dedicated departments constantly monitoring leading competitors, whereas smaller firms tend to collect information more informally through meeting customers and suppliers.

competitor profiling Sometimes referred to as 'competitive mapping'. ➤competitor analysis.

complementary asset An asset that, while not necessary to the core operations of a firm, enhances its performance. For example, to operate in any of the ➤packaged goods markets it is necessary to have access to effective distribution channels. These have almost become a necessary asset.

complementary good A product whose joint value is higher than its individual value. A left glove is a strong complement for a right glove; petrol is a complement

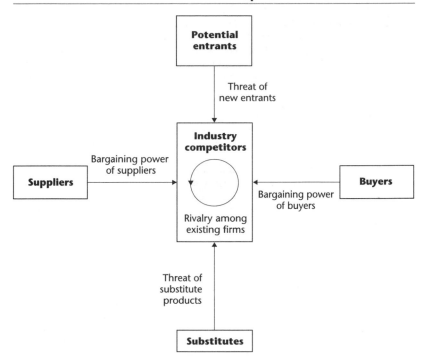

The Five Competitive Forces that Determine Industry Profitability Source: Porter, M. E., *Competitive Strategy: techniques for analysing industries and competitors* (Simon & Schuster, 1985)

for cars. Products are generally defined as complements in terms of cross-price effects between them. If, when the price of petrol goes up, sales of cars fall, cars and petrol are said to be complements. ➤substitute.

complex monopoly A notion of ➤monopoly used by the UK ➤Competition Commission, to characterize an industry even where a market is not dominated by one firm. Under section 7(1)(c) of the Fair Trading Act 1973, a complex monopoly situation arises if at least one quarter of services are supplied by members of a group of persons (not being a group of interconnected companies) who, whether voluntarily or not and whether by agreement or not, so conduct their respective affairs as in any way to prevent, restrict or distort competition in connection with the supply of those services.

compliance department, officer An official – particularly at a large company or ➤financial institution – responsible for ensuring that laws and regulations governing share dealing and ➤investment are complied with. Compliance officers may be required to investigate transactions carried out by their colleagues. ➤chinese wall.

comprehensive business income tax A type of ➤corporation tax in which there is no allowance for interest payments to be deducted from the profits on which tax is levied.

computer aided design (CAD) The use of computer software and hardware in the production of industrial drawings and designs. Prior to CAD, drawings were produced via drawing boards and pencils. The system enables designers to store and modify their work on a computer screen. Moreover, this can be linked to manufacturing machine tools facilitating the manufacture of components. ➤computer aided manufacturing.

computer aided manufacturing (CAM) The use of computer software and hardware in the production of industrial components and products. This involves not only the manufacture but also the testing, inspection, assembly and packaging prior to despatch. Frequently, CAM is linked to ➤computer aided design (CAD) to form an integrated design and manufacturing system, sometimes referred to as computer integrated manufacture. These systems allow information to be transmitted instantly between design machining and assembly stages of production. Since there are no time delays or intervening agents, there are few possibilities for breakdowns in communication, misunderstandings or misinterpretation between departments. Integrated computer systems require fewer staff and are faster, more reliable and more accurate than those based on manual labour. Duplication of effort is reduced and the implications of proposed alterations can be assessed immediately.

computer-assisted personal interviewing (CAPI) A form of interviewing where the market researcher carries a portable computer or electronic notepad and enters responses directly into the computer. CAPI improves the speed, efficiency and accuracy of survey based ➤marketing research because there is only one encoding stage. Moreover, if there are any ambiguous responses they can be clarified immediately during the personal interview. Web-based surveys also have the advantage of having only one encoding stage.

computer-assisted telephone interviewing (CATI) A form of interviewing where the market researcher follows a standardized script during an interview and enters responses directly into a computer using a precoded answer sheet. CATI improves the efficiency and accuracy of the ➤marketing research process.

computer numerical control (CNC) Manufacturing machine tools that may be programmed using numerical instructions. CNC machines may be programmed in advance to follow a set of instructions and then left to run for several hours. A single operator may be able to programme and supervise several of these machines. ➤computer aided manufacturing.

concentration A measure of the number of firms who dominate a market or industry. It is classically measured by the output of the biggest few firms in the industry, as a percentage of the whole market, the so-called *concentration ratio*. Concentration is widely viewed as a good proxy measure of the degree of competition that prevails in a sector.

concept generation One part of the early stages of ➤new product development. It is the stage at which an idea begins to take physical form as function and purpose are detailed. For example, a firm may have had an idea for a solar-powered miniature radio, but it is only at the product concept stage that the shape, size and power-supply considerations turn the idea into a physical concept.

conciliation The process of reaching agreement between two parties in a ➤negotiation. The process is often assisted by a conciliator – a trusted third party who acts as a 'go-between' and who is actively involved in suggesting and communicating solutions. Conciliation is similar to ➤mediation and distinct from ➤arbitration.

concurrent engineering A method for developing new products. It involves all activities in the ➤new product development process occurring simultaneously rather than in series. Indeed, it is sometimes referred to as 'simultaneous engineering'. The method centres on the idea of teamwork and that a new product team should comprise engineers, designers, accountants and marketers who should consider from the outset all elements of the product, including design, manufacture, marketing and disposal.

confidence interval A measure of the likely statistical error in the estimation of a ➤parameter based on a sample of data. For example, analysis of the relationship between the level of consumer spending and the level of consumer income may imply that consumption is on average equal to 0.8 times the level of income. But if this derived from a sample of consumers, it is subject to statistical error. The confidence interval attempts to quantify the likely magnitude of such error, and hence imply the degree of confidence one might have in the 0.8 figure that the sample provides. In general, the more variable the relationship in the sample, the less certain one can be about the true relationship. And up to a point, the smaller the sample, the less confident one can be about an estimate derived from it.

A confidence interval is expressed as a range of estimates within which it is likely the real relationship lies, e.g. 0.8, ± 0.1. Typically, that ± 0.1 would be calculated to mean that if other random samples had been taken similar to the one that was actually used, no more than 5 per cent of those samples would have generated an estimate outside the 0.8 ± 0.1 range. In other words, we can be sure that the estimate is within the range, with 95 per cent confidence. Unfortunately, to estimate the confidence interval, one has to assume the sample is representative of the whole population, bar random deviation. In practice, samples may not be truly representative. Hence, in some cases, the use of confidence intervals gives a spurious sense of statistical accuracy   opinion pollsters have expressed them, only to find their polling errors are far larger than the confidence interval implies because their samples have been biased.

Technically, for an estimate of a parameter in any large sample, the 95 per cent confidence interval can be calculated as the estimate ± 1.96 times σ, where σ is the standard deviation of the estimate. Confidence intervals are not purely of technical interest – all the points made here must be kept in mind when interpreting and using sample data from ➤marketing research, ➤attitude surveys and ➤operational research; otherwise, business decisions might be made that are incorrect and misleading.

conflict A condition where one party perceives that another party has negatively affected, or is about to negatively affect, the interests of the first party. For example, the decision by management to close a factory will be seen by employees as a threat to their jobs and livelihoods – this sows the seeds of conflict (whether conflict actually occurs will depend on how the decision is explained, whether employees are redeployed, whether they receive attractive redundancy payments, etc.).

Conflict starts when objectives and ideologies are in opposition to one another, or where they are incompatible. Management may see factory closure as a way to fulfil its formal objective to return a profit, whereas employees may focus on the responsibility management has for providing fulfilling jobs – these objectives appear to be incompatible in this instance. Given these conditions, people will think about the issues in relation to their own situation (through a process of cognition and personalization). Thus: 'What would a factory closure mean to me, given my ➤role?' Another source of opposition relates to territories and 'turf', e.g. 'Who owns the customer–marketing managers, sales staff or the database manager?' These factors may give rise to intended action (intentions) or actual conflict (behaviour).

A certain level of conflict is natural and inevitable within organizations. It may even be desirable if it stimulates people's thinking and leads to new ideas and new solutions ('creative conflict'). However, too much may give rise to 'felt conflict' in individuals (i.e. a level of emotional involvement that creates anxiety, tenseness, frustration or hostility) and may be 'dysfunctional' for the organization, i.e. it comes to hinder group and intergroup performance.

Early signs of impending conflict are where there is intergroup hostility and jealousy, interpersonal friction, low morale, and poor communication. This can give rise to one of three outcomes: (a) escalating frustration; (b) subversion of the conflict, or (c) some form of conflict resolution. Escalating frustration means more of the same – more hostility, jealousy and friction. However, this rarely continues unchecked. Either attempts are made to subvert the conflict (e.g. by withholding important information, distorting information, imposing rules and regulations on other groups, by controlling information channels and manipulating sources of power, and undermining or blaming opponents), or some form of conflict management is used. This entails the use of legitimate resolution techniques to achieve the desired level of conflict. Typically, some form of ➤negotiation technique is used. These techniques range from formal processes of independent ➤arbitration and ➤collective bargaining through to processes that encourage collaboration, co-operation and positive ways to get people to express their differences. Indeed, conflict should not be seen as the only way people express their differences of opinion in organizations; use is made of argument (or discussion) and competition. Like conflict, argument and competition can be productive or harmful and there may be too much or too little of it. Alternative policies, for example, might be discussed openly and frankly, but this should not be allowed to become disruptive, degenerate into conflict, or lead to interminable delays and indecision. ➤➤power.

conflict of interest A situation in which a financial institution is acting for the parties on both sides of a transaction, or where the institution itself has a financial interest in the outcome of the transaction (e.g. a ➤merchant bank both placing shares on the stock exchange on behalf of a client company and recommending the purchase of those shares to an investor client whose ➤portfolio it manages) or a securities house offering to an investor shares with which it is itself oversupplied and that it is under pressure to sell. ➤chinese wall.

conglomerate (UK) A business organization generally consisting of a ➤holding company and a group of ➤subsidiaries engaged in dissimilar activities.

congruency theory A theory that explains how things are seen to fit together.

For example, does an advertising message about a particular ➤brand fit with a person's prior beliefs about the brand? If it does, and if the person is involved in the purchase, the message will be regarded more positively than it actually is (this is known as the 'assimilation effect' in social judgement theory). ➤➤involvement theory. Questions of congruency– or fit – arise in many areas of management. There are applications in ➤brand management (where an issue is how product brands fit within the context of an umbrella brand, and whether elements of a dual-brand fit together) in the use of ➤agents (where the interests of agents and principals may not be congruent, ➤agency theory), in strategic alliance formation (where partners in an alliance must consider questions of fit), and in ➤integrated marketing communications (where thought must be given to how the different types of marketing communication fit together and whether they convey a single message or mixed messages).

conjoint analysis A ➤marketing research technique for evaluating new products, services and ideas. Consider the development of a new model of car. The goal is to elicit from potential consumers their evaluation of product attributes (doors, price, fuel efficiency), each at differing levels (e.g. two doors, four doors, four door hatchback). These attributes and levels are presented to respondents as sets of stimuli, and respondents are asked to evaluate alternative sets of stimuli. The evaluations enable the researcher to see how important each attribute is (doors relative to price), and the importance of each level (two doors relative to four doors). Armed with this information the ➤new product development team can simulate consumer interest in a range of alternative product designs ('what ifs').

With this technique an attempt is made to keep the decision-making context reasonably realistic for respondents. This is achieved through the careful selection of attributes and levels, and the design of stimuli. Different methods are used to present stimuli to respondents: trade-offs (all levels for just two attributes are presented and respondents rank-order these options in terms of their preferences), pair-wise comparisons (a pair of stimuli are presented and respondents state which they prefer) and full profiles (respondents are presented with a complete description of a single option and asked to rate this profile). The full-profile method gets closer to reality, although if there are many attributes the respondent starts to become confused and the analysis becomes less reliable. An extension of the full-profile method is choice-based conjoint analysis. Here respondents select a full profile from a set of profiles (the choice set), rather than simply rating each profile individually. There is no agreement over which method is best. ➤choice modelling.

conjunctive decision rule ➤decision rule.

consideration Something given in exchange for something else, i.e. the total amount of cash, goods or other property, or rights to cash or property, transferred from buyer to seller in settlement of a transaction. In ➤securities trading, the amount paid for securities before ➤commission and ➤taxation. In the UK, a transaction may not be legally binding until the consideration is paid.

consideration set The set of ➤brands from which a consumer makes a choice in a product category. Once formed, the set is presumed to be fairly stable. The process of forming the set in the first place is seen as deliberate, rational and utility maximizing. It envisages the gathering of information about brands (➤information search), but recognizes that as more brands are examined, so the utility of further search is likely to decline and that beyond a certain point it is not worth considering more brands. This is consistent with much ➤consumer behaviour theory of individual consumer decision-making, although empirical proof is limited. ➤➤evoked set.

consol (UK) Abbreviation for *consolidated stock*: irredeemable government stock, first issued in the eighteenth century and bearing a ➤nominal interest rate of 2.5 per cent.

consolidated account A financial statement that brings together the ➤balance sheet and ➤profit and loss account of a parent and subsidiary company so that the financial affairs of the group can be treated as a whole. Where the parent controls (i.e. owns more than 50 per cent of the equity of) a subsidiary, the balance sheet may include the ➤assets of the subsidiary at market value, with any premium paid for ➤goodwill included in the parent's balance sheet and written-off against earnings. This is called ➤acquisition accounting (US = *purchase acquisition*) or *full consolidation*. Adjustments are made to eliminate the double counting of purchases and sales, borrowing and lending between subsidiaries. Where subsidiaries are not wholly owned, the profits and assets attributable to the minority shareholders (minority interests) have to be shown separately. Under merger accounting (US = *pooling of interests*), assets of acquired subsidiaries are put in at historic cost (➤cost, **historical**); i.e. the balance sheets of parents and subsidiaries are added together line by line. Merger accounting gives a more favourable view, and this may be particularly desirable where the subsidiary has been acquired by an exchange of shares.

The term 'subsidiary' is usually reserved for companies controlled by the parent. Companies in which the parent has between about 20 and 50 per cent of the equity are *associate companies*, which it has influence over but does not control. The accounts of these associates may be partially consolidated by valuing them in the balance sheet at their investment cost plus the proportion of undistributed profits attributable to the parent. Companies in which the company has less than about 20 per cent of the equity are referred to as *trade investments*. ➤➤corporate control.

The techniques of financial consolidation are complex, and practices differ between countries. Generally, consolidation of earnings is less usual in Japan and continental Europe than in the UK and the US, and this may affect comparisons of ➤yield. The European Union's Seventh Directive harmonizes the requirements for the consolidated accounts of companies.

consortia ➤strategic alliance.

conspicuous consumption The purchase and display of luxury products and services to provide public evidence of a person's ability to afford them. The term was popularized by Thorstein Veblen (*The Theory of the Leisure Class*, 1899). The motives behind conspicuous consumption are relevant for an understanding of luxury ➤brands (e.g. Yves St Laurent, Rolex, Porsche, Bang & Olufsen) where the brand may symbolize and affirm a person's social status, especially among peers. Even non-luxury brands can come to be seen as status symbols within certain peer groups and certain societies, e.g. Nike, Marlboro, Levi's.

constant return to scale A situation in an industry where an increase in all the inputs into production leads to a proportionate increase in output, i.e. if you double the size of the factory, you double the output. ➤➤**production function.**

constraint theory   A concept developed by ➤Goldratt, Eliyahu to analyse capacity constraints of a production system, commonly referred to as ➤**bottleneck** parts of an operation. By identifying the location of constraints, trying to remove them and then addressing the next constraint, an operations manager is always focusing on the part of the production system that critically determines output. This approach is used in ➤**optimized production technology.**

consumer behaviour   A branch of ➤**marketing** that focuses on the purchasing of goods and services. 'Purchasing' is defined broadly to include attitude formation prior to purchase, expectations, and intentions, as well as the act of purchasing itself, and usage, consumption, satisfaction and dissatisfaction following purchase.

For the past forty years the core of the subject has been the 'consumer decision process', i.e. the process that is believed to lead to purchase (not only purchase itself). Characteristically, this starts with need/problem recognition. There then follows a process of information search from among a variety of sources (e.g. external sources such as advertisements, brochures, etc.). This will be undertaken with varying intensity (a single magazine advertisement may be skim-read, or many advertisements and other sources may be consulted). Alternatives are evaluated and a preferred alternative is selected. This might result in purchase, but usually there are many situational factors that mean the preferred alternative is not necessarily purchased, e.g. in-store stock-outs, service unavailability at the desired time and place, promotional deals that deflect attention to competing brands. Furthermore, purchasing may be far less pre-planned and deliberative than implied by the consumer decision process, notably in the cases of impulse purchasing and trial purchase. The final stage of the consumer decision process comes after purchase – postpurchase dissonance (➤**cognitive dissonance**), usage, evaluation, satisfaction and dissatisfaction (➤**customer satisfaction/dissatisfaction**).

The consumer decision process is seen as being influenced by a range of internal and external factors. Internal factors include: perception, ➤**learning** and memory, ➤**motivation**, ➤**personality traits**, ➤**emotion** and self-concept, lifestyle and ➤**attitude**. External factors include: cultural norms and ➤**values**, subcultural norms and values, and group influences. In addressing these themes, considerable reliance is placed on theories from psychology and sociology and, to a lesser extent, anthropology. Many similar considerations are regarded as important in the context of organizational buying. ➤**organizational buying behaviour.**

The systematic study of consumer behaviour has helped managers in many areas, notably ➤**marketing planning**, ➤**services marketing** and ➤**customer relationship management**. Furthermore, many aspects are amenable to formal modelling with ➤**choice modelling** and ➤**response models**. However, it has come under attack from a variety of directions on the bases that: (a) there has been a preoccupation with individual decision-making (when marketers normally work with aggregations of consumers); (b) that the focus has been too much on product category choice (whereas managers work with brands within product categories); (c) that the desire to examine prepurchase motives and attitudes has meant insufficient attention being given to revealed behaviour (but see ➤**buyer behaviour**); (d) that all too many studies have been based on ➤**experiments** using unrepresentative samples (raising doubts about the external validity of the results); and (e) that the assumed lines of causality may not be supported empirically. More fundamental criticism has come from postmodernists and those who subscribe to a consumerism viewpoint (that puts the interests of consumers first, rather than the interests of management). This has led, for instance, to an interest in non-mainstream consumption by people who have attempted to drop out of the prevailing consumer culture: 'home production', 'television smashing', 'shoplifting', 'dumpster diving'. It has also put a spotlight on the social responsibilities of organizations working within the framework of contemporary capitalism.

consumer credit Short-term loans to the public for the purchase of specific goods. Consumer ➤credit takes the form of credit by shopkeepers and other suppliers, credit accounts, personal loans and ➤hire purchase.

Consumer Credit Act 1974 (UK) Legislation introducing a licensing system for all agencies involved in ➤consumer credit. The Act provides protection for the borrower in consumer ➤credit business. The Act applies to banks and ➤hire purchase credit, to credit sales, ➤credit cards, private loans and ➤mortgages, and also to debt collectors. The Act principally provides for full disclosure of cost information, including the ➤annual percentage rate, for a ➤cooling-off period and for a written agreement, except in the case of ➤overdrafts.

consumer loyalty Persistent behaviour by consumers towards a product, ➤brand, service, store or activity. Despite the apparent simplicity of this statement, there is no universally agreed definition. Three distinct viewpoints are evident, with different implications for ➤marketing and ➤customer relationship management.
(1) Loyalty as primarily an ➤attitude. The strength of attitude to a brand (expressed in terms of people saying they like the brand, feel committed to it, will recommend it to others and have positive beliefs and feelings about it) is seen as the key predictor of its purchase and repeat purchase. These attitudes are formed through a process of cognitive learning. The appeal of this viewpoint is that if consumers have such strong attitudes, they will not only continue to buy the brand but recommend it to others, go out of their way to buy it (despite situational influences and the efforts of marketers to induce switching behaviour), and not be susceptible to negative information about the brand. One step on from this is to see strong attitudes developing into a relationship between consumer and brand. Implicit in this view is that over time, consumers have a small number of preferred brands in each product category (a ➤consideration set), which come to be bought exclusively ('monogamous behaviour').
(2) Loyalty as primarily ➤buyer behaviour. Loyalty is defined mainly with reference to the pattern of past purchases, with only secondary regard to underlying consumer motivations or commitment to a brand. Behavioural measures of loyalty include repeat buying, duplicate buying and share of category requirements. Evidence shows that few consumers are exclusive or 100 per cent loyal ('monogamous behaviour'), but nor are they completely indifferent to the range of brands on offer ('promiscuous behaviour'). Rather, most consumers are loyal to a portfolio of brands in a category ('polygamous behaviour'). A consumer buys the same brand not because of any strong prior attitude or deeply held commitment, but because it is not worth the time and trouble to search for an

alternative. If the favoured brand is unavailable (e.g. out of stock) then another functionally similar brand from the portfolio of acceptable brands will be purchased (➤substitute). This suggests minimal ➤information search and limited cognitive evaluation, although over repeated purchases, a weak commitment to the limited number of brands bought in a product category may form.

(3) Loyalty as the relationship between attitude and behaviour, moderated by various contingencies. Contingencies include the individual's characteristics (e.g. the consumer's desire for variety), her current circumstances (e.g. time pressures), and/or the purchase situation, e.g. product availability. Thus, even if there is a strong attitude towards a brand, this may only provide a weak prediction of purchase because any number of factors may co-determine which brand or brands are deemed to be acceptable. If attitudes are weak, then the influence of contingencies is even more apparent. In all cases, the contingencies are seen as playing key and inescapable roles in explaining the observed patterns of purchase behaviour. For the marketer this means any attempt to build or sustain loyalty must address the contingencies, as much as any core attitudes or behaviours with respect to the brand.

Confusion arises because the term 'consumer loyalty' is used in quite different contexts. Different assessments of loyalty arise depending on how many purchase occasions are studied, how long a time period is studied, how frequently a consumer buys, how involved the consumer is in the product category (➤involvement theory), etc. Thus, a person who only flies twice a year and on both occasions uses British Airways (BA) might (by some measures) appear more loyal than the person who flies ten times and uses BA half the time, but *ceteris paribus* the frequent flier is likely to be more profitable to BA and could be more attitudinally loyal (because she has had more opportunities to form an attitude). Or, a person could be attitudinally loyal to a particular brand of coffee (in contrast to most coffee buyers) but not feel this way about brands of tea, Cola, water, etc. Here the assessment of loyalty would depend on whether the focus was coffee buying in the population at large (where this person's attitude would be seen as exceptional) or products in general bought by this person (where coffee purchasing would appear as an exception).

consumer panel A sample of consumers who report their purchasing behaviour over time. Significantly, it is the behaviour of the *same* people that is assessed (in contrast to repeated surveys and ➤tracking studies). Aggregated data from consumer panels are used by marketers to assess the ➤market shares of brands in a product category, to study ➤buyer behaviour with respect to brand choice (e.g. repeat buying, consumer loyalty, duplicate buying), and also investigate the effects of marketing variables on brand choice such as prices, ➤promotions and ➤advertising spend. Many established markets are found to be fairly stationary in the short term, in that market shares and buyer behaviour do not change much from week to week, despite high levels of competitive marketing activity (one reason for this is the high degree of ➤competitive parity in these markets). However, if there are meaningful shifts in sales these might be modelled as responses to changing levels of advertising spend, salesforce activity, etc.

Traditionally, data were collected using self-completion diaries. On each visit to a store (a 'purchase occasion') the respondent would complete a diary sheet ticking off the brands bought, the time of purchase, the prices paid, etc. The diaries then would be collected together, and the information aggregated, by a marketing research agency on behalf of subscribing companies. While self-completion diaries are still sometimes employed, nowadays automated data collection is preferred. This takes the form of scanner panels (where the bar codes on products are scanned in-store and simultaneously matched with a panellist's identification card) or in-home diaries (where the panellist records all purchases at home using a hand-held scanner and the information is periodically downloaded to the marketing research company). Global leaders in this field are ➤A C **Nielsen Corporation** and ➤**Taylor Nelson Sofres.**

Consumer panels have several very attractive features: (a) the ability to record purchasing details (time and place, price paid, etc., as well as purchase incidence); (b) cost-effectiveness (on a per-unit-of-information basis panels are cheap), and (c) once-only recruitment on to the panel (whereas tracking studies require successive rounds of recruitment). Furthermore, a panel design reduces the time between the occurrence and the recording of an event, which should mean the information is more accurate. There are fewer problems to do with recall loss (the imperfect recollection of an event), recall distortion (ex-post justification of behaviour), and telescoping (over-reporting the number of events within a recall period). However, there are dangers: (a) problems can arise over initial recruitment (bias will arise if some types of people are more willing to be respondents than others); (b) the conditioning of respondents (those on the panel may become more self-aware and change their purchasing behaviour); (c) the loss of respondents with the passage of time (attrition), and (d) differential loss (if particular types of respondent are more inclined to leave the panel, such as the elderly and the more mobile). Panels then become unrepresentative of the population of interest.

Panels are also used to monitor people's viewing/reading/listening habits (➤**audience measurement**) and work behaviours, e.g. workloads, hours, overtime, income, ➤**pay** and other forms of ➤**compensation.**

consumer products companies   Those companies that produce goods and services for final consumers, rather than for business. The list includes producers of frequently bought items (soap, nappies, dog food) (which go under the more specific name of 'fast-moving consumer goods' (FMCGs), or ➤**packaged goods**), and infrequently bought items (which are described as 'consumer durables', and include 'white goods' such as refrigerators and 'brown goods' like hi-fi units). In practice, these distinctions are sometimes hard to sustain because many products are bought both by consumers and business (soup, detergents, paper); however, the decision-making and buying processes are likely to differ. ➤**consumer behaviour.**

consumer satisfaction/dissatisfaction   ➤customer satisfaction/dissatisfaction.

consumer surplus   The value a consumer derives from acquiring a product, over and above the price paid for it. It is perhaps best seen as the maximum amount a consumer would be willing to pay for the product. The total consumer surplus of sales in a market can be graphically depicted as the area under the ➤**demand curve,** above the horizontal price. In setting prices, firms would like to capture the consumer surplus for themselves. But they face a straightforward dilemma: charging higher prices to reduce the surplus of consumers who would be willing to pay a large

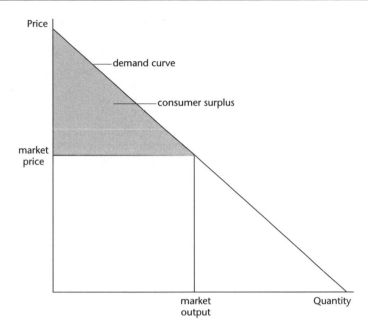

Graphical depiction of consumer surplus

amount may involve losing sales to customers who have less surplus, and may be only just motivated to make a purchase. The ideal solution to this dilemma is to charge more to high-surplus customers than the low-surplus ones, if it is possible to tell them apart. ➤**price discrimination**; ➤➤**segmentation**.

consumption function A mathematical expression of the factors affecting the amount consumers spend. For any particular item, consumer spending is typically related to the price of that item, the price of other items and income.

contango A situation in a ➤**commodity** market in which prices for future delivery are higher than those for immediate or very early delivery. Also known as ➤**for-wardation**.

contestability The degree to which firms can enter or leave an industry. Contestability provides a measure of the effect of potential competition in an industry. *Perfect contestability* implies there are no ➤**barriers to entry** into the sector at all. It requires that there are few ➤**sunk costs** of production, for these would imply that exit involves writing-off investment costs. In the early 1980s, the economist WJ Baumol drew attention to the power of perfect contestability to yield the results of ➤**perfect competition** in a market, without the huge number of small firms that that generally implies. The airline industry is generally held up as an example of a reasonably contestable industry.

contingent liability ➤**provisions**.

continuity programme A promotional programme that runs over several purchase cycles. ➤promotion.

contract 1. Any agreement under law, including an agreement to buy or sell a ➤security (➤contract note). **2.** Traded ➤options and ➤futures are agreements to buy or sell a security or commodity at a specified price and date and thus are referred to as 'contracts'. **3.** Any set of mutually understood obligations and entitlements governing the relationship between different parties. ➤➤implicit contract.

contracting out 1. (UK) The act of an occupational ➤pension scheme withdrawing from the State Earnings Related Pension Scheme (SERPS): subject to a guarantee of equivalent benefit, and attracting a reduction in contributions to the State. **2.** The decision of a company, or a public authority, to buy-in a service, rather than run it in-house. ➤make-or-buy decision.

contract note (UK) A document sent by a ➤broker soon after a transaction, showing the price at which a ➤security was bought or sold, a note of any benefits attached or excluded (e.g. ➤ex-dividend), the broker's ➤commission, tax charge, the ➤consideration and the terms of payment.

controlled coverage segmentation ➤segmentation.

conversion 1. Transfer of one type of ➤security into another, e.g. convertible loan stock or convertible bond, a fixed-interest security that on ➤maturity or at a specified date or dates may be exchanged for ➤equity at a fixed price. There may be an option to receive cash for those who do not wish to exercise their conversion rights. Convertibles usually carry a lower interest rate than similar fixed-interest securities, since the investor may make a ➤capital gain if the price of the underlying equity rises above the conversion price. ➤➤conversion premium; warrant. **2.** Change in legal form, e.g. conversion of a ➤building society to a public limited company (plc; ➤incorporation) under the Building Societies Act 1986.

conversion premium The difference between the current market price of a ➤share and the price at which a convertible security (➤conversion) or ➤warrant can be exchanged for the share. Expressed as a percentage of the market price of the convertible security, this is the conversion premium or, if the difference is negative, the conversion discount.

convertible 1. For a currency, a situation in which it can be bought or sold without restriction in exchange for other currencies. ➤exchange control. **2.** For a ➤security, a situation when it carries the right for the holder to exchange it at a fixed price for another form of security. ➤conversion.

cooling-off period (UK) A period, provided under the UK Insurance Companies Act and the Consumer Credit Act 1974, during which a person having entered into a long-term ➤life assurance policy or a ➤hire-purchase agreement has the right to withdraw from the commitment. The period is 10 days on effecting a life assurance policy and payment of the premium, and 5 days of receipt of confirmation of a hire-purchase agreement.

co-optition A term to describe the complex mix of competition and co-operation that exists between companies. This recognizes that companies can be competitors, customers, suppliers, collaborators and channels, and that these relationships will evolve over time, space and industrial sectors. Thus, within an established market, two companies traditionally might be competitors, but in an emergent area they may form an alliance and collaborate – something Sony and Philips have done to develop common optical media standards and to supply each other with components. Collaboration can also help to grow a sector, by offering consumers a bundle of products and services that might not appeal individually. This has been common in computer hardware and software and web applications, such as the way Netscape pulls together complementary technologies from competing firms in order to present consumers with something that has a strong overall-value proposition. The growth in alliances, networks, dual- and co-branding and co-operative exchange relationships is testament to the rise of co-option. This requires a mindset on the part of managers that can simultaneously cope with more competition and more collaboration. ➤➤**brand hierarchy**.

copyright An area of law that attempts to protect the work of its creator from being copied freely. Copyright is recognized by the symbol © and gives legal rights to creators of certain kinds of material, so that they can control the various ways in which their work may be exploited. Copyright protection is automatic and there is no registration or other formality.

This area of the law on intellectual property rights has changed significantly over the past few years, mainly because it now covers computer software. Computer software manufacturers are particularly concerned about the illegal copying of their programs. The music industry has also battled with this problem for many years. It has proved to be an exceptionally difficult area of law to enforce.

For the author of creative material to obtain copyright protection, it must be in a tangible form so that it can be communicated or reproduced. It must also be the author's own work and thus the product of his or her skill or judgement. Concepts, principles, processes or discoveries are not valid for copyright protection until they are put into tangible form, i.e. until they are written or drawn. To be valid for copyright protection, ideas must be presented in a particular way. If someone has written an article, you cannot simply rephrase it or change some of the words and claim it as your own. You are, however, entitled to read an article, digest it, take the ideas from that article together with other sources and weave them into your own material without any copyright problems. In most instances common sense should provide the answer.

Copyright may subsist in any of nine descriptions of work. These are grouped into three categories:

(1) Original literary, dramatic, musical and artistic works.

(2) Sound recordings, films, broadcasts and cable programmes.

(3) The typographical arrangement or layout of a published edition.

Each of these sections has more detailed definitions, e.g. 'films' includes videograms, and 'artistic work' includes photographs and computer-generated work.

The duration of copyright protection varies according to the description of the work. In the UK for literary, dramatic, musical and artistic works, copyright expires 70 years after the death of the author; in other cases, 50 years after the calendar year in which it was first published. The period was for 75 years in the US (but is now 50 years for all works created after 1978). ➤➤**intellectual property**.

core business The business that the firm sees as central to its survival and long-term strategy. Other businesses may be viewed as peripheral to the firm's purpose, and are therefore sold or closed. ➤competencies; competitive advantage.

core values The main or dominant values that are accepted throughout an organization. ➤values. ➤organizational culture.

corner A situation in which a particular trader in a market holds such a large volume of the asset being traded that he can set the price (➤price taking) and thus minimize the risk of his trades. For example, cornering allows a trader to engage in the ➤bear squeeze against other traders. Cornering the market is considered a dubious practice. It became notorious in the trading of agricultural produce in the late nineteenth-century US. In the novel *The Pit* (1902) Frank Norris describes an attempt by a wheat trader to corner the wheat market, driving himself and his wife into madness. To make a corner successful, the position has to be accumulated secretly so that other traders can't themselves counter the effect of the position.

corporate brand ➤brand hierarchy.

corporate control Generally, a situation in which one company owns more than 50 per cent of the ➤equity of another. However, in practice, considerable influence can be exerted with smaller equity stakes, especially where the share capital is fragmented into small units. In law in the UK, shareholders with over 25 per cent of equity can block a special resolution at an ➤annual general meeting to change the articles of association. ➤memorandum of association.

corporate finance ➤business finance.

corporate governance The selection of the senior officers of the organization and their conduct and relationships with owners, employees and other ➤stakeholders. The governance system concerns the monitoring systems of a corporation and consists of incentives, safeguards and dispute resolution processes used to control and co-ordinate.

Three main systems exist today; these are exemplified by the US, German and Japanese systems.
(1) The US system is founded on the 'one share one vote' principle where the shareholder is the sole owner of the firm. The board of directors is the corporate body and is accountable to society. Consequently, most directors are people from outside the firm and two thirds of directors are also chief executive officers. Relationships between employees, suppliers, lenders and the board are kept at arms length. Fifty per cent of shares are held by the public, the other 50 per cent are held by large institutions, with pension funds holding 25 per cent of this amount. The emphasis is on contracts (the law) rather than trust. Hostile corporate take-overs originated in this system and the courts are used to resolve disputes (such as after bankruptcies). This system seeks to maintain the accountability of corporate managers to corporate owners through the board of directors and the proxy voting mechanism.
(2) The German system is characterized by two boards of people: (a) the supervisory board (*Aufsichtstraat*) with employee representatives (the ➤trade unions are powerful), banks (*Hausebank*) and shareholder representatives, and (b) the man-

agement board (*Vorstand*) with the senior management team. The banks have large proxy voting power because they hold shares on deposit.

(3) The Japanese system is based on long-term consensus relationships with the emphasis on trust. Groups of companies (➤*keiretsu*) dominate and there is horizontal movement within them. The boards are dominated by inside directors and personal relationships are primary. There are almost no hostile corporate take-overs, and bankruptcies are informally resolved.

corporate identity ➤corporate image.

corporate image The overall set of associations that people have of an organization based not only on the image of specific products, but also pricing policies, service levels, support and assistance, salesforce conduct, communications, social responsibility, employee management, and business conduct. Thus, corporate image depends on the products made by a company, the actions it takes with regard to products and many other aspects of the business, and how it communicates these actions to consumers. These associations are based on general impressions, beliefs and feelings – they are not necessarily accurate in a factual sense. Typically, management will attempt to influence the formation of associations through its corporate communications. This takes the form of symbols, logos, brochures, annual reports, ➤advertising, etc. (collectively called 'corporate identity' material). The management of corporate image lies at the heart of corporate branding, as evident in such organizations as Sony, Shell, IBM, Ford, and Accenture, and of branding strategies more generally. ➤brand; brand hierarchy; ➤➤brand image; store image.

A closely related concept is 'corporate reputation', i.e. a person's overall evaluation of a company, given that person's prior beliefs about what is appropriate for the company in question. Evaluations summarize a person's respect for a company and the esteem in which it is held. Different people will have different prior values and therefore different evaluations, e.g. two people may share a similar image of Sony, but evaluate it differently because their prior values – or standards – differ. Although corporate image and corporate reputation are often discussed in terms of consumers, a variety of other ➤stakeholders and observers are of considerable importance, e.g. investors, financial analysts, regulatory bodies, service providers, suppliers. For these people, consumer issues are relevant (products, pricing policies, service levels, etc.), but so, too, are factors such as the quality of management, financial soundness and value of the company as a long-term investment. One way to have an impact on consumers, stakeholders and observers is through ➤cause-related marketing.

corporate planning ➤strategic planning.

corporate raider (US) An individual organization that makes hostile ➤take-over bids for ➤quoted companies. These bids may be financed by ➤junk bonds and involve 'greenmail' in which the target company may avert the take-over by buying in at a premium rate the ➤share stake built up by the raider or a risk arbitrageur. ➤arbitrage. The latter buys stakes in companies that are expected to be the subject of a contested bid (➤merger), selling the ➤stock of the acquiring company. In a take-over bid, the shares of the acquiring company usually fall on announcement of the bid, while those of the victim rise. The term 'greenmail' derives from the colour of dollar bills and the implication of blackmail in some threatened take-over bids. ➤➤poison pill; white knight.

corporate reputation ➤corporate image.

corporate social responsibility ➤business ethics.

corporate strategy ➤strategic management.

corporate venturing A technique to provide new fledgling businesses within a large corporation the freedom to grow outside the constraints of the existing large established organization. Conventional management thinking argues that new ventures should be sheltered from the normal planning and control systems, otherwise they will be strangled. Ideally, they should be given high-level sponsorship from senior management, but must be able to manage their own relationships with other companies. Many large organizations such as Du Pont, IBM and General Electric Company have long experience of corporate venturing stretching back to the 1960s. However, following some high-profile failures, most notably by Shell in the mid 1980s, corporate venturing fell out of favour. More recent research suggests that the record of corporate venturing compared to external venture capital shows that the latter do no better than the corporations.

Another form of corporate venturing is that in which the support is given to an external fledgling business. Large international companies sometimes acquire shares in smaller-growth companies, particularly in new technology-based industries, and may provide them with research and development (R&D), marketing or other support. This is done primarily to secure an interest in new markets or new technologies, and for that reason has been described as a low-cost form of R&D. The prime motives for corporate venturing are usually strategic in nature, but if the strategic objectives are met there will usually be financial rewards also.

corporation ➤incorporation.

corporation tax A tax levied on the profits of companies. It is typically calculated on profits after allowance has been made for all costs, including interest payments and depreciation (offered at some fixed rates, known as *capital allowances*). Corporation taxes generally can be modelled on one of a variety of forms; the *classical system*, for example (used in the US, UK and The Netherlands) charges tax on all profits, whether distributed as dividends or not. This means that shareholders receiving dividends and paying income tax on them, end up paying tax twice on the same profits. An alternative system is the so-called *imputation system* in which some income tax relief is offered to shareholders, to ensure that dividends are not subject to both income tax and corporation tax. The UK corporation tax was introduced in 1967 on the classical model; it was switched to the imputation system in 1973, only to revert to the classical form in 1997.

The rationale for corporation tax is not entirely clear. It was originally introduced in the classical form to encourage the retention of earnings by companies, in the hope that this would stimulate investment. The reversion to that system was partly justified on the same ground. Some economists argue that the allocation of capital resources is best determined by the capital market, and would prefer to see a higher proportion of dividends distributed and then rechannelled back to investment via the capital market.

correlation coefficient A measure of the degree to which variations in one variable can be used to track variations in another. Given a series of pairs of data for, say, income and consumer spending in different years, one can see how far movements in income correlate with movements in consumer spending. Given the usual notation, r, the coefficient equals 1 if there is a perfect correspondence in the variations, 0 if there is no correlation, and –1 if there is complete inverse correspondence (higher values of one variable perfectly correlate with lower values of the other).

More specifically:

$$r = \frac{\Sigma(x_i - \bar{x})(y_i - \bar{y})}{\sqrt{[\Sigma_i(x_i - \bar{x})^2]}\sqrt{[\Sigma_i(y_i - \bar{y})^2]}}$$

where x_i and y_i are the values of the two variables, and $\bar{x}$ and $\bar{y}$ are the mean values of each.

In business, correlation analysis is very widespread, both explicitly and implicitly. However, the temptation to infer causality from correlation analysis should be resisted, e.g. simply because income and consumer spending correlate does not mean one causes the other; to make that inference there needs to be causal analysis and underlying theory.

cost A sacrifice incurred in the pursuit of some activity. Seemingly simple, costs in fact come in a variety of forms. Cash costs (or explicit costs) accord with the popular notion of a cost, and enter the accounts of companies. However, an ➤**implicit cost** or an ➤**opportunity cost** have no cash flow associated with them, but are very real indeed. Even explicit costs can be divided up in a number of ways, e.g. the total cost of production of an item can be divided into fixed and variable components, the former being those costs that are incurred regardless of the volume of production, the latter varying with output. Fixed costs, or the equivalent accounting concept, ➤**overheads**, can themselves be subdivided in numerous ways, and a distinction can be made between short-run fixed costs, and long-run fixed costs, because costs that are fixed in the short run (such as the costs associated with a piece of capital equipment) may be variable in the longer run, as fewer such pieces of equipment would be purchased over time if lower output was desired. Finally, total costs of producing an item can be divided among the units produced to obtain average cost (a concept itself distinct from ➤**marginal costs**, which are the costs incurred by increasing output by one unit). The *cost function* maps the relationship between total costs and output, and from it average and marginal costs can be calculated.

cost accounting ➤management accounting.

cost–benefit analysis A specific set of techniques for weighing-up the benefits and costs of a particular project. Typically used by the public sector, it involves much of the financial analysis familiar in private ➤**capital budgeting**, plus some attempts to value the social impact of the project. In assessing a potential railway scheme, a private operator may simply forecast a set of cash flows, taking into account the revenue stream paid by passengers. A public sector operator may perform a cost–benefit analysis that would also take account of ➤**consumer surplus**, the value of lives saved on the road, the damage to the environment, etc. This form of analysis was first used to assess the building of London Underground's Victoria Line in the 1960s. The benefits considered in that case were convenience of travel for passengers and less road congestion. Set against these benefits were costs such as potential damage to buildings above ground and sewers underground. Some authors have criticized what they see as the spurious precision of attempts to value everything.

cost centre ➤management accounting.

cost elasticity A measure of the responsiveness of the cost of producing an item to the scale of production. It can be measured as the change in total costs that occurs from a 1 per cent change in the overall scale of output. If total costs rise by less than 1 per cent, then production enjoys ➤economies of scale. If total costs rise by more than 1 per cent, production is subject to ➤diseconomies of scale. ≫elasticity.

cost, historical Actual costs at the time incurred. An ➤asset in the ➤balance sheet at historical cost is shown at the price paid for it, even though it may be worth more or cost more to replace. ➤inflation accounting; ≫fair value.

cost leadership One of the three ➤generic strategies advocated by Michael ➤Porter. A firm that is leader in costs has developed a business that delivers the lowest cost in that industry, thus providing the business with an advantage over its competitors. To achieve such a position usually will require driving down costs in all areas of a business's operations including suppliers and driving up efficiencies. Such firms tend to offer no-frills products and services and maximize economies of scale.

cost of capital ➤capital, cost of.

cost of sales (UK) The cost of producing what is sold before making an allowance for contribution to general ➤overheads, i.e. material costs, manufacturing wage costs and production overheads.

cost per thousand (CPM) The cost to an advertiser to reach 1,000 listeners or viewers with a given message, obtained by dividing the cost of buying a particular time-slot (or segment) by the size of audience reached (in thousands). ≫advertising; audience rating.

cost-plus pricing ➤mark-up pricing.

counterparty risk The risk in securities trading that the counterparty to a purchase or sale may fail to discharge his obligation. If default occurs before settlement is due, the counterparty risk takes the form of *replacement risk*, i.e. the risk of incurring the cost of replacing the deal. Counterparty risk may also take the form of *settlement risk*, in which one side of the deal pays cash or delivers securities, but where the other side delays completing his part, causing illiquidity which may raise serious problems.

countertrading Another term for barter, i.e. the exchange of goods or services without any monetary consideration.

countervailing power Concept generally attributable to J K Galbraith to describe the emergence of large organizations as a natural response to the rise of big corporations. ➤Trade unions are thus seen to provide some countervailing power to large employers, for example. ≫collective action; conflict; power.

coupon **1.** A counterfoil or tag that, when detached from a ➤bond, serves as evidence of entitlement to interest. It is invariably used to refer to the rate of interest itself and, by extension, is also used to refer to the rate of interest on most financial

➤instruments, particularly ➤notes. **2.** A docket that consumers can use to obtain price discounts or rebates when buying goods and services. ➤promotion.

Covey, Stephen R Leadership guru and author of the best-seller *The Seven Habits of Highly Effective People* (1990). The seven habits are: (a) 'Be proactive' (choose your own response to people and situations); (b) 'Begin with an end in mind'; (c) 'Put first things first' (focus on what is important but not necessarily urgent); (d) 'Think win/win' (everyone can gain); (e) 'Seek first to understand, then to be understood'; (f) 'Synergize' (the whole is greater than the sum of the parts), and (g) 'Sharpen the saw' (seek continuous improvement and innovation). Stephen Covey is a very successful consultant and founder of the Covey Leadership Center near Salt Lake City.

CPM ➤cost per thousand.

crash A precipitate one-day fall in stock market prices.

credence qualities ➤evaluation process; ➤➤information search.

credit Granting the use or possession of goods and services without immediate payment. ➤consumer credit; double-entry bookkeeping; trade credit.

credit card A plastic, personal, magnetized card issued by an agency, bank or other institution against which purchases, up to a prescribed ceiling (*credit limit*) may be credited on signature of a voucher franked by the card. The vendor recovers the cash from the issuer of the card (less a percentage commission), and the purchaser pays the issuer on receipt of a monthly statement. If desired, the purchaser has the option of paying a minimum amount and settling the account in instalments plus interest. Credit cards are sometimes available free to creditworthy users; other cards, known as *charge cards*, are paid for by an annual fee and do not offer the option of a loan. A *debit card* works in the same way as the credit card but debits the purchaser's bank account immediately. Credit cards may be used to withdraw cash from an automatic teller machine, and the card may be magnetically inspected for authenticity. Credit cards are popularly referred to as 'plastic money'.

credit guarantee A type of ➤insurance against default, provided by a credit guarantee association, government body or other institution, to a lending institution, to allow small firms that lack collateral security, or are unable to obtain loans for other reasons, to obtain credit from banks. A government *loan guarantee* scheme of this type was introduced in the UK in 1980. Not to be confused with ➤deposit insurance.

credit line (US) ➤overdraft.

creditor One to whom money is due.

credit rating An assessment of the likelihood of an individual or business being able to meet its financial obligations. Credit ratings are provided by credit agencies or ➤rating agencies for sellers who wish to verify the financial strength of buyers, for lenders and for investors (ratings for specific ➤securities). The highest rating is Triple A. Banks also provide confidential trade references.

credit union A non-profit organization accepting ➤deposits and making loans, operated as a co-operative; a ➤**mutual** organization that is, in effect, a ➤**savings bank**. Similar credit associations exist in many countries.

CREST Electronic share register (➤**registrar** and ➤**settlement system**) introduced to the ➤**London Stock Exchange** in 1996. By recording titles to shares electronically it reduces the cost of the traditional system of ➤**share certificates** sent through the post. Title is recorded through ➤**nominee companies** set up by ➤**stockbrokers** and others. However, shareholders may continue to hold paper certificates if they wish. CREST is owned by Crestco, a company in which the London Stock Exchange has a minority holding along with other financial institutions.

critical incident An event in service delivery that contributes to, or detracts from, the customer's service experience in a major way. These events are studied using critical incident techniques (CIT). The techniques involve looking at employee responses to service delivery failures (e.g. unreasonably slow service in a restaurant), employee responses to customer needs and requests (e.g. special dietary needs of customers), and unprompted and unsolicited employee actions, e.g. attention paid to a customer. ➤➤**service encounter; services marketing**.

critical path analysis The process of dividing a project into a series of activities. These activities and their duration are then placed in the correct sequence. The critical path is the shortest possible time in which the project can be completed. This is illustrated in a diagram known as a 'critical path analysis network'. Special attention is given to those activities that are on the critical path as it is these that will affect the time of the project. A non-critical activity will have some slack time associated with it. ➤➤**Gantt chart**.

critical success factor (CSF) Part of the limited number of areas in which results, if they are satisfactory, will ensure successful competitive performance for the organization. They are the few key areas (usually between three and eight) where things must be correct. The CSF approach focuses on individual managers and their information needs. When first introduced by Rockart in 1979, its primary use was to help individual managers determine their information needs.

CRM ➤customer relationship management.

Crosby, Philip Quality management guru, formerly Vice-President for Quality at ITT, the US conglomerate. Proponent of Zero Defects who argued that the conventional policy of solving quality problems by rectification after the event, instead of preventing them in the first place, cost businesses very large amounts of money. Wrote *Quality Without Tears: the art of hassle-free management* (1984). He argued that newer ritualistic procedures like ISO 9000 and ➤**total quality management** (TQM, which he dubbed 'trivializing quality management') are ineffective substitutes for good management, which concentrates on getting transactions right and giving customers what they want. One of three famous American quality management exponents to emerge after the Second World War. ➤➤**Deming, W Edwards; Juran, Joseph**.

cross-border listing Shares and other ➤**securities** traded on exchanges in more than one country. Most such assets can only be traded freely where they are listed on an official ➤**stock exchange**.

crossed (US) A situation where one ➤**market maker** has a lower ➤**offer** price than another's ➤**bid price**. This is referred to as a locked or crossed market, and in the UK sometimes as ➤**backwardation**.

cross-functional teams A group of employees from a similar hierarchical level, but from different work areas, who come together to accomplish a task. ➤**group development; work groups**.

crossing The purchase and sale of a quantity of ➤**securities** by the same ➤**broker**. Stock exchange rules normally require such transactions to cross the market so as to ensure that the buyer or seller has the opportunity to get a better price if it is available. Where the two orders are for the same individual, or by another acting in collusion with him, a crossed sale is known in the US as a wash sale.

cross-price elasticity of demand A measure of the relationship between price movements in one product and the demand for another product. If an increase in the price of petrol has a large impact on the demand for cars, then there is a high cross-price elasticity of demand between petrol and cars. More specifically, the elasticity is the proportionate change in the quantity demanded of one item, divided by a proportionate change in price of another item. ➤**elasticity**. ➤➤**complementary good; substitutes**.

cross-section data The values of several variables at one period of time, each corresponding to one observation. A dataset consisting of height and weight for a large group of people at one point of time would be a cross-section data set. ➤**econometrics**.

cross-subsidy The practice of using revenues or profits of one activity, to support another activity. Common in the public sector, where it can be used as a form of hidden redistribution from some consumers to others, it is not uncommon in the private sector. Firms may cross-subsidize as a result of regulation, e.g. being compelled to provide loss-making rural phone boxes or to maintain a simple and uniform pricing structure (rural households paying the same phone rates as urban ones). Or to promote a new activity that requires start-up investment, or keep prices low in a competitive market, by using profits from one that is less competitive. For example, one reason Airbus chose to produce its large A380 airliner was to reduce the monopoly power of its rival Boeing in the large-plane sector as this had given Boeing the power to cross-subsidize smaller planes against which Airbus was competing. It is generally considered that the more intense competition is within an industry, the less the ability or inclination of producers to cross-subsidize.

CRP ➤capacity requirements plan.

CSF ➤critical success factor.

culture ➤national culture; organizational culture.

cum-dividend With-dividend; the purchaser of a security quoted cum-dividend is entitled to receive the next ➤**dividend** when due. The term 'cum' is used in a similar sense in relation to ➤**bonus issues**, ➤**rights issues** or ➤**interest** attached to ➤**securities**, etc.

cumulative preference shares (UK) ➤preference shares.

Curb Exchange ➤American Stock Exchange.

currency 1. Notes and coin that are the *current* medium of exchange in a country. **2.** In US and UK banking, all foreign currencies. **3.** In US ➤**money supply** terminology, currency refers to cash.

currency board A national body charged with maintaining a fixed ➤**exchange rate** by expanding or contracting the issue of domestic currency in line with holdings of foreign currency and other liquid assets. Unlike a ➤**central bank**, a currency board cannot simply issue new domestic currency without one-to-one backing, or act as a ➤**lender of last resort**. Currency boards link their domestic currency to a foreign currency, e.g. the exchange-rate peg to the US dollar maintained by the Hong Kong currency board.

current account 1. The most common type of bank account, on which ➤**deposits** do not necessarily earn ➤**interest** but can be withdrawn by ➤**cheque** at any time (US = *demand deposit; checking account*). **2.** That part of the ➤**balance of payments** recording current (i.e. non-capital) transactions.

current asset ➤asset.

current cost accounting ➤inflation accounting.

current liability ➤liability.

current ratio ➤working capital.

customer The word is sometimes used interchangeably with 'consumer', but formally it is reserved for the designation of those who directly buy from an organization. Thus, a manufacturer often has just a few wholesalers, distributors and retailers as customers, in contrast to the mass of final consumers who buy from retail stores. 'Customer' is used commonly in the context of ➤**business-to-business marketing**. ➤**customer relationship management**.

customer relationship management (CRM) A formal programme for the management of relationships between organizations, their staff and customers. Also termed 'client relationship management'. Required is an appraisal of all customers and the development of customized plans for managing them. For highly profitable customers this may result in adding value to the products and services offered already, whereas it may entail cutting back on services to low-profit customers. In financial services, for instance, high-net-worth customers might be offered loan and life ➤**insurance** services in addition to personal banking facilities, whereas low-net-worth customers may be charged fees for basic banking services and encouraged to use automated facilities. Among profitable customers a form of ➤**relationship marketing** often develops, but at the other end of the spectrum customer relationship management has more to do with cutting costs and the industrialization of services, with the substitution of capital for labour. ➤**key account management**; **services marketing**.

Many see tremendous potential for eCRM – electronic CRM. ➤**interactive electronic marketing**. One attraction of this is the ease with which aspects of the relationship can be measured (by evaluating clickthroughs, acquisition and retention costs and conversion rates) and kept up to date (using dynamic profiling).

customer satisfaction/dissatisfaction (CS/D) The overall attitude a customer has about a good or service after it has been bought and consumed. This post-purchase evaluation will relate to experience of processes (e.g. in-store sales and subsequent delivery) and outcomes, e.g. performance of the product. Satisfaction occurs when the customer feels his needs, desires and expectations have been met or exceeded. Dissatisfaction occurs when the feeling is that needs, desires and expectations have not been met. The norm would be to hope for satisfaction – with customers feeling contented and fulfilled – although sometimes it is possible to create an element of surprise and arousal, giving rise to 'customer delight'. CS/D is often discussed in the context of ➤**business-to-business marketing** and ➤**services marketing**, but it is also relevant to the post-purchase evaluation of consumer products, e.g. how easy the product was to obtain and use effectively, assessed against initial needs, desires and expectations. Having satisfied customers is seen as a way of retaining them, to reduce switching to competitors, and encourage positive word-of-mouth recommendations, but it is not equivalent to loyalty. ➤**consumer loyalty**. Many other factors besides satisfaction influence loyalty, e.g. product availability, price, and promotions. ➤➤**expectations**.

cyclical stock A share in a company expected to prosper particularly in times of economic boom, while its share price tends to fall most during recessions. Building companies and motor distributors, for example, are generally included as cyclicals while food retailers are regarded as *defensive stocks* least affected by the state of the economy.

D

DAGMAR An approach for setting goals and objectives for ➤advertising. DAGMAR is an acronym that stands for 'Defining Advertising Goals for Measured Advertising Results', an expression coined by Russell Colley in 1961. The main thesis of the approach is that advertising goals involve a specific and measurable communications task. There are four such tasks: (a) making consumers aware of a ➤brand ('awareness'); (b) helping them understand what the brand is and does ('comprehension'); (c) developing a disposition to buy the brand ('conviction'), and (d) enabling consumers to make a purchase ('action'). This approach is consistent with the ➤AIDA theory of how advertising works. ➤brand communication effects.

database marketing The use of information, held on computer systems, to undertake direct and pertinent communication with existing customers and/or prospects in the ➤target audience. Information may be purchased (e.g. for an accounting product, a list of accountants' names might be purchased from a professional society) or it might come from internal records, e.g. transaction records, names of those who have taken part in ➤promotions, details of those on ➤loyalty programmes and lists of those who have made enquiries in response to direct-response advertisements). Information on the database needs to be accurate and up to date if the communication is to be effective – this requires a major commitment to database maintenance and cleaning. Despite these problems, database marketing is widely practised and provides much of the input for ➤customer relationship management and ➤direct marketing. ➤personalization technologies.

data fusion In ➤marketing research, the merging of information from different sources. If a researcher has information about the television viewing habits of teenagers and, from a separate study, information about the buying behaviour of teenagers, it may be possible to merge the data. The samples used in these two studies would have to be matched, i.e. they have to be statistically equivalent. Fused data can be used to investigate aspects of ➤consumer behaviour and to model responses to marketing activities, e.g. if a product for teenagers is advertised on prime-time television, how many are likely to see the commercial, and does this have any subsequent impact on their buying behaviour?

dated security ➤Bond, ➤bill of exchange or other ➤security that has a stated date for redemption (repayment) of its nominal value. Short-dated securities are those for which the ➤redemption date is near; long-dated securities are those for which it is a long time ahead.

dawn raid (UK) The acquisition of a large block of shares on the ➤stock exchange, sometimes as a prelude to a ➤take-over bid. Usually purchases are carried out simultaneously by a number of ➤brokers first thing in the morning.

DAX (*Deutscher Aktienindex*) An index designed to reflect the movements in share prices of thirty companies listed on the Frankfurt Stock Exchange. It was given a base level of 1,000 in December 1987.

day after recall The number of viewers who can remember seeing a particular television commercial that was shown the previous night. This is a crude measure of whether a commercial is working. ➤➤brand communication effects.

DBS Database system. ➤database marketing.

DCF ➤discounted cash flow.

dealer Someone who buys and sells on their own account. ➤broker–dealer.

debenture, debenture stock (UK) A fixed-interest ➤security issued by limited companies (➤incorporation) in return for long-term loans. The former term is sometimes also used to refer to any title on a secured interest-bearing loan such as a bank loan. Debentures are dated for redemption between 10 and 40 years ahead. ➤redemption date. Debentures are usually secured against specific assets of the company (*mortgage debentures*) or by a floating charge on the assets. Debenture interests must be paid whether the company makes a profit or not. In the event of non-payment, debenture holders can force ➤liquidation, and they rank ahead of all shareholders in their claims on the company's assets. Convertible debentures carry an option at a fixed date to convert the ➤stock into ➤ordinary shares at a fixed price. ➤conversion.

debit ➤double-entry bookkeeping.

De Bono, Edward Proponent of 'lateral thinking', which he distinguishes from 'logical sequential thinking'. In *Lateral Thinking* (1970) he writes that this type of thought restructures the way situations are perceived, whereas logical, or vertical, thinking accepts there is perceptual pattern and develops it step by step. De Bono's ideas arose from a study of the way the mind works by making or recognizing patterns (*The Mechanism of the Mind*, 1969). This allows efficient interaction with the environment, but the patterns can become fixed in the mind and inhibit the creative use of new information. Since business is a creative activity, lateral thinking is needed in management (*Lateral Thinking for Management*, 1971) and de Bono has acted as a consultant to many large corporations. Born in Malta, he qualified in medicine there and went on to study psychology, physiology and medicine at Oxford. He lives in Venice.

debt A sum of money or other property owed by one person or organization to another. Debt comes into being through the granting of ➤credit or through raising loan capital. Debt servicing consists of paying interest on a debt. The term 'debt' is, by extension, used to refer to the total loan exposure of an enterprise or public authority or to the choice of ➤bonds rather than ➤equity in raising funds – 'to issue debt'.

debt instrument A medium for raising a loan, usually a short-term loan. ➤instrument.

debtor One who owes money to another.

decentralization A form of organizational design where decision-making, and responsibility for decisions, is passed to employees lower down the organizational hierarchy. Decentralization ensures that the expertise of employees who are close to the front-line is tapped – they should have the knowledge of, and proximity to, customers and markets to make better decisions. However, co-ordination and control across the decentralized units then becomes problematic, and each unit may start to duplicate functions that could be run more efficiently from the centre, e.g. with regard to the management of the payroll. ➤**personnel management; public relations.**

decision-making unit (DMU) In organizations, the group of people who are responsible for buying, purchasing and procurement decisions. ➤**organizational buying behaviour.**

decision rule The idea that when faced with a range of options people – consumers, employees, managers – select an option using a rule or a combination of rules. Typically, options are evaluated in terms of several criteria (e.g. five ➤**brands** of soft drink might be evaluated in terms of price, quantity, taste, fizz and 'coolness') and the rule refers to how the evaluative criteria are weighed up in reaching an overall decision.

There are five main rules.

(1) Conjunctive decision rule. This says: define minimum standards (cut-off points) for each evaluative criterion, and accept any option that is above *all* these cut-offs. Thus, the soft drink must be low price, be at least 330 ml, rate 4 or above in taste tests (on a 7-point scale), etc. Perhaps three brands fulfil these minimum standards. The rule does not say which of the three to choose, but if they all meet the minimum standards it is presumed the final selection is immaterial, i.e. the decision-maker is assumed to be indifferent between the remaining three brands.

(2) Disjunctive decision rule. This says: define high minimum standards (cut-off points) for each really important evaluative criterion, and accept any option that is above any *one* of these cut-offs. Taste and fizz might be seen as very important, so only those brands of soft drink that meet stringent requirements on these two criteria will be selected.

(3) Elimination-by-aspects decision rule. This says: rank the evaluative criteria, define cut-offs for each one, assess all options against the highest-ranked criterion. If more than two options are above the cut-off move on to the next criterion and evaluate the options against this next criterion. Keep repeating until only one option is left. Assume taste is most important, followed by fizz. Two brands may exceed the cut-off for taste, so then these two brands are evaluated for their fizz, at which point only one brand might exceed the cut-off. This decision-rule underlies 'the isolation effect' in ➤**prospect theory**.

(4) Lexicographic decision rule. This says: rank the evaluative criteria, define cut-offs for each one, assess all options against the highest-ranked criterion, and select the option that performs *best* (this is where the rule differs from (3) above). If two or more options tie for best position, the decision-maker moves on to

consider the surviving options against the next criterion – again, the aim is to select the option that performs *best*. If taste is most important, there may be two brands that exceed the cut-off (as in (3) above), but one may score better than the other and, therefore, this will be the one selected by the lexicographic rule.

(5) Compensatory decision rule. Here the decision-maker averages out good features and poor ones. The procedure is a little more complex than with non-compensatory rules (i.e. (1)–(4) above). First, one option is assessed on a single evaluative criterion, and this assessment is multiplied by the importance of the evaluative criterion (this weights the assessment by the importance of the criterion). This is repeated for all other evaluative criteria, and the results of these assessments are summed (giving a weighted sum). The procedure is repeated for all other options, resulting in a set of weighted sums. The highest weighted sum is selected. A particular brand may score very well in terms of taste and fizz, but be seen as too expensive. Another brand may be seen as cheap, but not so good for taste and fizz. A compensatory decision rule can be used to average out these varying performance levels across evaluative criteria, and help the consumer select the most appropriate brand of soft drink.

Different rules will result in different outcomes, so it is important to understand which rule is being applied in any given situation. In some contexts decision rules are made explicit. For example, employee recruitment guidelines might stipulate that each job applicant is evaluated using four key criteria (ranked in order of importance), following which an elimination-by-aspects rule is applied (this might be done to ensure an equitable treatment of all applicants). However, it is much more likely that the evaluative criteria and the rules are implicit, especially in informal contexts such as consumer decision-making. This makes it hard for an analyst to know which rule is being used. In ➤**consumer behaviour** and ➤**choice modelling** reasonable assumptions have to be made. For example, complex compensatory rules are more likely to be used when the decision is high-involvement (➤**involvement theory**), whereas simple conjunctive rules are probably good enough for low-involvement decisions (where the decision-maker is likely to want to minimize mental effort). Assumptions such as these are made by product designers when deciding which attributes to emphasize in a new product (➤**new product development**) and by advertisers when thinking of attributes to highlight in marketing communications. ➤**advertising**.

A problem with this view of individual decision-making is that it presumes people always weigh up a specific number of attributes, whereas it may be more realistic to assume an holistic assessment is made, perhaps followed by the weighing-up of attributes for a very limited set of choice alternatives. Thus, on looking at ten houses to buy, the person may dismiss eight alternatives based on first impressions. These impressions might be hard to articulate, but the person is quite sure the house is not suitable. Only with the final two options might specific features such as structure, decoration, number of rooms, garden quality, etc., be weighed up.

decision-support system (DSS) **1.** An information system to improve the overall efficiency and effectiveness of individuals within the organization. These particular information systems have, as their primary function, the processing of predefined transactions to produce fixed format reports at the necessary time. The principal use is to automate the basic business processes of the organization. Typical functions include: payroll, customer orders, purchase requests, etc. **2.** A system of guidelines to help managers make reasonably complex decisions, e.g. where there are trade-offs between one goal and another. Typically, these guidelines are grounded in a formal understanding of the underlying processes (which then can be captured in mathematical algorithms) and they use information from within the company, from the market-place, and from the judgement of managers. Applications include price-setting, product design, media buying, sales promotion, salesforce management, distribution strategies and logistics. ➤**management information system; management support systems;** ➤➤**marketing engineering; marketing mix.**

decreasing returns to scale A situation in an industry where an increase in all the inputs into production leads to a less than proportionate increase in output, i.e. if you double the size of the factory, you do not double the output. It is not to be confused with ➤**diminishing returns** (where successive increases in *one input taken in isolation* lead to smaller and smaller increments to output), nor is it to be exactly equated with ➤**diseconomies of scale**, which describe the disproportionately small increase in output as producing organizations become larger. Diseconomies of scale might result from management failure in large companies, while decreasing returns generally refer to specific characteristics of production technology. ➤➤**production function.**

dedifferentiation The removal of traditional barriers and distinctions between industries that were once quite distinct, e.g. the blurring of boundaries between broadcasting, entertainment, computing, telecommunications, information processes, etc. Popularized by authors such as George ➤**Gilder.** ➤➤**e-commerce; interactive electronic marketing; internet.**

deep discount bond Low-interest or no-interest ➤**debt** issued at a price well below ➤**par value.** This means that on ➤**redemption** at maturity, the holder will make a ➤**capital gain** which may be advantageous for tax purposes even though the running ➤**yield** is low.

deferred annuity An ➤**annuity** whose commencement occurs on a specified date after purchase.

defined benefits scheme Occupational ➤**pension** schemes promising a definite pension, usually as a percentage of final salary and based upon length of service.

defined contributions scheme ➤**personal pension** scheme in which the level of contributions is fixed, with no promise of a specific level of pension. In effect, a money purchase scheme. ➤**pension.**

deflation 1. A sustained reduction in the general level of prices. Deflation is often, though not inevitably, accompanied by declines in output and employment and is distinct from 'disinflation' which refers to a reduction in the rate of inflation. Deflation can be brought about by either internal or external forces in an open economy. **2.** A deliberate policy of reducing aggregate demand and output so as to reduce the rate of ➤**inflation** and the quantity of imports and lower the ➤**exchange rate**, thus improving export performance and the ➤**balance of payments.** Aggregate demand may be reduced by ➤**fiscal policy** (increasing taxes or reducing government expenditure) or ➤**monetary policy** (increases in the ➤**rate** of interest and slower growth or contraction in the money supply). **3.** In economic statistics, the adjustment of index numbers or economic aggregates to eliminate the effects of price changes, as in dividing an index of the gross domestic product (GDP) at current prices by a price index (➤**retail price index**) to give an index of GDP in real terms.

deindustrialization The process by which advanced economies have tended to shed large-scale manufacturing operations, and instead diverted resources to the services sector. In the UK, for example, in 1978, some 27 per cent of the workforce was employed in manufacturing; by 2000, this had almost halved to 15 per cent. While it is tempting to conclude this was the product of unique circumstances of the political climate in the UK, a similar trend was pervasive in the developed world. Part of the decline may be statistical mismeasurement – a cleaner employed by Imperial Chemical Industries (ICI) in 1978 would have counted as a manufacturing worker, but if the same cleaner was employed by a company contracting cleaning services to ICI in 2000, he would count as a service worker. Nevertheless, it seems clear that huge gains in manufacturing productivity have led to a shift out of manufacturing, or at least into higher value added, more specialist niche manufacturing. ➤➤**Baumol effect**.

delayering The removal of one or more layers of a management hierarchy from an organization's structure. In theory it provides greater responsibility to those staff below the layer that has been removed; however, it is sometimes a euphemism for removing people and making them redundant.

Delphi group forecast The use of a group of experts to provide forecasts for long-term planning. The name derives from a famous oracle, a place where Ancient Greeks would consult prophets, at Delphi. The method involves using knowledge and experience of experts in the field. Individual views are collected and then discussed and debated until a consensus emerges. More generally, the Delphi technique is a research method based on an interactive exchange of ideas and information among a panel of experts to arrive at a consensus with regard to a topic of interest (often involving a forecast, though not necessarily so). Questionnaires are used to elicit responses. Typically, several rounds of questioning are involved, with each round incorporating responses from earlier rounds of questioning. ➤**marketing research**.

demand curve A graphical depiction of the relationship between the different possible prices of an item, and the amount consumers would buy at each price. The demand curve is perhaps the first graph to which economics students are exposed, with price on the vertical axis, and quantity on the horizontal. The curve is held to slope down from left to right, as higher prices are associated with lower demand. It is possible to have a demand curve for an industry taken as a whole, and for individual firms within it and a different one for the short term or long term. The shallower the gradient of the curve, the more price-sensitive (➤**price elasticity of demand**) is demand for the product. The demand curve traces the pattern between price and demand on the assumption that all other factors affecting demand are held constant. ➤**consumer surplus**. In practice, it may be quite hard to calibrate the gradient of the curve because demand is only known at those price-points where an item is made available for sale or where a reliable estimate can be obtained from ➤**marketing research**. ➤➤**demand forecasting**.

demand deposit ➤current account.

demand forecasting The process of attempting to predict future demand for a product or service. All operations will be working to deliver a certain number of products or process a certain number of customers. In order to be able to do this some prior analysis would have been made of the number of products or services required. It is this analysis of the future, referred to as 'forecasting', that determines the number of products to produce. Some operations can make accurate forward provision because they have advanced firm orders from customers. This is known as 'dependent demand', and is a relatively predictable requirement for a product or service that is usually based upon some known factor. For example, the manufacturer of video cassettes is able to make reliable predictions of demand for new cassettes based upon sales of video cassette machines. Other operations, however, can only make predictions based on history. This is known as 'independent demand' and is a relatively unpredictable requirement for a product or service. For example, the operator of a fast-food outlet does not know how many people will arrive, when they will arrive, and what they will order.

Deming, W Edwards (died 1993) An American engineer, and later academic, who became famous as a ➤quality management guru. In the early 1940s, Deming established courses on statistical methods for quality control, i.e. using statistical process-control techniques to improve quality. He was invited to Japan by General MacArthur after the Second World War and was to have a major influence on Japanese thinking and achievements in quality management. Deming's approach is statistics-based and is founded on the need to reduce variation in output quality. His best-known book is *Out of the Crisis* (1986). Deming is the best-known of three American post-Second World War gurus on quality (➤➤Crosby, Philip; Juran, Joseph) and is credited with advancing the ➤total quality management movement.

demurrage Damages due to a shipowner where the contracted completion of loading or unloading is delayed.

denomination **1.** The value, as printed on its face, of a ➤security and the sum payable on ➤redemption. ➤face value. **2.** The specification in the ➤foreign exchange market, the international ➤money market and the ➤securities market of the currency to be used; often employed to refer to the currency itself.

departmentalization The organizational basis by which jobs are grouped together. Departments bring ➤work groups together into formal units, which invariably reflect functional activities (accounts, personnel, marketing, purchasing, property, finance and treasury, etc.). A danger, however, is that functional departments become isolated from one another or become territorial, and lose sight of broader organizational goals (the problem of 'functional silos'). In response more and more organizations have moved to project groups or customer service groups, both of which cut across functional boundaries. This can result in complex matrix structures, where employees belong to functional and project departments simultaneously.

Department of Trade and Industry (DTI) UK government department responsible for promoting trade with other countries and overseeing UK business and finance.

dependency ➤power.

dependent demand ➤demand forecasting.

dependent variable A variable, the value of which can be appropriately seen as conditional on the values of some other variable. For example, if consumer spending is conditional upon income, then spending is the dependent variable, and income is independent. In mathematics, statistics or ➤econometrics, for example, the dependent variable is the one that lies to the left of the equation:

$$C = a + bY,$$

where C is consumption and Y is income, and a and b are ➤parameters. ➤➤behavioural equation.

deposit 1. A sum of money lodged with a ➤bank, ➤discount house or other financial institution. 2. A sum of money proportionate to the total size of the transaction, lodged to secure a ➤forward, ➤futures or ➤option contract. Also termed a 'premium' or a 'margin'.

deposit account A bank account in which ➤deposits earn interest, and withdrawals from which require notice (US = *time deposit*). In France and other European countries deposit accounts are called 'savings accounts'.

deposit insurance A form of ➤insurance providing compensation to lenders with ➤deposits with ➤financial institutions in the event of failure of the bank or other institution. The Deposit Protection Scheme was set up in the UK under the Banking Act 1979; under this scheme the Deposit Protection Fund guarantees up to 75 per cent of the first £100,000 of a sterling deposit. In the US, the Federal Deposit Insurance Corporation provides protection for depositors with members of the ➤Federal Reserve System and other banks that choose to join.

Depository Institutions Deregulation and Monetary Decontrol Act 1980 (US) An Act that removed interest rate ceilings from passbook savings accounts, thus allowing these ➤deposit rate and borrowing costs to rise to market levels. Part of a process of deregulation of the banking system, the Act led to difficulties for many. ➤savings and loan associations.

depreciation 1. The reduction in the value of an asset through wear and tear. An allowance for the depreciation on a company's assets is always made before the calculation of ➤profit, on the grounds that the consumption of capital assets is one of the costs of earning the revenues of the business and is allowed as such according to special rules by the tax authorities. Annual depreciation provisions are normally calculated either by the *straight-line method* – where the estimated residual value of the asset (e.g. scrap) is deducted from its original cost and the balance divided by the number of years of estimated life to arrive at an annual depreciation expense – or by the *reducing balance method* – in which the actual depreciation expense is set at a constant proportion of the cost of the asset, i.e. a diminishing annual absolute amount. In periods of rising prices, the replacement cost of an asset may be very much greater than its original cost. This problem may be dealt with by revaluing assets at intervals and adjusting depreciation charges accordingly. This is called *replacement-cost* as opposed to *historic-cost* depreciation (➤inflation accounting). *Accelerated depreciation* occurs where the depreciation rate is faster than justified by the life of the asset, e.g. to benefit from tax credits designed to stimulate investment. **2.** A reduction in the value of a currency in terms of gold or other currencies in a free market. Also used to refer to a reduction in the purchasing power of any form of currency.

depth interview A lengthy and discursive one-to-one interview concerning an issue, good or service. ➤**qualitative market research.**

derivative A generic term for ➤**futures**, ➤**options** and ➤**swaps**, i.e. instruments derived from conventional direct dealings in securities, currencies and commodities. Trade in derivatives increased substantially in the 1990s, given their usefulness to company treasurers and fund managers as a ➤**hedge** against security price changes and currency fluctuations, particularly in the distributed currency markets of the period. ➤➤**Black–Scholes formula.**

developmental research A particular activity within a ➤**research and development** department that focuses on the use of known scientific principles with respect to particular products. Usually the activity will involve overcoming a technical problem associated with a new product. It may also involve various exploratory studies to try to improve a product's performance. For example, a new vacuum cleaner product would have several ➤**prototypes** that would undergo many modifications and enhancements before a commercial product was finally developed.

development capital Finance provided, usually by a specialized institution, in the form of ➤**equity** and loans to an established business. It is distinct from, though often used synonymously with, ➤**venture capital.**

differentiation The development of distinct and unique benefits or attributes in a product (specifically, a branded product or service) that is positioned in the market to appeal to a particular segment. This strategy requires a firm to offer branded products that meet the needs of customers better than other firms, or that are perceived to do this better. When this happens a firm is able to charge a price that is higher than the average price in the market and, hence, build for the firm above-average profits. These profits should enable the firm to re-invest so as to ensure it is able to sustain its competitive advantage for the future. Differentiation is a core concept in marketing (➤**segment–target–position strategy**) and is one of three ➤**generic strategies** advocated by Michael ➤**Porter** as a platform for business success. However, brands in established markets often show few differences from each other, and any innovative benefits or attributes are quickly imitated. Success in these ➤**competitive parity** markets is then a matter of achieving ➤**brand salience** in the minds of consumers (which may reflect weight of advertising, distribution, ease of purchase, etc., rather the possession of distinct and unique benefits or attributes).

diffusion of innovations ➤**innovation diffusion.**

dilution An increase in the number of shares in a company, e.g. by the exercise of ➤**warrants**, which reduces ➤**earnings per share.**

diminishing return The phenomenon in an industry that the more you increase the amount of one particular input into production, while holding the others constant, you tend to get less and less extra output as a result. For example, if we think of labour and capital as being the main inputs into production, then adding workers to a factory, while doing nothing to expand the number of machines, will yield less and less extra output. The extra workers will be less and less productive than the existing workers, who can more efficiently use the available capital (indeed, eventually they may get in the way of existing workers and have a negative return). It is distinct from ➤**decreasing returns to scale**, which imply a less than proportionate increase in output as *all* inputs are increased together.

direct investment Investment in the foreign operations of a company, e.g. by a ➤**multinational company**. Direct investment implies control, and managerial and perhaps technical input, and is generally preferred by the host country to portfolio investment. Direct investment can take the form of the purchase of an existing company or the establishment of a new operation – a greenfield site. ➤➤**balance of payments**.

directional policy matrix A ➤**portfolio planning** model developed by the oil giant Royal Dutch Shell. It is a development of the Boston Consulting Group (BCG) matrix, and uses the axes 'industry attractiveness' and 'business competitive position'. Industry attractiveness takes account of variables such as market size, market growth and industry profitability. The business competitive position axis includes variables such as market share, reputation, quality and market knowledge.

The principle behind the matrix is to provide a firm with a way of analysing its portfolio of businesses to help ensure that it invests in those businesses that are able to grow successfully, and divests itself of those businesses that have a weak competitive position and where future growth potential is weak.

Directives of the European Union Outline legislation prepared by the Commission of the European Communities (➤**European Union**), for enactment by member states when approved by the Council of Ministers. ➤**banking directive**; **Fourth Directive; Investment Services Directive**.

direct marketing Defined by the Direct Marketing Association (DMA) in the US as: 'an interactive system of marketing which uses one or more advertising media to effect a measurable response and/or transaction at any location.' Characteristics include: communication one-on-one with customers, quite personal communications, an outlook that is response-oriented and therefore something that can be directly measured against costs and revenues. This is in contrast to conventional mass-media advertising, where communications are impersonal, consumer actions may be hard to pin down, and where results are mostly measured against costs incurred without reference to revenue. Although popularly associated with 'direct mailing', the advertising media used in direct marketing also include electronic media, telemarketing, and forms of direct-response advertising. The ready accountability of direct marketing, together with the widespread creation of consumer databases, mailing lists and the use of ➤**personalization technologies**, has stimulated massive growth. In particular, these technologies enable communications to be targeted at specific individuals, with customized messages. However, major issues for the industry are data protection, privacy regulations and consumer protection.

direct response television (DRTV) commercials Television commercials that invite the viewer to respond by 'phoning a toll-free number or by going to a web site. More generally, direct response advertisements (in newspapers and magazines and on web sites, as well as on television) are a quick way to build a database of prospects from the ➤**target audience**. Having built the database, the advertiser is able to send out further information (using the same or different media), knowing that recipients have a self-declared interest in receiving the information. ➤➤**direct marketing; personalization technologies**.

Dirichlet model ➤buyer behaviour.

disclosure Enforced or voluntary publication of information. Under company law and other aspects of regulation, businesses are required to reveal information that they might otherwise wish to keep confidential, e.g. in the implementation in 1988 of the ➤**Financial Services Act 1986** brokers are required to reveal rates of ➤**commission** on certain insurance policies. ➤➤**Form 10-K; Fourth Directive**.

disconfirmation of expectations model ➤expectation.

discontinuous new product A product that makes a significant departure from previous products in the area. Such new products often launch a new generation of technology and sometimes create an entirely new market, whereas continuous product innovations involve improving existing technology. ➤**innovation; new product development**.

discount 1. Reduction in the ➤**face value** of a financial claim, such as a ➤**bill of exchange** or ➤**Treasury bill**, by the amount of money represented by the interest due on the claim during the remainder of its ➤**maturity**. The reduction involved is the discount. It also denotes the action of selling a claim at a discount, i.e. to discount. **2.** The term is used to refer specifically to the purchase of bills at a discount by the central bank, although ➤**rediscount** is more accurate. It is also used to denote direct lending to the commercial banks by the central bank, although more exactly an interest rate is charged rather than a discount deducted. **3.** The amount by which the future value of a currency is less than its ➤**spot** value; opposite of ➤**premium**. **4.** The amount by which a security's price in the ➤**secondary market** is less than the ➤**issue** price. **5.** The amount by which an ➤**option** trades below its ➤**intrinsic value**. **6.** ➤**discounting**. **7.** The amount (usually expressed as a percentage) by which the price of a share in an ➤**investment trust** is less than ➤**net assets**.

discounted cash flow (DCF) A sophisticated set of methods for ➤**investment appraisal** that take the time value of money fully into account. For example, £100 today is worth more than £100 in 1 year, risk apart, because if received today it could be invested for 1 year so that, at an annual ➤**rate of interest** or discount factor of 10 per cent we should receive £110 a year from now. For an investment to have a *present value* (PV) of £100 now, therefore, we should need to expect a return of £10 in a year's time from that investment, i.e. the *net present value* (NPV) of the investment – the total return minus the cost of the investment.

This principle can be used to calculate the NPVs of the ➤**cash flows** arising from more complex industrial and commercial investment projects where cash inflows and outflows are lumpy and spread over long periods of time. For two such projects, the one with the highest NPV will add most to the wealth of the business. An alternative method is to calculate the rate of interest that will equate the PV of the net cash flows and the cost of the investment. This is the *internal rate of return* (IRR), which will be the discount factor at which the NPV is zero, and can be compared with the firm's borrowing costs. ➤**capital, cost of.** If the IRR is higher than the cost of capital, then the project is worth undertaking. There are circumstances where the IRR method and the NPV method do not give the same result; in these circumstances the NPV method is generally to be preferred. Investment appraisal is not straightforward, since cash inflows and even cash outflows will be subject to uncertainty. An allowance for this can be made by choosing a higher discount factor for risky projects. DCF techniques will not necessarily rank investment projects in the same order of attractiveness as conventional accounting methods, such as ➤**payback** or ➤**return on investment**, which do not allow for the timing of receipts and payments.

discount factor ➤discounted cash flow.

discount house 1. A now defunct term for a ➤**bill broker** in a variety of ➤**debt instruments** in the ➤**money market**. Discount houses acted as principals for the purchase of ➤**market instruments** and of ➤**Treasury bills**, financed chiefly by borrowing from the banks with the support of the Bank of England as ➤**lender of last resort**. From March 1997 on a phased basis the term 'discount house' has ceased to be used and the institutions bearing that name have each become a ➤**bank** or other financial intermediary. **2.** A 'cut price' retail store selling goods at a ➤**discount**.

discounting 1. The application of a ➤**discount** or ➤**rate of interest** to a capital sum. Calculations of present value (➤**discounted cash flow**) or the price of a bill before ➤**maturity** are made by discounting at the current appropriate rate of interest. **2.** The future effects of an anticipated event (e.g. a decline in profit) are said to be discounted if selling leads to an adjustment of present prices in line with expected future changes in these prices.

discount market The ➤**money market**. ➤➤discount house.

discount rate The interest rate used in determining the ➤**discount** on the sale of a financial instrument. The term is frequently used in relation to a ➤**central bank**. The discount rate of the ➤**Bank of England** is the rate at which it will discount ➤**eligible bills** in the exercise of ➤**monetary policy**. In the US, the term has a more special meaning; the discount rate of the ➤**Federal Reserve System** is the interest rate at which it will lend, as ➤**lender of last resort**, to the commercial banks.

discretionary account (DA) Funds for investment placed with a ➤**stockbroker**, ➤**commodity** ➤**broker** or other authorized investment manager, with either no, or only general, instructions as to how they should be invested. The broker decides upon the distribution of the investments and keeps the client informed of purchases, sales and the value of the ➤**portfolio**. An account in which a ➤**broker** or manager may trade without the prior assent of the ➤**principal**.

diseconomies of scale Any factor which tends to increase the average costs of producing an item, as the size of the organization producing it tends to increase. If large companies tend to have higher costs of production than small ones, an industry might be said to exhibit diseconomies of scale. In practice, companies have tended to be optimistic about the potential ➤**economies of scale** they can achieve through growth. Bigger factories, for example, can be more efficient than smaller ones, and fixed costs can be defrayed over more units of output. However, diseconomies appear to be primarily managerial – larger organizations tend to be harder to control, and

103

require more formal mechanisms of accountability. ➤➤**decreasing returns to scale.**

disequilibrium ➤equilibrium.

disintermediation 1. Flows of funds between borrowers and lenders avoiding the direct use of ➤**financial intermediaries** whose normal role is to carry out the intermediation between the users of funds and the suppliers of funds. Disintermediation occurs, for example, when companies withdraw funds from the banks and lend them directly to each other or issue bills guaranteed (accepted) by the banks but sold to non-banks. Disintermediation may make it more difficult to measure and control the money supply and, indeed, is often motivated by a desire to avoid credit controls. **2.** The use of new technologies by consumers to bypass existing agents in a ➤**channel of distribution** (e.g. retailers, wholesalers, physical distribution companies, etc.) and buy direct from manufacturers or service suppliers. ➤**intermediary.**

disjunctive decision rule ➤decision rule.

distinctive capability ➤resource-based theory of strategy.

distributable profit, distributable reserve Current or net ➤retained earnings which are available to pay a ➤**dividend.** For public companies in particular, there are legal constraints on what is distributable. ➤➤**capital reserves.**

distributive bargaining ➤bargaining.

diversification The move by a firm into new areas of business where it has no current activities. This is usually referred to using the growth-share matrix (➤**portfolio planning**) which sees diversification as entering new markets with a range of new products.

dividend The amount of a company's ➤**profit** distributed to each ordinary shareholder, usually expressed either as a percentage of the *nominal value* (➤**par value**) of the ➤**ordinary share** capital, or as an absolute amount per share. A dividend is the same as a ➤**yield** only where the shares stand at their nominal value. The amount of the dividend is decided by the board of directors depending upon profitability and the need for ➤**retained earnings.** Where profitability is poor, if the outlook is good, then the dividend may be maintained at the previous year's level or even increased out of ➤**reserves.** The profits after tax from which dividends are paid are those after payments to holders of ➤**preference shares** and ➤**debentures** have been allowed for, the balance being split between dividends and reserves.

Dividends are paid to shareholders after deduction of income tax at the lower rate, ➤**corporation tax** where applicable having already been paid out by the company. The larger ➤**quoted companies** pay dividends quarterly or biannually (*interim dividends*). In these instances, the last dividend declared in the financial year is known as the final dividend. ➤➤**cum-dividend; ex-dividend.**

dividend cover (UK) The number of times the net ➤**profit** available for distribution exceeds the ➤**dividend** actually paid or declared. In US terminology the *pay-out ratio* is the dividend as a percentage of the profit available.

dividend mandate ➤mandate.

dividend stripping Buying ➤fixed-interest ➤securities when they have gone

➤ex-dividend and selling them before the next ➤dividend is paid, so as to avoid receiving dividends that in some countries are taxed at a higher rate than ➤capital gains. Also called *bond washing*.

dividend warrant The cheque by which companies pay ➤dividends to shareholders. US = *dividend check*.

dividend yield ➤yield.

division of labour The practice of achieving greater efficiency in production by dividing tasks up into smaller and smaller specialist operations.

DMU ➤decision-making unit.

domain address The internet address for an individual or an organization. Individuals and firms are linked up and identified through 'domain names'. These are essentially an address, it comprises four numbers, such as 131.22.45.06. The numbers indicate the network (131), an internet protocol address (22 and 45) and a local address (06). Numeric addresses, however, are difficult to remember. Internet authorities assigned and designated an alphanumeric designation. This mnemonic affords the consumer user-friendly information with regard to the identity and source of the domain name, and gives a measure of legal protection to the owner of the name, e.g. 'microsoft.com' and 'ports.ac.uk'. ➤➤dot com firm.

dormant company A company that indulges in no operations or accounting transactions that would require entries in its records and accounts.

dot com firm A description for internet-based firms. So-called because the ➤domain address of firms on the internet ends with 'XXX.com'. The '.com' represents commercial as opposed to academic institutions (denoted '.ac' or '.edu'), government institutions (denoted '.gov'), and professional organizations ('.org').

double-entry bookkeeping The accounting system in which every business transaction, whether a receipt or payment of money, sale or purchase of goods or services, gives rise to two entries, a debit and a corresponding credit, traditionally on opposite pages of a ledger. Since every debit entry has an equal and corresponding credit entry, it follows that the book will (or should) balance.

Dow-Jones index (US) One of several daily indices Dow-Jones & Co compiles of the closing prices of ➤securities quoted on the ➤New York Stock Exchange. The D J Industrial Average measures changes in the unweighted arithmetic average of thirty leading industrial shares (using a variable divisor to clean out the effect of ➤stock splits). Although it is probably not the best overall guide to movements in the stock market, its long history (it goes back to 1896) has earned it a place as the best-known index of any stock market in the world. There are similar indices for fifteen public utility stocks (D J Utility Average), twenty transportation stocks (D J Transportation Average) and an average for all sixty-five stocks called the D J Composite or 65 Stock Average.

downsizing Those activities designed to reduce expenses and make an organization more efficient, reflecting a 'lean and mean' mentality among senior management. Activities include reduction in the size of the workforce (voluntary and involuntary redundancies), hiring freezes, early-retirement incentives, a shift to

➤**out sourcing**, and the merging and consolidation of business units. Downsizing is seen as a purposeful course of action by management to improve efficiency, rather than as a response to organizational decline (which is seen as a quite separate issue). In the 1990s it was closely associated with ➤**re-engineering**. While downsizing ought to lead to greater efficiency (e.g. productivity gains, the removal of wasteful practices, and a simpler organizational hierarchy), its effectiveness has been questioned, e.g. among those employees who remain it may lower their morale, increase stress and result in dysfunctional conflict. ➤➤**conflict; role; stress.** Also, it will erode 'organizational memory', i.e. it will leave the organization with a smaller store of individual and group experiences and therefore limit the home-grown knowledge-base of the organization. This does not prevent ➤**organizational learning**, but it can mean that learning is less informed and less reliable. Also, in times of recession, the term 'downsizing' has been used as a euphemism for job losses unrelated to efficiency gains (typically, management is heard to argue that the shedding of employees is necessary to ensure the firm becomes the right size again; hence, the expression 'rightsizing').

downtime Time when production machinery or plant is not being used. It is usually regarded as a waste of resources and adds to fixed costs by limiting the potential volume available from the machinery or plant. It is most commonly associated with machinery or plant failure, but is also inevitable during periods of maintenance. The objective is to keep downtime to a minimum.

drip A ➤*d*ividend *r*e-*i*nvestment *p*lan where a company uses a planned dividend to buy its own shares at the stock exchange instead of issuing new shares by a ➤**bonus issue.** Shareholders pay dealing charges and stamp duty.

DRTV commercials ➤direct response television commercials.

Drucker, Peter The colossus of management gurus. In his copious writings are to be found anticipations of most of the ideas on management that have emerged in the past 50 years as well as insightful interpretations of some of the pioneers (he reckons that prior to the 1940s only about sixty or seventy books had been written on the subject in any language). Unlike many gurus, Drucker is easy to read, though he often strays from the point and repeats himself. With wide reading in history, politics, philosophy, economics and much else, Drucker is broader in his range and scope than all his contemporaries. He regards management as central to life and is equally concerned with management issues in government and not-for-profit institutions as well as in corporates and partnerships large and small.

Drucker was born in Vienna in 1909 and was educated there as well as in Germany and in the UK before taking up residence in the US in 1937. His first, short book, which appeared in 1933, was banned and burned by the Nazis. His first major book, *The End of Economic Man* (1939), predicted the Nazis' 'final solution', the plan to kill all Europe's Jews. With beginnings in merchant banking, he worked with Henry Luce at *Fortune* and later as a freelance writer and academic. In 1943, he was invited to make a study as a consultant for General Motors which led to his famous *Concept of the Corporation* (1946). Always outside the mainstream of management academics, he was Professor of Politics and Philosophy at Bennington College, then Professor of Management at the Graduate Business School of New York University and, since 1971, Clark Professor of Social Science at Claremont Graduate School, California.

Drucker has written some thirty books including a memoir about people he has known, *Adventures of a Bystander* (1978), and two novels. He has also written innumerable articles (many of his books are compilations of these). *The Practice of Management* (1954) introduced the concepts of ➤**management by objectives**. This book also, for the first time, fully developed the concepts of customer-driven marketing and the need to push risk-taking lower down in the organization, both current themes. *Managing for Results* (1964) anticipated another current theme, the importance of sticking to core competencies. *The Age of Discontinuity* (1969) and *Post Capitalist Society* (1993) anticipated most of current thinking on the knowledge-based economy. Drucker's work contains no graphs, no formulae, and he asserts that 'management is a practice rather than a science. In this, it is comparable to medicine, law and engineering. It is not knowledge but performance.' He distinguishes between the tasks of the manager, which are to do with purposes, objectives, strategies, performance and people, and managerial work, which is to do with skills and organization ('structure follows strategy'). It is around these distinctions that his 800-page summary manual, *Management: tasks, responsibilities, practices* (1973) is arranged. The consistent themes he identifies in his own work are diversity, decentralization, pluralism and the importance of social responsibility.

DSS ➤decision-support system.

dual branding ➤brand hierarchy.

dual capacity The situation where a ➤**market maker** can buy or sell shares to and from members of the public or other members of the stock exchange without the need for a ➤**broker**.

due diligence The analysis and appraisal of a business in preparation for a ➤flotation or ➤**venture capital** investment. Investors have a right to expect that these investigations are carried out thoroughly.

dummy variable In ➤econometrics, a variable which takes the value of 0 or 1, depending on whether some particular condition prevails or not. A dummy variable may be used to signify some qualitative feature of an observation. For example, one might want to look at income and car ownership as variables important in determining the distance a person lives from work: distance from work and income can be measured clearly on a continuous scale for each person in a sample, but car ownership would have to be a dummy variable, taking the value 1 if a car is owned, or 0 if not. ➤➤choice modelling.

duopoly A market in which there are just two suppliers. Duopoly is a special case of ➤oligopoly. ➤Game theory has been used to elucidate some of the strategic issues involved.

duopsony A market in which there are just two buyers.

duplicate buying ➤buyer behaviour.

dynamics of strategy A recognition that the environments in which a firm operates are continually changing. In some industries the level of change may be small, but for those firms operating at the forefront of scientific and technological developments or new emerging markets, developing strategy for the long term is fraught with difficulty. Attempting to forecast the future is extremely difficult and extremely risky. ➤**forecasting**.

E

early entrant A firm that enters a market ahead of the majority. There is a significant body of literature to support the view that pioneering firms that create a market or enter a market early have a substantial strategic advantage. However, like any form of pioneering, there are clearly risks attached. For example, prospective consumers of ➤**discontinuous new products** usually have to be taught the advantages of the new product and this may not be easy because of inertia, habit and a reluctance to change. ➤➤**barrier to entry**.

early stage investment Investment by ➤**venture capital** institutions in the provision of *seed capital* (funds to finance research and development before a business is operating) and start-up finance for new companies.

earnings per share (EPS) The total profits of a company after taxation and interest, divided by the number of shares at issue. EPS will usually be higher than the ➤**dividend** per share, because some earnings will be retained in the company and not distributed as dividends.

earnings yield ➤yield.

earn-out Tying the purchase price paid for a company to future earnings. If the company performs less well than expected, for example, a final instalment on the purchase price may not fall due. A *ratchet* is a similar arrangement sometimes used by ➤**venture capital** institutions to motivate the management of the companies they finance by giving them a large share in ➤**equity** if performance is better than expected.

EASDAQ ➤European Association of Securities Dealers Automated Quotation system.

ebitda Pre-tax earnings before interest, ➤**depreciation** and ➤**amortization**. A crude measure of ➤**cash flow** which can be compared with ➤**enterprise value**. The ratio of enterprise value to ebitda is considered by some analysts as more useful than the ➤**price–earnings ratio** as an indicator of how the stock market values a company. This is because it is not so sensitive to definitions of earnings intended to put the financial results of a company in a favourable light.

EBRD ➤European Bank for Reconstruction and Development.

e-business ➤electronic commerce.

ECGD (UK) ➤Export Credit Guarantee Department.

e-commerce ➤electronic commerce.

econometrics The use of statistical techniques to study the relationship between different variables, in particular to test hypotheses about the relationship, and to quantify the impact of variations in some variables on variations in others. For the uninitiated, econometrics is basically about mixing three things: (a) an equation that has some variables; (b) some data from the real world on those variables, and (c) some statistical techniques.

The equation, or system of equations, links a ➤**dependent variable** to one or more ➤**independent variables**, in the expectation that variations in the latter have some power to explain or predict variations in the former. An equation might take the form:

$$C_i = \alpha + \beta Y_i$$

where C_i and Y_i represent consumption and income for any given household, i. A dataset might consist of values of income and consumption for different households. The statistical techniques are used to estimate the size of α and β, known as *parameters*. For example, if β is 0.8, that would tell us that, on average in the sample of households, consumption was 0.8 times income, or 80 per cent of income. The equation can be said to form a simple ➤**model** of consumption, and typically the techniques of ➤**regression analysis** would be used to find the scale of the parameters.

Econometrics is a broad subject that can be used to test hypotheses such as $\beta > 0$; and a variety of techniques are used to check the robustness of estimates and the confidence with which estimates can be relied upon. ➤**confidence interval.** Econometrics tends to use data drawn over time – *time series data* – or from a sample of different individuals at any one time – *cross-section data*. Increasingly, use is being made of longitudinal data, i.e. data drawn over time from a single sample of individuals. ➤**consumer panel; marketing research.** ➤➤**response models.**

Economic and Monetary Union (EMU) An agreement reached under the Maastricht Treaty 1992 to establish a single European currency, namely the euro. The first stage of monetary union was for member states which met various convergence criteria (e.g. a budget deficit of 3 per cent or less of gross domestic product (GDP)) irrevocably to fix their exchange rates against each other and against the euro, and for the euro to take the place of the ecu. This was achieved on 1 January 1999. The currency became a full currency with notes and coins on 1 January 2002. The UK, Denmark and Sweden chose not to participate at the outset.

Under EMU, ➤**monetary policy** is conducted by the European Central Bank, based in Frankfurt. Member states are obliged to conform to the Stability and Growth Pact, which limits government borrowing under normal circumstances to below 3 per cent of GDP. The downside of the single currency, therefore, is that the ability of domestic authorities to use fiscal or monetary policy to stimulate or dampen economic activity is severely circumscribed. The upside is that ➤**transactions costs** of foreign transactions are reduced and exchange rate instability is removed for all those firms exporting and importing within the eurozone.

economic growth Expansion in national income over time. Growth is seen as perhaps the single most important measure of economic progress, even if there is plenty of evidence to suggest that beyond a certain income level, national happiness does not much increase with material consumption. The path of growth can be analysed in the short run (➤business cycle) or in the longer run. ➤trend growth. It has been observed that the fastest growth is associated with economies with lower levels of national income, who can enjoy sustained periods of 'catch-up' with richer counterparts (witness Ireland's economic 'miracle' in the 1990s). The richest economies have typically only sustained per capita growth rates of a little over 2 per cent. Theories explaining growth have tended to analyse the process by which business investment increases the productive capacity of an economy or, more recently, by which innovation and technology advance ➤productivity. ➤endogenous growth theory.

economic order quantity (EOQ) An approach to determining the quantity of any particular item to order when stock needs replenishing. It is the most common method used and essentially it attempts to find the best balance between the advantages and disadvantages of holding stock. For example, a firm may decide to order less frequently but in larger quantities; alternatively, it may decide to have many smaller deliveries throughout the year. This may reduce the level of stock held by the firm and reduce working capital costs, but there may be additional costs such as delivery. The EOQ formula seeks to establish what is the total cost of an ordering plan by adding together the holding cost of stock and the ordering cost.

economic profit ➤economic rent.

economic rent Term used by economists to refer to ➤profits or returns from an activity over and above those that would just be necessary to induce the participant into that activity. Economic rent may be thought of as abnormal, or super-normal profits. But it would be wrong to limit the term to companies – a rent can be any kind of surplus. For example, a footballer who earns £10,000 a week, and whose next-best occupation would be that of a plumber earning £600, makes a rent of £9,400. He would remain a footballer even if he were just paid £601. Economic rents tend to accrue to factors of production which face limited competition, or which are protected by ➤barriers to entry.

For a company, economic rent can also be referred to as *economic profit*. Both are distinct from the profit that a business might declare in its accounts, which might typically consist of some economic rent, plus ➤normal profit, a return that just compensates the producer for the ➤opportunity cost of the capital and entrepreneurship it provides.

Economists often ask why firms might be able to earn economic rents. In general, theories have to explain why new competitive entry into an industry does not occur, increasing competition, bidding down prices and profits to merely normal levels. ➤frictional profit theory; ➤➤quasi-rent.

economic value added A method for evaluating companies by comparing the rate of ➤return on investment with the ➤weighted average cost of capital. Companies which are seen to be earning less than their cost of capital are said to be destroying value, while those that have a rate of return above their cost of capital are creating value. In these calculations ➤assets in the ➤balance sheet are increased by writing back expenditure on research and development and adjusted in other ways, while profit is defined as ➤operating profits after tax (though there are variations in these definitions). An alternative approach is *market value added*. In this approach ➤**market capitalization** is compared with economic value measured by the capital it is using as defined above.

economies of scale Factors which tend to reduce the average costs of producing an item, as the size of the organization or industry producing it tends to increase. If large companies tend to have lower costs of production than small ones, an industry might be said to exhibit internal economies of scale (internal, because the economies accrue to inside the large firm). Such economies might derive from the greater potential for labour specialization in large operations (➤**division of labour**); technical factors which mean the costs of large items of equipment rise more slowly than the output they generate; flexibility in deployment, e.g. an airline might need spare planes to cover unforeseen contingencies, but doubling the size of the airline would not typically necessitate a doubling in the size of the contingency provision. In industries like automobile production, where it is widely accepted that economies of scale are huge, the main advantage of scale is in defraying over more vehicles the up-front fixed cost of establishing a platform of a range of models.

It is easy to overestimate economies of scale, as a well-run company may have low costs and grow large as a result. It may thus appear that large scale has lowered costs, even though, in fact, it was simply good management. Simply emulating a company's size will not necessarily allow a rival to emulate its low costs.

There are also *external economies of scale*, which reduce costs across an industry as the scale of the industry develops. ➤**clustering**. ➤➤**diseconomies of scale; increasing returns to scale**.

economies of scope Factors which tend to make it cheaper to produce different items in conjunction with each other than to produce the items separately. An example frequently cited is financial services, where selling and marketing costs are high and can be defrayed across more products if there is a diversified portfolio of products available.

ECR ➤**efficient customer response systems**.

ECU European Currency Unit. ➤**European Monetary System**.

Edgar (US) Electronic ➤**disclosure** system for the receipt, storage, retrieval and dissemination of public documents filed with the ➤**Securities and Exchange Commission**.

EDI ➤**electronic data interchange**.

EDLP ➤everyday-low-pricing.

efficiency wage hypothesis The idea that companies can raise the ➤**productivity** of their workforce by paying them wages above the going rate. ➤**pay**. There may be various reasons why wages feed into the productivity of staff. For one thing, higher-paid workers may be happier and better motivated, or they may be more scared of losing their job and having to get one that just pays a normal wage, so may work harder. ➤**employee retention**. Or, in very poor countries, well-paid workers may be better fed and thus more healthy and productive. And finally, companies who pay above the going rate will tend to have first choice of the best employees.

The hypothesis has been used to explain sustained unemployment, because it undermines the idea that companies will cut pay when there are spare workers trying to price themselves into jobs.

It is not only wages that may be affected by non-market pricing: a landlord may well choose to accept a lower than market rent in order to have a wide choice of possible tenants.

efficient customer response systems Systems for linking suppliers and buyers in business-to-business contexts, e.g. automated re-ordering of office supplies. These response systems are not only efficient for customers, but can reduce costs for all parties, speed up time to market, and streamline operations. However, a concern is that parties become 'locked-in' to one another; this may result in positive outcomes (➤relationship marketing) but can give rise to unhealthy levels of dependency. ➤➤vertical integration.

efficient market hypothesis (EMH) The idea that asset prices (e.g. ➤share prices) reflect the present value of the expected future returns from the ➤asset, on the assumption that all available information is incorporated in prices and that traders will bid prices up or down until assets are priced correctly. If it were true, EMH would mean that no investor could 'beat the market' for long. In its crude form EMH is not true, since it has been shown that, historically, share prices have fluctuated much more than ➤dividends, while ➤crashes have seen stock market prices fall by as much as one-third in a week – as in 1987 – without new information becoming available that could conceivably affect fundamental values to this extent.

EFTA ➤European Free Trade Association.

Ehrenberg, A S C Eminent British marketing academic who has contributed to our understanding of competitive markets, buyer behaviour, pricing, advertising, marketing research and business statistics. Unlike many marketers who focus on the decisions facing individual consumers or individual firms, Ehrenberg is interested in describing and understanding market-level phenomena. While this interest is shared with many economists, his empirically grounded approach and his reliance on market research have given his work a distinct edge. Seminal publications include *Repeat-Buying* (1972) and (with Gerald Goodhardt and Chris Chatfield) 'The Dirichlet: a comprehensive model of buyer behaviour' (*Journal of the Royal Statistical Society A*, 1984). Empirical support for this work is considerable, giving managers norms and benchmarks against which to assess their own situations. For many years, Ehrenberg was Professor of Marketing at London Business School.

80 : 20 rule The observation that 80 per cent of sales come from 20 per cent of customers. In a strict sense the rule often is not supported; however, it is approximately true in many situations (i.e. *most* sales, if not exactly 80 per cent, come from a *small proportion*, if not 20 per cent, of customers). This is sometimes called the Pareto principle after the nineteenth-century economist who showed that income is very unevenly distributed in society. ➤Pareto analysis.

EIS ➤Enterprise Investment Scheme.

elaboration likelihood model ➤involvement theory.

elasticity A measure of responsiveness of one variable, to a change in another. There are many elasticities in common use (e.g. ➤cost elasticity; **cross-price**

elasticity of demand; price elasticity of demand) to name but a few. The general equation for the elasticity of a variable x with respect to y is the percentage change in x divided by the corresponding percentage change in y. If a 2 per cent change in y is observed to cause a 4 per cent change in x, the elasticity is 2.

electronic banking The automated facility to call up bank account details, give instructions for payments and make use of other services by means of a computer, ➤**modem** and telephone line or ➤**viewdata** system. Used by businesses; retail customers appear to prefer telephone banking. More recently, several financial and other companies have set up *internet banking*. Unburdened by the need for a branch network, these low-cost services offer attractive ➤**rates of interest** for ➤**deposits**.

electronic commerce Also 'e-commerce' and 'e-business'. Any of a range of activities in different industries and business sectors that focus on commercial exchanges using new, electronic technologies. A typical exchange might entail on-line order-taking, on-line payment, and on-line delivery (as with the purchase and downloading of computer software). This has been made possible by the ➤**internet**, and associated hardware/software innovations and commercial developments. ➤**domain address; dot com firm; internet service provider; portal.** The growth of e-commerce has been very rapid as companies and governments have recognized the vast potential of this global technology to bring together customers and content in highly innovative and previously impossible ways. ➤➤**interactive electronic marketing; knowledge economy; new economy.**

One view of these developments is that the internet forces a rethinking of basic management and marketing principles. For example, emphasis shifts from the ➤**segmentation** of consumers to ➤**one-to-one marketing.** Whereas traditional marketing has relied on ➤**intermediaries**, now there are processes of ➤**disintermediation** and the deconstruction of supply chains. Off-line ➤**brands** thrived by delivering narrow solutions to limited customer needs; now, on-line brands are expected to meet a wider spectrum of needs and desires. In general, advocates of this view argue that:

(1) Totally new business models are required.
(2) Technological developments are so rapid that forward planning with any certainty is no longer possible. The name of the game is flexibility, adaptability and an acceptance of continual change.
(3) Markets, too, are more uncertain, if not chaotic. For instance, technology is lowering barriers-to-entry and therefore many more players can enter almost any market, be it local or global, mass or niche. In such a world it makes more sense to build 'share of wallet' with key customers rather than build ➤**market share.**
(4) Winning organizations will be those who can best capitalize on the interactive aspects of the internet. This means a change in emphasis from one-to-many communications ('talking at consumers') to many-to-many communications ('a dialogue with consumers'). Traditional media are ill-equipped for dialogue and those who rely on such traditional media will be at a severe disadvantage in the future.
(5) Power shifts from brand owners and distributors to consumers, reflecting the democratic character of the internet. Whereas classical branding creates infor-

mation asymmetries to the advantage of manufacturers, the internet enables dispersed access to information. If there are any asymmetries, they will be to the advantage of consumers.

(6) Location is irrelevant, changing our notions of the physical separation of buyers and sellers and greatly reducing transaction costs.

(7) New growth economics apply, based on the management of 'knowledge assets'. ➤knowledge management system. Old world notions of slow experience curves and lengthy depreciation cease to apply. Brand longevity counts for little. Indeed, it may be a handicap if it is associated too closely with traditionalism and a 'rear-view mirror' of markets.

(8) Consumers and businesses insist on customized products, services and solutions. Gone is the landscape of well-defined, relatively homogeneous mass markets served by standardized branded products. Buying is more akin to buying off a list – according to one's own specification – than choosing an all-purpose brand.

(9) Technology enables simultaneous competition and co-operation. ➤co-opption. Customers work with a network of alliances to agree on solutions – there is little room for dominant (and domineering) brands in this framework.

The alternative view is far more circumspect. Proponents of this view point out:

(1) Business fundamentals (liquidity, ➤economies of scale, cost control, profitability and growth) still apply. Attention must continue to be paid to costs, communication, fulfilment – these management fundamentals are ignored at one's peril.

(2) Traditional marketing practices are still very much alive. Indeed, 'dot.coms' have promoted themselves using conventional media such as newspapers, magazines and television, and they have faced familiar physical and logistic constraints when attempting to fulfil orders and deliver goods and services.

(3) A desire on the part of managers to build closer relationships with customers predates the internet. The story here is one of continuity, in that there has been a gradual rediscovery of ➤relationship marketing, based on the substitution of personal communication by capital-intensive technology-based communication, e.g. direct mail, call-centres, automatic teller machines, and automated bill payment systems. ➤personalization technologies. Similar concerns arise in both the old and new worlds, e.g. do customers want relationships, should they be expected to give permission, is technology-based communication quality communication?

(4) The future lies with 'clicks *and* mortar'. This development favours established brands that can extend their operations into the world of e-business, and e-business organizations that can build effective brands in a conventional sense.

(5) Many of the fears for the future of branding and brand management are not new. Brand managers have always had to contend with the pressure to commodify markets – the internet does not remove this pressure, but nor does it make the process of commodification inevitable. Balancing the demands of customization and standardization has always been a challenge for brand managers.

(6) Internet-like networks have been around for quite some time (20–30 years), nor is the internet the first technology to be commercialized with the result of imploding distance and enhancing communications. In their day, railways, automobiles, aircraft, the telegraph, fax machines and telephones, all had this effect.

electronic data interchange (EDI) An electronic exchange of instructions and documents between individuals and firms. The aim is to increase efficiency and reduce paperwork by streamlining the flows of information. It is being increasingly used by virtually all organizations. The main difficulty in EDI is agreeing on standards for these interchanges. The large software producers have solved many of the problems encountered in the early years of exchanging electronic data. The main advantage of EDI is its speed.

electronic funds transfer at point of sale (EFTPOS) A system that allows the automatic transfer of money from a buyer to a seller of goods or services at the time of sale. In the UK, EFTPOS is now widespread, e.g. using Connect and Switch cards.

electronic point-of-sale (EPOS) **system** Retail computer systems that record purchases at the point of sale, and which provide an enumerated receipt for customers and a stockholding record for the retailer. This has operational advantages in terms of inventory control and stock re-ordering. In addition, EPOS systems help retailers to gain a much better understanding of shopper behaviour. ➤➤**consumer behaviour**. This is particularly so where the EPOS information can be linked to specific customers, which is feasible when customers use credit, debit, or loyalty cards, or are on an in-store scanner panel. ➤**consumer panel**.

eligible bill 1. A bill issued by an authorized bank, which may be ➤rediscounted at the ➤Bank of England. **2.** US = *eligible paper*.

elimination-by-aspects decision rule ➤decision rule.

emergent strategy A strategy, the final objective of which is unclear and with elements developed during the course of its life as the strategy proceeds. The notion of emergent strategy has arisen among writers on the subject of business strategy who have rejected the rational dispassionate, long-term prescriptive approach to developing strategy. They argue that strategy is more complex than the prescriptive strategists would imply – this is because people and organizational culture and heritage all need to be taken into account. The concept of ➤**organizational learning**, whereby an organization undertakes a certain amount of trial and error to develop the optimal strategy, is a key part of emergent strategy development.

emerging industry A new industry that evolves from the development of new technology (e.g. digital communications, mobile telephony and biotechnology) or an industry that emerges in response to new social needs, such as counselling.

emerging markets (➤newly industrialized countries) in Eastern Europe and in other countries with ➤capital markets at an early stage of development, or the securities markets therein.

EMH ➤efficient markets hypothesis.

emotion ➤affect. ➤➤consumer behaviour.

empirical testing The use of real world data of one form or another, to validate an hypothesis. Commonly, this takes the systematic statistical approach typical of ➤econometrics. In business studies, it might involve a more anecdotal case approach. ➤validity.

employee attitude survey ➤attitude survey.

employee evaluation ➤assessment.

employee motivation ➤motivation.

employee retention The issue of how to keep employees from leaving an organization. Retention depends on maximizing job satisfaction (so employees do not wish to move) and/or making it harder for employees to move. Organizations can manage job satisfaction by focusing attention on: (a) ➤**pay** and conditions; (b) non-financial ➤**reward** (e.g. promotion prospects); (c) job variety ('job enrichment'); (d) supervisory arrangements (➤**empowerment**); (e) the provision of resources to do a job effectively, and (f) an employee's training and development needs. Impediments to movement also may be within an organization's control, e.g. employment contracts with penalty clauses in the event of premature resignation, non-transferable pension plans, and the development of organization-specific skills. However, many impediments are structural and reflect labour market conditions, e.g. 'turnover' – also called 'quit rate' or 'churn rate' – usually increases during an economic boom and declines in a recession. Retention is of major concern, given the costs of hiring new employees and the investment made in the socialization, training and development of existing employees. This is particularly true if the person who moves is productive and valued ('dysfunctional turnover'). There are, however, circumstances when turnover is desirable – 'functional turnover' is said to result where a poor performer quits or where it is easy to rehire someone as good or better. The challenge is how to minimize dysfunctional turnover, while tolerating or even promoting functional turnover, something that is especially important during a process of restructuring. ➤➤**downsizing; efficiency wage hypothesis.**

Employee Retirement Income Security Act 1974 (US) Law regulating private ➤**pension** plans. Provisions included the setting up of the Pension Benefit Guarantee Corporation, which protects beneficiaries in corporate pension schemes from loss in the event of insolvency or premature termination of a pension scheme.

employee share/stock ownership plan (ESOP) A scheme to allow employees to acquire shares/stocks in the company in which they work, thereby giving them a stake in the ownership and control of the organization. In the UK, ESOPs are employee share ownership plans that differ from Inland Revenue-approved profit-sharing schemes in that employees are liable to income tax when the shares are transferred at less than their market value. However, the costs of ESOPs borne by employers are deductible for ➤**corporation tax** purposes. A variant is the Employee Share Ownership Trust. These schemes can be viewed as a source of ➤**reward** and ➤**motivation** for employees.

employer branding ➤brand.

employment agency Brokers who help people to find jobs and employers to find people. The agency will keep a register of situations vacant, and another register of persons seeking employment. In some countries the State sponsors employment agency services, e.g. the Manpower Services Commission in the UK. This type of agency might also take on training activities for certain categories of person (e.g. youth training) and help to administer special programmes in areas of high unemployment, e.g. community programmes. Increasing reliance is placed on private agencies who charge fees for their services. These tend to have sector-specific expertise, especially those involved in the vetting and hiring of professional and managerial employees. The largest of these agencies will offer a range of services, including executive selection and search ('head-hunting'), human resource consulting, psychological consulting, out-placement services, and training and development services.

employment law Many laws affect the rights of employees and the responsibility of employers, e.g. the legal position of ➤**trade unions**, contracts of employment and termination of employment. Under the Employment Rights Act 1996 employees must receive a written statement giving details of remuneration, pension rights, holiday entitlement, notice period, disciplinary and grievance procedures, hours and place of work, and other matters. Employers may not make deductions from pay without the employee's written consent unless authorized by statute (as with taxation). The Employment Rights Act lays down minimum periods of notice for termination of employment. An *employment tribunal* can hear complaints about unfair dismissal from any employee with over 1 year's service. If dismissal is found to be unfair, then the tribunal may order reinstatement or compensation of up to £50,000. Discrimination in employment on the grounds of sex, race or disability (with exceptions) is unlawful under the Equal Pay Act 1970, the Sex Discrimination Act 1975 and 1986, the Race Relations Act 1976 and the Disability Discrimination Act 1995. There are commissions for equal opportunities, racial equality and disability rights which are charged with eliminating discrimination in the workplace. ➤**equal opportunities.**

Employment Rights Act (1996) ➤employment law.

employment tribunals ➤employment law.

empowerment The process where employees are put in charge of what they do. Empowerment is about the sharing of ➤**power** and responsibility with employees, rather than concentrating these attributes among a small cadre of managers. It requires coaching and nurturing skills on the part of managers. While empowerment has been in vogue for some time, it presumes a certain level of readiness on the part of employees to be empowered – this cannot be taken for granted. ➤➤**situational leadership theory.**

EMU ➤Economic and Monetary Union.

endogenous growth theory A set of economic models and ideas that have been used in attempts to explain both the rate of ➤**economic growth** and the degree of technological progress driving it. In this field, technology is interpreted very widely to include everything from new machines to a better understanding of efficient production methods or improved marketing techniques. The novelty of endogenous growth theory was in assuming that innovation can be affected by good policy and appropriate institutions. In the past, technology had been recognized as important in driving growth, but had been seen as 'beyond analysis' – an ➤**exogenous variable**, predetermined rather like the weather. Different models of endogenous growth focus on things such as the role of ➤**investment** in: (a) both physical and human capital; (b) the process of innovation; (c) the importance of ➤**intellectual property**, and (d) the ability of innovators to profit from it. They have stressed the need for institutions which nurture innovation, and provide incentives for individuals to be inventive. Indeed, ➤**competition policy**, industrial relations and the trade regime in place could all be said to be important. In general, these models have supported the conclusion that it may be sensible to subsidize education and research and development. They have also demonstrated that a far wider set of factors can affect growth than was traditionally supposed. But beyond that, they have not yielded a precision sufficient to offer useful prescriptions for policy.

endogenous preferences Consumer tastes that are not fixed as a matter of personal character, but which are to some extent dependent upon the experiences of the consumer. A clear example of endogenous preferences follows from addiction – an individual's taste for cigarettes is very much affected by whether the individual happens to have smoked many cigarettes or not. Acquired tastes, habits, the desire to justify past consumption all provide examples of ways in which previous spending decisions affect later preferences. The notion is destructive of much traditional economics, because once the assumption of exogenous preferences is removed, life is far more complicated than economics would imply. ➤**addictive consumption**.

endogenous variable A variable with a value determined by other variables within a system being studied. Studying the progress of the British economy, for example, one might say the exchange rate is endogenous, determined as it is by many factors, such as saving rates, which are likely to be included in any study of the economy. One could plausibly say, however, that saving rates themselves are not endogenous (i.e. are *exogenous*) because they can be determined by some factors that lie beyond the scope of most studies of the economy, such as the age profile of the population. For a firm, one might say endogenous variables are those within the control of the company; exogenous variables are those outside its control.

endowment life assurance ➤insurance.

enterprise agreement An agreement on ➤**pay** and conditions that results from ➤**bargaining** between employees (or their representatives) and management at the level of individual enterprise. ➤**collective bargaining**.

Enterprise Investment Scheme (EIS) (UK) A tax shelter aimed at encouraging ➤**business angels** to make direct ➤**equity** ➤**investments** in higher-risk small companies. Under the scheme a 20 per cent income tax relief is given for the initial investment in new ordinary shares. If held for at least 3 years, there is no ➤**capital gains** tax on any gain realized. Losses reduced by the income tax relief already given can be set against income or capital gains tax liability. The maximum annual investment by an individual taxpayer is £150,000. The EIS replaced the Business Expansion Scheme in 1994.

enterprise resource planning (ERP) **system** A software system used by companies to manage and plan business functions from order processing to manufacturing and from accounting to personnel. The use of ERP software grew rapidly during the late 1990s, reflecting the globalization of ➤**international business** and the premium this has placed on information technology systems which enable managers to control sprawling business operations. ➤➤**management information system**.

enterprise value The total value of a firm's assets, notwithstanding the financial liabilities of the firm. It is calculated by adding ➤**debt** to ➤**market capitalization**

and subtracting cash. The usefulness of the concept is in comparing similar companies which have chosen to finance their investments in different proportions of equity and debt. ➤➤**ebitda.**

entrepreneurship In general, the processes leading to any new venture creation. A new venture is a response to a new business opportunity, e.g. the creation of a new company to exploit business opportunities in an emergent market. At a minimum, this process has the following stages: (a) opportunity recognition; (b) strategy development; (c) specification of the venture's requirements and potential; (d) assembly of the resources and financing, and (e) starting the venture. A narrower definition sees entrepreneurship as concerned with developing *innovative* new ventures – with an emphasis on invention and innovation in response to changing environments. The new ventures may be developed by independent organizations or within established organizations, the latter being termed 'corporate entrepreneurship' or 'intrapreneurship'. Developments in industrial sectors such as telecommunications, media, e-business, computing and biotechnology have led to growing interest in entrepreneurship. In addition to these sector-based opportunities, there have also been geographical-based opportunities (e.g. new ventures in emergent Chinese markets) (termed 'international entrepreneurship'). ➤**international business.**

The person willing to take the necessary risks to transform an idea into an actual business that generates sales and profits is called an 'entrepreneur'. In economic theory, this person is seen as someone who brings together and harmonizes the two major factors of production – capital and labour. Considerable attention is paid to the role of the individual entrepreneur, with particular emphasis placed on the starting of small businesses and growing them into large and successful ones, e.g. the rise of the successful property entrepreneur, Minerva's Andrew Rosenfeld. He is responsible for building Minerva into a £200 million property business of which Rosenfeld has a £50 million stake. ➤➤**leadership.**

environmental scanning The systematic examination of each of the firm's environments to identify opportunities and threats created by external change. ➤**exogenous variable.** Not all environmental factors can be investigated – there are simply too many – so a handful of relevant external variables must be selected for research. Normally these variables concern:
(1) Marketing. The activities of competitors, trends in consumer taste, changes in structure and size of the market.
(2) Legislation. Government attitudes to the industry, impending statutes, licensing arrangements and possibilities of increased control.
(3) Technology. Production methods and their efficiency, new inventions, materials, processes and costs.
➤**change management; PESTL.**

EPOS system ➤electronic point-of-sale system; ➤➤automated stock ordering system.

Equal Opportunities Commission ➤employment law.

equal opportunity The principle that employees should not be subject to discrimination. Specific reference is usually made to discrimination based on gender, race, colour, religion, national origin, disability and age, and in some cases also marital status and sexual orientation. The principle may be embodied in legislation (e.g. the US Civil Rights Act 1964) and/or workplace policies. The aim is to ensure all qualified people have the same access to jobs, and will be treated the same way once in those jobs (especially in terms of ➤**pay** and conditions). Also embodied in the principle is that employees do not suffer 'harassment' as a result of their gender, race, colour, etc. European Union legislation has tended to focus on the prevention of discrimination and harassment (through, for instance, the British Equal Employment Opportunity Commission). ➤**employment law.** In the US, the process has been taken further to include ➤**affirmative action programmes**, where employers are required to take active steps to recruit and hire specific groups (notably women and members of minority groups). While this has made US human resource management extremely legalistic, equal opportunity remains something of an elusive goal.

equilibrium A situation in which the forces that determine the behaviour of a variable are in balance and thus exert no pressure on that variable to change. In business economics, equilibrium is perhaps most commonly applied to the price that prevails in a market, when the forces of supply and demand are matched. The opposite of equilibrium is *disequilibrium.*

In the field of ➤**game theory**, which has played an important part in the analysis of business strategy and tactics, the notion of equilibrium is rather different, and loosely refers to a set of mutually compatible strategies by players in a game such that, given the strategies of other players, each player would be content with his own strategy. ➤**Nash equilibrium.**

equity The residual value of a company's ➤**assets** after all ➤**liabilities** (other than those to holders of ➤**ordinary shares**) have been allowed for. The equity of a company is the property of the ordinary shareholders; hence, these shares are popularly called equities (UK). In a ➤**mortgage** or ➤**hire-purchase** contract, equity is the amount left for the borrower if the asset concerned is sold and the lender repaid.

equity gearing (UK) The ratio of borrowings to ➤**equity** or risk capital. ➤➤**capital gearing; gearing.**

equity kicker ➤mezzanine.

equity pair trade The adopting of offsetting positions in the equity of a company in different markets where there are small differences in the price of the stock. For example, if the price of Global Corporation shares in New York is slightly higher than in London, then an equity pair trade involves buying the shares in London and selling them short (➤**position**) in New York; thus, when the prices in New York and London converge, the trader wins, even if the overall price of the stock has fallen.

equity theory A theory that suggests people weigh up what they put into, and get out of, their jobs, compare this with what others put into, and get out of, their jobs, and then respond so as to eliminate any inequities. Comparison may reveal equity or inequity (a person could be under-rewarded or over-rewarded). The purpose in making the assessment is to eliminate any inequities, to the extent that these are seen as unfair or unjust. This can be achieved by: (a) changing what is put into a job (less effort is put into the job); (b) changing what is obtained from a job (higher pay/ status for the same amount of effort); (c) changing self-perceptions ('I now realize I work very hard'); (d) changing one's perception of others ('I now realize others work less hard than me'), or (e) quitting the job. A further response is to change the basis of comparison. An employee may base the comparison on his own experiences within the current organization or outside it, or on another person's experiences within the current organization or outside it. Depending on which basis of comparison is chosen, the assessment of equity will differ. These considerations have an important impact on employee ➤motivation.

ergonomics The consideration of physiological aspects of the human body and how it fits into its surroundings. For example, most cars are now manufactured to allow the driver to alter the driving position to suit that person's particular physique. The seat can be raised or lowered, moved towards the steering wheel and away from the steering wheel as required. The subject of ergonomics is now closely associated with workplace design, including environmental conditions of the workplace such as lighting and temperature, but the subject also includes the design of products to suit the human body.

ERG theory A theory of employee motivation. Three groups of core needs are proposed: (a) existence (E) (psychological and safety needs); (b) relatedness (R) (social needs, interpersonal relationships, and the external aspects of esteem), and (c) growth (G) (personal development, self-actualization needs, and the internal aspects of esteem). This is largely a reworking of ➤Maslow's hierarchy of needs, but there appears to be more empirical support for this theory. Policies and procedures that enable employees to become more involved in the organization can be viewed as a managerial response to ERG theory, e.g. ➤employee share/stock ownership plan; empowerment; quality circles; works council. ➤➤motivation.

ERP ➤enterprise resource planning.

escrow, escrow account A document of agreement held by a third party until one or both of the other two parties have fulfilled certain conditions. Thus funds on an escrow account will be released by a bank when agreed conditions are met.

ESOP ➤employee share/stock ownership plan.

ethical investing The practice by participants in the capital market of attempting to influence company behaviour by investing only in companies that observe certain standards of behaviour. The goal – apart from that of satisfying the consciences of the investors concerned – is typically to increase the cost of capital (➤capital, cost of) of firms whose ethical standards are low, and in doing so to make it harder for such firms to grow. Some proponents of ethical investing argue it represents a sensible investment strategy, as unethical firms invariably find their bad practices rebound on their long-term success.

ethics ➤business ethics.

Eurobond A ➤bond issued in a currency other than that of the country or market in which it is issued, i.e. a bond composed of claims in a particular currency but held outside the country of that currency. Eurobonds are identical in principle to

➤**Eurodollars** or ➤**Eurocurrency** and arose out of the Eurodollar and Eurocurrency market. The term predated the introduction of the euro currency.

Euroclear A settlement system, originally for ➤**Eurobonds**, more recently other securities, formed by a number of banks and securities houses in Brussels in 1968. It provides clearing house, accounting and dividend collection services as well as providing working capital to dealers. ➤*CEDEL* is a similar, competing organization.

Eurocurrency A currency used in the ➤**Euromarket**. ➤➤**Eurobond; Eurodollar.**

Eurodollar US dollars in bank accounts outside the US which are lent and re-lent in the form of dollar deposits and ➤**Eurobonds**. *Eurocurrencies*, by extension, are any foreign currency used in a similar way outside their country of origin.

Euromarket The generic term for all transactions in ➤**Eurocurrency**.

Euronext The cross-border ➤**stock exchange** created in 2000 by the merger of the Paris, Brussels and Amsterdam exchanges. For legal purposes – there being no licences for pan-European exchanges – Euronext operates through three separate national divisions, but the regulators of these are committed to harmonizing the rules governing their conduct.

European Association of Securities Dealers Automated Quotation system (EASDAQ) A pan-European ➤**stock exchange** for growth companies, especially technology companies, and modelled upon the ➤**National Association of Securities Dealers Automated Quotation system** in the US, which acquired it in the year 2000 to form NASDAQ-Europe.

European Bank for Reconstruction and Development (EBRD) Established in 1991, EBRD aims to facilitate the transition of the states of eastern and central Europe and the former USSR and Yugoslavia from centrally planned to market economies. Some fifty-eight countries, the European Union and the ➤**European Investment Bank** are members.

European Central Bank (ECB) The organization responsible for conducting ➤**monetary policy** in the eurozone. It was established in Frankfurt in 1998 and fully operational on 1 January 1999, when it became responsible for monetary policy in the euro area. The ECB is independent of national governments; it works with the national ➤**central banks** of the member states that have adopted the euro. All EU member states (➤**European Union**) except the UK, Sweden and Denmark have adopted the euro.

European Commission ➤European Union.

European Currency Unit ➤European Monetary System.

European Economic Area ➤European Union.

European Economic Community ➤European Union.

European Economic Interest Grouping A recognized form of grouping that allows companies incorporated in the ➤**European Union** to establish joint ventures employing up to 500 people throughout the EC without ➤**capitalization** and with the simplification of ➤**fiscal transparency**.

European Free Trade Association (EFTA)   A group of countries that have removed import duties (➤**tariffs**) on imports from each other. EFTA was formed in 1959 by Austria, Denmark, Norway, Portugal, Sweden, Switzerland and the UK. Finland effectively joined in 1961 and Iceland in 1970. Denmark and the UK left in 1973 and Portugal in 1986 on joining the European Community (EC). ➤**European Union.** After negotiations that began in 1984, EFTA and the EC reached agreement in 1992 for a European Economic Area that would include the member countries of both institutions.

European Investment Bank (EIB)   Set up in 1958 under the terms of the Treaty of Rome (➤**European Union**), the EIB finances capital investment projects to promote the integration and balanced development of EU member states. The EIB also implements the financial components of agreements concluded under European development aid and co-operation policies. The bank raises substantial volumes of funds in capital markets. The members of the EIB are the 15 EU member states who have subscribed the bank's capital of €10 billion. The EIB operates on a non-profit basis but in keeping with strict banking practice. The *European Investment Fund* (EIF) was established in 1994 to support the creation, growth and development of small- and medium-sized enterprises. The EIF is a public–private partnership owned by the EIB, the European Commission and some eighty European financial institutions.

European Investment Fund ➤European Investment Bank.

European Monetary System   The currency stabilization regime instituted by the European Community (➤**European Union**) in 1979 to link the currencies of member states and eventually forge them into a common monetary system. ➤**Economic and Monetary Union.** An Exchange Rate Mechanism was set up to keep European Community currencies within a fixed percentage to a central parity to the European Currency Unit basket of currencies. (The UK and Italy withdrew from these arrangements in 1992.) The European Monetary Co-operation Fund was set up to assist intervention operations aimed at maintaining parities.

European Union (EU)   A grouping of fifteen European member states, until 1992 known as the European Community (EC). The EC was founded in 1958 under the Treaty of Rome and includes the European Coal and Steel Community (ECSC), the European Economic Community and the European Atomic Energy Community (Euratom). The principal organs of the EU are the European Commission, the Court of Justice, the European Parliament, and the Council of Ministers. The Single European Act 1986 committed the EC to the complete unification of the internal market and the free movement of goods, persons and capital. That Act also foreshadowed ➤**Economic and Monetary Union.** The original members of the EC were Belgium, France, (West) Germany, Italy, Luxembourg and The Netherlands. The UK, Ireland and Denmark joined in 1973, followed by Greece in 1981, Spain and Portugal in 1986 and Finland and Sweden in 1995. Other countries have applied to join. The European Economic Area (EEA), which has preferential access to the EC, includes Norway, Iceland and Liechtenstein.

EVA ➤economic value added.

evaluation process   The way consumers assess goods and services. Three main evaluation processes are used, based on: (a) 'search qualities' (attributes of a good that consumers can assess prior to purchase and consumption, e.g. price, colour and style of an item of clothing); (b) 'experience qualities' (attributes of a good or service that customers can assess only during consumption, e.g. taste of a meal, ease of handling of a car and personal treatment during a haircut), and (c) 'credence qualities' (attributes of a service that customers find hard to evaluate even after purchase and consumption, e.g. investment advice, management consultancy advice, and technical repairs).

One of the main purposes of ➤information search is to gather data about the attributes that might be used in an evaluation process. Having obtained such data, a ➤decision rule can be applied to help select one option rather than another. The logic of this is most easily seen for search qualities. With credence qualities, by contrast, it is difficult to gather and interpret appropriate information, and therefore hard to apply a decision rule with any degree of accuracy.

everyday-low-pricing (EDLP) A strategic decision on the part of producers or retailers to offer low prices – on average. The emphasis is on long-run competitive pricing. This contrasts with strategies where low prices are offered as exceptions, such as short-run price ➤promotions and ➤sales (both of which are occasional drops in price to give consumers an added incentive to buy) or 'loss leaders', i.e. commodity products and staples – bread, milk, rice – dropped in price to draw consumers into a store and, once there, who purchase other, higher margin, items. To be credible, EDLP must be consistent with the overall positioning of the organization, i.e. consumers must trust the organization to offer generally low prices. This does not necessarily mean 'lowest pricing', but it should mean generally low prices. If costs can be kept under control, the organization can continue to obtain healthy margins, as shown by the examples of Wal-Mart in the US and Aldi in continental Europe.

evoked set The specific group of ➤brands which a consumer actively considers and sees as acceptable options in a given product category. Acceptability will depend on a variety of evaluative criteria, e.g. price, taste, performance, after-sales support, etc. The brands most likely to be evoked are either in memory because of previous purchase or use, or they are very prominent in the market-place because of wide distribution, ready availability, attention-getting publicity and other factors related to ➤brand salience. ➤➤brand communication effects.

The evoked set is only a sub-portion of all the brands known to the consumer (the 'awareness set'). Other brands either belong to the 'inert set' (brands towards which consumers are indifferent) or the 'inept set' (brands which are seen as unacceptable). In an attempt to minimize information overload, consumers will limit ➤information search to brands in their evoked set. This is closely related to the idea of consumers having a ➤consideration set.

Various strategies are suggested for brands in, or not in, a consumer's evoked set. A brand already in a consumer's evoked set will want to consolidate its position and become the preferred option – not just be seen as one of several acceptable brands. For a brand not in the evoked set, the aim will be to disrupt patterns of behaviour (where there is limited problem-solving) or gain acceptance (where there is extended problem-solving). For example, if new evaluative criteria are brought to the attention of consumers the list of acceptable brands might change. By carefully managing this process it may be possible for an inert brand to become an evoked brand, something that can occur when a salesperson invites a customer to consider an alternative that was not originally on the list of acceptable brands.

ex ante Expected, or intended before the event, as opposed to *ex post* which means after the event. One might, for example, say '*ex ante* prices were cut but as inflation turned out to be far lower than expected, *ex post*, prices turned out to be relatively high.'

exchange control   A method by which governments seek to control the ➤exchange rate of their national ➤currency and to preserve the national ➤reserves, consisting of the imposition of limitations or prohibitions on the movement of currency across national frontiers. There are now few exchange controls in the industrialized countries but many developing countries maintain them.

exchange rate   The price (rate) at which one currency is exchanged for another currency. The actual rate at any one time is determined by supply and demand conditions for the relevant currencies in the foreign exchange market, and most obviously driving such demand are trade flows and capital flows. ➤balance of payments. The latter can themselves be subdivided into ➤direct investment, portfolio investment, and ➤hot money (money speculation on rapid movements in exchange rates that can be turned into a quick profit). The demand for a currency tends to rise: (a) as demand for the products made by producers in the country of the currency rises, and (b) as interest rates in the relevant currency rise, or show signs of having to rise in the future, e.g. signs of a booming economy can send the exchange rate up, as that indicates a need for a rise in interest rates.

However, another way of viewing the exchange rate is as the economy's device for altering the relative prices of domestic produce – which does not trade internationally – and international produce, which is traded across borders. Take a hypothetical example. Oil is priced internationally, with prices set in dollars. Competitive forces ensure the UK price of oil is the same as the global price. ➤one price, law of. Haircuts, however, cannot be internationally traded, and are priced locally. They can cost more or less in Manchester than in Barcelona. Now, consider what happens to the price of oil and haircuts if the pound falls in value relative to other currencies. The price of oil remains constant in dollar terms, so automatically rises in pound terms. The price of haircuts remains constant in pound terms, so falls in dollar terms. Looking at it either in dollars or pounds, the relative price of haircuts has fallen. The signal sent by the exchange rate has now made oil a more valuable commodity in the UK than haircuts. It has, implicitly, given a price boost to oil exporters at the expense of hairdressers. Or, more generally, the falling pound has relatively hurt the primarily domestic sectors and helped the international sectors. This is important, because when the economy receives a 'shock', the relative size and profitability of the two sectors sometimes need to adjust, and the exchange rate is one means by which the necessary price signals can be transmitted to the two sectors.

For example, a 'shock' in this sense might include a big rise in domestic savings. In this event, consumption at home falls, and exports logically need to rise to keep the economy fully occupied. The exchange rate falls, making life easier for exporters, and increasing demand for their products. It is the means by which the need for the economy to switch away from domestic-oriented production, to export-oriented production, is transmitted. Or, to give another example, the government may make a sudden increase in its borrowing. That represents a large increase in domestic consumption, and in a fully employed economy necessitates a corresponding fall in exports. The exchange rate will rise. Or, further, there may be a sudden gain in ➤**productivity** in the tradable sector on account of, say, a new discovery, as was supposed of the US ➤**new economy** in the late 1990s. In this case, the non-tradable sector will want to expand so domestic consumption can rise as a result of the discovery – the exchange rate will rise.

In all these cases, the exchange rate is simply a price, albeit an important one, responding to the pressures set by preferences for domestic and foreign goods, and the flows of savings and investment funds across currencies. It follows that the value of the currency is obviously also determined by domestic ➤**monetary policy** – more money can imply more inflation, which tends to mean a lower exchange rate, as inflation hits the tradable sector more harshly than the non-tradable. (The tradable sector gets squeezed, as it has to hold its price constant in world markets, while the domestic sector can raise its local prices in an inflationary environment more easily.) The relative price changes embodied in a changing exchange rate could, and usually would, occur in a single currency area. The question is whether they would occur as painlessly and rapidly.

As an important economic variable, governments have often sought to control exchange rates. Sometimes that is because it seems to be the most effective means of stabilizing monetary policy, especially in smaller countries. ➤➤**purchasing power parity**.

Exchange Rate Mechanism ➤European Monetary System.

excise duty Taxes levied on goods (e.g. alcoholic drinks and tobacco) produced for home consumption, as distinct from customs duties or ➤**tariffs**, which are levied on goods entering the country.

ex-coupon ➤ex-dividend.

ex-dividend (xd) Without ➤**dividend**. The purchaser of a ➤**security** quoted ex-dividend does not have the right to the next dividend when due; this belongs to the seller. The prefix *ex-*, meaning 'excluding', is also used in a similar sense in several other ways, e.g. *ex-coupon* excludes the next interest payment on a fixed-interest ➤**security**, *ex-rights* means that there is no entitlement to a ➤**rights issue**, *ex-warrant* excludes rights to a forthcoming warrant issue, and *ex-all* (US) excludes all impending benefits. ➤**bonus issue**.

execution **1.** In finance, effecting a trade, as when a ➤**broker** buys or sells ➤**securities** in the execution of an ➤**order**. **2.** A legal term meaning that a ➤**contract** has been signed, witnessed if necessary, and delivered to the respective parties. **3.** In advertising, a specific version of a creative concept (for every creative concept there may be many executions, reflecting the opportunities presented by all the different media used in a particular campaign).

execution only The provision of a ➤**security** dealing service without advice, research or other services.

exit The realization of an ➤**investment**, usually in the context of ➤**venture capital**,

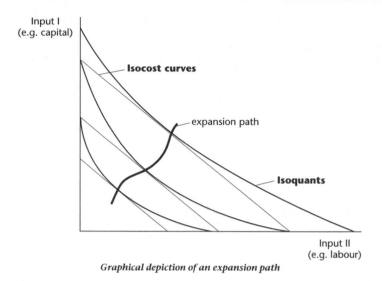

Graphical depiction of an expansion path

where an ➤**equity** investment in an ➤**unlisted company** may be realized by a trade sale (sold to a larger company or another venture capital company), by a ➤**management buy-out** or by ➤**flotation**.

exogenous variable A ➤variable whose value is not determined within the set of equations or ➤models established to make predictions or test a hypothesis.

expansion path A graphical depiction of the optimal combination of inputs used in the production of some item, as the scale of output is expanded. In simplistic terms, one might assume there are two different inputs to the production of widgets: labour and robots. The expansion path says how much of each one needs, as one plots different levels of total output. See above figure.

For those familiar with formal economic analysis of production in terms of ➤isoquants and ➤isocost curves, the optimum mix of inputs is typically where the latter provides a tangent to the former. The expansion path plots the tangent points on different isoquants, each a step further away from the origin.

expectancy theory A theory of ➤motivation. An employee will exert more effort when he believes increased effort will result in a good performance appraisal, that a good appraisal will lead to some form of tangible ➤reward (such as a ➤pay rise), and that it will also satisfy personal goals. There are three key relationships here: (a) an effort–performance relationship; (b) a performance–reward relationship, and (c) a reward–personal goals relationship. A problem in any one of these areas may result in demotivated employees, e.g. if a good appraisal leads to nothing more than a perfunctory pat on the back, while other employees receive bonus payments, this could lead to resentment and be demotivating.

Expectancy theory also goes under the name 'VIE theory'. This highlights that there are three components to consider: (a) 'valence' (the perceived value of an outcome, such as the perceived value of ➤**reward**); (b) 'instrumentality' (the perceived likelihood that one outcome will lead to another, e.g. that greater rewards will result in greater job satisfaction), and (c) 'expectancy' (the perceived likelihood that a behaviour will lead to an instrumental outcome, as in the perception that by working harder the rewards will be greater).

A knowledge of these components, and the relationships between them, helps in ➤**human resource management**, particularly where there is an attempt to influence employee motivation. Applications are also to be found in marketing, where the goal is to influence the purchase motives of consumers. ➤➤**expectations**.

expectations Anticipated levels of service and product performance prior to purchase. Anticipations will reflect previous experiences with the ➤**brand**, awareness of what competing brands have to offer, messages from marketing communications and information passed on by word-of-mouth. Expectations are important reference points when measuring ➤**customer satisfaction/dissatisfaction**. Thus, customers may be satisfied with mediocre performance if their initially low expectations were exceeded. Formally, these ideas are embodied in the 'disconfirmation of expectations model', whereby satisfaction is said to depend on the difference between a customer's prepurchase expectations and his perceptions of actual performance.

expected value A measure of the average value of a risky bet. For example, if an investment has a 50 : 50 chance of yielding a return of £1 million or nothing at all, the expected value is simply the mean return, i.e. £0.5 million. One might see the expected value as a measure of the fair price one would pay to buy a lottery ticket, if one was neither excited by the risk nor scared of it. Or one might see it as the insurance premium an insurer would charge a client if the insurer had no costs or profit.

experience curve The theory that an empirical relationship can be drawn between a cost reduction and the cumulative amount produced. This theory is based upon research conducted in the 1960s across a wide range of industries. It appeared to show dramatic reductions in costs. The relationship was explained by suggesting that in addition to economies of scale, there were other cost savings to be gained such as:
(1) Technical progress.
(2) Greater learning about processes.
(3) Greater skills from having undertaken the process over time.
These advantages can be seen at the firm level and the industry level. At the firm level, the market leader will, by definition, have produced cumulatively more than any other company. The leader should have low costs giving it a ➤**competitive advantage**. At the industry level, costs should fall as the industry overall produces more. Every firm should benefit from knowledge that is circulated within its industries.

One of the criticisms levelled against the benefits of experience curve effects is that the benefits will flow automatically whereas, in reality, organizations have to work extremely hard to gain the benefits suggested. Moreover, ➤**innovation** can overtake ➤**organizational learning** and may alter the cost profile of an existing operation. Finally, to achieve large-scale production, flexibility may have to be sacrificed. In some industries this may be a strategic mistake.

The concept was developed by Bruce D ➤**Henderson** and it forms the core of the growth–share matrix. ➤➤**portfolio planning.**

experience qualities ➤evaluation process.

experiment A type of research study in which conditions are controlled so that one or more independent variables can be manipulated to test hypotheses about their effect on a dependent variable. By controlling the external conditions, and focusing on the manipulation of one or a very limited number of independent variables, causal relationships between the variables can be tested. Manipulation of an independent variable is called a 'treatment'. In a full study there are likely to be several related experiments, comprising a number of treatments. These treatments are administered to 'subjects', also called 'test units' and 'respondents'. The specification of treatments, subjects, dependent variables and external conditions defines the 'experimental design'. A good design is one where any effect on the dependent variable can only be ascribed to the manipulation, i.e. there is no confounding effect from external conditions and extraneous variables.

Experimental techniques are used widely in management, notably in ➤**consumer behaviour** and ➤**organizational behaviour** studies. They are also used in applied ➤**marketing research**, including pricing experiments, willingness-to-pay studies, product attribute tests, and stated preference methods. ➤**choice modelling.** There is a tendency to think of experiments as laboratory-based, but many in management are field-based. However, in these contexts it may be very hard to control for external conditions and extraneous variables. Indeed, it may not be very meaningful to control for some of these. Experiments with consumer subjects may show a strong relationship between increased advertising exposure and higher levels of purchasing, but if the effects of competitive advertising are somehow controlled-out through the research design, the experimental conditions have to be regarded as artificial and contrived (given normal levels of competitive advertising and ➤**advertising clutter**). In these circumstances, the researcher must balance internal validity (from the experimental approach) against external validity (with respect to normal observable conditions). ➤**validity.**

A further problem with field-based experiments is that subjects may come to appreciate all the attention they have from being in an experiment and change their behaviour as a reaction to the attention, not in response to the manipulation – something discovered by Elton ➤**Mayo** in his work. The problem is known as the 'Hawthorne effect', named after a series of studies at the Hawthorne Works where improved performance was ascribed to the attention workers received from the researchers and not to the experimental manipulations. The effect was only noticed because the researchers gained counter-intuitive results. In many situations results are intuitive, but still might be explained by the Hawthorne effect. For instance, in a study of ➤**time management** techniques, does productivity improve because of the techniques, or because a spotlight has been placed on the employees and they respond to all the attention?

In a thorough study, several different methods are likely to be used. ➤➤**qualitative market research; quantitative market research.**

expert power ➤power.

expert system (ES) An information-processing technology, usually a computer, which stores large amounts of information on a specific area and then performs formal logic on responses to simple questions with the aim of 'solving problems'. The name comes from the ability of the system to represent an expert in that field. Typically, the system is based on simple mathematical equations such as 'if x then y'. The rules and data represent the knowledge base of the system, which is why ESs are sometimes called knowledge-based systems. The system asks the user a series of simple questions and eventually, through a process of elimination, a solution is offered.

Export Credit Guarantee Department (ECGD) (UK) Established in 1919, a government department for the provision of insurance cover against risks of default on export credit, and of cover against the risk of expropriation of assets invested abroad. Since the ECGD also covers against official payment and licensing restrictions for the foreign purchase of UK goods and services, it may be said to be the only significant insurer of long-term ➤**sovereign risk**. The ECGD's short-term credit insurance operations were privatized (➤**privatization**) in 1991.

ex post ➤*ex ante*.

exposure The placement of ➤advertising or ➤promotion so that a person in the ➤**target audience** can see/read/hear the message. Without being exposed to the message a consumer cannot respond to it. This means space or time must be bought in media that members of the target audience are likely to view/read/hear. Not all those who are exposed to an advertisement or promotion will notice it (the problem of 'attention'), let alone understand it, associate it with the ➤**brand** and take action, but careful placement is the first step in the process of successful marketing communication.

ex-rights ➤ex-dividend.

extended group ➤qualitative market research.

external constraint A factor outside the control of the organization that hinders its plans in some way. Organizations try to consider all possible constraints when developing and planning strategy (➤**marketing planning**). The acronym ➤**PESTL** is frequently used to group together the most common external influences on the organization.

external economies of scale ➤economies of scale; clustering.

externality A cost or benefit from some activity, which affects those other than the agent who makes decisions relevant to that activity. Externalities represent a problem for decentralized, market-led resource allocation, as companies and individuals are likely to neglect them when choosing how much or how to produce or consume. Classic examples are pollution and congestion. But externalities can be positive as well as negative – the benefits of a piece of new technology might extend beyond the extra profits it gives to the inventor. ➤**intellectual property**. Or, when a popular store opens a new branch, it yields benefits to the stores nearby.

One special case is the *pecuniary externality*, which is an effect that works through prices. A company that buys a big property in Luton may push up property prices in

Luton, having a negative and positive effect on other property buyers and property owners. ➤cost–benefit analysis.

extraordinary items ➤below the line.

extrinsic rewards ➤reward.

F

face value ➤par value.

facility A generic term denoting a bank loan in various forms, e.g. ➤acceptance; overdraft.

factoring A business activity in which a company takes over responsibility for collecting the ➤debts of another. Typically, the client debits all its sales to the factor and receives immediate payment from it, less a charge of about 2–3 per cent and interest for the period of ➤trade credit given to the customer. There are a number of different types of factoring: the simplest is invoice discounting. In its most elaborate form the factor maintains the company's sales ledger and other accounting functions and does not seek recourse to its client if unable to obtain payment from that client's customers (*non-recourse factoring*). The customer need not know that a factor is being used.

failure analysis The activity of analysing why production and operational failures have occurred. There are many different techniques and approaches used to uncover the root cause of these failures (➤fault tree analysis). Broadly, the three key areas of failure analysis are:
(1) Accident investigation. Large-scale disasters such as aircraft crashes will usually be investigated by experts trained in the detailed analysis of such incidents.
(2) Product liability. Any failures associated with a product can be traced back to the process that produced it, or the suppliers who provided it.
(3) Complaint analysis. Customer complaints are increasingly being used as a method for investigating errors or potential errors. Usually customer complaints will represent the 'tip of the iceberg' as many customers would not complain. Organizations should be able to use complaints to try and rectify product defects. ➤customer satisfaction/dissatisfaction.

fair value The practice of valuing assets and liabilities in company accounts at the amount at which they could be exchanged in an arms length transaction between informed and willing parties. Fair value is not established under conditions of a forced or liquidation sale. The world's ➤accounting standards setters are moving towards the mandatory adoption of fair value accounting in place of ➤historic cost. The International Accounting Standards Committee already requires the application of fair value to some financial assets, such as derivatives, but its extension to other financial assets is controversial. It would mean, for example, that the value of bank loans would fluctuate with interest rates and changes recognized in the ➤profit and loss account.

133

FASB ➤Financial Accounting Standards Board.

fast-moving consumer goods ➤packaged goods.

fault tree analysis A particular technique for analysing production and operational failures. This is a logical procedure that starts with a failure or potential failure and works backwards to identify all the possible causes and therefore the origins of that failure. The fault tree is made up of branches connected by AND nodes and OR nodes.

Fayol, Henri (died 1925) Generally credited as the first thinker to codify the functions in a business (production, commercial, accounting, finance and security) and the role of management. The five management activities were: planning, organizing, command, co-ordination, and control. Fayol was a French mining engineer and became managing director of a coalmining company. A contemporary of Frederick ➤Taylor, Fayol was born in 1841 but his book *General and Industrial Management*, published in France in 1916, did not appear in English translation until 1949, long after his death.

FCB planning grid Foote Cone Belding planning grid. ➤involvement theory.

FDI ➤foreign direct investment.

Fed (US) ➤Federal Reserve System.

Federal funds rate (US) Rate of interest charged on ➤Fed funds loaned by and to ➤commercial banks. The rate is regarded as an important determinant of bank ➤liquidity.

Federal Reserve Bank (US) ➤Federal Reserve System.

Federal Reserve System (Fed) (US) The central banking system of the US, established by the Federal Reserve Act 1913 and organized on a regional basis, given the large area involved and the multiplicity of small- and medium-sized banks. The system is composed of twelve regional *Reserve banks*, twenty-five branches and eleven offices under the control of a board of governors located in Washington, DC (the Federal Reserve Board). The board of governors consists of seven governors appointed by Congress on the nomination of the President, each serving for 14 years, with one reappointment falling due every 2 years. The regional Reserve banks are controlled by boards of nine directors, of whom three are appointed by the board of governors; the president and vice-president of each Reserve bank are drawn from the last three. The chairman of the board of governors is the head of the Federal Reserve System, appointed for a term of 4 years.

The regional Reserve banks supervise banking practice and management, act as ➤lenders of last resort, provide common services in cheque clearing, statistics and research, and apply monetary policy at the instance of the board of governors. Monetary control is exercised chiefly through open market operations and is determined by the board of governors' Federal Open Market Committee, day-to-day transactions in pursuance of this being handled by the Reserve Bank of New York. The board of governors' constitutional independence is guaranteed by the long-term appointment of the governors and by the fact that the system generates a surplus (mostly paid as a dividend to the Treasury), relieving it of financial dependence on

Congress. The chairman, members and staff of the board frequently explain Federal Reserve policy to congressional committees and maintain close contact with the US administration, but retain final responsibility for their policy.

Since the Monetary Control Act 1980, all US banks are members of the Federal Reserve System. The system was modified by the Banking Act 1935. ➤➤**Federal funds rate; Fed funds.**

Fed funds (US) Deposits made by ➤**commercial banks** in their local Federal Reserve Bank. ➤**Federal Reserve System.** Fed funds include cash balances in excess of the reserve requirement, which may be loaned to other banks overnight to enable them to meet their reserve requirement. ➤➤**Federal funds rate.**

fiduciary A person or legal body acting on behalf of others who have a beneficial interest in investments or other property. An *executor.*

Fiedler contingency model The theory that effective groups depend upon a proper match between a leader's style of interacting with subordinates and the degree to which the situation gives control and influence to the leader. Developed by F E Fiedler (*A Theory of Leadership Effectiveness*, 1967), the model explicitly recognizes three situational criteria: (a) leader–member relations; (b) task structure, and (c) position power. These criteria can be manipulated to create a match with the behavioural orientation of the leader. ➤**leadership.**

final dividend ➤dividend.

final salary scheme An alternative term for an occupational pension scheme in which pension benefits are established not with reference to how much a person has contributed to the scheme, but to his salary on leaving the scheme. ➤**pension.**

finance The provision of money when and where required. Finance may be short term (usually up to 1 year), medium term (1–7 years) or long term. Finance may be provided in the form of loan finance, i.e. ➤**debt**, or ➤**equity**, or as a grant. Finance may be required for consumption or for ➤**investment.** When provided for the latter, it becomes ➤**capital.** ➤➤**business finance; consumer credit.**

finance house (UK) A financial institution engaged in the provision of ➤**hire purchase** and other forms of instalment credit for customers and business, sometimes known as *industrial banks* (US = *small loan company*) for ➤**consumer credit**, and *commercial credit company* for business credit. Some suppliers (e.g. motor manufacturers) have their own finance houses, known in the US as *captive finance companies.*

financial accounting The process of preparing the ➤**profit and loss account** and ➤**balance sheet** for an enterprise, usually on an annual or 6-monthly basis. ➤➤**audit; management accounting.**

Financial Accounting Standards Board (FASB) (US) The non-governmental body which sets the accounting rules for US companies. Although formal responsibility for rule-setting lies with the ➤**Securities and Exchange Commission**, the latter leaves the task in the hands of the FASB, rarely intervening.

financial future A ➤future in a financial ➤**asset**, i.e. a contract for the purchase of a specific standard quantity of a financial asset at a specific price on a specific future date.

financial institution A major commercial and public organization engaged in exchanging, lending, borrowing and investing money. The term is often used as an alternative for ➤financial intermediaries.

financial intermediary An institution that holds money balances of, or borrows from, individuals and other institutions, in order to make loans or other ➤investments. Hence, it serves the purpose of channelling funds from lenders to borrowers. ➤Banks, ➤building societies, ➤hire-purchase companies, ➤insurance companies, ➤savings banks and ➤investment trusts are financial intermediaries, but it is usual to distinguish between bank and non-bank financial intermediaries because of the role of the former in determining the money supply.

financial ratio 1. A measure of creditworthiness such as the current ratio (➤working capital), ➤gearing, ➤dividend cover, ➤interest cover and the ratio of long-term ➤debt to ➤net tangible assets. **2.** A calculation based on company accounts and other sources to indicate the profitability or other financial aspects of a business. ➤price–earnings ratio; return on investment.

financial reporting standards ➤accounting standards.

Financial Services Act 1986 Legislation enacted in November 1986 but which came into force in April 1988 to regulate the investment business in the UK. The Act followed a report on investor protection commissioned in 1981 from Professor Jim Gower and completed in 1984. The Gower Report recommended that the new regulatory system should cover ➤insurance, ➤unit trusts and other forms of investment business in addition to stock exchange ➤investments. The Act set up a Securities and Investment Board (SIB) run and paid for by investment professionals, but with statutory powers and reporting to the Department of Trade and Industry. Investment businesses had to be registered with the SIB directly or with *self-regulating organizations* (SROs), some of which were replaced by the Personal Investment Authority in 1994. In mid 1997 the UK government announced that the SROs would be absorbed into the SIB, which was renamed the Financial Services Authority.

At the same time, it was announced that the Authority would take over the regulation of the ➤insurance industry (until then regulated by the Department of Trade and Industry), the ➤building societies industry (until then regulated by the Building Societies Commission) and also friendly societies, ➤credit unions and industrial and provident societies. The Authority also took from the ➤Bank of England the supervision of the banking system. The Financial Services and Markets Act 2000, which came into force in December 2001, superseded the 1986 Act and established the FSA as the single regulator for virtually the entire financial sector in the UK.

Financial Services and Markets Act ➤Financial Services Act.

Financial Services Authority ➤Financial Services Act.

***Financial Times* share indices** *FTO (Financial Times (Industrial) Ordinary)* or *FT 30 Share Index*, an unweighted (➤weighted average) *geometric* average of 30 leading ➤blue chip issues quoted on the ➤London Stock Exchange, was introduced in 1935 and calculated hourly. The FT 30 has been superseded by the FT/SE 100 ['*Footsie 100*'] *Index*, a ➤market capitalization weighted average calculated minute by minute (real time). The ➤**base period** for the FT 100 is 3 January 1984 = 1,000 and its constituents are the 100 largest quoted industrial and commercial companies by free capitalization (➤**free capital**), reviewed quarterly; ➤**investment trusts** are excluded. The *FT/SE Mid-250 Index*, also calculated minute by minute, covers the next 250 companies, ranked by market value, and the *FT/SE/Actuaries 350 Index* includes all the constituents of the 100 and 250 indices.

The 350 Index covers about 92 per cent of total market value and the 100 Index about 72 per cent. The *FT/Actuaries All Share Index* has been published daily since 10 April 1962; it now covers some 800 shares and fixed interest ➤**stocks** and covers some 98 per cent of total market value, and has indices for industry *baskets* and subsections. The *FT/SE Small Cap Index*, introduced in 1993 and calculated daily, covers those shares within the FT/A All Share Index but not within the 350. In 1987 the *FT/Actuaries World Share Index* was introduced, based on a weighted sample of 2,400 share prices, initially from 24 countries. In 2001, new global sector indices were introduced. The *FT/Actuaries Fixed Interest Indices* measure the prices and ➤**yields** of UK ➤**gilts**, index-linked (➤**indexation**), ➤**debentures** and loans. Total return figures are calculated for all the UK indices and published daily. These figures, which are gross of tax, take account of both price performance and income received from ➤**dividends**. ➤➤**index number**.

financial year A 12-month period in respect of which financial accounts are kept. Years of account for financial purposes often do not coincide with calendar years and hence are referred to as 'financial years'. A financial year 2002/3, for example, might run from 31 August 2002 to 1 September 2003. Government financial years are called *fiscal years*.

firewall Used on ➤**internet** web sites to prevent unauthorized users from accessing certain parts of the site. A so-called wall of fire is established around certain pages of information, thereby protecting some parts but allowing access to unprotected parts of the site. This is important if proprietory business information is to be kept secure and confidential.

first-mover advantage The advantage that flows from being the first ➤**brand** to enter a market or to meet the needs of a consumer segment. Also called 'order of entry advantage'. The advantage is manifest in several ways: (a) the first-mover establishes a position in the market; (b) it can lay down the ground-rules for doing business in the market; (c) it can set expectations in terms of product features and service levels, and (d) it can set standards which any competitor then has to follow. The main advantage comes from making a link in the mind of customers between the innovation and the brand. This provides a basis for making ➤**sales**, building ➤**consumer loyalty** and retaining customers. Those who claim to have a first-mover advantage talk of 'owning' the market or consumer segment. That, having made the connection in the minds of consumers between the innovation and the brand, the market or consumer segment is largely theirs. These advantages might be consolidated by erecting ➤**barriers to entry** for followers and ➤**switching costs** for consumers.

However, the reality of so-called first-mover advantages can be very different. The first-mover will face considerable business risk. Inexperience in the area may give rise to costly mistakes. To derive advantage, consumers and observers must perceive the brand to be the first – it must be seen as a pioneer. Simply being first is not enough. Furthermore, if the innovation has merit for consumers and is profitable for producers, there will be followers – this is only to be expected in open free-market economies. It may be second-movers who gain most advantage, especially if they are perceived as innovators and if they have been able to learn from the mistakes of the pioneer.

Whether first-movers, second-movers or other followers gain most advantage partly depends on the type of innovation and the.type of organization making the first move. Thinking in this area tends to assume the innovation is a really new product and possibly a one-off purchase for which a price premium is justified, such as a DVD player. In this context the first-mover logic may stand up to scrutiny. But the logic is not so clear where an organization develops a product for an established market, launches a line extension, or tries to carve out a new submarket by changing a few product attributes, e.g. by adding an extra ingredient to a canned product. Here it may be relatively easy for a follower to imitate the innovation, a price premium may be hard to justify, and it would make little sense to talk of 'owning' the market or consumer segment. The problem is compounded if the first-mover is small. Initially it may gain advantage from the minor innovation, but it is unlikely to sustain its position once a competitor with a significant share in the overall market enters the submarket. The large competitor will have advantages in terms of brand awareness and brand familiarity, perceived quality and trustworthiness, and marketing support, i.e. the amount it can spend on advertising, distribution, etc. These factors will tend to outweigh the small company's ability to benefit from its innovation, especially longer term. ➤➤**early entrant; new product development.**

fiscal policy Government management of its spending and taxation decisions. Fiscal policy has important, but much-debated effects on the short-run behaviour of the economy. If governments choose to tax more than they spend (i.e. run up a surplus) then the impact of policy is broadly to depress the overall level of spending in the economy. The reverse occurs if government runs up a deficit.

Arguably, however, fiscal policy has only marginal effects on the economy, as any fiscal measure spawns offsetting measures elsewhere. For example, more government borrowing may cause higher interest rates and, in turn, lower investment. Or, it may prompt the private sector to increase its level of saving in anticipation of the higher taxes that will be needed in future to repay the borrowing. More government borrowing can push the exchange rate up, as foreign lenders send money into the currency, to lend to the government, thus depressing exports.

Fiscal policy enjoyed its golden years in the three decades following the Second World War. However, once ➤**inflation** became embedded in the Western world in the 1970s, fiscal measures seemed impotent to cure it, and the power of ➤**monetary policy** was rediscovered. Moreover, it now appears accepted that fiscal measures are slower to enact than monetary ones; thus, fine-tuning the economy by cutting or raising taxes or government spending is decidedly unfashionable.

fiscal year ➤financial year.

five factor model of personality A model of personality. It is also known as the 'Big Five' model. Five basic personality dimensions are seen as underlying all others:
(1) Extraversion (a personality dimension describing someone who is sociable, talkative and assertive).

(2) Agreeableness (describing someone who is good-natured, co-operative and trusting).

(3) Conscientiousness (describing someone who is responsible, dependable, persistent and achievement oriented).

(4) Emotional stability (describing someone who is calm, enthusiastic and secure).

(5) Openness to experience (describing someone who is imaginative, artistically sensitive and intellectual).

Research shows that these personality dimensions are related to job performance; therefore, they are of interest in ➤human resource management in the contexts of hiring and selection, job placement, ➤work design, and ➤group development. ➤➤Myers–Briggs Type Indicator; personality traits.

five forces framework ➤competitive strategy.

fixed asset ➤asset.

fixed interest Generally, refers to ➤securities such as bonds on which the holder receives a predetermined and unchanging rate of interest on the nominal value (➤par value) as opposed to the non-guaranteed, variable return on ➤equities.

flexible manufacturing systems (FMS) The integration and arrangement of several production operations that use process technologies to form a self-contained 'micro-operation', which is capable of manufacturing a whole component. A distinct feature of such systems is the use of ➤numerical control, automated loading and unloading and movement of components between work stations, often using robotics. This is usually co-ordinated by a central computer control system. In theory, such systems once set up should be able to produce a range of components with minimal disruption to the whole manufacturing system – it is this flexibility that gives the system its name. For example, an FMS may be set up to manufacture 10,000 injection moulded tennis rackets; with the necessary changes in tooling and materials such a system may then be able to produce 20,000 chairs.

flighting An ➤advertising technique for interspersing periods of concentrated advertising with periods of inactivity. Commonly associated with the management of television advertising because of the prohibitive cost of continuous activity, but applicable to any form of marketing communication. ➤media planning.

floating capital Capital invested not in fixed assets (e.g. such as buildings) but in work in progress, wages paid, etc. ➤working capital.

floating charge An assignment of the total ➤assets of a company or individual as ➤collateral security for a ➤debt; as opposed to particular assets, when such an assignment is known as a 'fixed charge' or 'mortgage'. ➤➤debentures.

floating rate 1. A ➤rate of interest that varies with the market, more particularly with an agreed reference standard, e.g. the ➤London interbank offered rate. ➤variable rate security. **2.** An ➤exchange rate that is not fixed by the national authorities but varies according to supply and demand for the currency.

floating rate note ➤variable rate security.

floor broker (US) **1.** A member (or employee of a member firm) of the ➤stock exchange who buys or sells ➤securities on the ➤trading floor on behalf of clients, as distinct from floor traders (who do so on their own account). **2.** The representative of a member of a ➤**commodity** market, authorized to deal on the trading floor of the market. A full member of the market and thus also called a floor member.

flotation The issue of shares in a company on a stock exchange or ➤**unlisted securities market** for the first time. The method may be an ➤**introduction**, an ➤**intermediate offer**, a ➤**placing** or an ➤**offer for sale**. When a private company (➤**incorporation**) becomes a public company and has its shares listed in this way, the process is known as *going public*.

flow chart A diagram used to identify the main elements of a process. Flow charts usually include symbols to indicate decision points and activities. They are usually presented using a linear cause-and-effect style, with lines linking activity boxes or decision diamonds. They are useful in simplifying and thereby helping to understand what may often appear to be a complex system. A criticism of flow charts is that they sometimes fail to take account of all the inputs and can oversimplify a process. ➤➤**blueprinting**.

flow-charting the customer experience A listing of each step in the customer's experience of a service, identifying front-stage activities at each of these steps, and mapping on to these steps all the supporting back-stage activities. Flow-charting helps managers to appreciate service provision and service quality from the viewpoint of customers. Shortfalls in service delivery become apparent, too. For example, the manager may be focused on bill-payment systems (back-stage), but not have considered how easy it is for a consumer to read her bill (front-stage). Also called 'service mapping' (when describing an existing service) and 'service blueprinting' (when planning a new or revised service). ➤➤**blueprinting; services marketing**.

flow production A continuous production process, where a plant is set up to run continuously for days, weeks or even years. It offers the benefit of large economies of scale, but requires large-scale investment and has limited flexibility in terms of the product produced.

FMCGs Fast-moving consumer goods. ➤**packaged goods**.

FMS ➤**flexible manufacturing systems**.

FOB ➤**free-on-board**.

focus group A small group of ➤**target audience** individuals who are invited to express views and opinions on an issue, good or service. ➤**qualitative market research**.

focus strategy One of the three ➤**generic strategies** advocated by Michael ➤**Porter** that are available to a business. Sometimes referred to as 'niche marketing'. ➤**niche brand**. Such an approach is characterized by offering products or services to a specific market segment. In theory, this enables the firm to develop a competitive advantage by tailoring its strategy to serve this particular market segment. A firm may also adopt a cost-leadership approach or a differentiation strategy.

Follet, Mary Parker (died 1933) An early thinker on management and, with Elton ➤**Mayo**, one of the founders of the Human Relations School which reacted against the Scientific Management School of Frederick W ➤**Taylor** and others.

Foote Cone Belding ➤involvement theory.

Ford, Henry (died 1947) Car manufacturer who led price-cutting for volume and mass-production techniques and who paid high wages. A natural mechanic born in a farming family, he had little formal schooling. He built his first car in 1896 and started his famous company in 1903. As one of only two businessmen management gurus included in this book (the other is another car executive Alfred ➤**Sloan**), Ford is a paradoxical choice for inclusion because he did not believe in management in the sense of delegated, decentralized functions. Ford ran his business and no one else was expected to take significant decisions. This led to the downfall of his company in the 1920s, though since Ford was enormously rich the company did not go bust and was to be revitalized by his grandson Henry Ford II after the Second World War.

Ford wrote several books, including *My Life and Work* (1926). The term 'Fordism' has gained currency when referring to the mass-production, assembly-line-based industrial landscape which is now giving way to batch and fully automated production where workers have more control over their activities.

forecasting The art or science of predicting the future behaviour of a variable. Usually the predictions will be based upon past events, e.g. using statistical methods to extrapolate past trends in plotting a future one. ➤**barometric forecasting; growth trend analysis**. Or they can be derived from ➤**econometric** analysis to instil a degree of scientific method. ➤**demand forecasting**. Often, however, they involve pure speculation, especially when there are no data on relevant previous occurrences. Thus, forecasting has to be seen as a judgemental and inexact practice.

Forecasts tend to be divided into short-term and long-term projections, the latter being subject to greater uncertainty. Often the forecaster's task is to identify connections between variables (i.e. what causes what) and, hence, to generate predictions of future outcomes. This can be achieved by drawing on the expertise and judgements of managers, advisers and forecasters. ➤➤**Delphi group forecast; scenario planning**. Hopefully, this enables management to determine the consequences of its intended policies and thus select the best course of action.

foreign direct investment Investment in the foreign operations of a business. ➤➤**direct investment**.

foreign exchange market The activity of exchanging currencies through purchase and sale. The market is mainly conducted by ➤**dealers** in ➤**commercial banks**, and much of the ➤**turnover** is accounted for by speculation on exchange rate movements.

forfaiting A form of export finance in which the forfaiter accepts, at a discount from the exporter, a ➤**bill of exchange** or *promissory note* (➤**note**) from the exporter's customer; the forfaiter in due course collects payment of the debt. The notes are normally guaranteed by the customer's bank. Maturities are normally up to 3 years.

forming ➤group development.

Form 10-K (US) An annual return made to the ➤**Securities and Exchange**

Commission by companies listed on one of the national stock exchanges, giving financial and other information. A public document available on ➤**Edgar**.

forward A prospective amount of a currency or a commodity obtained by a contract between a buyer and a seller. Under this, the seller undertakes to provide the client with a fixed amount of the currency or commodity on a fixed future date at a fixed rate of exchange, or price. This differs from a ➤**futures** contract in that each forward contract is a once-only deal between the two parties, while futures contracts are in standard amounts traded on exchanges.

forwardation ➤contango.

4 Ps Shorthand for '*p*roduct, *p*rice, *p*lace and *p*romotion' – the four Ps of marketing. The 4Ps were devised by E Jerome McCarthy as a quick way to summarize the key elements of the ➤**marketing mix** (*Basic Marketing: a managerial approach*, 1960). While a handy catch-phase, the 4Ps give an incomplete view of the functional aspects of marketing. For this reason several other 'Ps' have been suggested, including 'people' (e.g. the salespeople who interact with customers in a ➤**service encounter**) and 'processes', e.g. a consulting organization offers processes to clients, rather than fixed and tangible products. Moreover, the notion of 4Ps conveys no sense of marketing being a business philosophy (as embodied in the ➤**marketing concept**). For this reason it has been heavily criticized in recent times, particularly by those who see marketing as a business philosophy based on understanding customers and building relationships (➤➤**relationship marketing**).

Fourth Directive The most prominent of a series of European Union (EU) directives (➤**Directives of the European Union**) leading to the harmonization of company law in member states. The Fourth Directive introduced detailed schedules for the form and content of company accounts and was implemented in the UK in the Companies Act 1981. ➤➤**incorporation**. ➤➤**consolidated accounts**.

Frankfurt Stock Exchange ➤German stock exchange.

free capital (UK) That proportion of the ➤**equity** of a ➤**company** available for trading by the public on a stock market (US = *free float*). It excludes equities held by controlling shareholders.

free float ➤free capital.

free-on-board A term of sale stating who is to pay transport/shipment costs, who is to control the transportation/shipment, and the stage at which title passes from seller to buyer. Originally, it simply meant the goods were 'free-on-board'.

free-rider problem A problem associated with linking an incentive to pay for a benefit, where the benefit is to all and no one can be excluded, such as a public good. Public parks and street lighting are examples where everyone benefits (free ride) and it is difficult to exclude people (who might not have paid). In such circumstances it is usually the State that provides these goods and uses taxation to pay for them.

Freiverkehr (Ger.) The unofficial or ➤**unlisted securities market(s)** of ➤**German stock exchanges**.

frequency ➤media planning.

frictional profit theory The idea that abnormally high profits for a firm or an industry (➤**economic rent**) can often be explained as a temporary phenomenon associated with the lag between some new innovation occurring, and the arrival of more intense competition resulting from it. For example, if Direct Line insurance finds it can use direct telephone selling as a new way of transacting business at far lower cost than methods used by rival suppliers, then it will be able to make large profits. However, those 'frictional profits' will not last for ever, as new firms overcome the ➤**barriers to entry** and enter the market, attracted by the profits to be made, and as existing firms switch to the new technology. Eventually, more intense competition will drive profits back to the levels previously prevailing and consumers will benefit from the lower prices the new innovation can sustain. Under this account, 'frictional profit' can be seen as a disequilibrium phenomenon.

fringe benefit One of a range of extra benefits given to employees, e.g. company cars, childcare support, staff discounts on goods and services, membership of associations and professional bodies, subsidized travel for self and family. Fringe benefits are usually designed to lure potential employees or ➤**reward** existing employees. The idea of offering fringe benefits is related to the notion of benefits-in-kind, where employees receive benefits in lieu of additional pay. However, generally it is illegal to force employees to take benefits-in-kind. A key piece of British legislation in this regard was the Truck Act, 1831 which abolished the system of paying employees with tokens that only could be used at the company's own factory shop ('tommy shops'). The practice is still observed in some developing countries. Fringe benefits and benefits-in-kind are often thought of as non-financial rewards and tax-exempt, but most Western governments have moved to tax these disguised forms of ➤**compensation**.

FSA **1.** ➤**Financial Services Act**. **2.** Financial Services Authority. ➤**Financial Services Act**.

FT/Actuaries World Share Index ➤*Financial Times* share indices.

full listing (UK) The inclusion of a company in the ➤**Official List** of the ➤**London Stock Exchange**.

fund A sum of money, as in an amount of savings, handed to a ➤**stockbroker** for investment and management (➤**discretionary account**), or subscribed to a savings scheme or invested by a ➤**life assurance** company to meet the claims of policyholders. Fund management consists of carrying out administration such as the receipt of ➤**dividends** and ➤**interest**, subscribing to ➤**rights issues** and adjusting the ➤**portfolio** by purchases and sales with the objective of maximizing capital growth or income. The term is frequently used to denote the institution managing the fund, e.g. a pension fund. ➤**pension**. Also used generally to describe any investment vehicle such as a ➤**unit trust** or an ➤**investment trust**.

fundamental analysis ➤technical analysis.

funded debt Generally, short-term ➤**debt** that has been converted into long-term debt. ➤**funding**.

funded pension scheme ➤pension.

funding The process of converting short-term to long-term ➤**debt** by the sale of long-term ➤**securities** and using the funds raised to repay short-term debt. In public finance, *overfunding* occurs when the government is selling more debt to the non-bank sector than is necessary to meet the public sector's need for borrowing, and *underfunding* when it is selling less than is necessary for that purpose. Under *full funding*, purchases of government paper by the banks do not count towards the financing needs of public borrowing, which are fully met by sales to non-banks, i.e. to other ➤**financial intermediaries**, and the personal and corporate sectors.

fungible A class of good or ➤**security** that has the property of being substitutable or interchangeable with another in the same class. ➤**Bearer securities**, ➤**ordinary shares** and money, such as £5 notes, are fungible because, if of the same denomination, one can be replaced by another without loss or gain. Fungibility is important because it allows the pooling and offsetting of classes of items without the need to identify them individually by serial numbers or other means.

future A vehicle for the purchase and sale of ➤**commodities** and financial ➤**instruments** at a date in the future. Futures take the form of a fixed and binding contract for a standard amount to be sold at a fixed price at a fixed future date. In the precise obligation involved, the future differs from an ➤**option** and a ➤**forward** transaction. A future is a ➤**negotiable** ➤**instrument**. ➤➤**financial future**.

futures market A market dealing in ➤**futures** and ➤**options** on shares, ➤**bonds**, foreign currencies and ➤**commodities**.

G

game theory A branch of economics useful in the study of business behaviour, concerned with representing economic interactions in a highly stylized form, with players, pay-offs and strategies. In much of business economics outside game theory, firms are assumed to be so small that any decision they make has little material effect on the actions of other firms. In real life, however, the behaviour of one firm does prompt a reaction from rivals. Game theory has been found to provide a neat set of tools to ➤**model** those interactions. Many business situations lend themselves to caricature as a kind of generic 'game'. ➤➤**battle of the sexes; chicken; prisoners' dilemma**. In general, understanding the behaviour of an industry as the interaction of different strategies, given different pay-offs in different states of the world, is very helpful.

The games companies play can be classified in several different ways: (a) co-operative games in which collusion is possible, and non-co-operative games where it is not; (b) ➤**zero sum games**, where the winnings of one player come at the direct expense of another, versus ➤**variable sum games**, where there are some outcomes in which the total pay-offs available are bigger than in others, and (c) ➤**repeated games**, where the interaction described reoccurs regularly, thus making it possible for players to shape a strategy in later rounds of the game, dependent on the behaviour of other players in earlier rounds. ➤➤**equilibrium; pay-off matrix**.

gamma stocks alpha securities, ➤**stock**.

Gantt chart A chart that shows the scheduled start date and the progress of each job compared to its scheduled delivery date. ➤**critical path analysis**.

gap analysis A planning technique. It compares projections of current activities assuming that present circumstances continue. Divergences are then analysed, and measures implemented to bridge the gap. For example, a firm may project sales will continue at the current level for the next 5 years, but it also projects that costs are likely to rise at current rates causing a gap between income and expenditure. Measures that could be taken to reduce this gap could be to: (a) increase prices; (b) increase sales volume, or (c) reduce costs.

GDP ➤**gross domestic product**.

gearing (UK) The relative importance of loans in the ➤**capital structure** (US = *leverage*). There are several ways of measuring gearing. The usual way is the ratio of fixed-interest ➤**debt** to shareholder interest plus the debt. ➤**net asset**. A corporation may borrow capital at fixed interest, and if it can earn more on that capital than it has to pay for it in interest, then the additional earnings accrue to the ➤**equity ➤shareholders**. Thus, a firm with high gearing will be able to pay higher ➤**dividends** per share than a firm with lower gearing earning exactly the same return on its total capital, provided that return is higher than the rate it pays for loan capital. However, the contrary is also true; so the higher the gearing the greater the risk to the equity shareholder. ➤➤**capital gearing; equity gearing; gearing effect.**

gearing effect (UK) **1.** The impact upon ➤**earnings per share** of ➤**capital** structure. ➤**gearing. 2.** The multiplication of a change in the price of a ➤**warrant** compared with that of a share that may be exchanged for it, or in the price of a share compared with an ➤**option**.

General Agreement on Tariffs and Trade (GATT) ➤World Trade Organization.

general insurance Insurance against fire, accident, theft, etc., as distinct from life insurance.

generally accepted accounting principles (GAAP) (US) Rules for ➤accounting standards. The ➤**Securities and Exchange Commission** requires audited accounts for ➤**quoted companies** to comply with GAAP.

generic An unbranded product sold by retailers. Generics are distinct from producer ➤**brands** and retail ➤**private labels**, in that they are sold primarily on the basis of low price. They are displayed in minimal 'no frills' packaging, are given no/little promotional support, and are likely to have cheaper ingredients/attributes. Some generics are made by producers of branded products, especially if the producer's equipment is not working to full capacity and the company is looking for an additional source of sales.

generic strategy Based on some very simple economic and marketing principles, Michael ➤**Porter** has argued that there are three basic strategies open to firms: (a) ➤**cost leadership**; (b) ➤**differentiation**, and (c) ➤**focus**. According to the theory, every business needs to follow one of these strategies in order to compete successfully and gain sustainable ➤**competitive advantage**. Porter argued that there were potential dangers for firms that engage in more than one of the generic strategies and fails to achieve any of them, i.e. a firm that attempts to be a low-cost producer and differentiate its products may find that it loses out to those firms that concentrate on either of the other two strategies. This is usually portrayed using the figure opposite.

Many researchers have since argued that there is empirical evidence to show that some firms have successfully followed more than one of the generic strategies, such as Toyota automobiles. Moreover, many would argue that the dynamic technology-intensive firms of today do not and should not adopt the generic strategy approach for fear of missing major market opportunities. Furthermore, Porter's approach focused only on the market positioning aspect of strategy and for many firms the real difficulties lie in deciding in which technology to invest and which skills are required for the firm to develop new products and services for the future.

geodemographic segmentation The grouping of people on the basis of the demographics of an area, region or administrative unit. It is assumed that people

COMPETITIVE ADVANTAGE

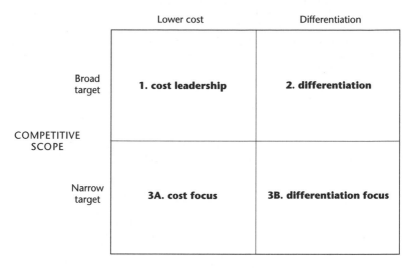

	Lower cost	Differentiation
Broad target	**1. cost leadership**	**2. differentiation**
Narrow target	**3A. cost focus**	**3B. differentiation focus**

COMPETITIVE SCOPE

Three Generic Strategies Source: Porter, M. E., *Competitive Strategy: techniques for analysing industries and competitors* (Simon & Schuster, 1985)

within an areal unit not only share demographic characteristics, but also have similar values, resulting in similar behaviour with respect to product choices, media usage and responsiveness to promotions, coupons, direct mail, advertising, and so forth. Such information is used for market ➤**segmentation** and the targeting of marketing communications and promotional offers. ➤**direct marketing**.

The areal unit in commercial studies is the post code, enumeration district or census district. In general, it is best to work with the finest disaggregation allowable under privacy regulations, and aggregate up to larger reporting units. The most well-known areal unit in the UK is CACI's ACORN classification. This profiles people in each areal unit into one of six broad categories (thriving, expanding, rising, settling, aspiring or striving), seventeen groups and fifty-four types (plus one unclassified residual type). For example, within the thriving category there are three groups: (a) wealthy achievers in suburban areas; (b) affluent greys in rural communities, and (c) prosperous pensioners in retirement areas. These groups are further divided into, for example, the prosperous pensioners, who are then divided into home-owners and occupiers of private flats.

In the US, the most well-known system is PRIZM, operated by Claritas. This system enables each areal unit (ZIP code, census tract or census block) to be profiled in terms of forty lifestyle clusters. These clusters reflect twelve underlying social groups. As an example, one social group comprises the unskilled living in the urban US, for which there are four lifestyle clusters labelled 'Heavy Industry', 'Downtown Dixie-Style', 'Hispanic Mix' and 'Public Assistance'. An array of demographic measures and consumption data are used to form the clusters and profiles.

A problem with these systems is keeping them up to date. National census data only appear at 10-year intervals in many countries and even then take time to be released publicly. Therefore, it is usual to supplement census data with information from other sources (postal services, public utilities, electoral registers, etc.). Another problem arises from the 'ecological fallacy', i.e. relationships found at one level of resolution are not found, or are contradicted, at another level of resolution. A further problem is that if the areal definition is changed, differing results might be produced ('the modifiable areal unit problem'). Thus, different clusters and profiles could result from changing the (arbitrary) areal units used in geodemographic segmentation studies. ➤➤lifestyle segmentation.

geregelter Freiverkehr (Ger.)   Second-tier official ➤unlisted securities markets operating at the stock exchanges in Germany. There is also an unregulated third tier called the *ungeregelter Freiverkehr*. Finally, there is an ➤over-the-counter telephone market in which both listed and unlisted shares are dealt, the *Telefonverkehr* (literally, 'telephone traffic').

German stock exchange   One of the numerous ➤stock exchanges in Germany grouped under *Deutsche Borse AG* with a Federal Securities Supervisory Office in Frankfurt. Frankfurt is by far the largest exchange, accounting for over 75 per cent of volume. A new electronic ➤order driven trading system, 'Xetra', went live in November 1997.

Gesellschaft (Ger.) ➤company.

Gesellschaft mit beschränkter Haftung (*GmbH*) (Ger.) A private limited company. ➤incorporation.

get-up ➤look-alike; visual equity.

Giffen good A product which consumers tend to buy more of, as its price rises. Giffen goods are those with a ➤demand curve that is upward sloping. The observation that such goods could exist was originally made of staple items in the budgets of the poor in the nineteenth century. As the price of bread rose, for example, the poor could not afford to buy as many luxurious foods, and were thus forced, perversely, to buy more bread despite its higher price.

Gilder, George Independent writer and technology guru. His bestselling book *Wealth and Poverty* (1981), which exalted free market capitalism and the 'irrational' entrepreneur (risk is incalculable and depends upon blind leaps into the unknown) was a favourite of President Reagan. In his *Microcosm* (1989) he foresaw the implications of the ever-falling cost of computer processing power and the potential of the internet. In *Telecosm* (2000) Gilder argues that the cost of bandwidth will fall even faster as the capacity of fibre optics and wireless communications continues to expand. All this, he says, has profound implications. Digital technology will allow all media communications and information processing to be delivered via the internet, thus removing the barriers between different parts of these industries (a process of industrial ➤dedifferentiation). ➤➤e-commerce; interactive electronic marketing; new economy.

Gilder evangelizes his religious beliefs into his talks and writings, and early in his career wrote controversial books about feminism and race. He publishes a monthly newsletter.

gilt, gilt-edged security (UK) Fixed-interest UK ➤**government securities** traded on the ➤**London Stock Exchange**. They are called gilt-edged because it is certain that ➤**interest** will be paid and that they will be redeemed (where appropriate) on the due date. Some gilts are ➤**dated securities**, some are ➤**undated securities**, and some are index-linked. ➤**indexation**. Gilts are not a risk-free investment, of course, because of fluctuations in their market value. Gilt-edged securities do not include ➤**Treasury bills**. The prices of gilts, hitherto quoted in fractions of £1, are now quoted in decimals in line with European practice. ➤➤**gilt strip**.

gilt repo The market in agreed sales and repurchase of ➤**gilts, gilt-edged securities** introduced by the ➤**Bank of England** in January 1996. Within 2 months of launch the open gilt repo market was already much larger than the ➤**bill market** (➤**money market**), the restricted size of which had recently hampered ➤**open market operations**. The gilt repo market was launched to increase the attractiveness of gilts to foreign investors and to reduce the cost of funding the government deficit but may be used by the Bank of England for open market operations, as repos are used by the ➤**Federal Reserve System**.

gilt strip (UK) A form of gilt-edged stock issued by the ➤**Bank of England** as from December 1997. No interest is paid, but the stock is issued at a discount to provide the equivalent of the interest when the bond is repaid at maturity. The bond is divided into a series of annual 'gilt strip' issues where the amount of discount is fixed in relation to the present value, in the year in question, of the interest due at maturity.

giro A means by which money is transferred from one bank account to another without the use of a cheque. Also termed *bank giro*.

Glass–Steagall Act 1933 (US) Legislation prohibiting ➤**commercial banks** from acting as ➤**investment banks** or owning a firm dealing in securities. The Act has been challenged by banks offering ➤**money market mutual funds** and other investment services and is the subject of reform.

global bond A ➤fixed-interest ➤security issued simultaneously in the US, Europe and Asia. Principal issuers are sovereign governments and international organizations such as the ➤**International Bank for Reconstruction and Development** but also ➤**multinational companies**.

global custody A service provided by ➤**investment banks** and other ➤**financial intermediaries** to local fund managers for cross-border ➤**settlement** and administration.

globalization The expansion by firms into all corners of the world both in terms of sales and sourcing of materials and components. The environment in which large multinational firms now operate means that a firm may seek investment from one continent, source raw material from another continent, assemble and manufacture in another and sell the products and services in the remaining two continents. ➤global product company; international business.

global product company A firm that has products that are distributed and sold all over the world. ➤➤globalization.

goal-setting theory A theory of motivation. Specific and challenging goals are claimed to lead to higher performance. These goals give people a clear sense of purpose and direction, i.e. they provide something for which to strive and ultimately attain. This idea is operationalized through the management of people's intentions, or ➤management by objectives. ➤motivation.

GNP ➤gross national product.

going concern value ➤goodwill.

going public ➤flotation.

gold This precious metal ceased to have a significant monetary role in 1971 when the US abandoned its commitment to buy or sell gold at a fixed price. However, the non-monetary rise of gold, especially in jewellery, has expanded rapidly and gold also remains in demand as a store of value as well as a means of adornment. In the very long run, gold has retained its value in real terms, though recent sales by some ➤central banks have depressed sentiment in favour of gold.

Goldratt, Eliyahu Responsible for the development of the concept of ➤optimized **production technology** (OPT). Goldratt wrote two books developing and promoting the concept: *The Goal* and *The Race*. He also became particularly well known as he marketed the OPT software around the world.

goodwill (UK) The value of a business to a purchaser over and above its ➤net **assets** (US = *going concern value*). It is normal practice to show goodwill in the balance sheet but to write it down for ➤depreciation. ➤➤consolidated accounts.

Goshal, Sumantra ➤Barlett, Christopher A.

government securities All government fixed-interest paper, including ➤funded debt and ➤Treasury bills. ➤➤gilts.

government stock A ➤bond issued by government; a term most commonly used to refer to central government stock or, in the UK, ➤gilts.

gravity model A model used in store location planning founded on Newton's Law of Universal Gravitation, i.e. that two bodies attract each other in proportion to the product of their masses and inversely as the square of their distances apart. The 'force' is seen as consumer movements or trips between locations, while the 'masses' are trip-generators and trip-attractors (households, stores, shopping centres, etc.). 'Distance' can be physical distance, or expressed in terms of costs, time or psychic-distance. From this simple analogy a large number of gravity and spatial interaction models have been proposed. These are used to help retailers and other service providers locate new stores/facilities and rationalize existing chains/networks. Information from geographic information systems is used to calibrate the models. ➤anchor stores; channel of distribution.

greenfield site A location for the construction of a new building. Such sites enable firms to design factory and other commercial premises to suit their needs rather than trying to convert and refit existing buildings which may not be appropriate. Interestingly, the site is not always a green field and may be an urban piece of land, e.g. disused railway sidings. The term is also associated with making a completely new start and shedding old practices, hence its association with the removal of restrictive labour practices.

greenmail ➤corporate raider.

grey market   A term describing a market in a ➤new issue of shares before the shares have been received by subscribers.

gross domestic product (GDP)   The money value (at market prices) of the goods and services produced by the economy in a period of time, usually a year or a quarter. No allowance is made for expenditure on the replacement of capital assets. Only goods for final consumption or investment are included, since the value of intermediate goods (e.g. raw materials) is included in the prices of final goods. GDP is distinguished from *gross national product* by the exclusion of income from abroad. These national accounts aggregates, as they are called, may be valued at current prices or in real terms, i.e. after adjustment for inflation.

gross national product ➤gross domestic product.

gross rating points (GRPs)   The 'weight' of media advertising (across all media) for a given advertiser during an advertising cycle. GRPs are calculated as the sum of the percentage reach of each advertising insertion in the advertising cycle. Thus, one GRP means an insertion reached 1 per cent of the target audience. If there are lots of insertions in many different media, the GRP will quickly rise, e.g. 1 per cent from one insertion, plus 1 per cent from another insertion, etc. Note that this is a simple summation – no account is taken of whether it is the same or different people seeing the advertisement; it is purely a measure of 'weight'. ➤media planning.

group development   The stages through which people go when they come together as a group to perform a particular task or achieve a particular objective. Four stages are described: (a) forming; (b) storming; (c) norming, and (d) performing. The first stage, 'forming', is characterized by uncertainty – individuals are unsure of the issues they face, their roles and how best to interact. Individuals seek to make an impression, but in the absence of clear objectives, procedures and norms for the group, this may be without focus. The second stage, 'storming', is characterized by intragroup conflict where individuals attempt to put across their view of the issues, roles and interactions. Very often preliminary views about issues, roles and interactions are challenged and rethought. At this stage realistic objectives, procedures and norms begin to emerge. The third stage, 'norming', is characterized by close relationships and cohesiveness, which help to establish and formalize the norms. Finally, with 'performing', the group starts to be productive and deal with the task at hand. While these stages are necessary and often prove to be creative, the group must move beyond the largely procedural matters that dominate the early stages if it is to perform effectively. However, if the group becomes too cohesive it may lapse into ➤group-think. ➤➤role.

group-think   The condition where the desire for consensus within a group overrides the realistic appraisal of alternative courses of action, downplays the risks involved in the favoured course of action, and becomes very selective in its use of information to support decisions. A group might commit to a policy because it ensures harmony, gives individuals a cosy and comfortable feeling and maintains morale within the group, rather than because it is the most appropriate policy. Irving L Janus (*Victims of Group-Think*, 1972) describes the condition and some of the telltale signs of group-think, e.g. over-optimism about a policy, an inclination to explain away any evidence that would undermine the favoured policy, disregard for moral or ethical implications of a policy and reluctance even to suggest alternative policies. The use of non-executive directors, advisory boards, independent assessors, and outside consultants are all ways to prevent groups from lapsing into group-think. ➤group development.

growth ➤economic growth.

growth--share matrix ➤portfolio planning.

growth stock A share in a company, usually in expanding sectors in the economy, which is expected to enjoy a high rate of growth in ➤earnings per share and therefore has a high ➤price : earnings ratio.

growth trend analysis A simple ➤forecasting technique based on the assumption that a variable grows by a constant percentage rate over time. If a company wants to predict its sales over time, for simplicity it may assume they will grow by an absolute amount each year (a series running from £100 million, £110 million, £120 million, £130 million, for example). But this implies that, as time goes on, the percentage growth rate declines, as £10 million of growth is a smaller percentage of £120 million than it is of £100 million. Growth trend analysis makes the simple assumption that growth proceeds with a constant percentage – £100 million, £110 million, £121 million, £132.1 million, etc. A simple equation allows the company to see what its sales will be in any year, t years from now:

$$\text{Sales in time } t = \text{sales now} * (1 + \text{growth rate})^t.$$

GRPs ➤gross rating points.

guesstimate An estimate based largely on experience, intuition and guesswork. Firms investing large sums of money would want to make decisions based on reliable factual information, but this is not always possible. Sometimes precise information takes time to acquire and a decision may need to be made quickly. In such circumstances experienced people may be asked to give their views based on the limited information available.

H

Hamel, Gary Californian-based strategy guru with his own consulting firm, Stategos, and who is Visiting Professor of Strategic and International Management at London Business School. Hamel first built his reputation, which continues to grow, at the University of Michigan Business School where, with C K Prahalad, he wrote *Competing for the Future* (1994). The themes of the book are that management is in transition from the classical control model (see, for example, Alfred ➤**Sloan**) to an entrepreneurial model in which the challenge is to identify and stake out a leading position in new market opportunities. These ideas are part of the new wave of thinking on the management of change inaugurated by Tom ➤**Peters** in the 1980s and are in contradistinction to the business process re-engineering school, which is concerned more with innovation in processes rather than in markets (Michael ➤**Hammer**).

Hamel, in his latest book *Leading the Revolution* (2000) says that in the digital age he wanted to emulate the pioneers of the quality movement (W Edwards ➤**Deming**) who 'invented the tools and methods that turned quality into a ubiquitous capability' and to do the same thing for innovation, '. . . to turn it from a hit-or-miss kind of thing into a deeply embedded capability.' Hamel is particularly interested in encouraging 'grey-haired revolutionaries' to continuously re-invent their companies and their industries. Part of the key to this is to harness creative employee activists to change the business. 'Where Silicon Valley is a vibrant market, the average big company is a centrally planned economy . . . Silicon Valley is nothing more than a refugee camp for revolutionaries who couldn't get a hearing elsewhere.'

Hammer, Michael Joint author with James Champy of the bestselling *Re-engineering the Corporation: a manifesto for business revolution* (1993). ➤**Re-engineering** was the management fad of the mid 1990s, creating new work for management consultants who were called in to re-examine all business processes and often redesign companies as a result. Re-engineering forces companies to look anew at functional departments which may cut across and slow down essential processes. Management layers are compressed to achieve faster horizontal, instead of vertical, communication, and processes which were once split up to achieve scale economies are recombined, e.g. to improve customer service. The origins of corporate re-engineering lay in attempts in the mid 1980s by a consulting firm, CSC Index (where Champy worked), and the MIT Sloan School of Management (where Hammer was lecturing on computer science) to understand what the computer revolution would mean for management. One of their discoveries was that the benefits of IT were not fully realized if existing processes were simply computerized; it was necessary to change the processes. In 1990 Hammer published an article in the *Harvard Business Review* entitled 'Re-engineering work: don't automate, obliterate'.

Re-engineering has more recently been seen as a form of digital-age Taylorism (➤**Taylor**) and is now, perhaps somewhat unfairly, associated with the negative aspects of ➤**downsizing**.

Handy, Charles Popular British writer on ethics, organizations and society. Likes to characterize his ideas by symbols. For example, in *The Age of Unreason* (1989) he likened the modern organization to a shamrock (the Irish national emblem – Handy was born in Ireland) – one leaf for the small and contracting professional core, one for the contractual fringe in which functions are put out to specialists, and one for part-time and temporary workers in the flexible labour force. The pace is hot in the core and some, especially older people, move out to build portfolios of different, part-time activities. This is the direction in which the knowledge society is moving – less security but richer lives. Handy worked for Shell, the oil company, and became a professor at the London Business School.

Hang Seng An index designed to reflect movements in the share prices of thirty-three companies listed on the Hong Kong Stock Exchange. It was set at 100 in July 1964.

harassment Unwelcome advances, requests and other verbal or physical conduct in the workplace. Often of a sexual nature, but may also be related to race, colour, etc. ➤**equal opportunities**.

Hawthorne effect ➤experiment.

head and shoulders A pattern seen in a graph of share prices against time which ➤**chartists** claim can provide signals of a significant downturn in price.

heavy share (UK) A share that has a high unit price in relation to the average price of shares in the market. On the ➤**London Stock Exchange** many shares are priced around £4, but a few are £20 or more. For companies with similar earnings and prospects the ➤**yield** may be the same but the price may be very different. In the UK, investors seem to prefer to buy large numbers of shares at low prices, but in the US average unit prices are much higher. For this reason, to improve the marketability of its shares, a company that has experienced a rapid growth in earnings may decide to make a ➤**bonus issue** to reduce the price of its shares. ➤➤**penny share**.

hedge A transaction tending to the opposite effect of another transaction, engaged in to minimize a potential loss on the latter. Hedging usually relates to commodity, currency and financial transactions. Thus, an anticipated liability in a currency can be covered, where a rise in its price is expected, by a ➤**forward** purchase of the same currency at a fixed price. Commodity and ➤**security** transactions can be hedged by ➤**futures** and ➤**options** contracts, sometimes *put* and *call* simultaneously. ➤➤**hedge fund**.

hedge fund An investment vehicle which speculates on fluctuations in ➤**securities**, currencies and other ➤**assets**. They operate in a flexible way, often making use of ➤**futures** and other hedge devices. Largely unregulated.

Henderson, Bruce D Founder of the Boston Consulting Group (BCG). Developed the concept of the ➤**experience curve**, which relates unit costs to cumulative output of a product. Where one competitor is further down this curve than another then the former must prevail if the products and margins are similar, hence the need for differentiation. He derived from these ideas the well-known growth-share matrix (➤**portfolio planning**) which has been used to distinguish between: (a) business activities in a diversified company that generate cash that can be invested elsewhere (cash cows); (b) those that are self-sufficient in cash flow (stars), and (c) cash traps (dogs).

Henderson was a graduate of Harvard Business School and worked in industry and at Arthur D Little, the consulting firm, before establishing BCG. He is the author of *The Logic of Business Strategy* (1984).

Herstatt risk The risk of loss in the capital value of a currency transaction, where one side of the bargain is completed, but completion on the other side is delayed. Named after the Herstatt Bank of Germany, which suffered loss in 1974 having settled the D-mark side of a transaction before closing for the night, leaving the dollar side unpaid in North America.

Herzberg, Frederick Guru on employee ➤**motivation** who coined the phrase 'job enrichment'. ➤**job description; job satisfaction.** Through empirical research Herzberg found that the factors associated with job satisfaction and dissatisfaction were essentially different. Job satisfaction was associated with motivational factors (achievement, responsibility, recognition, level of interest in the content of work, and personal advancement). Job dissatisfaction was associated with hygiene factors (company policy and administration, working conditions, ➤**pay** and job security). Herzberg explained that the two sets of factors reflect two ranges of human needs: to avoid pain and to grow psychologically. The implications of his findings were that job dissatisfaction could be reduced by better pay and working conditions and that it was necessary to meet good standards in these respects. Job satisfaction, however, could be increased by providing more opportunities for personal growth and development. In contrast to ➤**Taylor,** therefore, Herzberg advocates enriching jobs by giving more responsibility and scope for skill and initiative rather than rationalizing and simplifying work processes. He concluded that it was possible to achieve both efficiency and job satisfaction. ➤➤**Maslow; McGregor.**

Frederick Herzberg is Professor of Management at the University of Utah and author, among other books, of (with F Mausner and B Snyderman) *The Motivation to Work* (1959).

heuristics A technique for applying *ad hoc* rules of thumb to the solution of complex problems. Results are regarded as provisional and subject to alteration as circumstances change. The game of chess is an example.

hierarchy-of-effects model A theory of how some forms of marketing communications work, e.g. ➤**advertising**. It is envisaged that a consumer must pass through the following steps if he is to respond to a communications stimulus: (a) initial awareness of a product; (b) knowledge about it; (c) liking and then preference for it; (d) conviction to buy it and, finally, (e) purchase. These steps are spread over a period of time, so the marketer needs to consider how best to influence the consumer at each stage over time. This theory is similar to the ➤**AIDA model.**

hierarchy of needs ➤Maslow's hierarchy of needs; McClelland's theory of needs; motivation.

high yield bond ➤junk bond.

hire purchase (UK) A form of ➤consumer credit in which the purchaser of a good or service pays the ➤principal and interest in regular instalments over a period of 6 months to 2 years or more; usually an initial deposit is required, and full ownership passes to the purchaser at the end of the period. US = *instalment credit*. ➤➤finance house.

historic cost ➤cost, historical.

historic-cost depreciation ➤depreciation.

Hofstede, Geert Cross-cultural management guru. The identification of national cultural differences is a constant preoccupation of those who work in international organizations such as the Organization for Economic Co-operation and Development (OECD) and the United Nations, and recognition of these differences stretches back in literature to ancient times. Hofstede was the first to analyse cultural differences systematically and apply them to business management, and his work has made managers in international companies more sensitive to cultural differences as they affect both employees and customers in a globalizing economy.

Culture's Consequences (1980) was based on a major survey of employees in forty subsidiaries of IBM. Hofstede identified four basic dimensions of the differences between national cultures: (a) power–distance in relation to superiors; (b) uncertainty–avoidance in dealing with novelty; (c) individualism–collectivism, and (d) masculinity–femininity. Countries fell into eight clusters: e.g. More Developed Latin, Germanic and Anglo shared broadly common values on the four dimensions. The US, Australia and the UK (in the Anglo group) were high on masculinity and individualism, low to medium on power–distance and uncertainty avoidance, and so on. Later, following further research, Hofstede found that long-term versus short-term orientation was a more appropriate dimension for Chinese cultural values than uncertainty avoidance, though the other three applied equally to Eastern and Western cultures. His other work includes *Cultures and Organizations: software of the mind* (1991). The implications of all this are that management styles need to be adapted to different cultures (e.g. a more participative approach is needed in Germanic countries where individualistic values are weaker than in Anglo countries); however, transnational organizations also need a common corporate culture if they are to be effective. Although Hofstede's empirical work is quoted widely, there are many unresolved issues in the analysis of culture, not least the relationship between ➤national culture and ➤organizational culture in a business context.

Hofstede was Professor of Organizational Anthropology at the University of Limburg, Maastrict, in The Netherlands until his retirement. His other published work includes *Cultures and Organisations* (1995) and *Uncommon Sense about Organisations* (1997).

holding company A company that controls one or more other companies, normally by holding a majority of the shares of these ➤subsidiaries. It is possible for a holding company to control a large number of companies with a combined ➤capital very much greater than its own, since it needs to hold only half or even less of the shares of its subsidiaries. This is known as *pyramiding*. ➤➤consolidated accounts.

Hong Kong stock exchanges The four ➤stock exchanges in Hong Kong were modernized and unified in 1986, to become the Stock Exchange of Hong Kong. They are regulated by the Securities and Futures Commission. Structural reforms, including dependence for the commission, were recommended in a report by Ian Hay Davison following the October 1987 market crash and were implemented. The Hang Seng Index of thirty-three leading stocks provides the basis for ➤options and ➤futures contracts on the futures exchange. There is also a more broadly based index, the Hong Kong Stock Index.

horizontal integration The combination of firms operating in the same industry at the same stage of the production–distribution channel. The most common reason for adopting this approach would be to gain ➤economies of scale in either production or bulk purchases. ➤➤vertical integration.

hostile take-over The acquisition of a firm where the acquired firm did not want to relinquish control. The predatory firm needs only to acquire a majority shareholding to gain management control. In many ➤take-overs firms usually try to structure an arrangement that is beneficial to the directors of both firms. Frequently, this will involve dividing the directorships in the new firm between the directors of the predatory and target firms, allowing for early retirements and 'golden goodbyes'. Sometimes, however, ➤predator firms may seek to acquire another firm and be rejected, hence the hostile nature of the activities.

hot-desking The sharing of office space. Hot-desking reflects wider changes in patterns of work, including the growth of job-sharing, the acceptance of flexible working hours, the rise in out-sourcing and other forms of arms-length employment. In principle, technology is enabling more people to work from home, which is another reason for hot-desking in the workplace. However, this is to ignore the social–psychological reasons for why people work (human interaction, friendship, companionship, etc.).

Hotelling's law A simple model of ➤positioning, designed to demonstrate that in some competitive markets of two competing players, both will tend to offer similar products. The law was derived from the simple example of ice-cream sellers on a beach. Assuming that customers go to the nearest ice-cream seller, both sellers will end up positioned in the middle of the beach, right next to each other. This gives both half the market. If either deviates from the middle, the other can obtain more than half the market by positioning himself just next to the first. In the parlance of ➤game theory, the middle market positioning is a ➤Nash equilibrium. The law has been used to account for the positioning of political parties, the scheduling of rival buses or planes, and the choice of music played on radio stations.

hot money Short-term flows of speculative capital, across national borders. Primarily aimed at drawing profit from possible changes in the exchange rate of different countries, hot money can be a problem for policymakers as it can destabilize the exchange rate in the process.

HRM ➤human resource management.

hub-and-spoke arrangement A technique for co-ordinating complex distribution of products. The technique was first developed by Federal Express, the parcel delivery company, whereby all parcels are routed through a central hub in Memphis to provide overnight parcel delivery anywhere in the US. This technique is now replicated by many different firms in a variety of industries.

human capital The stock of valuable know-how embodied in the labour force. Such know-how can be seen as surprisingly analogous to physical capital, such as machines and buildings. Human capital typically requires ➤**investment** to be created, in the form of education or training (➤**human resource management**); it has a market value; it can depreciate with time. In accounting for differences in economic performance (➤**economic growth**), economists have become increasingly more preoccupied with human, rather than physical, capital. ➤➤**endogenous growth theory.**

human resource management (HRM) Policies, plans and procedures for the effective management of employees ('human resources'). Specific areas of interest include: (a) employee recruitment and selection; (b) staff training and development; (c) employee ➤**reward**, appraisal and ➤**evaluation processes**, and (d) internal communications. Generally, the aim has been to instil employee commitment – to create shared values, encourage innovation, promote flexible and adaptable behaviours, foster communication and shift emphasis away from control of employees to ➤**autonomy** and ➤**empowerment**. It has become the mantra of hi-tech and e-business firms. It has also become important for multinational corporations wishing to take account of cultural sensitivities in the management of their international workforces. ➤**culture**. In more traditional organizations, HRM normally sits side-by-side with established ➤**industrial relations** practices, despite the two having very different underlying assumptions. Some view HRM as a repackaging of traditional 'personnel management', although it is claimed that the development of HRM has led to a more proactive and strategic role for human resource planning than ever before.

HUT Households using television. ➤**audience measurement.**

hygiene factor In an organizational context, a factor that, when adequate in a job, placates employees, e.g. company policies, supervision arrangements, salary levels. When these factors are adequate, people will not be dissatisfied. In a competitive context, hygiene factors are those things that have to be provided adequately in order to maintain acceptable standards, but they are unlikely to give rise to a distinct competitive advantage, e.g. the provision of in-flight entertainment and in-flight catering by airlines, both of which have become part of the standard offering to air travellers. ➤**motivation-hygiene theory.**

Hypertext A database format in which information related to that on a display can be accessed directly from it. This enables large amounts of information on a particular subject to be accessed quickly from the database if and when required by the reader. A good example of where this technology works well is in the electronic production of encyclopaedias either in the form of CD-ROM or 'on-line'. This enables the reader to access quickly additional information related to the entry, or simply to see a picture or a video clip of relevant information.

I

IASC ➤International Accounting Standards Committee.

IBBR ➤London interbank offered rate.

IBEX 35 An index designed to reflect movements in the share price of thirty-five companies traded in the Spanish Continuous Market, the Joint Stock Exchange System of four Spanish stock exchanges. It was given a base value of 3000 in December 1989. It is not the most comprehensive or theoretically accurate index of Spanish stocks (i.e. the Madrid General Index) but it is the index chosen to serve as an underlying asset for futures and options trading.

IBRD ➤International Bank for Reconstruction and Development.

iconic rote learning A form of cognitive ➤learning.

idea generation ➤new product development.

idle time The amount of time a machine or producer is not operational. In its simplest form it can be a telephone switchboard operator without any telephone calls to direct. Within complicated production plants there will be machines that are not always running at full capacity. ➤➤downtime; bottleneck.

IFA ➤independent financial adviser.

IFC International Finance Corporation. ➤International Bank for Reconstruction and Development.

imperfect competition ➤monopolistic competition.

implicit contract A commitment generally understood and agreed, but not written into a legally enforceable form. Implicit contracts are seen to play an important part in many business relationships, where legally binding contracts would be too inflexible, or too complicated to embrace all possible circumstances. Japanese business culture is held to use implicit contracts more widely than, say, the more legalistic Anglo-Saxon equivalent. Such a contract might be that of lifetime employment for the workers, for example (although this particular implicit contract has become increasingly harder to honour even in Japan). Or the understanding that any surpluses in an employer's pension fund will be used to pay more generous benefits than the minimum specified in the employee's pension contract. Implicit contracts can be understood as the outcome of a 'you scratch my back and I will scratch yours'-type arrangement, possible where the parties involved are interacting regularly and repeatedly. In the parlance of ➤**game theory**, they can be the rational outcome of selfish players interacting in a ➤**repeated game**.

implicit cost A sacrifice incurred in the pursuit of some activity, but which does not involve an explicit cash payment. A business may be familiar with accounting for cash costs, such as wages. But it may have implicit costs, too. For example, if a project requires the use of scarce management time that could be devoted to other profitable activities, the profits forgone are an implicit cost of the project. Or, if a new product line carries the risk of damaging an established ➤**brand** name, then that damage is an implicit cost. ➤➤**cost**.

impression management (IM) The process of trying to control the impression that others have of you. It is assumed impressions of you by others have an impact on their willingness to co-operate, to avoid conflict and to reward and punish. Rather than leave this to chance, these impressions are self-consciously managed using a variety of techniques. For instance, admitting responsibility for a poor decision in the hope of being pardoned for the decision (apologies), or agreeing with another person's opinions to gain his/her approval (conformity). Successful IM can help a person fulfil his ➤**role** and exercise ➤**power**. ➤➤**politicking**.

impulse purchasing The purchase of an item without prior deliberation or preplanning, often in response to prominent display in the retail environment or as a result of short-term ➤**promotions**.

imputation system ➤corporation tax.

income effect The impact of a change in price of a product on the real income, or buying power, of its customers. When the price of bread changes, it has two distinct effects on the desire of consumers to buy bread: (a) the income effect – that consumers are poorer than they were, and so can afford to buy less than before, and (b) that bread is relatively more expensive than other items, making it less attractive than its ➤**substitutes**. This relative price effect is labelled the *substitution effect*. Income effects can make consumers buy more or less of a product. ➤**income elasticity of demand**. ➤➤**Giffen good**.

income elasticity of demand The responsiveness of the amount consumers buy of a product to changes in the consumers' real income. More specifically, the income elasticity of bread, for example, is the percentage change in the amount of bread consumers choose to buy divided by the corresponding percentage change in consumers' income (with prices held constant). Products can be classified into groups depending on their income elasticity. An elasticity between 0 and 1 implies that a 1 per cent increase in incomes leads to an increase in demand between 0 and 1 per cent (items of this sort are labelled *normal*). An elasticity greater than 1 suggests buying disproportionately more of a product as our income rises, perhaps relating to a more luxurious item (labelled a *superior* good). A product with a negative income elasticity is one that we buy less of as our income rises, such as tinned meat. (These are labelled *inferior goods*.) ➤➤**elasticity**.

income gearing A measure of ability to service ➤**debt**. It is calculated by dividing ➤**profit** before ➤**interest** by total interest costs. Also referred to as *times covered*, i.e. the number of times profits exceed interest payments.

income statement (US) ➤profit and loss account.

incomplete contract A contract which does not have provisions setting out obligations or entitlements for all possible situations. Most contracts are obviously incomplete, unable as they are to list all possible states of the world and, hence, many problems that arise in contract enforcement occur when unforeseen contingencies emerge.

incorporation The act of forming a company by carrying out the necessary legal formalities. ➤memorandum of association. A company is a legal person separate and distinct from the people who own it, usually with ➤limited liability. In the UK under the Companies Act 1985 there are three classes of company: (a) limited; (b) unlimited, and (c) *public limited companies* (plcs). All companies are obliged to file certain information for public inspection and to circulate accounts to their shareholders, though these ➤disclosure requirements are less onerous for smaller private companies. ➤abbreviated accounts. A plc may have an unlimited number of shareholders and may offer shares for public subscription. ➤offer for sale. Only plcs may qualify for listing on the ➤London Stock Exchange or the unlisted securities market. Private companies may place certain restrictions on the transfer of shares but may not offer shares to the public. ➤close company. The European Union's *Twelfth Directive* providing for single-member limited liability companies is now implemented in the UK. Company law sets out other provisions dealing with the powers, appointment and terms of directors, the protection of investors (including *minority interests*) (➤consolidated accounts), ownership and control, the regulation of shares, the disclosure of interests in shares, accounts, winding up (➤bankruptcy; liquidation) and other matters. The Companies Act 1981 allowed companies to acquire their own shares under certain circumstances, a practice known as 'buying in' shares, which may be carried out to improve the dividend ➤yield. ➤➤European Economic Interest Grouping.

The broad outline of company law is similar in most countries, though there are important differences in detail, e.g. in Germany, public companies (*Aktiengesellschaft* (AG)) are required to have two-tiered boards. In the US, the term for an incorporated business is corporation (Inc.), but there are not separate *legal forms* for private companies and public companies. Other business–legal forms include the ➤company limited by guarantee, ➤partnership and ➤sole proprietorship. ➤➤*Gesellschaft mit beschränkter Haftung*; partnership; *société anonyme*; *société à responsabilité limitée*.

increasing return to scale A situation in an industry where an increase in all the inputs into production leads to a more than proportionate increase in output, i.e. if you double the size of the factory, you more than double the output. ➤decreasing returns to scale; ➤➤production function.

incremental innovation ➤innovation.

indemnity The sum in compensation paid by an ➤insurance company in the event of loss or damage under the contract.

independent demand ➤demand forecasting.

independent financial adviser (IFA) A firm licensed under the Financial Services and Markets Act (➤**Financial Services Act 1986**) to advise on, and to transact investment business on behalf of, clients, acting on a wholly independent basis with no commitment to any producer of investment products. IFAs are legally obliged to give 'best advice', i.e. to offer the product best-suited to the circumstances of their clients. Relevant investment products include ➤**life assurance**, ➤**pension**, ➤**unit trust**, investment management and investment advice.

independent variable A variable with a value appropriately seen as conditioning the values of some other variable. For example, if consumer spending is thought to be conditional upon income, then spending is the dependent variable and income is independent. In mathematics or statistics, the independent variable is the one that lies to the right of the equation, e.g.:

$$C = a + bY$$

where C is consumption (dependent variable), Y is income (independent variabale), and a and b are ➤**parameters**. ➤➤**behavioural equation**.

indexation The indexation or automatic linkage between monetary obligations and the price level; ➤**securities** may be index-linked. The UK government introduced an index-linked security in 1981 for financial institutions and has subsequently issued others for private investors as well as institutions. e.g. the 2.5 per cent *index-linked* Treasury stock 2011 in which both the interest and the ➤**principal** are adjusted in line with changes in the ➤**retail price index**. Some ➤**National Savings** certificates are also index-linked (US = *inflation proofing*). General indexation, including the index-linking of bank and other loans, has been used in some countries (e.g. Brazil) to help control inflation in the past. ➤➤**indexing**.

index fund ➤indexing.

indexing Weighting a ➤**portfolio** in the same proportions as the components of a ➤**share index** such as ➤**Standard and Poor's 500**. The performance of a fund consisting of company shares weighted in this way will mirror that of the index, thus ensuring that an index fund will not perform worse (or better) than the market as a whole. Not to be confused with ➤**indexation**.

index number An ➤**average** of a group of observations of a price or some other variable, expressed as a percentage of the average of the same variable in the ➤**base period** against which the comparison is being made. In price indices, the ➤**variables** may be ➤**weighted averages** or unweighted averages.

indifference curve A graphical depiction of combinations of different commodities, each of which gives a specified consumer an equal amount of utility. If a consumer thinks four Mars bars and two Diet Cokes yield the same pleasure as three Mars bars and three Diet Cokes, then these two combinations of Coke and Mars would lie on one indifference curve. Another indifference curve – perhaps yielding higher utility – might link five Mars bars and three Diet Cokes, and four Mars bars and four Diet Cokes. In the figure opposite, all the combinations of Mars and Coke on indifference curve II would be preferred to those on indifference curve I. Economists have used such curves to derive plausible characteristics of consumer demand. The intellectual motivation for devising them was that indifference between different combinations of commodities is something consumers can meaningfully reveal, even if, in practice, market research rarely requires them to do so.

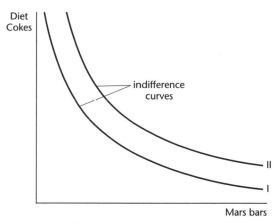

Graphical depiction of indifference curves

➤**marketing research**. Prior to the conception of indifference curves, the economic theory of demand relied on a theoretical consumer being able to specify how many units of utility different commodities yielded (not something that most consumers can do very easily). ➤➤**choice modelling**.

individual retirement account (US) A pension plan (➤**pension**) under which employed people not covered by another retirement plan and whose income is below a specified minimum make tax-deductible contributions to a fund of ➤**securities** and other forms of investments. Contributions are subject to a limit, and withdrawals before age 59.5 years are subject to a penalty. ➤➤**personal pension**.

individual savings account (ISA) A new tax shelter for personal savings which the UK government introduced in April 1999. ISAs, like the personal equity plan (PEP) and tax exempt savings account (TESSA) which they replaced, are exempt from income tax and capital gains tax. There are annual limits on what may be invested in them, e.g. £5,000 in ➤**stocks** and shares.

industrial dispute ➤**collective action**.

industrial espionage Nefarious attempts by one firm to obtain access to the unpublished and secret information held by another firm. In this age of technology-intensive industries and multinational corporations, this is a growing area of concern for all firms. The increasing use by all aspects of business of the ➤**internet** means that it is theoretically possible for firms to gain access to another firm's computer systems and data, unless there is an effective ➤**firewall**. Preventing espionage is extremely difficult and there have been several high-profile cases of so-called advanced technology-intensive firms such as Microsoft falling victims to such activities.

industrial organization A branch of applied economics dealing with industry structure and industry performance and, in particular, the relationship between the two.

industrial relations In principle, the study and practice of all aspects of employment relations. However, the focus has tended to be on collective employment relations, including ➤**trade unions**, ➤**collective bargaining**, and ➤**collective action**. An underlying assumption is that conflicts of interest between employers and employees are endemic, and therefore collective action by both parties is inevitable and natural. ➤**Conflict** is deemed to arise because of an imbalance of ➤**power** between employees and management. Therefore, industrial relations can be seen as a way to study and understand these imbalances of power in an attempt to control conflicts – to the advantage of employees, managers or both. Industrial relations is distinct from ➤**human resource management**, which is more concerned with areas of co-operation within the organization (including individual employee management through recruitment and selection policies), training and development programmes, and systems of ➤**reward** and appraisal and ➤**evaluation processes**.

industry life-cycle A concept that suggests all industries go through a cycle similar to other living organisms. A typical industry life-cycle has four key phases:
(1) Introductory phase. New products are introduced and their technologies are in their infancy and may be unreliable. Customers may be enthusiasts. This phase may last a few months or many years.
(2) Growth phase. The product starts to become established, and there may be improvements in the product and process technology used to produce it. Demand may be so high that firms face difficulties keeping up with it. New firms may enter to take advantage of the opportunities.
(3) Mature phase. The rate of industry sales slows and this often coincides with a settling down of technological progress so that product and process technologies become more stable. Firms can now invest in large production facilities with less risk.
(4) Decline phase. Sales in the industry fall, perhaps because of saturation of the market or ➤**substitute** products have become more attractive.
Industry life-cycles are likely to be influenced by wider economic forces. ➤**business cycle**. Also, the experiences of individual firms within an industry are likely to differ from one another. ➤**product life-cycle**.

inept set ➤evoked set.

inert set ➤evoked set.

inferior good A product that consumers tend to buy less of, the richer they get. ➤**income elasticity of demand**.

inflation A sustained tendency for the general level of prices to rise. Inflation typically results when the level of spending, or overall demand, in an economy exceeds the ability of the economy to deliver matching output. ➤**output gap**. Economists generally talk of inflation as having one of three different causes: (a) excess demand (or too much spending); (b) relaxed monetary policy, and (c) rising costs. However, the three accounts often amount to much the same thing. Excess demand can be a monetary phenomenon, caused by the authorities allowing the supply of money to grow too fast, thus encouraging too much spending (as occurred when medieval kings debased their currency by minting coins in non-precious metals or in the hyperinflation of post-First World War Germany). Sometimes, inflation does not have a monetary cause, e.g. when some specific prices rise, such as world oil-prices (so-called cost–push inflation). But even in these cases, a general inflation would not result unless there was sufficient total demand and spending to allow companies to raise prices. Thus, the different theories of inflation are hard to disentangle from each other.

Inflation has tended to come in waves; over long periods of time, prices have been remarkably stable, but at times of particular social and economic upheaval, there have been rapid price rises. In the late 1990s, it was commonly felt that 'inflation was dead'. ➤new economy.

For business, inflation gives rise to various problems, e.g. the mechanics of price adjustment (sometimes referred to as *menu costs*). Since the 1970s, however, few firms have chosen to print their prices on their products in indelible ink. The biggest problems, however, arise from unanticipated inflation. This means the prices that firms set are lower in real terms (relative to the value of money generally) than the firms had intended. Unanticipated inflation also has an effect on ➤interest rates, or more accurately *real* interest rates. By devaluing the spending power of money, unanticipated inflation hurts lenders of money, who find they are not getting as much spending power back from their savings as they might have expected. The large unanticipated inflation of the 1970s did hurt lenders, often driving real interest rates below 0. As a result, in the 1980s, the risk of inflation eroding the value of savings led to increases in real interest rates as lenders applied a risk premium to their lending rates.

inflation accounting Methods of keeping a record of financial transactions and analysing them in a way that allows for changes in the purchasing power of money over time. In periods of rapidly rising prices, with accounts maintained on a historical cost basis (➤cost, historical), the replacement cost of assets may be much higher than their recorded costs, and ➤depreciation provisions may be inadequate and profit overstated. *Current cost accounting* (CCA) is a form of replacement cost accounting that involves revaluing assets from historic costs to current costs.

inflation proofing ➤indexation.

influence ➤power.

infomediary ➤intermediary.

infomercial Television commercials in which an organization states or advocates a viewpoint. In some cases the infomercial may be as long as a programme. ➤➤advertising.

informational/transformational theory ➤involvement theory.

information search The process of gathering information about products and services prior to, or during, purchasing. Information is needed about evaluative criteria (a friend tells you what features to keep in mind when buying a four-wheel-drive-all-terrain vehicle), the alternative options (available four-wheel-drive vehicles are listed in a car magazine), and the performance of options against these criteria (advertisements in the car magazine make certain performance claims). Using this information, consumers have the ability to make more informed decisions (➤consumer behaviour) and reduce any attendant risks. ➤perceived risk. However, for reasons of efficiency, and in an attempt to minimize information overload, consumers will normally focus their attention on only the most important evaluative criteria and confine themselves to brands in the ➤evoked set.

External information may come from personal sources (e.g. the opinions of friends) and from impersonal sources, e.g. messages from mass media advertising. A further division is into: (a) non-commercial personal sources (recommendations from family, friends and colleagues); (b) commercial personal sources (meetings with experts and professional advisers); (c) non-commercial impersonal sources (information from professional society listings, consumer groups and government advisory services), and (d) commercial impersonal sources (messages from mass or selective media, classified listings, electronic interactive media).

While external information search can be extensive, in practice the process is often quite limited, even for the purchase of new and expensive products and services. There is cost in terms of time, physical effort, psychological strain and money that has to be expended to acquire information. Also, there is a risk of the information being biased, partial or unreliable. How impartial is a magazine advertisement going to be in which performance claims are made for a brand of four-wheel-drive vehicle? Furthermore, in some markets it is very hard to evaluate or judge the quality of the information– in technical and professional services this can be difficult to do even after purchase and consumption (the problem of assessing 'credence qualities'). ➤evaluation processes. For these kinds of reasons, considerable use continues to be made of word-of-mouth information from friends or business associates, despite the amount of money spent on commercial impersonal sources.

For familiar products that consumers have previously bought, used, experienced or heard about, a process of internal information search is most likely to be at work. This will be based on memories of past experiences and past searches, together with some low-involvement learning. ➤involvement. In these circumstances, sources of external information search may only play a supporting role, e.g. advertising, an external source of information, may help to capitalize on the memory consumers have of previous product usage. ➤➤brand communication effects. For these reasons, a distinction is often drawn between 'habitual behaviour' (automatic purchasing with no/little search), 'limited decision-making' (which mainly relies on internal search) and 'extended decision-making' (where external search is that much more important).

initial charge ➤unit trust.

initial public offering (IPO) (US) The offering of the shares in the ➤equity of a company to the public for the first time. ➤➤new issue.

initial yield ➤yield.

innovation The process of developing and commercializing something new, usually a product, service or manufacturing process. The management of innovation is a growing and significant subject in its own right. While there is continued debate about the range of activities covered by the term, there is broad agreement that successful innovation management involves research, technology development, marketing and manufacturing. It is the successful co-ordination of these activities that gives competitive opportunities (or competitive problems) to firms and managers. Many writers distinguish 'product innovation' from 'process innovation'. Process innovation refers to the development of new production processes or the improvement of existing ones. Product innovation refers to the development of new products and improvements to existing ones (inevitably, there is considerable overlap here with the field of ➤new product development). The creation of a completely new product can lead to the creation of a new business, as was the case for Dyson appliances with their development of the first bagless vacuum cleaner. Some firms such as 3M have developed a reputation for being able to continually develop innovative products. It should be apparent that these innovations may represent major discontinuities, or quite minor incremental technological advances.

Most writers distinguish innovation from invention by suggesting invention is the conception of the idea, whereas successful innovation entails both idea conception and its subsequent translation into something of commercial and practical value. The following simple equation helps to show the relationship between the two terms:

Innovation = theoretical conception + technical invention + commercial exploitation

The *conception* of new ideas is the starting-point for innovation. A new idea by itself, while interesting, is neither an invention nor innovation; it is merely a concept or a thought or collection of thoughts. The process of converting intellectual thoughts into a tangible new artefact (usually a product or process) is an *invention*. This is where science and technology usually play significant roles. At this stage, inventions need to be combined with hard work by many different people to convert them into products that will improve company performance. These later activities represent *exploitation*. However, it is the complete process that represents innovation. This introduces the notion that innovation is a process with a number of distinctive features that need to be managed. Hence, innovation depends on inventions, but inventions need to be harnessed to commercial activities before they can contribute to the growth of an organization.

Successful commercialization of the innovation may involve wider organizational changes. For example, the introduction of a radical technological innovation, such as Polaroid's Instamatic camera, invariably results in substantial internal organizational changes. In this case, substantial changes occurred with the manufacturing and marketing and sales functions. The business decided to concentrate on the Instamatic camera market, rather than on the traditional 26 and 35 mm-film camera market, thus forcing changes on the production function. Similarly, the marketing department had to employ extra sales staff to educate and reassure retail outlets that the new product would not cannibalize their film processing business. Furthermore, a new business had to be established to produce and distribute the unique film required by the Instamatic camera – a service innovation. Hence, technological innovation can be accompanied by additional managerial and organizational changes that are often referred to as innovations in their own right. This begins to widen the definition of innovation to include virtually any organizational or managerial change (but, in so doing, may render the concept of less practical use). The table on page 168 shows a typology of innovations.

A typology of innovations

Type of innovation	Example
Product innovation	The development of new or improved products, with new attributes and features
Process innovation	The development of a new manufacturing process such as Pilkington's float glass process
Organizational innovation	A new venture division, a new internal communication system; introduction of SAP R3
Management innovation	TQM (total quality management) systems, BPR (business process re-engineering) systems, and the introduction of SAP R3
Production innovations	Quality circles, JIT manufacturing system, new production planning software (e.g. MRP II) and new inspection systems
Commercial/marketing innovations	New financing arrangements, and new sales approach, e.g. direct marketing
Service innovations	New services, such as web-based and telephone-based financial services

It is also worthy of note that many studies have suggested that product innovations are soon followed by process innovations in what is described as an industry innovation cycle. Furthermore, it is common to associate innovation with physical change, but many changes introduced within organizations involve very little physical change. Rather, it is the activities performed by individuals that change. A good example of this is the adoption of Japanese-inspired management techniques (e.g. ➤**total quality management**) by automobile manufacturers in Europe and the US.

innovation diffusion The process by which innovations, ideas and new products spread through a market or through a social system. Getting a new idea adopted, even when there are obvious advantages, is often very difficult. There is a wide gap in many fields between what is known and what is actually put into use. Many innovations require a lengthy period, often some years, from the time they become available to the time they are widely adopted. Many technologists believe that advantageous innovations will sell themselves. Unfortunately, this is seldom the case.

Much attention in diffusion studies is paid to the shape of the diffusion curve, the rate of adoption and the points of inflexion. The curve is typically S-shaped, describing an initially slow uptake of the product, followed by very rapid growth as more and more new consumers make a purchase, and then reaching a plateau once the market has been saturated with the product. The rate of adoption will be greater where the product: (a) has a relative advantage over existing or competing products; (b) is compatible with existing norms, values and behaviours; (c) is communicable, (d) is divisible, i.e. it can be tried and tested on a limited basis. By contrast, we must add (e) as a complex product that will diffuse at a slower rate (because it is difficult to understand, use or accept). It is common for analysts to attempt to model these diffusion curves, rates and points of inflexion.

An extension is the suggestion that different types of consumer are involved at each stage. In the initial stage, it is lead users, early adopters and opinion leaders who drive the process. The mass of consumers drive the process in the middle stages. Laggards bring up the rear. These groups are predisposed to innovations in different ways, reflecting demographic and psychographic factors. Recent research has emphasized the crucial role of lead users, not only as those who are first to adopt, but also as sources of innovative ideas in their own right and as facilitators of further sales growth because of the recommendations they make.

The diffusion process best describes the uptake of new consumer products and technologies, where the goal is to secure one-off purchase (rather than trial and repeat purchase). A classic study was of the adoption of hybrid corn, and more recent examples would be the adoption of computer hardware, telephony equipment, kitchen appliances, high-definition and digital television. Furthermore, as these examples show, it is mainly descriptive of the uptake of products, not ➤brands within categories, e.g. a new brand may dominate a new market initially, but as other brands enter the market the growth has to be shared among all competitors. The concept, therefore, has some of the same strengths and weaknesses as the idea of the ➤product life-cycle and the ➤industry life-cycle.

An analogy would be the spread of diseases through communities, and most of the diffusion models used in management have their genesis in epidemiological research. The seminal work outside of epidemiology is by E M Rogers (*Diffusion of Innovations* (1962)).

innovator Someone who continually generates new ideas and sees new and interesting ways of doing things. Sometimes referred to as a 'technical innovator', as they are usually an expert in one or two fields. They are also colloquially referred to as 'mad scientists' or 'Heath Robinsons'.

input An item that is used in the production of another item. Economists traditionally distinguish four main categories of input: (a) labour; (b) capital; (c) land, and (d) 'entrepreneurship', or organization. But economists use somewhat strange terminology, so 'land', for example, is held to include any natural raw materials (not just 'land').

input–output analysis Analysis of an economy based on tracking the production of each sector through its uses in other sectors. The output of steel, for example, is used as an input into cars, and into construction. Steel itself requires as inputs the output of energy and mining sectors. If one wanted to divide the economy into, say, a hundred sectors, it would be possible to draw up a huge 100 × 100 square input–output table, collating the volumes of each sector's outputs and inputs drawn from all other sectors. This kind of analysis can be useful in ➤forecasting, anticipating bottlenecks in an economy and also for the authorities in planning.

insider dealing (US) The buying and selling of shares while in possession of price-sensitive information obtained unlawfully, e.g. through employment in the company whose shares are being dealt with (US = *insider trading*). Insider dealing is illegal in the UK, the US, France and other countries.

insider trading (US) ➤insider dealing.

insolvency ➤bankruptcy.

instalment credit ➤hire purchase.

institutional investor An organization, as opposed to an individual, that invests funds arising from its receipts from the sale of ➤securities, from ➤deposits and from other sources, i.e. ➤insurance companies, ➤investment trusts, ➤unit trusts, ➤pension funds and trustees. ➤trust. Institutional investors own over 70 per cent of the shares of quoted UK companies.

instrument A term used to denote any form of financing medium, most usually those for the purpose of borrowing in the ➤money market, e.g. ➤bill of exchange, ➤bond, ➤certificate of deposit, ➤Treasury bill and *promissory notes*. ➤notes. Normally used to denote the document itself. A financial instrument is acquired, or bought, by payment to the existing owner of the ➤face value of the instrument, normally less a ➤discount. By the same token, the owner transferring the instrument is the seller. On original sale, or ➤issue, the instrument is a means of raising a loan and thus of acquiring an ➤asset. The term also applies to ➤derivatives.

instrumental conditioning A form of behavioural ➤learning, also called 'operant conditioning'.

instrumental learning A form of behavioural ➤learning.

insurance A contract to pay compensation in certain eventualities (e.g. death, fire, theft, motor accident) in return for a ➤premium. The premiums are so calculated that on average, in total, they are sufficient to pay compensation for policyholders who will make a claim, together with a margin to cover administration costs and profit. ➤actuary; underwriter. In effect, insurance pools risk so that loss by an individual is compensated for at the expense of all those who insure against it. The traditional forms of insurance are *general insurance* (e.g. marine and other property insurance against theft, fire and accident) and *life insurance* (strictly assurance, because the cover is given against the occurrence of an event which is inevitable). There are also many other kinds of insurance including public or professional liability, sickness and unemployment insurance, some of which (like National Insurance and private healthcare) are not, or not always, carried out by the traditional insurance companies. There are over 800 authorized insurance companies in the UK which the Financial Services Authority now regulates. ➤Financial Services Act. The bulk of the assets of insurance companies consist of investments made out of premium income against their liabilities to 'pay out' on life policies; only about 10 per cent of their assets are in respect of general funds. These companies, and the ➤pension funds they manage, control a large proportion of ➤quoted company shares. Life insurance is a popular way of providing for old age and house purchase as well as protecting the financial position of dependants. In *endowment insurance*, policyholders benefit from a share in the appreciation of the life fund. The lump sum payable is increased by bonuses, called *reversionary bonuses*, annually, plus a *terminal bonus* on death or termination of the policy. The UK is an important centre for the world insurance industry.

Lloyd's of London is an incorporated society of private insurers established by Act of Parliament in 1871. Much of the capital is provided by a large number of individual members, or 'names', organized into syndicates. Each syndicate is led by an underwriter (➤**underwrite**) who writes policies on behalf of the members, each of whom bears unlimited liability. Lloyd's also provides a comprehensive system of shipping intelligence.

intangible assets ➤Assets on which a value is placed in the ➤**balance sheet** but which do not have a physical form, e.g. ➤**brand equity; goodwill; patents**.

intangible resources The resources of a firm that have no physical presence. This may be in the form of expertise, knowledge, patents, research programmes (all of which can be regarded as ➤**intellectual assets**), and reputation, brand loyalty, databases, etc. While physical ➤**assets** are readily displayed on a firm's balance sheet, intangible resources are more difficult for the accountancy profession to recognize. ➤➤**knowledge management system**.

integrated marketing communication (IMC) The planning and execution of all types of marketing communication to meet a common set of communication objectives for a ➤**brand**. For example, the objective might be to develop a certain level of brand awareness and instil certain brand attitudes among consumers in the target audience. This can be achieved using a range of marketing communications, from mass media (e.g. television, radio, newspapers and magazines) to direct communications (e.g. direct mail and e-mail), and also ➤**sales** and ➤**promotion**, ➤**public relations** and ➤**direct marketing**. The virtue of integrated marketing communications is that it offers a planned and disciplined approach, which provides clarity, consistency and focused communications. In particular, this supports a single ➤**positioning** for a brand. In the absence of IMC there is a danger that different types of marketing communication do not support a common set of communication objectives for a brand. Thus, television commercials might be instilling one set of brand attitudes and direct mailings could be developing a totally different, and contrary, set of brand attitudes. Such an outcome would suggest the organization is unclear about the positioning of its brand, resulting in consumer confusion. ➤**advertising**.

integrated services digital network (ISDN) Provides a communication network, which can carry all types of digital-based information. This is achieved through the use of shared protocols, which allow communication and the compression of digital information into a given space.

integrative bargaining ➤bargaining.

intellectual assets Non-physical assets that represent the firm's knowledge. This includes expertise, knowledge, patents and research programmes. Frequently, such assets have a high ➤**tacit knowledge** content. ➤**knowledge management system**. They can be regarded as a subset of a firm's ➤**intangible resources**.

intellectual property (IP) An asset with a prime value which derives from the product of human knowledge, discovery, invention or mental creativity. Intellectual property covers a host of different types of product, e.g. a new drug, film or pop song, piece of computer software, book, cooking recipe, photograph, television game show format, the television rights to a football game, an innovative steel manufacturing process. Most output in the economy embodies some intellectual

171

property and some material property. A computer program may come on a disk, but its value will lie in the material on it. It has been argued that as the economy increasingly becomes less industrial, value is *dematerializing* (➤**weightlessness**), and intellectual property is increasing in importance.

Intellectual property has some important characteristics. Firstly, unlike material property, the enjoyment of it by one person does nothing to damage or exclude the enjoyment of it by other people. Intellectual property does not get 'used up'. This means that pricing of intellectual property is challenging, and typically has to deviate from ➤**marginal-cost pricing**. A second feature is that intellectual property is hard to appropriate for private gain – inventions can be copied, pop songs pirated. The existence of ➤**patents**, ➤**copyright** law, ➤**trade marks** and ➤**registered designs** can provide some legal protection, but enforcement is hard and litigation can be protracted. Arguments over intellectual property appear to be increasing. A third feature is that markets in intellectual property do not function well. If an individual tries to sell a television game show format to a large television network, he faces the challenge of either persuading the network to buy the format without knowing what it is, or persuading it to pay for the idea once he has told them what it is, when there is little practical method of proving they had not thought of it themselves. Some of these problems also arise when trying to estimate ➤**brand equity**.

interactive electronic marketing The use of digital and interactive technologies in marketing. The best-known of these technologies, and the most widely used to date, is the ➤**internet** – a massive global network of interconnected packet-switched computer networks that facilitates interactive multimedia many-to-many communication between users. Communication is achieved through specific applications and environments, of which the World Wide Web is one example. The internet also supports discussion groups (e.g. moderated and unmoderated mailing lists), brand communities and anonymous consumer profiling, communication systems (e.g. Internet Relay Chat), file transfer, electronic mail and global information access and retrieval systems.

The most visible aspect of this technology for marketers has been the creation and use of web sites. These sites have provided a platform for the provision of information, ➤**advertising** (e.g. ➤**banner advertisements; interstitials**), communication, dialogue, and order placement. ➤**electronic commerce**. For some products, they allow direct order fulfilment, e.g. news services and online music. The organizations behind these web sites are a mixture of dedicated on-line businesses and dual-purpose on-line/off-line businesses. Some are new ventures (e.g. ebay.com, and handbag.com), others have quite a heritage of techno-branding to draw upon (e.g. ibm.com, and dell.com), and a few are providing textbook cases of integrated on-line/off-line branding, e.g. orange.com, and gap.com. Added to this list of sites are many new ➤**intermediaries** – search engines, shopping robots and one-stop web portals, e.g. yahoo.com, excite.com, aol.com. Also a new array of ➤**marketing research** and ➤**audience measurement** services, e.g. mediametrix.com.

interbank market The ➤**money market** in which banks (➤**banking**) borrow or lend money among themselves either to accommodate short-term ➤**liquidity** problems or for the lending-on of surplus funds. These loans may be arranged either direct or through ➤**money brokers**. ➤**London interbank offered rate**.

interest 1. Payment for a loan. ➤**rate of interest. 2.** A share in ownership, e.g. company A may have an interest (own shares in) company B.

interest cover The number of times the interest payments made by a company to service its loan capital are exceeded by the income of the business.

interest rate ➤rate of interest.

interest rate future A ➤futures contract on a ➤bond, thus allowing the buyer to know exactly what rate of interest will be paid on that type of bond at some future date.

interest rate option An ➤option to pay or receive a particular rate of interest on a loan should the market rate move out of a prespecified range. Interest rate options allow borrowers to borrow at variable rates of interest, subject to a maximum or cap. Similarly, they allow lenders to receive rates subject to a floor. Interest rate options started appearing around 1983, as options on ➤bonds. If a trader has the right to sell a bond at a particular price at some future date, he effectively has the right to borrow at the rate of interest implied by the price of the bond at that date.

interest rate swap A deal between two parties in which one borrows money in one market, and the other borrows money in another market, and in which each agrees to pay the other party's interest. For example, if Global Corporation has ready access to the dollar ➤bond market in New York, and Swiss Corporation has ready access to the Swiss franc bond market, through a swap, Global Corporation can pay Swiss franc interest at the rate secured by Swiss Corporation, while Swiss Corporation can pay interest in dollars at the rate secured by Global Corporation. The swap is designed to allow each party to borrow in the market which offers it the best terms and to then effectively convert the loan into some other form which it might have found it harder to secure. In 1981, Salomon Brothers organized a swap between IBM (borrowing in dollars) and the World Bank (borrowing in Swiss francs), and from then on the swap market grew into a large-volume business. Often, swaps involve one party giving up interest payments on a loan at a fixed rate of interest, in return for a loan of another party at a variable or floating rate of interest.

interim dividend A ➤dividend paid during the year instead of at the end of the year. Some large companies pay dividends quarterly.

interim financial statement A summary financial statement issued part-way through a ➤financial year.

intermediary Organizations which help producers/providers/vendors to sell their goods and services to final consumers. Where producers do not directly sell to consumers they work through a distribution chain that is external to their organization. ➤channel of distribution. Examples are retailers, wholesalers, physical distribution companies and service agencies (travel agents, real estate agents), colloquially called 'middlemen'. In a single distribution chain there may be several intermediaries (producer–wholesaler–retailer–customer). There are also ➤**financial intermediaries**.

New technologies can provide a means for consumers to bypass existing intermediaries and buy direct from manufacturers or service suppliers – a process of ➤**disinter-mediation** (in a business sense). Companies like Dell Computers have gained competitive advantage by selling direct to consumers, thereby avoiding retail mark-ups and reducing distribution costs (although they still face shipping, handling and servicing costs). Software, information, publishing and music providers can distribute digitized material via the internet at much lower cost than in a hard-copy format. Businesses that do not sell information, but are heavily reliant on it such as financial services and travel agents, are also vulnerable to disintermediation because of the cost savings to providers or buyers of going direct. However, technology also creates opportunities for new intermediaries to flourish. Virtual retailers are an example – the classic case being Amazon.com with over a million titles but few of the costs associated with a traditional book retailer. 'Infomediaries' collect and sell information, helping consumers search for suppliers, make comparisons and conclude transactions on the internet. It is a role that traditionally might have been undertaken by an informed retailer or adviser, and can be described as 're-intermediation'.

intermediate offer A ➤new issue of ➤shares in which shares are placed with financial intermediaries. ➤placing. Private investors may apply for these shares through a ➤stockbroker; offer for sale.

intermediation ➤disintermediation.

intermercial A web advertisement with dialogue and motion video. These may last for several minutes. ➤➤advertising; interactive electronic marketing.

internal rate of return ➤discounted cash flow.

international accounting standards (IAS) Rules for the preparation of company accounts. Developed by the ➤International Accounting Standards Committee, the IAS conforms to the Fourth and Seventh EU Company Law Directives. ➤Fourth Directive.

International Accounting Standards Committee (IASC) A London-based body working to reach agreement on worldwide ➤accounting standards. Publishes *International Accounting Standards*. The IASC works with accounting bodies in all the major countries and its standards have been adopted by the ➤London Stock Exchange but not as yet by the regulatory authorities in Canada, Japan and the US.

International Bank for Reconstruction and Development (IBRD, World Bank) Founded, together with the ➤International Monetary Fund (IMF), by the Bretton Woods Conference of 1944 as an international bank to finance the reconstruction and development of member countries. Operations started in 1946. The bank is financed partly by contributions paid by member countries, partly by bond issues. The national contributions constitute the World Bank's capital and relate to the individual countries' share of world trade. The bond issues finance the lending operations of the bank. Operational revenues have come to be supplemented over the course of time by receipts of interest on, and repayment of the capital of, loans. In financing the economic needs of member countries, the IBRD complements the IMF, which finances temporary balance of payments difficulties. Loans are made to governments or government-guaranteed entities. At first devoted to the reconstruction needs of industrial countries, the World Bank by the 1950s had focused its attention on the developing world.

In 1956, the IBRD formed the *International Finance Corporation*, the purpose of which was to promote growth in the private sector of ➤**developing countries** and to mobilize domestic and foreign capital for this purpose. In 1960, the IBRD formed the *International Development Association* in order to assist the poorer developing countries.

international business 1. The activity of engaging in business operations across national borders. Strategic decisions have to be made about: (a) in which countries to operate; (b) whether to export or licence; (c) whether to establish new facilities or enter into ➤**joint ventures** or acquire local businesses, and (d) how to remain competitive internationally. **2.** The field of study that concerns itself with the development, strategy and management of multinational enterprises in the global context of complex and dynamic business environments. Interest lies in multinational enterprises, ➤**culture** and communications, and the special skills that are required to operate in the global business environment, e.g. country risk analysis.

International Development Association ➤International Bank for Reconstruction and Development.

International Finance Corporation ➤International Bank for Reconstruction and Development.

International Monetary Fund (IMF) Organization established by the Bretton Woods Conference in 1944, with the purpose of fostering international monetary co-operation through the stabilization of exchange rates, the removal of ➤**foreign exchange** restrictions and the facilitation of international payments and of *international* ➤**liquidity**. At the outset, member nations declared their ➤**exchange rates**, or ➤**par values**, to which, within a margin of 1 per cent in either direction, they held their currencies. The par values were quoted in terms of the US dollar, which was itself valued in terms of gold. However, following the breaking of the dollar's link with gold in 1971 and the abandonment of national fixed parities from 1972 onwards, the IMF rule was abolished in 1976.

The major function of the IMF has been lending in support of countries in ➤**balance of payments** difficulties. For this purpose, the IMF has been funded by contributions, or quotas, from member countries. Countries in difficulties obtain foreign currencies in exchange for their own, which they must repay within 3–5 years. Members in severe balance of payments difficulties are obliged to consult with the IMF on remedial domestic policies, as a condition of further assistance. The funds of the IMF have been progressively increased over the years.

International Organization for Standardization (ISO) A worldwide quality certification organization. It awards certificates based on reviewing the applications made by firms. Firms use these certificates to demonstrate to customers and suppliers they have met the minimum standards necessary. ISOs 9000–9004 are particular certificates. They are being used worldwide to provide a framework for quality assurance. Most countries have their own quality system standards, which are equivalent to the ISO 9000 series. The ISO 9000 registration requires a third-party assessment of a company's quality standards and procedures and regular audits are made to ensure the systems do not deteriorate. The ISO 9000 series provides detailed recommendations for setting up quality systems.

175

internet An international network of computer networks, which in turn link together individual personal computers. More formally, a global network of inter-connected packet-switched computer networks that facilitates interactive multi-media many-to-many communications between users. Its origins lie in local area networks that were used to link together all the personal computers in, say, a military establishment or a university. During the 1970s more and more of these networks were linked up for multi-site and multi-organization communication, e.g. JANET, the British joint-academic network. Only since the early 1990s has there been serious commercial interest in these networks. However, in recent years the growth of ➤electronic commerce, ➤dot com firms and ➤interactive electronic marketing has been phenomenal. ➤new economy.

internet banking ➤electronic banking.

internet service provider (ISP) A firm that provides access to the ➤internet usually via a telephone connection to a server, or more recently, a broadband connection. In the traditional UK model, the service provider generated an income from part of the telephone call fee while the user remained connected to the internet.

interstitial A web advertisement that appears to a user while a browser is download-ing a page within a web site. ➤advertising; interactive electronic marketing.

intrapreneurship Adoption of entrepreneurial attitudes and approaches to man-agement by employees of large organizations. For example, the traditional ➤brand management system encouraged individual managers to behave as if they were enterpreneurs, often in competition with other brand managers from the same parent organization. ➤entrepreneurship.

intrinsic reward ➤reward.

intrinsic value 1. The value believed by some to attach inherently to a natural object (e.g. a precious metal) regardless of its price at any given time. In economics, value is determined only by demand and is denoted by price; hence, intrinsic value is inapplicable. **2.** In the ➤options market, the amount by which the striking price (➤offer for sale) differs from the current price of the underlying asset, i.e. in a *call option* the intrinsic value is an amount in excess of the current price; in a *put option* it is an amount below that price.

introduction (UK) A means of initial entry to a stock market for companies whose shares are already widely held but, until the introduction is effected, are not quoted or listed. ➤offer for sale; placing.

invention The act of developing something new. It usually involves creativity in the form of conception and development. It need not involve any commercialization. Indeed, most of the ➤patents that are registered each year are not developed further. However, where there is subsequent communication, the process of invention trans-mutes into ➤innovation and/or ➤new product development.

inventory A term for stock, popular in the US. It includes items available for sale to customers and raw materials, parts and supplies to be used in production. They can be reported as the cost incurred to either purchase or produce them. If the cost of replacing such items has declined, then the inventories may be recorded as such to reflect the decline in value. There are times when it is necessary to record inventory as all the money the system invests in things it intends to sell (thus including all labour costs invested during a process after purchase).

inventory planning and control The task of setting the effective capacity of the operation so that it can respond to the demands placed upon it. This usually means deciding how the operation should react to fluctuations in demand. Typically, operations managers are faced with a ➤**forecast** of demand, which is unlikely to be either certain or constant. Before any decisions can be made, quantitative data on both production capacity and demand are required. This will usually involve measuring the aggregate demand and capacity levels for the planning period. The next step will be to identify the alternative capacity plans, which could be developed in response to demand fluctuations. The final part of the process is to decide the most appropriate capacity plan for any given circumstances. ➤**inventory smoothing**.

inventory smoothing A technique to try to balance capacity leads and capacity lags through using ➤**inventory**. Essentially, this is achieved by introducing production capacity such that demand can always be met by a combination of production and inventories, and capacity is fully utilized. The cost of this technique is that of carrying additional inventory. ➤➤**economic order quantity**.

inverse elasticity rule A rule that suggests, if prices are to deviate from ➤**marginal cost**, they should be highest in those markets where the ➤**price elasticity of demand** is lowest. Imagine an electricity company trying to decide what prices to charge business and residential customers. If the company needs to charge above the marginal cost for power, the rule suggests it should apply the biggest mark-up in the market which is least price-sensitive. This will ensure that any drop in sales relative to those that would prevail with marginal cost pricing will be as small as possible.

investment 1. The act of placing monetary resources into the creation of ➤**assets**, in the manufacturing and service sectors of the economy. Only real *capital formation*, such as the production of machinery, adds to the stock of investment goods. **2.** The act of placing monetary resources into financial assets, i.e. the purchase of shares or ➤**bonds**. Shifting money from a bank account to ➤**securities** in this way simply moves savings from one form to another. **3.** The sum of money itself so invested, or the total of financial assets so acquired.

investment analyst Someone who studies companies and financial ➤**securities** and makes recommendations to buy and sell shares and other securities. Analysts work not only in investment banks and stockbroking firms (the *sell-side*), but also in the financial institutions such as pension funds (the *buy-side*) which own the majority of stocks and shares. ➤➤**investment approaches**.

investment appraisal ➤discounted cash flow.

investment approach One of a variety of strategies for choosing the allocation of different types of assets in a ➤**portfolio**. *Bottom-up* refers to the selection of companies considered promising according to various criteria (e.g. ➤**price/earnings growth factor**) but without much regard to geographical or sectoral origin. *Top-down* refers to the selection of countries and industries which are believed to offer good prospects. A portfolio manager is said to be *underweight* or *overweight* in a stock or a market if the share of the ➤**market capitalization** of the stock or market in his portfolio is less or more than its share in total market capitalization. In practice, of course, both these approaches are generally used, but one may be emphasized over the other. *Contrarian* refers to the practice of buying shares when their prices have fallen to lows by historical standards, while *momentum investing* involves buying shares whose prices are rising. *Value investing* is an approach in which shares are sought which have prices below ➤net asset value or where there are unexploited or undervalued assets. ➤➤cyclical stocks; efficient market hypothesis; technical analysis.

investment bank A ➤financial intermediary that offers many of a range of different services to corporate or large individual customers, such as purchasing new issues and placing them in smaller parcels among investors or giving advice on ➤take-overs. The investment bank is now seen as something of a financial services conglomerate, and the term and institutions have come to supersede the UK ➤merchant bank. Many ➤commercial banks have an investment banking arm.

Investment Services Directive (ISD) ➤Directive of the European Union (1993) on the provision of investment services such as savings products and cross-border share issues. Its main feature is that of a 'mutual recognition passport' whereby accredited providers of specified services can access regulated markets of other member states without the need for accreditation in each country.

investment trust A company which has the sole object of investing a fixed volume of ➤capital in a wide range of ➤securities, i.e. a ➤closed-end fund. An investment trust issues shares and uses its capital to buy securities and shares in other companies. A ➤unit trust, in contrast, issues units that represent holdings of shares; it expands or contracts with the total number of subscribers. Unit holders thus do not share in the ➤profits of the company managing the trust. Investment trusts can also raise part of their capital by issuing fixed-interest securities, and the yield on the ➤ordinary shares of the trust can thus benefit from ➤gearing. The price of a share in an investment trust may be above (➤premium) or more likely below (➤discount) the value of the underlying shares and other assets, i.e. the ➤net asset value per share.

investors in industry (3i) A public limited company operating in the field of venture capital. Originally this firm was the venture capital department of the Industrial and Commercial Finance Corporation set up in 1945 to aid small- and medium-sized businesses in the UK, hence its name. It was owned and financed by the UK banks including the ➤Bank of England.

involvement theory The idea that people are more or less engaged with things. In a consumer context, these things might be products, people, media, messages or purchases. Typically, a distinction is drawn between high and low involvement. Thus, a high-involvement purchase is deemed to be very important to the consumer, it has some perceived financial and/or social risk ('will it be too expensive?' and 'what will my peers think?'), and there is likely to be a complex process of problem-solving prior to purchase. This extensive and thoughtful (cognitive) problem-solving requires external information search, information processing and evaluation of alternatives. For most people, the purchase of a house or a wedding dress would be classified as high-involvement (although it should be noted that involvement is a feature of people in a situation, not an inherent characteristic of the product). By contrast, a low-involvement purchase is not very important – it is seen as low-risk, requiring limited or no problem-solving. Some information may be drawn from memory, but the consumer is not going to exert much thought (low cognition). Repurchase of laundry detergent or the reordering of photocopying paper in an office would be classified as low-involvement. ➤➤**information search**.

The idea of involvement makes intuitive sense. However, it is not easily defined and measured. One reason for this is that there are several facets (importance, risk, information processing, etc.) which relate to slightly different concepts. Researchers have not been entirely consistent in their use of these concepts. Furthermore, it is possible to be involved with different things (products, people, media, etc.) in different ways – so, a consumer who is involved in product usage is not necessarily involved with the purchase of that product ('I use a computer, but have never bought one'). Also, this may change over time. A consumer may be very involved in the first-ever purchase of a laundry detergent, but subsequent purchases are routine and not involving. This gives rise to variations in observed levels of involvement across consumers.

Despite measurement problems, involvement theory is widely applied in ➤**advertising**, ➤**brand management**, ➤**sales** and ➤**consumer behaviour**. Some particularly well-known examples are in the following areas:

(1) Social judgement theory. People who are highly involved in something will come to have firm beliefs about it. This, in turn, means they will see a message that supports their beliefs more positively than it actually is (an assimilation effect). A message that does not support their beliefs will be seen more negatively than it actually is (a contrast effect). The argument follows that a brand manager should attempt to raise levels of involvement with the brand – not only will consumers have firmer beliefs about it, but they will give extra weight to any advertising messages about it, and downplay any messages about competing brands. The theory also has applicability in sales and ➤**service encounters** where salespeople question customers, find out their prior beliefs and then playback information that is congruent with these prior beliefs. The information will be seen more positively than it actually is.

(2) Central and peripheral routes to persuasion. For high-involvement purchases advertisers should encourage consumers to think about the product (the central route to persuasion). This might be achieved by discussing product attributes or by making the message more personally relevant to consumers. In these cases the advertiser elaborates on why a consumer should wish to buy the brand (termed the 'elaboration likelihood model' (ELM)). By contrast, for low-involvement purchases advertisers should not attempt to get consumers to think – they should simply get them to learn the brand name and/or brand attributes (the peripheral route to persuasion). This can be achieved through simple repetition, without elaboration. Given that there is no elaboration about the brand itself, ploys are needed to capture people's attention, such as the use of music, visuals and celebrity presenters.

(3) The Foote Cone Belding (FCB) planning grid. The 2 × 2 creative planning grid from the FCB advertising agency draws a distinction between high- and low-involvement purchases, and thinking-based (cognitive) and feeling-based (affect) purchase motives. In contrast to the central and peripheral routes to persuasion,

it is possible to have both motives under each level of involvement. Thus, a 35mm camera purchase might be classified as high-involvement thinking-based (with the creative guideline to offer specific information using long-copy advertisements, as in the elaboration likelihood model). A sports car purchase is also high-involvement, but plays on affect (the creative guideline here is to have large advertisements with impact and dramatic effects). Typical of the low-involvement thinking-based category are insect repellents and insecticides (remainder advertisements are deemed to be appropriate). Finally, in the low-involvement feeling-based category are ➤packaged goods such as brands of beer, soft drinks and snacks (attention-getting creative work is needed).

(4) Informational/transformational theory. In its simplest form this can be seen as another 2 × 2 creative planning grid. Again, there is a distinction between high and low involvement and two categories of motivation. These categories describe informational motives (which are essentially negative motives for making a purchase) and transformational motives (positive motives). For example, a consumer buys Colgate toothpaste to clean his teeth (problem removal), or to avoid the accumulation of plaque (problem avoidance), or because stocks of toothpaste are low (normal depletion) – all these are informational motives in the context of a low-involvement purchase. These motives contrast with the purchase of a Swan-Hellenic cruise, a high-involvement transformational purchase, where the goal is to see wonderful sights (sensory gratification), be informed about the past (intellectual stimulation) and impress peers (social approval). This theory was proposed and developed by John Rossiter and Larry Percy (*Advertising and Promotion Management*, 1987). ➤➤brand communication effects.

Apart from the problem of defining and measuring involvement, a further danger with all these applications is to use them unquestioningly for prescriptive purposes. If all advertisers in a product category are using the same theories, and drawing the same implications for creative planning, the resultant advertising may be too predictable and too similar, e.g. all four-wheel-drive car advertisements show the vehicle facing up to the challenges of driving over rugged, mountainous terrain. ➤competitive parity.

IP ➤intellectual property.

IPO ➤initial public offering.

IRA ➤individual retirement account.

IRR internal rate of return. ➤discounted cash flow.

irredeemable security ➤redemption date.

irrevocable letter of credit ➤letter of credit.

ISA ➤individual savings account.

ISE International Stock Exchange. ➤London Stock Exchange.

isocost curve A graphical depiction of combinations of inputs used in the production of an item, that each cost the same amount. Imagine a company employs robots and people in some combination to make widgets: if the company can employ either one robot and three people, or two robots and two people, and either way the cost of doing so is the same, then that pair of combinations would lie on one isocost

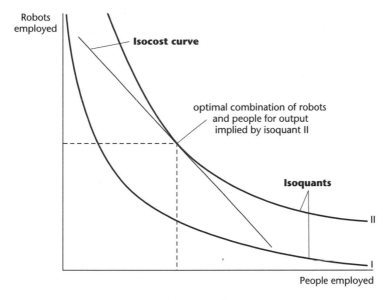

Graphical depiction of isoquants

curve. Typically, an isocost curve is used in the economic theory of production, in conjunction with an ➤isoquant in deriving certain properties of the ➤production function.

ISO 9000 ➤International Organization for Standardization.

isoquant A graphical depiction of combinations of inputs used in the production of an item, such that each combination produces the same final output. Imagine a company employs robots and people in some combination to make widgets: if the company can employ either ten robots and fifteen people, or twelve robots and twelve people, and either way the total number of widgets produced would be the same, then that pair of combinations would lie on one isoquant. Typically, isoquants are used in the economic theory of production, in conjunction with an ➤isocost curve in deriving certain properties of the ➤production function. In general, the assumed shape of isoquants and isocost curves is as shown in the above figure. Optimal-point combination of inputs is that marked on the graph where the gradient of an isocost curve equals the gradient of the highest isoquant curve it touches. ➤➤expansion path.

issue The initial sale of a ➤security.

issued capital The part of a company's ➤capital that has been subscribed by shareholders. It may or may not be paid up. ➤paid-up capital.

issuing house (UK) An ➤investment bank, ➤stockbroker or other ➤financial institution that organizes a ➤new issue of ➤securities. The issuing house or securities house, in conjunction with the issuing ➤broker, will advise the client on the timing and form of the issue and in return for a ➤**commission** will ➤**underwrite** or arrange underwriting for all or part of the issue. The issuing house is nowadays often referred to as a *sponsor* because it lends its reputation to the issue.

J

Jacques, Elliott A Canadian medical doctor and psychologist. A founder member of the Tavistock Institute of Human Relations in London after the Second World War and later an academic at Brunel University. In the late 1940s and 1950s he worked on the long-term Glacier Metal project on worker behaviour. Jacques was interested in the interaction of people in organizations. In *The Measurement of Responsibility* (1956) he elaborated his 'time-span of discretion' concept which was based on the observation that the lowest-paid staff have their actions monitored at frequent intervals, which become longer and longer the higher the person is placed in the hierarchy and the higher the pay. In *A General Theory of Bureaucracy* (1976) he developed these ideas and in all wrote some ten books. In *Requisite Organization* (1997) he deals with the relationships between individuals, organizations and society. Jacques has made many contributions to current management thought in his long working life, including his emphasis on 'empowering' employees.

JDI Job Description Index. ➤job description; job satisfaction.

JIT ➤just-in-time.

jobbers A now obsolete term for ➤market maker.

job description A written statement of what an employee is expected to do, how it is done, and why it is done. This statement arises from the process of job analysis, whereby a detailed description is prepared of the tasks involved in a job, the relationship of a given job to other jobs, and an assessment of the knowledge, skills and abilities necessary for an employee to perform the job successfully. The process is most necessary at the time of making an appointment or when making a reappointment; however, periodic review may be necessary because of organizational change. Review may result in 'job enlargement' – the horizontal expansion of a job – or 'job enrichment' – the vertical expansion of a job. The practice of 'job rotation' (i.e. the periodic shifting of an employee from one task to another) also may demand renewed job analysis. However, if the review is part of a wider re-evaluation of ➤work design and business processes (➤re-engineering) the employee may be given fewer responsibilities or even lose her job altogether.

job enrichment ➤Herzberg; job description.

job production A production process that deals with high variety and low volumes. Each product being produced within a job production environment has to share the operation's resources with many others. The resources of the operation will process a series of products but, although all the products will require the same kind of attention, each will differ in its exact needs. A good example of a job production environment is that of a specialist furniture restorer. Typically, this will involve similar tools, equipment and skilled labour but the products may differ considerably. ➤➤mass production.

job satisfaction An overall assessment of how an employee feels about her job. It is not, therefore, a description of the job, but a description of the emotional feelings an employee has about a job, i.e. the focus is on ➤affect. Within this overall assessment the employee will have distinct feelings about specific components of the job (working conditions, colleagues, supervision, tasks, promotion, etc.). In measuring job satisfaction it is usual to probe employees' feelings about these components, although there is then some dispute over how to sum or combine the results from these separate components. Typically, some form of employee ➤attitude survey is administered. Two of the most respected surveys are the Minnesota Job Satisfaction Questionnaire (JSQ) and the Job Description Index (JDI), both of which report component-level results as well as overall measures.

Job satisfaction is influenced by an employee's ➤motivation to work and her ➤expectations of work, as well as how well the organization treats the person and others against whom the person assesses herself. In other words, there are internal, personal factors (personality, attitudes, levels of self-esteem, etc.) and external, environmental factors (➤autonomy; **equity; pay; roles**, working conditions). The list of suggested influences is very long and has been heavily researched, partly because job satisfaction is seen as an important influence on performance, productivity, ➤absenteeism, ➤employee retention and turnover.

joint and several liability A ➤liability that falls at the same time on each one of two or more parties, and on all together. A claimant can choose to sue one or more of the parties (severally), or all together (jointly).

joint-stock company The early term for an incorporated business (➤incorporation), in which investors contributed funds and received ➤shares in the firm. The term probably originated in arrangements for pooling stocks of goods or raw materials by merchants in a single trading unit.

joint venture The establishment of a separate business by two or more parties that will be operated jointly. This would usually involve a separate firm with joint equity stakes. It is important to distinguish a joint venture from other forms of ➤strategic alliance. Frequently, they are formed between larger and smaller companies where the larger company seeks technology and the smaller one seeks market share. While the advantages are clear – such as access to technology or markets – the disadvantages include reluctance to share proprietary information and a clash of management styles. Many joint ventures are not successful; indeed, over 70 per cent do not progress. Joint ventures are a common form of market entry for firms seeking to enter new markets, especially internationally. ➤international business.

junior debt ➤subordinated.

junk bond (US) Company bonds of low-quality ➤security backing sold with high ➤coupons, rated below investment grade by the two US rating agencies, ➤Standard and Poor's 500 and ➤Moody's Investors Service, and giving a ➤yield of at least

200 ➤basis points above the yield on ➤Treasury bonds. Junk bonds were pioneered in the mid 1970s by the New York house Drexel Burnham Lambert; however, this was a revival of a market dating back to at least the 1920s (➤leveraged buy-out). Junk bonds are also known as *high-yield bonds*.

Juran, Joseph (died 1994) A quality management guru. Juran, an engineer, worked at Western Electric and AT & T in the 1920s. His *Quality Control Handbook* (1951) established his reputation and he was invited to Japan (where he subsequently had considerable influence) to lecture on quality management in 1953, and where he was preceded by W Edwards ➤Deming. There are several parallels between the careers of Juran and Deming: both were trained as electrical engineers, both worked at Western Electric and both initially had far more influence in Japan than in the US. Juran emphasizes the need for companywide quality management, commitment by senior management and the human aspects of quality improvement. ➤total quality management.

just-in-time (JIT) A manufacturing system that is designed to minimize the cost of holding stocks of raw materials, components, work-in-progress and finished goods by very carefully planning the scheduling of resources through the production process. The traditional approach to manufacturing was to hold large stocks of raw materials and components to ensure the production plant was able to keep running. It was a form of insurance. The disadvantage of this approach was that it led to very high costs of maintaining these stocks. Providing a firm could ensure the efficient and reliable delivery of materials and components it was not necessary for the manufacturing firm to maintain these high levels of stock. A supermarket store is an example of a simple JIT system. The store does not keep large stocks of food – these are delivered daily. The system is dependent on efficient ordering and delivery systems, and there is particular emphasis placed on relationships with suppliers.

JIT is often also described as a business philosophy. The philosophy was founded in Japan and is based upon doing the simple things well, on slowly improving the ways they are done and removing waste. The Toyota Motor Corporation is recognized as a founder and leader in this business philosophy. Its principles are based upon the need to minimize waste, improve efficiencies and add value through manufacture. This is often attributed to the cultural and economic situation in which Japan found itself after the Second World War. With few natural resources and a relatively crowded country, the economy and firms in particular were forced to '*make every grain of rice count*'.

Commonly cited advantages of JIT systems are as follows.
(1) Reduced space requirements.
(2) Reduced inventory investment in purchased parts, raw materials, work-in-process, and finished goods.
(3) Reduction in manufacturing lead times.
(4) Increased productivity of direct labour employees, indirect support employees and clerical staff.
(5) Increased equipment usage.
(6) Reduction in paperwork and simplification of planning systems.
(7) Sets valid priorities for production scheduling.
(8) Encourages the participation of the workforce.
(9) Increased product quality.

Commonly cited disadvantages (which, in some cases, may be viewed as advantages, depending on your vantage point) are as follows.

(1) Requires workers and supervisors to take responsibility for shopfloor production control and productivity improvements.

(2) Requires an atmosphere of close co-operation and mutual trust between the workforce and management.

(3) Requires actual daily production to approximate the daily schedule (closely).

(4) Cannot respond rapidly to changes in product design, product mix or large demand volumes.

(5) Requires a large number of set-ups and frequent shipments of purchased items from suppliers.

(6) Requires parts to be produced and moved in the smallest containers possible.

(7) Not well suited for irregularly used parts or specially ordered products.

(8) The layout of the factory may have to change to a cell-based or product-based system, rather than a process-based system.

(9) JIT by definition takes safety out of the process by reducing buffer stock; this causes stress on operators which can be extreme.

K

kaizen A Japanese term meaning 'continuous improvement'. The importance of this ethos towards manufacturing production cannot be overstated. In the 1960s Japanese motor vehicles were ridiculed as inferior to their European counterparts. Using the approach of slowly and continually improving their manufacturing techniques the Japanese motor industry soon became the world leaders in the industry. The important consideration in this approach to manufacturing is that frequently the improvements are small. Suggestions (e.g. from shopfloor operators) while being perhaps in themselves not very significant, can, when many such small improvements are combined, effect significant improvements. Moreover, this approach offers additional advantages when compared to the European one of large-scale technology-based improvements.

kanban A technique for controlling the flow of ➤inventory through a manufacturing system. It is closely linked to the ➤just-in-time system. The term is Japanese for 'card' or 'signal'. Indeed, in its simplest form the technique may be viewed as a card used by operators to instruct their suppliers to forward more materials. *Kanban*s are used to minimize the amount of inventory in a manufacturing system and thereby improve the speed at which ➤work-in-progress is processed. It gives the impression of pulling inventory through the manufacturing processes; whereas the alternative system of ➤material requirements planning is referred to as a 'push system'.

Kantar Group, The (TKG) A leading market research company, operating in roughly sixty countries. It is a full-service research company, conducting both quantitative and qualitative ➤marketing research. The company includes Millward Brown (a global leader in continuous brand tracking and brand equity evaluation) and Research International (which undertakes customized research across the globe). TKG's main competitors are ➤A C Nielsen Corporation and ➤Taylor Nelson Sofres, although there are many smaller players in specific markets.

Kanter, Rosabeth Moss Influential academic and consultant. Described in *Men and Women of the Corporation* (1977) how the bureaucratic structures of modern corporations impaired the quality of life and opportunities for personal development and creativity. In *The Change Masters* (1984) she showed how empowerment of employees could promote change and innovation, and in *When Giants Learn to Dance* (1989) how big companies were learning to become more entrepreneurial by adopting flatter hierarchies and delegating more to small autonomous units, while at the same time still capturing the efficiencies and resources attributable to their large scale.

Kanter is Professor of Business Administration at Harvard and was editor of the *Harvard Business Review*. She is much respected by many other distinguished gurus, but a critic of the 'managementese' which characterizes most writing on the subject.

Kaplan, Robert S Professor at Harvard Business School who writes and consults on advanced management accounting and the relationship between accounting and corporate strategy. His book *Relevance Lost: the rise and fall of management accounting* (1987) with H Thomas Johnson, argued that after the First World War the management accounting function became subservient to the needs of financial reporting and did not report costs accurately, and that this is still true in many cases, especially in large diversified companies.

Advanced Management Accounting (1998) by Kaplan and Anthony A Atkinson, is a textbook on overcoming these and other deficiencies. For example, 'activity-based costing' has been developed to more accurately assign the costs of indirect and support services using cost-drivers, not only to products but to all the resources used for activities that support the production and delivery of products and services to customers, such as materials handling and after-sales service.

Kaplan believes that in the information era the mobilization and exploitation of intangible assets such as ➤intellectual property rights and employee skills are more important than the deployment of physical assets, and that financial accounting models must be supplemented to take account of this. He has developed the ➤balanced scorecard which brings the attention of management to these important non-financial factors. The scorecard covers three perspectives in addition to the usual financial data and ratios: (a) the market/customer perspective, e.g. ➤market share; (b) the internal process perspective, e.g. percentage of sales from new products, and (c) the ➤organizational learning and growth perspective, e.g. employee turnover, percentage of customer-facing employees with on-line access to customer information. ➤➤marketing metrics.

Katz's functional theory of motivation A model of social and psychological needs. A distinction is drawn between: (a) cognitive needs (related to gathering information and understanding the environment); (b) affective needs (related to strengthening aesthetic, pleasurable and emotional experiences); (c) personal integrative needs (related to building the credibility, confidence, stability and status of an individual); (d) social integrative needs (related to contacts with family, friends and the rest of the world), and (e) escapist needs (related to escape, tension release and the desire for diversion).

Marketers have used this classification of needs to think about the way people consume media and products. This resulted in the suggestion that there are four 'functional attitudes' to products: (a) ego-defensive (does the purchase of this product reflect the desire to fulfil my ego?); (b) knowledge-oriented (does this product relieve me of having to process detailed information about the product?); (c) value-expressive (are my values embedded in the purchase decision for this product?), and (d) utilitarian (does the purchase of this product rely mostly on obtaining functional benefits?). The theory was first described in a paper by Daniel Katz ('The Functional Approach to the Study of Attitudes', *Public Opinion Quarterly*, 1960).

Kay, John A Independent British economist, author and consultant on business strategy. Like ➤**Porter, Michael E**, Kay explains the success of businesses in terms of competitive advantage. This in turn results from three sustainable and distinctive capabilities: (a) innovation; (b) reputation, and (c) the system of relationships within the firm, or between it and its suppliers and customers, which he calls the 'company's architecture'. Other factors often identified as underlying success, such as large size, market share and attractive (e.g. fast-growing markets) are more likely to be symptoms of success rather than causes: these factors are not in themselves sources of sustainable advantage, since they will attract competitors. Size in particular should not be pursued for its own sake; mergers fail more often than not; the European Union will encourage specialization, not necessarily giant companies. The purpose of business is to add value, which is achieved by exploiting unique combinations of strengths in the architecture which makes up the firm. He is a proponent of the ➤**stakeholder** concept of corporate governance which predominates in France and Germany and in which the firm is perceived as operating within the wider social context. At the conclusion of *Foundations of Corporate Success* (1993) Kay writes: 'The search for generic strategies, for recipes for corporate success, is doomed to failure. There can be no such recipes because their value would be destroyed by the very fact of their identification.'

Kay has held chairs at London Business School and at Oxford.

keiretsu A Japanese term for a group of companies that have minority shareholdings in each other. This forces them to discuss long-term strategy. Well-known *keiretsu* include Mitsubishi. ➤➤**corporate governance**.

key account management ➤customer relationship management.

key performance measures (KPMs) Measures used to assess the performance of something that is actively managed. Thus, if customer care is actively managed, relevant KPMs might be measures of customer satisfaction, number of complaints and repeat patronage. For a brand manager, measures might include volume/value ➤**market share**, brand awareness, perceived price, perceived quality, or a measure of ➤**buyer behaviour** (such as repeat-buying). Wherever possible, measures should be related to a benchmark; this might be a theoretical norm (e.g. from a formal model of repeat-buying), an empirical norm (e.g. average repeat-buying), or a temporal norm, e.g. repeat-buying for the same period last year. Some of the measures are, by definition, relative: market share, relative perceived quality, relative price. Where these measures are based on consumer perceptions, it is important to find out how familiar and experienced consumers are with the alternatives (it is hard for people to comment on relative perceived quality if they do not know or have not used the alternatives). ➤**balanced scorecard; marketing metrics; marketing performance measures**.

know-how The knowledge of techniques and skills acquired by a company over time through working on particular projects. This is often coupled to research and development and/or manufacturing, where a firm learns from its experiences. The key point here is that much of this knowledge and know-how will be in the form of ➤**tacit knowledge** that is difficult to codify or capture in ➤**intellectual property**. For example, a firm manufacturing cameras may have gained much know-how in the area of precision assembly of components. The ➤**patents** and designs for such cameras may be widely available, but the manufacture of such products may be difficult to replicate because of the skills necessary to assemble the product. Such tacit knowledge is frequently overlooked by firms when they attempt to move into new product areas, only to find out later that they do not have the skills required.

knowledge economy A label describing societies that have the ability to turn information into productive knowledge. These economies are characterized by: (a) the dominance of service organizations, where the supply of products is just one aspect of service provision; (b) the primary resource of these organizations is intellectual capital; (c) competitive advantage accrues to those organizations that can acquire, deploy and manage knowledge strategically; (d) organizations exist which can adapt themselves to create, accumulate, protect, apply leverage and use knowledge, and (e) where culture and technology work together as organizational mechanisms for conserving, enhancing and making knowledge available for use. ➤**knowledge management systems**. A premium is placed on innovations and a capacity to harness innovations. People in these sectors are called 'knowledge workers'.

Knowledge economies are described as 'post-industrial'. However, despite their apparent novelty, the focus on knowledge is not new – consider the role of tertiary institutions (universities, colleges, research laboratories), the professions (accounting, law, medicine), and ➤**marketing research** agencies (to the extent that they do not simply collect data but also interpret and use it). The viewpoint is also in danger of trivializing the amount of knowledge that had to be developed and harnessed in earlier periods of industrialization, e.g. in eighteenth-century Britain.

knowledge management system A process and procedure for capturing, organizing, analysing, interpreting and adding value to information as part of a wider set of managerial goals. If access to raw materials was the mainstay of industrial societies, access to information is said to be the mainstay of post-industrial ➤**knowledge economies**. However, the mere possession of information is not enough, it must be accumulated, protected, leveraged and used to address specific managerial goals; this requires systems as well as appropriately skilled employees ('knowledge workers'). Together, these add value to the information and, thus, to the organization. This has led to detailed analyses of the skills and ➤**know-how** that firms and their employees possess, these being referred to as 'capabilities' and ➤**competencies**.

The area of knowledge management has grown tremendously in the past two decades, often in association with developments in telecommunications, information technology, software engineering and management consulting. This has underscored the importance of hiring and retaining skilled employees (➤**intellectual assets** and ➤**human capital** are seen as the key assets of knowledge-based organizations, not capital plant and equipment). It has also led to rethinking of organizational structures (such as the formation of adaptive and flexible project teams, not rigid functional hierarchies). Indeed, the whole subject of knowledge management is linked closely to the subject of ➤**organizational learning** and ➤**learning organizations**. It is argued that successful firms are able to acquire knowledge and learn from experience. This is then shared among the employees and managers, thereby enabling the organization to learn. It is the management of these processes that lies at the heart of effective knowledge management. ➤➤**resource-based theories of strategy**.

Kotler, Philip Professor of International Marketing at the Kellogg Graduate School of Management, Northwestern University. Arguably, the most well-known exponent of marketing principles, concepts and practices in the international arena. His textbook *Marketing Management: analysis, planning, implementation and control* (1967) is the most widely used marketing textbook in graduate schools. He has written extensively on marketing planning and control, and marketing in not-for-profit, social and health-care contexts. ➤**marketing concept**.

Kotter, John P Professor of Leadership at the Harvard Business School and successful writer on management. His books, which deal with leadership, business culture and managing change, are full of practical insights and advice. In *A Force for Change*, Kotter distinguishes the many differences between management and leadership. For example, the leader establishes direction – the manager plans and budgets; the leader aligns people, which means communicating the vision for the future – the manager establishes organization and staffing; the leader motivates and inspires – the manager controls and solves problems. Most leaders had experience of leading and risk-taking early in their career and learned by mistakes how difficult leadership is. The prime function of leadership is to produce change. In *Leading Change*, Kotter emphasizes the importance of communication – not simply issuing documents, but by action, e.g. bold action to re-base remuneration of the senior management towards performance and results and making more people lower down accountable for performance. (Get rid of the company jet aircraft, sell the corporate headquarters, and demonstrate weaknesses against competitors to staff to convince them of the challenges faced.)

L

labour union (US) ➤trade union.

Lagrange multiplier A mathematical device, developed by the Frenchman Joseph Louis Lagrange (1736–1813), for calculating the optimal value of a variable subject to some constraint, in order to maximize or minimize another variable. The technique can be used to solve a problem of the form in this example: what combination of labour and capital should a firm use in order to minimize costs, given that output has to equal some particular level. Solving the problem without the constraint of achieving a target output is mathematically straightforward, but typically uninteresting in the real world. The Lagrange technique involves writing an equation expressing the objective of cost minimization, with another equation expressing the constraint, and combining the two. Or, to take a simple example, suppose we wish to set X and Z at a level that maximizes Y, where:

$$Y = X * Z$$

and is subject to the constraint that $(X + Z)$ is equal to 10, or:

$$X + Z - 10 = 0.$$

We construct a new, 'artificial' objective function of this form:

$$L = X * Z + \lambda(X + Z - 10).$$

This is, in fact, the same as the old one, but it has had the constraint added on. It has been added on, however, in such a way that it equals 0, if it holds. The constraint is also multiplied by a new ➤**parameter**, λ, called the Lagrange multiplier.

It turns out that maximizing this new objective function is the same as maximizing the old one subject to the constraint. So we then maximize L by setting X, Y and λ using the mathematics of calculus. The resulting values of X and Z are the values we want.

laundering The conversion of money obtained illegally (e.g. from drugs) into apparently legitimate bank accounts or businesses. There are now elaborate regulations obliging banks to determine the origin of funds deposited with them.

law of diminishing return ➤diminishing return.

law of one price ➤one price, law of.

lay-offs ➤collective action.

leader–member exchange theory (LMX) The theory that leaders create 'in-

192

groups' and 'out-groups', and that subordinates with in-group status will have higher performance ratings, less turnover and greater satisfaction with their leader. However, selection of in-group members may reflect levels of performance and satisfaction that are higher in the first place. ➤leadership.

leader-participation model A leadership theory that provides a set of rules to determine the form and amount of participative decision-making in different situations. ➤leadership.

leadership The ability to influence a group of people towards the achievement of goals. This ability is brought about through the process of 'leading' – this includes motivating subordinates, directing others and earning the respect of superiors. Leadership may arise from formal rank/status (as with appointment to a managerial position, ➤role), or from non-sanctioned authority (as with a leader who emerges from a group). ➤➤leadership types. Effective leadership is seen as depending on 'leader–member relations', i.e. the degree of confidence, trust and respect subordinates have in their leader. These relations have to be earned and therefore not all managers can be regarded as effective leaders; nor are all leaders managers.

Conventionally, the emergence of leaders has been viewed through two different lenses, i.e. one puts the emphasis on selection, the other emphasizes development. Selection takes into account personality, social, physical and intellectual traits that differentiate leaders from non-leaders (the 'trait theory of leadership'). ➤➤personality traits. Thus, successful leaders are said to be self-assured, show initiative, capable of solving problems, have 'helicopter vision', be in good health, etc. Development, by contrast, is the process of building confidence, trust and respect with subordinates and superiors using particular styles of leadership, and this is more directly based on an understanding of behaviour and deeds (the 'style theory of leadership'). ➤➤managerial grid. For example, the style might be autocratic or democratic. However, experts now tend to take a more contingent view. This suggests that while personality traits and behaviour *can* be important in accounting for the emergence of leaders, much depends on specific contingencies (notably, the specifics of a particular situation). Theories that recognize the importance of contingencies include the ➤Fiedler contingency model, ➤situational leadership theory, ➤leader–member exchange theory and the ➤leader-participation model.

Several leadership gurus have had an influence on popular thinking in this area, including Warren ➤Bennis and John P ➤Kotter.

leadership types Many different leadership types have been described. The variety of types arises because attention may be focused on the personality traits of leaders, the behavioural characteristics of leaders, or a range of contingent factors. ➤leadership. However, there are two very broad types: (a) transactional, and (b) transformational, leaders. 'Transactional leaders' are those who guide or motivate their subordinates in the direction of established goals by clarifying what has to be done by whom, i.e. task and ➤role requirements are made clear. 'Transformational leaders' are those who inspire their followers, provide intellectual stimulation, create opportunities for employees to develop, and who have a certain amount of charisma (in the sense of providing vision, creating a sense of mission and instilling pride, respect and trust). Evidence suggests that truly effective leaders build transformational leadership on top of transactional leadership. By contrast, a purely transactional approach may fail to inspire, and a purely charismatic approach may come to focus unhealthily on the leader. ➤➤**empowerment**.

lead manager A bank, ➤**company** or other financial institution which co-ordinates a *syndicated loan* or the underwriting (➤**underwrite**) of ➤**securities**. The institutions share in the provision of funds for a syndicated loan, but the lead manager does much of the work and receives a larger fee than the others. Once completed, syndicated loans or ➤**new issues** are announced for the record in the press. The advertisement is called a *tombstone*. ➤**syndicate**.

lead time The length of time from receiving an order to the delivery of the finished product. In some industries (e.g. the aircraft industry) this may be many years. In other industries this may be much shorter and can be an area in which firms compete.

learned helplessness model ➤**attribution theory**.

learning The process of acquiring experience, information and knowledge that comes to be lodged in long-term memory, and which might then be used to assist in decision-making. The experiences, information and knowledge might relate to ➤**attitudes** and behaviour, ➤**values** and beliefs, preferences, skills and ➤**know-how**. The psychological concept of learning has been applied widely in ➤**marketing**, ➤**consumer behaviour** and ➤**human resource management**. For example, a study might consider how consumers come to know about a ➤**brand** and its attributes, or how they come to know about the process of buying goods on the ➤**internet**. Armed with these insights, marketing and communications campaigns can be planned to exploit the way people learn.

Theories of learning fall into two categories: (a) 'behavioural learning theories', and (b) 'cognitive learning theories'. Behavioural learning by individuals refers to cases where people are exposed to a stimulus (external information) and they see a corresponding response (observed behaviour), such that they come to learn that the stimulus and response occur together (association). Within this category of learning theories there are two main types.

(1) Classical conditioning. A response elicited by one object will be elicited by a
    second object if both objects frequently occur together.
(2) Instrumental (operant) conditioning. A response that is given reinforcement is
    more likely to be repeated when the same situation arises again in the future.
Cognitive learning relates to 'thought-based' processes, where the person is engaged in gathering information, thinking about ideas and concepts and solving problems. This occurs in the realm of the mind, rather than through direct experience. Within this category of learning theories there are three main types:

(3) Reasoned learning. People use thought-processes to restructure existing infor-
    mation to form new associations, ideas and concepts.
(4) Vicarious learning. Behaviours are learned by watching the outcomes of other
    behaviours or by imagining the potential outcome of other behaviours.
(5) Iconic rote learning. Two or more concepts become associated without con-
    ditioning.
Roughly speaking, behavioural learning and iconic rote learning are linked to low-involvement learning situations, where people are not very engaged in the process, i.e. where people do not expend much mental effort. Reasoned cognitive learning theories, by contrast, are mostly linked to high-involvement learning situations,

where people are more engaged in the process, i.e. where people are consciously thinking about, and reflecting on, what they are doing. This means behavioural learning and iconic rote learning are likely to be most relevant when the decision is relatively unimportant, e.g. in buying ➤**packaged goods**. By contrast, reasoned cognitive learning will be more relevant when the decision is relatively important, e.g. the choice of where to live and work or the hiring of key personnel. It should be kept in mind that this is the way the theories tend to be used, but there are exceptions.

In practice, it is not always clear which process of learning is at work, nor whether the decision is important or not. ➤➤**involvement theory**. Part of the difficulty is that theories of learning are abstractions. For example, when brand choices are being made it is unlikely that a purely thought-based process would operate; while consumers may not have direct experience of buying the brand, they may have used it, know people who have bought it, bought/used brands like it, etc. Also, learning does not take place in a vacuum, devoid of the influence of others. This suggests a sixth form of learning:

(6) Social learning. How people come to deal with their environment and the situations they find themselves in. Thus, a single person may come across as extrovert *or* introvert, depending on the particular circumstances and who she is with.

While learning theories are expressed at the individual level, it is possible to envisage forms of group learning. Businesses, for instance, have the opportunity to learn from employee and organizational experiences through processes of ➤**organizational learning**. However, systems need to be in place to record and review these experiences, e.g. ➤**knowledge management systems** and ➤**learning organizations**. Otherwise, the learning may only reside in individuals and be lost when those individuals change job or change ➤**role**.

learning curve The process of gaining experience and knowledge over time, invariably partly due to learning from one's mistakes. Individuals and firms that have been operating in an industry for many years will have gained much insight and learned from others about how the industry operates. Successful firms move up the learning curve quickly, enabling them to compete with established firms.

learning organization A concept developed in the 1990s that argues that successful companies have an ability to acquire knowledge and skills and apply these effectively, in much the same way as human beings learn. The concept of the learning organization has received considerable attention in the management literature. The emphasis of much of the early literature on this subject has been on the past history of the organization and the strong influence of an organization's previous activities and learning on its future activities. That is, the future activities of an organization are strongly influenced by its previous activities and what it has learned.

Unfortunately, the term 'organizational learning' has been applied to so many different aspects of corporate management – from ➤**human resource management** to technology management strategies – that it has become a particularly vague concept. At its heart, however, is the simple notion that successful companies have an ability to acquire knowledge and skills and apply these effectively, in much the same way as human beings learn. Arguably, companies that have been successful over a long period have clearly demonstrated a capacity to learn. Cynics have argued that this is just another management fad with a new label for what successful organizations have been doing for many years. However, according to Chris Argyris (1977), organizations can be extremely bad at learning. Indeed, he suggests that it is possible for organizations to lose the benefits of experience and revert to old habits. It is necessary for organizations to engage in double-loop learning rather than single-loop learning, argues Argyris. For it is the second loop that reinforces understanding. At its most simple level, single-loop learning would be the adoption of a new set of rules, each to improve quality, productivity, etc. Double-loop learning occurs when those sets of rules are continually questioned, altered and updated in line with experience gained and the changing environment.

The accumulation of knowledge and the effective assimilation and application of this knowledge is what appears to distinguish innovative firms from their less successful counterparts. This capability is popularly referred to in the management literature as ➤**organizational learning**. However, it is the internal processes that lead to this ability that need to be the focus of management attention. One would expect that a review of the organizational innovation literature would help in revealing these activities. However, this body of literature tends to use a structural approach when exploring the ability of organizations to innovate. Hence, discussions are dominated by how organizational structures and management strategies affect an organization's ability to innovate. For example, Burns and Stalker supported the view that flexible organizational forms will sustain innovation but bureaucratic firms will not. Igor Ansoff suggests the need for forecasting and environmental analysis techniques at the strategic management level. Other writers have discussed the importance of key individuals in the process – in this case the business innovator. All of these writers emphasize the presence or absence of certain factors rather than describing the actual activities or processes that are required by them. Recent studies by Japanese scholars on the development of new products have shown that to develop ➤**competencies** companies have to uncover and understand their 'dynamic routines' which will invariably be built on ➤**tacit knowledge**. ➤➤**knowledge management system; market orientation**.

leaseback A contractual arrangement in which an asset is sold and immediately leased back (➤**leasing**) to the seller. It is a means of raising ➤**finance** from an institution such as an insurance company and then renting it back on a long lease.

leasing An agreement between the owner of a property (lessor) to grant use of it to another party (lessee) for a specified period at a specified rent. Leasing of business equipment, for example, may have tax advantages because the leasing company may receive tax relief on ➤**depreciation** or investment tax allowances (➤**corporation tax**) that it can pass on to the lessee. Leasing may in effect be a form of ➤**hire purchase**, because ownership of the ➤**asset** may be transferred to the lessee for a small sum at the end of the lease, and the distinction between the two becomes blurred. Leasing is also a form of ➤**off-balance-sheet finance**.

least squares regression A technique used in ➤**econometrics** for estimating the magnitude of a relationship between different variables. For example, an equation might take the form:

$$C_i = \alpha + \beta Y_i$$

where C_i and Y_i represent consumption and income for any given household, i. A dataset might consist of values of income and consumption for different households.

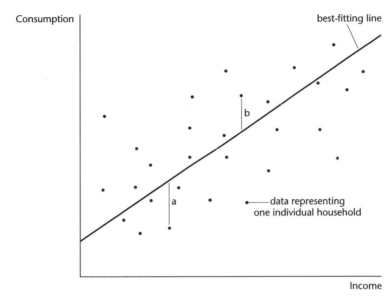

Least Squares Regression Line

Least squares regression can be used to estimate the size of α and β. Imagine values of C and Y existed for a hundred households. A graph could be created, with all hundred combinations plotted as dots. The goal is to 'fit' a line through the scatter of dots that best reflects the underlying relationship between C and Y.

Of course, any line you draw will involve a gap between itself and the actual observations (like a and b in the above figure). The least squares technique says the best-fitting line minimizes the total distance between individual observations and the line itself. It finds this by taking the squares of the gaps and setting a value for a and β that minimizes the sum of those squares. Relatively simple computer programs can perform this kind of regression.

legal person ➤incorporation.

legitimate power ➤power.

lemon problem ➤adverse selection.

lender of last resort An institution, normally a ➤central bank, that stands ready to lend to the commercial banking system when the latter is in overall shortage of funds. The latter position will arise when extra large payments out of the banking system, such as seasonal tax payments (e.g. periodic ➤corporation tax payments by companies) reduce the banking system's holdings below the level appropriate to its ➤reserves. The central bank will, in such cases, lend at short term to the banking system until such time as funds return through normal depositors. Lenders of last resort in the US and the UK are the ➤Federal Reserve System and the ➤Bank of England, respectively. The Federal Reserve normally lends through ➤repurchase

agreements. As part of its function as a regulator of ➤**credit** and money supply a central bank will, on occasion, induce a shortage in the commercial banking system so as to force the system to resort to it ('into the bank') and to require commercial banks to borrow from it at high rates of interest, so bringing about a general rise of interest rates and discouraging subsequent lending.

letter of credit A non-negotiable (➤**negotiable**) order from a bank to a bank abroad, authorizing payment to a named person of a particular sum of money or up to a limit of a certain sum. Letters of credit are often required by exporters who wish to have proof that they will be paid before they ship goods, or who wish to minimize delay in payment for the goods. A confirmed letter of credit is one that has been recognized by the paying bank. Letters of credit may be irrevocable or revocable, depending on whether or not they can be cancelled at any time.

leverage (US) ➤gearing.

leveraged buy-out (US) The acquisition of one company by another, financed mainly by bank loans and ➤**bonds**. ➤**Corporate raiders** in the US launched ➤take-overs using ➤**junk bonds** and bank loans on many occasions in the 1980s.

Levitt, Theodore A business academic and early proponent of the role of market-ing in corporate strategy and the prime importance of consumer orientation. His famous article, 'Marketing Myopia' (*Harvard Business Review*, 1960), distinguished between selling and marketing, which 'view(s) the entire business process as con-sisting of a tightly integrated effort to discover, create, arouse and satisfy customer needs.' Selling focuses on the need of the seller to shift a product or service; marketing focuses on the needs of the buyer, which alone will determine the survival of the selling corporation. He gave the example of the buggy-whip industry in the early days of the automobile: 'No amount of product improvement could stave off its death sentence. But had the industry defined itself as being in the transportation business rather than the buggy-whip business, it might have survived. It would have done what survival entails, that is, change.' Levitt went on to write several books on marketing and foresaw the growing strength of global ➤**brands** like Coca-Cola. He has been associated with Harvard Business School for 40 years and was editor of the *Harvard Business Review* in the second half of the 1980s. ➤**marketing concept**; **market orientation.**

lexicographic decision rule ➤decision rule.

liability **1.** An obligation to make a financial payment, namely repayment of a bank loan, redemption of *loan stock* ➤**stock**, payment of a ➤**commercial paper**, payment of a business invoice. It may be either direct or implicit, i.e. the implicit obligation of a bank to repay the ➤**deposits** held with it. The liabilities of a company include its ➤**bank loans** and ➤**overdraft**, its short-term ➤**debts** for goods and services received (*current liabilities*) and its loan capital and the ➤**capital** subscribed by shareholders. Antithesis of ➤**asset**. Most frequently used in ➤**money markets**, banking and business accounting. **2.** Of insurance, the insurance of the risk of claims in respect of misjudgement and incompetence to which employers and the professions (e.g. doctors and accountants) are exposed. The term also used to denote such exposure.

licensing An agreement between the owner of ➤**intellectual property** to lease to a third party the right to use their intellectual property in return for a royalty or fee. Commonly this is for the right to use a patent, whereby a manufacturer uses another firm's knowledge and technology during the manufacture of a product. For example, Coca-Cola licenses the right to manufacture and bottle its beverage products to drinks manufacturers all over the world. This enables Coca-Cola to concentrate on developing and building the brand and to leave manufacturing to local producers. Another common form of licence agreement is that in which an author assigns copyright of his work to a publisher in return for royalties from the sale of the book. Similarly, firms who own brands frequently license the right to use their brand to other firms in return for a royalty.

life assurance ➤insurance.

lifestyle segmentation The grouping of people by how they live. 'How they live' is defined in terms of people's activities and interests, likes and dislikes, ➤**attitudes** and ➤**values**, consumption and usage patterns and expectations about the future. Because of a correlation with lifestyle, account is usually taken of people's demographics (age, sex/gender, income, etc.). In ➤**marketing research**, measures of all these dimensions of how people live are used to form segments. ➤**segmentation**.

Many lifestyle segmentations are extremely general. The most famous of these is VALS – the Values and Lifestyles Program. This was launched in 1978 by SRI International and updated in 1989 as VALS 2. Respondents are asked to show their level of agreement or disagreement with forty-two lifestyle questions. This enables respondents to be classified along two dimensions: (a) 'self-orientation', and (b) 'resources'. Self-orientation is seen as comprising three types: (a) a person is principle-oriented (guided by beliefs); (b) status-oriented (influenced by the opinions of others), or (c) action-oriented (given to physical activity and risk-taking). The resources dimension runs from minimal resources (low income, little wealth, poor education, etc.) to abundant resources (high income, skilled, educated). Resources govern a person's ability to realize their dominant self-orientation (thus, a person may seek to be guided by strong beliefs but not have the wherewithal to meet this goal).

Using these two dimensions, eight generic lifestyle segments are derived: (a) 'believers' (principle-oriented with minimal resources); (b) 'the fulfilled' (principle-oriented with abundant resources); (c) 'strivers' (status-oriented with minimal resources); (d) 'achievers' (status-oriented with abundant resources); (e) 'makers' (action-oriented with minimal resources); (f) 'experiencers' (action-oriented with abundant resources); (g) at the base are 'strugglers' (they have extremely limited resources and are concerned with the basic need for safety and security) and (h) at the apex are 'actualizers' (they have very abundant resources and successfully take charge of their own and others' lives). In marketing, VALS segments (or variations of them) are used widely in thinking about product category choices, to assist in media selection and to suggest ideas for creative advertising copy. For example, 'believers' are claimed to do more gardening than the norm, are more likely to read *Reader's Digest* and respond to an advertisement that conveyed conventional family values.

Despite its popularity, VALS is criticized for being too general. It says, for instance, that believers do more gardening, but does not suggest how a specific ➤**brand** of gardening product might differentiate itself from another. Moreover, 'the fulfilled', 'achievers', 'makers', and 'actualizers' may all do more gardening than the norm – this is not, therefore, a very discriminating segmentation. For these reasons, it is often necessary to prepare very specific lifestyle segmentations. Questions are asked about activities and interests, likes and dislikes, attitudes and values, consumption and usage and expectations for the future with respect to a specific product category: gardening products, or pet foods, or air travel. This is more likely to uncover brand-specific issues and help in the development of ➤**line extensions** and brand repositioning. ➤**positioning**.

lifetime value The value of a customer over that customer's whole purchase history. The history is with respect to ➤**brand** purchases (e.g. a specific brand of paint) or purchases from a portfolio of products and services that an organization offers, e.g. a range of paints, fillers, glues, tools and after-care services. The aim is to determine who are the most profitable customers over the whole purchase history, and then perhaps offer value-added services, rewards or incentives to ensure these customers are retained. ➤**relationship marketing**.

Likert scale A verbal scale where respondents indicate the degree of agreement or disagreement with a number of statements about an object of interest, such as a ➤**brand**, service or organization. For each statement there will be a score, and these are summarized for each respondent across all statements. This summary measure can be used indirectly to infer a person's ➤**attitude**, particularly the cognitive component of an attitude. For instance, it might be argued that responses to the following statements capture a person's attitude to an airline: 'airline X is safe', 'airline X has friendly staff', 'airline X offers value for money'. For each of these three statements respondents are asked to say whether they 'strongly agree', 'agree', 'neither agree nor disagree', 'disagree' or 'strongly disagree'. If 'strongly agree', the response is given a score of 1, 'agree' 2, etc. then a summary score can be obtained for each respondent across all three statements. (Technically speaking, only statistics appropriate for ordinal data should be used with Likert scales; however, many analysts treat the data as interval. Researchers remain divided on this matter.) ➤**rating scales**.

limited company ➤incorporation.

limited liability The restriction of an owner's loss in a business to the amount of capital that he has invested in it. Should a company be put into ➤**liquidation**, the owner as ➤**equity** ➤**shareholder** can lose, at most, only the value of his shares, although director shareholders may be subjected to other liabilities such as personal guarantees for bank borrowing. ➤➤**incorporation**.

limit order ➤order.

linear programming A mathematical method of solving practical problems (e.g. the allocation of resources) by means of linear functions where the variables involved are subject to constraints.

linear relationship Any relationship between two variables that can be graphed as a straight line. For example, if $x = 2y$, then it would be straightforward to plot corresponding values of x and y on a graph, and the line joining them would be straight. If however, $x = y^2$, then the equivalent graph would be a curved line and known as non-linear.

line extensions The use of an established ➤brand name to introduce additional items in the existing product category. The items – lines – are variants of the established brand in the given product category, such as new features, flavours, colours, pack sizes or ingredients. The gains from having line extensions are incremental; the target audience might be expanded a little or existing customers might be offered somewhat more choice. This contrasts with ➤brand extensions where the gains, and risks, are usually much greater. ➤stock-keeping unit.

line of credit 1. An agreed amount of loan arranged between a bank and its customer, normally to be drawn down in stages. ➤overdraft. **2.** A loan from the ➤International Monetary Fund to a member country, the total amount of which is fixed, but normally available in stages.

liquid asset An asset which consists of cash or other asset such as ➤Treasury bills which can be quickly turned into cash.

liquidation The termination, dissolution or winding up of a limited company. ➤incorporation. Liquidation may be initiated by the shareholders or directors (voluntary liquidation) or by its creditors. If the company is solvent (➤bankruptcy) the ordinary shareholders will receive any surplus after the company's liabilities have been met.

liquidity 1. In general, availability of funds to meet claims. An economic agent is considered to have high liquidity, or to be highly liquid, if all its financial holdings, or ➤assets, are in cash, and to have low liquidity if its holdings are all in forms such as property, commodities and long-term securities, that are difficult to convert into exact amounts of ready cash. **2.** In banking, liquidity refers to a commercial bank's ability to meet withdrawals of deposits, and relates to the bank's holdings of cash and short-term assets. **3.** In ➤balance of payments contexts, liquidity relates to a country's ability to cover a shortfall on its overall external accounts, and refers essentially to that country's ➤reserves. International liquidity is the total of all national reserves. **4.** In monetary control terminology, liquidity denotes the total amount of money and very short-term financial assets in the economy. **5.** In ➤securities markets, liquidity refers to the quantity of tradable ➤instruments available. The greater the number of ➤stocks at issue, the more ➤market makers there are; the more widely held the stock, the greater the liquidity of the market in any given stock is likely to be. In a liquid market a trader can buy and sell stock without moving the price. Stocks on the ➤London Stock Exchange are classified into *liquid* and *less liquid* categories. ➤➤normal market size.

liquidity ratio 1. The proportion of the total assets of a bank that are held in the form of cash (➤cash ratio) and ➤liquid assets. There is no longer a mandatory liquidity or reserve asset ratio for UK banks, although all larger banks are required to deposit 0.5 per cent of eligible liabilities with the ➤Bank of England. ➤➤capital adequacy; Federal Reserve System. **2.** The ratio of liquid assets to the current ➤liabilities of a business. This is also called the 'cash ratio'.

liquid ratio ➤acid ratio.

LISREL ➤path analysis.

listed company A company with its shares listed on an official stock exchange. Thus, a *quoted* company.

listed security A ➤security that has been officially accepted for trading and ➤quotation on a recognized stock exchange. The term 'listing' comes from the published list issued by the stock exchange authorities and known in the UK as the *Stock Exchange Daily Official List.* ➤official list.

listing ➤listed security.

Lloyd's ➤insurance.

LLP ➤partnership.

LMX theory ➤leader-member exchange theory.

loading 1. Of insurance, that part of the premium that provides for administrative expenses, contingencies and profit. **2.** Of banking, an additional charge made to the customer's account to recover the cost of additional services or account-handling difficulties. **3.** Of unit trusts, the charge incorporated in prices and premiums to defray administrative expenses. **4.** Of loans, the charging of interest.

Loan Guarantee Scheme (LGS) ➤credit guarantee.

lock-out ➤collective action.

logical incrementalism An approach to strategic management that is based on learning from experience and making incremental changes. James B Quinn argued that managers do not develop strategies from conscious once-and-for-all decisions and/or a grand master plan, but rather are formulated step by step via an interactive process of experimentation, probing the future, learning from experience and then adding knowledge on to existing policies. It is because of the complexity of the business environment and modern management control processes that the supporters of logical incrementalism argue that it is not possible to develop future scenarios for all possible outcomes. Hence, in practice many managers adopt an incrementalist approach. ➤strategic management.

logistics The movement and storage of goods together with associated information flows from the beginning to the end of the supply chain. For a manufacturing firm, the supply chain extends from the procurement of raw materials and components through all production processes to the final distribution of finished goods to either end-users or retail ➤intermediaries. ➤channel of distribution.

logo A visual symbol of an organization or a ➤brand. This may be a badge on the bonnet of a motor vehicle, a stylized form of lettering, a coat of arms or some device, which in the mind of the public becomes precisely and unmistakably identified with a particular organization. The logo type is often produced in a distinctive colour. It will usually be registered as a ➤trade mark of the firm.

London interbank offered rate (LIBOR) (UK) The rate of interest offered on loans to first-class banks in the London ➤interbank market for a specified period (usually 3 or 6 months). Owing to the heavy volume of interbank dealing, the 3-month and 6-month rates have come to be widely used as a basis of reference for the setting of many other rates. It is closely related to ➤base rate but is closer to *prime rate* in US terms. The rate may apply to sterling or ➤Eurodollars.

London International Finance Futures Exchange (LIFFE) An exchange established in London in September 1982 for trading in ➤financial futures and ➤options. The decision to set up a London market followed the success of the financial futures market in Chicago and of that started in Sydney in 1979. Originally based on floor trading (➤floor broker), the LIFFE exchange is now screen based. It trades in index, currency and interest futures and, from 2001, in single equity stock futures.

London Stock Exchange (LSE) (UK) The London market in which ➤securities are bought and sold. Its correct name is the London Stock Exchange Ltd. Members are formed into a declining number of firms that, following the ➤Big Bang, now include major ➤investment banks, ➤clearing banks and other financial intermediaries, some of which are foreign owned. Business is now conducted by telephone through an automated screen trading system, and the ➤trading floor is no longer used. The ➤Stock Exchange Automated Quotation system (SEAQ) allows ➤market makers and others to see competing quotations on their screens, and ➤stockbrokers to select the best ➤bid price or ➤offer price for their clients. Member firms operate in ➤dual capacity. An ➤order driven electronic *Stock Exchange Trading System* (SETS) was introduced in 1997, initially for the Financial Times Stock Exchange 100 Index companies. ➤*Financial Times* share indices. SETS handles transactions of more than 1,000 shares (500 where worth more than £5 each); other share bargains continue on SEAQ. ➤➤alternative investment market; CREST; Financial Services Act; normal market size; offer for sale; stock exchange; stocks.

long-form report (UK) A detailed confidential report for the ➤sponsor (➤issuing house) of a company being prepared for ➤flotation by the reporting accountants. The long-form report is intended to satisfy the sponsors so that they can lend their names to the issue and identify matters that need to be rectified before going public. The report will provide the basis for the *short-form report* included in the ➤prospectus.

look-alike A ➤brand that appears to the consumer to be like another brand in the same product category. Some look-alikes are deliberate attempts to imitate a leading brand, and even the name and packaging ('get-up') may appear to be similar. The goal is for the look-alike to benefit from consumer confusion. Colloquially, these are termed 'copy-cats'. In many jurisdictions it is illegal to 'pass-off' products in this way, although to prove a case it is necessary to show that consumers would confuse the look-alike with the branded product (which is not always easy). A more common situation is that in which functionally similar brands come to look alike because they all take on the 'design norms' of the product category, e.g. most Cola is sold in red cans, including retail own brands and private labels. Colloquially, these are termed 'me-toos'. ➤visual equity.

loyalty ➤consumer loyalty; employee retention.

loyalty ladder ➤relationship marketing.

loyalty programme Schemes offering some type of delayed, accumulating economic benefit to consumers who buy the brand. Usually this is in the form of points that can be exchanged for gifts, free products or aspirational rewards such as air miles. The airline frequent-flier programmes have been a prototype for many of these schemes. Such schemes are distinct from ➤**affinity programmes**, where there is no direct economic benefit to the promoter. A hybrid format is that in which all customers receive the same offer, or even pay for club membership, in return for access to special events and offers. This format is prevalent in countries like Germany, where privacy and trading laws prohibit incentive-based schemes, e.g. Volkswagen Club, Swatch the Club, Mercedes Mastercard. ➤➤**customer relationship management**.

LSE ➤London Stock Exchange.

M

Machiavellianism A term used to describe the ruthless use of power, particularly coercive power, and manipulation to attain personal goals. The name comes from the Italian Renaissance writer and diplomat, Niccolo Machiavelli (1469–1527), who condoned questionable tactics for obtaining and holding on to political power. His most famous book *The Prince* (1513) suggests that whether a policy was brutal or treacherous in the pursuit of power was immaterial, unless this affected the success of the policy, which was more likely to occur if the policy was regarded as honourable and fair. Many textbooks discuss Machiavellianism as the pursuit of power by any means when, in fact, Machiavelli never advocated such an approach, but analysed its political uses objectively.

Machiavelli's views on the State, human nature and power were largely based on the assumption that greed and egoism are the primary human motivations. He believed successful government thrives on human weakness, control of the conflict that grows out of human self-interest, and the State's capacity to counteract the natural aggression of its citizens. Since the objective of the State was to preserve its reputation, property and assets, it could not survive without popular support. A ruler or ➤**leader(ship)** should therefore strive to be both loved and feared, but if one could not be both, it was better to be feared than loved. ➤**managerial grid**.

macroeconomics The study of whole economic systems, aggregating over the functioning of individual players within them. More specifically, it is usually the study of national economies and the determination of national income, ➤**economic growth**, the ➤**balance of payments**, and the ➤**exchange rate**. It is distinct from ➤**microeconomics**, which looks at understanding the decisions of individual agents. In classical macroeconomics lay a presumption of the efficiency and effectiveness of free markets, and all macroeconomic variables were seen as the sum of the variables as they applied to individual firms or consumers. Macroeconomic mechanisms were largely embedded in macroeconomics. Since the time of John Maynard Keynes, however, economists have allowed for ➤**disequilibrium** in macroeconomic variables and therefore the macroeconomy can almost follow a life of its own. For example, individual households may choose to save and we may understand the motivation of that saving with a microeconomic analysis, but if all households choose to save too much at the same time, the economy can dive into ➤**recession** – a topic for the macroeconomist.

For many businesses, macroeconomics has one dimension: forecasting the path the economy will follow, as that can be such an important factor in determining the right level of prices, output and investment. ➤**quantity theory of money**.

main market The market dealing in ➤**stocks** and shares on the ➤**official list** of the ➤**London Stock Exchange** and not including second-tier or ➤**unlisted securities market(s)**.

make-or-buy decision A decision by a firm to purchase products, components or services from a supplier rather than create them itself. Very often this is a difficult decision and involves cost and quality analyses. The purchasing function is usually responsible for determining whether the firm is better-served purchasing products and services or choosing to create them itself. Even if it appears to be economically sensible to buy-in products and services, there are strategic issues to consider such as: (a) will the firm become dependent on another firm, and (b) will it lose the skills necessary to produce the products and services in question? ➤➤**transaction cost**.

make-to-order A type of response to demand that is triggered only when the customer requests the product or service. The planning and control necessary for this type of operation will only begin on receipt of the request – this is also known as resource-to-order planning and control. ➤➤**demand forecasting**.

make-to-stock A type of response to demand that produces goods or services prior to any firm order from the customer. This is usually done because substantial economies of scale can be achieved by producing in bulk. For example, a cinema offers performances irrespective of the actual level of demand. This type of operation requires make-to-stock planning and control.

management accounting Business accounting practice concerned with the provision of information to management for control and decision-making purposes, as opposed to ➤**financial accounting**. Management accounting techniques have developed considerably since the nineteenth century, when firms had few locations and products. Modern multinational enterprises may have hundreds of *profit centres* in which managers have operational discretion and are evaluated on the basis of their financial results. Not only are financial accounts produced for these centres, but measures such as ➤**return on investment** are used for the purpose of allocating capital between them. These large enterprises may have thousands of *cost centres* which are established where output and related inputs can be measured. In *cost accounting* for these centres, costs are related to outputs for the purposes of pricing, departmental budgeting and the control of production methods, material and labour usage. Some costs vary with output (e.g. material or labour costs) while others (e.g. overheads) do not. Overheads may be allocated to outputs using the measures of *standard costing* or *absorption costing*, where unit overheads are costed at levels which will cover total overhead costs at budgeted output by means of percentage rates such as percentages of direct labour cost. In *activity-based costing* more sophisticated methods are used to allocate overheads in a way that reflects cost-drivers. For example, the cost of the after-sales service overhead is allocated to products according to the number of guarantee claims received or the number of sales engineer-related visits in connection with the product in question. Management accounting may be concerned simply with the production of management accounts prepared on a more frequent basis (e.g. quarterly) than financial accounts, and show gross profits for profit centres, i.e. their contribution to overheads and the overall financial result for the enterprise after overheads. Or management accounts may be very similar to the audited financial results, with adjustments for ➤**depreciation**, ➤**work-in-progress**,

➤**foreign exchange** gains and losses, etc. With modern information technology and full data capture throughout the organization it should be possible to produce management accounts at shorter and shorter intervals – indeed, one large IT company claims to produce them on a daily basis!

management buy-in (MBI) The purchase of a business by one or more outside managers with the help of a group of financial backers. It is an offshoot of the management buy-out industry. The term was applied indiscriminately in the late 1980s to any bid involving a well-known city figure, on the grounds that a buy-in sounded more constructive than the ➤**hostile take-overs** they usually were. Buy-ins are now seen as being considerably riskier than buy-outs, because they involve an outside management team which does not know the company as well. Many deals are neither pure buy-ins nor buy-outs, but are a combination of the two. A buy-in management buy-out combines interests of both existing and new outside management.

management buy-out (MBO) When managers of a business buy the necessary number of shares (share ➤**capital**) to gain control of it. Usually this occurs when a business is struggling and the owners are considering selling or closing the business. The managers of that firm may believe that they would like the opportunity to own and run the business, and that given the necessary incentive of access to the profits of the firm, they would be able to operate a viable business. Competitive pressures upon large companies since the 1980s have led to the disposal of many weak or peripheral subsidiaries in this way. The management are usually assisted by loans from a venture capital (➤**risk capital**) or other financial organization, and both may expect to seek public ➤**flotation** in due course. Also, this type of purchase of a business occurred in the UK when the government decided to sell State-owned industries to the private sector. ➤**privatization**. For example, there are several examples of managers of local bus companies buying and running the privatized bus business.

management by objective (MBO) A method of co-ordinating and motivating a firm's workforce by dividing the organization's goals into specific objectives for each section, department and individual. Managers and subordinates jointly agree targets, for an explicit time period, and then monitor progress towards their attainment, with feedback as the programme unfolds. For individuals it can provide a means for discussing their role in the organization and can be linked to reward systems. Managers will often review the performance of an individual in light of their progress towards the agreed objectives. At the highest level there will be organizational objectives, e.g. to achieve an annual 10 per cent growth. This is then broken down into targets and objectives for each section and department. It is often used as a way of delegating authority from the highest level in the organization to all other levels.

Two of the strengths are that managers are forced to state the organization's aims and discuss these with subordinates. Whereas critics argue that it is a very time-consuming process to agree targets with divisions, departments and employees and the agreed targets are quickly out of date.

A useful technique for evaluating business objectives is the so-called SMART method. Which is a useful acronym for five questions concerning the objectives. Are the objectives:

(1) Specific. Are they as clear and specific as possible?
(2) Measurable. How will you know that the objective has been reached?
(3) Achievable. Is the objective do-able?
(4) Relevant. Do you really want to do this?
(5) Time-based. What are the milestones and when will they be reached?

management consultant An individual or firm who/that specializes in offering management advice to organizations. Typically, on making more effective use of resources employed, organization of activities and the implementation of new technology. During the 1980s and 1990s this was an area of rapid and enormous growth. Many large firms regularly employ the services of management consultancy firms for specific projects and to undertake major internal reorganizations on their behalf.

management guru A well-known writer, adviser and preacher on management theory and practice, usually challenging accepted wisdom. Gurus can help to advance and change thinking, but more recently some have been criticized for selectively over-emphasizing simple notions about business and for leading fashions and fads in management practice that are ultimately unhelpful and even destructive. Probably the first was Frederick W ➤**Taylor**, but some contemporary gurus have derived management insights from much earlier writers such as Clausewitz (*On War*, posthumous 1833) and Machiavelli (*The Prince*, 1513) and from nineteenth-century commentators, e.g. Samuel Smiles (*Self-Help*, 1859). Many are academics in business schools; only a few are academics in other disciplines, e.g. economists who think that on the whole, management science is even less of a science than their own subject. Some gurus are, or were, chairmen or chief executive officers of businesses, e.g. Lee Iacocca of Chrysler, Jack Welch of General Electric and Andy Grove of Intel ('only the paranoid survive'). Businessmen achieve guru status through a combination of pithy sayings and the evident success of their company, though success alone is not a qualification. Many successful business leaders are not management gurus, e.g. Bill Gates of Microsoft who is, none the less, an information technology guru. Business managers love to read about management. Global stardom as a management guru is a phenomenon of the last 25 years or so and some (e.g. Tom ➤**Peters**, Michael ➤**Hammer** and Michael ➤**Porter**) command very large speaking engagement fees and their books have achieved bestseller status.

management information systems (MIS) The integration of computer hardware and software applications for collecting, manipulating and presenting information so that it can be used in the management of organizations. Such systems can be vast, indeed, if they attempt to manage all the information coming into and leaving the organization. They have been critically important for the effective use of ➤**enterprise resource planning systems**, ➤**decision-support systems**, ➤**expert systems**, ➤**electronic data interchanges**, ➤**database marketing** and ➤**customer relationship management** systems. However, critics point out that significant sums of money have been wasted by firms over the past 10 years on MISs that have failed to meet expectations. All MISs must be judged against the revenues they generate and not their cost. If the cost of generating the information is used as the basis of evaluation, then a strategic misallocation of information resources is likely to result. The usefulness of the information is the paramount factor to take into account.

management support systems (MSS) A set of tools that a manager can call upon to assist in making better decisions. These tools might help the manager to analyse a situation, diagnose problems and suggest solutions. The tools are often seen as providing answers ('the optimal number of units to produce is X'); however, this can be misleading. The real benefit of MSS is to help managers think about their problems in a structured way, to force them to make their assumptions explicit, to quantify their beliefs, to consider the context in which decisions are made, and to stimulate new thoughts and new solutions. Traditionally, this has been achieved using data-driven MSS. Data-driven systems make use of existing databases to help explore relationships between variables. ➤response models. Having done this, the models can be used to assist managers in making decisions. ➤decision support systems. However, recently greater attention has been paid to knowledge-driven systems. Drawing from cognitive science and artificial intelligence, knowledge-driven systems focus on learning, with a view to helping managers learn and adapt. ➤expert systems.

managerial grid A view of leadership styles based on behavioural theories, i.e. based on the behaviours that specific leaders have shown. There are two dimensions (each with a number of different levels): (a) 'concern for people', and (b) 'concern for production'. Different types of style can be located on the resulting grid. The grid comprises a 9 × 9 matrix, giving eighty-one different leadership styles, e.g. 'country club management', 'team management', 'organizational management', 'impoverished management' and 'authority–obedience management'. Developed by R R Blake and J C Mouton (*The Managerial Grid*, 1964), the managerial grid has been used descriptively, but cannot be relied upon as a predictive tool. ➤leadership.

mandate A written document authorizing a named person to write cheques on a bank account or to receive dividends, as in *bank mandate*, *dividend mandate*.

manufacturing resource planning (MRP II) An integrated system for planning and monitoring all the resources of a manufacturing company. The objective is to link the production, engineering, marketing and finance functions to optimize the efficiency and profitability of the firm. Essentially, MRP II is a large single database and links sales figures with the firm's operations and finance rather than having three or four separate databases. The objective is to provide consistent and reliable information for everyone in the firm. For example, engineering should be able to modify designs to products that will automatically be noted and recorded for all to see (without the need for all functions to change and update their records). It relies on the accurate input of information by all who use it. ➤management information systems. It was developed by Oliver Wight in the early 1980s. It has since been used by many manufacturing organizations all over the world. ➤Enterprise resource planning systems extend the concept of linking operational functions further by linking all functions and operations of the firm.

margin 1. Generally in finance, the *gross margin* is the difference between the price at which something is bought and the price at which it is sold; thus, the contribution towards ➤overheads and other costs. **2.** In banking, the difference between the interest rate paid to depositors or for funds on the ➤money market and the rate charged to borrowers. **3.** A deposit as partial surety that a ➤contract will be fulfilled, as in ➤commodity markets and ➤financial futures markets. Expressed as a percentage of the price paid (or sold), the *margin requirement* may necessitate further payments by the client if prices move against them. **4.** (US) The proportion of the price of a ➤security paid when giving an ➤order to a ➤broker, the rest being on ➤credit.

marginal analysis The study of ➤variables in terms of the effects that would occur if they were changed by a small amount. For example, rather than analyse whether or not it is in the interest of an individual to spend money on food at all, attention can sensibly be focused on whether or not welfare could be enhanced by spending slightly more or less on food. Nothing better demonstrates the concept than the so-called *paradox of value*: although water is more necessary to man than diamonds, it has a much lower price – this is because man usually has so much of it that extra water is worthless. This is not true of diamonds.

The marginal value of a variable is equivalent to its rate of change: marginal cost is equal to the change in total cost as output increases; or for those who prefer to see things expressed in the mathematics of calculus, marginal cost is the first derivative of the ➤cost function. For those who prefer to visualize things graphically, marginal cost is the gradient of a curve depicting the relationship between total cost and total output.

The margin is important in economics as it is the impact of small changes in variables, rather than their level *per se*, that determines whether rational economic agents change them. For business, marginal analysis is important as decisions on price and the level of a firm's output can be shown to be appropriately determined by the level of ➤marginal cost and ➤marginal revenue.

It is worth understanding the key relationship between ➤average costs and marginal costs. If average costs fall as the level of output rises (➤economies of scale), then marginal cost will be below average cost. If average costs rise as output rises, then marginal cost will be greater than average cost.

marginal cost The increase in the total costs of a firm caused by increasing its output by one extra unit. If all costs are fixed, the marginal cost of the first unit of output will be very high, but all subsequent units can be made for next to nothing. Economists normally assume firms to be producing at a point at which marginal costs are positive and rising. ➤marginal analysis.

marginal-cost pricing The setting of the price of an item equal to the cost of producing one extra unit of the item. There are good reasons to believe that marginal-cost pricing sends efficient price signals to consumers. That is because ➤marginal cost represents the ➤opportunity cost, or the total sacrifice to society from producing an item. The price represents the cost to consumers of buying it, and if price is equal to marginal cost, then consumers will buy an item if and only if they value it at least as much as the extra cost of producing it. If price is below marginal cost, consumers will be happy to buy an item even if they perhaps value it less than the amount it cost to produce it. If, on the other hand, price is greater than marginal cost, some consumers who value the item more than it costs to make will still be deterred from buying it.

There are, however, factors which undermine the case for marginal-cost pricing. Primarily, any company enjoying ➤economies of scale will have average costs in excess of marginal costs (➤marginal analysis), and with marginal-cost pricing, average costs will exceed price. A company in such a position will therefore make a loss. Only if production is at a point at which marginal and average costs are equal will marginal-cost pricing be sustainable.

Marginal-cost pricing provides a major advantage of ➤**perfect competition** over ➤**monopoly** or ➤**monopolistic competition**, because in more competitive industries, prices tend to be driven towards marginal cost. Attempts to impose it on firms outside competitive markets – especially nationalized industries – have been made, with limited success. ➤➤**inverse elasticity rule**.

marginal efficiency of capital ➤marginal efficiency of investment.

marginal efficiency of investment The rate of interest at which an investment project just breaks even, i.e. in ➤**capital budgeting**, the discount rate at which the ➤**net present value** of the project just equals 0. It is equivalent to the internal rate of return. ➤**discounted cash flow**.

marginal physical product ➤marginal product.

marginal product The extra output created by the employment of one additional unit of an input to production. It might, for example, be the extra number of widgets produced by employing one extra worker in a widget factory. In general, it is believed that the marginal product of a particular input rises when the factor is employed in small quantities, but eventually falls as the amount of the input employed increases. Marginal product is measured in the physical units of the output produced and it is thus sometimes called 'marginal physical product'. ➤➤**diminishing returns**.

marginal profit The extra profit earned by a company for each extra unit of output produced.

marginal propensity to consume (MPC) The extra spending on consumption that consumers engage in, for one extra unit of income. If a person spends 80 pence of an extra pound of income and saves 20 pence, their marginal propensity to consume is 0.8, and their marginal propensity to save is 0.2. It is an important variable in economic management. For example, if a government cuts taxes, it will be interested in whether the extra disposable income put into consumers' pockets will be spent or saved. In principle, however, the MPC should really depend on whether consumers believe any extra income is permanent or just temporary.

marginal propensity to save ➤marginal propensity to consume.

marginal rate of substitution (MRS) The rate at which a consumer needs to substitute one commodity for another in order to maintain constant total utility from the commodities taken together. If a consumer values two boxes of Daz equally to one of Persil, the marginal rate of substitution between them is 2, because if one box of Persil were taken away from the consumer, two boxes of Daz would have to be provided to compensate. The marginal rate of substitution between commodity A and B usually diminishes as consumption of commodity A increases. If at consumption of twenty apples and twenty bananas the consumer is indifferent between one or other, at consumption of thirty apples and ten bananas he is likely to start demanding more than a mere one apple before giving up a scarce banana. In ➤**indifference curve** analysis, the MRS is the slope of an indifference curve.

marginal revenue The increase in the total revenue received by a firm from the sale of one extra unit of its output. For a small firm which cannot influence the market price of its output (➤➤**perfect competition**), the extra revenue gained from an extra sale is simply equal to the price of the sale. For a firm with a large share of

211

the total market,however, marginal revenue is more complicated. If a large firm sells more, it will be likely to drive down the market price slightly, so that the true revenue gain from the extra sale equals the cash gained on the new sale minus the loss that occurs on all the sales that would otherwise have been made at the previously higher price.

marginal revenue product (MRP) The revenue gained by a firm when it sells the output generated by the employment of one additional unit of an input to production, e.g. it is the extra revenue a widget company makes by employing one more worker in its factory. In this case, the MRP is influenced by three factors: (a) the number of extra widgets produced by the worker (➤**marginal product**); (b) the sale price of the extra physical output, and (c) the rate at which the price of widgets falls as extra widgets are put on to the market. To calculate it, ➤**marginal product** must be multiplied by ➤**marginal revenue**.

marginal tax rate The rate of tax paid on extra units of income. An individual may pay no tax on the first £1,000 of income, and 50 per cent tax on all pounds earned thereafter. Those individuals earning more than £1,000 will thus face a marginal tax rate of 50 per cent, even though their overall tax rate will be less than 50 per cent, e.g. someone earning £1,001, will only pay 50 pence of tax – a tiny proportion of his total income. The marginal tax rates facing economic agents are often considered important in determining how far taxation impinges on incentives to work, invest, save or spend money.

marginal utility The extra satisfaction a consumer enjoys from consuming one extra unit of a particular item. While economists have, on occasion, found it useful to talk of marginal utility – and, in particular, have speculated that the more one consumes of an item the less utility one gains from it (the tenth Mars bar is always less pleasurable than the first, a phenomenon known as *diminishing marginal utility*) – its practical usefulness as a concept is decidedly limited as utility is not measurable.

marginal utility, diminishing ➤marginal utility.

market capitalization The total value at market prices of the ➤**securities** at issue for a company or a stock market or sector of the stock market. Calculated by multiplying the number of shares issued by the market price per share.

market definition The way a market, comprising buyers and sellers who are engaged in exchange, is defined. Market definition is simple where the market occupies a physical location – a market square or a commodity exchange. However, most are markets in name only, and questions of definition arise (even more so with the growth of virtual on-line markets). A common assertion is that markets must be defined by consumers (buyers) – it is how they see markets and the language they use to describe them that matters. If consumers describe Mars bars as a snack food then that is the market Mars bars are in, not the confectionery market. Its competitors will be snack foods, only some of which will be confectionery brands.

But markets are also defined by producers (sellers). It is the producer who delimits the market, and says which ➤**brands** are direct competitors and which are not. Thus, manufacturers may see themselves in the confectionery market, which might have a number of submarkets (chocolate-coated confectionery, assortments, etc.).

On this basis, ➤**marketing research** agencies are commissioned to gather information about the purchasing of brands in these markets and submarkets. Over time, the producer's definition becomes ingrained – the agency always reports the data that way, the marketing plan relies on this definition (especially where ➤**market share** is a key performance indicator), and direct competitors also come to see the market in a similar way (a shared language develops).

It is possible for the consumer and producer views to be quite distinct – Mars bars seen as a snack versus confectionery. To reconcile the two it is necessary to look at patterns of buying – to see which other brands are being bought and whether these are seen as competitive ➤**substitutes**. In frequent-purchase markets, this is reasonably easy to do because consumers typically buy a repertoire of brands and therefore it is possible to observe which other brands are bought. ➤➤**cross-price elasticity of demand**.

Some of the same difficulties exist with the definition of submarkets. A consumer view would see submarkets being developed to meet the needs of particular segments, e.g. within the toothpaste market a 'sensitive teeth' submarket might be defined in response to the desire by some consumers for toothpaste that is suitable for sensitive teeth. But submarkets – like markets – are often created by producers to meet their own goals (which are not necessarily coincident with those of consumers). In an established and mature market such as toothpaste, producers may invent submarkets to create 'news' – simply to enliven the market and have something new to say to consumers. At various times over the past 50 years, toothpaste producers have emphasized the cosmetic and therapeutic aspects of their toothpastes; introduced mint and spearmint flavours; added fluoride, baking soda and whitening agents; emphasized tartar control, protection against tooth decay and gum disease; stressed the merits of powders, pastes, gels, tubes and pump pack, as well as introducing flosses and prebrushing dental rinses. Each wave of activity has created new submarkets – at least in the eyes of producers. Certainly there is more choice for the mass of consumers, but whether there are distinct consumer segments whose needs are being met by this array of products is more questionable. ➤**segmentation**.

market-driven organization This is an organization that has the pursuit of customer value at the heart of its business strategy. This strategy would be supported by a ➤**market orientation**.

market failure A situation arising from the self-interested behaviour of individuals in the economy – unimpeded by government regulation or other action – in which economic efficiency does not prevail. Market failures provide a ubiquitous argument for intervention of some form or other. But they have two main sources.

(1) They derive from the fact that many transactions which would need to occur for the sake of economic efficiency simply do not occur. This may be on account of frictions in the system, such as the cost of transacting business (➤**transactions costs**) or the costs of setting a price at the efficient level. Or there may be a deficiency of information to the parties involved, or perhaps asymmetric information between participants in the market (with the corresponding problems of ➤**adverse selection**, ➤**moral hazard** and ➤**agency costs**). Or, there may be *strategic behaviour* by the individuals involved, who fail to engage in a trade, in the hope that they might extract a better deal from their adversary if they 'play it tough'. A large number of 'missing trades' are those involving the many

resources over which no properly defined property rights exist (such as clean air) and thus over which no trade can occur. ➤➤**intellectual property**. Similarly, there are ➤**externalities**, which are costs or benefits associated with someone's behaviour, for which no corresponding price or charge is levied.

(2) There are sometimes collective interests that are unable to be served by self-interested, individual behaviour. There are goods or services that have to be consumed collectively (public goods like defence); there are so-called *free rider problems* in which, for example, citizens hope to avoid paying for a service on the ground that someone else will pay (why should I give to charity if others will do so for me?); there can be ➤**prisoners' dilemma**-type situations, in which selfish behaviour leads to sub-optimal outcomes. There can be industries subject to ➤**increasing returns to scale**, in which ➤**monopoly** is inevitable, which carries large efficiency costs unless there is a collective effort to regulate.

marketing ➤marketing concept.

marketing communication ➤advertising; integrated marketing communication; promotion.

marketing concept The process of planning and executing the conception, pricing, promotion and distribution of ideas, goods and services to create exchanges that satisfy individual and organizational goals. This definition, based on that provided by the ➤**American Marketing Association** (AMA), highlights the importance of 'exchange'. The discipline of marketing has this in common with economics. However, exchange is not the endpoint – it is undertaken to satisfy individual and organizational goals. This requires a thorough understanding of consumers and customers, their goals, needs, wants, motives, habits, thoughts and feelings, etc. In addition to drawing upon economic theory, marketers seeking to learn more about consumers draw from theories in psychology and sociology. ➤**consumer behaviour**. The AMA definition also highlights the process of planning and executing the conception, pricing, promotion and distribution of ideas, goods and services. Here, the emphasis is on business functions and management processes. ➤**competencies**. In order to bring about meaningful exchange, marketers spend time developing new products and services, thinking about price levels, deciding how to promote, publicize and distribute products and considering ways to ensure customers are satisfied. This is rather inadequately described as the ➤**marketing mix** of ➤**4Ps** – 'product', 'price', 'place' and 'promotion'. Management theory is used in understanding these aspects of marketing, as well as knowledge of specific functional areas (➤**brand management**, design, ➤**advertising**, ➤**media buying**, supply chain management, sales, retailing, distribution, international trade, customer relations). ➤**marketing planning**.

The AMA definition highlights the importance of exchange, consumers and competencies. However, a further dimension must be recognized. Exchange takes place in markets, therefore marketers have a keen awareness of the markets in which they operate. Typically, these markets are competitive and a great deal of brand management activity is devoted to building share in a competitive market. ➤**market share**. For example, in many markets advertising and publicity are mainly intended to maintain or build a brand's share, not stimulate sales of a product category. By contrast, in a ➤**monopoly** the goal may be to grow the product category – the question of market share does not arise. It should be noted that many of the principles continue to apply in monopolies (e.g. the need to understand customers), although there may be less incentive to implement the marketing concept, e.g. dissatisfied customers will have no alternative source of supply.

An understanding of exchange, markets, consumers and competencies requires information. Managerial experience is one important source of information, and there may be other informal sources, e.g. feedback from the salesforce. Implicit in the marketing concept, however, is the need to gather formal and systematic information as well. In other words, for the manager not to rely on a 'sample of one' (herself), but to use formal and systematic market research in making plans and decisions. ➤**marketing research**. The collection, analysis and use of such information is facilitated by a variety of tools and techniques, ranging from surveys, through experimental methods, to ➤**depth interviews**. Increasingly, attempts are being made to harness both managerial experience and formal sources of information, e.g. in the use of decision-support tools and expert systems. ➤**marketing engineering**.

In summary, the marketing concept describes a management function and business philosophy. It emphasizes exchange, markets, consumers and competencies, and all this is underpinned by formal and informal sources of information. Because of the breadth of marketing, the skill-set of successful marketers tends to be wide, operating at both conceptual and practical levels and thinking creatively but also having good analytical skills. Equipped with these skills, marketers have applied the marketing concept in product markets, services markets, and not-for-profit markets (including charities and government services), and they have done so at local and international levels. ➤➤**services marketing**.

In general terms, articulation of the marketing concept extends back to the later nineteenth and the early years of the twentieth centuries. Wharton Business School appointed the first Professor of Marketing in the 1880s and by this time European and North American trade schools were teaching some key aspects of marketing (sales, retailing, purchasing, etc.). Melvin T Copeland ('Relation of Consumers' Buying Habits to Marketing Methods', *Harvard Business Review*, 1923) wrote a notable synthesis of early thinking, although his was by no means the first. However, the spirit behind the concept is evident in the writings of such classical authors as Adam Smith, and the practice of marketing is as old as the process of exchange.

Many of the essential features of modern marketing are seen in the writings of Peter ➤**Drucker** (*The Practice of Management*, 1954). He took a managerial perspective, describing marketing as a core business function. This idea became embodied in the teaching and practice of marketing through two very influential textbooks: E Jerome McCarthy (*Basic Marketing: a management perspective*, 1960) and Philip ➤**Kotler** (*Marketing Management: analysis, planning, implementation and control*, 1967). Both brought a sense of order to what seemed to be a very diffuse area of management. Also during the 1960s, the marketing concept was popularized by Theodore ➤**Levitt** ('Marketing Myopia', *Harvard Business Review*, 1960). He drew a clear distinction between a sales mentality and a marketing mentality, arguing that marketing is a philosophy of business and not simply a business function.

The contributions of these authors continue to be widely recognized, but a number of different perspectives have emerged recently. One view is to see marketing as a ➤**market orientation** – a sense of direction that considers customers, competitors and competencies, that makes full use of information sources and has measurable and demonstrable benefits for the organization. The latter feature is important because it sets out to show that companies which adopt the marketing concept have superior business performance (the ➤**profit impact of marketing strategy** project was an earlier attempt to do this, too). Another viewpoint is that of ➤**relationship marketing**. This defines the marketing concept in terms of the establishment, maintenance and enhancement of relationships with customers and other partners to meet each party's goals. It is a process of 'mutual exchange'. Not 'them and us' (customers and marketers), but 'we' (interacting parties). The relationship viewpoint has grown in significance over the past decade, although it traces its roots to the Copenhagen School of economists in the 1930s.

marketing engineering An approach to marketing decision-making based on formal modelling, optimization and simulation. The goal is to provide decision-support and improve outcomes in all functional areas of marketing management (product strategy, product design, price-setting, advertising budgeting, copy testing, media selection and scheduling, sales promotion, salesforce management, etc.). Typically, a response model is specified and estimated, whereby outcomes (e.g. sales to final consumers) are seen as a function of marketing inputs (e.g. advertisement spend in specified media) as in ➤**econometrics**. The approach employs mathematical and statistical tools and techniques (including ➤**regression analysis**, causal modelling, and optimization algorithms), but also draws heavily on ➤**consumer behaviour** theory, management science, and economic theory, e.g. in its conceptualization of utility, risk, uncertainty and ➤**equilibrium** conditions. The adoption of marketing engineering has been spurred-on by the widespread availability of high-performance computers, by increasing amounts of quantitative data, and by the analytical literacy of professionally trained managers. Despite these developments, the approach should be seen as a *support* for managers, not a substitute – experience and judgement remain important in making any managerial decision. ➤**decision-support system**.

marketing metrics The measurement of the effects of marketing activities. Measurements are made at three levels.
(1) Metrics for gauging the effectiveness of specific programmes and activities, such as the effectiveness of a media advertising campaign, or a loyalty scheme, or a continuous promotion, or a direct mailing. Formal mathematical modelling of effectiveness can be traced back 40 years to early articles in the *Journal of Marketing Research* and monographs published in the 1960s and 1970s. Also influential have been the various effectiveness awards and associated books, notably the Institute of Practitioners in Advertising awards in the UK and the EFFIES in the US.
(2) Product and service level metrics that are concerned with brand health and customer satisfaction, including brand audits, ➤**brand equity**, and customer-focused measures (➤**brand**). Using ➤**consumer panel** data, brand audits have been possible in packaged goods markets for over 40 years. Recently, interest in metrics at this level has been stimulated by brand equity studies – especially where attempts have been made to put brands on the balance sheet.
(3) Metrics that relate general investments in marketing and marketing-related activities to overall measures of company or ➤**SBU** performance. For example,

➤**market orientation** studies, assessment of ➤**innovation** activity, evaluation of the relationship between marketing, ➤**entrepreneurship**, ➤**organizational learning** and business performance.

Over the past decade there has been renewed interest in marketing metrics. Three sets of drivers can be distinguished.

(1) Marketing-specific reasons, such as to assist in the process of resource allocation, e.g. whether to invest scarce marketing resources in traditional media advertising or web-based communications. Also, to help organizations learn and understand more about their own business (to know which controllable elements of the business are responsible for financial outcomes), their own customers (to know who are the most profitable customers), and their own markets (to appreciate who are the key competitors). This sees marketing as a research-driven activity, based around the marshalling of information (akin to ➤**knowledge management systems**).

(2) General business reasons, mainly to do with making marketing more accountable. Marketing is seen as generating a stream of revenue (sales), and therefore it should be possible to pay for marketing activities by results. Underlying motives here may be to control costs and achieve efficiency savings, as distinct from improving effectiveness – this is of concern to many managers.

(3) ➤**Politicking** and posturing are also important drivers. Metrics can be used to support a special plea (that one form of marketing activity (e.g. advertising) is more deserving of additional resource than another); they can be used to impress other managers (to gain their respect at the boardroom table), and they can be part of a process of 'making the numbers' within the context of a procedurally-based marketing planning exercise, i.e. metrics are presented merely for the sake of appearances.

A range of challenges face those using marketing metrics. The basic decision of which ➤**key performance measures** (KPMs) to use is a matter of contention. Consensus seems unlikely because of differing levels of analysis and the different purposes for which metrics are used (we would not expect a marketing manager and a main board director to need exactly the same information, ➤**marketing performance measures**). Although, in practice, the range of KPMs is quite limited. At a brand level, the list includes volume/value market share, brand awareness, relative price, customer complaints and customer satisfaction. Wherever possible, measures should be related to a benchmark or norm, or expressed relative to a competing alternative. In addition, there is a question over whether KPMs should be grouped into composite measures or kept as sets of measures – managers tend to work with sets of measures, e.g. share of category requirements, duplicate buying, repeat-buying – all these relate to customer loyalty/retention, but they are not grouped into a composite measure.

Some academics, by contrast, argue for multi-item constructs, drawing on psychometric theory that would suggest they are more valid and reliable. Measurement error will be associated with any metric used in business, e.g. typically we are reliant on perceptions, impressions, recollections and estimates, not precise measurements.

Any formal modelling of the relationship between marketing activities or inputs and KPMs raises standard econometric and forecasting issues (the effects of omitted variables and seasonality, interactions between the variables at only one time, and the deterioration of the signal–noise ratio as the time horizon is increased). Apart from measurement issues, there are also challenges for those charged with the implementation of marketing metrics systems: how to hire staff with the required analytical skills; securing the agreement of different divisions to share information; changing business practices to focus on effectiveness, accountability and efficiency. These changes are not without their dangers, in that an over-reliance on metrics can lead to 'analysis paralysis', unintended changes in behaviour ('what isn't measured doesn't get done'), and a tendency to ignore or sideline important factors that are not easily measured, e.g. creativity, inspiration, emotions and politicking.

marketing mix The components of marketing. Conventionally described as the ➤4Ps – 'product', 'price', 'place' and 'promotion'. 'Product' refers to brands, packaging, product attributes, new product development and performance characteristics. 'Price' not only relates to the final selling price, but also the setting of trade prices, and agreement of trade margins and credit terms. 'Place' is related to distribution and is concerned with ways of getting goods to market (some of which are not particularly bound by place, e.g. web-based delivery). Finally, 'promotion' concerns the best way to communicate or publicize the product. Several variants on the 4Ps have been proposed, notably the 7Ps of services (i.e. to the standard 4Ps are added 'people' (staff, personnel, employees), 'physical evidence', and 'processes'). A functional view of marketing underlies the concept of the marketing mix, with its emphasis on marketing activities, e.g. marketers are seen as researching consumers' needs and wants with a view to launching ➤line extensions, ➤brand extensions, and ➤new product developments. While this functional view remains significant, the ➤marketing concept is broader in scope.

marketing myopia ➤marketing concept.

marketing performance measure (MPM) Any marketing performance measure that top management should review. It is a measure that matters to the whole business, not simply those in the marketing department. Measures may be financial (usually from the profit-and-loss account), from the market-place (market share, volume/value sales, customer satisfaction, loyalty/retention measures), or from non-financial internal sources (such as innovation and new product development activity). ➤marketing metrics; ➤➤balanced scorecard.

marketing planning A formal process that is designed to assess an organization's situation and, on the basis of this information, plan marketing activities for the future. Typically, the process is undertaken as part of an annual planning cycle and results in a written document. This document is seen as having a number of sections:
(1) Executive summary.
(2) Situation analysis ('audit').
(3) Marketing objectives.
(4) Marketing strategy.
(5) Action programmes.
(6) Budgets and financials.
(7) Monitors, controls and evaluation.
(8) Contingency plans.
Within the situation analysis (or 'audit') are sections on industry analysis (market size and potential, market activity, sales, costs and gross profits, product and process technology, market trends, government and social climate, industry attractiveness),

sales analysis (market area performance, trends by area, product, channel, etc.), competitor analysis (competitor strategies, relative performance, benchmarking, evaluation of relative resources), customer analysis (an understanding of customers – who, what, how, why, where, when, so what?), planning assumptions (explicit statement of underlying assumptions) and forecasts (by industry and product).

Situation analysis also goes by the title of ➤3Cs analysis ('consumers', 'competitors' and 'competencies'), although this ignores wider environmental factors; hence, there is usually a need for ➤PESTL analysis as well (where the 'PESTL' acronym stands for political, economic, social, technological and legal issues). Another popular label is to refer to situation analysis as a SWOT analysis (the acronym stands for strengths, weaknesses, opportunities and threats).

All these forms of situation analysis show the need for looking at external factors (opportunities and threats with regard to customers, competitors, markets, the wider environment) and internal factors (strengths and weaknesses with regard to performance, organizational capabilities and constraints, resources and so forth). These considerations then feed into the rest of the planning process.

Marketing objectives follow from the situation analysis – this refers to specific objectives for the brand (sales and shares). Market strategy describes how the objectives will be achieved, especially in terms of customer targets, competitor targets and core business strategy. Specific programme details come next (product developments, pricing decisions, distribution plans, direct marketing activity, advertising and promotion, service plans and trade marketing). Here are listed the various actions that must be completed over the coming year: who does what, when, where, how. These programmes then must be budgeted and financial statements prepared (listing costs, forecasting revenues and estimating profits). Monitors, controls and evaluations are put in place. This requires having plans for the gathering together of pertinent information: in-house data (sales, orders and re-orders), customer data (trade stocks, retail sales, customer attitude tracking, satisfaction studies), and customized research. ➤marketing metrics. Finally, various contingency plans should be prepared (in case key assumptions change, or market conditions alter, or there is an unexpected crisis: product contamination, sabotage, a medical scare or an environmental disaster).

The sections are described as a linear, sequential, sequence (1–8 in the example above); however, it is possible for there to be feedback loops. Thus, a budget squeeze (in stage 6) would impact on the action programmes (stage 5) and may lead to a revision of the marketing objectives (stage 3).

The purpose of the marketing plan is to do one or all of the following: (a) provide direction in terms of customers to be served and markets to be entered; (b) secure the commitment of staff to the agreed direction and reward those who show appropriate levels of commitment; (c) allocate resources to move effectively in the agreed direction, and (d) control marketing activities so that performance targets are met. In fulfilling these purposes it may be necessary to benchmark the performance of staff and activities against other divisions or competitors. An integrated and consistent approach can be achieved using a marketing plan rather than by making an *ad hoc* set of decisions. An integrated approach also should ensure that strategy formulation and action programmes are linked, that broad longer-term goals are met by taking relevant and appropriate actions in the short term. The ethos of marketing planning has become central to marketing thought, reinforced in particular by the writings of Philip Kotler (*Marketing Management: analysis, planning, implementation and control*, 1967), Malcolm McDonald (*Marketing Plans*, 1984) and Don Lehmann and Russ Winer (*Analysis for Marketing Planning*, 1988).

Desirable as these features of marketing plans are, they have been subject to much criticism. The 'ideal' plan is seen as too formal and linear (rather than lateral and creative), largely about content (whereas much of management is concerned with process), zero based (when no business is faced with a clean slate), overly rational (when emotions and ➤**politicking** are known to characterize managerial decision-making), and grandiose (with a focus on grand strategies, not the nuts and bolts of practical implementation). However, in practice, many marketing plans fall short of the ideal. Commenting on actual plans, managers typically complain that they are not realistic enough, are not specific enough, are not taken seriously, concentrate too much on the short term, and lack adequate performance measures. Managers also point out the difficulty of gaining consensus and of not having enough time to prepare properly. As a result, the planning process can become ritualized and meaningless; plans are prepared, but they are not used as working documents.

This has led some to dismiss marketing planning completely. This is rationalized in various ways: 'we need to be flexible', 'we value opportunism', 'our market is too volatile or too competitive to give us any fixed reference points'. The alternative is to rethink the nature of marketing planning. We could start, perhaps, with current strategies and action programmes, evaluating these and questioning the underlying assumptions, involving staff in the process in order to build consensus, looking forward to make forecasts and consider different future scenarios, and only then agreeing measurable objectives and targets. With such plans, direction and control emerges from a realistic assessment of where the organization is and how it might evolve. ➤**emergent strategy**. This approach also emphasizes the planning process in its own right, i.e. that the process of engaging employees in planning may be of as much benefit as the writing of the report.

Another change has been the move to separate strategic marketing plans (covering a 3–5 year time horizon), from 1-year operating plans. Operational plans are considered to be very practical, having some specific and detailed actions that can be monitored and controlled quite simply. Compared to strategic plans, it is much easier to ensure operational plans are clear, quantified, focused, realistic and agreed, and with these characteristics the chances of successful implementation are that much greater.

marketing research That branch of marketing concerned with gathering data about consumers, markets and organizations, and the analysis of such data to support management decision-making. Typical applications include demand forecasting, product testing, price setting, willingness-to-pay studies, advertisement copy testing and advertising evaluation. Professional market researchers emphasize the *systematic* nature of data gathering and the need for *formal* and *objective* analysis. This is achieved through a four-stage research design: (a) specification of the management goals; (b) development of a data collection procedure; (c) sampling plan and data collection, and (d) data analysis and reporting.

Many data collection procedures are available, notably: focus groups, in-depth interviews, large-scale surveys, consumer panels, and experiments. Some procedures generate qualitative data (e.g. verbatim comments from a focus group), others provide quantitative data, e.g. tabulations from a large-scale survey. The type of data has implications for analysis and reporting. Quantitative data can be analysed using statistical and mathematical techniques, from simple descriptive statistics to multivariate data analysis (factor analysis, ➤cluster analysis, multidimensional scaling, regression, analysis of variance, ➤path analysis). These techniques are formal in the sense of having agreed rules and conventions (e.g. in regard to appropriate levels of significance when using a statistical test), although the analyst must take into account how the data were obtained (whether from a random sample or stratified sample, say) and make quite a few subjective decisions (choices about the technique, the algorithm, the variables to include, etc.). ➤validity. With qualitative data, the content must be interpreted by the analyst, and while this sounds very subjective, various principles and guidelines now exist. There is a tendency to classify marketing research as either 'quant' or 'qual', but in practice a management problem may demand both and adopt a pluralistic approach. Thus, an initial exploratory study ('qual') might be followed by a more extensive survey ('qual'). ➤qualitative market research; quantitative market research.

Ethical standards and rules governing interviewing protocols, data protection, privacy, 'sugging' (selling in the guise of conducting marketing research) are embodied in industry ➤codes of practice. However, not all marketing research is collected by industry professionals. Managers will have access to internal sources, company records, customer files, feedback from the sales staff, advice from consultants, and – possibly – industrial espionage. The value of these other sources has to be weighed against questions of their reliability, representativeness, unbiasedness, and also the ethics of the methods used to collect the information.

market instrument Short-term ➤debt instrument.

market maker A ➤broker–dealer who is prepared to buy and sell specified ➤securities at all times and thus makes a market in them.

market order An instruction from a client to a ➤broker–dealer to buy or sell a ➤security or commodity at the price prevailing at the time of execution of the transaction ➤order.

market orientation The processes and activities associated with creating and satisfying customers by continually assessing their needs and wants, and doing so in a way that results in a measurable impact on business performance. Information and market intelligence-gathering are key activities for any organization that purports to be market-oriented. In this sense, market orientation is closely allied to the ➤marketing concept and the idea of the ➤market driven organization. However, market orientation is also concerned with interfunctional co-ordination, and questions of ➤organizational competencies, ➤organizational decision-making, ➤organizational culture and ➤organizational learning.

In the early 1990s two operational definitions came to dominate thinking. Ajay Kohli and Bernard Jaworski ('Market Orientation: the construct, research propositions, and managerial implications', *Journal of Marketing*, 1990) described market orientation as a set of behaviours and activities in an organization. Specifically, they saw market orientation as the organization-wide generation of market intelligence relating to current and future customer needs, dissemination of the intelligence across departments, and the organization-wide responsiveness to it. Drivers (antecedents) of market orientation were hypothesized to be: (a) senior management factors, e.g. whether they are risk-averse; (b) interdepartmental dynamics, e.g. whether there is conflict between departments, and (c) organizational systems, e.g. the extent to which reward systems are market-based. Consequences were threefold: (a) customer responses; (b) business performance, and (c) employee responses. These elements were brought together in what then came to be called the MARKOR scale (a scale based on a battery of questions asked of managers). In their alternative definition, John Narver and Stanley Slater ('The Effect of a Market Orientation on Business Profitability', *Journal of Marketing*, 1990) saw market orientation as comprising three behavioural components: (a) customer orientation; (b) competitor orientation, and (c) interfunctional co-ordination. They also argued that it is organizational culture that effectively and efficiently creates these behaviours, thereby lifting the discussion to a more strategic level. These ideas were reflected in the MKTOR scale (also based on a battery of questions asked of managers).

These and subsequent authors show a clear link between market orientation and business performance, although in some cases the link is moderated by other factors, such as technological turbulence and levels of competitive intensity. Thus, it is harder to show a link when technology is changing very quickly and competition is intense – under such conditions it may be achievement enough to stay in business. Despite much research, there remain unresolved questions, e.g. do market-oriented organizations take enough risks; are their skills and capabilities rare and difficult to imitate, and does the concept really lead to sustainable competitive advantage or simply competitive survival? Furthermore, measurement issues continue to be hotly debated. There is no universally agreed operational definition; the popular MARKOR and MKTOR scales are related, but not equivalent, nor interchangeable. The question of which performance measures to use has not been resolved, and probably it cannot be resolved in a definitive way. ➤**key performance measures; marketing metrics**. Virtually all studies rely on self-assessed business performance, where an element of self-delusion is quite likely, although this problem might be overcome by using financial, operational and customer-related performance measures as well. Different studies work with different units of analysis and different levels of management, making cross-study comparison difficult. More fundamentally, the emphasis given to process suggests the need for methods that directly explore dynamics, feedback and hysteresis effects, yet most studies to date have relied on cross-sectional surveys – a very imperfect way to investigate business processes.

market power The degree to which a firm exercises influence over the price and output in a particular market. Under intensely competitive conditions – such as under the paradigm of ➤**perfect competition** – all firms are assumed to have zero market power: they have to take the going price and cannot hope to alter it on their own. Wherever firms represent a significant portion of the whole market, however, their own actions will be very likely to influence price. (In the parlance of the economics of demand theory, instead of facing a flat ➤**demand curve**, they will face a downward-sloping one.) In a less than perfectly competitive market, a large player could expect to raise their price and not lose all their sales. It also means, however, that if they wish to increase their sales they have to lower their price. The stronger this relationship, the greater the market power.

Where market power exists, the producer has such influence on the market that the amount he decides to produce affects the market price, and so in deciding on how much to produce the large firm must think not just about the going price at which the extra output will sell, but also about the consequent fall in price on the existing output. ➤**marginal revenue**. Market power is related to the availability of substitute items. Those items which are highly differentiated from those of competitors will give more market power to the producer than those which are standard. ➤➤**monopoly**.

market pull A concept describing the ability of buyers to create demand for their wants. The concept suggests that 'the market' can demand products and services from firms, thereby 'pulling' products and services from them. There is, however, much debate in the literature about whether a market can pull products from firms or whether firms use their operations and technology to push products and services into the market; hence, the term ➤**technology push**. The concept is fraught with difficulty and many would argue that with most developed new products there is an element of both market pull and technology push. ➤➤**marketing concept**.

market segmentation ➤segmentation.

market share The sales of a brand relative to the rest of the market. Brand sales are expressed as a percentage of (volume or value) sales for the whole market. If 20 million DVD players are sold each year and Sony accounts for 5 million of these, Sony's market share is 25 per cent. Market share is very widely used as a ➤**key performance measure** in marketing. The rationale for this is that certain benefits tend to be associated with leading brands: (a) consumer awareness levels of the brand are higher; (b) consumers are more familiar with the brand and many will have direct experience in buying/using it; (c) the brand name is more likely to be seen as an indicator of quality and trustworthiness; (d) distribution is easier to secure, and (e) it is possible to outspend competitors (enabling greater use of expensive communications media such as television). Furthermore, ➤**profit impact of market strategy** analysis shows that high market share is correlated with higher levels of profitability. These factors are best seen as interrelated, not causal, e.g. high market share implies good distribution in the first place and makes it easier to secure further distribution.

Moreover, for those involved in framing business strategy, market share has often been seen as a highly desirable goal, yielding any of a number of different ➤**competitive advantages**, such as ➤**economies of scale**, for example. The pursuit of market share, even sometimes at the expense of profit, has been a ubiquitous feature of expansionist business strategies for decades. Its logic is that in a market which can only sustain a few large players, having a large share is a ticket to a long-term presence there. With the rise of ➤**new economy** businesses, selling ➤**intellectual property**, or trying to establish themselves as large players in the world of the internet, the idea that all that mattered was market share took hold. In fact, however, many businesses found the cost of acquiring share – against other firms intent on the same purpose – was unsustainably high. ➤➤**chicken**.

Across different geographical and product markets, market shares vary considerably. Also, while in marketing the goal often is to increase market share, the goal may conflict with anti-trust rules and regulations if the increase brings about market dominance. Market dominance confers on the brand a responsibility to shape and develop the whole market, and it becomes the reference point for all consumers and smaller competitors in the market, but it may also be prone to ➤**monopoly** imperfections, e.g. an influence over prices and output that is not in the interest of consumers. Indeed, for economists, market share has been seen as important in determining the degree of ➤**market power,** ➤**concentration** and ➤**monopoly** in an industry. Shares are regularly used by the ➤**Competition Commission** in the UK, for example, to assess whether a company is dominant.

Two assumptions underlie the calculation of market share. First, there must be accurate knowledge of each brand's (volume or value) sales. This is feasible in most ➤**packaged goods** markets, but may be difficult in fragmented emergent markets and under-researched markets (textiles being an example). Even in packaged goods markets discrepancies arise because research agencies use somewhat different monitoring procedures. ➤**A C Nielsen Corporation**. Some organizations measure factory shipments, others measure warehouse or retail stocks; yet others measure sales at the point of purchase (using in-store scanners) or shortly after purchase (in-home scanning). Second, the calculation assumes there is a clearly defined market – an assumption that may be hard to make in practice. ➤**market definition**. What constitutes 'the market' may differ depending on whether a consumer or producer view is taken. Different producers may have legitimate reasons for defining the market differently from one another. Added to which, markets change and old distinctions can blur. Telecommunications, computing, broadcasting and information services have become blurred because of technological changes and new demands from consumers – a process of ➤**dedifferentiation**. In theory, the problem can be solved by assessing whether the brands are competitive ➤**substitutes**. But, in practice, it is more common to find markets defined by management, industry conventions and market research agencies than by formal economic analysis.

market structure The organizational and other characteristics of a market and, in particular, those which affect the nature of competition and pricing. Traditionally, the most important features of market structure are the number and size distribution of buyers and sellers, which reflect the extent of ➤**monopoly** or ➤**monopsony**; these, in turn, will be affected by the existence or absence of ➤**barriers to entry**. ➤➤**concentration; contestability; market definition**.

MARKSTRAT ➤business simulation.

mark to market accounting A means of keeping track of the value of ➤**derivatives** contracts prior to those contracts finally being exercised. For example, suppose a trader sells a ➤**futures** contract at a particular price to deliver a barrel of oil at $30 in 3 months time. If the price of oil rises during the 3-month period, the value of that futures contract falls. Mark to market accounting would involve taking into account the change in value of the futures contract during the 3 months, even though no cash or oil necessarily changes hands during the period.

mark-up pricing A method by which firms determine the price to charge by looking at their average costs, and simply adding some profit margin. Surveys indicate this is the most commonly used form of pricing technique, notwithstanding the sophisticated techniques economists have developed for deriving the optimum price to charge. Mark-up pricing typically involves estimating the direct costs of production (variable costs), the indirect costs (or overheads, such as administrative functions and marketing) and a reasonable profit, which is, of course, partly determined by what the market will bear. In practice, mark-up prices will often be close to the more sophisticated 'optimum' prices, particularly where a firm only has a rough idea of its ➤**marginal revenue**. Moreover, when a firm is operating at full capacity, it is not inappropriate to charge a price reflecting all costs of production. However, when a producer has a lot of spare capacity, it can be useful to sell at a price closer to incremental or ➤**marginal cost** than average cost. Or it can be useful to find ways of engaging in ➤**price discrimination**, i.e. charging different mark-ups to different kinds of customer.

martingale A betting strategy that involves repeating a bet on a particular outcome, doubling the stake on each recurrence, until the bet is won. For example, the martingale strategy might involve repeated bets on a toss of a coin coming up heads. The first bet might be £1; if the coin comes up heads, the strategy is completed, and the bet won. If the coin comes up tails, then a repeat of the bet is made at £2. If the coin now comes up heads, the total outlay is now £1, and the total winnings £2 – the martingale strategy is complete, and the gambler has won. If the coin comes up tails, then the bet is repeated at £4. If this pattern of repetition is continued, as long as heads eventually comes up, the gambler wins £1 over the whole series of bets. The martingale is a safe and guaranteed means of winning a bet – but only as long as the gambler is willing and able to continue doubling the stake as recurrences proceed. If the gambler has to drop out of the game before winning the bet, then of course the losses can be extremely large, representing a series of increasing stakes, each with no return. The existence of martingales has been seen as important in finance theory: the strategy of maintaining a portfolio of perfectly hedged ➤**positions** using derivatives and offsetting holdings of underlying assets (➤**replicating portfolio**) can itself be considered a kind of martingale.

Maslow, Abraham (died 1970) Psychologist and behavioural scientist who developed the theory of the hierarchy of human needs which need to be fulfilled in sequence. Once basic food and shelter needs are satisfied, higher needs for social esteem and personal fulfilment are released. Wants are not absolute; once satisfied they become taken for granted.

Maslow criticized Douglas ➤**McGregor**'s Theory Y – that workers' psychological need for participation, responsibility and achievement meant that they would be motivated to perform better under non-authoritarian management – on the ground that it neglected the fact that some people need structure and direction if they are to feel secure. Some people cannot handle too much responsibility or uncertainty. Maslow himself was later criticized for not recognizing, as Frederick ➤**Herzberg** did, that economic rewards and all wants can become a source of dissatisfaction as needs are met. Wants can change as they are satisfied. As Marilyn Monroe said, 'After you get what you want, you don't want it.'

Maslow's hierarchy of needs A theory of human needs. It is claimed that there is a hierarchy of five human needs: (a) psychological (hunger, thirst, shelter, sex); (b) safety (security, protection); (c) social (affection, friendship); (d) esteem (self-respect, autonomy, achievement), and (e) self-actualization (growth, achieving one's potential, self-fulfilment). As each need is satisfied, in turn, so the next becomes dominant. Those needs that are satisfied internally – social, esteem and self-actualization – are described as higher-order needs. It has been suggested that this theory of needs has a bearing on employee ➤**motivation**. For example, one way to interpret ➤**theory X and theory Y** is that theory X assumes lower-order needs dominate, and theory Y assumes higher-order needs dominate. This theory has entered the popular imagination, but empirical proof is thin. Moreover, there are several competing needs-based theories of motivation, of which this is only one. ➤**Maslow**.

mass production Production processes which produce goods in high volume and relatively narrow variety. Most ➤**fast moving consumer goods** are produced using this method. Such operations are characterized by many repetitive and predictable activities. Examples of mass production processes include beer bottling plants and automobile plants. An automobile plant, for example, might produce several thousand variants of car if every option of engine size, colour, etc. is taken into account. Yet, essentially it is a mass operation because the different variants of its product do not affect the basic process of production.

master production schedule (MPS) An expression of the operational plan of production by a time period, indicating the time and size of end-term quantities. The MPS is arguably the most important schedule in a business's planning and control system and is a key driver in ➤**material requirements planning** systems. The MPS contains a statement of the volume and timing of the end products to be made; this schedule drives the whole operation in terms of what is assembled, what is manufactured and what is bought. This is based on firm orders and forecast demand. It is the basis of planning the utilization of labour and equipment and it determines the provision of materials and cash flow.

matched bargain or bid A method of ➤**securities** trading in which bids and offers (➤**bid price; offer price**) are matched together. Used on the German stock exchanges, it is said to have greater transparency than the more common ➤**quote-driven** systems. ➤➤**order driven**.

material requirements planning (MRP I) A system for taking manufacturing planning information and calculating the volume and timing requirements which will satisfy demand. It enables a firm to calculate how many materials of particular types are required and at what times they are required. To do this it uses a sales order book which records known future orders and also a forecast of what sales orders the business is reasonably confident of securing. The MRP then checks all the ingredients which are required to make these future orders and ensures they are ordered in time. The three key inputs to MRP are the ➤**master production schedules**, ➤**bills of materials** and ➤**inventory** records. With these inputs it can produce a production schedule.

matrix structure An organizational structure that creates dual lines of authority, e.g. functional and product departmentalization. Thus, a member of the finance department also might be a member of a project management team.

maturity The period between the creation of a financial claim and the date on which it is to be paid. Often refers to the date of payment, e.g. the date on which a ➤**bond** becomes due for repayment.

maximin strategy A technique of selecting a course of action from a range of options, designed to ensure that of the worst-case scenarios associated with each course of action, the least bad is the one chosen. For example, imagine a company has to choose one of three different strategies: (a) cut its price; (b) hold its price, or (c) raise its price. In each case, the result of the decision is a little uncertain, depending as it does on the reaction of competitors. (Will the rival cut, hold or raise its price?) The maximin approach says: First estimate all the different outcomes associated with each of the three strategies, and then compare just the three worst-case scenarios. Choose the strategy on the basis of getting the best of the worst cases. It is a simple decision rule used in ➤**game theory**, but is a naïve approach, in the sense that it ignores the possible gains from choosing alternative strategies. It makes most sense for an extremely risk-averse person, or in a ➤**zero-sum game**, where it does make sense to concentrate on worst-case scenarios.

Mayo, Elton (died 1949) Remembered principally for his role in the Hawthorne Investigations which transformed understanding of worker ➤**motivation** and its effect on performance. The experiments were carried out at Western Electric's Hawthorne plant in Chicago from 1927 to 1932, when they were terminated by the Depression. At the point where Mayo joined the project, six female workers assembling telephone relays were segregated in a room with researchers so that working conditions could be varied and the results for output monitored. Later, fourteen men wiring and soldering banks of telephone terminals were isolated, and in this case the effects of individual and group incentive payments monitored. The general finding was that output in the first of the two groups rose over a period of years irrespective of the changes made, and in the second group, output did not seem to be related to the incentive payments. Mayo eventually concluded that spontaneous co-operation in informally organized social relationships among employees in the work situation was what counted. For workers the 'logic of sentiment' was dominant, in contrast to the 'logic of cost and efficiency' which ruled management. ➤**experiment**. The Human Relations School of organizational theory built upon Mayo's findings, which have proved to be of great importance as well as consistent with, or foreshadowing, work organization developments in several countries. Examples of these include Japan's Quality Circles and Sweden's experiments in group car assembly as a substitute for the Fordist assembly line. Often contrasted with Frederick W ➤**Taylor**, Mayo was not against scientific management as such, provided the human dimension was taken into account.

Elton Mayo was born in Australia in 1880, educated there and in the UK, and taught at the University of Queensland before emigrating to the US in 1923. He became Professor of Industrial Research at the Harvard Graduate School of Business Administration.

MBI ➤management buy-in.

MBO ➤management buy-out; management by objectives.

MBTI ➤Myers–Briggs Type Indicator.

McCarthy, E Jerome One of the first to provide a systematic treatment of marketing as a formal management discipline. His text *Basic Marketing: a management perspective* (1960) was extremely influential. ➤**marketing concept**.

McClelland's theory of needs A theory of human needs. People are categorized in terms of their need for: (a) achievement (their drive to succeed); (b) power (their need to have others behave in ways they would not otherwise have behaved), and (c) affiliation (their desire for friendly and cordial interpersonal relations). Practical applications in the area of employee ➤**motivation** are claimed to follow from this. For example, those with a need for high achievement will be motivated if they are given responsible jobs; however, they do not necessarily make good managers because their need is self-centred, rather than other-oriented.

McGregor, Douglas (died 1964) Famously distinguished two management styles which were based on ➤**theory X and theory Y** on the nature of workers. Theory X holds that workers are lazy and need authoritarian management (which was Frederick W ➤**Taylor**'s approach), while Theory Y holds that workers are creative and have a psychological need for participation and achievement. The distinction helped to reinforce the shift from authoritarian to participative management that prevails today. ➤➤Frederick **Herzberg**; Abraham **Maslow**.

McGregor was Professor of Management at the Massachusetts Institute of Technology where he inspired and influenced other young researchers including Edgar ➤**Schein** and Abraham Maslow.

McKinsey, James (died 1937) Founded the firm of McKinsey and Company, the management consultants, in 1925. Peter ➤**Drucker** credits James McKinsey and Lyndall ➤**Urwick** as being the first consultants to work on basic management concerns, such as business policy and management organization, as distinct from technical problems.

After a few years, McKinsey left his firm to others to develop, but it is now a multinational operation, not the largest but the most profitable of the international consultancies. Several management gurus, as well as industrial and political leaders, are former McKinsey employees, e.g. Tom ➤**Peters**, Kenichi ➤**Ohmae** and Christopher A ➤**Bartlett**.

MDS Multidimensional scaling. ➤**perceptual mapping**.

means-end value chain The set of links between product or service attributes (the 'means') and desired benefits for the consumer (the 'ends'). For example, inclusion of airbags for passengers in a car (attribute), makes the car more attractive (consequence), because the buyer can be reassured about the safety of his passengers (end value). End values are regarded as the ultimate basis of consumer choice and determinants of post-purchase satisfaction. Thus, car buyers ultimately want reassurance about the safety of their passengers, and are not interested in airbags *per se* – they will be satisfied only if they gain this reassurance (irrespective of whether, objectively, airbags are provided). Analysis of means-end value chains is important in ➤**new product development** and in the management of ➤**customer satisfaction/dissatisfaction**.

media buying The activity of buying space in media, such as space and insertions in a newspaper/magazine, time slots/segments on television/radio, etc. Although expressed as space or time, it is the audience that is bought and sold; hence, the significance of ➤**audience measurement** and ➤**audience rating**.

media planning The process of co-ordinating media selection and scheduling. At a broad level this entails selection of media types (press, television, web, etc.) and then specific media vehicles (television day-parts, particular magazines, certain web sites). Precise scheduling is a function of the available budget – this demands a trade-off between 'reach', 'frequency' and the number of 'advertising cycles'.

An advertising cycle is a flight of advertising within a planning period, e.g. a 4-week flight of advertising undertaken within the context of a 1-year planning period. There may be several advertising cycles over the entire planning period. These cycles may run into one another, or be organized into blocks of activity ➤flighting. The task of determining the number and duration of these advertising cycles is a key decision in media planning. The decision partly depends on how many cycles are needed to meet the marketing communication goals, and on how many can be afforded. With the growth of ➤integrated marketing communications, it is perhaps more relevant to refer to 'communication cycles', not simply advertising cycles.

Reach is the number of target audience individuals exposed to marketing communications in a communications cycle. Used primarily in the context of ➤exposure to advertising during an advertising cycle, but can equally apply to other types of communication. Reach tends to be reported as a percentage (i.e. the proportion of the total ➤target audience that is exposed to marketing communications in a communications cycle), e.g. 40 per cent of individuals may be exposed to a particular television commercial. While reach is important, of greater importance is 'effective reach' (i.e. the number or proportion of target audience individuals reached at the effective frequency level in an advertising cycle), e.g. 40 per cent of individuals may be exposed to a particular television commercial, but only 5 per cent may see it enough times for action to be taken.

Frequency is the number of times a target audience individual is exposed to a form of marketing communication in a communications cycle. Specifically, in advertising, the number of exposures per individual target audience member in an advertising cycle, e.g. a person might be exposed twice to a particular television commercial in a 4-week advertising cycle. While frequency is important, 'effective frequency' is of greater significance (i.e. the number of exposures, in an advertising cycle, to have the target audience individual take action), e.g. a person might be exposed twice to a particular television commercial in a 4-week advertising cycle, but would need to be exposed four times before taking any effective action. The lower boundary is called 'minimum effective frequency' (MEF); in the example here the MEF is four exposures.

Another trade-off in media planning is between the high cost of precision versus the lower cost of being flexible. This is made clear in the notion of 'run of paper' (ROP)/'run of station' (ROS). ROP means that an advertisement may be placed on any page of the newspaper. This helps to lower the advertiser's media costs, but is a less precise way to reach the target audience than the purchase of specific media space. Similarly, ROS means that a commercial may be placed anywhere in the television schedule. This helps to lower the advertiser's media costs, but is a less precise way to reach the target audience than through the purchase of specific time slots/segments. Also, competitors may pre-empt the best slots/segments.

The data for media planning come from ➤audience measurement (also ➤gross ratings points; ratings).

media relations ➤public relations.

media selling The task of selling space in media. ≫media planning.

mediation The process of using a neutral third party to resolve an industrial dispute or ➤conflict. Mediators have no legal powers and cannot coerce or compel parties to reach a negotiated settlement; therefore, they must suggest, reason and convince the parties to make an agreement. This is similar to ➤conciliation and contrasts with ➤arbitration. ➤negotiation.

media vehicle ➤media planning.

membership programme ➤loyalty programme.

memorandum of association The document that forms the basis of registration of a company, listing the subscribers to the ➤capital and the number of shares, the name and address of the company and, where appropriate, its powers and objects. The memorandum also states that the ➤liability of its members (shareholders) is limited (➤incorporation) (US = *articles of incorporation*). The *articles of association* set out the rules by which the company will be administered, e.g. the voting of directors and the calling of meetings (US = *corporate bylaws*). ≫corporate control.

mercantilism The belief that economies thrive by running up surpluses in the ➤balance of payments (which allows them to build up reserves of global money supply) and that measures to promote exports and restrain imports are thus appropriate. Mercantilist ideas were popular 300 years ago, when running up a balance of payments surplus allowed a nation to hoard precious metals – as the surplus implied foreigners were furnishing payment that way – in excess of the levels of payment going abroad to pay for imports. Mercantilists thought the accumulation of monetary assets was a measure of national success. Conventional economics since Adam Smith has been opposed to mercantilist ideas, which can be shown to be self-defeating. Increasing the supply of gold in the economy tends to create ➤inflation, and thus render exports less competitive in the long run. In a modern economy, where gold is not the universal currency, a balance of payments surplus will often lead to an appreciation of the ➤exchange rate, thus making exports more expensive in foreign markets. Notwithstanding these faults, mercantilist thinking is frequently evident in public debate in calls for protection against free trade; it was labelled *neo-mercantilism* by economist Harry Johnson.

merchant bank An institution that carries out a variety of financial services, including the acceptance of ➤bills of exchange, the issue and ➤placing of loans and ➤securities, ➤portfolio and ➤unit trust management, ➤foreign exchange market dealing and some banking services. Several houses, often through subsidiaries, provide ➤risk capital, deal in gold bullion, ➤insurance and ➤hire purchase, and are active in the ➤Euromarket. Merchant banks advise companies on ➤mergers and other financial matters. There has been a recent trend, especially following the ➤Big Bang, for merchant banks, including London firms on the stock exchange, to participate in financial ➤conglomerates, so as to be able to offer a full range of financial services, including retail services. The term 'merchant bank' is now giving way to ➤investment bank as its activities are absorbed into large global concerns. ➤accepting house.

merger Creation of a new legally recognized firm by the bringing together of two or more previously independent companies. It often implies a consensual element to the arrangement, where the firms agree to combine activities and equality in the size and strength of the combining firms. This, however, is not always the case. Experts frequently question so-called mergers and argue they are, in fact, take-overs, sometimes ➤hostile take-overs. Many analysts regard the so-called merger of Daimler Benz and Chrysler as a euphemism of the take-over of Chrysler by Daimler. ➤➤acquisition.

merger accounting ➤consolidated accounts.

method study ➤work measurement study.

mezzanine A term signifying an intermediate stage in a financing operation. It usually refers to ➤unsecured ➤debt and ➤equity in ranking for payment in the event of default. ➤➤subordinated. It may carry an ➤option on some other claim to a stake in equity (an *equity kicker*). A form of *quasi-equity* combining features of both debt and equity.

MIB 30 (Milano Italia Borsa 30 Index) An index designed to reflect movements in the share prices of thirty companies traded on the Milan Stock Exchange. It was given a base value of 10,000 in December 1992.

microeconomics The study of economics at the level of individual consumers, groups of consumers or firms. No very sharp boundary can be drawn between microeconomics and the other main area of the subject, ➤macroeconomics, but its broad distinguishing feature is its focus on the choices facing, and the reasoning of, individual economic decision-makers. The general concern of microeconomics is the efficient allocation of scarce resources between alternative uses, but more specifically it involves the determination of price through the optimizing behaviour of economic agents, with consumers maximizing their utility and firms maximizing profit. It covers behaviour of individual sectors and sector interaction in ➤equilibrium and disequilibrium in individual markets. ➤consumer behaviour.

Miller, Merton H (died 2000) A pioneer in modern financial economics. With Franco Modigliani, he developed the proposition that the market value of a firm and its cost of capital is unaffected by its chosen method of financing (debt relative to equity, ➤gearing) or whether it distributes its profits in dividends or retains them. He showed, for example, that what matters is the profit made by the business: if dividends stop being paid but earnings are wholly reinvested, then *ceteris paribus* the shares will be revalued to reflect the money retained in the business. The two propositions on capital structure and the irrelevance of dividends depend upon simplifying assumptions about perfect capital markets. These do not necessarily hold in the real world and the M & M Theorem, as it is called, abstracts from such issues as taxation, which typically favours debt over equity. ➤efficient market hypothesis; perfect competition.

Merton Miller spent some 40 years as a professor at Chicago University. He was awarded a Nobel prize in 1990 jointly with Harry Markowitz and William Sharpe, who pioneered the ➤capital asset pricing model.

minority interest ➤consolidated account.

Mintzberg, Henry Professor of Management at McGill University, Montreal, and at the European Institute of Business Administration in France. Mintzberg is original and iconoclastic, with a lively presentational style. He first gained attention with a book, *The Nature of Managerial Work* (1973), based on research carried out for his doctoral dissertation in the late 1960s. This research used diaries to record how five successful chief executives actually used their time. He asserted that if asked to describe what they do, executives usually say they plan, organize, command, co-ordinate and control, the five key elements of management delineated by Henri ➤Fayol. In practice, Mintzberg found, managers were less reflective and organized than this. In his sample of executives, half their activities lasted less than 9 minutes: they were responding to the pressures of their job, they relied on oral, not written, communication, and placed much importance on soft, up-to-date and forward-looking information such as gossip, hearsay and speculation. Their activities were fundamentally indistinguishable from their counterparts of 100 years previously before the emergence of the new technologies and management theories.

Mintzberg distinguishes six elements or parts of the organization: (a) an ideology or culture which pervades the entire system; (b) a strategic apex where the system is overseen; (c) an operating core which does the basic work of producing products and services. Then, as the organization grows: (d) middle line management; (e) support staff, and (f) a techno-structure of analysts and planners outside the hierarchy of line authority. He goes on to say that there are six configurations which explain much of what can be observed in organizations. The configurations are the outcome of basic pulls that are exerted by each of the six elements, e.g. the apex pulls to lead, the operating core to professionalize, the ideology to unify, and a seventh element, politics, tends to pull the organization apart. In each of the six configurations one of the six elements predominates: in the entrepreneurial organization, for example, it is the strategic apex, in the machine organization, the techno-structure (the other configurations are: professional, diversified, innova-tive and missionary organizations). Mintzberg also distinguishes six types of co-ordinating mechanisms including mutual adjustment, direct supervision and standardization, which glue each of the various organizations together. In the entrepreneurial organization, for example, the prime co-ordinating mechanism is direct supervision; in the machine organization it is standardization of work processes.

Whereas Max ➤Weber was clear that the machine bureaucracy was the most efficient large-scale organizational form, from his modern perspective Mintzberg recognized that bureaucracy is best only for certain mass-producing activities such as airlines, oil extraction and distribution. Even then, these organizations can only work satisfactorily in the long run if pressures for excessive standardization, insensi-tivity to the environment, internal politicization and the inhibition of innovation can be resisted.

Mintzberg's work is, in his own words, 'a celebration of intuition' which 'was at odds with the mainline management literature that emphasized, almost to the point of obsession, the role of analysis in organizations . . .'. He argues that good managers use the right (intuitive) side of the brain as much as, if not more than, the left (analytical) side. Strategy, for example, should involve much more than deliberate planning; it should be emergent, adapting with action and experience. The error is the common assumption that thought must be independent of (and precede) action. Hence, he coined the phrase 'crafting strategy': '. . . no craftsman thinks some days and works others.' His work is conveniently brought together in *Mintzberg on Management* (1989). ➤**logical incrementalism; muddling-through theory; politicking.**

mission statement A concise summary of the fundamental purpose of an organization. It should provide the sense of common purpose to direct and stimulate the organization. Usually it focuses on growth targets and desired quality levels and attitudes towards the environment, customers, shareholders and suppliers. Critics argue that such statements are public relations exercises and are often meaningless. Others argue that they help employees to share a common understanding of the organization's long-term aims and objectives.

mixed strategy A means of selecting one choice from a set of options, with a degree of random selection, on the basis of pre-assigned probabilities attached to each option. It is a concept used in ➤**game theory** where, in certain situations, your best strategy is to behave unpredictably in order to prevent an opponent guessing your behaviour. It can be a good idea to adopt a mixed strategy in the game tic-tac-toe (sometimes referred to as paper–scissors–stone) for example. Or imagine running a movie channel on television, for example, with the goal of inducing viewers to watch as many commercials as possible. If a movie is scheduled at 8 p.m., you could run 3 minutes of advertisements beforehand, but the problem with doing that regularly is that viewers can get wise to your plan and simply turn on the 8 p.m. movie at 8.03 to avoid the commercials. Equally, the problem with running no commercials at all at 8 p.m. is the loss of a good advertising opportunity. Instead, then, by adopting a mixed strategy, so that sometimes you run commercials and sometimes you do not, you can induce viewers to turn on at 8 p.m., and at least to watch some advertisements on the days you run them. A mixed strategy is the opposite of a *pure strategy*, in which there is no random element. In formal terms, a mixed strategy is beneficial when, given your opponent's reaction, you are indifferent between two pure strategies, and when your opponent can benefit from knowing what your next move is. An important finding in game theory is that anyone facing a mixed strategy will always find a pure strategy to be among the best responses.

model A representation of a real-life system, relationship or state, that can take any of a variety of forms. At its most informal, a model can be said to consist of a verbal description or analogy of some real-world phenomenon. Or it may take the form of a diagram or a set of equations setting out the relationship between different variables (➤**econometrics**). In applied economics or business, a model is likely to be expressed in a computer program or spreadsheet in which data (the 'input') are processed and manipulated to produce results (the 'output'), e.g. as in ➤**decision-support systems** and ➤**marketing engineering**.

Model-building usually consists of two main stages: (a) to work out the basic relationships and to develop the structure of the model, setting out what factors affect which variables (often as far as model construction goes), and (b) to estimate the actual magnitudes or strengths of the relationships postulated, often using statistical techniques. ➤**parameter.**

Models have a variety of uses: (a) they can simplify and clarify the behaviour of the real world by illuminating and describing systems clearly, stripped of all unnecessary complications; (b) computer models in particular are useful for simulation, e.g. modelling traffic flows allows a planner to see the effect of changes to road patterns (in this case, the model would not want to strip out the complexity of the real world, but to incorporate it for as accurate a representation to be constructed as possible); (c) models provide forecasts (➤forecasting) of the behaviour of variables, based on past observations, and (d) the specification of models is a prerequisite to the testing of different theories. ➤➤business simulation.

modem A device providing an interface between a computer and a telephone line or other line used for transmitting data.

Modigliani–Miller theorem ➤Miller, Merton H.

momentum investing ➤investment approaches.

monetary policy Central government policy with respect to the supply of money in the economy, the rate of interest and usually the ➤exchange rate. Monetary policy is now broadly accepted as having the predominant role in the control of total spending in the economy, and through that, of ➤inflation. In choosing to conduct an anti-inflationary strategy, there have been various fashions as to the appropriate techniques: (a) targeting the volume of money in the economy, measured in various ways; (b) targeting the exchange rate against some other currency, or (c) more recently targeting inflation directly, using interest rates to encourage or discourage spending.

Because various of these fashions have produced disappointing results, the most common development world-wide has been to take monetary policy from day-to-day political control and pass it over to an independent central bank which has no other purpose than to maintain low inflation or, more broadly, economic stability. ➤Monetary Policy Committee.

It is worth understanding that it is not possible for the authorities simultaneously to set the money supply, the exchange rate and interest rates independently, because the three are simultaneously determined. If the money supply is increased, for example, the exchange rate tends to fall unless interest rates are raised.

Monetary Policy Committee The nine-person committee of the ➤Bank of England, charged with setting interest rates in the UK. The committee consists of the Bank's governor, the two deputy-governors, two other officials of the Bank, plus four economists nominated by the government. It is accountable to the Court of the Bank of England, and to MPs through the House of Commons Treasury and Civil Service Select Committees. It meets monthly, and the minutes of its proceedings are published with a lag of 2 weeks. The Committee is charged with setting interest rates to meet the government's explicit inflation target. The US equivalent is the Federal Reserve's Open Market Committee (the ➤Fed), which consists of the seven governors of the Fed., plus five of the twelve presidents of the Federal Reserve district banks around the US. In the Eurozone, the equivalent is the Governing Council of the ➤European Central Bank, consisting of six executive directors of the Bank, plus the governors of each national central bank in the zone.

money broker A ➤broker operating in the ➤interbank market, acting as intermediary between banks wishing to borrow and banks wishing to lend. Money brokers also operate in the ➤foreign exchange and ➤Eurocurrency markets.

money illusion The phenomenon of failing to account for ➤inflation and, hence, believing that some effect which merely compensates for higher prices is of real significance. A worker who believes he is better off with 4 per cent pay rise, with 4 per cent inflation, than with no pay rise and no inflation is said to suffer money illusion.

money market The market in short-term (normally up to 1 year) financial claims, e.g. ➤bills of exchange, ➤Treasury bills and ➤interbank market. The market is wholesale (i.e. in large quantities traded not by individuals but by banks or finance houses, the ➤Bank of England, the ➤Federal Reserve Bank and others) and most transactions are by ➤discount.

money market mutual fund A type of ➤mutual fund created in the USA in the early 1970s, designed to take advantage of the rise in interest rates by investing in short-term ➤money market ➤instruments.

money purchase ➤Pension schemes in which contributions to a fund are used to buy an ➤annuity, as distinct from a ➤defined benefits scheme.

monopolistic competition Competition in an industry in which there are many firms, each producing products that are similar to each other, but which are not identical. Washing powder might be said to be such an example. In economic analysis, monopolistic competition can be seen as having some features in common with intense competition (➤perfect competition) and some in common with ➤monopoly. Three key features can be said to characterize monopolistic competition.
(1) The firms make products between which consumers slightly differentiate and consequently some consumers will prefer one product to those of its competitors sufficiently to exhibit a limited amount of loyalty to that brand when its price rises. This means that each firm has a small amount of ➤market power. In this regard, a monopolistic competitor is similar to a monopoly, but not to a firm in an intensely competitive industry.
(2) Firms are able to enter the industry if the level of profits is attractive. This is a feature shared with the perfectly competitive industry, but not the monopoly.
(3) Like both perfectly competitive and monopolistic firms, producers in monopolistic competition are assumed to maximize profits.
In economics, monopolistically competing firms are assumed to set their outputs at a level at which the ➤marginal cost of production is equal to ➤marginal revenue. The selling price at the specified output is determined by the firm's demand. Profits are assumed to be zero in the long term, on account of new entry occurring whenever they are positive, driving up total supply in the industry and cutting the demand for each company's product.

It can be shown that generally, in a monopolistically competitive industry, output will be rather lower than it would be under perfect competition, with price above marginal cost and, thus, rather higher. Moreover, output will not tend to occur at the lowest possible levels on average, as each firm will tend to operate with some excess capacity.

monopoly A market in which there is only one supplier. Monopoly has been a concern of governments throughout the developed world for decades, with ➤com-

petition policy aimed at preventing it from emerging (through ➤**merger** or ➤**acquisition**, for example) and at ensuring it is not unduly exploited.

In its theoretical caricature, three features characterize a monopoly market: (a) the firm in it is motivated by profits; (b) it stands alone and barriers prevent new firms from entering the industry (➤**barriers to entry**), and (c) the actions of the monopoly itself affect the market price of its output – the monopoly is sufficiently big in the market-place to find an increase in output depresses the market price. The monopoly is said to enjoy ➤**market power**.

In economic analysis, a monopoly will tend to set its output at a level that ensures ➤**marginal revenue** is equated with ➤**marginal cost**. If marginal revenue were any higher it would pay the monopoly to increase production because the additional costs generated would be lower than the revenue and profits would rise. The reverse would be true if marginal revenue were any lower than marginal cost. The price the monopoly gets for its product at the chosen level of output is determined by demand in the market-place; the firm cannot set both output and price – if it could, it would set both very high!

A monopoly will make profits in excess of those merely necessary to keep it in business (➤**economic rent**) and as new entry is, by assumption not possible, there will be no pressure for price to fall and cut profit. Theory suggests that under monopoly, prices tend to be higher and output lower than they would be under the intensely competitive conditions of, say, ➤**perfect competition**.

The power of the monopolist derives from the fact that demand for his product is not as price-sensitive as it would be if good competing substitutes existed for it. Thus, when price rises, sales largely hold up. This is not the case for a competitor in a commodity business where many suppliers compete in the sale of identical products, because there, if a firm raises its price even a fraction above the going rate, it can expect to sell nothing. The degree of monopoly power a firm enjoys can be measured by how insensitive demand for its product is. The more insensitive demand is, the more the monopoly can raise its prices without losing sales.

Monopoly is held to be inefficient and undesirable for two reasons: (a) because price will be higher than otherwise, and almost certainly higher than marginal cost, so that even if some consumers value an item more than it costs to make, they may not choose to buy it (➤➤**marginal-cost pricing**), and (b) in the long term, there is no tendency for costs to be at their lowest possible level because the pressure of more efficient, incoming, competitors does not bear down on costs. It is not surprising, given these results, that most nations choose to control monopolies, which are usually defined as any firm dominant in a particular industry, e.g. with a ➤**market share** in excess of 25 per cent.

However, in some industries, efficient production requires a single dominant supplier (➤**economies of scale; increasing returns to scale; natural monopoly**). Moreover, a distinction has to be made between a monopoly that has earned its dominance by developing better products than rivals, and a monopoly which inherited its status or which acquired it by less than benign means of ousting rivals. It is possible that consumers benefit from monopoly in the long run if the profits generated act as a spur to ➤**innovation**. And in any event, defining monopoly is a more subtle process than it looks – almost no company really has a monopoly. Even what appears to be a monopoly gas company faces some competition from, for example, electricity suppliers. ➤➤**contestability**.

monopoly, discriminating A company that charges different prices for more or less the same product to different types of customers. ➤price discrimination; monopsony; segmentation.

monopsony A market in which there is only one main buyer of the item sold, e.g. the UK government is a near monopsonist in the market for teachers. The features of monopsony are rather like those of monopoly. Unlike individual consumers in most markets, the decisions of the monopsonist will have an impact on the market price prevailing. When it purchases an extra unit of the item, market demand perceptibly increases and the market price rises. This means that to buy one extra item costs the monopsonist not only the price of that item, but also the extra price that has to be paid for all the items that were previously being bought at the lower price. ➤➤bilateral monopoly.

Monte Carlo method A method of simulating (➤simulation) real-world predicaments, using randomly generated hypothetical data in a ➤model. The Monte Carlo method is so-called, because it requires some kind of roulette wheel – actual or figurative – to generate repeated random numbers according to some preset distribution. These numbers then need to be translated into some real-world phenomenon that needs modelling (e.g. traffic flows, customer arrivals, daily revenue figures, etc.) and then repeated simulations of the experience randomly generated can be performed to analyse alternative likely outcomes. Because the data used are random, statistical techniques are required in interpreting the results of a Monte Carlo simulation to ensure that any conclusion is the result of the practice being modelled, not the particular random configuration of data thrown at it.

mood state ➤affect; ➤➤consumer behaviour.

Moody's Investors Service ➤Standard and Poor's Ratings.

moral hazard The incentives for people to behave recklessly, because they do not expect to face the cost of their actions. A typical case arises out of insurance, because once someone has, say, insured his house against burglary he does not have the incentive to be as careful as he otherwise would be to protect his property. Another example would be the incentive to find a job – perhaps a rather less than satisfying one – given the existence of State benefits to the out-of-work (as with job-seeker allowances). Another oft-quoted example is that of irresponsible lending: large banks have been accused of pumping money into risky investments in emerging markets, simply because they expect the International Monetary Fund will bail the country out if it faces bankruptcy. Moral hazard is one of those important market distortions based upon imperfect information, as it is the inability of, say, the insurer to distinguish the well-behaved claimant from the badly behaved one that creates the problem.

mortgage A legal agreement conveying conditional ownership of ➤assets as ➤security for a loan and becoming void when the debt is repaid. A common form of loan for home purchase in most countries, the home being the asset providing the security.

mortgage-backed security A ➤bond that represents a bundle of small mortgage loans. An individual mortgage is typically too small for a large-scale investor to be

237

interested in financing, but it is to the detriment of the mortgage market that big players, able to buy and sell loans in a liquid form (➤**liquidity**), are absent. The solution, pioneered by the US government in the form of the Government National Mortgage Association (GNMA), was for a package of mortgage loans to be bought from mortgage providers and sold in the form of bonds, whose return was simply the combination of mortgage-holders' interest payments. The GNMA bonds were nicknamed 'Ginnie Maes', and they allowed housing developers to organize mortgage finance for house-buyers before building or selling their homes. The process of creating paper assets of this form out of a package of smaller loans is known as ➤**securitization**.

motivation The effort and drive to satisfy an individual need, e.g. a person might work, and work harder, because of a need for money and status. Motivation is conceptualized as a process: starting with an unsatisfied individual need, giving rise to tension, this stimulates drives and search behaviour, finally resulting in the satisfaction of the need and a reduction of tension. Early theories of motivation focused very much on needs. Four of these are particularly well known and have intuitive appeal: Alderfer's ➤**ERG theory**, ➤**McClelland's theory of needs**, ➤**Maslow's hierarchy of needs**, and ➤**motivation–hygiene theory**. However, nowadays, their validity is seriously questioned, and management theorists have increasingly turned to other theories. Specifically: ➤**equity theory; expectancy theory; goal-setting theory; reinforcement theory**. Motivation theories such as these are used to analyse ➤**absenteeism**, turnover, performance in the job, productivity, ➤**employee retention** and ➤**job satisfaction** of employees. Some theories are more suited to particular analyses than others. Thus, goalsetting theory is useful in productivity studies but not elsewhere; by contrast, equity theory is useful for studies of productivity, absenteeism and turnover, and has some bearing on satisfaction studies, too.

Motivation–hygiene theory A theory of employee motivation. A distinction is drawn between internal factors that are rewarding and motivating, and external factors that are nice to have but not necessarily motivating ('hygiene factors'). In an employment context, things that people find intrinsically rewarding are achievement, recognition, the nature of the work itself, responsibility and growth. Employees need to feel satisfied about these if they are to be motivated. While with external factors (e.g. company policies, supervision, interpersonal relations, working conditions and salary) it is nice if employees are not dissatisfied, but just getting these things right will not be motivating. ➤**hygiene factors**.

MRP I ➤material requirements planning.

MRP II ➤manufacturing resource planning.

MSQ Minnesota Job Satisfaction Questionnaire. ➤**job satisfaction**.

Muddling-through theory A view that suggests in practice much decision-making is the result of compromises and trying to satisfy many different parties. Linbloom ('The Science of Muddling Through', *Public Administration Review*, 1959) argued that, contrary to popular belief, many strategic business decisions are not based upon a strong rationale. Even ➤**logical incrementalism** might appear to develop from conscious strategic decisions, yet in reality organizations have to appease strong advocates and develop compromises. This is especially the case in public sector organizations or where decision-making is committee-based. ➤politicking.

multi-attribute attitude model ➤attitude.

multidimensional scaling (MDS) ➤perceptual mapping.

multi-echelon inventory support A system for storing stock outside the operation but away from the customer. Such a system allows a producer to store goods in warehouses often close to customers, e.g. in regional centres. These serve as distribution points for other ➤**channel of distribution**. This type of multilayered distribution of inventory is common in the food industry, for it allows the producer to supply many retailers who are then able to hold inventory in regional centres.

multimedia A device encompassing several communication media such as sound, pictures and text. This area of technology has developed rapidly around personal computers and in particular the technology that enables personal computers to interact on the ➤**internet**. Whereas software for a personal computer manufactured in 1990 would facilitate text and drawings only, 5 years later it was possible to use pictures and sound. Today, most personal computers are sold with software that enables them to display, send and receive moving images in the form of video, still images in the form of photographs, books in the form of text, and music in the form of sound.

multinational company (MNC) A company having production and other facilities in a number of countries outside the nation of origin. Also, and more correctly, called multinational enterprise or *transnational corporation.* ➤Bartlett, Christopher A.

Murphy's law 'If anything can go wrong, it will.' Arthur Bloch's book of this title (1977) quotes a letter from a manager at NASA attributing the law to a Captain Ed. Murphy, a development engineer, although the notion of the perversity of fate is lost in antiquity; 'Sod's law' is another formulation. Murphy's law is a useful guide not only for safety and space engineers but for all managers. Bloch gives several corollaries, including: 'Whenever you set out to do something, something else must be done first', and: 'If there is a possibility of several things going wrong, the one that will cause the most damage will be the one to go wrong.'

mutual 1. A company without ➤**issued capital** stock, legally owned by those who have deposited funds with it, perhaps by paying premiums on an endowment policy. Common among ➤**savings banks** and ➤**insurance** companies. Profits, after retention of reserves, are distributed to depositors in contrast to a proprietary company. **2.** In the US, also an open-ended investment trust. ➤**mutual fund.**

mutual fund (US) A pooled system of group investment, equivalent to a ➤**unit trust** in the UK, first developed in the US in the 1930s. The funds are invested chiefly in ➤**stocks** (company shares) and bonds, both of companies and of the public authorities. A major category emerging in recent times has been the ➤**money market mutual fund; open-ended fund.**

MVA ➤economic value added.

Myers–Briggs Type Indicator (MBTI) A widely used personality test that classifies individuals according to four characteristics, which are then combined into sixteen personality types. The four characteristics are extroverted or introverted (E or I), sensing or intuitive (S or N), thinking or feeling (T or F) and perceiving or judging (P or J). Example personality types include 'ESTJs' who are 'organizers', 'ENTPs' who are 'conceptualizers', and 'INTJs' who are 'visionaries'. The indicator is used to aid employee recruitment and appraisal by many large corporations, educational institutions and armed forces. However, it is not as well tested as the ➤five factor model of personality. ➤personality traits.

N

NAPF ➤National Association of Pension Funds.

NASD ➤National Association of Securities Dealers.

NASDAQ ➤National Association of Securities Dealers Automated Quotation system.

NASDAQ composite An index of price movements consisting of all stocks traded on the NASDAQ exchange. It was established in February 1971, with a base value of 100. Given the composition of the exchange, it became accepted as the best measure of movements in the value of stocks of high-tech companies.

Nash equilibrium A concept central to ➤game theory, which characterizes any situation where all the participants in a game are pursuing their best possible strategy given the strategies of all the other participants. It is a notion of ➤equilibrium because, given the behaviour of everybody else, no one has any incentive to change his own behaviour. Everybody's strategies are self-reinforcing.

A game is any situation in which there are participants, rules of conduct and pay-offs. One might imagine a simple game in a two-person country where both the people have to decide the side of the road on which to drive. The pay-offs are either 'no crash' (when both drive on the left or right) or 'crash' (when one drives on the left and the other on the right). In this situation, two possible Nash equilibria could be said to exist: (a) either both driving on the left, or (b) both driving on the right. If one drives on the left and the other on the right, it is not a Nash equilibrium because, given the choice of the other, each would change their own policy. Popular examples of Nash equilibria arise in ➤Hotelling's law and the ➤prisoners' dilemma. The Nash equilibrium is not necessarily the most likely outcome of a game as, in some cases, Nash equilibria can involve players choosing strategies that can easily be bettered. In other cases, a Nash equilibrium can be upheld by the use of an implausible threat by one player. Even though the threat would not be likely to be carried out, it can influence a Nash equilibrium. For these reasons, economists have searched for other notions of 'solving' games. Nash, nevertheless, represents the starting-point for all discussion on the subject.

National Association of Pension Funds (NAPF) The representative organization of providers of occupational pension schemes. ➤pensions.

National Association of Securities Dealers (NASD) (US) ➤National Association of Securities Dealers Automated Quotation system.

National Association of Securities Dealers Automated Quotation system
(NASDAQ) (US)   A series of computer-based information services and an ➤order
execution system for the US ➤over-the-counter market. The system was set up in
1971. NASDAQ provides quotations by over 500 active ➤market makers on the
➤securities of over 4,000 companies that are actively traded, an average of eight
dealers for each security and a minimum of two.

There are some 180,000 NASDAQ terminals in use, of which 25,000 are outside
the US. NASDAQ was designated a UK *recognized investment exchange* in 1988.
➤**Financial Services Act**. Brokers and institutional traders, having selected the
market maker who offers the best price on their screens, may execute their deals by
telephone or teletype or, since 1984, may enter orders directly through the Small
Order Execution System (SOES). The SOES allows dealers to fill orders for 500 shares
or less and 1,000 shares for NASDAQ ➤**National Market System** issues. NASDAQ
International has operated from London since early 1992 and allows investors to
trade US stocks before the ➤**New York Stock Exchange** opens.

The National Association of Securities Dealers is a self-regulatory organization
(under delegated powers from the ➤**Securities and Exchange Commission**) that
set up and now regulates NASDAQ and the ➤over-the-counter market.

national culture   The set of values, norms, motives and beliefs held by a majority
of people in a nation that can be used to describe and predict people's behaviour.
This draws on anthropological and psychological notions of culture as 'shared
meanings, values, attitudes and beliefs', e.g. A L Kroeber and C Kluckholm, *Culture:
a critical review of concepts and definitions* (1952).

In a business context, the most quoted sources are the cross-cultural studies by
Geert ➤**Hofstede** (*Culture's Consequences*, 1980; *Cultures and Organisations: software
of the mind*, 1991). He identified four dimensions:
(1) Power distance. The equality of power distribution between senior managers and
    subordinates.
(2) Individualism–collectivism. The sense a person has of being psychologically
    separate from, and independent of, others, versus the sense of being linked to
    others through close personal networks and social bonds.
(3) Uncertainty avoidance. The desire to avoid uncertainty by trying to control the
    future.
(4) Masculinity–femininity. The case where gender roles are distinct, versus the case
    where gender roles overlap.
(5) A fifth dimension has been added: Long-term versus short-term orientation.
Hofstede placed countries in this cultural landscape (e.g. small power distance
(Denmark), large power distance (Indonesia), collectivist (Pakistan), individualist
(US), weak uncertainty avoidance (Hong Kong), strong uncertainty avoidance
(Japan), feminine (The Netherlands), masculine (Germany)). Another major cross-
cultural study was completed by Michael ➤**Porter** in *The Comparative Advantage of
Nations*, 1990.

Most of these studies have focused on national culture as manifest within companies – IBM in the case of much of Hofstede's work, and a wider pool of companies
in the case of Porter. In these studies, elements of national and ➤**organizational
culture** are interlinked. While the two are conceptually distinct, operationally it is
hard to treat them as such – to a degree, employees of a particular nationality will

self-select their employer, thereby confounding the two forms of culture, e.g. a particular type of Frenchman will choose to work for Microsoft in Paris. A further problem is that there is likely to be much variation within national and organizational cultures (therefore only looking at the mean, or dominant, culture could be very misleading). For example, particular subcultures may have more in common *across* countries or corporations than *within*, e.g. those belonging to 'Generation X' in the UK may share many characteristics of the same subculture in the US, perhaps overriding differences in uncertainty avoidance among the dominant cultures.

National Market System (NMS) (US) A system providing information on the quoted price of ➤stocks, the latest price paid, the high and low for the day and the current ➤volume. NMS brokers are required to report this information through the system within 90 seconds of the trade. Congress mandated the creation of a NMS in its amendments to the 1934 Securities Exchange Act in 1975, which created the ➤Securities and Exchange Commission. The purpose of the NMS was to increase competition by linking the US stock exchanges together in a way that would ensure that prices for any given stock would be the same at all of them.

National Savings (NSB) (UK) A ➤savings bank administered by the Department for National Savings and operating through the post office network. Formerly known as the Post Office Savings Bank.

natural monopoly An industry in which technical factors preclude the efficient existence of more than one producer. ➤monopoly. An example might be local refuse collection, where it is uneconomic to have two companies each driving up the same street to collect rubbish from every second home. In the past, the notion of a natural monopoly was interpreted quite widely to include the public utilities such as water, gas and electricity, as well as post and telecommunications. In order to prevent these natural monopolies exploiting consumers, public ownership of the dominant companies was designed to promote the public interest. However, as privatization saw the ownership of many companies transferred, regulators (➤regulation) saw opportunities for introducing competition in what were previously natural monopolies. In the case of telecoms, the UK regulator in the 1990s even promoted the construction of a second tier of cable phone networks to compete with the incumbent British Telecommunications (BT) network. It has to be said, however, that the pendulum has swung back somewhat and the existence of natural monopoly has been re-emphasized. In the telecommunications case, it transpired to be hard for the cable companies to profit from their extensive investment. Instead, the dominant regulatory model is that of separating the naturally monopolistic segment of the industry – usually the network of pipes or cables – from the potentially competitive parts such as retailing or feeding material into the network. Thus, electricity has been subdivided into a separate natural monopoly in the form of the national grid and competing generators of electricity, and competing retailers of it. In telecommunications, the emphasis has been on setting terms by which competitors to BT can connect to its cables, to provide competing services, so-called 'unbundling of the local loop'. This promotes competition without the true benefits of natural monopoly being lost.

negotiable 1. Subject to agreement between the parties involved in a transaction.

2. A negotiable instrument (e.g. an endorsed ➤**cheque** or ➤**bearer security**) is one in which the title to ownership is transferred freely from hand to hand.

negotiation   The process of bargaining over a set of issues for the purpose of reaching an agreement. This definition presupposes there is a willingness by each party to negotiate. This will only occur if both parties believe they will be better off as a result of negotiating than they would be otherwise. Hence, the importance of seeking 'win–win' outcomes. The definition also alludes to 'a set of issues', which emphasizes the fact that most negotiations are about a combination of issues or agenda items. So, it is important to understand what these issues are and their importance to both parties (the importance will differ among the parties). Concessions and compromises will be easier to reach over relatively unimportant issues. Viewpoints on some issues will be convergent (reflecting common interests) and on others, divergent (reflecting conflicting interests). Finally, the definition stresses the ultimate goal – an agreement that is acceptable to both sides. Without this outcome the negotiation is said to have failed (a solution may be imposed through coercion, manipulation or deception, but then this is not a negotiated settlement).

The process of negotiation has several stages: preparation, positioning, reflecting, ➤**bargaining** and problem-solving, and closure. Preparation is a crucial first step. Why is the negotiation taking place? Is there a ➤**conflict**, and over what? What does *each* and *every* party want from the negotiation? Positioning – at this stage a formal proposal – is presented by one or both parties, e.g. a seller submits a proposal to the potential buyer, an employer makes a pay offer to trade union representatives, a line manager gives a subordinate a suggested work plan. This is discussed, clarified and justified. There then follows a period of reflection – both parties have revealed their positions and each understands what the other would like to achieve. Where there are differences (and there usually are differences), bargaining and problem-solving ensue. The aim at this stage is to remove or reconcile any differences that stand in the way of getting agreement. This usually means making adjustments and reaching a compromise. While it is important to secure a 'win–win' outcome, an equally beneficial 'win–win' is rare and should not be expected (rather than 50 : 50, the outcome may be 60 : 40 or 70 : 30). Finally, the agreement must be signed-off and implemented. If the settlement has not been fully accepted this will become apparent during implementation; parties will deviate from the agreement or attempt to undermine it or allow conflicts to resurface.

The skilled negotiator not only knows how to bargain (e.g. by fostering openness and trust), but has a thorough understanding of the whole process. He will have a thought-through strategy, including a view on his and the other side's best alternative to a negotiated agreement (BATNA). This is the lowest outcome acceptable to him for a negotiated agreement. Below this level there can be no resolution and no agreement, but anything above this level is at least better than a stalemate. The other side's BATNA needs to be considered, too; there will be no agreement if their minimum level is not reached.

Considerable use is made of third-party negotiators. In commercial negotiations, consultants are employed to negotiate prices and terms between suppliers and buyers. In international trading contexts, this requires an appreciation for cultural factors as well as negotiation skills. In industrial relations settings, mediators, conciliators and arbitrators are used. Mediators are completely neutral third parties who are able to reason with both parties. They do not coerce or compel, they merely suggest, reason and convince the parties. Conciliators take on a similar role, operating as a 'go-between', but they may be known to both parties and may become involved directly in suggesting and communicating solutions. ➤conciliation. Arbitrators, by contrast, have the authority to dictate an agreement. The parties may have voluntarily agreed to go to ➤arbitration and stand by the decision, or they may have been compelled as a result of legal processes. ➤collective bargaining; industrial dispute.

negotiation-based strategy The development of a strategy for a firm through discussions with a variety of groups. The idea with this approach is that politics and negotiations are part of all organizations and whatever routes are devised they need to have the support of everyone in the organization. This approach helps to achieve this, but also links it to optimal decision-making through microeconomics and mathematical modelling. Consideration must be given to factors internal and external to the firm. The theoretical background can be considered as being through three conceptual areas:
(1) Human resource strategy. This focuses on negotiations with people within the organization.
(2) Network-based strategy. This explores the degree of co-operation and competition present in related organizations.
(3) Game theory strategy. This examines the way the actual strategic negotiations are conducted and suggests guidelines for optimal decisions.

net asset, net asset value (NAV) The value of a company according to its ➤balance sheet. It is calculated by taking fixed assets plus current assets less ➤liabilities owed to all except the owners of the company, and therefore is the same as ➤shareholders' equity and is also called *net worth*. Where long-term liabilities (e.g. bank loans) are not deducted in arriving at net assets, then this term is synonymous with ➤capital employed. Assets are valued at *historic cost*. ➤costs, historical; depreciation. The market value may be greater than the net asset value. NAV for an ➤investment trust is the market value of shares owned by the trust plus cash, usually divided by the number of shares at issue to give NAV per share. The price of investment trust shares may be at a ➤discount or at a ➤premium to the underlying NAV. ➤balance sheet; investment trust; working capital.

net current asset ➤working capital.

net present value ➤discounted cash flow.

net profit (NTA) ➤profit.

net tangible asset Fixed ➤assets plus current assets minus intangible assets, such as ➤goodwill, and minus current ➤liabilities.

net worth ➤net asset.

Neuer Markt ➤German stock exchange.

new economy The label given to the development of generally benign economic conditions in much of the developed world (especially the US) in the second half of the 1990s, typically attributed to the permeation of information and communications technology. The phrase took off as conventional economic forecasts of inflation, unemployment and output were consistently shown to be too pessimistic. A solid uplift in the rate of growth in US productivity in the late 1990s, coinciding with an investment boom focusing on the new technologies, led many to suggest the constraints of economic growth (➤**trend growth**) had been eased. As long as fast productivity growth continued, growth generally could continue without any danger of rising prices.

The term 'new economy' is sometimes used narrowly, to refer to the effect of IT. At other times, it is used more broadly, to refer to a whole plethora of economic changes, including increased global trade, labour market flexibility, stability oriented economic management and corporate ➤**re-engineering**. A distinction, implicit or otherwise, could be drawn between: (a) those who think the new economy is simply a mirage, created by a soaring US boom that had to end at some time – certainly, the ➤**speculative bubble** in the shares of technology companies that peaked in March 2000 played a large part in generating new economy hype; (b) those who think new economy effects give a temporary boost to growth, allowing gross domestic product to reach a higher level than it would otherwise have obtained before continuing to grow at the old economy rate, and (c) those who think it allows the Western world permanently to grow faster. ➤➤**electronic commerce; knowledge economy.**

new entrant ➤early entrant, ➤➤barriers to entry; first-mover advantage.

new issue The sale of ➤securities (e.g. loan ➤stock or ➤equity) to raise new or additional ➤**capital**, either by way of a ➤**placing**, an offer for *subscription* (➤**offer for sale**) or a ➤**rights issue**. The term may also refer to the ➤**flotation** of the existing securities of a company on a stock exchange or an ➤**unlisted securities market** for the first time, though such an issue may also involve the raising of additional capital. ➤new issue market.

new issue market That part of the ➤**capital market** that provides new long-term capital, specifically the ➤**stock exchange**. Borrowers in the new issue market may be raising capital for new investment or may be converting private into public capital; this is known as *going public*. ➤**flotation**; ➤➤**new issue; rights issue.**

newly industrialized countries (NICs) Not counted as developing or Third World countries, although they have not yet achieved the status of an advanced country. The term is applied to countries which achieved rapid rates of industrial growth in the 1970s, e.g. Hong Kong, Mexico and Taiwan.

new product development (NPD) The process of developing and bringing to market new products and services. A complete process involves the following stages: planning and market definition, idea generation and opportunity identification, positioning and segmentation, forecasting, product design and quality checks, product advertising tests, pretesting of the product prior to launch, test marketing, introduction and commercialization, monitoring of the launch, improvements and enhancements, and life-cycle management and product portfolio planning. Strictly, the latter two stages have more to do with product management than new product development, but even at the outset of the process it is prudent to think about longer-term management issues.

The NPD process may be proactive or reactive. Proactive NPD is driven by a formal assessment of opportunities, looking at customer needs and buyer behaviour, identifying ideas with high potential, and relating this to organizational factors, e.g. the organization's competitive advantage, its distinctive competencies, and its goals for sales and profit growth from new products. This is likely to entail market research (➤qualitative market research, brainstorming, lead-user analysis, ➤means–end value chain) and self-assessment, e.g. ➤SWOT (strengths, weaknesses, opportunities and threats), ➤PESTL (political, economic, social, technical and legal forces) etc. There then follows a formal design phase. The aim is to create a product that will offer certain benefits to the target audience, and do so in a way that positions the product distinctively in the minds of consumers. Further market research is required to develop and design the product (typically, ➤conjoint analysis, stated-preference ➤choice modelling, ➤perceptual mapping, concept testing). These product ideas must be integrated with other aspects of ➤marketing mix (pricing, advertising, promotion, distribution, selling, delivery and post-purchase servicing). The process continues with further research and analysis, e.g. 'beta testing' prior to a national roll-out and evaluation of trial and repeat rates post launch.

With reactive NPD the organization needs to be able to sense changes in the market, read competitive signals and move quickly. It must also be able to decide whether a competitive threat or opportunity is significant. Where it is significant, the reaction might be to copy the concept (possibly resulting in a look-alike or 'me-too') or improve on the concept (by offering features which are better able to meet market needs). While this will often mean adding features, it could also entail simplifying the product, especially with technological products (this has been the case with pocket calculators, VCR tapes, and DVD systems). If the reactive organization does any market research at all it is by stealth. Where reactive NPD is common, competitors may deliberately send mixed signals to the market ('competitive signalling'); this keeps consumers interested but gives a confusing picture to competitors who may find it hard to respond appropriately.

There are various inputs to the NPD process, notably investment in NPD (absolute and as a proportion of turnover for a defined time period) and the number of employees engaged in NPD activities, e.g. teams. General outcomes are measured in terms of the contribution of new products to company profits, company growth, current revenue and current sales volume/value. The success of a specific new product will be assessed using one or more of the following criteria: financial measures (➤net present value, ➤return on investment, ➤internal rate of return, contribution to company profit), sales measures (volume/value sales, percentage of sales contributed by the new product, market share contributed by the new product), customer measures (customer satisfaction, feedback, complaints) and qualitative factors (the belief by management that the market potential has been realized).

A problem in thinking about NPD is that the term 'new product' is used to describe very different things. A distinction can be drawn between different types of new product. Using ➤H I **Ansoff**'s opportunities matrix (1957) a common distinction is between:

(1) Existing products in existing markets (NPD merely involves minor changes, such as new varieties and flavours, in known markets).
(2) Existing products in new markets (NPD entails minor adaptations for the new markets).

(3) New products in existing markets (the full process of NPD is required for the focal organization, although others already have products in the market).

(4) New products in new markets (NPD involves diversification, with new-to-the-world products in a totally new area).

A further distinction relates NPD to types of brand development, following E M Tauber ('Brand Franchise Extension: New Product Benefits from Existing Brand Names', *Business Horizons*, 1981):

(1) Development of an existing product category and existing brand name gives rise to line extensions.

(2) Existing product category and new brand name defines a flanker.

(3) New product category, with existing brand name, is a franchise extension or brand extension.

(4) New product category and new brand name can be seen as a really new product/brand.

Another popular classification is that suggested by Booz, Allan & Hamilton (*New Product Development for the 1980s*, Booz, Allen & Hamilton, 1982):

(1) New-to-the-world products. These products represent a small proportion of all new products introduced. They are the first of their kind and create a new market. They are inventions that usually contain a significant development in technology (e.g. a new discovery) or manipulate existing technology in a very different way leading to revolutionary new designs such as the 'Sony Walkman'. Other examples include Polaroid's Instamatic camera, 3M's Post-It Notes and Guinness' In-can-system.

(2) New product lines (new to the firm). Although not new to the market-place, these products are new to the particular company. They provide an opportunity for the company to enter an established market for the first time. For example, Canon was able to enter the paper-copying market when they launched their own range of copiers to compete with Xerox, who were the originators of the product.

(3) Additions to existing lines. This category is a subset of new product lines above, the distinction being that while the company already has a line of products in this market, the product is significantly different to the present product offering, but not so different that it is a new line. The distinction between this category and the former is one of degree, e.g. Hewlett Packard's Colour Ink Jet-Printer was an addition to its established line of Ink-Jet Printers.

(4) Improvements and revisions to existing products. These new products are replacements of existing products in a firm's product line, e.g. Hewlett Packard's Ink-Jet printer has received numerous modifications over time and with each revision performance and reliability have been improved. Also, manufacturing cost reductions can be introduced providing increased added value to the company. This classification represents a significant proportion of all new product introductions.

(5) Cost reductions. This category of products may not be viewed as new from a marketing perspective, largely because they offer no new benefits to the consumer other than possible reduced costs. From the firm's perspective, however, they may be very significant. The ability to offer similar performance while reducing production costs provides enormous added value potential. Indeed, frequently it is this category of new product that can produce the greatest financial rewards

to the firm. Improved manufacturing processes and the use of different materials are key contributing factors. The difference between this category and the improvement category is simply that a cost reduction may not result in a product improvement.

(6) Repositionings. These new products are essentially the discovery of new applications for existing products. This has more to do with consumer perception and branding than technical development. This is none the less an important category of new products. A well-known example in the UK is the repositioning of Lucozade by SmithKline Beecham from a refreshing drink for sick children and pregnant mothers into a health and sports drink. Similarly, following the medical science discovery that aspirin thins blood, aspirin has been repositioned from an analgesic to an over-the-counter remedy for blood clots, and may help to prevent strokes and heart attacks.

In practice, the vast majority of 'new products' are minor changes and line extensions of existing brands, which tend to be low-risk. Really new products, where both the brand and the product category are new, are far less common and higher risk. This, however, will differ by sector (new technology-based sectors, such as digital television, mobile telephony, genetic engineering and DNA profiling, will have more really new products than established sectors). The subject has been researched thoroughly by management consultants, notably by Booz, Allen & Hamilton, whose studies in the 1980s drew worldwide attention to both the importance of new products (e.g. accounting for almost a third of company growth over a 5-year period) and the high failure rates (most new product ideas are never commercialized and, of those that are, a third do not succeed). MIT has been a catalyst for academic research (Glen Urban & John Hauser, *Design and Marketing of New Products*, second edition, 1993).

Studies show that NPD success is correlated with an ability to: match customer needs, offer something that has high value (or high perceived value) to customers, be innovative, build technical superiority, offer quality, make full use of market research before (e.g. pre-testing) and after (e.g. customer satisfaction surveys), have product screening processes (to select winners), use decision support systems, choose favourable competitive environments, offer something that is a good fit with internal company strengths and capabilities, foster good communication among different functions (➤research and development (R & D), marketing, production, etc.), secure top-management support and commitment, put in place product champions, use formal NPD processes, avoid unnecessary risk, achieve a short time to market, and devise a coherent product portfolio plan (including migration paths if customers need to be guided through different models and upgrades). ➤first-mover advantage.

Reasons for NPD failure are equally numerous, but are essentially the reverse of the success factors, e.g. the market is not there or is too small ('a phantom market'), the product is a poor match for the company given its capabilities, there is no real consumer benefit, etc. The importance of internal factors is apparent here. The traditional view of new product development was that the R & D function would develop new technology that would be transformed by the engineering function into a product and this would later be passed to the marketing function to promote. Such a linear process is no longer valid as most new products now involve consumer testing of new product concept at an early stage. ➤concurrent engineering.

249

Moreover, there is recognition that to be successful the process of developing a new product needs to have a more integrated approach between the functional groups of the organization.

New York Stock Exchange (NYSE) (US) The leading New York ➤**stock exchange** and largest in the world in terms of ➤**market capitalization** (➤➤**American Stock Exchange**). Some 2,000 companies and 5,000 ➤**securities** are listed on the NYSE. It is the oldest exchange in the US dating from 1792, and is also referred to as the 'Big Board'. There are about 500 broking firms, with some 1,366 members or seats. These members trade as specialists in particular ➤**stocks** on the ➤**trading floor**, as ➤**floor brokers** on behalf of clients or as floor traders on their own account. The NYSE is a self-regulating body, though it has to ensure compliance with the requirements of the ➤**Securities and Exchange Commission**. ➤➤**Dow-Jones index**.

niche brand A brand that appeals to a specific group of committed, heavy and/or frequent buyers. Typically, niche brands are targeted at a minor segment within the wider context of the whole market. ➤**segmentation**. For a smaller organization or a start-up company, niche branding is seen as a way to concentrate resources and gain a foothold in a market. Niche brands may also exist in immature markets, perhaps before mainstream brands enter. For several years, Body Shop was seen as a niche brand in the immature environment-friendly toiletries and cosmetics market; however, as the market grew, and as established retailers moved into the sector, Body Shop had to decide whether to become more of a mainstream brand itself or stay as a small player. Despite the intuitive appeal of niche branding, there are severe obstacles in practice. Business risks are usually high in immature markets. Small fledgling brands are often extremely vulnerable to competitive incursions. Moreover, there is evidence to suggest that most so-called niche brands are merely small – they do not secure an exceptional number of committed, heavy and/or frequent buyers. The usual pattern of behaviour associated with small brands (compared to larger brands) is that most will have fewer buyers who will buy somewhat less. The exception to this may be in certain geographical markets, where distance may 'protect' a small brand (however, the truth of this will partly depend on how trading areas are defined and which brands are included in the competitive set). ➤**market definition**; ➤➤**generic strategy**.

Nikkei 225 An index designed to reflect movements in 225 stocks traded on the ➤**Tokyo Stock Exchange**. It was first published in 1949.

NMS ➤**National Market System**; **normal market size**.

nomad Nominated adviser. A stockbroking firm (➤**stockbroker**) approved by the ➤**London Stock Exchange** to advise and sponsor companies on the ➤**Alternative Investment Market**. ➤➤**issuing house**.

nominal interest rate The ➤**rate of interest** on a ➤**fixed-interest** ➤**security**, expressed as a percentage of the ➤**par value** as opposed to its market price. ➤**yield**.

nominal value ➤**par value**.

nominal yield ➤**yield**.

nominee A person or company holding ➤**securities** on behalf of another in order to preserve anonymity or to simplify ➤**settlement**. Many ➤**stockbrokers** have set up *nominee companies* in which their clients have *nominee accounts* recording their beneficial interests in shares legally owned by the nominee companies. Such a system avoids the necessity for the broker to send ➤**share certificates** through the post and has allowed *paperless settlement systems.* ➤➤**CREST**.

nominee account ➤nominee.

nominee company ➤nominee.

non-cumulative preference shares ➤preference shares.

non-linear relationship Any relationship between two variables that can be graphed as a curved line. For example, if $x = y^2$, then it would be straightforward to plot corresponding values of x and y on a graph, and the line joining them would be curved. If, however, $x = 2y$ then the equivalent graph would be a straight line, and known as linear.

non-recourse ➤recourse.

non-recourse finance A loan with servicing and repayment dependent solely on the profitability of the underlying project and not on other funds potentially in the possession of the borrower. ➤➤**factoring**.

normal market size (NMS) (UK) A system for classifying ➤**stocks** quoted on the ➤**London Stock Exchange** by ➤**liquidity**. NMS for each stock is calculated by multiplying the value of the average daily customer ➤**turnover** in the previous year by 2.5 per cent to give an estimated average value of the normal institutional ➤**bargain**; this is then divided by the price of the stock to give that normal bargain size in terms of the number of shares. This number of shares is allocated to 12 NMS *bands* indicating the degree of liquidity. The system is used to set the size of transactions for which ➤**market makers** quote prices and for the publication of market data.

normal profit The level of profit a firm has to make to just compensate its investors for the cost of the capital tied up in the business. Anything above normal profit can be referred to as ➤**economic rent**. It is not an accounting concept, but useful in judging the impact of business decisions on shareholders. Imagine, for example, that shareholders can save money in the bank earning a rate of interest of 5 per cent. Imagine a company they own earns some large profits, and the company decides to invest these in a project that is expected to earn a return of 4 per cent. In this case, making the investment will cause the volume of the company's profits to grow, but because the investment makes less than a normal profit, the shareholders would have been better off taking the money out of the company and putting it in the bank for themselves. The normal profit in this case would have to be 5 per cent, and that provides a good benchmark for executives to decide whether they are creating ➤**shareholder value** or not when they invest.

Normal profit can be seen as the ➤**opportunity cost** of capital but, in practice, it is not easy to measure accurately. Adjusting for the risk of an investment, the effect of taxes and the different opportunity costs of different investors is important.

norming ➤group development.

North American Free Trade Agreement (NAFTA) An agreement for a tariff-free area arising out of the Free Trade Area established between the US and Canada in 1989 and extended to Mexico.

note 1. An ➤instrument recording a promise to pay a specific sum of money by a given date; a *promissory note*. ➤➤commercial paper. **2.** A banknote.

not invented here (NIH) The tendency of a project group of stable composition to believe it possesses the monopoly of knowledge in its field, leading it to reject new ideas from outsiders to the likely detriment of its performance. One of the most well-known barriers to technology transfer is the NIH syndrome. It is general folklore among ➤research and development (R & D) professionals that groups of scientists and engineers who have worked together for many years will begin to believe that no one else can know or understand the area in which they are working better than they do. In some cases, this attitude can spread across the whole R & D function so that the effect is a refusal to accept any new ideas from outside. This syndrome has been so widely discussed since it was first uncovered that, like many diseases, it has been virtually wiped out. R & D managers need, however, to be vigilant to ensure that it does not recur.

NPD ➤new product development.

NPV Net present value. ➤discounted cash flow.

NSB ➤National Savings Bank.

numerical control (NC) A method for storing instructions for a machine tool using numerical data, which can then be used to control its movements during a manufacturing process. The first such machines – developed in the 1950s – used punched paper tape. Today, the machine tools have their own microprocessor and computer, and are referred to as ➤computer numerical control machines. The operator is now able to input instructions directly to the machine, thereby eliminating the need to produce punched-tape instructions. In addition, an operator is able to operate several machine tools simultaneously. The principle of operation, however, remains the same as the first machines.

O

OB ➤organizational behaviour.

observation techniques ➤qualitative market research.

occupational pension scheme ➤pension.

OEIC ➤open-ended investment company.

OFEX An ➤unlisted securities market trading in shares in companies (not ➤quoted companies) on the ➤London Stock Exchange.

off-balance-sheet finance A business ➤asset that is not purchased and subject to ➤depreciation, but is acquired by ➤leasing or ➤hire purchase, and thus does not appear on a company's ➤balance sheet. Rental payments will, of course, be taken into account in the ➤profit and loss account, but the indebtedness of the company and ➤capital employed will be understated. However, in the US and the UK, companies may be required to capitalize leased assets.

offer for sale (UK) A means of selling new shares to the public at a fixed price in an advertised offer (US = *public offering*). Those who purchase the shares are said to have subscribed, i.e. it is an offer for subscription. More rarely, an offer for ➤tenders will be called-for. In a tender, potential investors are invited to specify the number of shares they are prepared to buy at a specified price at or above the issuer's stipulated minimum price. The ➤issuing house will set a price (the offer for sale) at which the whole issue can be sold at the highest price. Those who have made a tender offer at or above the striking price will receive the number of shares they asked for (unless the issue is ➤oversubscribed); those whose offer price is below the striking price will receive no shares. Issues over a certain size (£50 million) have to be offered to the public in their entirety, under the rules of the ➤London Stock Exchange, instead of by a ➤placing or an ➤intermediate offer. ➤➤introduction.

offer price The price at which a ➤dealer or ➤market maker will sell ➤commodities or shares (US = *asked price*). ➤Unit trust managers also quote an offer price at which they will sell units to the general public. ➤bid price.

Office of Fair Trading (OFT) The agency responsible for promoting competition and consumer welfare in the UK, under the charge of the Director-General of Fair Trading. The OFT has two important front-line divisions: one for consumer affairs and another for competition policy.

The Consumer Affairs Division has – through the Director-General – a variety of responsibilities under a range of different Acts of Parliament. The Director-General advises government on consumer policy and monitors the markets for goods and services in order to analyse trends and identify potential problem areas for further investigation. The Director-General is responsible for regulating consumer credit and issuing licences to businesses which lend money to consumers.

Under the Estate Agents Act 1979 the Director-General can ban people from engaging in estate agency work if they are unfit to do so. Under the Control of Misleading Advertisements Regulations, the Director-General supports and re-inforces the role of the Advertising Standards Authority, where it has been unable to take effective action. Under Part III of the Fair Trading Act 1973, the Director-General has the power to ask traders who persistently neglect their responsibilities to give written assurances about their future behaviour. The Unfair Terms in Consumer Contracts Regulations give the Director-General the power to ask the courts to stop traders using unfair terms in the standard contracts they use in their dealings with consumers.

It is, however, in upholding ➤competition policy, particularly under the tough provisions of the Competition Act 1998 (which took effect in 2000) that the OFT is best known, acting as the 'first base' in the conduct of UK anti-trust policy. The Director-General is the guardian of the Act, and essentially has the right to investigate on a preliminary basis ➤mergers, ➤monopolies or anti-competitive behaviour, and to decide whether they should be referred to the ➤Competition Commission (through the Secretary of State for Trade and Industry) for full scrutiny. The 1998 Act itself is designed to mimic EU law (discussed under ➤competition policy). It prohibits agreements which 'prevent, restrict or distort competition and may affect trade within the United Kingdom' (known as a Chapter I prohibition), a breach of which can attract a fine of up to 10 per cent of annual turnover. The Act lists specific examples to which the prohibition is particularly applicable. These include:

(1) Agreeing to fix purchase or selling prices or other trading conditions.
(2) Agreeing to limit or control production, markets, technical development or investment.
(3) Agreeing to share markets or supply sources.
(4) Agreeing to make contracts subject to unrelated conditions.
(5) Agreeing to apply different trading conditions to equivalent transactions, thereby placing some parties at a competitive disadvantage.

The Act also prohibits the abuse of a dominant position, usually defined as having a ➤market share exceeding 40 per cent but, more specifically, 'conduct by under-takings which amounts to an abuse of a dominant position in a market and which may affect trade within the United Kingdom', (a so-called Chapter II prohibition). Abuse might include ➤predatory pricing, charging excessive prices or imposing unfair contract terms on customers.

The 1998 Act replaced or amended a number of pieces of legislation, including the Restrictive Trade Practices Act 1976, the Resale Prices Act 1976 and the majority of the Competition Act 1980. It aimed to have more bite and less bureaucracy about it. For example, under the old legislation, all potentially restrictive agreements between firms had to be registered with the OFT (which could then refer them to a *Restrictive Practices Court*, to ascertain whether they were in the public interest). This was a burden to some firms whose agreements were entirely benign. The new approach is not to register all agreements but to punish heavily those caught out as being anti-competitive.

official list (UK) The daily list of ➤**securities** admitted for trading on the ➤**London Stock Exchange**. It does not include securities quoted on the ➤**unlisted securities market(s)**.

Ohmae, Kenichi Japanese business guru and global strategist. In *The Mind of the Strategist* (1982), Ohmae interpreted the success of Japanese-based companies abroad as based on a long-term view which avoided direct competition, initially with large international firms and using design and productivity approaches that would meet identified customer needs in a wide range of markets. He made it clear, however, that there are no formulae for getting things right. Effective strategy does not result from analysis – this is useful only to stimulate creativity and to test ideas – but rather from a state of mind, intuition and seeing customer needs clearly. In *The Borderless World* (1990) and *Triad Power: the coming shape of global competition* (1985), Ohmae argued that global communications meant that customers were now dominant, increasingly free to choose, and that they knew what products were best value. Companies must establish a presence in Europe, North America and Japan (The Triad) if they were not to be overtaken by others with global reach. Joint ventures and global strategic alliances could serve to support and protect innovative strategies.

Partly educated in the US, Ohmae became Head of ➤**McKinsey**'s Tokyo office and is the only Japanese business thinker to have achieved international recognition.

oligopoly A market which is dominated by a few large suppliers. Oligopolistic markets are often characterized by heavy ➤**product differentiation** through advertising and other marketing ploys, with long periods of price stability intermittently disrupted by keen price competition. Petrol sales and soap powder are notable oligopoly industries in the UK in which free offers, competitions and advertising are often more heavily used than price competition for attracting custom.

There is no single theory of oligopoly equivalent to that of ➤**perfect competition** or ➤**monopoly** because the behaviour of oligopolistic firms is crucially determined by the reaction and behaviour of their rivals and the assumptions they make about those reactions. Instead, there are a number of alternative theories:

(1) The first was developed by Cournot and assumed that each firm sets its price and output on the assumption that its rival does not react at all. In such a situation, each firm will leap-frog past the other, lowering price and increasing output to gain a higher ➤**market share**. The result is, nevertheless, a market in which prices are higher and output lower than they would be if the firms behaved as perfect competitors.

(2) The so-called *Bertrand competition*, in which keen price competition drives firms to ➤**marginal-cost pricing**, the outcome that prevails in intensely competitive industries.

(3) That firms recognize their interdependence, and one among them leads in price-setting with others following. In this case, the leader enjoys higher profits than any followers, but all firms benefit from the stability and predictability of the industry.

(4) All firms attempt to act as leader, then they all earn lower profits than they would under Cournot's solution. ➤➤**prisoners' dilemma**.

(5) Firms assume their rivals will follow their prices down, but not follow their price if it rises; in this situation, firms will be very reluctant to change their price (it is as though the ➤**demand curve** the firm assumes it faces, is kinked). It could

account for the fact that prices are often stable in oligopolistic industries despite large changes in costs.

(6) Firms collude and between them achieve the outcome that would occur if a monopoly existed in the industry. However, if one firm colludes, it always pays another to cheat and sell more than agreed, so that maintaining collusive agreements may be difficult in situations where firms cannot monitor each other's behaviour. Otherwise hefty State penalties for collusion can deter oligopolists from making agreements that have negative effects on consumers.

Other approaches to oligopoly exist, notably ➤game theory, which has been used to simulate the reactions of firms to each other's behaviour.

omnibus survey A general-purpose survey periodically sent to a large sample. This enables information to be gathered about brands bought and viewing, listening and reading habits of respondents, i.e. 'single-source' data. Also, an individual client can ask that a particular survey include one or two additional questions on topical issues. An example is the Target Group Index.

one price, law of The rule that says in any one market, at any one time, there can only be one prevailing price for identical products. If this was not the case, people would buy at a low price, and resell at a high price, until the prices converged.

one-to-one marketing A form of marketing that emphasizes the relationship between an organization and each customer, one by one. The aim is to build 'share of wallet', rather than the traditional goal of mass marketing – the building of market share. This can be seen as an extreme form of microsegmentation. ➤direct marketing; interactive electronic marketing; permission marketing.

open-ended fund An investment company in which units may be purchased from, or sold to, the fund manager, i.e. a ➤unit trust or ➤mutual fund company. The fund is open in the sense that its size depends upon its success in selling units, in contrast to an ➤investment trust. Units are bought and sold at a price that reflects the market value of the securities they represent, plus a management charge equal to the difference between the ➤bid price and ➤offer price.

open-ended investment company (OEIC) An ➤open-ended fund listed on a stock exchange at a single unit share price; like an ➤investment trust but it can issue or redeem (➤redemption) shares to match demand in a similar way to a ➤unit trust. Common in continental European countries and the US. OEICs have recently been permitted in the UK.

opening price The price at which a ➤security is quoted when a stock exchange, or other market, opens for business in the morning. ➤Market makers will adjust their prices from the level they reached when trading stopped on the previous day (➤closing price) in line with their expectations of the strength of supply and demand.

open market operations Dealings in the ➤money market by a ➤central bank, with the object of influencing short-term interest rates in pursuit of ➤monetary policy.

operant conditioning A form of behavioural ➤learning, also called 'instrumental conditioning'.

operating profit (or loss) Profit (or loss) before tax and interest, usually on the principal trading activities of the business and excluding extraordinary items. ➤**below the line.**

operational research (OR) Applied mathematics devoted to the study of an organization's operations. It is a set of techniques that help to organize and plan operations such as production, scheduling and resource allocation. Some of the techniques (e.g. ➤**critical path analysis** and ➤**queuing theory**) are well known and have proved to be very successful in optimizing an organization's resources. Operational research techniques were devised during the Second World War and use quantitative techniques to study qualitative factors (e.g. risk) using statistics and probability. The techniques are extremely well suited to computers and many computer software packages enable people with limited mathematical training to utilize OR techniques. Given the widespread use of computers, it is increasingly the case that OR techniques are finding applications in all aspects of business (not simply production and scheduling), e.g. in marketing, in the guise of ➤**marketing engineering.**

Previously known as 'systems analysis' it originally sought to bring together ideas from engineering and economics to help improve the performance of project managers in large organizations. The process focused on the analysis of organizations, use of resources and information flows in order to improve performance.

operations function ➤operations management.

operations management The methods, tasks and techniques firms use to produce goods and services. It concerns all the activities involved in planning and controlling the materials, people and machines to produce and deliver all the goods and services we consume. All operations are concerned with the transformation of input resources (i.e. labour, materials and machines) into output resources, i.e. goods and services.

opportunity cost The value of something that has to be given up – a lost opportunity – as a result of a decision. Opportunity cost is a ubiquitous concept, useless in terms of the accountant's practice of collating the cash cost of an activity but often significant in terms of understanding true costs and benefits. For example, a company with some capital to invest in a project should not simply look at what profits it can make from it; it should look also at the opportunities foreclosed by tying up the capital in one particular way. ➤➤**normal profit.** Or, in assessing whether to take over a rival, a company must take into account the potential lost opportunities of other take-overs that would not be practical if this one proceeds. A farmer who owns his land should not just look at how much money he makes from it each month, he should also be assessing how much rent or income the land could attract in alternative uses. It may be, for example, he would be better off selling his plot, investing the money in the building society and living off the interest.

The conventional view of costs as a cash outlay only equates to opportunity costs where competition ensures that the price of every input to production is charged at a price equal to its value in its best alternative use.

optimized production technology (OPT) A concept for planning a production system to known capacity constraints. The basic principle underlying this approach is the recognition that capacity constraints in a production system, known as 'bottle-necks', determine the rate of throughput for any production system. Production systems are scheduled around known bottlenecks because, it is argued, it is these that limit the flow of production. Eliyahu ➤Goldratt developed and promoted this concept and later developed and marketed appropriate software for production systems. The basic principles of OPT are:

(1) Balance flow not capacity.
(2) The level of utilization of a non-bottleneck is determined by some other constraint in the system, not by its own capacity.
(3) An hour lost at a bottleneck is an hour lost for ever.
(4) An hour lost at a non-bottleneck is a mirage.
(5) Bottlenecks govern both throughput and inventory in the system.
(6) Schedules should be established by looking at all constraints simultaneously.

option **1.** A contract giving its beneficiary the right to buy or sell a financial ➤instrument or a commodity at a specified price within a specified period. The option can be exercised freely or disregarded, there being no obligation to transact. Where the right is to buy, the contract is termed a *call option*; where the right is to sell, it is termed a *put option*. The holder of the option is able to take advantage of a favourable movement in prices, losing only the premium payable for the option should prices move adversely. The writer, or seller, of the option is correspondingly more exposed to risk. **2.** In the ➤foreign exchange market, a binding contract to buy or sell a currency at a specific price, the date of the transaction being left to the choice of the holder of the contract.

order An instruction from a client to a ➤broker–dealer to buy or sell a ➤security. An order may be a market order to buy or sell at the best price the dealer can obtain at the time of execution. Alternatively, the client may impose a stop order to buy or sell only if the price rises or falls to a specified level; ➤stop-loss orders are intended to protect the client from loss or to limit the client's loss in a falling market (US = *limit order*).

order driven A ➤stock exchange system in which prices react to orders, as in the *auction system* in the ➤New York Stock Exchange, where ➤brokers and dealers bid for stock (*open outcry* or *auction*) around a *specialist* who maintains a market in chosen stocks by buying and selling for their own account and for broker clients. As distinct from ➤quote driven. An order-driven system may be automated so as to match bargains (➤matched bargains or bids) electronically, as in the ➤London Stock Exchange.

ordinary least squares ➤least squares regression.

ordinary share (UK) A share in the ➤equity ➤capital of a business, holders of ordinary shares being entitled to all distributed ➤profits after the holders of ➤debentures and ➤preference shares have been paid (US = *common stock*).

organic growth Where a firm develops as a result of its internal efforts, e.g. by increasing market share. This form of 'growing' a firm differs from that of expanding through external acquisition of other businesses. ➤Conglomerates use the acquisition of additional businesses to grow rapidly. Organic growth is usually a slower form of growth and implies that the firm raises the finance for growth rather than using external finance. In many ways, this is viewed as a traditional form of growing a business and there are many examples of well-known firms, such as Tesco and IBM, that have used this approach to grow steadily over the past 50 years.

organizational behaviour (OB) A field of study that investigates the impact that individuals, groups, structures and systems have on activities within organizations. Specific areas of study include: (a) individuals in organizations (their values, attitudes, beliefs and motives; decision-making and behaviour; satisfaction and performance); (b) groups in organizations (teams, roles, and leadership; control, power, conflict, co-operation, negotiation and politics), and (c) structures and systems (hierarchies, structures, rules and regulations, practices and policies; organizational cultures and values; organizational learning, change and development). The purpose is to apply such knowledge in an attempt to improve the performance of individuals within an organization and enhance an organization's effectiveness. OB invariably relates to the study of business organizations, but it may also consider not-for-profit and government organizations – in essence, any organization that requires formal management.

OB arose out of management thinking from the early decades of the twentieth century. Arguably the most influential thinker was Frederick W ➤Taylor (*Principles of Scientific Management*, 1911), whose focus was the scientific study of work on the shopfloor. Through the analysis of practices and procedures on the shopfloor, Taylor believed it was possible for management to make more profit and workers to earn more pay. Gains were achieved by being more efficient and productive – this meant workers had to be trained properly and given incentives for extra effort and it also meant managers had carefully to plan and control the activities of workers. At a broader level, OB has drawn heavily from sociology, notably the writings of Max ➤Weber (*The Theory of Social and Economic Organisation*, 1947). Weber described the structures and systems of organizations, using this as a basis for a theory of the ideal organizational system ('the ideal bureaucracy'). ➤➤Barnard; Bartlett.

Contemporary concepts in this area are described by Stephen P Robbins (*Organizational Behavior*, 1979 and subsequent editions) and in Nigel Nicholson (ed.), *The Blackwell Encyclopedic Dictionary of Organisational Behaviour*, 1995.

organizational buying behaviour The way organizational purchases are made. Many of these purchases will be straight rebuys, in which case reordering can be automated or delegated to a single (junior) procurement/purchasing officer. Examples include automatic replenishment of stationery, office furniture, beverages, etc. Other purchases are complex, one-off, high-involvement decisions that may occupy a team of people (known as a ➤decision-making unit) and requiring wider consultation (with advisers, influences and gatekeepers). Examples are the acquisition of a new factory or the purchase of an expensive piece of specialist equipment. In these circumstances, the decision-making process can be involved and protracted, with perhaps several suppliers asked to pitch or tender for the business. Just as managers attempt to understand ➤consumer behaviour in a business-to-consumer context, so they also need to understand the forces at work in a business-to-business context, e.g. gaining an understanding of ➤attitudes and ➤buyer behaviour, and ➤values and beliefs, of those directly and indirectly involved in the purchasing process.

organizational competency ➤competency.

organizational culture Sets of values, norms and beliefs that are reflected in an organization's structures and systems, including its customs, stories, symbols, traditions and rituals, and the language in which all these facets are expressed. In common parlance, we talk of the differing atmospheres and differing ways of doing things in different organizations ('the way we do things here'). One company may be very sales oriented, another in the same industry may be more profit focused. Others, again, may be more people oriented, or innovation oriented. Intuitively, therefore, organizational culture is easily appreciated, but it is hard to define in a formal sense. It can be described as a system of shared meaning, which ensures everyone is working to the same goals. But this definition remains rather vague.

All organizations will have some form of culture, and it can be regarded positively or negatively. On the positive side, it delineates an organization (from other organizations), gives those in an organization a sense of identity and purpose (beyond narrow self-interest), provides a social fabric (helping employees to see where they fit in) and helps to define and enforce the 'rules of engagement' in an organization (employees come to know what they can or cannot do). If all these aspects are well-defined (i.e. there is a strong culture), it is easier to see whether an employee will 'fit' into the organization or not. This has an impact on selection and recruitment, promotion and status, and employee retention. It is also easier for suppliers, customers and consumers because they will tend to be treated consistently by all employees. However, there may be negative consequences. A strong culture may act as a powerful barrier to change (a serious problem if the business environment demands change, as senior managers have found at corporations such as IBM and the BBC). It also may be unhealthily risk-averse and conformist, e.g. employees hiring only in their own image, rather than thinking about the requirements of the job and who best meets these requirements.

The system of shared meaning that underlies an organizational culture must be sustained. For existing employees, this is achieved through customs, stories, symbols, traditions and rituals. These are formal (e.g. regular executive meetings) and informal, e.g. informal groupings over lunch. Culture is also sustained through the selection and socialization process – potential employees are assessed in terms of 'fit' and, once hired, are exposed to the culture which they will gradually make their own. The fully socialized employee is one who has internalized the system of shared meaning. Many of these processes are organic – they occur as a result of the interplay between people in an organization. However, many corporations have managed cultures – often taking on the personal values and business philosophies of the founder or chief executive officer, e.g. the imprint of Richard Branson on the Virgin Group or, in an earlier era, that of Walt Disney on his corporate namesake. Culture can be seen as the organizational equivalent of personal ➤values, and nowhere is this clearer than where a corporation takes on the persona of its founder.

Despite path-breaking studies such as those by Geert ➤Hofstede, many important questions are still unresolved. For example, how do organizational and personal values interrelate?, is the appropriate unit of analysis the whole organization or some division of it?, how stable and widespread should we expect a culture to be?, and how explicit does the culture have to be? What is the effect of subcultures on an organization's dominant culture? Stability will be important for some large and established organizations but, in parallel, there may be a need for innovative units (a situation faced by 'telecoms' who need to service existing customers but also bring new products to market) – how can these cultures be reconciled? In a multinational context, how do organizational and ➤national cultures interrelate? The common assumption is that national overrides organizational culture. But the problem is compounded by employee self-selection (a particular type of Frenchman will choose to work for Microsoft in Paris).

organizational knowledge ➤intellectual assets; knowledge management system.

organizational learning Ongoing capacity of an organization to record and review individual and group experiences, learn from these, and then make appropriate adaptations and changes. Peter Senge (*The Fifth Discipline*, 1990) made a strong case for organizations to think about how they learn and for employees to be more open with one another so that they might learn from one another's experiences. Learning then becomes the basis for thinking about tackling problems and responding to opportunities – not in isolation, but in the wider context of changing goals, rules, procedures and processes.

It is possible to envisage a ➤learning organization, where there is a commitment to (or a culture of) learning. This is achieved by having certain organizational values (e.g. openness, supportiveness, trust, respect for employees, etc.) and the use of specific techniques (e.g. consultative processes, team-building approaches, etc.). A particularly creative approach is to have employees 'visit the future' – different scenarios are presented and possible courses of action explored, giving employees a sense of what experiences *might* eventuate and what *might* be learned from them. This approach draws from the fields of scenario planning and military strategy.

Attention has also turned to how best to record and review experiences. Typically, this requires a ➤knowledge management system to be in place, otherwise organizational memories may be quite short and the wisdom that could flow from previous experiences is lost. During the 1990s, the loss of organizational memories became an acute problem; organizations became consumed by the need for change (as a result of ➤change-management programmes, ➤re-engineering, and organizational learning) and (through ➤downsizing) lost many employees who might have had a valuable store of experiences. It is now acknowledged that effective learning needs a knowledge-base, as well as a capacity to adapt and change.

organizational structure ➤architecture.

Organization for Economic Co-operation and Development (OECD) A large, Paris-based official 'think tank' representing the interests of the developed countries. The purposes of the OECD are to promote growth and high employment consistent with financial stability in its member countries, to foster international trade and to contribute to the economic progress of the developing countries and of non-member countries. The OECD operates through a number of major committees attended by ministers of the member countries. An early achievement was the further promotion of the code of liberalization adopted by its predecessor, which contributed substantially to the removal of ➤exchange controls. The Economic Policy Committee has latterly become an important venue for international consultation and agreement on policy response to the economic situation. The OECD publishes a wide range of reports, among them regular assessments of the worldwide economic situation and of the economies of individual members. The Development Assistance Committee centralized the OECD's activities in respect of the developing world and established, among other things, a standard of aid contributions to which all members should aspire.

output gap The difference between the actual level of activity in an economy, and the sustainable amount of activity given the capacity of the economy. The output gap has become a fashionable and simple way of understanding the state of the economy, and its short- or medium-term prospects. An output gap is measured as a percentage: it may be a negative gap of 2 per cent, which would imply the economy was operating at 2 per cent below its true capacity or potential. It may be plus 2 per cent, which would imply the economy was operating unsustainably fast, that it was overheating. The usual assumption made is that a negative gap implies falling inflation, as companies seek to raise demand for their products and their output by raising their prices below the existing inflation rate. A positive gap implies rising inflation.

The output gap is expressed as a percentage of the *level* of gross domestic product (GDP). Note that GDP may grow very quickly for several years, but if the growth commenced at a time of a large negative gap GDP may still be below its potential and inflation thus still falling. The gap is useful in assessing ➤**monetary policy** because it assumes that any increase in demand in the economy will generate extra output if actual GDP is below potential, and it will generate pure inflation if actual output exceeds potential.

In practice, it is not possible to observe the potential output of an economy. Indeed, it is hard enough for statisticians to record actual activity. Thus, proponents of output-gap analysis typically have to estimate potential output on the bases of simple assumptions about ➤**trend growth** rates.

The output gap is probably best seen as a helpful device for framing discussion of the economy rather than as a strong, predictive theory of economic life.

outsourcing A term used to describe the process of using external organizations to provide the firm with the necessary services it requires and that it previously supplied from within, e.g. maintenance, cleaning, catering, computer support, telecommunications services. The benefits of outsourcing include reduced costs and improved service levels, and also the freeing-up of resources to enable the firm to focus on its core business and its most profitable areas of activity. ➤➤**make-or-buy decision**.

overdraft (UK) A loan facility on a customer's current account at a bank permitting the customer to overdraw up to a certain limit for an agreed period. Interest is payable on the amount of the loan facility taken up, and it may therefore be a relatively inexpensive way of financing a fluctuating requirement. ➤➤**line of credit**.

overfunding The practice by government of borrowing from the private sector more money than it requires to meet the difference between its income and outgoings. Overfunding implies the government sells bonds, or hands out long-term debt, in return for cash. In doing so, it draws cash out of the private sector and reduces the supply of money. It has thus been seen as a tool of ➤**monetary policy**.

overhead   A cost that does not vary with output in the short run, e.g. rent, administrative salaries.

overseas bank (UK)   **1.** A bank operating in the UK but foreign-controlled. There are over 600 such banks in the UK. **2.** A UK-owned bank that conducts its business mainly abroad.

oversubscribed, oversubscription   A ➤new issue in which investors are prepared to purchase more shares at the offered price (or the ➤striking price) than are available. In these cases, the ➤issuing house either conducts a ballot or lucky draw in which the successful applications are selected at random, or it scales down applications for above a certain minimum quantity of shares. ➤offer for sale.

over-the-counter (OTC) **market**   **1.** A group of licensed dealers who provide two-way trading facilities in company ➤securities outside the stock exchange. The term originated in the US in the 1870s when ➤stocks were first bought across bank counters. The term is sometimes used to refer generally to ➤unlisted securities markets. **2.** More generally, any securities-trading activity carried on outside stock exchanges (e.g. OTC ➤options, which are options written by a single seller for a single buyer under a private and confidential arrangement) as distinct from *traded options* which might be in the form of a standard contract traded on an exchange.

overtrading   A situation in which a business has insufficient ➤working capital to meet its debts when they fall due.

own brand   ➤private label.

P

packaged good A tangible product that is packaged or canned. Typically, packaged goods are branded, nationally advertised, and widely distributed via retail outlets to final consumers. Examples are toothpastes, laundry detergents, ready-to-eat (RTE) breakfast cereals, and over-the-counter (OTC) pharmaceuticals. Also called fast-moving consumer goods (FMCGs) because most consumers buy these products and purchase cycles are reasonably short, therefore large volumes of product can be shifted from the shelves of retail outlets within quite brief periods of time. Given high levels of product and brand familiarity and in-use experience, consumers of packaged goods may engage in very limited decision-making processes or simply buy out of habit. Nevertheless, competition in established packaged goods markets is intense and some of the most archetypal marketing-driven companies are to be found in this sector, e.g. Heinz, Procter & Gamble, Unilever, Kao, Henkle. ➤consumer products companies; services marketing.

paid-up capital That part of the ➤issued capital of a company that has been paid-in by the shareholders. *Partly paid shares* are those on which only a proportion of the issue price of the shares was paid on subscription. This may arise where shares are issued in partly paid form, the second part being payable a few months later to increase the attractiveness of the issue.

P & L account ➤profit and loss account.

panel data A dataset that consists of entries both for a cross-section of a population, and for different periods of time. Panel data thus combine the two more typical kinds of dataset: (a) the time-series (e.g. average household spending through a number of years), or (b) cross-section, (spending by different households in a particular year). ➤consumer panel.

paper A vernacular term for any ➤security, most generally applied to those in the ➤money market. Used more specifically for ➤notes issued by companies for trading at a ➤discount, namely ➤commercial paper.

paradigm shift A fundamental change in the understanding of how something works. The concept was first discussed by the philosopher Thomas S Kuhn (*The Structure of Scientific Revolutions*, 1962).

parallel import One of a flow of imports from one market into another, outside the formal trade arrangements made by the company responsible for the product in question. It is a common practice that undermines ➤price discrimination when a company tries to charge different prices in different jurisdictions. For example, if

GlaxoSmithKline try to sell their drugs at a low price in poor countries, and at a high price in the richer ones, parallel trade might occur, as people try to buy the drug in the poor country to resell it in the rich one. Parallel trade is a form of ➤arbitrage.

parallel money market A market in short-term securities other than ➤Treasury bills, ➤bills of exchange and ➤bonds and including ➤Eurocurrency, ➤certificates of deposit, loans to local authorities and interbank loans. ➤interbank market.

parameter ➤econometrics.

parent company 1. The corporate headquarters of a firm with subsidiaries. Some firms have many different subsidiaries operating in a variety of different markets and industries. Such firms are called ➤conglomerates. The headquarters of a conglomerate is often referred to as the 'parent' company, where the subsidiaries are viewed as 'offspring'. The parenting resource of corporate headquarters can offer:
(1) Corporate functions, e.g. central human resources and finance.
(2) Corporate development initiatives, e.g. research and development.
(3) Additional finance for opportunities, on the principle of ➤portfolio planning.
(4) Development of linkages between subsidiaries for ➤technology transfer.
2. A company that owns 50 per cent or more of the ➤ordinary shares of a ➤subsidiary company.

Pareto analysis A simple technique for identifying the important from the trivial. It is based on the frequently occurring phenomenon of relatively few causes explaining the majority of defects. It is sometimes referred to as the ➤eighty : twenty rule, this is because frequently 80 per cent of a firm's business is likely to come from 20 per cent of its customer base. Similarly, this principle is found in many walks of life, e.g. relatively few of a doctor's patients will occupy most of his time. It is named after the nineteenth-century economist who showed that income is very unevenly distributed in society.

Paris *Bourse* (Fr.) The principal ➤stock exchange in France, from 1991 incorporating the regional stock exchanges in Bordeaux, Lille, Lyons, Marseille, Nancy and Nantes. A member of the stock exchange in France is called an *agent de change* and will be a member of the Chambre Syndicale des Agents de Change which, with the official Commission des Opérations de Bourse, supervises the securities markets. The *bourse* has three main segments: (a) the *Marché à Règlement Mensuel* and the *Marché au Comptant*, which comprise the first segment, or *premier marché*; (b) the *second marché* for small and medium enterprises, and (c) the *nouveau marché* for hi-tech growth stocks. In addition, there is an unregulated *Marché Libre OTC*, formerly the *Marché Hors Cote*. In 2000, the Paris, Brussels and Amsterdam stock exchanges merged to create a single cross-border institution, Euronext.

Parkinson's law An unofficial law proposed by C N Parkinson in his book *Parkinson's Law*, which has been generally accepted as a very relevant half-truth. It claims that work often expands according to the time available in which to perform it.

participating preference share (UK) ➤preference share.

participation rate The proportion of a population that is *economically active*, i.e. working or unemployed and seeking work.

partly paid share ➤paid-up capital.

partnership An ➤**unincorporated business** based on a contractual relationship between two or more people who share risks and profits. Each partner, unless a limited partner, is liable for the ➤**debts** and business actions of the others, to the full extent of their own resources (although they are taxed as individuals). A new form of partnership, limited liability partnership (LLP), was introduced in the UK in 2001. Unlike ordinary partnerships, LLPs have to file accounts for public inspection.

par value The *nominal* or *face* value at which a security is first traded. It may thereafter trade above or below par, or still at par.

passing off ➤look-alike.

patent A legal monopoly offered by the State to inventors giving them the sole right to make, use or sell their invention during the period the patent remains in force. This period is for a maximum of 20 years from the date of filing. The theory behind patents is to offer some economic reward for inventors that will enable them to profit from their ingenuity. Without such potential protection, inventors would be at the mercy of unscrupulous copiers. ➤**innovation; invention; new product development**.

The UK Patent Office was set up in 1852 to act as the UK's sole office for the granting of patents of invention. The origins of the patent system stretch back a further 400 years. The word 'patent' comes from the practice of monarchs in the Middle Ages conferring rights and privileges by means of 'open letters', i.e. documents on which the royal seal was not broken when they were opened. This is distinct from 'closed letters' that were not intended for public view. Open letters were intended for display and inspection by any interested party. The language of government in medieval England was Latin and Latin for open letter is *litterae patente*. As English slowly took over from Latin as the official language, the documents became known as 'letters patent' and later just 'patents'.

Patents are granted to individuals and organizations who can lay claim to a new product or manufacturing process, or to an improvement of an existing product or process which was not previously known. The granting of a patent gives the 'patentee' a monopoly to make, use, or sell the invention for a fixed period of time – which in Europe and the US is 20 years from the date the patent application was first filed. In return for this monopoly, the patentee pays a fee to cover the costs of processing the patent and, more importantly, publicly discloses details of the invention. The idea must be new and not an obvious extension of what is already known. A patent lasts up to 20 years in the UK and Europe, but heavy annual renewal fees have to be paid to keep it in force. Discoveries (as opposed to inventions), scientific theory and mathematical processes are not patentable under the Patent Act 1988. ➤➤**intellectual property**.

The earliest known English patent of invention was granted to John of Utynam in 1449. The patent gave Mr Utynam a 20-year monopoly for a method of making stained glass that had not previously been known in England. For a patent to benefit from legal protection it must meet the following strict criteria:

(1) Have novelty. The Patent Act 1977, Section 2(1): 'An invention shall be taken to be new if it does not form part of the state of the art.' A 'state of the art' is defined as all matter, i.e. publications, written or oral, or even anticipation (*Windsurfing International* v. *Tabar Marine* 1985) will render a patent invalid.

(2) Be an inventive step. Section 3 of the Patent Act: 'An invention shall be taken to involve an inventive step if it is not obvious to a person skilled in the art.'

(3) Have industrial applications. Under the Patent Act an invention shall be taken to be capable of industrial application if it can be a machine, product or process. Penicillin was a discovery which was not patentable but the process of isolating and storing penicillin clearly had industrial applications and thus was patentable.

path analysis A technique used in management analysis to model how a set of constructs relate to one another. The relationship between constructs is normally depicted graphically in a 'path diagram' (thus constructs A, B and C may be shown converging on D, which in turn points to E). This path then can be specified as a series of regression-like equations that can be estimated simultaneously. At root, the technique is a complex form of correlation analysis. Path analyses, and higher-level techniques such as structural equation modelling, have become popular in management research because they acknowledge the complexity of managerial relationships and because of the availability of software such as LISREL. Although described as causal modelling, the 'causal' status of path analysis is questionable – it would often be more appropriate to see the analysis as a tentative description of hypothesized relationships based on correlations between constructs. ➤**regression analysis**; ➤**experiment; validity.**

pathfinder prospectus ➤red herring.

pay Monetary compensation to employees for work rendered. Typically, this is given as a fixed wage or salary; however, there are other forms of payment. A 'bonus' may be paid in addition to the fixed salary; while not necessarily based on performance, this is usually the case. Performance-related pay is where a portion of an employee's pay is some function of an individual and/or organizational measure of performance, e.g. ➤**profit-sharing** is one example. An alternative system is 'piece rates', whereby employees are paid a fixed sum for each unit of production completed. Non-monetary compensation often forms part of an overall pay package; this might include employer superannuation contributions, private health insurance, daily travel and living allowances or ➤**employee share/stock ownership plans.** For taxation purposes, these may be categorized as ➤**fringe benefits.** With changes in the organization of business (e.g. deregulation, federal organizations, the growth of networks and alliances, increased outsourcing and the informal economy), the traditional focus on wages and salaries is shifting more to a focus on fees and commission, i.e. payments for specific services rendered. The people involved are not strictly employees, but there may be very close business, personal and social ties. Thus, whereas a telephone engineer may have previously received a wage from a State-run telecoms company, she may now negotiate a fee with the privatized and deregulated telecoms company in exchange for services rendered. This, together with more varied forms of compensation for employees within an organization, has implications for traditional ➤**industrial relations** and particularly the role and purpose of ➤**trade unions.**

Various other forms of pay may be received under special circumstances. Notably, statutory sick pay is paid to those who are absent from work due to sickness and ill health, and who have made appropriate contributions.

payback, payback period The period over which the cumulative net revenue from an investment project equals the original investment. Its main defects are that it does not allow for the time value of money or for ➤**cash flows** over the whole life of the project. ➤➤**discounted cash flow.**

pay-off matrix A table, commonly used in ➤**game theory**, depicting a range of strategic choices facing someone, and the outcomes associated with each choice. In this context, a game is defined as a highly stylized set of players and choices. By analysing the pay-off matrix, it is relatively easy to determine the likely strategy of each player. For example, imagine the pay-offs depicted in the table.

Pay-off matrix

		Fred's widgets	
		Cut price	Hold price
Bloggs' widgets	Cut price	2,2	6,1
	Hold price	1,6	5,5

The correct way to read this is as follows: Bloggs' Widgets has two choices: (a) to cut the price, or (b) hold the price of his product; the same choices face Fred's Widgets. That means there are four possible outcomes, one associated with each combination of strategies of the two 'players'. Each outcome yields a return to each player – the cell (2,2) in the top left describes what each of the two players gets, with Bloggs' return first.

If Bloggs was to analyse this business predicament in the simplified form of this game, he first might ask: 'What would I do if Fred cuts his price?' (this involves analysing the two choices offered in the first column, associated with Fred's cutting price; as it is a choice between 2 or 1 for Bloggs, the choice would be to cut price). And second: 'What would I do if Fred held his price?', i.e. a choice between 6 and 5, again pointing to the need to cut price.

The pay-off matrix, if properly defined, is evidently a useful way of simplifying strategic choices. ➤➤**Nash equilibrium; prisoners' dilemma.**

payroll A list of employees, stating their pay details for a specified period, i.e. gross pay, basic pay, supplements, special duty payments and overtime payments, deductions for tax, insurance, pension contributions, net pay. Standard payment periods are a week, a fortnight and a month.

peak pricing The policy of raising prices at times of high demand, common in transport and utility industries. Peak pricing is sometimes seen as a classic form of ➤**price discrimination**, enabling producers to obtain higher margins from price-insensitive customers who choose to use the peak times, and undoubtedly this does explain a lot of peak pricing. For example, business travellers tend to use peak transport, and they also have a higher willingness to pay than other customers, so it makes sense for airlines and rail companies to charge them more. However, there is another good rationale for peak pricing, i.e. the peak usage necessitates a higher level of capacity in an industry to be maintained than would be the case if the same total amount of demand was spread evenly through time. In the electricity industry, for example, the peaks require the existence of power stations that lie idle in the off-peak hours. The cost of keeping those stations is high, as they are not defrayed across as many customer hours; thus, it is both efficient and, in some sense fair, that the customers who demand peak services should bear the cost they incur. For the sake of efficiency, the appropriate price is one that reflects the ➤**marginal cost** of production (➤**marginal-cost pricing**). In an off-peak period, when there is spare capacity, that will be a price not reflecting the cost of the capital incurred in the business; at a peak time, when capacity is all utilized, it will be a higher price that reflects the cost of adding extra capacity should yet more demand be forthcoming.

PEG ➤price : earnings growth factor.

pendular arbitration A form of ➤arbitration in which each of the two sides in dispute makes a claim against the other, and the arbitrator chooses one of those claims. The key feature of pendular arbitration is that the arbitrator cannot 'split the difference' between the two sides. One side gets its way. The idea is to induce the disputants to make reasonable demands rather than pitching their claims as extremely as possible in the hope that that will shift the eventual solution their way.

penetration ➤buyer behaviour.

penny share (UK) A share (➤**quoted company**) on the ➤**London Stock Exchange** priced at less than £1, e.g. 18 pence. Penny shares seem cheap and are therefore popular with some speculators, but what is really important is the ➤**yield** of a share and the prospects for the company. ➤**heavy share**.

pension Regular income after a certain age and usually after retirement from work, provided by a State scheme or private scheme. Most countries have a mix of State and private pension schemes. In the UK the flat-rate retirement pension is paid to men over 65 and women over 60 who have paid appropriate National Insurance contributions. In addition, most people are expected to have some top-up private second pension; for those who do not, there is a second State pension, the State Earnings-Related Pension Scheme.

There are two broad types of private scheme: (a) *occupational pension schemes*, provided by employers, either contributory or non-contributory, and (b) *personal pensions*, for the self-employed or others not members of an occupational scheme. The former are often (but decreasingly) *defined benefit schemes* in that the pension benefits are specified in terms of the final salary of the recipient. The latter are *defined contribution schemes*, or ➤**money purchase** schemes under which individuals pay contributions into a fund, probably managed by an ➤**insurance** company or other ➤**institutional investor**, and which pays out an amount reflecting the contributions paid in plus interest. These schemes typically provide a cash lump sum at retirement age, but if it is to qualify for tax relief, the accumulated fund must be used to purchase an ➤**annuity** although a proportion of it may be taken in cash. Occupational pension schemes may also be *self-administered*, i.e. managed by the employer. *Stakeholder pensions* are low-cost defined contribution schemes, regulated by the State, which must be made available by all employers. Employers are obliged to provide similar pension entitlements to men and women and to part-time employees. Pension schemes may be *funded* (a capital-reserve system), with contributions paid into a fund that is invested in ➤**securities** and other ➤**assets** and from which pensions are ultimately paid. Such funds, which receive special tax treatment, are important operators in securities markets (➤**institutional investor**). Pension schemes may also be *unfunded*, as in the UK National Insurance scheme and most other State schemes, where pensions for retirees are paid out of the contribution of those in work. An ageing population and a fixed (or falling) age of retirement pose threats to pension schemes. ➤➤**Employee Retirement Income Security Act 1974; individual retirement account; personal pension; superannuation.**

P : E ratio ➤price : earnings ratio.

perceived risk Consumer judgements of the likelihood of negative outcomes, and the degree of negativity of these outcomes. Types of risk include: (a) physical risk (where a product is deemed to be unsafe or insecure); (b) performance risk (where a product fails to function in the way expected); (c) financial risk (where a consumer believes he has lost money or feels he has paid too much), and (d) psychosocial risk (where, for example, peers might question the use of a particular product or the outcome from a particular service). Consumers can reduce these risks by confining purchase to tried and trusted brands, looking out for guarantees and warranties, gathering more information and taking advice from well-trained sales staff. Attempts to reduce perceived risk are especially important in the context of new situations, e.g. purchasing a new product, engaging a new service provider and entering a new market. ➤➤**evaluation processes; information search.**

perceived service quality (PSQ) The judgement of an organization's overall excellence or superiority in service performance. Perceived service quality serves as a global value judgement made by consumers, and it therefore has some of the properties of an ➤**attitude**. This perception of quality differs from the more objective notion of technical quality in manufacturing. In part, this is because of the intangible, inseparable and multifaceted nature of services. The management of service quality requires the organization to meet the ➤**expectations** of customers, and to do so consistently across ➤**service encounters**. This is achieved by attempting to close any gaps that might exist between the initial expectations of consumers and their perceptions of actual performance. ➤**SERVQUAL.**

perceptual mapping A technique used in marketing to depict how brands are perceived relative to one another, when mapped in two or more dimensions. Also called 'position mapping'. A list of brands is specified, e.g. say, ten brands of curry paste. Respondents are asked to say how similar they think these brands are to one another (A is similar to C, D is similar to E, etc.). It is respondents' perceptions of similarity that are captured – these might not accurately mirror objective similarities, e.g. people may think A is similar to C when, in fact, the two brands of curry paste have quite different ingredients. A statistical procedure is employed to obtain spatial positions of the brands in multidimensional space to reflect these perceptions. A common procedure is multidimensional scaling, for which there is off-the-shelf software, e.g. PREFMAP, INDSCAL. Output is depicted as a map. This conveys the relative position of the brands, but does not relate to any absolute measure of distance.

The number of dimensions (two, three, etc.) depends on how many are needed to plot the data without incurring an intolerable level of stress. The dimensions themselves are derived without labels, and great care must be taken in labelling them. A formal way to label dimensions involves the use of attribute ratings. At the same time as similarity data are collected, the researcher asks respondents to rate (on a ➤**ratings scale**) each brand for a number of attributes (taste, quality ingredients, price and so forth). Each attribute is assessed for how closely it corresponds with the dimensions (low–high price may be closest to dimension 1; thus, dimension 1 is labelled the price axis). Although formal, the selection of attributes is subjective.

In marketing, a popular alternative to the use of similarity data is the use of preference data, i.e. data where an evaluation of one item dominates another. Data may be in the form of paired comparisons (is A preferred over C?) or rankings (A is most preferred, followed by C, etc.). Similar procedures apply, but with preference data it is possible to investigate 'ideal points', e.g. by including a hypothetical brand X into the preference comparisons or ranking. The word 'ideal' here is misleading because X may be far from ideal. It is also possible to locate ideal combinations of attributes on the map – either for individual consumers or segments – and see which brands (if any) are close to the ideal. Various marketing implications might follow, including the possibility of designing a new product for an unmet market (seen as an empty quadrant on the perceptual map) or repositioning an existing product to be closer to the ideal point of a segment than competitors. This form of analysis is very beguiling but it can be very misleading, e.g. an empty quadrant may represent an unmet need or a phantom market, and a new brand may get closer to the ideal point of a segment but, in so doing, change the whole configuration of the map (including a relative shift in the ideal point). One of the most popular business games, MARKSTRAT, uses these facets of perceptual mapping to simulate the dynamic interplay of competing firms in established and new markets.

The technique is applied in product and brand positioning studies. ➤**new product development; positioning; segment–target–position strategy**. Informally, the ideas behind perceptual mapping are reflected in the thinking of many marketing managers, even though they may never make use of the formal techniques.

perfect competition   A simplified model of an industrial structure in which many small firms compete in the supply of a single, homogeneous product. Perfect competition is useful as a practical guide to the workings of a limited number of real-world sectors, particularly those of agricultural commodities where a large number of farmers produce almost identical items. More generally, it is a useful theoretical extreme that helps illuminate an understanding of less than perfectly competitive markets in simple form.

Three primary features characterize a perfectly competitive industry.
(1) There is a multitude of firms (buyers as well as sellers) all too small to have any individual impact on market price. Therefore, for each producer, ➤**marginal revenue** and price are equal.
(2) All firms aim to maximize profit.
(3) Firms can costlessly enter and exit the industry.
In addition, it is assumed that the outputs traded are homogeneous.

Perfect competition is economically efficient in three ways.
(1) In the short run, maximization ensures that each firm will set its output so that its ➤**marginal cost** is equal to its marginal revenue. To produce when marginal cost exceeds marginal revenue implies that cutting back production would save more than the revenue lost, and to produce when marginal revenue exceeds

marginal cost implies that expanding production would increase revenue more than costs. Thus, marginal revenue will equal marginal cost. Under the assumption that for each firm, price equals marginal revenue, perfect competition implies that marginal cost equals price. This is efficient for the allocation of resources, because it ensures that no consumer will be deterred from buying something which he values more than it cost to make. ➤**marginal-cost pricing**.

(2) In the long run, freer entry and exit ensures new entrants will be attracted into any industry where high profits are made. The effect of these new entrants is to increase supply and bid down price until no excess profit is made (apart from a ➤**normal profit**). That implies the average revenue (i.e. the price) derived from each sale equals the average cost of producing it.

(3) Again, in the long run, as average cost equals average revenue – which equals price, which equals marginal cost – we can deduce that average cost equals marginal cost. The only point on the average cost curve for which this is true is at the bottom of it, i.e. at the lowest cost point.

Finally, therefore, perfect competition ensures minimum-cost production. ➤➤**contestability; monopolistic competition; monopoly.**

performance evaluation ➤assessment.

performance-related pay ➤pay; productivity.

performing ➤group development.

permanent income hypothesis The theory proposed by Milton Friedman which suggests that however variable their income over time, consumers will attempt to smooth out the pattern of their consumption. If, for example, someone's income varies between 0 and £20,000, a year, averaging £10,000, he will more or less spend at a rate equivalent to a constant £10,000 a year. It is manifestly sensible to transfer spending from bountiful times to times when one is poor, simply because we tend to value things more, the less we have of them. By saving in some periods and 'dissaving' in others, this can be achieved. In this sense, the theory is no more sophisticated than making the obvious argument that if someone wins the lottery, they will not generally spend all their money at once, but will save some for future periods when their income is likely to be far lower.

The theory was important in explaining consumer spending patterns. People receiving windfalls should be less inclined to spend them than people receiving permanent gains in income. It provided a breakthrough in accounting for an important real world mystery: that rich people save more than poor people, although as society as a whole gets richer, people do not tend to save more. The hypothesis reconciled these two observations, because on any given day the rich would be in a bountiful period of their lives, who need to save; the poor would be those with low incomes, needing to dissave. But through time, as people's permanent expectations of income rise, savings would have no need to change.

permission marketing The idea that marketers must obtain the trust of customers as a prelude to developing a close relationship. Trust is gained when the organization promises to safeguard personal information about a customer as well as meeting basic product and service requirements. Having earned trust, the organization is in a better position to gain permission from the customer for personalized mail, e-mail, phone calls and relationship-building initiatives. The organization is also able to invite the customer to help promote the product or service through word-of-mouth and word-of-mouse ('viral marketing'). Permission marketing has its genesis in ➤direct marketing and the use of ➤personalization technologies. It takes on board some of the logic of ➤pyramid selling. However, it has been observed that many people see these forms of contact as invasive, a violation of personal privacy and often irrelevant and misdirected. Poorly targeted mail-shots, or 'junk mail', are an example. So, too, are many of the uses to which 'cookies' are put. ➤personalization technologies. By contrast, permission marketing uses these technologies through consent. Customers opt-in.

personality trait One of a set of enduring characteristics that describe an individual's behaviour across a wide range of situations. Knowledge of an individual's personality traits is used in the selection, appraisal and management of employees. ➤assessment. The most well-known distinction is between type A and type B personalities. Type A people are described as 'strivers' – they want to succeed in whatever they do, will work long hours, put pressure on themselves (with tight deadlines and punishing work schedules), take work home, dislike being reliant on others, become frustrated easily, find it hard to relax and unwind, and neglect other aspects of their life, e.g. home, family, etc. ➤Stress is a common outcome. Type B people, by contrast, are more content and at ease with themselves and others.

The practical use of personality traits is beset with problems, including the large number of potential traits, variations in the extent to which traits are enduring, and the lack of hard evidence for some of the predictive claims. ➤➤psychological testing. Nevertheless, some measures of personality traits are very widely used, notably the ➤Myers–Briggs Type Indicator and the ➤five factor model of personality. These measures reduce potential traits to a manageable number of types or dimensions. Related research shows that in business contexts just a few personality attributes are powerful predictors of behaviour in organizations. These can be expressed as a series of self-awareness questions: What is your locus of control (is it within you or external to you)? How Machiavellian are you (do you believe the ends justify the means)? What level of self-esteem do you possess (do you like yourself)? Are you a self-monitor (can you adapt easily to new situations and change)? Are you a risk taker (do you take chances)? Are you type A (aggressively and impatiently trying to achieve success)?

These personality traits have predictive power, and for this reason they are seen as particularly useful in selecting business leaders. ➤leadership. However, this must be viewed cautiously. For example, while type A people are found in senior management positions they are not necessarily the best managers – they have drive and energy, but may be insensitive and too 'stressed-out' to be effective with others. Furthermore, it is unclear whether type A people seek out senior positions or whether those with senior positions have to adopt type A behaviour whatever their underlying personality traits, i.e. their ➤role dictates that they have to work, for example, to tight deadlines and punishing work schedules, and it is a consequence of their role that they become stressed.

personalization technologies The use of various tools to communicate directly, by name, with consumers. Traditionally, in ➤direct marketing, this has meant the creation and use of databases to send personalized letters or personalized e-mail messages. A standard reason for doing this is to target advertising and promotional offers at specific consumers, in contrast to the scattergun approach of mass communication methods and non-personalized direct mail ('junk mail'). There also may be a ➤**relationship marketing** goal (e.g. the provision of pertinent information for existing customers) based on the organization's understanding of the likes, interests and purchase histories of these customers. This at least creates the *appearance* of a more personal relationship between an organization and its customers. Developments in ➤**interactive electronic marketing** have introduced new tools for personalization, including:

(1) 'Cookies', i.e. targeted but unsolicited advertising. Cookies store a user's identification and web-usage information (the web site accessed, items purchased, etc.), and if a user revisits a web site the cookie information can be accessed to send an instant and personalized message. The hope is that any message is seen as relevant because it relates to something in which the user has already expressed an interest. However, because cookies are unsolicited and can be obtained by third parties (notably advertising agencies) there is potential for abuse.

(2) 'Standard on-line mailing lists', i.e. where users elect to have their names and details on a computer mailing list, and copies of an e-mail message are sent to all individuals on the list.

(3) 'On-line mailing lists using push technology', i.e. criteria are used so that messages are sent only to customers who fit the desired criteria. Typically, criteria are those used as ➤**segmentation** bases, e.g. demographics, geodemographics, etc.

personal pension A ➤pension deriving from a pension account in the name of a single individual, as compared with an occupational pension or company scheme. Personal pensions were made available to UK employees under the Social Security Act 1985; until then, employees had access only to occupational pensions. Personal pensions are all ➤**money purchase** schemes; taxation and contribution rules are the same as pension schemes for the self-employed. Personal pensions can be taken with individuals when they change jobs, thus the term *portable pensions*. In the US, personal pensions were introduced in 1975 as ➤**individual retirement accounts**.

personnel management The management of people at work, including recruitment and selection, pay and remuneration, training and development, terms of employment and working conditions, consultative processes and employer–employee negotiations. The more contemporary term ➤**human resource management** is very often preferred. ➤**Industrial relations** is a distinct aspect of personnel management that sits side-by-side with human resource management. Professionally represented by the Institute of Personnel Management.

PESTL An acronym for the components of an environmental analysis: *p*olitical, *e*conomic, *s*ocial, *t*echnological, and *l*egal forces. The analysis is commonly used during the process of developing an organization's strategy and in ➤**marketing planning**. It is a simple and easy-to-remember acronym to help managers consider the main groups of constraints that affect a firm. Frequently, these are ➤**external constraints**, beyond the control of the firm. ➤**exogenous variable**. For example, under the first group of constraints – political – a firm would need to consider what the likely effect would be of any forthcoming government legislation. ➤**environmental scanning**.

Peters, Tom Joint author with Robert Waterman of *In Search of Excellence* (1982) who emphasizes the importance of customers, people and innovation. His work is focused mainly upon corporate cultures and values. Peters has done much to enliven and shake-up management thinking and his message is delivered with enthusiasm, passion and a genuine anger directed at dull or wrong thinking. His seminars are theatrical events, with Peters striding about the platform or among the delegates, microphone in hand, multicoloured audio-visual presentations on all sides, rather like a night-club entertainer. His recent books are similar to his seminars in style, with multiple typefaces, photographs, quotes, sketches and large exclamation marks.

In Search of Excellence analysed the reasons for the 20-year financial outperformance of 43 of *Fortune*'s Top 500 companies. The authors found that all these companies shared eight characteristics: (a) a bias for action; (b) closeness to customer; (c) autonomy and entrepreneurship; (d) productivity through people; (e) hands-on, value-driven; (f) stick to the knitting; (g) simple form, lean staff, and (h) simultaneous loose–tight properties. This last meant that autonomy is pushed downwards in decentralized operations but corporate values are tightly controlled. A strong leader had formed the culture of excellence at an early stage in almost every case. The book sold many millions of copies and is still in print. The majority of the companies ran into difficulties in subsequent years and Peters learned from this: things change. In *Thriving on Chaos* (1987) he embarked on a new direction which emphasized and analysed change and obsolescence and the need for flatter, open management structures to cope with it.

Peters himself changes his thinking all the time and likes to shock. In *The Circle of Innovation* (1997) he writes 'I cherish inconsistency. A lot of what I say here contradicts what I said 15 years ago. Some of what I say here contradicts what I say in other places. S-o-o-o? The world is inconsistent. All bets are off . . . and they never were on.'

Peters worked with Waterman at ➤**McKinsey** and their book grew out of a major programme of research carried out by the firm. Peters wrote a sequel with Nancy Austin, *A Passion for Excellence* (1985) and Waterman went on to write several books on his own, including *The Renewal Factor* (1987). Peters, who served in Vietnam, worked in government before joining McKinsey in 1974, qualified in civil engineering and gained an MBA at Sandford later. He is currently based in Silicon Valley.

picketing The process of manning entrances to a place of work to inform employees, contractors, etc. of the details of an industrial dispute, usually with the intention of persuading these people not to cross the picket line. To be deemed legal, picketing must be non-aggressive, conducted at one's own place of work (i.e. not at a secondary place of work), and must not prevent those who want to work from exercising their right to work. 'Flying pickets' from outside the workplace are regarded as illegal, being both secondary and aggressive. An injured employer may bring a civil action against those individuals or trade unions who/that engage in illegal picketing. ➤**collective action**; ➤➤**industrial relations**. However, recourse to civil action and/or the involvement of law enforcement agencies will inflame the situation and are unlikely to resolve the cause of a dispute.

piece-rate Pay related to the number of units produced ('pieces') over a set time-frame. Common where it is relatively easy to measure the number of units produced by each person, e.g. on a production line or in an 'industrialized service'. This form of pay contrasts with fixed payments over a set time-frame (a wage paid for a 40-hour working week). ➤**pay**.

PIMS ➤profit impact of market strategy.

pipeline principle Inventory that has been ordered but is not yet available to the customer is said to be in the pipeline. Pipeline inventory exists because inventory cannot be transported immediately from the point of supply to the point of demand. When stock runs out and an order is placed, that stock is in the pipeline until it is available to the customer.

placing (UK) The sale of new shares to institutions or private individuals, as distinct from an ➤**introduction** or ➤**offer for sale** (US = *placement*). The placing of shares is common for private companies, where it may be carried out by the company directly with investors (a private placing) or with the help of a stockbroker. For public companies wishing to place shares as a route towards a ➤**listing**, a ➤**sponsor** will be used; this is sometimes called a 'public placing'. Stock exchange authorities allow listed companies to use placing only for small issues, since not all investors have the opportunity to buy at the same price. For larger issues an offer for sale is required, but this is a more costly means of raising capital. ➤➤**vendor placing**.

planning ➤marketing planning; strategic planning.

planning and control ➤inventory planning and control.

planning cycle ➤marketing planning; strategic planning.

planogram A 'map' showing the layout of a store, warehouse or factory. Designing the layout is of importance for operational reasons (storage of stock, inventory control, stock replenishment), but it also may be of wider significance, e.g. in a supermarket, the layout is used to steer customers through the store, ensuring they are drawn to the back of the store and past high-margin items.

PLC ➤product life-cycle.

plc ➤incorporation.

poison pill A defence technique used by a firm under threat of ➤**take-over** to ensure that it is no longer such an attractive target. For example, the firm would purchase a poorly performing business or sign an agreement with its employees that would give itself a financial burden. This would clearly be unattractive to the bidding firm, thus hopefully forcing it to decide against the take-over.

politicking Behaviour within an organization designed to influence decision-making processes, goals or criteria, which rests on the exercise of power beyond one's formal job specification. The aim is to obtain favourable outcomes in terms of greater rewards or less punishment. In some circumstances, politicking is subversive or unethical (such illegitimate political behaviour would include industrial sabotage and whistle-blowing); however, it must be recognized that there is a natural level of political behaviour in all organizations. Examples include camouflaging your self-interest, making yourself appear indispensable, developing powerful allies, avoiding those on the fringe, and so forth. While some of these are proactive forms of political behaviour (e.g. developing powerful allies), many are defensive, e.g. avoiding action ('passing the buck', stalling, playing dumb), avoiding blame (covering your rear/ass, playing safe, scapegoating, kissing up), and avoiding change (resisting change, protecting turf). Politicking is described by Henry ➤Mintzberg (*Power In and Around Organization*, 1983) as a set of political games that are common to all organizations to varying degrees. These games are designed to resist authority, counter resistance, build power bases, defeat rivals and change the organization. ➤➤impression management; muddling-through theory; power.

polluter pays principle The idea that polluting emissions should be taxed in order that those who create them bear the costs of their actions. The principle of allowing pollution to occur, but taxing it, derives from the economist, Arthur Pigou in 1932. It is an approach which contrasts with banning pollution outright or, restricting it to certain limits. The advantage of taxing it is that if the tax rate covers the damage or suffering caused by the pollution – it will pay firms to pollute only if the benefits of them so doing outweigh the costs. The tax will also generate revenue that can be used to compensate those who suffer most. In the UK, examples of pollution taxes are the climate change levy on fossil fuel use, and the landfill tax on the dumping of waste.

portal An ➤internet site that operates as a gateway to other internet sites. Such sites also provide general internet capabilities. The advantages to these internet gateways is that they can direct users to certain sites – who can take the opportunity to advertise and promote products and services– and offer additional services to users. All of which will usually involve income generation for the operator of the portal.

Porter, Michael E Professor of Management at Harvard University and business strategy guru. His first major work, *Competitive Strategy* (1980) set out five forces which drive competition: (a) existing rivalry between firms; (b) the threat of new entrants; (c) the threat of substitute products and services; (d) the bargaining power of suppliers, and (e) the bargaining power of buyers. The sources of *competitive advantage* are to be understood by analysing a firm's activities which create value for its buyers. The ➤value chain consists of five ➤primary activities: (a) inbound logistics (transport and storage of inputs); (b) operations (production); (c) outbound logistics (transport to buyers); (d) marketing, and (e) sales and aftersales service, together with support activities, i.e. research and development, procurement, human resource management, and finance and planning. Firms compete by cost leadership or differentiation (rarely both) and by focusing on particular geographical, product or buyer groups. ➤generic strategy. A firm's value chain is embedded in the *value system* which includes the value chains of its suppliers upstream and its distributors, retailers and buyers downstream.

A criticism of this work was that Porter concentrated on market positioning, i.e. what firms should do once they have a product or service. It focused on issues like market attractiveness, competitors and, in particular, which market to enter. Little attention was paid to the problem of what firms should do to achieve this position in the first place, e.g. in terms of stimulating ➤innovation.

In *The Competitive Advantage of Nations* (1990) Porter extended his analysis to attempt to explain the success or failure of countries and international companies, emphasizing the importance of clusters of mutually supporting industries in national value systems. Porter constantly reminds his readers of the importance of competition, a word which appears in the titles of most of his books and articles. National economic performance depends upon the success of a wide range of individual firms at the microeconomic level. In *Can Japan Compete?* (2000), written jointly with Takenchi and Sakakibara, he challenged the widespread belief that the postwar success of Japan was attributable to a unique model of government intervention. On the contrary, Porter argues, Japan's recent long recession reveals deep-seated structural problems stemming from its system of bureaucratic capitalism which reflect the effects of harmful intervention and a mistrust of competition.

Porter's notions on competitive advantage and the value chain and system have endured and provide a useful framework for thinking about corporate strategy. Some aspects of his work have proved controversial, however. For example, it has been pointed out that some Japanese companies have gained competitive advantages in both cost and quality, while the largest multinational companies are increasingly independent of national value systems. Moreover, Porter's commitment to formalized strategic planning has been criticized as impractical, inappropriate or unrealistic, though the debate has become a semantic one since all businesses must think and plan for the future. ➤Mintzberg. Porter rebuts his critics in his latest book, a collection of essays, *On Competition* (2000).

portfolio **1.** A group of ➤securities held as an investment. ➤portfolio theory. **2.** A branch or class of insurance business.

portfolio planning A management planning technique developed by the Boston Consulting Group (➤Henderson, Bruce D) which involves management plotting each of the businesses on a simple chart. These are then rated as 'stars', 'dogs' or 'cash cows' and invested in, divested out of, or profits harvested from accordingly. 'Problem children' comprise a fourth category.

Portfolio planning recognizes that a diversified company is a collection of businesses, each making a distinct contribution to the overall corporate performance and which should be managed accordingly. Putting the portfolio planning philosophy into place takes three steps in the typical company.
(1) Redefine businesses for strategic planning purposes as ➤strategic business units (SBUs), which may or may not differ from operating units.
(2) Classify these SBUs on a portfolio grid according to the competitive position and attractiveness of the particular product or market.
(3) Use this framework to assign each a 'strategic mission' with respect to its growth and financial objectives and allocates resources accordingly.
Benefits:
(1) Companies gain a better understanding of each of their businesses. This allows them to make appropriate strategic decisions.
(2) Allows verbal, as opposed to purely financial, analysis of the business and thereby aids business understanding.
(3) Improves allocation of resources.
(4) Improves operations because it encourages focus, objectivity and commitment.
Limitations include:

(1) Assumes market share is more significant than profit.
(2) Allocation of resources tends to focus on investment rather than other resources, e.g. people, research, etc.
(3) Tends to overlook long-term issues in favour of today's performance.
(4) Tends to inhibit diversification.

portfolio theory Economic analysis of the means by which investors can minimize risk and maximize returns. Central to portfolio theory is the notion that risk can be reduced by diversifying holdings of assets while returns are a function of expected risk. Statistical analysis of share prices is used to provide guidance on portfolio composition. ➤➤**alpha coefficient; beta coefficient; capital asset pricing model.**

POSB Post Office Savings Bank. ➤**National Savings Bank.**

position 1. The extent of a person's financial commitment to a ➤**stock**, commodity or currency. If a dealer, for example, sells 100 shares he does not own, he has sold short or has a short position of 100 in the shares ➤**short-selling**. If he owns 100 shares, he has a long position of 100 in the stock on his books. He will take a ➤**bear** position (i.e. a short position) if he expects the price of the stock to fall and can buy the stock to meet the sale more cheaply later on, and a ➤**bull** (i.e. long) position if he expects the price to rise. **2.** The acquisition by the arranging bank of one half of a ➤**swap** deal in order to complete the deal with the intention in due course of finding a counterparty.

positional good A good that is necessarily scarce, and the scarcity of which cannot be reduced by increased productivity, e.g. original paintings by famous artists, or holidays on empty beaches. These are things rich people might expect to have, but however rich society becomes, it would not be possible for everyone to have them. They were described by Fred Hirsch in his book *The Social Limits to Growth* (1977). He distinguished those positional goods – the value of which derived from their intrinsic usefulness but which are limited in their supply (like prime-location city-centre homes) – and those which do not yield pleasure from their absolute qualities but from their pure scarcity value (like original paintings by famous artists). Allocation of these goods is a ➤**zero-sum game**. Their importance is in explaining the observation that, as people become richer, their levels of material frustration do not appear to diminish.

positioning The process of creating and maintaining a distinctive place in the market for an organization and/or its individual brands. The aim is to put some distance between an organization and its competitors by offering something different (e.g. a special technological feature) or doing something differently (e.g. faster service than others); also called ➤**unique selling proposition**. To be effective the differences must be important, relevant, noticed and understood by consumers; otherwise, they will not have a decisive role in determining brand choice. In practice, many points of difference are non-determining. The *perceptions* of consumers are of primary importance in the positioning process, e.g. an organization may believe its new press-button can-opener is distinctive – that this feature differentiates the brand from the competition – but if consumers do not perceive any difference, the positioning cannot be regarded as effective. Even effective positioning tends to erode over time, as competitors copy or improve upon the points of difference or as the needs of the ➤target audience change. In these circumstances, an organization may have to *reposition* itself.

In a strategic sense, positioning is seen as the outcome from two earlier stages: (a) segmentation, and (b) targeting. ➤segment–target–position strategy.

The concept of positioning is central to marketing, but all too often is defined very narrowly, with a sole focus on distinctive *product* attributes that offer benefits to consumers. This fails to recognize that many organizations and/or brands succeed in the market place because of non-product-based advantages, including supply-side factors (e.g. wider distribution, strategic alliances and sheer weight of communication spend) and organizational capabilities (e.g. managerial talent, quick-footedness, etc.). Thus, a particular digital television may be perceived as having beneficial distinctive features and yet not be bought because it is not readily available to members of the target audience. ➤➤competitive parity.

power Capacity of one person to influence the behaviour of another, so that the other person does things she would not otherwise do. In an organizational setting, a manager might wish to increase productivity (a legitimate and positive use of power), or she might withhold important information from a colleague so as to influence a decision (an illegitimate and negative use of power). The successful exercise of power will normally result in compliance – the thing that otherwise wouldn't be done, is done. Alternatively, the other person internalizes the idea and sees any change in behaviour as arising from her own initiative.

Power comes from five sources or bases:

(1) 'Coercive power', based on fear, the infliction of pain, or the threat of punishment. Those with physical strength are in a better position than most to exert this type of power. The school bully exercises physical power in the schoolyard.

(2) 'Reward power', arising from the ability to grant benefits, offer money, facilitate promotion or provide interesting work, e.g. in a retail franchise operation the franchisor can offer incentives and bonuses to high-performing franchisees. Also termed 'resource power' because the ability to grant benefits depends on the possession of resources (the franchisor possesses the money and information to offer incentives and bonuses).

(3) 'Legitimate power', based on a person's position in the formal hierarchy of an organization, e.g. a manager is likely to be able to influence the behaviour of subordinates because of her status and ➤role, regardless of any ➤leadership qualities (also called 'position power').

(4) 'Expert power', arising from a person's acknowledged expertise, knowledge or skill, e.g. the authority with which doctors, planners, scientists, etc. speak influences the behaviour of people.

(5) 'Referent power', based on the possession of personal traits that are desired or admired by others, e.g. charisma. Thus, a sporting icon might command attention because of her athleticism; this partly explains the use of such people in product endorsements.

For power to be exercised there must be 'dependency' in the relationship, i.e. one party must possess and control something that others want (e.g. monetary rewards) making others dependent on the one party. The 'thing' must be seen as important, scarce and non-substitutable. This often is not the case in organizations, e.g. status may be substituted for monetary rewards, giving power to those who control promotion committees as well as to those who control remuneration committees.

Power is the capacity to influence, and dependency creates the conditions, but 'influence' is the method by which power is exercised. Four influences are recognized: (a) force or the threat of force (deriving mainly from coercive power); (b) exchange of favours, promotions, rewards (associated with any source of power but especially reward and legitimate power) ➤➤bargaining; (c) rules and procedures (based on authority from legitimate power and backed by reward power), and (d) persuasion (associated most with expert and referent power) (this influence is most closely associated with ➤trust). Finally, having a keen awareness of power and influence is also a form of power and influence in its own right, a point underlying the writings of organizational thinkers from Machiavelli to Charles ➤Handy.

Prahalad, C K ➤Hamel, Gary.

predator firm A firm seeking to purchase another firm in a ➤hostile take-over.

predatory pricing Setting prices at very low levels with the objective of weakening or eliminating competitors or to keep out new entrants to a market. Since it could only make sense to engage in this practice if prices are to be raised again once these objectives have been achieved, there is no permanent benefit to the consumer. Predatory pricing is generally regarded as an abuse of ➤monopoly power, and is not used to describe the practice of many young entrants to a market who will legitimately price below cost to establish themselves in the market and develop familiarity and a reputation. The authorities are generally suspicious of below-cost pricing where it is practised by a large firm (➤Office of Fair Trading), although some economists have argued that it rarely makes sense to invest so much expense in knocking-out competitors, because if they are viable in the long term, they will surely invest in remaining in business. Predatory pricing can simply spark a price war, in which case it simply becomes a game of ➤chicken to see who can hold out the longest in a costly struggle. The UK authorities have investigated claims of predatory pricing against oil companies (accused of knocking independent petrol retailers out of business) and against certain newspapers.

pre-emptive right (UK) The right of shareholders of a ➤company to have first refusal to purchase any new shares issued by the company. These rights have legal backing in the UK. ➤➤rights issue.

preference data ➤perceptual mapping.

preference share (UK) Holders of preference shares precede the holders of ➤ordinary shares, but follow ➤debenture holders in the payment of ➤dividends and in the return of ➤capital if the issuing company is liquidated. ➤liquidation. Preference shares (US = *preferred stock*) normally entitle the holder to a fixed rate of dividend (i.e. are *non-participating*) but *participating preference shares* also entitle the holder to a share of residual profits. Preference shares carry limited voting rights and may be redeemable or not. ➤redeemable securities. *Cumulative preference shares* carry forward the entitlement to preferential dividends, if unpaid, from one year to the next, while *non-cumulative preference shares* do not.

preferred stock (US) ➤preference share.

premium 1. In ➤insurance, the sum of money paid, either once (single premium) or continuously (regular premium), to buy an insurance policy. **2.** In the ➤forward and ➤futures currency and commodity markets, the amount by which a later-date price exceeds an early-date price. **3.** Of ➤securities, the amount by which the ➤secondary market price exceeds the ➤issue price or ➤par value. **4.** Of ➤options, the initial down payment, normally 10 per cent, required. **5.** The amount by which the price of an ➤investment trust share exceeds the ➤net assets.

prescriptive corporate strategy An approach to developing strategy where the objective has been defined in advance and the main elements have been developed prior to commencement. For example, a prescriptive strategy would be that in which an automobile manufacturer states that its main objective is profit maximization (to create a return for its investors) and this will involve ensuring the firm develops products for markets that deliver the highest possible return.

present value ➤discounted cash flow.

price discrimination The selling of similar items to different buyers at different prices. The goal of price discrimination is to charge a high price to buyers who are willing to pay a high price, while still making sales to more price-sensitive buyers who would otherwise not make a purchase. The airline industry is probably the most effective at discriminating between different customer types: the well-to-do business executive who will pay a lot, and the backpacking traveller who cannot afford very much. If the airline charged one price to all, it would either be too high a price for the backpacker (in which case the planes would fly half empty, and the limited profit the airline makes on the budget traveller would be lost altogether), or the price would be low enough to keep the budget traveller on board, but the executive would get a flight at a fraction of the cost she was willing to pay. The airline would thus lose profit. ➤➤yield management.

For price discrimination to work, several conditions must prevail. First, there must be a separation between markets that does not allow buyers in one to resell the item in another (no parallel trade must be possible). Secondly, the seller must possess some degree of ➤market power in at least one market, for under competitive conditions, prices will be driven down to the level of costs in all markets. Thirdly, buyers in different markets must have a different level and elasticity of demand for the good. ➤price elasticity of demand. The profit-maximizing firm that discriminates will sell in each market such that ➤marginal cost is equal to the ➤marginal revenue in that market. Sales will be at a higher price in markets in which price sensitivity is generally low than where it is high. In perfect price discrimination the monopolist charges a different price to every consumer. In terms of the economics of demand and supply, this ensures the supplier has sales revenue equivalent to the area under the ➤demand curve for his product. ➤➤market segmentation; ➤inverse elasticity rule.

price/earnings growth (PEG) **factor** A financial ratio used to assist in share selection. The PEG factor is calculated by dividing the prospective ➤price/earnings (P/E) **ratio** of a share by the estimated future growth rate in ➤earnings per share. A share with earnings growth of 15 per cent and a P/E of 25 would have a PEG factor of 1.67 (25 divided by 15). Jim Slater, who devised this measure, says that on this measure alone shares may be attractive at a PEG factor of 1 or less, but he warns that other factors need to be taken into account, while the method is designed only to measure ➤**growth stocks** and not ➤**cyclical** or ➤**recovery stocks**. It will also be noted that the method relies upon earnings forecasts by ➤**investment analysts** which may prove incorrect.

price/earnings (P/E) **ratio** (PER) The quoted price of a share divided by the most recent year's earnings per share, also known as the *multiple*. In the UK, the net distribution method is usually used in calculating the PER, in which earnings are defined as the net-of-tax dividends plus ➤**retained earnings**. High P : E ratios reflect favourable investors' assessments of the future earning power of the company.

price elasticity of demand A measure of the sensitivity of demand for a product to changes in its price. ➤**Elasticity** is a concept much used by economists in a variety of forms; the demand elasticity (sometimes known as the price elasticity) is measured by the percentage change in quantity demanded for an item divided by the corresponding percentage change in price that generated the change in demand. In general, a price elasticity will be negative (a higher price leads to lower demand). An elasticity of –1 would indicate that a 1 per cent increase in price leads to a 1 per cent fall in demand. An elasticity of –2 would indicate the product is more price-sensitive. In terms of the economist's theory of demand, a higher elasticity equates to a ➤**demand curve** which is on a less steep gradient. A perfectly flat demand curve amounts to demand which is of infinite elasticity, and this implies that even a minuscule increase in price would drive sales to zero. In the intensely competitive conditions assumed of so-called ➤**perfect competition**, it is assumed that each firm faces demand of that kind. ➤➤**market power**. Price elasticity may not be constant for all prices or levels of demand for an item – a product may be more price-sensitive at higher prices than low ones, for example. ➤➤**marginal revenue**.

price elasticity of supply A measure of the sensitivity of supply for a product to changes in its price. ➤**Elasticity** is a concept much used by economists in a variety of forms; the supply elasticity is measured by the percentage change in quantity supplied of an item divided by the corresponding percentage change in price that generated the change in supply.

price leadership A pattern of behaviour in an industry by which one leading firm sets its prices and others follow in its wake with theirs. It is seen as one outcome in ➤**oligopoly**-type industries. Price leadership may be exhibited by the dominant firm, which acts rather as a ➤**monopoly** with ➤**market power**. In this case, smaller rivals act as firms who take the market price as given. ➤**price taking**. Leadership may, alternatively, be exhibited by a 'barometer firm' (*barometric price leadership*) in which case a more representative supplier finds itself leading the pack, announcing price changes in response to changing cost or demand conditions. In increasingly global markets, it is often the case that within any individual country, a large domestic player acts as a price-setter, with importers tending to follow. For example, it has been suggested that in the UK car market, Rover acted as a price leader.

price promotion ➤promotion.

price regulation A form of ➤**regulation**, common for public utilities in the UK, in which the prices of the supplier are not allowed to rise above a certain level. The regulation is designed to prevent the abuse of a ➤**monopoly** position. UK price regulation has applied to telephone, gas, electricity and water providers. In each case the design has shared certain common features: (a) allowed price rises are set out for a few years in advance, typically 4 or 5; (b) there is a review at the end of each period, at which the regime governing the next period is decided, and (c) allowed price rises are specified relative to the ➤**retail prices index** (RPI), and might be RPI – 4.5 per cent each year, for example. (This protects the regulated firm against inflation.) Under this form of price regulation, if firms can keep their costs low they can earn big profits, at least until the pricing formula is next reviewed. This gives firms an incentive to be efficient that does not exist under ➤**rate-of-return regulation**. But it has been suggested that, in each periodic review, the regulator looks at the rate of return to decide what new price formula should be applied, thus reducing the difference between the two types of scheme. ➤➤**Averch–Johnson effect**.

price taking The situation in which a firm with limited ➤**market share** and little or no ➤**market power** sets its price – and level of output – according to the prevailing market price. A price-*taking* firm is one that is too small to find that increasing its own output depresses the market price. A price-*making* firm is one with market power, that finds it comprises a significant enough proportion of the market for its own decisions on output to affect the price it fetches for its product. In economic language, for a price taker, price and ➤**marginal revenue** are identical.

pricing policy The area of business decision-making that involves setting price. A formal starting-point is the economics of price-setting. Here, the assumption is that a profit-maximizing firm will determine how much to produce according to costs and revenues of production. In economics, however, firms do not look at their overall costs or revenues, but only those associated with marginal (or incremental) increases in production. More specifically, the firm will choose how much to produce so that ➤**marginal revenue** equals ➤**marginal cost**. If marginal revenue exceeds marginal cost, then the firm can benefit from increasing output (as incremental revenues exceed incremental costs). If marginal revenue is less than marginal cost, then the firm will cut production because the cost saved will be larger than the revenue forgone. Once the firm has chosen how much to produce according to this rule, it will then let the market determine the actual price of output. In business economics, this type of pricing is ubiquitous across different industry structures (➤➤**monopolistic competition; monopoly; perfect competition**) although in ➤**oligopoly** more complicated pricing behaviour is recognized.

In practice, pricing can be both more complicated and more simple. For example, firms often strive to engage in ➤**price discrimination**, charging different amounts in different markets. Or firms may find that they are subject to ➤**regulation** of some kind, or that they need to follow some kind of ➤**inverse elasticity rule**. Moreover, firms often do not have sufficiently accurate information to make precise estimates of marginal costs or revenues, and follow rules of thumb such as ➤**mark-up pricing**, cost-plus pricing, and competition-oriented pricing. Finally, price can act as a signal of the quality of a product, and thus setting a price becomes a tool of marketing the product.

Prices are often set by marketers who will employ a variety of pricing strategies, depending on specific circumstances rather than formal economic analysis. With new products a choice is made between the two main alternative strategies of price skimming (high initial price), and penetration pricing (low initial price). Price skimming is recommended when: (a) demand is price-inelastic; (b) where there is little chance of quick competitive entry (because of innovative technology and protective patents); (c) where consumers are unaware of production and marketing costs, and (d) where sizable margins are needed (perhaps because volume sales will not be possible in the short term). Penetration pricing, by contrast, is recommended where: (a) demand is elastic; (b) competitors are likely to enter quickly; (c) there is no prestige or status attached to the product, and (d) where the size of margins is not so important (because of volume growth of the market). However, it is easier to reduce prices from skimming, than raise prices from penetration.

For existing products, pricing strategies are developed: (a) to influence demand over time (e.g. ➤peak-pricing and ➤sale-pricing); (b) to cross-sell products (e.g. bundling-pricing); (c) to achieve volume goals (e.g. quantity discounting and price promotions to achieve ➤yield management goals); (d) to tie-in buyers (e.g. relationship pricing), and (e) as a response to competitors (reference pricing and ➤predatory pricing).

primary activity Part of Michael ➤Porter's ➤value chain. According to Porter, every organization consists of activities that link together to develop the value of the business. He suggests that the primary activities of a business are:
(1) Inbound logistics. The areas concerned with receiving the goods from suppliers, storing and distributing them.
(2) Operations. This is the production area or service delivery area. ➤operations management.
(3) Outbound logistics. These distribute the goods and services to the final customer.
(4) Marketing and sales. This analyses customers' requirements and brings them to the attention of the organization.
(5) Service. Aftersales service.

primary demand The level of consumer demand for a product category, e.g. total demand for new cars. This is distinct from the secondary demand for specific manufacturers, brands, models and makes, e.g. Ford, BMW, Mazda. For new-to-the-world products (e.g. innovative biotechnology applications) the forecasting of primary demand is of huge importance and promotional activities are undertaken to stimulate interest in the category. ➤new product development. By contrast, for an established product category (e.g. personal banking) the forecasting of ➤market share assumes importance and most of the promotional activity is brand-specific, e.g. Barclays, HSBC, Abbey National.

primary market ➤new issue market.

prime cost A cost of production that is directly associated with the output. These would include labour and raw materials, plus the fixed costs of maintaining production that would disappear if production ceased but the firm remained in business.

principal 1. A person acting on his own account and buying and selling at his own risk, as distinct from someone acting as an ➤agent for another, e.g. a ➤broker. **2.** The amount of a debt (i.e. the capital sum) excluding any ➤premium or ➤interest.

principal agent theory The body of economics concerned with the incentives and behaviour that characterize the relationship between those hiring representatives to perform tasks and those they hire. In this field, the employer is known as the 'principal', and the person hired as the 'agent'. Examples of principals and their agents would include: (a) the owners of companies and the executives who are employed to manage them; (b) customers of professional service firms and the professionals they employ, or (c) employers and their employees. On the realistic assumptions that: (a) principals cannot observe, monitor or assess every action by the agent, and (b) that the agent defines her own interests differently to those of the principal, then the structure of relationships, contracts and outcomes associated with these situations is ripe for analysis. ➤➤agency costs; agency theory.

prisoners' dilemma A situation in which it pays each of several economic agents individually to behave in a particular way, even though it would pay them as a group to behave in some other way. The prisoners' dilemma is a classic and fundamental concept in ➤game theory. It is best exemplified by the fable from which it derives its name, in which a sheriff picks up two suspected criminals and needs to secure evidence to convict them of a serious crime. So he puts them in separate cells, and gives each the chance to confess to having committed the crime with the other, and tells them their fate will be as follows.

(1) If you don't confess and your partner doesn't confess, you will get 3 years in gaol for a minor offence for which evidence is already available.
(2) If you confess and your partner confesses, you will each get 6 years in gaol.
(3) If your partner confesses and you don't, you will get 12 years in gaol.
(4) If your partner doesn't confess and you do, you will get 2 years in gaol.

These outcomes can be summarized in a ➤pay-off matrix, where the left-hand number in each pair is criminal 1's sentence, and the right-hand number is criminal 2's.

Pay-off matrix

		Criminal 2 Confess	Don't confess
	Confess	3,3	2,12
Criminal 1			
	Don't confess	12,2	6,6

Given the choice of confessing or not, the best one from the point-of-view of the prisoners taken together is for both not to confess, giving them 3 years each in gaol. However, if they each believed the other was to behave in this way, it would pay them to confess in the hope of getting 2 years instead. Indeed, scrutiny of the choices shows that if one believes his partner is going to confess, he ought to confess also (avoiding the 12 years), and if one believes his partner is not going to confess, he still ought to confess in order to get 2 years instead of 3. This compelling logic will drive both criminals to confess unless they genuinely have as much concern for each other as they do for themselves. The logic of the situation is that they end up getting 6 years, even if they can see they could get away with 3.

Situations for which the prisoners' dilemma stands as an analogy are ubiquitous within business and within life generally. In business in particular, it is often seen as a way of characterizing ➤**oligopoly**. Here, it may pay firms to collude and jointly act as a monopolist, but it will pay individual firms to cheat on the colluding deal and produce more than they agreed to. ➤➤**cartel; Nash equilibrium; repeated game.**

private company (UK) ➤incorporation.

private equity Institutional investment in ➤**unlisted companies.** ➤➤**venture capital.**

private finance initiative (PFI) A programme of the UK government designed to encourage the private sector to design, finance, build and operate assets providing services to and for the public sector. The PFI is a specific subset of the more general concept, the ➤**public private partnership.** It was launched in November 1992 by the then Chancellor of the Exchequer, Norman Lamont, who repealed a number of Treasury rules which had had the effect of restraining private involvement in public projects. With these restrictions swept away, it was open to government departments to use the PFI as a means of contracting-out. Any capital which was provided by the private supplier (e.g. for building prisons, roads, new hospitals or buying new hospital equipment) would not count as government borrowing. In order to induce private providers, the public sector would have to sign contracts to purchase services from them once the assets were constructed. The fact that government was signing contracts to buy services without spending any upfront cash on their provision led critics to argue that it was simply a form of 'buy now, pay later' scheme, designed to reduce immediate pressure on public spending by getting the private sector to pay. The Treasury has always insisted that such contracts cannot be signed, unless a sizable amount of risk is borne by the private provider. In practice, that, and the government's desire to avoid paying market rates of return, has meant the process of negotiating such contracts is a tortuous one. Nevertheless, the PFI remains an important policy initiative, designed to limit the problems of the public sector's inability to finance capital spending very effectively in the belief the private sector can manage assets more effectively.

private label Products bearing the retailer's own name, rather than a manufacturer's. Also called 'own-labels'. Traditionally described as cheap inferior products (perhaps with poorer quality ingredients). However, in the UK, in particular, retailers have launched innovative private labels, supported by national advertising campaigns, and priced only fractionally below brands. In the minds of consumers, these private labels are closer to ➤**brands** than ➤**generics**, i.e. closer to distinctive premium products than low-price commodities.

privatization The sale of government-owned equity in nationalized industries or other commercial enterprises to private investors. It may involve the retention of either a majority or a minority holding by government, though the UK government in several cases has retained a golden share which is intended to give it power of veto in an unwelcome take-over bid, e.g. one from overseas. With few obvious large-scale enterprises left to privatize, the UK government has tended to direct its efforts to reform public services, not through privatization, but through ➤**public private partnerships.** ➤➤**private finance initiative.**

PRIZM ➤geodemographic segmentation.

process groups ➤qualitative market research.

process innovation ➤innovation.

process layout Where the layout of the production operation is dominated by the activities involved in the process. In process layout, similar production processes are located together. For example, in an aircraft manufacturing plant all machine tools would be located together as they require similar specialist technical support. Another example could be a supermarket where all frozen food products are grouped together because it is convenient to restock if they are grouped together. One limitation of this type of layout is that different products or customers may require different needs. Hence, the flow pattern for different machined components for an aircraft may take different routes around the machine tool section. Similarly, customers take very different routes around a supermarket as they purchase different items from the shelves. ➤➤mass production; job production.

process re-engineering ➤re-engineering.

process theory An approach to understanding situations that examines the activities and how they interact with each other. In terms of strategic management, the emphasis is on understanding how a strategy is developed and how it is implemented. Many writers argue that process theories, and subsequent process models, indicate lower aspirations about explained variance, but a richer explanation of how and why the outcomes occur when they occur.

procurement A formal word for 'acquisition', but commonly used in the US to cover the activities of buying and purchasing. ➤organizational buying behaviour.

product The generic title for items bought and sold as part of the exchange process – the first P of the ➤four Ps (4Ps). Typically, products are seen as tangible goods (e.g. toothpaste, computers, filing cabinets), but the term also extends to services, e.g. pension plans, fast food meals, air travel. These will vary in the degree to which they are tangible. ➤services marketing. Many products are branded; however, the two are not equivalent. ➤brand. A distinction should be drawn between a product (salt) – the generic term – and a branded product (Tate & Lyle salt) – the specific product. In new markets, the goal may be to grow the product and the brand (primary and secondary demand respectively), but in established markets much marketing effort is on maintaining brand sales/share (a focus on secondary demand within the product category).

product attributes ➤choice modelling; decision rules.

product champion A person in an organization who is enthusiastic and knowledgeable about a specific product or initiative. This person is likely to be instrumental in rallying support for the product among line managers, as well as ensuring continued support and commitment from senior management. This is of particular importance in ➤new product development – such a person will 'sell' the new product idea and steer it through the long and arduous development and commercialization process.

product concept An idea for a new product that has been matched to a market need, has a physical form and its technology is known. Usually, there are many ideas for new products but few can be transformed into product concepts. For a product idea to become a new-product concept, three inputs are required: form, technology and need.

(1) Form. This is the physical thing to be created (or in the case of a service, the sequence of steps by which the service will be created). It may still be vague and not precisely defined.

(2) Technology. In most cases there is one clear technology that is at the base of the new product.

(3) Need. The benefits gained by the customer give the product value.

product development ➤new product development.

product differentiation ➤differentiation.

product innovation ➤innovation.

production function The mathematical relationship between the output of a firm or economy and the inputs used to produce that output:

$$Q = f(L, K, t \ldots)$$

where Q is the ➤**dependent variable** (output) and L, K, t ... are independent variables or inputs. The amount of inputs (e.g. labour, capital, raw materials, etc.) required to produce a given output depends on the fundamentals of production technology and this will be reflected in the form of the function. For example, it may be linear (➤**linear relationship**) or non-linear. An example of the latter is the *Cobb–Douglas function* which takes the form:

$$Q = aL^b K^c$$

where a, b and c are parameters. ➤**econometrics**.

One important feature of a production function is whether it implies that output tends to grow more or less proportionally as inputs are expanded. A production function in which both inputs and outputs tend to grow by the same amounts is said to enjoy ➤**constant returns to scale**, i.e. if inputs are doubled, output is doubled, too. Similarly, a function may exhibit ➤**increasing returns to scale**, if output grows more than proportionally, or ➤**decreasing returns to scale** if it grows by less. The form:

$$Q = aK.L$$

exhibits increasing returns, because if inputs are, for instance, doubled, output increases by $2 \times 2 = 4$ times. More generally, in the Cobb–Douglas form above, constant returns to scale are implied if $b + c = 1$; increasing returns are implied if $b + c > 1$, and decreasing returns to scale are implied if $b + c < 1$.

A production function was estimated for the US economy of the Cobb–Douglas form:

$$Q = 1.1K^{0.25}L^{0.75}$$

where K is the capital stock and L a measure of the labour input. This implies constant returns.

The above functions are sometimes termed 'homogeneous of degree n', when a given increase x in each of the inputs increases output by $x \times n$. For example, a function homogeneous in degree 3 is one such that if the inputs are scaled-up by a factor of 2, the outputs are scaled up by a factor of 2×3. If n is > 1, the function reflects increasing returns to scale, if < 1, diminishing returns to scale; if it $= 1$, constant returns to scale.

production line The arrangement of a ➤**flow production** system so that parts move systematically from one stage to the next. Such systems lend themselves to the ➤**division of labour** and high degrees of automation.

production scheduling A timetable of production operations. Schedules detail when each task should commence. Schedules of work are used in operations in which some planning is required to ensure that customer demand is met. Other operations (e.g. rapid-response service operations where customers arrive in an unplanned way) cannot schedule the operation in the short term.

productivity In general, the relationship between the output of goods and services and the inputs of resources used to produce them. The word is frequently used to refer to the average output per worker in a company or country, which should more accurately be labelled *labour productivity*. The term ➤**total factor productivity** is then used to refer to the output per unit of all inputs combined.

At a macroeconomic level, productivity growth is generally seen as the basis for ➤**trend growth** in the economy, and the long-term tendency towards more affluence. It is clearly affected by technology (indeed, in the productivity growth boost of the late 1990s in the US, information technology was said to have played a big part). ➤➤**new economy**. Labour productivity is also affected by the size of the capital stock in a country or a company – better-equipped workers would naturally be more productive. No matter how hard a farm labourer works in Africa, a farmer in Europe would always produce more because of the use of other resources, e.g. equipment, fertilizers and fuel. It is the application of resources other than labour that enables the farmer in Europe to be more productive. However, labour productivity can also be affected by the ➤**participation rate**. If one country employs a higher proportion of its population than another, it is only natural that average productivity might be lower, simply on account of ➤**diminishing returns**.

At a business unit level, productivity is usually seen as an employee's level of output, given certain resource inputs (time, materials, skills, etc.), i.e. labour per hour or per dollar. Productivity is measured to ensure the business is using its scarce resources efficiently. It also may be measured to benchmark the performance of employees one against another, e.g. as part of a work study (using, say, time and motion reports). Productivity is a common issue in enterprise bargaining, where employers may be willing to offer pay rises in exchange for productivity or performance-related agreements. In theory, such agreements should not be inflationary because the wage rise only results from an increase in output, with constant or even falling unit costs. This means such agreements are popular during periods of prices and incomes control. At other times employees may argue for a rise in basic pay, without committing to productivity or performance gains. ➤➤**assessment; pay.**

product liability ➤failure analysis.

product life-cycle (PLC) A model of how sales of a product grow through time. For a new product, sales growth is slow at first, then more rapid, reaching a peak and then declining. These four stages are: 'introduction', 'growth', 'maturity' and 'decline'. Profits follow a similar cycle: non-existent in the introductory phase, growing rapidly to a peak in early maturity and thereafter declining.

Each stage will take on certain characteristics, associated with which will be a number of management implications.

(1) Introduction. Innovating consumers are high-income, channels and competitors are few, the price is high and so, too, are margins; the product design is basic, often with poor product quality, the purpose of advertising is to build awareness but this may not be on a sufficient scale to prevent over-capacity. Management must make the best consumer prospects aware of the existence of the new product. They must decide whether to pursue a high price (skimming) strategy or a low price (penetration) strategy. The process of getting from prototypes and beta versions to fully functional commercial products must be managed.

(2) Growth. A mass market of high-income consumers develops with many channels, but also many more competitors, prices fall and so, too, do margins; product design and product quality improve, the brand and its attributes are advertised and there may now be under-capacity. Management must establish the brand name in the face of competition, improve the product and ensure there is enough manufacturing capacity. It may be necessary to reduce the price. Also, distribution must be secured to make sure the product is available.

(3) Maturity. A truly mass market exists, with many channels and many direct competitors, price falls even further, squeezing margins, product quality continues to improve and may result in a range of differentiated products; advertising focuses on price, and capacity is much easier to predict. Management faces fierce competition, having to work hard even to maintain levels of buying. There can be more and more product differentiation in an attempt to claim a share of more specific consumer segments. ➤➤**segmentation**.

(4) Decline. Laggards buy the product for the first time and specialists continue to buy, the number of channels and competitors falls, prices rise, but margins remain low, the design of the product does not change, advertising support focuses on the main buyers or is withdrawn altogether, and there may be over-capacity. Management can use price to maintain buying levels or to milk the market, i.e. continue to derive revenue without investing in the source of the revenue stream. Weak products will be eliminated, others will be milked or relaunched.

This model has pedagogic value, but empirical support for the existence of PLCs is very mixed. In response, the basic PLC model has been elaborated. Further stages have been proposed: turbulence between growth and maturity, saturation aftersales have peaked, and petrification when sales stabilize at a low level after a period of decline. Also, other patterns have been described, e.g. the cycle–recycle pattern where a product enjoys a second lease of life, or the scalloped pattern where new markets are added to existing ones.

However, some problems with the PLC model are deep-seated. One issue is ambiguity about whether the 'product' in question is the product category, a subcategory, an umbrella brand or a single product brand. ➤**brand hierarchy**. Intuitively, we would expect the growth patterns for toothpaste (product category), whitening toothpaste (subcategory), Macleans (umbrella brand), and Macleans whitening (product brand) to differ. Within product categories, there is some support for the idea of a PLC in the early stages, but the maturity stage can be very long-lasting, i.e.

without reaching a period of decline unless there is some major technological shift. Product subcategories tend to be less long-lasting and therefore more likely to exhibit PLC features. However, it is very difficult to gauge the duration of each stage. Umbrella brands might cover quite a diverse range of product areas, so these are less likely to enter a decline phase (they have specifically spread the risk in order to avoid this outcome). Single product brands, by contrast, may go through all stages. This would be consistent with the view that new brands describe an S-shaped growth curve over time, finally reaching market saturation. ➤➤**diffusion of innovations**.

A further problem is that the PLC may become a self-fulfilling prophecy. If a manager believes a brand is about to decline, she may withdraw advertising and promotional support and fail to push it with trade customers, thereby helping to bring about its demise, whereas the correct strategy may have been to rebuild, relaunch and/or reposition the brand. A final difficulty is that most brands in most markets are in the mature stage, which means the recommended course of action is unclear, other than to continue competing.

product platform A robust design that forms the foundation for a series of closely related products. The automobile industry is the classic example of this idea where several individual models may share the same basic frame, suspension and transmission. The Sony Walkman gives another illustration, with its 160 variations and four major technical innovations between 1980 and 1990, all of which were based upon the initial platform. Black & Decker rationalized its hundreds of products into a set of product families, with consequent economies throughout the chain from procurement to distribution and aftersales service. In all these cases, the evolution of the product platform, along with the evolution of the requisite capabilities, is central to the product development strategy.

This notion may have originated in engineering but it can be applied widely. Food, cosmetics, clothing and furniture manufacturers can be seen to have product platforms and families. Johnson & Johnson and its development of the Acuvue disposable contact lenses provides another example. Many people needing vision correction did not wear traditional hard or soft contact lenses because of the discomfort and the cleaning requirements. Acuvue uses high-quality soft contact lenses sold at a sufficiently low price to allow disposal after a week, without cleaning. This distinctive advantage, which was clearly relevant to many consumers, led to the successful launch in 1987 that defined a new market segment. The original product became the basic platform for continuing innovation that is leading to other new offerings in Johnson & Johnson's vision care product family.

Sometimes entirely new platforms and entirely new capabilities are required. Step changes in the product or manufacturing technology, in the customer need or in what the competition offers, and how it offers it, can demand ➤**discontinuous new products** rather than incremental change. The risk is all the more great if that means the adoption of new technologies, outside the firm's traditional arena.

product proliferation The tendency for the number of brands, brand extensions and product lines to increase to such an extent that the product portfolio is suboptimal, i.e. greater profit would be obtained by having fewer products. This can arise from: (a) companies offering products in more and more narrowly defined submarkets; (b) overzealous and unchecked ➤**new product development** activity, and (c) a desire to match all the competitive offerings ('if they have an orange-flavoured biscuit, so must we'). Left unchecked, ➤**brand management** systems can result in product proliferation. The problem must be resolved through product rationalization, something that for many consumer products organizations was stimulated by the shift to ➤**category management**.

professional indemnity insurance ➤Insurance providing compensation against damages incurred on grounds of negligence, available to those in professional occupations, such as doctors, lawyers and accountants.

profit A measure of surplus by a company from some activity or project over some time period. While simple at first sight, profit has a number of definitions, and is far from simple in practice. Two important concepts of profit are: (a) *net profit* before tax (or pretax profit), which is the residual after deduction of all money costs, i.e. sales revenue minus wages, salaries, rent, fuel, raw materials, interest payment on loans, and ➤**depreciation**, and (b) *gross profit*, which is net profit before depreciation and interest. ➤➤**ebitda; economic rent; margin.**

profit and loss account (UK) (P&L) A financial statement showing revenue, expenditure and the ➤**profit** or loss resulting from operations in a given period.

profit centre ➤management accounting.

Profit Impact of Market Strategy (PIMS) A systematic and exhaustive research study to find out why some strategic business units (SBUs) within companies are more profitable than others. Information was collected from SBUs concerning their profitability, measured as return on investment (ROI). The research study looked for correlations between ROI (the dependent variable) and a wide range of independent variables.

PIMS was started in the General Electric Company in 1960, moved to Harvard in 1972 and in 1975 the Strategic Planning Institute was formed to give it a permanent home. The early focus was on US companies, but the database was subsequently expanded to include European companies and others. Initially, only cross-sectional data were collected, but the study was expanded gradually to include longitudinal information.

To an important extent, results were sensitive to the definitions and measures used by the PIMS researchers. SPI offered guidelines for the definition of SBUs, but these could not be regarded as hard-and-fast rules. ➤**strategic business unit.** Similarly, the way markets were defined would have an impact on results. ➤**market definition.** ROI was defined as pretax net income, including special non-recurring costs, minus corporate overhead costs, as a percentage of average investment (including fixed and working capital at book value, but excluding corporate investment not particular to this business). The factors influencing profitability were threefold: (a) competitive position (market share, relative quality, patent advantages); (b) product structure (investment/sales, investment/value added, use of capacity, productivity, vertical integration), and (c) market attractiveness (growth in served market, market concentration, fixed capital intensity, marketing expense/sales, purchase amount, customer characteristics). In total, 100 pieces of data were collected for each business unit.

PIMS researchers claimed, by means of a 37-factor regression model, to explain roughly 70–80 per cent of the variance in ROI in the sample of several thousand

SBUs. Typical results were that, on average, market share has an important, positive influence on profits, higher relative product quality (whether actual or perceived) increases rates of return, and investment intensity is a drag on profitability (because productivity does not improve enough to pay for the heavier levels of investment). These results gave managers a model or framework of how the various components of their activities interrelated. It provided opportunities for simulation ('What would be the effect on ROI of using 10 per cent more of our capacity?') and benchmarking ('How does our performance compare with our closest competitors?'). Thus, an output of PIMS studies was the 'par ROI report', showing the normal rate of return on investment for a business, given the profile of its strategic characteristics.

Despite these uses, the validity of PIMS analyses has been called into question. ROI is not necessarily a suitable global measure of success and it certainly is not the only measure. Some components of ROI (the dependent variable) also appear as independent variables, e.g. fixed capital intensity. Variables (e.g. product quality) are sometimes hard to measure. Partly because of being hard to measure, important variables are omitted, e.g. management goals, synergy and organizational learning. The temptation is to infer causal relationships between the independent variables, but the analysis rests merely on correlations. Any causal study would have to make allowance for changes in the environment and technology. Thus, the result quoted above – that investment intensity is a drag on profitability – might not hold in turbulent markets.

The spirit of PIMS lives on through ➤**market orientation** studies and ➤**marketing metrics**. Many of the same analytical concerns remain; there is still debate about which are the most appropriate measures of performance and how best to take account of dynamic factors.

profit-sharing Organization-wide programmes that distribute ➤**compensation** and ➤**reward** based on some established formula designed around a company's profitability.

programme evaluation and review technique (PERT) A widely known technique in project management for applying probability theory to time estimates. It had its origins in military planning and was used to plan very complex projects. Its success in military project planning made it popular in more general industry. The technique recognizes that activity durations and costs in project management are not fixed, and that probability theory can be applied to estimates. Usually time estimates are given three values: (a) an optimistic value; (b) a pessimistic value, and (c) a likely value. A probability distribution can be applied and statistics calculated for each activity in a project.

programme trading (UK) US = *program trading*. Computer-generated purchases or sales of ➤**securities**, particularly that occur when large premiums open up or disappear between the prices of securities and the prices of the same securities on the ➤**futures market**.

project finance The assembly of funds necessary for large-scale civil engineering and construction operations, including large housing projects. These are chiefly loan funds, with possibly some admixture of ➤**equity** finance, of a ➤**maturity** matched as far as possible to the duration of construction, together with such government grants and credits as may be available and backed, particularly in the case of foreign operations, by public or private ➤credit guarantees and political risk insurance.

Where projects on foreign soil are concerned, optimum use of foreign exchange is necessary. Significant finance is invariably obtained from international sources such as the International Development Association (➤International Bank for Reconstruction and Development), the Export–Import Bank, the development banks and the ➤Eurobond and ➤Eurodollar markets. Project finance is normally conducted by a consortium of banks, contractors and investment vehicles.

promissory note ➤note.

promotion 1. The generic title for marketing communication – one of the Ps of the ➤4 Ps. This usage is somewhat loose, including, as it does, all forms of impersonal communication, e.g. advertising, public relations and incentives. Conceivably, it might also include personal communication (e.g. personal selling and direct marketing), although this is also categorized under 'place'. The term has more pedagogic than practical value. **2.** The advancement of an employee, usually involving higher levels of ➤pay and ➤reward, a redefinition of ➤roles and responsibilities, as well as a change in title and status.

promotion A form of marketing communication in which incentives are used to stimulate sales or bring sales forward in time. Promotions are either consumer-based or trade-based.

Price promotions, discounts and sales typify consumer-based incentives. They are undertaken for several reasons: (a) to bring forward purchasing in markets where capacity is fixed and time-dependent (airlines, hotels, sporting fixtures and artistic performances); (b) to help achieve decycling in markets prone to peaks and troughs in demand (seasonal demand in the travel sector, the diurnal demand for public transport in cities); (c) to shift stock and reduce the inventory-holding costs associated with old (low margin) stock and release space for new (high margin) stock, and (d) to secure greater prominence for a brand (more shelf space in a store, or a position next to cash registers). Less worthy reasons include: (a) to help catch up on missed sales targets (by 'buying sales'); (b) to reduce the hard graft of promoting and selling products/services (by giving away low-price, or even free, samples); (c) matching the competition in an attempt to achieve parity pricing, and (d) giving the appearance of being active in the market place (in lieu of any other newsworthy things to say about a brand, price promotions can be featured in advertisements, mail-drops, in-store posters, etc.).

Evidence shows that consumers will respond to short-run price promotions ('people like a bargain') unless they do not know, trust or like the product (in which case no level of incentive may be successful). However, this response will not necessarily be profitable (the additional sales volume may bring in less revenue than the revenue lost due to the price cut). In the longer term, evidence for repeat-purchase markets suggests that there are no enduring effects in terms of gaining new customers. Other longer-term problems include: (a) low price is not the attribute marketers most want to emphasize (especially if it is seen as a 'promotional bribe' that fails to distinguish the brand from competitors); (b) consumer expectations are set by frequent bouts of price promotion, and trade expectations may be influenced in an adverse way, e.g. they see the product as a commodity, not as a well-supported quality brand. The alternative is to shift attention away from low price, offer a clear justification for the recommended price (rather than the promotional price), support the recommended price with brand-building activities, use more sophisticated forms of promotion, or use more positive forms of communication that stress the merits of the product itself.

More sophisticated forms of consumer promotion offer an economic reward, but not one based on price. These include sweepstakes, competitions, coupons/dockets and continuity promotions. Relationship building, rather than promotion, is claimed to be the main factor behind ➤**loyalty programmes** and ➤**affinity programmes**. However, the emphasis on direct and indirect rewards and incentives in these programmes means that many take on the appearance of sophisticated forms of promotion.

Many promotions are trade incentives, designed to capture the interest of sales people who will then be motivated to push the brand on behalf of the producer.

prompted recall In ➤**marketing research**, where a respondent is asked about something after being prompted by the researcher, e.g. 'Thinking of BA' (the prompt) 'do you recall seeing a commercial for them last night on television?' This contrasts with 'unprompted recall' ('Tell me what commercials you recall seeing last night on television').

prospect theory A theory of individual decision-making under risk that became popular in management from the 1970s onwards. Until that time, the study of decision-making under risk had been dominated by expected utility theory – a model that described how decisions ought to be made by rational people, i.e. a normative model of rational choice. This, however, came to be questioned by behavioural scientists who looked at decision-making through a psychological lens rather than a purely economic one. These scientists pointed out that people do not always follow the rules of rational choice.

Three effects were described to illustrate the line of argument.

(1) The certainty effect. In which people over-weight outcomes that are certain, relative to outcomes that are merely probable; thus, there is a risk-averse preference for a sure gain over a larger gain that is merely probable.

(2) The reflection effect. This describes what happens when the signs of the outcomes are reversed so that gains are replaced by losses. Again, there is an over-weighting of certainty. This leads to a risk-seeking preference for a loss that is merely probable over a smaller loss that is certain. This can be seen in the way people buy insurance packages or the way people respond to product pricing and promotions.

(3) The isolation effect. This occurs when people simplify problems by disregarding the components that are common to alternatives and focus only on the differences. This implies that inconsistent preferences are obtained when choices are presented in different, decomposed, forms. This can be seen in consumer decision-making, e.g. functionally similar products might have the same price, but if one brand presents the price in a distinctive way it may be seen very differently. It is also evident in job selection interviews, e.g. where discussion focuses on something quite minor, but which seemingly distinguishes one applicant from another.

Prospect theory takes account of these effects. Decisions are seen as comprising two phases: (a) an editing phase (a preliminary analysis of the prospects involved, often resulting in simplified representations of the prospects), and (b) an evaluation phase (where the edited prospects are evaluated and the one with the highest value is chosen). The value function is generally concave for gains and convex for losses, and steeper for losses than gains, i.e. the effect of a loss is greater than the effect of a gain of similar magnitude. Path-breaking work was published by Daniel Kahneman and Amos Tversky ('Prospect Theory: an analysis of decision under risk', *Econometrica*, 1979). There followed many laboratory experiments to test specific propositions about decisions that could be seen as showing signs of 'systematic irrationality'. The method has been criticized for being highly artificial, but applications in market research, consumer behaviour, pricing and promotions research, and insurance analysis are numerous. ➤behavioural decision theory; choice modelling; decision rules.

prospectus A document containing company information in connection with a ➤new issue. With only a few exceptions, it is unlawful for a company to invite anyone to apply for shares unless the application form is accompanied by a prospectus containing certain information set out in the Companies Act 1985 (➤incorporation) or, in the case of a ➤London Stock Exchange company, in compliance with the regulations.

Protestant work ethic ➤values.

protocol analysis ➤qualitative market research.

prototype The representation of product designs in a physical form. Prior to launching full production, firms will usually develop a series of prototypes to test. Product prototypes may include card or clay models and computer simulations, for example. Many automobile manufacturers will create computer simulations on-screen to develop the first generation of prototypes. Following lengthy evaluation, a few will be transformed into clay models, which will then be shown to customers for feedback. Those that generate positive response may be developed into a lifesize wooden replica; this represents the third phase of the prototyping process.

provision A sum set aside in the accounts (and charged against profits) to provide for anticipated loss or expenditure, e.g. a bad debt. Provisions may not be made where the loss or expenditure is highly uncertain, as in a possible lawsuit, but noted as a *contingent liability*. Where losses do not materialize, the provisions may be *written back*. Where, for example, a bad debt has proved impossible to recover it will be *written off*, i.e. removed from asset book values.

proxy The use, by a shareholder unable to be present at a shareholders' meeting, of an authorized person (possibly the chairperson or other director) to vote on his behalf, either as thought fit or according to specific instructions.

prudential ratio ➤capital adequacy.

PSQ ➤perceived service quality.

psychographic segmentation The grouping of people according to psychological factors – specifically, their activities, interests and opinions. Information about activities (work, hobbies, sports, holidays, etc.), interests (family, home, food, media, etc.) and opinions (about self, politics, business, education, etc.) is obtained using an Activities, Interests and Opinions questionnaire (an AIC questionnaire) where hundreds of questions are asked to build a profile of the respondent. Respondents with similar profiles are grouped together as a basis for ➤**segmentation**. Segments are offered different products, or subjected to different marketing communications. Psychographic segmentation has given way to ➤**lifestyle segmentation**, although the two are very closely related and are sometimes seen as interchangeable. Lifestyle segmentation is probably a more accurate term given the focus on activities, interests and opinions, rather than psychological determinants *per se*, e.g. motives, personality, emotions, etc.

psychological testing Tests of a person's intelligence, ability and aptitude, personality and interests. Ability and aptitude are seen as components of intellectual performance – they indicate what a person is capable of now and potentially capable of in the future. However, a person may be capable of something, but not do it routinely, e.g. a bright manager who is lazy might not be as useful as a manager of moderate ability who perseveres and has well-honed people-management skills. Personality is a guide to how a person of given intelligence will perform routinely. These tests are used in the selection and recruitment of employees as a component of promotion assessments, and in team-building. ➤**assessment**. Tests rely on an understanding of psychological theory, e.g. theories of ➤**personality traits**. They are formal in character, in that certain rules of psychological measurement are observed (termed 'psychometrics'). These rules are designed to ensure the testing is reliable (i.e. the results of the test are consistent over time), valid (i.e. the test measures what it claims to measure), objective (i.e. scoring is based on an agreed system, rather than reliant on *ad hoc* judgements), standardized, i.e. the test conditions are similar for all people taking the test. Results of a test are compared against a norm or benchmark; thus, the manager being tested is compared to an appropriate norm such as other managers in the industry. Although used widely, psychological testing has its critics – they point out that some tests are more rigorously composed than others, that some may suffer from bias (e.g. favouring particular racial or ethnic groups, ➤**equity**), that the underlying psychological theories are not universally accepted (so the tests may not be well grounded), and/or that tests are open to abuse in the way they are administered.

psychometrics ➤psychological testing.

public affairs An aspect of ➤**public relations** that involves working with governments and groups that help determine public policy and legislation. The purpose is to ensure the legitimate interests of an organization are not overlooked when public policy is being reformulated.

public good An item that cannot meaningfully be consumed by individuals, but which is instead necessarily consumed by society or groups within society. Defence is the archetypal public good. In general, though, public goods have two defining characteristics: (a) they yield non-rivalrous consumption – one person's use of them does not deprive others from using them (if you are defended against foreign invasion, so am I); (b) they are non-excludable – if one person consumes them it is impossible to restrict others from doing so, e.g. public television has traditionally been non-excludable, but the technology of scrambling television pictures has changed that. Between them, these characteristics ensure no proper market can exist for a product, and provision must probably be made by government, financed by taxation.

Many items are partly public and partly private goods. A developed patent system, for example, has public-good properties, benefiting not only the community as a whole, but especially inventors who take out patents.

public limited company (plc) ➤incorporation.

public offering ➤offer for sale.

public placing ➤placing.

public private partnership (PPP)   One of a range of co-operative ventures between government and the private sector in the UK, including the ➤**private finance initiative,** joint ventures and concessions, outsourcing, and the sale of equity stakes in State-owned businesses. The goal of PPPs has been to extend the perceived quality of private management to the delivery of public services. The UK government's sale of a large stake of its National Air Traffic Control System to a consortium of private airlines is a classic example.

public relations (PR)   Activities and communications undertaken to monitor, evaluate, influence and adjust to the attitudes, opinions and behaviours of various publics of an organization. 'Publics' include, but are not confined to, customers, consumers, investors, the media and government. Individuals in each of these groups are linked together by common interests, e.g. product developments, investment prospects and social policy issues. Often a contrast is drawn between paid-for advertising in media and unpaid-for publicity through PR, the former being easier for an organization to control. However, in practice, the distinctions are not precise and hybrid approaches are common. Public relations is *not* synonymous with media relations; nevertheless, an important goal is to manage the media to obtain publicity for an organization or to respond to media interest in an organization. This is facilitated by issuing 'media releases', or brief one-page reports, in which all key points on an issue are itemized conveniently.

purchase cycle The time from one purchase to the next, where goods and services are repeatedly bought by an individual or organization.

purchase repertoire ➤buyer behaviour.

purchasing ➤organizational buying behaviour.

purchasing power parity A level of ➤exchange rate between two currencies such that the buying power of each is the same in their domestic markets. For example, if £1 buys the same amount in the UK that $1.50 buys in the US, then purchasing power parity holds at the exchange rate of $1.50 to the pound. In principle, exchange rates should tend to converge towards purchasing power parity, because if they do not it would pay to convert one currency into another and buy goods in the foreign market. The switch in demand would raise prices in the cheaper market, and the purchase of the foreign exchange would alter the exchange rate towards parity. In practice, rates can deviate from purchasing power almost indefinitely.

put option ➤option.

pyramid investment scheme An investment in which generous returns are paid to one set of investors, financed by the deposits of a later set of investors. Such schemes are dangerous for those involved, because unless an endless flow of new depositors is forthcoming, there will be one generation of investors whose money, having been disbursed to earlier generations, cannot be repaid. As there is not, in most cases, an infinite queue of later investors, disappointment is inevitable at some stage. Pyramid schemes are outlawed in the UK and other economies, but the principle behind them is more ubiquitous than one might first imagine. The notion of a ➤speculative bubble has pyramid-like features, and the construction of unfunded pension schemes (➤pensions) has that air about it: the first generation of recipients pay nothing in, but get a pension out, financed by the next generation. As long as there always is a next generation, these pension schemes work. But if there was to be a collapse in population, there would be one generation who become pensioners, only to find no young working generation large enough to finance their pension.

pyramid selling A form of sales technique involving the creation of an hierarchy of agents. Agents at each level of the hierarchy pay commission to agents at the level immediately above. Greatest rewards are reaped by the individual at the pinnacle of the hierarchy. Pyramid selling has had a chequered history because sales growth depends on gaining more and more agents further down the hierarchy, something that logically cannot continue indefinitely.

Q

q-theory A theory of investment behaviour which suggests that firms tend to invest as long as the value of their shares exceeds the replacement cost of the physical assets of the firm. Developed by economist James Tobin, q-theory is attractive because it encompasses other theories of investment in a simple framework. The q referred to is the ratio of two numbers. The first is the value of a firm to its shareholders, which in well-functioning markets approximates to the value of the expected future profits of the firm. The second number is the replacement cost of the assets of the firm, machines, buildings, etc. If the first exceeds the second (i.e. $q > 1$) the firm would want to expand, as the profits it expects to make from its assets are greater than the cost of its assets. If $q < 1$, the shares of the firm are worth less than the assets and it will pay the firm to engage in divestment to sell the assets rather than try to use them. What should happen is that firms invest or divest, or the share price itself moves, until $q \approx 1$. q can be used as a gauge of stock market valuations, i.e. when $q > 1$, shares can be interpreted as looking quite expensive.

qualitative market research A way to collect, analyse and interpret data that involves observing what people do and listening to what they say. Characteristically, the process is unstructured. This can generate a large amount of detailed information in a short space of time, but this information must then be interpreted, summarized and synthesized by the researcher – a subjective and time-consuming task. The type of information will relate to people's behaviour (➤**consumer behaviour**), ➤**attitudes**, ➤**beliefs**, and/or ➤**values**, usually in answer to 'why?' questions (in contrast to ➤**quantitative market research** that usually answers 'how much?' questions).

Traditionally, qualitative research is used at two stages of the market research process.

(1) In an exploratory phase – to get a 'feel' for the issue of interest, to establish the vocabulary people use when talking about the issue, to discover some of the key factors associated with it and generate some initial hypotheses. For example, in a study of retail shrinkage it may be unclear how employees regard the issue (do they see it as theft from their employer?), and they may use a variety of euphemisms (referring, perhaps, to 'benefits' and 'perks of the job', rather than using language that highlights the illegality of shrinkage). This exploratory phase helps researchers begin to understand an issue. It also provides a basis for more structured and formal quantitative research (in a follow-up survey on retail shrinkage questions might refer to 'perks of the job', not pejorative words such as 'theft'). This phase is commonplace in advertising development, new product

development, and where new practices are being introduced (when, for instance, a new IT system is being introduced that could have an impact on the way secretarial staff work together).

(2) In a diagnostic phase after qualitative research. It helps to flesh-out numerical information obtained from quantitative surveys by seeking to uncover reasons, motives and feelings that may lie quite deep in people's minds. Thus, a survey might reveal that 20 per cent of casual employees help themselves to the goods of their employer, whereas only 5 per cent of full-time employees do so; with qualitative research it may be possible to find out why there is this difference, e.g. is it a reflection of poor pay and conditions, or greater opportunity, or lower levels of commitment to the job?

Various techniques are used:

(1) Observation techniques, where the researcher observes and records behaviour but does not intervene or question those being observed.

(2) Focus groups typically comprise six to eight people who are invited to discuss a topic of interest to the researcher – the discussion can be quite free-ranging, with the group developing a line of argument of its own and with little intervention or prompting from the interviewer-cum-moderator.

(3) Extended groups are focus groups that meet on several occasions.

(4) Process groups are another variant of focus groups, but in this case participants are invited to solve problems, create something, propose solutions and brainstorm.

(5) Depth interviews are lengthy, discursive, one-to-one interviews and are suited to researching sensitive topics, such as an analysis of drug taking, sexual behaviour, fraud, diseases and human conditions that people are ordinarily reluctant to discuss, e.g. AIDS, cancer, mastectomy.

With groups and depth interviews a number of elicitation procedures are used to tap into people's thoughts and ideas. Conversation is the most common procedure. Where the conversation is between an interviewer and respondent, it tends to be non-intrusive and open-ended, e.g. 'Tell me about web-based grocery shopping services', 'Can you elaborate on what you have just said?' Other approaches include: projection ('what would a retiree say about this service?'), stereotypical drawing ('sketch a typical user'), personification ('if the service was a person, what sort of person would it be?'), role-play, games and simulations ('act out how you might use the service').

Despite their popularity, groups are heavily criticized. Concerns are raised about the representativeness of people willing to participate in groups, e.g. are they more extrovert, gregarious and vociferous than average? The problem of ➤**group-think** can become acute, especially where there is a dominant member of the group. The technique depends on the ability of group members to express themselves verbally, graphically and symbolically (note that the aim is to uncover people's thoughts and ideas, not test their ability to communicate). Consciousness of the interviewing context can become a problem, too, if group members become aware of videos, tape-recorders, microphones, the moderator and each other (the artificiality and strangeness of the context may bias people's comments). The technique also depends on the skill and ability of the interviewer/moderator to draw meaningful interpretations, often where information is contradictory, ambiguous or incomplete, e.g. how is silence to be interpreted – that people don't know, don't care or don't want to hurt the feelings of others in the group? There is a high cost per group discussion, which often severely limits the number commissioned. Depth interviews avoid the problem of group-think, but they by no means avoid all the other problems. Skilled researchers will be sensitive to these issues and have ways to minimize their impact.

quality circle A team established to improve the quality of manufactured products. The concept is based on the premise that those working closest to the process are likely to have greatest insight into improving the way it's produced. This will be further enhanced if people work together as a team rather than as individuals. The nature and composition of the team will depend on the particular circumstances. In Japan, quality circles seem to work well, but their success in Europe and the US has been mixed. Other similar improvement groups have been used, often involving management, which seem to have had more success.

quality function deployment (QED) A technique developed in Japan for ensuring the needs of the customer are considered in ➤**product development**. This technique is used extensively by Toyota and its suppliers to check that what is being proposed for the design of the product or service will meet the needs of its customers.

quality management Ensuring quality issues become an integral part of the firm's operations rather than something that is checked at the end of the process. Today, issues of quality are viewed in terms of the context of business performance. It is argued that superior perceived quality is achieved by developing a set of product specifications and service standards that more closely meet customer needs than competitors. In addition, superior conformance quality is achieved by being more effective than competitors at conforming to appropriate product specifications and service standards (why invest in quality if the customer won't pay for it?). The management of quality should be an ongoing process and is often embraced by firms with the implementation of ➤**total quality management** programmes.

quality of work life (QWL) A movement focusing on employee perceptions of job satisfaction and job challenges, health and safety at work, job fulfilment and working conditions and the balance between work and non-work. The movement has promoted such things as flexitime, autonomy, employee participation in decision-making, etc. QWL is used as a measure of organizational effectiveness, looked at from the perspective of employees (in contrast to financial performance as a measure of organizational effectiveness from a manager's or shareholder's perspective). Underlying this use of QWL is the belief that it enhances employee performance and productivity; however, empirical proof of this relationship is not conclusive.

quango An acronym for quasi-autonomous non-governmental organization. There was a substantial increase in the use of such semi-permanent public commissions or agencies during the 1990s. These organizations are usually established by government departments and are funded from the public purse and may have substantial powers, but their members are unelected officials.

quantitative market research A way to obtain quantitative information about customers, businesses and markets using a variety of formal tools and techniques. Typically, quantitative market research is used to answer questions about 'how much' and 'how many'. This is most easily appreciated by thinking about studies of

➤**consumer behaviour**, where a count is made of purchases or usage occasions, e.g. the relative frequency of internet users in Tokyo compared to Beijing and Seoul. However, counts of ➤**attitudes**, perceptions and ➤**beliefs** are common, too, e.g. the relative frequency of people in Tokyo, Beijing and Seoul who believe the Internet will reduce the costs of procuring goods and services. In quantitative studies, questions are carefully and precisely defined by the researcher. Thus, it is the researcher who may decide to ask a question about the belief that the internet will reduce the costs of procuring goods and services. This contrasts with ➤**qualitative market research**, where the approach is more open-ended and (arguably) more respondent-oriented, e.g. the interview might have started with a general remark ('from personal experience, tell me about the impact of the internet') and from this might have flowed a conversation in which the costs of procuring goods and services were mentioned.

Quantitative information is used by managers to help them understand their customers, business and markets, to make forecasts and predictions, to provide data for business planning, and to assist in decision-making. ➤➤**decision-support systems; forecasting; management support systems; marketing planning**. The information is used for model-building by researchers, analysts and consultants. ➤**choice modelling, response models**.

The most common forms of data collection are:

(1) Surveys, where respondents are presented with a list of structured questions. Surveys are administered in different ways: through face-to-face interviews, mail-drops, telephone calls, and on line. Each method has its strengths and drawbacks, and sometimes it is necessary to use a combination of methods. Many surveys are customized to enable a client to investigate a particular set of issues. An alternative is to use a syndicated survey, where a group of clients share the cost of administering one combined questionnaire and where each client is allocated a portion of the questionnaire for its own purposes.

(2) ➤**Consumer panels** also present respondents with a list of structured questions, but in this case the same respondents are surveyed repeatedly. Traditionally, respondents would complete diaries, mail these back to the researcher, and from this a record of responses would be built up over time. Nowadays, automated ways are used to collect much of this data. ➤**scanner panel**. Tracking studies are another means of looking at trends and patterns over time; however, the data for these studies usually come from repeated surveys, not panels, i.e. the questions are kept the same, and the respondents are matched in terms of their demographics and so forth, but they are not the same respondents.

(3) ➤**Experiments** enable hypotheses about the effect of one thing on another to be tested under controlled conditions. The degree of control varies. At one extreme are laboratory experiments – the conditions might be quite artificial, but the researcher can focus on the effect of interest and control-out other things that might influence the results. Field experiments are at the opposite end of the scale – the researcher will attempt to focus on the effect of interest but there are likely to be many other things confounding the results. Most experiments are administered face-to-face, partly as a check on cheating and to be sure that the conditions are controlled.

In using these methods experienced market researchers give particular attention to:

(a) sampling (the selection of target respondents from a population of interest);

(b) response rates (the proportion of those asked to participate in the research who agree to do so); (c) questionnaire design (the wording of questions, the order in which questions are asked, the use of scales, etc.) (➤**Likert scale**); (d) pre-testing and piloting (to check different aspects of the research before starting the main study); (e) data cleaning and coding, and (f) analysis (the way the data will be looked at, which might involve descriptive statistics, univariate analysis and multivariate analysis). An underlying concern is the extent to which a study is free from systematic and random error. ➤**validity**. Many of the procedures used by market researchers are designed to minimize error; however, it is not possible to remove all sources of error.

quantity discounts ➤pricing policy.

quantity theory of money The theory that changes in the money supply have a direct influence on prices, and nothing else. The theory is derived from the identity $MV = PT$, where M is the stock of money, V the velocity with which the money circulates, P the average price level and T the number of transactions. All this equation says is that the amount of money spent equals the amount of money used, and is not so much a theory as a truism. The theory itself has two key elements: (a) that the velocity of money circulation is stable, at least in the short term, and (b) that the number of transactions (which is closely related to the level of physical output) is fixed by the tastes of individuals and the real behaviour of firms in equilibrium. In this case, increases in M can only lead to increases in P, i.e. money supply increases cause ➤**inflation**. The theory provided the basis for ➤**macroeconomics** prior to J M Keynes's General Theory, and had a plausibility about it in the eyes of early economists, who strongly believed in the power of markets to settle at equilibrium points. Keynesian economics attacked both pieces of the theory. Increases in money supply M were potentially held to lead to falls in the speed with which money circulated, V. And, in some circumstances, increases in M could lead to increases in real activity T, not just increases in prices.

quasi-equity ➤mezzanine.

quasi-rent A profit earned by an asset, over and above the amount just necessary to make it worth keeping the asset in its use but insufficient to merit replacing it. A quasi-rent is a form of transient ➤**economic rent**. Imagine a steel company has a blast furnace that cost £10 million to build or replace. Imagine, also, that the cost of supporting the capital tied up in the blast furnace is £1 million a year. Imagine, too, that by running the blast furnace and making steel, the company makes a profit, ignoring the cost of the blast furnace itself, of £500,000 a year. The firm will make a loss, because its profits do not cover the cost of the capital it employs, but – because the blast furnace has already been built, and the costs of creating it have been incurred regardless of whether it is used or not, and because it cannot be transferred usefully to any other activity than making steel – it still pays the firm to keep using it, even though it would not pay to build it if it didn't exist already. The profit, net of the cost of the blast furnace, is a quasi-rent. The cost of the blast furnace can be described as a ➤**sunk cost**, and when the firm calculates whether to produce steel that cost should be ignored.

queuing theory Analytical models using mathematical formulae that can predict the steady-state behaviour of different types of queuing system. The ➤capacity planning and control problem faced by all service operations is to forecast their expected average level of demand. This enables the provider to supply adequate capacity, usually in the form of additional personnel. For example, food retailers have to try to ensure they have sufficient numbers of cashiers to deal with customers and avoid long queues; similarly, it does not want cashiers sitting idle. Too little capacity (i.e. insufficient servers) and queues build up; too much capacity (i.e. sufficient servers) and there are no queues but servers sit idle. The analytical queuing theory models help to predict the levels of queues and waiting time. ➤➤operational research.

quick ratio ➤acid ratio.

quit rate ➤employee retention.

quotation A price for ➤securities at which a ➤market maker will trade. ➤➤bid price; offer price.

quoted company A company (➤incorporation) whose quoted shares are listed on an official stock exchange. Compare ➤unlisted company.

quote-driven A stock market system (usually in relation to an electronic system) in which prices are initially determined by quotations of dealers or ➤market makers, as used on the ➤National Association of Securities Dealers Automated Quotation system and until, in part, recently the ➤London Stock Exchange. Ultimately, prices are determined by supply and demand as in any other market, but it is useful to distinguish between that system and those in use on, for example, the ➤New York Stock Exchange, which are ➤order driven.

QWL ➤quality of work life.

R

random walk The path followed by a variable in which each successive step is determined by a chance event. For example, imagine that you have an investment I of £1,000, and that at the end of each month you get a return added to that sum, which is the outcome of a random event: in your total investment in time t, I is governed by:

$$I_t = I_{(t-1)} + v_t$$

where v_t is a random variable, such that the values in any period t are independent of the values in any other. Your investment then follows a random walk. You might imagine that v is determined by the toss of a coin. A random walk can have some drift – it might be that v has a general tendency to be positive, but nevertheless bounces around.

The importance of the random walk is in the finding that in efficient markets for company stocks, share prices follow a random walk. Why? Because if they did not, we could predict that the share price will rise or fall, and if we could do that, we could make a profit by buying or selling the shares to take the gain or avoid the loss. The very process of buying or selling shares to capture that gain or loss would ensure the price of the share rose or fell until the expected gain is eroded. ➤**efficient market hypothesis**.

rate of interest The proportion of a sum of money that is paid over a specified period in payment for its loan. It may be a fixed rate of interest or a ➤**floating rate**

rate of return ➤return on investment.

rate-of-return regulation A form of ➤regulation, common for public utilities in the US, under which firms are prevented from earning too high a rate of return. Under such a regime, price rises are capped to levels at which the target rate of return will not be exceeded. This price will invariably be lower than the price which a profit-maximizing monopolist would charge. ➤**Averch–Johnson effect; price regulation**.

rating ➤Standard and Poor's 500 Ratings.

rating agency A firm or organization set up to rate issuers of ➤**commercial paper**, or ➤**securities**. In the UK, US and other countries, there are many rating agencies. In France the *Agence d'Evaluation Financière* was set up as a joint venture between the government agencies and institutional investors. In Australia, rating is done by Australian Ratings. ➤**credit rating**.

rating scale A scale used by respondents to indicate their evaluation of an object, e.g. a brand, service or organization. Rating scales are used widely in ➤**attitude** research, especially in the context of ➤**marketing research**, the study of ➤**consumer behaviour** and in ➤**human resource management**. They are particularly widely used for measuring the cognitive and affective components of attitude, e.g. 'What is your evaluation of the design of a brand: very favourable, somewhat favourable, indifferent, somewhat unfavourable, very unfavourable?' The prompts can be graphic (e.g. a smiling face to indicate very favourable) or verbal (e.g. the words 'very favourable'), and numbers can be assigned to these ordered categories for purposes of data analysis, e.g. a 'very favourable' response is labelled '1'.

In principle, rating scales can be ordinal (where an ordered relationship is presented to respondents: $0 < 1 < 2 \ldots < 7$), interval (where distances among the numbers on the scale correspond to distances between the objects on the characteristics being measured and intervals between the numbers are equal: $2 - 1 = 7 - 6$) or ratio (these are like an interval scale, but there is an absolute 0 point and ratios are equal: 10 divided by 5 = 6 divided by 3). In practice, rating scales often provide only ordinal data. Respondents to a rating scale indicate their evaluation by marking the appropriate position among ordered categories (for ordinal scales) or on a continuum (for interval and ratio scales). Although very common, users need to be aware of the problems associated with ratings scales, e.g. responses can be influenced by the number of points on a scale (whether it is a 5-, 7- or 9-point scale), whether there is a midpoint or not (7-point scale versus a 6-point scale), the choice of prompt (graphic images or words) and so forth. Choice of technique can have an impact, too. In one technique respondents are asked to indicate their evaluation in response to a scale with bipolar adjective (➤**semantic differential scale**); in another, they are asked to indicate their strength of agreement or disagreement with a series of statements. ➤**Likert scale**. Both are verbal scales but they will not give exactly the same result. A further danger is the temptation to treat ordinal data as interval or ratio data (semantic differential scales and Likert scales generate ordinal data, but it is not uncommon to find analysts treating the data as if they are interval). Researchers remain very divided about this matter, partly because it has major implications for the type of statistical analysis that can be undertaken with ratings data.

rational expectation The assumption made in certain economic ➤**models** that economic agents base their behaviour on forecasts of future events which are not systematically falsified by actual economic events. Of course, nobody can predict the future with perfect foresight because unforeseen, random happenings are bound to occur. Rational expectations do not equate to perfect foresight. However, someone with rational expectations will construct their expectations so that *on average* they are correct, i.e. they will be wrong only because of those random, non-systematic errors. For example, imagine trade unions bargaining for higher wages. Under the assumption of rational expectations, unions will build into their demands sensible forecasts of inflation. Imagine what an assumption of less than rational expectations might look like: perhaps the unions demand wage increases based on this year's inflation rate, even though at a time of increasing inflation, the wage demands would perpetually lag behind the actual inflation rate. On the old assumptions made prior to the common use of rational expectations in models, unions would carry on forecasting inflation this way, despite its manifestly poor performance.

The theory of rational expectations has stimulated debate in economics because it has controversial implications.

(1) It undermines a case for government policy aimed at stimulating demand in the economy: if the government attempts to increase overall spending in the economy, by itself spending more, or increasing the money supply, the public may simply believe that prices will rise as a consequence. Then, wage demands and prices will automatically reflect the anticipated inflation and the extra spending will feed straight into higher prices, not higher real output.

(2) Markets behave efficiently. ➤efficient market hypothesis. The price of the shares of a company reflects the profits the company is expected to make. If expectations are rational, the price at any time is based on expectations which have taken into consideration all possible information about the company. This has two consequences:

(a) if some 'news' arrives that indicates the company's fortunes are likely to change, that information will cause the price to change immediately;

(b) however, as the 'news' that arrives can reflect only random, not systematic, events, the price of the company's shares must follow a random path. ➤random walk.

The interesting implications of rational expectations should not necessarily make them appear a plausible description of people's behaviour. Nevertheless, like ➤perfect competition in ➤microeconomics, rational expectations provide a model of an extreme form of human behaviour that provides a useful benchmark against which the behaviour of people in the real world can be judged. Moreover, in the very long term, the hypothesis that systematic forecasting errors are not made appears by no means implausible.

reach ➤media planning.

reasoned action theory ➤attitude.

reasoned learning A form of cognitive ➤learning.

rebate ➤pricing policy.

receivables Amounts due to a business, i.e. owed by ➤debtors.

receivership ➤bankruptcy.

recession Technically, two consecutive quarters of a year in which an economy shrinks, i.e. exhibits negative ➤economic growth. A recession is more often a looser concept, describing a serious economic downturn. A more serious and sustained period of economic stagnation is termed a *depression*. Recessions are usually caused by a drop in the overall amount of spending in an economy – a fall in demand for the outputs of firms. They most typically follow a period of sustained growth, at which point ➤inflation begins to occur, and the authorities then choose to apply higher interest rates (➤monetary policy) to reduce spending and make it harder for companies to raise prices. But not all recessions occur as a counter-inflationary tool. They might follow an investment boom, in which case companies might find they have built-in too much productive capacity; they consequently reduce their investment spending, thus taking overall spending down as a result. Or recessions might follow the collapse of a ➤speculative bubble, in which over-optimism caused people to feel richer than they really were, with consequent popping of the bubble, causing reality to bite, and forcing retrenchment and reduction in spending. In most cases, if there is no worry about inflation, the authorities can act to raise spending, although in most serious cases (e.g. Japan in the 1990s) policy can be ineffective against the natural forces of retrenchment.

recourse The right to claim indemnification from the seller of a financial instrument if the originator of that instrument does not honour the commitment given on it. A ➤**bill of exchange** stamped *non-recourse* or *without recourse* is not endorsed for payment. ➤**factoring**.

recovery stocks Shares in companies which have suffered a re-rating downwards and which are now recommended in the hope or expectation that they will recover.

recursive model A system of equations in which ➤**endogenous variables** in one equation appear as ➤**exogenous variables** in others, but in which there are no subsets of equations which each cross-refer to endogenous variables. For example, imagine a ➤**model** consisting of the following two equations:

$$a = f_1(z)$$
$$b = f_2(a)$$

This is recursive, while the following system is not:

$$a = f_1(b)$$
$$b = f_2(a)$$

The significance of a recursive model is the ease with which it can be solved in terms of exogenous variables: values for all the endogenous variables can be found straightforwardly if the equations are solved in the right order.

redeemable security ➤Stocks or ➤**bonds** that are repayable at their ➤**par value** at a certain date, dates or specified eventuality. Most fixed-interest ➤**securities** are redeemable, though ➤**consols** bear no redemption date.

redemption The repayment of a loan or the ➤**par value** of a ➤**security** at ➤**maturity** on the repurchase of a security such as a ➤**unit trust** certificate.

redemption date The date at which a loan is repaid.

redemption yield ➤yield.

red herring (US) A preliminary ➤**prospectus** issued to test the market for a ➤**new issue**; it does not include a firm price. (UK = *pathfinder prospectus*)

rediscount The act of a ➤**central bank** in ➤**discounting** paper submitted to it by ➤**money market** operators. So-called because the paper has already been discounted in the market, and the central bank is acting in its capacity of ➤**lender of last resort**; often referred to simply as *discounting*.

reducing-balance methods of depreciation ➤depreciation.

redundancy The situation in which an employee is dismissed without having violated any contract of employment and without being offered any alternative employment by the same employer. In developed nations, statutory systems are in place to ensure that those made redundant are given redundancy payments based on length of continuous service, age, experience and so forth.

re-engineering The process of taking apart the organization in order to design a better (more efficient and more effective) one. Also termed 'business process re-engineering'. The process starts by identifying the organization's strengths, relative to its competitors. This defines its distinctive competencies. For example, these strengths might be technologically superior products or a more highly trained workforce. The second step is to assess those business processes that contribute to the development of these distinctive competencies. This step is known as 'process value analysis'. Thus, a new product development process might explain success in launching technologically superior products. However, other processes may add little or nothing, and are best cut or changed. The final step is to reorganize business processes around cross-functional and self-managed teams, to best support the organization's distinctive competencies. An example would be to have a cross-functional new product development team, involving marketing, production and ➤**research and development**, and led by a project controller; this reorganization should enable the organization to maintain its success in launching technologically superior products.

In many respects, re-engineering is simply an amalgam of existing management practices. The first and second steps are integral to any strategic ➤**marketing planning,** and a third goes to the core of ➤**change-management programmes** (based on an understanding of ➤**organizational behaviour**). It has also been likened to the ➤**total quality management** (TQM) movement of the 1980s. However, TQM tended to focus on very specific and incremental technical changes to achieve quality goals and targets. By contrast, with ➤**re-engineering**, the degree of reorganization is presumed to be far more radical. Also, ➤**enterprise resource planning** systems can be viewed as adopting a similar approach to re-engineering.

Re-engineering became a vogue topic after Michael ➤**Hammer** and J Champy published their manifesto (*Re-Engineering the Corporation: a manifesto for business revolution*, 1993). In part, its popularity reflected other trends, e.g. dissatisfaction with functional departments, bureaucracies, hierarchical structures and traditional ways of organizing business. These have been replaced by cross-functional teams, fewer managers, flatter organizations, the outsourcing of activities, and a willingness to use new technologies and new communications methods. In its wake, however, many employees have lost their jobs through ➤**downsizing**, and those that remain have had to contend with increased workloads and tremendous change, causing much anxiety and ➤**stress**.

reference pricing ➤pricing policy.

referent power ➤power.

registered design A design as protected by registration and referring to the outward appearance of an article. Only the appearance given by its actual shape, configuration, pattern or ornament can be protected, not any underlying idea. The registered design lasts for a maximum of 25 years. Initially, the proprietor is granted the exclusive right to a design for a fixed term of 5 years. This can be renewed for up to five further 5-year terms.

A new product may be created which is not sufficiently novel or contain an inventive step so as to satisfy the exacting requirements for the granting of a ➤**patent**. This was the situation faced by the UK's textile manufacturers in the early nineteenth century. Manufacturers would create new textile designs, but these would be copied later by foreign competitors. The designs registry was set up in the early 1800s in response to growing demands from the UK's textile manufacturers for statutory protection for the designs of their products. Today, designs that are applied to articles may be protected by design law. There are two systems of design law in the UK: (a) one similar to that used for patent law and requiring registration, and (b) design right provided along copyright lines. There is a large area of overlap between the two systems.

The registered designs system is intended for those designs intended to have some form of aesthetic appeal. For example, electrical appliances, toys and some forms of packaging have all been registered.

To be registered a design must first be new at the date an application for its registration is filed. In general, a design is considered to be new if it has not been published in the UK (i.e. made available or disclosed to the public in any way whatsoever) and if, when compared with any other published design, the differences make a materially different appeal to the eye. For example, if a company designed a new kettle that was very different to any other kettle that had been made before, the company could register the design. This would prevent other kettle manufacturers from simply copying it. Clearly, the kettle does not offer any advantage in terms of use; hence, a patent cannot be obtained, but a good design is also worth protecting.

registered security ➤bearer security.

registrar A person or company appointed by a company to keep a record of the ownership of its shares and to communicate with shareholders (US = *transfer agent*, where the registrar is not the company). The *share register* is a list of shareholders' names and addresses and the quantity of stock each one holds.

regression analysis A mathematical technique for estimating the ➤**parameters** of an equation from sets of data of the independent and dependent ➤**variables**. It is used widely in ➤**econometrics**. For example, in the demand equation, $q = aY + bP + c$, in which q = quantity bought of a good, Y = income and P = price, the parameters a, b and c can be estimated provided there is a sufficient number of corresponding observations of the variables, q, Y and P. Regression analysis finds the values of a, b and c, such that when substituted in the expression $aY + bP + c$, it yields the 'best' prediction of q, compared to the actual observations of q. ➤**beta coefficient; least squares regression.** ➤➤**response models.**

regulation The application of enforced standards of behaviour in a market. Most commonly it is associated with general regulation (e.g. minimum wage or health and safety regulation) or the price regulation of public utilities and natural monopolies. ➤**natural monopoly.**

One can distinguish between external regulation by a government agency, e.g. the Financial Services Authority, or self-regulation of a kind that has been common in the professions. The advantage of self-regulation is that it implies those most familiar with a field end up regulating it; the disadvantage is that an industry regulating itself may have interests that conflict with those of the public at large.

Another form of regulation is co-regulation, which is a hybrid of the self and external variety.

The regulation of natural monopoly has tended to take one of two different forms: (a) in the US, ➤rate-of-return regulation, in which the profits of the provider are capped to a reasonable level, or (b) more commonly in the UK, ➤price regulation, in which the price of the provider is capped to a reasonable level, with the provider allowed to make big profits if it can do so within the capped price. In general, price regulation offers better incentives to cost efficiency. Rate-of-return regulation provides the incentive to inflate costs, knowing that profits will be the same regardless of how efficient production is. In practice, the two approaches converge: price caps have to be reviewed periodically, and the regulator obviously has to take account of rates of return in reaching a judgement as to what makes a reasonable price. And rate-of-return regulation can involve some assessment of what costs incurred should be allowed or disregarded in reaching an assessment of a reasonable profit. ➤➤Averch–Johnson effect; regulatory capture.

Regulation Q (US) A ➤Federal Reserve regulation setting ceilings on rates of interest paid by banks on their deposits. The Regulation stimulated the development of the ➤Eurodollar market.

regulatory capture The idea, from the field of government regulation of business activity, that a regulator can begin to become an advocate for the interests of the businesses it is meant to be regulating. For example, it has been argued that the then Ministry of Agriculture, Fisheries and Food in the UK abandoned the idea of prescribing acceptable standards of behaviour for the food industry and, instead, began to define its role as defending the industry against attack from outside. This may be because a regulator recognizes that its own self-interest requires a healthy industry to regulate, or because the social and business context within which the regulator operates is close to that of the industry. Or because the regulator is simply seeking a quiet life. In extreme cases, industry itself can seek its own regulation, as it may have the effect of legitimizing certain features of a cartel by, for example, maintaining very high standards of practice or by enforcing barriers to competitive entry. ➤barrier to entry.

reinforcement theory A theory of behaviour. In a personnel context, higher performance is achieved by nudging people in a particular direction – through a process of behavioural reinforcement. For example, an employee works on a project and receives praise for the budget statement (positive reinforcement) but is admonished for the lack of strategic thinking (negative reinforcement). Over time, the employee learns to build on her budgetary skills and to change her approach to strategic thinking. In practice, positive reinforcement (with ➤rewards) tends to be more effective in shaping behaviour than negative reinforcement. ➤motivation. Reinforcement theory also has been used to explain how marketing communications influence people in a ➤target audience. ➤➤ATR + N model.

reinsurance The practice of insurers of passing-on some of the risks they assume to other parties in return for a proportional share of the premium income. The reinsurance market grew significantly from a premium income of between \$5–6 billion handled by a small number of conservatively minded professional reinsurers in the 1960s, to one of some \$56 billion in the early 1980s handled by many more professional reinsurers, direct insurers entering into the business, and also by ➤**captive** insurers. This strong growth was occasioned by an imbalance of capacity as against demand. In the late 1980s, with a revival of profitable direct insurance, reinsurance growth eased. Reinsurance normally accounts for some 10–15 per cent of direct business.

reintermediation ➤intermediaries.

relationship marketing A view of marketing that has at its core the mutual exchange and fulfilment of promises between organizations, their staff and consumers. Emphasis is given to: (a) connections between people; (b) mutual benefits, and (c) interactions that are continuous or take place over successive occasions. It is not the organization 'doing something to' a customer, but specific individuals engaging in a joint activity over time to achieve a 'win–win' outcome. Apart from economic features of an economic relationship (e.g. the creation of value), there are likely to be more intangible features, notably the agreement of promises and the development of trust and social bonds (or friendships). Ideally, the relationship develops to such an extent that consumers are no longer seen as prospects, customers and clients, but as advocates or even evangelists. This describes the so-called 'loyalty ladder', whereby trust and social bonding become stronger and stronger, and ultimately lead to advocacy or evangelism. Although it is appealing to believe that advocates and evangelists can be created in this manner, this is an idealistic idea and shows a lack of understanding of most consumers and most markets. ➤➤**competitive parity**.

Relationship marketing has long been recognized in business-to-business and industrial contexts, typically taking the form of ➤**key account management** systems and ➤**customer relationship management** programmes. As a concept, relationship marketing traces its origins to the Copenhagen School of economists of the 1930s. However, only in the past decade has it become widely recognized outside of these narrow contexts popularized by Scandinavian writers such as Christian Gronroos and Evert Gummesson. Developments in the general business environment have been driving this process, e.g. the development of new interactive communications, the growth of strategic alliances and networks, increasing levels of outsourcing and federalization – all of which suggest the existence of weblike relationships, rather than traditional mass marketing exchanges.

Although intuitively appealing, there are hazards in adopting relationship marketing. The costs of maintaining relationships can be considerable. Procedures, such as ➤**lifetime value** calculations, help managers to address these issues, e.g. lifetime value calculations enable the profitability of each customer to be estimated, making it easier to decide how much money should be spent on maintaining each relationship. A further problem is that expectations are created which may be hard to fulfil. Also, some customers are reluctant to form relationships, even if the latter buy regularly and are profitable to the organization; this has given rise to ➤**permission marketing**.

Finally, in practice, the *appearance* of a relationship is easier to foster than the creation of a true and authentic one, e.g. the use of databases to send personalized letters or e-mail messages, or reliance on promotional rewards to sustain the interest of customers. ➤**personalization technologies**. This has been a criticism of many ➤**loyalty programmes** and ➤**affinity programmes**.

rent ➤economic rent.

renunciation The assigning by a shareholder, of the rights granted in a ➤**rights issue**, to another person. A shareholder can sell the rights to someone else by signing a renunciation form. She may decide to do this, where the rights issue is at a ➤**deep discount** or where she does not wish to increase her stake in the firm offering new shares.

repeated game A strategic interaction between a small number of players that occurs in the same form many times. The repeated game is a concept drawn from ➤**game theory**, which characterizes real-life situations as simple games. The distinguishing feature of repeated games, however, is that the players can learn about the strategies of the other players by looking at what they do in earlier rounds. Moreover, the players can punish or reward co-operative behaviour in early rounds by adopting certain strategies in later rounds, substantially changing the nature of the interaction. The general logic of a repeated game is that players can find it rational to co-operate with each other more than they might without repetition. For example, imagine a game where one can play 'nice' or 'nasty' (➤**prisoners' dilemma**); in a repeated game, players might display 'tit-for-tat'-type behaviour – being 'nice' to other players if they are nice in earlier rounds, or playing 'nastily', if they play nastily in earlier rounds.

However, repeated games come in two varieties: (a) those that are repeated a finite, known number of times, and (b) those that go on being repeated indefinitely. In the academic analysis of games, the indefinitely repeated game fosters co-operation and characterizes many real-life situations, e.g. competition between companies that may find it convenient to co-operate. But the finite repeated game can be shown to end up looking rather like the one-shot game. This is because a self-interested player will treat the last round of the game as a one-shot game, as no subsequent punishment or reward can occur thereafter. Knowing how the last round will be played, however, means that in the penultimate round players will disregard the last round as having bearing on the punishment or rewards facing them. Thus, the penultimate round looks like a one-shot game, too; one can apply this logic backwards to show all rounds end-up looking like a one-shot game if the players are sufficiently 'rational' in their calculation of the outcomes.

repeat purchase ➤buyer behaviour.

repetitive strain injury (RSI) Physical injury as a result of the continuous repetition of a very narrow range of movements. The overuse of some parts of the body (especially the arms, hands and wrists) can result in pain and reduction in physical capability. There is some controversy surrounding the extent of physical injury through repetitive work but it is none the less an accepted condition.

replacement-cost depreciation ➤depreciation.

replicating portfolio A portfolio of assets constructed to ensure that its value changes with market prices in a way that offsets precisely the changes of value in a ➤**derivative** contract. For example, if a ➤**hedge fund** sells an ➤**option**, the value of the option rises or falls with the value of the asset underlying the option. The replicating portfolio represents holdings of the underlying assets to ensure that the sale of the option is a safe offer to have made. So, if HedgeCo sells an option to Jane to buy two shares in Widget Corp at £10 each in 3 weeks, and the value of the shares goes up to £11, then the option becomes a burden to HedgeCo, as Jane can buy two shares at £10 when they are worth £11 each. HedgeCo loses £2. If the price of Widget Corp shares falls to £9, Jane makes nothing at all as the option is worthless. Clearly, HedgeCo wants the shares to fall in price. However, suppose HedgeCo constructs a replicating portfolio by buying one share in Widget Corp. Now, whatever happens to Widget Corp shares, HedgeCo faces the same outcome. A rise in price to £11 would make HedgeCo lose £2 on the options and make £1 on the share, thus yielding a loss of £1. If the price falls to £9, then HedgeCo loses nothing on the options but loses £1 on the share so, again, the overall loss is £1. It may be a loss, but it is a predictable and safe one. The single share thus offsets the movement in price of the two options, and represents a replicating portfolio. The certain loss of £1 on the option and its replicating portfolio can be used to tell you how much the option should be sold for in the first place. If the seller is guaranteed to lose £1 by constructing this portfolio, then each option has to be worth 50 pence to make it a break-even package. The replicating portfolio provides a neat way of deriving option prices, which in practice can be a very complicated business. ➤**Black–Scholes formula**.

reporting accountant One of a firm of accountants reporting to the ➤**sponsor** of a ➤**new issue** on the financial affairs of a ➤**company**. ➤➤**long-form report**.

repositioning ➤positioning.

repurchase agreement (repo) Short for *sale and repurchase agreement*. A transaction in which funds are borrowed through the sale of short-term securities on the condition that the instruments are repurchased at a given date. Used principally between the ➤**central bank** and the ➤**money market** as a means of relieving short-term shortages of funds in the money market (perhaps overnight, hence *overnight repo*) and thus as a means of monetary control by the central bank. Interest is paid on the instrument in the meantime. Repurchase agreements are also utilized in ➤**open-market operations** by central banks.

resale price maintenance (RPM) The practice by which manufacturers attempt to fix the price at which retailers (or other distributors) sell their products. RPM used to be ubiquitous, but was largely outlawed in the UK, for example, after the Resale Prices Act 1964 under which all resale price agreements were assumed to be against the public interest unless it could be proved otherwise to the Restrictive Practices Court. RPM is an example of a so-called ➤**vertical restraint**. The key question to ask is, for example, why a multivitamin or perfume manufacturer might want to fix retail prices. After all, usually one might assume that the manufacturer would choose to sell the product at a proportionately high price to the retailer and then hope the retailer sells it at a low price, thus generating lots of sales. RPM can be seen as a device by which manufacturers limit competition and uphold the profit margins not of themselves, but of the people to whom they sell. In reality, there are many reasons why such behaviour may be beneficial to the manufacturer, but it turns out to be so most often for those for whom the retailing ambience is important. Books, medication, perfume are the kinds of products in which manufacturers have a keen interest in upholding retailing standards and in ensuring that high-cost retailers do not get pushed out by low-quality ones who might damage a brand or its reputation.

It is possible to imagine less benign motives for RPM. It could, for example, be used by groups of competing manufacturers to help sustain a ➤**cartel** by making price information more public, and enforcement of price discipline more effective.

research and development (R & D) Commonly linked together to describe the research and technical function within an organization. In industry, R & D is a generic term for all the activities associated with discovering new knowledge and applying it to new products. It is sometimes difficult to determine when research ends and development begins. It is probably more realistic to view industrial R & D as a continuum with scientific knowledge at one end and physical products at the other. In most R & D departments the range of activities undertaken is usually divided into ➤**applied research; basic research; developmental research** and ➤**technical service.**

After the Second World War, R & D played an important role in providing firms with competitive advantage. The technical developments of firms in industries such as chemicals, electronics, automobiles and pharmaceuticals led to the development of many new products, which produced rapid growth. For a while, it seemed that technology was capable of almost anything. The traditional view, then, of R & D has been to overcome genuine technological problems, which subsequently leads to business opportunities and a competitive advantage over one's competitors.

President Kennedy's special address to the US Congress in 1961, in which he spoke of 'putting a man on the moon before the decade was out', captured the popular opinion of that time. Many believed anything was possible through technology. This notion helps to explain one of the major areas of difficulty with R & D as follows. Traditionally, R & D has been viewed as a linear process moving from research to engineering and then manufacture. That R & D was viewed as an overhead item was reinforced by Kennedy who pledged to spend 'whatever it costs' and, indeed, enormous financial resources were directed towards the project. But this was a unique situation without the usual economic or market forces at play. Nevertheless, industry adopted a similar approach to that used in the space programme. Vast amounts of money were poured into R & D programmes in the belief that the interesting technology generated could then be incorporated into products. In many instances this is exactly what happened, but there were also many examples of exciting and interesting technology developed purely because it was interesting technology, without any consideration of the competitive market in which the business operated. Hence, many business leaders began to question the value of R & D.

There is no single best way to manage R & D. There is no prescription, no computer model that will ensure its success. Each company, every competitive environment is unique and in its own state of change. Hence, R & D needs to be managed according to the specific heritage and resources of the company in its competitive industry. While the management of R & D in the aircraft industry is very different to the textile industry, there are, none the less, certain factors and elements that are common to all aspects of R & D management, almost irrespective of the industry.

One may be tempted to think that research, by definition, is based around exploring things that are unknown. It cannot, therefore, be managed and organizations should not try to do so. There is, however, overwhelming evidence to suggest that industrial technological research can, indeed, be managed and that most of those organizations who spend large amounts of money on R & D (e.g. Microsoft, IBM, Sony, Siemens and GlaxoSmithKline) do it extremely well.

Large organizations with greater resources can clearly afford to invest more in R & D than their smaller counterparts. Therefore, in order to present a more realistic comparison than that derived from raw sums invested, R & D expenditure is frequently expressed as:

R & D as percentage of sales = (R & D expenditure/total sales income × 100)

This not only allows comparisons to be made between small and large firms, but also gives a more realistic picture of R & D intensity within the organization. Indeed, across industry sectors there are great differences in expenditure. The table shows typical levels of R & D expenditure across different industrial sectors. This shows clearly how some industries are regarded as technology-intensive with relatively high levels of R & D expenditure.

R & D expenditure across industry sectors

Industry sector	R & D expenditure as percentage of sales
Pharmaceuticals	14
Computers	10
Chemicals	8
Electrical & electronics	7
General manufacturing	6
Aerospace	5
Automotive	5
Food	1.5

The fact that some of the largest and most successful companies in the world spend enormous sums of money on R & D should not be taken as a sign that these companies have mastered the process. It is important to acknowledge that R & D management, like innovation itself, is part art and part science. Industry may not be able to identify and hire geniuses like Faraday, Pasteur or Bell, but many of these companies would argue that they already employ people who, year after year, develop new patents and new products that will contribute to the future prosperity of the organization. These same companies would also argue that they cannot justify spending several millions of dollars, pounds or marks purely on the basis of chance and good fortune. This would clearly be unacceptable, not least to its shareholders. So while companies appreciate that there is a certain amount of serendipity, there are also formal management techniques that, over the years, have been learned, refined and practised and which are now a necessary part of good R & D management.

On a global scale, R & D investment increased by an average of 23 per cent from 1991 to 1996. R & D expenditure now consumes a significant proportion of a firm's funds across all industrial sectors. This is principally because companies realize new products can provide a huge competitive advantage. While it is relatively easy to measure inputs, it is far harder to measure outputs in terms of quality.

Many international companies, including Unilever, ICI and British Aerospace have conducted numerous studies attempting to justify R & D expenditure. This has not been easy because there is not a satisfactory method for measuring R & D output. Many studies have used the number of patents published as a guide. This is mainly because it is quantifiable rather than it being a valid measure. It is, however, quality not quantity of output that is clearly important. It is worthy of note that most companies would like to be able to correlate R & D expenditure with profitability. At present, there is a lack of conclusive evidence to connect the two. Edwin Mansfield has undertaken many studies concerning the relationship between R & D expenditure and economic growth and productivity. He concludes that 'although the results are subject to considerable error, they establish certain broad conclusions. In particular, existing econometric studies do provide reasonably conclusive evidence that R & D has a significant effect on the rate of productivity increase in the industries and time periods studied.' Furthermore, a study by Morbey (*Journal of Product Innovation Management*, 1988) did reveal a positive relationship between R & D expenditure and *long-term* growth. This raises an important point: R & D expenditure should be viewed as a long-term investment. Indeed, R & D expenditure may reduce short-term profitability. Company accountants increasingly question the need for large sums to be invested in an activity that shows no obvious and certainly no rapid return. Many argue that public money should be used for 'pure research' where there is no clear application. Its outputs could then be taken and used by industry to generate wealth. However, the UK government's recent initiatives to couple science to the creation of wealth through such programmes as Technology Foresight, seem to suggest that even public money is being directed towards applied research.

R & D activity is allied closely to the management of ➤**innovation** and ➤**new product development**. ➤➤**scientific freedom**.

reservation price ➤pricing policy.

reserve 1. Of countries, the central bank's holdings of gold and foreign currencies and International Monetary Fund drawing rights, for the purpose of providing for fluctuations in the country's ➤**balance of payments**; commonly referred to as the gold and foreign currency reserves. **2.** Of banks, cash and short-term claims, held as backing for the bank's ➤**deposit** liabilities; commonly referred to as ➤**reserve assets**. **3.** Amounts set aside from profits in company accounts for an unspecified purpose. Reserves are part of ➤**retained earnings**, i.e. they are undistributed profits and belong to the ordinary shareholders of the company. In the US, the term *reserves* is often used in the UK sense of ➤**provisions**, which are sums set aside for specific anticipated purposes. **4.** Of ➤**insurance**, amounts set aside to meet underwriting liabilities; commonly referred to as *technical reserves*.

reserve asset A holding of a commercial bank, not used for loans or other transactions and therefore available for use in the last resort to meet a shortage of funds. In most countries, the level and constitution of reserve assets and their ratio to ➤deposits are prescribed by the regulatory authorities. ➤➤**liquidity ratio**.

resource-based theories of strategy A view of strategy that focuses on the resources of the firm. This is distinctive from previous dominant approaches, as advocated by Michael ➤**Porter** and others, which have emphasized the importance of the market and a firm's position in it. During the 1980s and early 1990s, numerous writers were critical of the market-based view of strategy. They argued that if a firm's position in an industry was the key determining criterion for success why, then, did firms in the same industry and similar market positions differ considerably in their performance? The resource-based view of strategy focuses on the individual resources of the firm. In particular, it suggests that a firm's competitive advantage is dependent on its ability to develop and acquire knowledge, skills and technology.

resource requirements planning (RRP) A long-term plan to project the future needs of the firm's operations. Typically, this will involve assessing the need for larger or additional resources such as machines or production plants. Sometimes these plans are referred to as 'infinite capacity plans' as they assume infinite ability to increase production.

response models A formal way to express the effect of one variable on another. For example, we might believe sales rise in response to increases in advertising expenditure, and use a response model to describe this relationship. In this instance, the sales level is the dependent (response) variable and advertising expenditure is the independent variable. Models of this type are very common in all areas of management – with response variables such as sales, profit, ➤return on investment, ➤market share, time saved, cost reduction, ➤employee motivation, ➤productivity, user satisfaction, and perceived value. These models are implicit in the thinking of managers and consumers – managers are likely to believe that by increasing advertising expenditure, sales for their brand will rise, although they may recognize that because of poor advertising, competitive responses and external conditions, sales actually may be static.

The relationship between one variable and another can take a number of characteristic forms or shapes. There might be a simple linear relationship where, for example, a rise in advertising expenditure is matched by a one-for-one rise in sales. Alternatively, there may be decreasing returns to scale and eventual saturation (where extra advertising expenditure has no impact on sales), or increasing returns (where the weight of extra advertising expenditure has a growing impact on sales), or an S-shaped curve (where there are first increasing and then decreasing returns to scale). These shapes can be expressed mathematically, and this is a particularly important step in developing response models. Often, use is made of ➤regression analysis and ➤econometric techniques.

Another step is to decide whether to use a static or dynamic model. Static models provide a snapshot of how one variable is related to another. However, responses to management actions do not always take place immediately. The effect of increasing advertising expenditure may not be apparent at first (a delayed-response effect), or the effect on sales might last well beyond the end of the campaign (a customer-holdover effect), or a quick sales rise might be followed by a slow decline after the campaign (a hysteresis effect). There are also competitive reactions to consider. Dynamic models aim to capture these and other responses over time.

Restrictive Practices Court ➤Office of Fair Trading.

restructuring A means of reorganizing with a view to improving efficiency. This may involve changing the management hierarchy or altering the way the organization processes information, goods or services. ➤business process re-engineering. In some instances, the word 'restructuring' is used as a euphemism for large-scale redundancies. ➤downsizing.

retail banking ➤retail deposit; wholesale banking.

retail deposit 1. A ➤deposit placed by an individual customer, normally in relatively small amounts, with a bank, in contrast to a ➤wholesale deposit. **2.** In money supply terminology, deposits held for expenditure purposes (*transaction balances*), as against those held for savings (*investment balances*). **3.** In ➤hire purchase, funds received by ➤finance houses from individual investors rather than from the wholesale ➤money market. **4.** In the mortgage business, funds raised by mortgage banks (building societies) from individual depositors, rather than through wholesale borrowings from the money market or from other sources.

retail gravitation principle ➤gravity model.

retail prices index An index of the prices of goods and services purchased by consumers to measure the rate of ➤inflation or the cost of living. The weights used in the index are revised annually and are based on the proportion of household expenditure spent on each item, information on which is obtained in the UK from the Family Expenditure Survey. The prices of these items are collected, and the index updated, monthly. Changes in thee index have an important effect on the economy because they may influence wage and salary awards and may affect the value of index-linked assets and pensions. ➤➤indexation.

retained earnings An undistributed profit that may simply be a ➤reserve or may be used for investment in ➤fixed assets. When a company finances its capital expenditure from retained earnings rather than borrowings, it is said to be self-financing.

return on capital employed ➤return on investment.

return on investment (ROI) A financial ratio showing profit as a percentage of total ➤assets or ➤capital employed or ➤shareholders' equity. The numerator and denominator of the ratio need to be defined carefully, e.g. profit after interest and ➤depreciation as a percentage of total assets at *historic cost*. ➤cost, historical.

return to scale The proportionate increase in output produced as a result of making proportionate increases in all inputs. If the number of workers, raw materials and machines used by a firm are all doubled, three situations can result: (a) ➤decreasing returns to scale would hold if output less than doubled; (b) constant returns to scale would exist if output exactly doubled, and (c)➤increasing returns to scale would hold if output more than doubled. Decreasing returns to scale should not be confused with the law of diminishing returns (➤diminishing returns) which traces the response of output to an increase in one individual input with all others held constant. ➤➤economies of scale; production function.

revaluation reserve Capital reserves created when the book value of existing assets is revalued to bring it into line with replacement costs, or when new shares are issued at a ➤premium over ➤par value.

Revans, Reg W Original but little-celebrated British thinker on management training who worked as a local government education official and in industry as a consultant. In her *Guide to the Management Gurus* (1991), Carol Kennedy writes that Revans was the:

inventor of Action Learning in which working teams of managers educate each other amid the real risk, confusion and opportunity of the workplace itself. The idea has become an accepted part of management education, though only the Japanese have fully acknowledged the importance of Revans' early work as a foundation stone of their quality circle philosophy.

Revans' writings include *Developing Effective Managers* (1971) and *Action Learning* (1979).

revealed behaviour ➤buyer behaviour.

revealed preference method ➤choice modelling.

reverse engineering Taking apart a product to understand how it has been manufactured. Firms frequently undertake this activity when analysing a competitor's product. It enables firms to analyse closely the design of a product, in particular the materials used, the number of parts and the assembly techniques. As a result, a firm may decide to amend and incorporate the key features into its own products. It may consider applying for a licence to incorporate patented technology that seems to be advantageous.

reversionary bonus ➤insurance.

rewards The payoff from doing something, e.g. working, joining, buying or consuming. An understanding of rewards is crucial if a manager is to motivate employees, members or consumers. It is argued that people will not do certain things unless there are rewards (except where there is compulsion or coercion). The payoff will be financial (monetary), psychological (personal growth) and/or social (social esteem). Depending on the circumstances, these different types of payoff will be more or less effective as motivators, e.g. a wealthy person may be more motivated by social esteem than further monetary rewards, or an employee may be more motivated by special recognition ('salesperson of the year') than by the provision of something that is available to all (such as a pension plan). ➤**motivation**.

A distinction is drawn between intrinsic and extrinsic rewards.

(1) Intrinsic rewards. These arise from doing the thing itself. Work can provide intrinsic satisfaction and fulfilment. There are various ways to enhance intrinsic rewards in an organizational context, e.g. by giving people more interesting work, offering people greater freedom and discretion over what they do, increasing the variety of tasks in a job, granting more responsibility and encouraging people to participate in decision-making, and creating opportunities for personal growth and development. With intrinsic rewards, psychological factors dominate financial and social ones.

(2) Extrinsic rewards. These come from beyond the thing itself. In an organizational context, ➤**pay** is the most evident extrinsic reward. It is the possession of money, and what money can buy, that is rewarding, not the work itself. Pay is a financial reward, and is a form of direct compensation, other forms of direct compensation being performance bonuses, overtime payments, profit-sharing schemes and stock/share options. Organizations are also able to offer various forms of indirect compensation, including private health insurance, pension and superannuation contributions, employee privileges and ➤**fringe benefits**. Although these rewards are indirect, they, too, can be seen as forms of financial reward (hence

they are not necessarily given tax-exempt status). Other extrinsic rewards are social in character, e.g. high-status job titles, designated parking spaces, flexible working hours, discretionary patterns of work, a personal secretary, more attractive working conditions, etc. These symbolize status as well as provide satisfaction in their own right, both of which are likely to be valued by an employee and provide motivation.

In the consumer context, the purchase of some goods and services may bring intrinsic pleasure (e.g. having a formal dinner, choosing a dress), as well as offer extrinsic rewards, e.g. the social cachet that comes from dining at certain restaurants or from the possession of certain clothing brands. This is particularly important in the management of services. ➤services marketing. More generally, marketers use an understanding of rewards to provide incentives for consumers to buy one brand rather than another, and as a way to maintain customer loyalty. Thus, price ➤promotions are designed to offer a small financial reward to consumers who try the brand. Loyalty, affinity and membership programmes may offer financial, psychological and social rewards. ➤reward schemes.

reward power ➤power.

reward scheme A special marketing scheme designed to reward consumers for their continued patronage and loyalty to an organization. These take the form of financial/economic ➤rewards that accumulate as more use is made of the product or service. They also include non-economic rewards. For example, a British Airways (BA) executive club member has the economic benefit of free flights (through the frequent-flier scheme), the psychological satisfaction that comes from being seen as a valued customer and the social esteem of belonging to a privileged club. These rewards provide additional reasons for a customer to continue using BA, over and above the fact that the airline can convey a person from one place to another. This mix of rewards is also the basis for ➤affinity programmes with trade customers and final consumers. More broadly, all these schemes can be seen as forms of ➤customer relationship management.

rights issue An offer of new shares to existing shareholders, to raise new capital. A company will offer the rights in a certain proportion to existing holdings, depending upon the amount of new equity capital it wishes to raise. Thus in a one-for-one rights issue, shareholders will be offered a number of new shares equal to the number they already hold. The key feature of a rights issue is that it protects the existing shareholders from the potential danger of newly issued shares diluting their existing holding. To ensure that the issue is taken up, the new shares are offered at well below the market price of the existing shares (i.e. at a discount) which will usually result in some fall in the price of existing shares, but this does not matter as long as the existing shareholders are getting the new cheap shares anyway. Rights issues are a relatively cheap way of raising capital for a quoted company, since the costs of preparing a brochure, ➤underwriting, commission and press advertising involved in a new issue are avoided. ➤new issue market.

risk A state in which the number of possible future events exceeds the number of events that will actually occur, and in which some measure of probability can be attached to each possible outcome. This definition distinguishes risk from *uncertainty*, in which there are multiple possible future events, but in which the

323

probabilities attached to each are too vague to have numbers attached to them. A roulette player, for example, faces risk rather than uncertainty – because she could either be very much richer tomorrow than she is today or (more likely) slightly poorer, depending on whether a roulette wheel spins the ball into the right hole – but she knows the odds of the roulette wheel landing in each hole. It is normally assumed that economic agents dislike risk. ➤➤**risk aversion**.

The study of risk has been most intensely applied in the analysis of financial market returns, which often have an inherent degree of riskiness about them. The usual assumption is that risky assets yield higher returns than safer ones on average, but with less degree of certainty in any particular case. Unfortunately, the notion of risk has proved too complicated for theoreticians to describe fully. For example, most simple financial ➤**models**, assume there are only two periods – this year and next year – and that all the uncertainty surrounds next year. Under this assumption, shares are risky because no one knows what price shares will sell at next year, and cash and ➤**bonds** are safe because we know how much they will be worth next year. In practice, though, the world is far more complicated than this in ways that undermine the usefulness of these simple models. For one thing, over the long term, shares are safer than they look in the short term, as good times tend to be followed by bad, and vice versa, so that long-term performance is often more predictable than short-term performance, and less risky. As for cash, it may look safe for next year, but if you want to invest for 5 years, and if interest rates tumble next year, then the return you will get investing in cash repeatedly year after year may not be as high as you want or expect. ➤**Inflation** adds risk to the different assets as well, as shares tend to be more inflation-proof than some other assets. ➤➤**strategic asset allocation**.

risk assessment A measure of the risks of a course of action, and the costs and benefits of reducing those risks. Risk assessment has been promoted as a means of preventing economic activity which creates more dangers than are reasonable. But perhaps more importantly, it can prevent the error of creating 'too much safety' – the imposition of costly safety mechanisms that reduce risks less than is worth while given the cost. Economists argue that it is not worth investing millions of pounds in, say, a rail safety system if it is expected to save one life a year, if the money could have saved more lives invested elsewhere. Those involved in risk assessment acknowledge the wide variety of different valuations it is reasonable to place on human safety. ➤**cost–benefit analysis**.

risk aversion The placing of a higher value on a prospect arriving with certainty, than on an uncertain prospect which has the same expected outcome but with some ➤**risk** or uncertainty attached. If you would prefer to be given £10 with certainty, than to have a 50 per cent chance of winning £15 and a 50 per cent chance of winning £5 (which after all gives an average of £10) then you are risk-averse. Economists normally assume that consumers are risk-averse because of what is called *diminishing marginal utility*, which says the more money we have, the less we value each extra pound we have, i.e. the utility we get from the marginal unit of money diminishes. The consequence of this is that we suffer more from a drop in income than we benefit from a gain in it; the displeasure of losing £5,000 outweighs the pleasure of winning an extra £5,000. That means a fair bet which offers the prospect of losing and gaining the same amount overall probably diminishes total welfare (unless we derive pleasure from gambling).

Risk aversion explains why people normally insure against disaster. Gambling, on the other hand, is risk-loving behaviour; people at casinos on average pay out more than they win back.

While human beings are naturally assumed to be risk-averse, it may not be that companies are; with ➤**limited liability**, firms can find that by taking risks they enjoy potential benefits, but at the same time face the possibility of losses that are limited.

risk capital Long-term funds invested in enterprises particularly subject to risk, as in small or new ventures. Hence, the alternative term ➤**venture capital**, a somewhat more precise term meaning capital provided for a new or young business by people other than the proprietors. Venture capital is usually provided by specialized venture capital institutions, including ➤**captives**, and specialized venture capital funds.

risk-free rate of return The rate of return earned on an asset that can be assumed to have no risk of default. Typically, the risk-free rate is the real rate of interest paid on a government bond.

risk management The identification and acceptance or offsetting of the risks threatening the profitability or existence of an organization. ➤**Insurance** provides protection against death, fire or flood (➤**hedge**) against fluctuations in exchange rates and accelerated ➤**depreciation** against the risk of obsolescence of fixed assets; also, management by a company of events and activities so as to minimize the degree to which damage or loss may occur, so reducing dependence on insurance.

ritual A repetitive sequence of activities that expresses and reinforces the key ➤**values** of the organization, what goals are most important, which people are important, and which are expendable.

road-blocking Where, in an advertising campaign, space is bought in all the media used by members of a particular ➤**target audience**. This maximizes the chances of members of the target audience being exposed to the communication; metaphorically, their exposure is road-blocked.

ROCE Acronym for return on capital employed. ➤**return on investment**.

ROI ➤return on investment.

role A set of expected behaviour patterns attributed to a person in a given position within a business organization, family or other social unit. The particular individual is called the 'focal person', and surrounding him is a 'role set' of people who interact with the focal person (colleagues, business associates, clients, managers). Members of the role set will have expectations about how the focal person should act and behave ('role expectations'). The focal person also will have a view of how he should act and behave and usually will develop certain attitudes and behaviours consistent with the role ('role identity'). ➤➤**impression management**. There is an element of self-fulfilling prophecy in this – a person who is given the label 'manager' is expected to become like a manager and invariably does so when at work (a 'halo effect'). Role identity may change according to the context; thus, a manager at work may feel it is appropriate to behave differently in the office and with a client.

To assist people in decoding role expectations and role identities we rely on certain cues, symbols, signs and ➤**rituals**, e.g. job titles, clothes and uniforms, office size.

However, in practice, there is often confusion. Focal persons may suffer from five role-related problems:

(1) Role ambiguity. It is unclear exactly what a person is expected to do, e.g. is a particular manager responsible for simply agreeing tasks with staff, or is he also expected to develop staff?

(2) Role incompatibility. The role is clear but the tasks expected of the person are incompatible, e.g. is a manager expected to motivate and inspire staff while also ➤downsizing the workforce?

(3) Role conflict. A person has several well-defined roles that are in conflict, e.g. being a senior manager who works long hours, and being a parent.

(4) Role overload. The number of roles a person is expected to fulfil becomes hard to manage, e.g. a person may find it difficult to cope simultaneously with being a manager, mentor/teacher, parent, etc.

(5) Role underload. The role is seen as insufficient, e.g. where a frustrated junior clerk believes he could be an effective senior administrator.

These problems can give rise to tension, anxiety and insecurity, and may affect a person's morale and motivation to work and his ability to perform effectively. Collectively, this is described as 'role stress'. ➤stress. In such circumstances, however, organizations can try to manage role stress, e.g. by preparing for role transitions such as when a manager takes on higher-level responsibilities.

Tension might also arise if there is lack of fit between the focal person's view of her role and the views of those in the role set ('role incongruence'). ➤➤congruency theory. This can arise in service encounters, e.g. if a waiter believes he should behave in a very formal manner but the customer expects more informal and relaxed service. Without a resolution of this incongruence, neither party will feel his expectations are being met. ➤Script theory is used to anticipate and rehearse the responses needed in different situations and/or with different customers.

role ambiguity ➤role.

role conflict ➤role.

role overload/underload ➤role.

role perception How others are perceived, taking into account the other person's ➤role. In forming these perceptions we rely on certain cues, symbols, signs and rituals. For example, a judge will be perceived in a particular way, not only because of her role as a judge, but also because of the trappings (the wearing of a wig and gown, the court rising as she enters, etc.). A danger is that inappropriate stereotyping occurs, e.g. judges are often *seen* as conservative because of the trappings, not that they necessarily *are* conservative.

round tripping Occurs when a non-financial company can borrow at lower than current and short-term market ➤rates of interest and can therefore borrow and on-lend at a ➤profit.

r^2 A statistical measure of the proportion of variations in one variable explained by variations in other variables. For example, suppose we do some ➤econometrics and discover that variations in consumption spending C can be 'explained' by variations in consumers' income Y so that:

$$C = 0.8Y$$

(➤**regression analysis**). It is highly unlikely that we would find the relationship held exactly; other things than income would determine consumption, even though we might have estimated a decent relationship between the two. The statistic r^2 is literally the proportion of variation in C that our simple ➤**model** of C and Y has explained; for that reason, r^2 is often referred to as a measure of 'goodness of fit'. r^2 allows us to compare the actual values of C from real world data, with the values that our model produces, where C is taken as 0.8 times Y and the Y is taken from the real world data. The statistic takes a value between 0 and 1; a value of 1 would imply that the actual data and the model's 'predictions' of the data are identical. A value of 0 would imply that the model generates numbers for C that have no correlation whatsoever with the actual data. Simple computer packages for performing regression analysis will routinely produce an estimate of the r^2. The formula for it is, however, just the square of the ➤**correlation coefficient** of the predicted values of C and the actual values. r^2 is known as the coefficient of determination. In the case of more complicated models, where instead of one explanatory variable, such as Y, there are many variables, r^2 is written as R^2 and is known as the coefficient of multiple determination.

running yield ➤yield.

S

SA ➤*société anonyme.*

safety stock ➤buffer stock.

sale and leaseback ➤leaseback.

sale and repurchase agreement ➤repurchase agreement.

sales The function of selling a good or service. One view of sales is to see it as making the sale now, without much regard to the cost of achieving success. A parody of this is the 'hard-sell', where the salesperson heavily pushes a product (even when the consumer is evidently reluctant to buy) and where inducements such as price cuts are very readily given (even if they harm revenues and margins in the short run and undermine the brand image in the longer term). Aggressive selling is found in discount retailing and, in the past at least, in some consumer sectors, e.g. door-to-door selling, insurance, automobiles. ➤**pyramid selling**. However, this is a partial and unhelpful view of sales in general. Far from 'pushing' the product, the astute salesperson will listen carefully to the customer, finding out what she wants and what reservations she might have. Only after having done this will the salesperson direct the customer to specific products, and in so doing show how the product meets her needs and overcomes any reservations. This approach is more likely to result in sales without costly inducements, and ensure the customer is satisfied (which, in turn, minimizes the risk of customer complaints and maximizes the opportunity for repeat-purchase or positive word-of-mouth recommendation). Social judgement theory offers some conceptual basis for this. ➤**involvement theory**.

A broader view is to see it as the task of building relationships, variously described as the ➤**business development function** (where the emphasis is on securing new customers) and ➤**customer relationship management** (where the emphasis is on managing existing customers). Also related is ➤**key account management**, where there may be just a few key customers or clients in, for example, a business-to-business context. ➤➤**services marketing**. Despite new technologies, the face-to-face meeting remains important in these contexts. ➤➤**call plan**.

The word 'sales' has at least two other meanings in business: as in seasonal retail sales (➤**promotions**) and as a measure of performance. ➤**key performance measure; marketing metrics**.

sales call ➤call plan.

sampling The selection of a (small) proportion of individuals from the total population. Sampling theory is used in ➤**marketing research** (e.g. in selecting respondents for a survey) and ➤**statistical process control**, e.g. for quality checks and ➤**work sampling** on a production line. There are several different forms of sample. In the 'random sample' every individual has an equal chance of being selected. In 'probability sampling' individuals are selected in such a way that the chance that any particular member of the population will be selected for the sample is known (this enables the researcher to calculate the chances that the sample accurately represents the population from which it was selected). With a 'stratified sample' the population is divided into strata (groups or subpopulations with common attributes) and the sample chosen contains the same proportion of desired attributes as the population strata from which it is drawn.

satisficing Behaviour which attempts not to achieve the best possible outcome, but some reasonable outcome. The most common application of the concept in economics is in the ➤**behavioural theory of the firm**, which does not assume companies strive to make the most possible profit but, instead, postulates that producers strive to make a reasonable profit. In this sense, profit is less an objective and more a constraint to which the firm must direct itself, so that, although at least a critical level of profit must be achieved by firms, thereafter priority is attached to the attainment of other goals. ➤➤**Simon, Herbert A.**

savings and loan (S & L) **associations** (US) Savings banks that, like ➤**building societies**, receive savings deposits and make mortgages. The deregulation of interest rates by the Depository Institutions Deregulation and Monetary Decontrol Act 1980 created difficulties for S & Ls because they had commitments for long-term loans at fixed rates of interest, so that as deposit rates rose, they were sometimes paying more to depositors than they were receiving from their borrowers. Also referred to as *savings and loan institutions* and ➤**thrifts**, they exercise some banking functions such as operating cheque accounts (US = *checking accounts*) and providing ➤**consumer credit** and high-yield investment vehicles. S & Ls are largely ➤**mutual** organizations, though many have incorporated (➤**incorporation**) so as to broaden their access to ➤**capital markets**. S & Ls are regulated either by the Federal Home Loan Bank Board or, in the case of state chartered S & Ls, by each state.

savings bank A bank that accepts interest-bearing deposits of small amounts. The earliest savings banks were established in the private sector, but later they were set up or supported by governments to encourage individual savings. In the UK the two main forms of savings bank have been the ➤**National Savings Bank** and, before ➤**privatization**, the Trustee Savings Bank (TSB). The TSB, however, is now part of Lloyds TSB. The ➤**building societies** share the basic objectives of the savings banks.

savings ratio The proportion of household income which is not spent, usually expressed as a percentage of total household disposable income. It may be calculated *gross* or *net*. In the latter case, a deduction is made for the ➤**depreciation** of household fixed assets. The savings ratio in the UK has fluctuated enormously: it increased from an average of about 2 per cent in the late 1940s and early 1950s to around 8–10 per cent in the 1960s. It peaked at 15 per cent in 1980 at a time of high inflation, fell in the boom in the late 1980s, recovered to about 11 per cent in 1996, and fell again as the economy enjoyed a sustained period of growth. In late 2001, it was 5 per cent.

The savings ratio does not take account of capital gains made by households that add to overall wealth. Thus, if house prices or share prices go up, households may save less but still be richer.

SBU ➤strategic business unit.

scale economies ➤economies of scale.

scanners ➤consumer panel.

scenario planning A technique to help firms plan for the future. The ability to predict the future accurately will give any organization an advantage. ➤Forecasting, while helpful, is also unreliable; the construction of a number of scenarios each describing a possible future state is another way of helping organizations prepare for the future. Scenario building is said to stimulate creative thinking and help identify major opportunities and threats. It is a highly practical approach to forecasting and enables the combination of an extensive range of political, social, economic and technological factors into predictions of the future. There are, none the less, limitations with this technique; it is a time-consuming and costly exercise and scenarios do not indicate the best course of action.

Schein, Edgar H Professor of Management at the Massachusetts Institute of Technology who has made important contributions to knowledge on employee–employer relations and corporate culture. He demonstrated that not only the Rational Economic and Social Models relating to Douglas ➤McGregor's ➤theory X and theory Y, but the self-actualizing model which developed beyond them (Abraham ➤Maslow and Frederick ➤Herzberg) were oversimplifications of human needs and behaviour in the workplace. Schein proposed a complex model that recognized that things vary with people at different stages in their careers and from person to person. Correct diagnosis was the key to successful management of relations with subordinates. Schein introduced the concept of the two-way 'psychological contract' which determines the motivation of people in organizations. This contract goes far beyond written employment agreements on pay, notice period, etc., to cover autonomy, self-esteem and opportunities for personal development as well as the preservation of trade secrets and other aspects of employee loyalty. Elements in this contract, particularly affecting personal development, amount to a career anchor which promotes stability in employment as well as affecting the type of work employees are happy to perform. All these things are related closely to corporate culture, the management of which is the key to leadership, and particularly in merger situations where different cultures come together. Schein's books include *Organizational Psychology* (1980); *Career Dynamics: watching individual and organizational needs* (1978), and *Organizational Culture and Leadership* (1985).

science park An industrial area or district close to an established centre of excellence, often a university. The underlying rationale behind this is that academic scientists will have the opportunity to take laboratory ideas and develop them into real products. In addition, technology or science-based companies can set up close to the university so that they can utilize its knowledge base. In the US, where science parks have been around for 40 years, the achievements have been difficult to quantify. Examples are Silicon Valley, which is a collection of companies with research activities in electronics, and the 'research triangle' in North Carolina, which has several universities at its core. In the UK, one of the first science parks to be established was the Cambridge Science Park. Over the past 20 years, this has grown into a large industrial area and has attracted many successful science-based companies. Many other universities have also set up their own science parks, such as Southampton, Warwick and Cranfield. ➤➤**technology transfer.**

scientific freedom The time necessary for the autonomous spirit of enquiry found in scientists, which is necessary for research. The popular view of research is that, by definition, it is concerned with uncovering new things and discovering something that previously was unknown. And to try to introduce any form of planning would surely stifle creativity and innovation. This leads to one of the most fundamental management dilemmas facing senior managers: how to encourage creativity and at the same time improve efficiency.

➤**Research and development** (R & D) managers will argue that the technologist's and scientist's spirit of enquiry must be given room and freedom to exercise. Without the freedom to work on projects that may not appear of immediate benefit to the company, the laboratory may become conservative and uncreative. Furthermore, it may be difficult to attract and retain the best scientists if they are not allowed to pursue those areas that are of interest to them. Indeed, there are many disputes between research and technology managers and other senior functional managers concerning the amount of time scientists and research teams should be allocated for personal research programmes.

However, R & D managers are realistic, they recognize that few companies, if any, are going to invest large sums of money solely as an act of faith. There are many formal management techniques that are employed to help to improve the effectiveness and productivity of R & D without necessarily destroying the possibility of serendipity.

'S' corporation ➤subchapter S corporations.

screening The use of a mechanism that allows someone to judge the characteristics of someone or something even though they cannot see those characteristics directly. Screening has become a fashionable area of economics, used to explain many different phenomena. For example, an employer may wish to know some feature of a job applicant (e.g. how hard-working she is) but may not be able to observe that directly. A screening device is one that can be observed and which correlates with the unobservable characteristics. For example, if hard-working people enjoy school and spend many years there, and lazy people hate it and leave as soon as possible, the number of years spent at school may provide a device for screening hard-working people from lazy ones. Other examples of screening devices are advertising used as a screening device by consumers to determine which products are the ones producers truly believe are going to be around for some time (and are thus worth investing in) and dividend payments by companies, used as screening devices by investors to determine how confident executives are about the long-term sustainability of their company's profit levels. ➤**signalling.**

screening of product concept The evaluation of new product ideas. Not all new product ideas will be capable of further development into a finished product. Scientists, designers and product managers need to be selective as to which ➤**product concepts** they progress to the point of developing prototypes and further investment. In effect, the screening of ideas is a continual process that occurs at every stage of the ➤new product development process. However, over the years, three significant screening stages have emerged as significant activities in their own right.

(1) Marketing screen. The marketing team will need to ensure that any product concept will work in the market-place, that it offers something different to what is already available and fits-in with existing marketing strategy.

(2) Operations screen. The operations function is primarily concerned with the feasibility of being able to deliver the product. It will need to ensure the firm has the capacity within the operations and the expertise in terms of commercial and technical knowledge.

(3) Finance screen. The finance department would wish to examine all the financial implications of any new product idea. This would include capital and investment requirements, likely profit margins and likely return on investment details.

screwdriver plant A manufacturing plant that assembles product parts into a finished product. This is typically a pejorative term implying that such plants are largely low-skilled operations. It is argued that many multinational firms set up so-called screwdriver plants in low-wage economies to benefit from the low-cost labour. Such plants are relatively simple to establish and equally simple to close. It is argued that such operations do not develop the knowledge base of an economy.

scrip issue ➤bonus issue.

script theory The idea that people have a set of standard responses to different situations when carrying out a particular ➤role. An airline attendant, for example, would have rehearsed how to respond in the event of an emergency landing, or a hijacking, or simply as a result of spilling coffee on a passenger. The analogy is with a drama or play, where actors do not spontaneously act out a role but rehearse it in advance of the performance.

The theory has application in the management of ➤service encounters, where employees who deal directly with customers have to act appropriately given different situations and/or different customers in department stores, government offices, banks, travel agencies, hotels, personal services agencies, etc. By providing scripts, the organization has some control over the consistency of service provision and prepares employees for a range of situations (some of which might be quite rare, but where it would be unwise to leave the response to chance). The provision of a script can also give the employee a greater sense of control and confidence, giving rise to higher levels of performance. A danger, however, is that it becomes evident to customers that a person is mindlessly following a script. In some service encounters this may not matter much (e.g. in buying fast food), but in other instances it will matter to the customer that the experience is authentic and that service provision is genuinely meant, e.g. in dining at a local family-run restaurant.

SEAQ ➤Stock Exchange Automated Quotation system.

search quality ➤evaluation process.

secondary bank (UK) A bank that has relatively few branches and therefore does not play a major role in the payments system as far as the general public is concerned. Included in the term are ➤merchant banks, the UK ➤overseas banks and some ➤finance houses.

secondary market A market in which ➤securities or other assets are resold and repurchased, as distinct from a primary market in which assets are sold for the first time. ➤new issue market. The ➤stock exchange is a secondary market, though it is also a primary market. The term is sometimes wrongly used to refer to *second tier* or ➤unlisted securities market(s).

secondary picketing ➤collective action.

second best, theory of An argument about achieving the best in an imperfect world, that says we may not improve things by trying to emulate some of the conditions of the perfect world. It is an argument used in economics, where one might be able to identify, say, ten conditions that ensure a particular situation is optimal. The theory of the second best says that if, for some reason, one of those ten conditions cannot be satisfied and we are thus short of optimality, then it may not be best for all the other conditions to apply. Quite possibly, the second-best world would be one where none of the ten conditions of perfection are satisfied but that each of them is nearly satisfied. For example, suppose in a simple world with ten different products that the most efficient achievable situation would involve the price of all products being equal to their marginal cost of production. ➤marginal-cost pricing. Suppose that for some reason, one product cannot have its price equal to marginal cost. Should the other nine prices be set to marginal cost? According to the theory of the second best, not necessarily.

second marché (Fr.) Second-tier ➤unlisted securities market in Paris, with regional markets established in February 1983.

second-tier market ➤unlisted securities market(s).

secular trend A long-term movement in the trend of a phenomenon, as distinct from the effects generated by short-term fluctuations of the ➤business cycle or the seasons. Such movements could, for example, be due to slow, long-term changes in affluence or productive technology or globalization.

Securities and Exchange Commission (SEC) (US) Federal agency for the ➤regulation of the markets in ➤securities set up in 1934 to administer the Securities Exchange Acts 1933 and 1934, which require most securities offered for sale to be registered. The SEC regulates the stock exchanges and ➤brokers, including those on the ➤over-the-counter market, investment advisers and others in industry. ➤➤Form 10-K.

securitization The substitution of ➤securities for bank loans, i.e. a bank may, instead of lending to a customer, purchase or accept (➤acceptance) a ➤bill of exchange, a ➤note or other security from them. Alternatively, a would-be borrower – rather than apply to a bank – may issue a bill of exchange, note or other debt instrument to a non-bank purchaser or acceptor. Securitization was, in part, a revival of the capital markets, much impaired by the economic crisis of the 1970s and early 1980s, and in part a development of short-term security forms that give the lender ➤negotiable ➤instruments and enable banks to raise funds more easily. Securitization also relieves banks of reliance on the traditional interest rate differences on deposits and advances, and it enables them, in times of pressure on capital ratios, to avoid balance sheet additions. On a requirement to manage or ➤underwrite the security issues by the banks, a fee-earning opportunity is also opened to the banks. Since many of the securities have been short term, with ➤**floating rates** of interest, investors have been more ready to buy them than fixed-rate bonds, whose return or capital value would have fallen with any rise in general market interest rates. ➤➤**disintermediation; mortgage-backed securities.**

securitized paper The ➤**instrument** resulting from the conversion of a bank loan into a *marketable (negotiable)* ➤**security.** ➤**securitization.**

security 1. A pledge of financial or physical property to be surrendered in the event of failure to repay a loan. **2.** Any medium of investment in the money market or ➤**capital market**, e.g. a money-market instrument, a ➤**bond**, a ➤**share. 3.** A term used to refer only to bonds, and shares, as distinct from ➤**money market assets.**

seed corn capital Sometimes referred to as 'seed capital', it is a minimal amount of money necessary to set up a new business venture. ➤**venture capital.**

segmentation The process of dividing the mass of consumers into distinct groups, with the aim of treating these groups differently. Different products may be targeted at distinct groups, e.g. luxury automobiles for wealthy individuals and sedans for middle-income families. Or different marketing methods can be used to sell products to distinct groups, e.g. magazine advertising to reach new automobile buyers and direct mailings to existing customers to invite them to upgrade their model. It is for the organization to decide whether it develops strategies for all groups (a differentiated full-coverage strategy), a portion of the groups (a multiple segment strategy), or whether to focus its effort on just one group (this might be a niche strategy or a core strategy, but would not be both).

It is assumed that the organization will secure performance gains (i.e. higher profits) by treating these groups differently than if it sold the same products using the same marketing methods to the mass of consumers. Therefore, the idea of segmentation contrasts with mass marketing. The performance gains from a segmented approach are assumed to outweigh any loss of production and distribution economies of scale.

The concept of segmentation has been a cornerstone of ➤**marketing** for over 50 years. Particularly influential was a paper by Wendell Smith ('Product Differentiation and Market Segmentation As Alternative Marketing Strategies', *Journal of Marketing*, 1956). However, many practical and methodological difficulties remain. First, often the purpose of segmentation is not made clear. Analysts might refer to their wish to 'gain insights', but this is a vague and imprecise goal. From a managerial standpoint, the first main purpose ought to be to define groups that can be treated differently in order to achieve performance gains. This means having segmentations that are actionable, not vague.

Three criteria are used to assess whether a segmentation scheme is actionable: (a) differential strategy development; (b) accessibility, and (c) measurability. Differential strategy development means having a segmentation that gives rise to specific products and marketing methods for each of the groups, e.g. differently designed products, at various price points. Accessibility refers to the ability to use the differential strategy, e.g. that the differentially designed products can be brought to the attention of the various groups, using appropriate communications and channels of distribution. In addition, the groups must be measurable – there is a need to know how many consumers are in each, their sales potential, the costs of accessing them and their contribution to profit. This requires thorough ➤marketing research, as well as internal financial assessment.

A second major issue is the choice of which segmentation variable ('base') to use. The most commonly used bases for segmentation come from ➤consumer behaviour studies, including: (a) behavioural variables, e.g. volume/value of purchase, product and media usage, consumer need and benefits sought; (b) demographic variables, e.g. age, gender, marital status, income, purchasing power, education, nationality, ethnicity, culture and social group membership; (c) geographic variables, e.g. urban/rural, administrative area, ethnic region and climatic zone (➤geodemographic segmentation); (d) psychographic variables, e.g. opinions, attitudes, values, beliefs and personality type (➤psychographic segmentation), and (e) lifestyle variables (activities and interests). ➤lifestyle segmentation. The focus of all these bases is consumers (the demand side of marketing). It is also possible to think of bases that are associated with organizational issues (the supply side of marketing). For example, segmenting on the basis of the cost to service different customers – banks and financial institutions have pursued just such a strategy, by having special programmes for highly profitable customers and, at the other end of the spectrum, by demarketing to unprofitable customers. Another example is to segment in terms of the costs of communicating with different customers (for a subscription service, it may be cheaper to send renewal notices to current subscribers than to use sales representatives to talk to new prospects, even though some of the prospects might gain more benefit from the service).

Faced with this choice, it is hard for anyone undertaking segmentation studies to know whether they are using the most appropriate base, and yet generally it is too expensive to test out more than half-a-dozen bases. In practice, the default base has been 'benefits sought'. This has been particularly so since the publication of a formative paper by Russell Haley ('Benefit Segmentation: a decision oriented research tool', *Journal of Marketing*, 1968). It is claimed that consumers do not buy products as such, rather they buy the bundle of benefits that characterizes a product, e.g. the consumer looks for certain levels of safety, reliability, performance, etc. when buying a car. Therefore, it makes sense to segment people in terms of benefits sought (those who want high performance and a set of related benefits are distinguished from those who are unconcerned with performance and the related benefits). Despite its intuitive appeal and popularity, this is not necessarily the most useful base and it is only one among many possibilities.

Third, another difficult issue is the choice of method. Historically, use has been made of fairly simple classification and clustering techniques (notably Ward's method and the k-means algorithm). But over the past two decades, the focus has shifted to formal statistical models, e.g. latent class conjoint analysis. These methods approach the job of segmentation in different ways, giving rise to different segmentations. Moreover, there is no consensus among analysts, although each method has its adherents and detractors. For this reason there is a large subjective element to the process of segmentation, despite all the effort that has been put into refining each of the methods.

A further complicating factor is whether or not there are distinct groups with respect to the base of interest. Most analysts assume that there are small numbers of underlying groups ('natural segments' or 'latent populations'). Individuals within these groups are believed to be similar to one another (homogeneous) and distinct from those outside the group. Hence, the use of statistical techniques that maximize within-group homogeneity, such as cluster analysis and latent class analysis. But it is entirely possible for there to be no latent populations, merely a mass of consumers. Statistically, this mass of consumers might be described by a smooth continuous distribution (e.g. by the Normal distribution) where there are no natural clumps or groupings.

A pragmatic response to these issues is to select bases and methods that improve an organization's performance, regardless of whether they are optimal ('the best') and regardless of whether there are latent populations. In other words, the segmentation may not result in optimal performance, but it should at least improve performance. And, while the grouping of consumers may be artificial, it nevertheless can be thought of as useful for the purpose of designing and targeting marketing strategies. Any organization taking this pragmatic stance needs to double-check that the artificial grouping is indeed useful, not merely fragmenting a market and increasing the costs of doing business. For example, it may be doubted that we really need so many magazine titles and that the proliferation of titles is merely fragmenting subscriptions and advertising revenues.

Fourth, many segmentation schemes relate to ➤**product** category usage rather than ➤**brand** choice. While product category usage may be of interest to analysts, marketing managers are usually more concerned with brand choice in competitive markets (where weakly differentiated brands directly compete with each other). Consider the example of petrol: the market may be segmented into those who buy unleaded petrol and those buying leaded, but the marketing manager will be responsible for a brand – Shell, for example – which has unleaded and replacement leaded variants, just like BP, Esso/Exon, etc. In this instance, segmentation by product category usage is not very useful, whereas brand choice factors are likely to be crucial, e.g. accessibility of the petrol stations and relative prices. The failure to consider brand choice and competitive effects is a severe criticism of many segmentation schemes, including the vast majority of benefit and lifestyle segmentations. For example, a lifestyle segmentation may colourfully describe 'achievers' and 'strugglers' and suggest that golfing equipment should be promoted to achievers, not strugglers, but this tells us nothing about the situation facing brands (more than likely there will be several competing brands of golfing equipment, all targeted at achievers). ➤**lifestyle segmentation.**

This is not an easy problem to solve. An economic approach to it might be to assess ➤**cross-price elasticity of demand** for groups of brands. If a fall in price of one group of brands has no effect on the demand for another group of brands, it is assumed the two groups of brands are in different segments. This, however, may be to place too much emphasis on price. Market researchers, therefore, tend to look at the buying patterns of consumers – whether those who buy one brand also buy another. These buying patterns will reflect the effects of price, but also other aspects of the marketing mix (notably distribution/availability).

Ideas about segmentation are now being challenged by the shift to ➤**one-to-one marketing.** Traditionally, segments have been seen as quite substantial – something less than a mass market, but going beyond a single customer. The costs of tailoring products and marketing methods to a particular group have had to be justified in terms of performance gains, and this has meant groups being of a certain critical size. The logic of one-to-one marketing differs from this. With advances in technology and flexible manufacturing methods (which have reduced costs) it is possible to envisage microsegments and even 'segments' of one. These can be targeted very precisely and offered highly customized products. While this may have been possible in the past (e.g. when servicing highly profitable customers) it is now possible for a much broader spectrum of consumers.

Also, the classic definition of segmentation assumes a controlled coverage strategy. That is, the organization looks at the mass of consumers and places them into a distinct segment, e.g. an automobile manufacturer might place a consumer in the family sedan segment and promotes directly to that consumer. This contrasts with the situation in which consumers self-select their membership of a group (family sedans are offered and some consumers choose to buy them). The spirit behind one-to-one marketing is more interactive than implied by either of these strategies. It suggests organizations and consumers codetermine outcomes.

segment–target–position (STP) **strategy** A marketing strategy that suggests managers should first segment consumers into distinct groups, evaluate the attractiveness of these groups, decide which group or groups to target and then offer differentiated products so the needs of the target group or groups are met. Needs can best be met through the careful positioning (or differentiation) of existing products or the development of (differentiated) new products. This has direct implications for the allocation of marketing resources across an organization's portfolio of products. ➤**differentiation**.

Several key assumptions underlie the STP strategy. It is assumed there are distinct groups of consumers, i.e. 'natural segments' or 'latent populations'. Further, these groups have needs that can be formulated as 'ideal' products, and organizations can come up with products that approximate to these. Finally, in coming up with these products, organizations not only have an offering that is differentiated by segment but is also differentiated from the products of competitors. Unfortunately, these assumptions may not hold true. There may not be distinct groups. ➤**segmentation**. Even where there are distinct groups, or where they have been artificially created, it may be hard for consumers to articulate what an ideal product would look like. ➤**new product development**. If that can be achieved, it may prove unprofitable to offer the product or the window of opportunity during which profits can be derived may be very short lived (because group membership changes, or the needs of consumers change or competitors undermine any initial advantage). Indeed, if there is a major unmet need all competitors are likely to see this and position (or reposition) their products in broadly similar ways. ➤**competitive parity; positioning**.

In the light of these problems, an STP strategy that also takes account of supply-side factors and organizational capabilities stands a better chance of enhancing performance.

self-esteem Individuals' degree of liking or disliking for themselves. ➤**personality traits**.

self-financing ➤retained earnings.

self-regulating organizations ➤Financial Services Act.

selling short ➤short selling.

sell-side ➤investment analyst.

semantic differential scale A seven-point rating scale used by respondents to indicate their evaluation of an object such as a brand, service or organization, and bounded at each end by bipolar adjectives. The bipolar adjectives define opposite ends of a continuum. For example, consumers might be asked to indicate whether they believe a brand 'tastes nice' (at one end of the scale) or 'tastes awful' (at the other end of the scale). Between these bipolar adjectives are a number of intermediate points, allowing respondents to check off more neutral positions. It is common to give the seven-point scale a zero midpoint (+ 3, + 2, + 1, 0, –1, –2, –3), and treat the resultant data as coming from an interval scale (which enables arithmetic means to be reported). However, the scale is, in fact, ordinal and, strictly speaking, only statistics designed for ordinal scales should be used (which allows medians to be reported, but not arithmetic means). Researchers are very divided on this matter, partly because it has major implications for the type of statistical analysis that can be undertaken with these types of data. Semantic differential scales are a form of verbal ➤rating scale, and are widely used to measure ➤attitude, particularly the cognitive component of attitude.

Senge, Peter Author of *The Fifth Discipline* (1990), a bestselling book on the ➤learning organization. ➤organizational learning. The book is about how organizations can achieve success by learning to cope with continuous change. Five disciplines have to be practised: (a) *personal mastery* or self-discipline on the part of all members; (b) *continual challenge* of stereotypical mental models; (c) the creation of a *shared vision*; (d) commitment to *team learning* rather than conflict, and (e) *systems thinking*, which leads to the understanding that information about problems generates action, which has results, which in turn creates new information and problems, often with long delays, in a continuous feedback loop. It is not possible to understand complexity by breaking the whole down into parts: the dynamic system has to be understood as a whole. Senge identifies a number of systems archetypes to illustrate this. For example, a successful group is given more resources at the expense of other, less successful groups, which further diminishes the chances of success of the other groups.

Peter Senge is Director of Systems Thinking and Organizational Learning at the Sloan School of Management, Massachusetts Institute of Technology (MIT). He studied with Jay W Forrester of MIT – who invented random access magnetic-core memory – and was a pioneer in the development of systems dynamics.

senior debt ➤subordinated.

sensitivity analysis A method whereby critical parameters in a model are systematically modified to determine the effects on the solution.

separation of ownership from control The feature of modern corporations, i.e. that their owners do not participate actively in their management. In its earliest form, business was owned and managed by the same people. Economic and technological development led to the advent of the ➤joint-stock company in the seventeenth century to meet the need for larger amounts of capital to be injected. This began the process of the separation of ownership from control that continued with the introduction of ➤limited liability for both ➤incorporation and ➤private

companies, and the gradual emergence of the modern giant corporation in which none of the directors or managers have more than a minority financial interest. This process has given rise to the possibility that the interests of those who control business and those who own it may conflict. ➤**principal agent theory**. The task of overseeing the executives and their stewardship of the shareholders' assets has challenged investors, executives and politicians, all striving for the right balance between applying too much accountability, killing nimble and strong decision-making, and applying too little control, leaving the executives too much freedom to run companies as though they own them. ➤**agency theory; corporate governance**.

serial correlation A ➤correlation coefficient, not between two different variables, but between successive values of one variable. It creates a potential problem in ➤**regression analysis**, in particular in ➤**least squares regression**, when the residual of the regression (i.e. the difference between the actual observed values of the ➤**dependent variable** and the predicted values from the regression) is itself serially-correlated, e.g. it appears to behave in a systematic pattern over time. That is because the regression methods most commonly adopted assume that the residual is random for some of their desirable properties. Autocorrelations, or serial correlation, can be measured by a Durbin–Watson statistic (a value of 2 implies the absence of the problem). If it does exist, it can sometimes be solved by transforming the data used from absolute levels of different variables for each period, into the change in the value of the variables between periods.

service encounter The specific time and place where customers meet and interact with service personnel and sales staff. These encounters are experiential in character, i.e. customers experience an interaction and this gives rise to various feelings about the service, the service personnel, the place and also the customer's own frame of mind. The customer's frame of mind describes *a feeling state* (or *affect*). This in turn encompasses both *mood* (temporary feelings that are independent of the service encounter) and *emotion* (intense feelings prompted by aspects of the service encounter). For example, a customer may be in a negative mood on entering a post office, and then, because of the length of the queue, become frustrated and angry (emotions). These feeling states have a direct bearing on customer behaviour, e.g. whether a customer becomes argumentative with service personnel or complains to other customers. These encounters are experiential for service personnel, too. Thus, if an employee is in a negative mood, this might influence the way he deals with customers (as evident in the employee's tone of voice, friendliness, mannerisms, levels of stress, etc.). Feeling states have a significant impact on overall levels of ➤**customer satisfaction/dissatisfaction**, and often attempts are made to manage and control them in service encounters. ➤**critical incidents**.

service level agreement (SLA) A formal agreement to establish internal customer relations. Some organizations formalize the internal customer concept by requiring different parts of the operations to agree SLAs. These establish the dimensions of service and the relationship between two or more parts of an organization. They are useful in establishing boundaries of responsibility, especially if there have been internal management difficulties in the past.

servicescape The physical layout of a service facility, ambience, background music and comfort. The design of these elements can affect a customer's impressions of, and satisfaction with, the service. Careful management of these elements can help to reduce ➤**perceived risk**, especially risk arising from the ➤**experience qualities** or ➤**credence qualities** of the service.

services marketing The marketing of professional services, banking and financial services, telecommunications, restaurants and hotels, airlines and other forms of transportation, etc. Typically distinguished from goods marketing because of a focus on: (a) the intangibility of services; (b) their heterogeneity (i.e. one service encounter differs from another); (c) the perishability of the output (making services time- and place-specific), and (d) simultaneity of production and consumption, i.e. production and consumption are inseparable. This gives rise to several distinguishing features, e.g. people (service personnel) are central to service performance, customers often are actively involved in helping to create the service, consistent quality control is harder to achieve than with goods, it can be harder for customers to evaluate service performance, inventories tend to be absent and many services are delivered in real time. In practice, a continuum exists from pure services that are dominated by intangibles and high levels of contact between customers and staff (such as professional services) through to pure goods (➤**commodities**) that are tangible in character, e.g. the purchasing of salt, oil and cocoa. In some sectors there has been a tendency to industrialize services by giving them more tangible features by taking advantage of developments in information technology, e.g. in banking, the introduction of automated teller machines and telephone and web-based services. Management of services requires attention to be paid to the ➤**service encounter**, ➤**servicescape** and ➤**critical incidents**. To do this effectively, the services manager has to work with marketing, operations and human resources. ➤➤**knowledge economy**.

SERVQUAL A popular service quality research questionnaire. The questionnaire is used to measure five broad dimensions of service quality: (a) tangibles (appearance of physical elements such as layout of facilities, appearance of staff and newness of equipment); (b) reliability (dependable, accurate performance by staff and the organization); (c) responsiveness (promptness and helpfulness of the organization and its staff); (d) assurance (competence, courtesy and credibility of the staff, and security of the facilities), and (e) empathy (easy access to staff, good communications and customer understanding). For each item in the survey, respondents are asked to rate on a seven-point 'strongly agree – strongly disagree' scale their initial expectations and their assessment of actual performance. Where performance ratings are lower than expectations, quality is deemed to be poor, while the reverse indicates good service quality. SERVQUAL was originally proposed by V A Zeithaml, A Parasuraman and L L Berry (*Delivering Quality Service: balancing customer perceptions and expectations*, 1990).

SETS ➤London Stock Exchange.

settlement 1. Payment of an obligation, e.g. payment in cash for ➤**securities**. Hence, ➤**account day** on the ➤**London Stock Exchange** is also known as settlement day or the settlement date. **2.** The transfer or intended transfer of property after a legal agreement or on the ➤**execution** of a will after death.

set-up time The time taken to change over the production process from one to another. In some manufacturing operations, this time is a significant element of the total manufacturing time for ➤batch production. For example, consider the time it takes to change the wheel on a car; if this has to be undertaken many times during the day it would be essential that the set-up time was kept to a minimum.

seven S framework A framework for analysing the core determinants of the performance of an enterprise. It was developed by the ➤McKinsey management consultancy and has been extensively used for auditing the strategic and operational configurations of organizations. It is essentially a checklist with each element beginning with the letter S to aid memory. It is argued that these seven areas are key components of any organization. These are:

(1) Strategy. How the organization allocates its resources to achieve its aims. Crucial here is the interface between strategy formulation and its implementation.
(2) Structure. Organization structure, level of centralization, authority and responsibility arrangements. The relationship between strategy and structure.
(3) Systems. The organization's ➤management information systems, budgetary and other control mechanisms. Internal communications. Efficiency and cost-effectiveness of operations.
(4) Style. Leadership style, type of supervision, level of autonomy, etc.
(5) Staff. Human resource programmes, e.g. induction, recruitment, training, etc. Promotion systems and calibre of staff.
(6) Skills. The capabilities of the enterprise in all areas.
(7) Shared values. Morale of the workforce and group cohesiveness.

SGML An acronym for Standardized General Mark-up Language. This is a standard for the exchanging of sophisticated information (in the form of documents) between computer applications and platforms. ➤Hypertext; Multimedia.

shadow price The ➤opportunity cost to society or company of engaging in some activity, where the price actually charged for the activity cost does not reflect the burden it creates. For example, you might imagine that if petrol were rationed and the price kept low, then the true cost of using petrol would be higher than just the price spent on it because, quite apart from the amount spent on the petrol, would be the fact that the ration was depleted and other opportunities for using petrol forgone. In this example, a shadow price would be the amount you would be willing to pay for extra petrol were the ration to be increased by a small amount. Or suppose there is unemployed labour in the economy: the cost of using that labour to society is virtually zero; by employing it no sacrifice is made in terms of other goods produced. The shadow price of labour is zero, even though the workers, if employed, would have to be paid a wage. Alternatively, suppose there is excess demand for labour and at the going wage rate, labour is in short supply. In this case, employing a worker may cost a firm only the going wage, but the cost to society of that firm employing that worker is the production the worker could have produced in an alternative occupation; this will be worth more than the wage rate if labour is scarce. The shadow price of labour in this case is higher than the wage rate. In effect, it reflects the benefit that would result from relaxing the constrained supply of workers by one unit.

More generally, shadow prices are used in valuing any item which is implicitly rationed or constrained in some way. Shadow prices can be derived using linear programming techniques and used in social ➤cost–benefit analysis.

share One of a number of equal portions in the nominal ➤**capital** of a company, entitling the owner to a proportion of distributed profits and of residual value if the company goes into liquidation; a form of ➤**security**. Shares may be fully or partly paid (➤**paid-up capital**), ➤**voting shares** or non-voting (sometimes called ➤'**A**' shares). ⤜**ordinary share; preference share; separation of ownership from control; shareholder value; stock.**

share certificate A document issued by the ➤**registrar** or his agent confirming legal title to the ownership of a stated number of ➤**equity** ➤**shares**. ➤**CREST**.

shareholders' equity *Shareholders' funds.* The total assets of a company minus its external liabilities, i.e. except those to ➤**equity** shareholders. Put another way, the ➤**balance sheet** will show shareholders' equity as ➤**paid-up capital**, ➤**revaluation reserve** and *undistributed profits.* ➤**retained earnings;** ⤜**net asset.**

shareholder value The economic returns generated by a firm for its shareholders. A popular term associated with the concentration by companies on their core activities and the disposal of unwanted subsidiaries. Shareholder value is created when companies invest in activities that yield a return in excess of the cost of capital (➤**capital, cost of**) or dispose of activities that earn less than that. Rapaport has controversially argued that the purpose of a business is essentially to increase the wealth of its owners, i.e. its shareholders. Such a view dismisses the roles of other ➤**stakeholders** of the firm. ➤**business ethics.**

share index An index number indicating changes in the average prices of shares on the stock exchange. The indices are constructed by taking a selection of shares and (usually) weighting the percentage changes in prices together as an indication of aggregate movements in share prices. Roughly speaking, a share index shows percentage changes in the market prices of a ➤**portfolio** compared with its value in the base year of the index. ⤜**Dow-Jones index; Financial Times** *share indices;* **Standard and Poor's Ratings.**

share of category requirements (SCR) ➤buyer behaviour.

share premium Where shares are sold at a premium to their ➤**face value**. The excess proceeds of sales of its own shares by a company at a premium are credited to a share premium account and shown as such in the balance sheet as part of the permanent capital of the business. The share premium account may not be used to pay dividends (though it may be used for a ➤**bonus issue**).

share register ➤registrar.

Sharpe ratio A measure of the extra reward that is given to risky assets in financial markets. It is the ratio of the average 'excess' return made by an asset (over the ➤**risk-free rate of return**) over a number of periods, to the standard deviation of those returns over those periods. Higher excess return implies higher reward; higher standard deviation implies higher risk. A high Sharpe ratio implies high reward given the risk absorbed. W F Sharpe, after whom the ratio is named, is one of the original inventors of the ➤**capital asset pricing model**, which attempts to predict the prices of assets given a particular notion of their risk.

shelf registration (US) The allowance that, since 1983, larger companies may register advance details of securities with the ➤**Securities and Exchange Com-**

mission (SEC) without any date of issue, so that when they need to raise capital they make an issue 'off the shelf' without the delay involved in waiting for clearance of an application to the SEC.

short selling Selling assets without actually owning them. It is a trading strategy for those who believe the price of the asset will fall; hence, by the time they have to deliver the asset, it will be possible to buy it at cheaper price than that at which it has just been sold. It is a particularly popular strategy of ➤**hedge funds** which can typically borrow the asset in question, sell it and then buy it again to repay the lender. ➤**position.**

short squeeze ➤bear squeeze.

sight deposit A bank ➤deposit, all or part of which may be withdrawn without notice, i.e. on sight. US = *demand deposit.* ➤**current** account.

signalling The use of a mechanism by which someone indicates to someone else that they have certain characteristics, even though these characteristics are not directly observable. A signal is the converse of a screen (➤**screening**). Advertising is seen as signalling the quality of a product to consumers because it is only those firms who have faith in their product, and who think it will be in production for many years, who will find it worth engaging in expensive advertising. The engagement ring is a signal of commitment to the fiancé for, as long as it is expensive enough, it would not pay the man to buy the ring unless he was serious about getting married. Economists have been increasingly inclined to explain economic and non-economic phenomena as signals.

Simon, Herbert A Nobel prizewinner who has made important contributions to the theory of managerial decision-taking. For Simon, all managerial action comes down to making decisions. In the economic theory of the firm, the basic assumption is of a rational 'economic man' maximizing revenues and minimizing costs. In reality, business decisions are taken in uncertainty and ignorance. Simon developed a theory of administrative man in which decision-takers 'satisfice' (➤**satisficing**), i.e. seek out actions which are good enough to deal with known circumstances without attempting exhaustive analysis. He called this 'bounded rationality'. Individuals modify their behaviour continually in the light of experience. Some decisions can be programmed, i.e. subjected to computerized mathematical analysis.

Professor Simon is a graduate of the University of Chicago and has held posts at the University of California, Illinois Institute of Technology and the Carnegie Mellon University. He was awarded the Nobel prize in economics in 1978. His books include *The New Science of Management Decisions* (1960), *Models of Discovery* (1977) and *Models of Bounded Rationality and Other Topics in Economics* (1982).

simulation The practice of using data and a ➤**model** to represent the behaviour of the real world. Simulation is a substitute for experimentation in real life, where such experimentation is impractical or costly. In judging the efficacy of traffic systems, for example – rather than just trying various schemes to see what happens – it pays to have a model of traffic flows and to simulate the effect of different road schemes to gauge which is likely to work best. In judging how many counters to keep open at different times of day, a supermarket manager might find simulation usefully lets him estimate the length of queues that would result from different decisions. The increasing power of computers has made simulation an easier and more frequently adopted management technique. Good simulation requires a good model, a clear question to be answered, a set of practices to be simulated and some data to mimic the occurrences the real world might throw at the situation being modelled. The data may be drawn from historical experience or random generation. ➤business simulation; Monte Carlo method.

simultaneous engineering ➤concurrent engineering.

single capacity A term used to describe a situation where a ➤market maker on a stock exchange deals only with other professionals and not with the investors. ➤dual capacity.

single market 1. The name given to the objective of the European Union's (EU's) 1985 initiative to foster free trade in goods, services and capital within the EU, culminating in the Single European Act 1986. The idea was to limit the degree to which technical, fiscal and physical barriers limit the flow of commodities across borders. The initiative aimed to create a single market by 1 January 1993; in reality, the programme consisted of specific measures that did have the effect of reducing ➤barriers to trade but could not abolish them; some natural barriers, such as differences in national tastes, will obviously remain. In this regard, the term 'single market' is not used in its strict economic sense. **2.** A trading zone in which roughly homogeneous items are traded in roughly uniform conditions of supply and demand. It is likely that in a single market the law of one price (➤one price, law of) will prevail.

sinking fund Provision for the repayment of debt, including the ➤redemption of a ➤security by the issuer, by accumulating a fund through regular payments that, with interest, will *amortize* the loan.

situational leadership theory A contingency theory of leadership that focuses on the readiness and maturity of followers. In essence, it says 'leaders are as good as their followers'. At an early stage of readiness (R1), employees are both unable and unwilling to take responsibility and they are unlikely to be capable or confident. Employees may then go through two intermediate phases: unable and willing (R2) and able and unwilling (R3). At a later stage (R4), employees are both able and willing to do what is asked of them. In the R3 case, a 'telling' style is appropriate, whereas in the R4 case an appropriate style would be 'delegating'. Developed by Hersey and Blanchard in 1974 and widely used in large corporations and the US military.

SKU ➤stock-keeping unit.

skunk work A term describing a covert research project undertaken within an industrial organization. Technology-intensive companies recognize that if they are to attract and retain the best scientists they have to offer ➤scientific freedom. Moreover, experience has shown that scientists will undertake covertly these projects if autonomy is not provided. There are many examples of exciting technology and successful products that were initiated by scientists operating in a covert manner. In the US, such research projects are referred to as 'skunkworks'.

The name 'Skunk Works' can be traced back to the US aircraft manufacturer

Lockheed. The name was originally used by Al Capp's 'Li'l Abner' comic strip which featured the 'Skonk Works' (later to be called 'skunk') where Appalachian hillbillies ground up skunks, old shoes and other foul-smelling ingredients to brew fearsome drinks and other products. Lockheed engineers identified the secret jet aircraft assembly facility as the place where Clarence Johnson was stirring up some kind of 'potent brew'. The Skunk Works was created by Clarence Johnson to design and develop the F-80C Shooting Star, America's first production jet aircraft. The nickname stuck, although 'skonk' became 'skunk' in deference to the non-hillbillies working at the Lockheed facility and because Al Capp objected to anyone else using his unique spelling. Cartoonist Capp and the 'Li'l Abner' comic strip departed many years ago, but Skunk Works is now a registered service mark of Lockheed, along with the familiar skunk logo (Lockheed Martin Corporation, 1998).

sleeping partner A person who contributes to the financing of a business partnership but who takes no active role in the firm and can therefore arrange to have limited liability status.

Sloan, Alfred P (died 1966) Author of *My Years with General Motors* (1963), which describes how General Motors (GM), a sick holding company of acquired car firms in the early 1920s, was transformed into the world's largest automotive company. Sloan became president of the company in 1923 and, learning from the experience of Pierre Du Pont who, as the largest shareholder had brought Sloan in from one of GM's subsidiaries to save the business, adopted a new structure. Autonomous divisions for automobile lines and components were created, each with their own design, production and sales functions and controlled by a small central policy and finance staff. It will be noted that Sloan did not invent the federally decentralized structure (which Du Pont had used before GM and indeed which was, and is, essentially the decentralized structure of the Roman Catholic Church), nor did he decentralize GM; in fact, he introduced more standardization and centralization into the holding company. Although long, Sloan's book (on which he had the help of a writer from *Fortune* magazine) is readable enough but now largely of historical interest. Peter ➤Drucker, who helped to popularize Sloan's notions in his own book *Concept of the Corporation*, which appeared a decade and a half before Sloan's, later recognized that the federal structure no longer met current needs and realities. GM was a one-product, one-country manufacturing company – very different from the multi-technology, multiproduct multinational companies that emerged after the 1950s.

slotting allowance A form of trade promotion where the manufacturer pays a retailer to feature the product in a distinctive way in store (e.g. in a supermarket), by placing the product at eye level, featuring it at the end of an aisle, or giving it more shelf space.

small business investment company (SBIC) (US) A company set up with low-cost funds and taxation advantages from the US federal government to invest in small businesses, authorized under the Small Business Investment Act 1958. Elsewhere ➤venture capital companies and ➤investment trusts or their investors may be eligible for tax incentives. ➤➤business investment; venture capital trust.

small cap stock (US) Shares in smaller ➤quoted companies which have a low market capitalization compared with ➤blue chip issues and mid-cap stocks. There are no generally agreed definitions, but small caps have capitalization of around $250 million or less, and big caps $2 billion or so. The attraction of small cap stocks to some investors is that they have in aggregate tended in some periods to outperform big caps, despite being not fully researched and individually risky.

smart card A plastic card incorporating a microchip. Invented in France, where it is called a *carte à mémoire*; a smart card can be used as plastic money, a credit facility being drawn down as it is used and recharged by the issuing bank or store, or used at automatic teller machines (cash dispensers). ➤**credit card.**

SMI (Swiss Market Index) An index designed to reflect movements in the share prices of twenty-one companies traded on the Swiss stock exchange (*Schweizer Borse*). It was given a base value of 1500 in June 1988.

social judgement theory ➤involvement theory.

société anonyme (*SA*) (Fr.) Public limited company. ➤**incorporation.** Also in some non French-speaking countries, e.g. Greece.

société à responsabilité limitée (*SaRL*) (Fr.) Private limited company. ➤**incorporation.**

sociodemographic segmentation The grouping of individuals by certain concrete personal characteristics, e.g. age, sex/gender, income, marital status, family size, ethnicity, nationality, language group, highest educational achievement, etc. These are measured routinely in both national censuses and commercial market research studies, and are widely used as bases of ➤**segmentation.** Other bases of segmentation tend to be less routinely measured and/or harder to measure, e.g. psychological characteristics, customer profitability.

soft loan A loan made at below market rates of interest.

sole proprietorship An ➤**unincorporated business** owned by a single person and not benefiting from limited liability. ➤**incorporation.**

solvency The ability to pay one's debts in full on the due date.

solvent A condition in which total assets exceed total liabilities.

sources and uses of funds (UK) Statements of flow of funds within a company during a period. Now a required element in the published financial accounts for all but the smallest companies, alongside the ➤**balance sheet** and the ➤**profit and loss account.** Also known as sources and applications (or disposition) of funds and, in the US, as a statement of *changes in financial position*. There are various forms of flow of funds statements, but typically they show all the capital flows of a business between balance sheet dates. *Sources of funds* are profits from trading operations, ➤**depreciation** provisions, sales of assets and borrowing including equity and other capital issues. *Uses of funds* are purchases of fixed or financial assets, cash and distribution of income.

sovereign risk The hazard that political risk may arise in a country, threatening overseas investments or trading.

spatial interaction model ➤gravity model.

special drawing right (SDR) A form of international ➤reserve ➤currency created by the ➤International Monetary Fund. The SDR is a weighted average of the five leading currencies according to their share in world trade.

specialist (US) A member of the ➤New York Stock Exchange who makes a market in a number of stocks by buying and selling on his own account and for commission brokers. ➤➤order driven. The role of specialists is similar to that of jobbers under the system that operated on the ➤London Stock Exchange before the ➤Big Bang. A specialist operates from a *trading post*, a location on the trading floor where particular securities are bought and sold.

speculative bubble A deviation between the price of an ➤asset in the market and the price justified by its inherent value sustained by a belief on the part of buyers that they will be able to sell at an inflated price. The interesting thing about a bubble is that as long as everyone believes in it, the bubble need not burst. The price can almost indefinitely deviate from fundamental value. Indeed, money is almost by definition an asset with a bubble-type characteristic, i.e. its value in exchange deviates from its inherent value. Unfortunately, for other assets, the people holding the asset when it does burst – or revert to fundamental value – sustain a large loss equivalent to the difference between the asset's inflated price and the actual value. They can be likened to ➤pyramid investment schemes because bubbles can carry on growing, and making profits for speculators, as long as there is a willing queue of new buyers. While some have suggested they are a sign of irrationality in the financial markets – creating more variability in the price of assets than is merited by fundamental swings in values – attempts have been made to account for them as rational phenomena.

split capital investment trust An ➤investment trust with two categories of investment; either: (a) dividends from the shares held by the trust, or (b) the capital growth from the shares. This allows different types of investor to choose which form of return to make.

sponsor ➤issuing house.

spot Immediate or now, as in a spot market which deals in the trading of assets for imminent delivery.

spot price The present value of an asset, as opposed to ➤forward, ➤futures or ➤option prices. It is applied to dealings in currencies, securities and commodities, and synonymous for the latter with *cash*, *physical* or *actual* prices.

spread 1. The difference between the interest rate charged by a bank or banks on a loan and that paid by them for their funds. Most used in connection with syndicated international credits and Euromarket loans. The bank's funding rate is normally assumed to be a reference rate, such as ➤London interbank offered rate or *London interbank bid rate*. **2.** The difference between the selling price asked by dealers in foreign exchange or securities and the price at which they have bought them. **3.** The difference between the price at which an underwriter buys securities from an insurer and the price at which they sell them to the general public. **4.** The distribution of risks taken on by an insurer. **5.** The sale of a contract in the commodity, ➤options or ➤financial futures market, and the purchase at the same time of a contract for a different item – or of a contract with different terms for the same item – the object being to achieve a profit on the movement in prices between the contracts. ➤**straddle. 6.** The difference between the ➤**bid price** and ➤**offer price** of units in a ➤**unit trust**.

SRO Self-regulating organization. ➤**Financial Services Act.**

SSAP Statement of Standard Accounting Practice. ➤**accounting standards.**

stag A speculator who subscribes to new share issues, in the expectation that they will rise to a quick premium over their issue price, so that they will be able to sell their allotment at a profit when dealings in them begin. Some people make multiple applications where there is a likelihood that the issue will be oversubscribed and a ballot or scaling down is expected, though multiple applications may be proscribed and illegal.

stagflation An economic environment in which ➤**unemployment** and ➤**inflation** coexist. In the early postwar era, it was believed that stagflation would never occur. Either there would be an inflation or a deflation, with rising prices or unemployment, respectively, but never the two together. That analysis was based on the premise that inflation is typically a problem of excess demand in the economy (too much spending, making it easy for companies to raise prices without suffering), and that unemployment was a problem of too little demand (meaning companies do not need to hire workers). You could not simultaneously have both too much and too little spending. But in the 1970s the problem of stagflation emerged. While that seemed like a mystery, it can be explained in two ways: (a) not all unemployment is caused by deficient spending and can be caused by structural problems, e.g. there may be jobs in the south of England, but unemployed workers in the north, and (b) if inflation takes off, expectations of price rises get built into people's behaviour and inflation can be self-fuelling. If everybody expects prices to rise by 10 per cent next year and acts to put 10 per cent on to wage demands and prices accordingly, then a neutral level of demand in the economy will be consistent with 10 per cent inflation. Getting inflation from 10 per cent to 2 per cent would require deficient demand to hammer out built-in inflationary expectations. ➤**output gap.**

stakeholder People or groups of people with a vested interest in the behaviour of a company. Examples of stakeholders are: employees, customers, shareholders, government, suppliers, etc. They may or may not hold formal authority, but usually they will have invested something in the organization, whether it be time, finance or other resources. Accordingly, every stakeholder will expect a reward from the enterprise and will wish to influence the decision-making within the organization. For example, customers will want lower prices, suppliers will want prompt payment of invoices, employees will want higher wages and shareholders will want a return from their investment of capital. The task facing the managers of an organization is to try and meet the expectations of all the stakeholders. They need to establish good relations with each group and try to represent each party. Some stakeholders are far more powerful than others and managers recognize this and will devote their energies accordingly. ➤**shareholder value.**

stamp duty A form of taxation that involves, or used to involve, the fixing of prepaid stamps on legal or commercial documents. Stamp duty is levied on share transactions in the UK and on the transfer of real property.

Standard and Poor's 500 (STP 500) (US) A share index measuring price changes in five hundred securities quoted on the ➤New York Stock Exchange; four hundred company stocks, forty financial, twenty transportation and forty public utility issues are included, each weighted in accordance with the number of stocks at issue.

Standard and Poor's 500 Rating (US) A classification of preferred stocks (➤preference shares), ➤bonds and ➤ordinary shares according to risk. 'AAA' represents the highest-quality investment grade, in which the risk of default is minimal; 'BBB' is medium grade, and 'Bb' predominantly speculative; 'C' is the lowest quality of bond, paying no interest, and 'DDD' in default or in arrears; 'D' is of questionable value. A similar service is provided by Moody's Investor Services, a subsidiary of Dun & Bradstreet.

standard costing ➤management accounting.

start-up A new independent business venture.

start-up company A new or recently formed company.

stated preference method ➤choice modelling.

Statement of Standard Accounting Practice ➤accounting standards.

statistical process control (SPC) The use of statistics to check and monitor a product during its production. It is used extensively in ➤mass production operations. Samples (➤work sampling) of products produced over time are taken and compared to control charts to see if the process is performing as it should. If the process seems to be moving out of tolerance levels or out of control, steps can be taken to bring it back within tolerance before there is a serious problem or faulty products are produced. SPC is an essential element within ➤quality management and ➤total quality management.

stock **1.** A particular type of security, usually quoted in units of £100 value rather than in units or proportion of total ➤capital, as in shares. Stock, or stocks, and shares have now become synonymous, and the original distinction between stocks and shares has become blurred. The term 'stock' in UK usage is now coming to mean exclusively a fixed-interest security (e.g. loan stock) but in the US, fixed-interest securities are referred to as ➤bonds, while other securities are called 'stocks' as in ➤ordinary shares. **2.** An accumulation of capital. **3.** An accumulation of a commodity or of finished or semi-finished goods or materials. ➤inventory.

stockbroker A member of a ➤stock exchange who buys and sells ➤securities as an ➤agent for clients in return for a commission (US = *commission broker*). ➤➤broker; floor broker; market maker.

stock dividend ➤bonus issue.

stock exchange A market in which ➤securities are bought and sold. There are stock exchanges in most capital cities, as well as in the large provincial cities in many countries. The ➤New York Stock Exchange (NYSE), ➤London Stock Exchange and ➤Tokyo Stock Exchange (TSE) are the largest in terms of ➤market capitalization and ➤**turnover,** although London lists the securities of more companies, particularly overseas companies, than either the TSE or the NYSE. ➤➤**German stock exchange; Paris** *Bourse.*

Continental European exchanges are often referred to as *bourses* (Fr.). Stock exchanges facilitate savings and investment by making it possible for investors to dispose of securities quickly if they wish to do so (in the ➤**secondary market**) and for companies, governments and other organizations to raise new capital in the primary market. ➤**new issue market.** Ready marketability requires that: (a) new issues should be made and backed by reputable borrowers or institutions; (b) information should be available on existing securities; (c) competition should exist among ➤**market makers,** and (d) there should be adequate ➤**liquidity.** There should be both a legal framework and market rules to prevent fraud and sharp practice. There are various trading systems on stock exchanges (➤**order driven; quote driven**), but many ➤**trading floors** have given way to automated screen trading and telephone markets. These new technologies and deregulation have permitted the consolidation and mergers of stock exchanges (➤**Euronext**) and the development of new systems for trading securities outside stock exchanges. ➤➤**unlisted securities markets.**

Stock Exchange Automated Quotation system (SEAQ) (UK) A screen-based quotation system for securities that allows ➤**market makers** on the ➤**London Stock Exchange** to report their price quotes and trading volumes to users of the system. SEAQ was introduced in preparation for the ➤**Big Bang** and has allowed all transactions on the exchange to be carried out by telephone rather than as formerly on the trading floor. ➤➤**normal market size.**

Stock Exchange Daily Official List (UK) ➤official list.

Stock Exchange Trading System ➤London Stock Exchange.

stockholding costs The overheads resulting from the stock levels held by a firm. These include:
(1) Warehouse rental and insurance costs.
(2) Energy costs.
(3) Manpower costs.
(4) Interest charges on money tied up in the stock.
Stock levels can be minimized using a ➤**just-in-time** system of managing stocks. For example, many firms develop very close working relationships with suppliers, especially when that relationship has existed for many years. This is not, however, a joint venture.

stock index futures ➤Futures contracts based on ➤share indices.

stock-keeping unit (SKU) An individual item or line in a retail outlet. SKUs are specified at the sub-brand level, therefore there are likely to be many SKUs for each ➤**brand,** reflecting different varieties, flavours, pack sizes, etc. ➤**line extensions.** They have an important role to play in stock and inventory control for producers, wholesalers and retailers. They are not expressly known to consumers – unlike brands – although it has been suggested people may be as loyal to particular SKUs as brands (the consumer always chooses 330 ml cans, although the brand may be Coca-Cola, Pepsi-Cola or Tango). ➤**UPC.**

stock market ➤stock exchange.

stock split (US) A ➤bonus issue of shares that reduces the unit quoted price but not the ➤yield or market value of the investor's holding.

stop-loss **1.** The price at which a security is automatically sold to protect the investor against further loss. **2.** Insurance against losses on the Lloyd's market. ➤➤insurance.

stop order ➤order.

store image The holistic impression that people have of a single store or, more often, of a retail chain, often expressed in relative terms ('store A has a better image than store B'). This overall impression will reflect the way people perceive the store, their attitudes to, and any behaviour they exhibit towards, it, e.g. patronage, shareholding, etc. Store image is allied to the similar concepts of ➤brand image and ➤corporate image. A challenge in managing store image is how to ensure consistency across what may be quite a diverse range of individual retail outlets (varying in size, product assortment, physical structure, age of construction and markets served).

storming ➤group development.

storyboard Art and graphical work that displays a television commercial as a sequence of images, like a cartoon strip.

STP strategy ➤segment–target–position strategy.

straddle Used interchangeably in the ➤commodities, ➤options and ➤financial futures markets with the term ➤spread. A straddle often signifies the simultaneous sale and purchase of ➤call options and ➤put options or of different terms in the same financial futures or commodity market. ➤equity pair trade.

strategic alliance An agreement between two or more partners to share knowledge or resources, which could be beneficial to all parties involved. The term is used to cover a wide range of co-operative arrangements. Furthermore, alliances can range from a simple handshake agreement to mergers, from licensing to equity joint ventures. They can involve a customer, a supplier or even a competitor. There are three generic types of strategic alliance:
(1) Joint venture. A joint venture is usually a separate entity, with the partners to the alliance normally being equity shareholders. With a joint venture, the costs and possible benefits from a ➤research and development (R & D) research project would be shared. They usually are established for a specific project and will cease on its completion. The intention of establishing a joint venture is generally to enable the organization to 'stand alone'.
(2) Collaboration (non-joint ventures). The absence of a legal entity means such arrangements tend to be more flexible. This provides for the opportunity to extend the co-operation over time if so desired. For example, many manufacturing firms are increasingly entering into long-term relationships with their component suppliers. Often such agreements are for a fixed term (e.g. 5 years) with the option of renewal thereafter. British Aerospace adopt this approach when negotiating component suppliers for its aircraft.

351

(3) Consortia. A consortium describes the situation in which a number of partners come together to undertake what is often a large-scale activity.

Faced with new levels of competition, many companies, including competitors, are sharing their resources and expertise to develop new products, achieve economies of scale, and gain access to new technology and markets. Many have argued that these strategic alliances form the competitive weapon of the twenty-first century. One of the major factors that prevents many firms from achieving their technical objectives and, therefore, their strategic objectives is the lack of resources. For technology and R & D, the insufficient resources are usually capital and technical 'critical mass'. The costs of building and sustaining the necessary technical expertise and specialized equipment are rising dramatically. Even for the largest corporations, leadership in some market segments they have traditionally dominated cannot be maintained because they lack sufficient technical capabilities to adapt to fast-paced market dynamics.

In the past, strategic alliances were perceived as options reserved only for large international firms. Intensified competition, shortening product life-cycles and soaring R & D costs mean that strategic alliances are attractive strategies for the future. Many argue that strategic alliances provide an opportunity for large *and* small high-technology companies to expand into new markets by sharing skills and resources. They argue it is beneficial for both parties, since it allows large firms to access the subset of expertise and resources they desire in the smaller firm, while the smaller company is given access to its larger partner's massive capital and organizational resources.

Technology partnerships between, and in some cases among, organizations are becoming more important and prevalent. From 1976 to 1987, the annual number of new joint ventures rose sixfold; by 1987, three-quarters of these were in high-technology industries. As the costs, including risk associated with R & D efforts, continue to increase, no company can remain a 'technology island' and stay competitive.

Businesses are beginning slowly to broaden their views of their business environments, from the traditional go-it-alone perspective of individual firms competing against each other. The formation of strategic alliances means that strategic power often resides in sets of firms acting together. For example, the success of the European Airbus strategic alliance has been phenomenal. Formed in 1969 as a joint venture between the German firm MBB and the French firm Aerospatiale, it was later joined by CASA of Spain and British Aerospace of the UK. The Airbus A300 range of civilian aircraft has achieved great success in the 1990s securing large orders for aircraft, ahead of its major rival Boeing.

strategic asset allocation The choice by investors of the broad categories into which they will put their money, and in what proportions. The classic portfolio choice is between shares (equities), bonds, cash and one or two other classes, e.g. venture capital investments or property. Strategic asset allocation does not involve any decision-making at the level of the particular share or particular property. In general, the key factor in strategic asset allocation is the risk-preference of the investing institution. More risky portfolios, or those that have more time to hold assets without needing to take cash out, tend to be more geared towards shares.

strategic business unit (SBU) An organizational unit within a company. The

Strategic Planning Unit suggests the following three guidelines for defining an SBU: (a) less than 60 per cent of each unit's expenses should be arbitrarily allocated joint costs; (b) less than 60 per cent of the revenues should come from captive markets within the same company, and (c) if a unit sells its products in more than one market, it must be treated separately unless it is similar in terms of competitors, growth rates and market share. Inevitably, there is some arbitrariness about the way SBUs are defined, e.g. it depends partly on how narrowly the market is defined. ➤market definition. ➤➤Profit Impact of Market Strategy.

SBUs are features of large organizations who need, somehow, to maximize their effectiveness across a range of activities and markets. Typically, they are embedded within multifunctional and multidivisional organizational structures, which are likely to be complex. As a concept, therefore, SBUs are attractive because they allow for diversification and flexibility within the complex overall structure. They can be changed and new ones formed. They can cross divisions and functional areas. And, importantly, they allow for business benchmarking and analysis.

strategic fit The relationship between business strategy and organizational structure. For an organization to be economically effective, there needs to be a matching process between the organization's strategy and its structure. Organizations need to adopt an internally consistent set of practices in order to undertake the proposed strategy effectively. This usually involves more than just structure and covers things such as information systems, recruitment and training.

strategic management The totality of management decisions that determine the purpose and direction of the firm. It involves ➤strategic planning and eventually implementation. The selected strategy will determine its *raison d'être*, the direction, its goals and the activities it pursues to achieve its objectives. The strategies adopted will establish the internal character of the organization, how it relates to the external environment, the range of products and services, and the markets in which it operates. There is much confusion in the strategic management literature concerning vocabulary, in particular, for example, 'plans', 'policies', 'objectives' and 'aims' are often interchanged. The key point here is that any strategy should consist of a series of actions to enable the firm to compete.

Organizations are groupings of people and resources created for the purpose to produce a product, provide a service or a mixture of the two. It is complex because a lot of information needs to be considered in order to understand the organization and the situation it finds itself in and take the necessary action. There are not only the interests of the firm to consider (e.g. profits) but also outside interests from ➤stakeholders, e.g. government and customers and suppliers. However, the leaders of the organization are responsible for its sense of purpose and overall direction. This would normally be the directors. In small businesses, this will mean the livelihoods of the owners and their families; in larger organizations it will be the financial investments made by ➤pension funds, as well as the jobs of many thousands of people around the world who might be affected by decisions made. Commentators on the subject of strategic management such as Peter ➤Drucker and Igor ➤Ansoff argue that strategy is about mapping-out the future directions that need to be adopted against the resources possessed by the organization.

When it comes to operationalizing strategy it is most usual to consider this in terms of levels of strategy. There are three distinctive levels of strategy:

(1) Corporate strategy. This will consider long-term issues and fundamental questions, e.g.: What business should we be in?, and: What should be our portfolio of businesses?

(2) Business strategy. This should consider the long-term plans of that particular business and concentrate on improving its competitiveness in the short and long term.

(3) Functional strategy. At the functional level, strategy should focus on the activities of the function to improve competitiveness and quality of performance.

Prior to any implementation of a strategy, organizations need to ensure comprehensive ➤strategic planning is undertaken to help deliver effective decision-making. ➤➤business strategy.

strategic planning A top-down approach to business planning, with an emphasis on long-term businesswide issues. Strategic planning gained popularity in the 1970s, particularly with the development and application of portfolio models, growth-share matrices, studies of business synergy, the search for competitive advantage, experience curve analyses, product life-cycle analysis and research studies, e.g. the ➤Profit Impact of Market Strategy. The approach was driven by general management consultancies, notably the Boston Consulting Group, McKinsey, Arthur D Little, Bain & Co. and the Strategic Planning Institute. ➤➤Boston Consulting Group matrix.

Strategic planning models encouraged the view of markets as aggregations of competitors rather than as aggregations of customers (in contrast to the ➤marketing concept). They also tended to emphasize general management solutions to problems, often at the expense of ignoring implementation issues in specific functional areas (e.g. finance, marketing, human resource management, etc.) though each of these areas may have its own planning processes, as is the case with ➤marketing planning). While general management solutions continue to be put forward (e.g. ➤total quality management, ➤re-engineering, total performance management, ➤customer relationship management, ➤knowledge management systems, ➤organizational learning) there is now wider recognition of the need to consider implementation issues, to think about bottom-up as well as top-down approaches, and to create processes that are flexible and allow for adaptation. With this view, it is as relevant to consider 'how' management should plan as to decide 'what' should be planned.

Strategic planning, by its nature, is very analytical and is dependent on the preservation and rearrangement of established categories of the firm. For example, it usually analyses the existing levels of strategy (corporate, business, and functional), the established types of products (identified as ➤strategic business units) overlaid on the current structure (divisions, departments, etc). In large organizations this type of work is undertaken by planners, who lack managers' authority to make commitments and access by managers to soft information that is so critical to strategy-making. However, they do have time to undertake analyses and are therefore critical to the process.

Closely linked to the planning of strategy is the creative process of strategic thinking; indeed, it is often difficult to disentangle the two activities. The two terms are linked together under the umbrella of ➤strategic management. This involves the softer concepts, e.g. intuition, vision and creativity. The outcome of any strategic plan should be an integrated perspective of the enterprise, and a general vision of its future direction.

stress An anxiety-state that is both psychological and physiological in character. A state of anxiety arises when an individual is striving for something important, but where the outcome is uncertain and where obstacles are placed in the way, e.g. too little time to complete a task, too many constraints against getting the job done well, etc. These obstacles may be real or imagined. For example, a desirable house is for sale, but because it is to be auctioned, the outcome is uncertain ('Will we be able to afford it?', 'Will there be lots of other bidders?'), yet whether you buy the house or not will affect where you live, how you travel to work, your social ties, etc. Stress is dynamic in that the condition will change in response to mood swings, the re-evaluation of opportunities or constraints, or new information. However, it can build up and become acute, posing medical problems.

In the workplace, stress arises where ➤**roles** and expectations are unclear, when changes are being introduced, where people have to work on the boundaries of one function and another, where responsibility has to be taken for other people's work, where there is responsibility for decisions but little discretion, and where there are relationship problems. Some people are better at tolerating these stresses than others. In particular, investigations of employee ➤**personality traits** show that Type A personalities are more prone to stress than those categorized as Type B. In a managerial position, those who are more sociable, more strong-minded and reasonably sensitive (they cannot be insensitive, but nor can they be highly emotional) are less likely to be stressed or create stress for others.

If stress persists, a number of symptoms are likely to appear (e.g. high blood pressure, high cholesterol levels, hypertension, a tendency to smoke and drink to excess, loss of sleep and a tendency to take little exercise) all of which are associated with a greater risk of coronary heart disease. Apart from the personal tragedy of this, it is in the interests of an organization to manage stress because of its impact on productivity, absenteeism, and employee effectiveness. Stress-reducing measures include: (a) better management of business uncertainties (e.g. clarification of ➤**roles** to minimize 'role ambiguity' and 'role incompatibility', especially during periods of change, and the review of ➤**work designs** to ensure everyone is clear about what to do); (b) greater control of the obstacles (e.g. improved ➤**time management** and more delegation of responsibility); (c) the development of workplace support systems (e.g. counselling and medical examinations, and the use of ➤**work groups** to address these problems), and (d) preventative action unrelated to the job, e.g. aerobic exercise such as yoga and lifestyle changes. While stress is invariably seen as harmful, a low level of stress may be stimulating and provide some pressure to perform.

strike ➤collective action.

striking price, strike price ➤offer for sale.

stripping The separate trading of the capital and interest of a ➤bond. ➤➤gilt strip.

structural equation modelling ➤path analysis.

structured query language The most popular high-level language for manipulating data stored in databases.

subchapter S corporations (US) Under subchapter S of the Internal Revenue Code, corporations with thirty-five or fewer non-corporate shareholders may elect to be subject to income tax instead of ➤corporation tax. This allows a business to choose whichever tax regime is most favourable to it, e.g. where it would be advantageous to offset losses in the company against other personal income. When a company is taxed in the normal way it may be referred to as a *C-corporation*.

subcontracting ➤outsourcing.

subordinated Of a liability, ranked below another liability in order of priority for payment. *Junior debt* is ranked after *senior debt* for repayment in the event of a default.

subsidiary Generally, a company controlled by another, parent, company. ➤consolidated accounts. Also referred to as an *affiliate*.

substitute A different product which at least partly satisfies the same need of consumers, e.g. butter and margarine. Capital is a substitute for labour as ➤inputs to production. Products are generally defined as substitutes in terms of cross-price effects between them. If, when the price of minidiscs goes up, sales of compact discs rise, compact discs are said to be a substitute for minidiscs, because consumers can, to some extent, satisfy the need served by minidiscs with compact discs.

This account is complicated by the fact that, when the price of an item changes, it affects both the real income of consumers and the relative prices of different commodities. Strictly, one product is a substitute for another if it enjoys increased demand when the other's price rises and the consumer's income is raised just enough to compensate for the drop in living standards caused by the price rise. One product is a gross substitute for another if it enjoys an increase in demand when the price of the other rises and no compensation is made.

Substitution is not a relationship that only holds between individual commodities – groups of commodities can also be substitutes for each other. Benson and Hedges cigarettes may be a substitute for Marlboro, while cigarettes in general may be a substitute for alcoholic drink. Both together may be a weak substitute for restaurant meals. Substitution (but not gross substitution) is a symmetric relationship: if apples are a substitute for bananas, bananas are a substitute for apples. ➤➤complementary goods; cross-price elasticity of demand.

substitution effect The rate at which consumers switch spending to or from a commodity when its relative price changes but the total living standard of consumers is left constant. The substitution effect measures how much consumers would switch their spending away from (or towards) an item whose price has risen (fallen), if the resultant fall (rise) in purchasing power was offset by a compensating transfer of income that would allow them to maintain their total living standard. It thus isolates the impact of a change in relative prices from the ➤income effect. In terms of ➤indifference curve analysis, the substitution effect represents a swivel of the budget line around a single indifference curve while the income effect represents a parallel shift of the budget line on to a new indifference curve. ➤➤cross-price elasticity of demand.

sunk costs A cost incurred in the past which is irretrievable and which is therefore irrelevant to any future decision-making. For example, a small bakery might buy an oven at a fixed cost. Because this could be sold at some future date, this is *not* a sunk cost. But the baker might also pay out a large amount in advertising his services; this could not be recovered later on – once paid for, the advertising has gone, whether or not the promotion is successful, so this *does* represent a sunk cost. The finding that sunk costs should not influence future decisions is a very important one. The Channel Tunnel, for example, is a sunk cost. The economics of it suggest that it was not a good commercial investment. However, that does not mean it should not now be open – once dug, the tunnel might as well be used. Sunk costs represent a ➤**barrier to entry** in an industry because they scare potential entrants from entering – should it fail, they would have wasted all the sunk costs. ➤➤**contestability**.

superannuation Regulation payments by an employee and/or employer to a pension fund. ➤**pension**.

SUPERCAC ➤Paris *Bourse*.

superior good An item which enjoys disproportionately large increases in demand, as consumers' incomes tend to rise. ➤**inferior good**.

super-normal profit ➤economic rent.

supplier quality assurance Programmes to monitor and improve levels of supplier quality. In some industries (e.g. aircraft manufacturing) it is necessary to have a rigorous quality supplier programme. This will involve an assessment of a supplier's capability in terms of equipment, systems, procedures and training. In these industries, extensive efforts are made to ensure suppliers are able to deliver the desirable quality. In other industries, suppliers can confirm their capability by having their systems and processes certified as conforming to internationally recognized standards, such as ➤**ISO 9000**.

supply The quantity of a good (or service) available for sale at any specified price. Supply is determined by a number of influences: (a) price itself: the higher the price, the more profitable it is (other things being equal) for producers to sell a good, and the more they will attempt to sell; (b) the cost of ➤**inputs**: the lower are costs, the more profitable it is to sell a good at a given price and more will be offered for sale, and (c) the price of other goods: when the prices of other goods rise, the supplier of a good may find it advantageous to switch his production to the supply of the newly high-priced goods rather than stay in the relatively less-profitable industry, where supply will fall.

It should be noted that supply in this context is *planned* supply, not necessarily what is actually sold. The latter depends on ➤**equilibrium** in the market. The conditions of supply constitute but one aspect of the determination of the quantities sold and market price, the other being the conditions of ➤**demand curve**.

supply curve A graphical representation of the quantity of a good or service supplied at different price levels. ➤**supply**. With price on the vertical axis and quantity supplied on the horizontal axis, supply curves normally slope upwards for two reasons: (a) higher prices allow profits to be made at higher levels of production for firms already in the market, and (b) if profits are made, new entrants are attracted into a market.

Supply curves can be drawn for the short and the long term. In the short term, new firms do not have time to enter a market and higher output results only from an increase in production by market incumbents. In the long term, however, new entry can occur. The long-term supply curve links demand–supply equilibrium points on different short-term curves and will be less steep than the short-term curves.

supply-side economics The area of economics concerned with the capacity of the economy to deliver outputs, rather than with the level of spending or demand for those products. Supply-side economics is most often used to describe the preoccupation of those in the profession who are sceptical of the power of conventional economic policy-making (e.g. ➤**fiscal policy** and ➤**monetary policy**) to increase living standards in the long term, without provoking ➤**inflation**.

Supply-side economics is based roughly on a positive and negative thesis. On the negative side, supply-side economists tend to deny an important role to demand management. Because, they believe, economic agents are only concerned with their real income and because markets have a tendency to clear at their ➤**equilibrium** levels, an artificial increase in aggregate demand cannot achieve anything. When demand is boosted, the price of all goods rises, and out of a desire to feed the extra demand, more labour will be sought, requiring an increase in wages. Out of all this, nothing changes in real terms: real wages are the same as they were, as are relative prices; all economic agents behave in the same way as they did before, even though the absolute price level might have changed, and possibly some temporary aberration from market equilibria occurred.

The positive views of such economists relate to the policies they believe can be effective in influencing the performance of an economy. Anything that attempts to influence the supply of labour or the supply of goods can be called a supply-side measure. Such policies could include: (a) cutting taxes to improve incentives (affecting people's personal trade-off between going out to work and staying at home); (b) heavily legislating against ➤**monopoly** in order to encourage free competition, low prices and incentives to be efficient; (c) diminishing the ability of trade unions to inhibit the workings of a free labour market; (d) restricting the growth of the money supply to control inflation, improve economic stability and encourage investment; (e) enacting measures to increase the mobility of labour, and (f) cutting the benefits available to those out of work to improve their incentive to take a job.

It would be wrong, however, to believe that supply-side measures are only the concern of free-market economists. Almost any form of government intervention in the economy can be classed as on the supply side, and measures of this sort might include: (a) increases in spending on education; (b) the introduction of ➤**profit-sharing** as a means of removing industrial conflict, and (c) the establishment of a State investment bank for subsidizing high-risk, new-technology firms.

Free-market supply-side economics emerged as a body of thought in the early 1980s as a doctrine complementary to monetarism, which first provided a macroeconomic case against demand-management; it was strengthened by the theoretical revolution that arrived in the form of ➤**rational expectations**.

survival-based strategy This approach is based on Darwin's theory of the survival of the fittest. Such an approach takes the view that strategy is primarily about competing and winning in the market-place. This approach focuses solely on survival and has little time for ➤**prescriptive corporate strategies**, which state an aim. The key point here is survival, and that may mean continually changing the strategy. The driving force is the market place, which will force weak firms out of business. Critics of the survival-based strategy argue that it is too pessimistic and cautious;

sometimes major investment decisions are required, yet such bold steps would be ruled out.

sustainable competitive advantage ➤competitive advantage.

swap 1. A transaction whereby a security of a certain value is sold to a buyer in exchange for the purchase, from the buyer, of a security having the same value, the purpose being to obtain an improvement, in the eyes of either of the parties, in the quality of the security, or to anticipate a change in yield. **2.** In foreign exchange, the purchase/sale of a currency in the ➤spot market against the simultaneous purchase/sale of the same amount of the same currency in the ➤forward market. **3.** In international monetary regulations, the opening by one ➤central bank of a ➤line of credit in its own currency against the opening of an equivalent line of credit in another currency by the relevant central bank.

sweepstake ➤promotion.

SWIFT Society for Worldwide Interbank Financial Telecommunications. A credit-transfer system between banks operated on a non-profit basis from Brussels. The system links some 1,500 banks in 68 countries.

switch ➤swap.

switching cost A cost that buyers face in changing products, services or suppliers. They arise because, among other things, a buyer's product specification ties it to particular suppliers, the buyer has invested heavily in specialist ancillary equipment, the new product requires new learning or its production lines are connected to the supplier's manufacturing facilities. In addition, buyers may have developed routines and procedures for dealing with a specific vendor that will need to be modified if a new relationship is established. The effect of both types of switching costs for a buyer is that there is a disincentive to explore new vendors. All else being equal, buyers will be motivated to stay in existing relationships to economize on switching costs.

SWOT analysis The acronym for the components of a situation analysis ('audit') in marketing and business strategy: strengths, weaknesses, opportunities and threats. It is a very simple and, hence, useful framework for analysing the environment in which a firm is operating. Opportunities and threats are usually found in the external environment, whereas strengths and weaknesses usually exist within the firm. A meaningful SWOT analysis needs to involve far more than merely listing of factors. It is necessary to examine each one in depth to see what needs to be done in practical terms to deal with each factor. Above all, it is necessary to place all the factors under each heading in some order of priority. This will focus attention on the most important issues in each area. The weaknesses of the analysis include the time and cost of collecting accurate information and, potentially, the enormous list of factors. ➤marketing planning.

syndicate 1. A group of banks or other financial institutions formed to provide credit or to underwrite or manage an issue of a security. **2.** The operating unit into which the ➤Lloyd's insurance market is divided.

syndicated research ➤marketing research.

synergy A beneficial result of combining the activities of more than one player. It is sometimes said to imply the whole is greater than the sum of the parts, or that 2 + 2 = 5. The concept is based upon some sort of ➤**economies of scale** or scope. ➤**economies of scope**. This may occur, for example, because the parts share overheads, ➤**transfer** their technology or share the salesforce. Claims are often made for this approach when an ➤**acquisition** is made, but this synergy is not necessarily achieved in reality. ➤➤**Ansoff, Igor.**

systemic risk A situation in which problems in any one financial institution or market may spread, widely endangering the whole system. ➤**alpha coefficient.**

systems theory A view of organizations as a number of interrelating subsystems that jointly convert inputs into outputs. It looks at the organization as a whole and considers all aspects of its relations to suppliers, customers, etc. However, while it may be useful to think in systems terms, the abstract nature of systems theory makes it difficult to apply in practice. Also relationships and environments can be extremely complex and almost impossible to analyse systematically.

tacit knowledge Knowledge that is context-specific and deeply rooted in actions and skills. It is difficult to formalize, codify and therefore communicate to others. It is embodied by the term 'know-how'. It is sometimes referred to as knowledge that you know but can't tell to others. A simple but useful example is the tying of a shoelace. Most people know how to tie a shoelace and can tie a shoelace, but if you try to communicate this to someone using words and drawings it becomes extremely difficult. ➤➤**knowledge management systems; intellectual assets.**

Taguchi method A method for testing the robustness of a design as advocated by Genichi Taguchi. The principle of the idea is that the product or service should continue to perform in extreme conditions. For example, one does not expect a mobile telephone to be thrown down the stairs but, many certainly will suffer this fate. It is the task of a product designer to achieve a design that can cope with extreme conditions and treatments. The major problem facing designers, however, is the number of design factors which they could vary to try to cope with all eventualities. The Taguchi procedure is a statistical technique for carrying out relatively few experiments and yet remaining able to determine the best combination of design factors.

take-over The acquisition of a firm through the purchase of a majority of the shareholding. Public companies with freely traded shares have a market value given by the current share price. The purchase of 51 per cent of the total number of shares would give the purchaser a controlling interest and would, in theory, have taken control of the business. Sometimes take-overs can be welcomed by the firm, especially if there is the promise of investment. This is often termed a friendly take-over; however, many acquisitions involve ➤**hostile take-overs.** The EU has yet to reach agreement on a pan-European code for take-over activity. ➤**corporate raider; merger; take-over panel.**

take-over panel (UK) The Panel on Take-Overs and Mergers is a committee responsible for supervising compliance with the City Code on Take-Overs and Mergers, a non-statutory code instituted in 1968 (though with earlier origins) and revised in 1987. The Code is intended to protect the interests of shareholders and requires *inter alia* that any company acquiring more than 29.9 per cent of the shares in another company must make a full bid at a price not lower than the highest price paid for its shareholding.

target audience The specific individuals at whom marketing activities (e.g. communications) are aimed. Audiences may be final consumers or the trade, e.g.

retailers, wholesalers, brokers, agents, intermediaries and search engines. Various criteria are used to define target audiences, e.g. purchasing behaviour, levels of involvement, media consumption (➤**sociodemographic segmentation; geodemographic segmentation; psychographic segmentation**), lifestyle and personality traits. The choice of criterion depends on having available data and the purpose at hand. Many of the criteria help to describe target audiences in terms of product category consumption, not specific brand choices. For example, listeners to a particular type of popular music might be described as aged 18–25, living in high-density urban areas and regularly visiting nightclubs, i.e. demographic, geodemographic and lifestyle criteria, respectively. These characteristics are likely to be common to the target audience of all artists offering this particular type of popular music. Thinking of the target audience in this way is important where the goal is to grow ➤**primary demand** for the whole product category. However, for established product categories (where ➤**competitive parity** may have become a norm among directly competing brands) it is relevant to use criteria that distinguish the target audiences of differing brands, e.g. not whether an individual buys petrol, but which brand of petrol the person will buy. The target audience for a brand may be considered in terms of purchasing behaviour (or intended behaviour), i.e. ➤**average purchase frequency; duplicate buying; penetration; repeat purchase** rates, etc. For example, one brand of petrol may have a much higher penetration and a somewhat higher average purchase frequency than competitors' brands. Such brand-level behavioural differences are likely to arise from a combination of ➤**marketing mix** factors (also ➤**brand salience**). (They are unlikely to come from one brand appealing to 18–25 year-olds and another directly competing brand appealing to 48–60 year-olds.) ➤➤**segmentation; target audience action.**

target audience action   The actions by specific individuals (➤**target audience**) in response to marketing activities. Typical activities include types of marketing communication, product development, and pricing decisions, all of which are intended to give rise to specific actions. Actions take four forms: (a) purchase by consumers (either trial or repeat purchase); (b) purchase-related behaviour by consumers (recommending the brand to friends, making a sales enquiry); (c) purchase by the trade (stocking or re-ordering a brand), and (d) purchase-related behaviour by the trade (displaying and promoting the brand).

targeting   ➤segment–target–position strategy.

tariffs   Taxes imposed on imports, either on an ➤*ad valorem* basis or as a specific amount per unit of imports.

TARPS   Target audience rating points. ➤audience rating.

task force   A ➤work group established for a special, investigative purpose. Once it has reported, the task force would most likely be wound up.

taxation   A compulsory transfer of money from private individuals, institutions and commercial enterprises to finance government expenditure. It may be levied on wealth or income, or in the form of a surcharge on prices. In the first case it would be called a *direct tax* (e.g. ➤income tax), and in the second an *indirect tax*, e.g. ➤value added tax. ➤➤corporation tax; excise duty; stamp duty; tariffs.

Taylor, Frederick W (died 1917) 'The father of scientific management' – these words are inscribed on his tombstone. A most important figure in the history of management. Peter ➤**Drucker**, in *Post-capitalist Society* (1994) credited America's productive efficiency which won the Second World War to Taylor's influence and reasserted that Taylor, not Karl Marx, warranted a place in the trinity of makers of the modern world, along with Darwin and Freud. Taylor's life was devoted to finding *The One Best Way* of performing each industrial task. Robert Karrigel's biographical study of Taylor with that title says that Taylor took 'currents of thought drifting through our time – standards, order, production, regularity, efficiency – and codified them into a system that defines our age.'

Born in Philadelphia in 1856, Taylor became an apprentice in the machine shop at a steelworks, later to become Midvale. After 20 months he was made a gang boss and eventually became chief engineer. In 1883, he gained a degree in mechanical engineering. In the machine shop he was aware that workers held back their output for fear of having piece-rates reduced (the practice of 'soldiering'). He realized that output could be increased enormously and that if better ways could also be found of performing functions, both company and workers could be much better off. Very early on, he developed not only techniques of time measurement but also found ways of rectifying deficiencies in machines and improving productivity through greater specialization, e.g. by removing responsibility for tool sharpening from machine tool operators. He also paid attention to flows of materials and the development of jigs, templates and gauges to reduce the work of inspection, approaches which were soon to form the basis of ➤**Fordism** (Henry ➤**Ford**) and, much later, the quality movement. ➤**Deming**, W Edwards.

As Taylor's ideas gained influence, he began to attract criticism. He wrote a number of papers during his working life: in some of them, and in his book *The Principles of Scientific Management* (1911) he claimed that his personal methods had never precipitated a strike in 30 years of practising them. Whether that claim was true or not, there was a strike at Watertown Arsenal in 1910 at which it was asserted that his methods were in use and Taylor had to defend them at an official inquiry. Taylor was accused by trade union representatives of treating workers as less than human, and that reputation has stuck to this day. ➤**organizational behaviour.**

Taylor Nelson Sofres (TNS) A leading market research company, operating in over forty countries. Services include consumer panels, television audience measurement and specialist research in the automotive sector, health care, telecoms, media monitoring and information technology. The company was formed when UK-owned Taylor Nelson AGB acquired the French-owned Sofres Group. Its main competitors are ➤**A C Nielsen Corporation** and ➤**Kantar Group**, although there are many smaller players in specific markets.

team building ➤group development.

technical analysis The study and prediction of price movements in security and commodity markets, based on the analysis of charts of share prices and trading volumes; hence, the practitioner's title: *chartist*. Contrasted with practitioners of *fundamental analysis* – which involves the study of financial accounts and other information about companies – the chartist tends to believe that all the necessary information is in the share price. ➤➤**efficient markets hypothesis.**

technical service A particular activity within a ➤**research and development** (R & D) department that focuses on providing a service to existing products and processes. This frequently involves cost and performance improvements to existing products, processes or systems. For example, in the bulk chemical industry this means ensuring that production processes are functioning effectively and efficiently. This category of R & D activity would also include design changes to products to lower the manufacturing costs.

technology The application of knowledge to the needs of humanity through products, manufacturing processes and artefacts. The ➤**Organization for Economic Co-operation and Development** (OECD) defines it more narrowly as 'the first application of science in a new way with commercial success'. For business it is important that technology is embraced, for the solutions to many of its problems are increasingly provided in the form of technology. The learning curve in technology is, in fact, a series of separate curves linked by periods of saturation and bursts into new periods of growth.

technology push ➤market pull.

technology strategy The development of long-term plans for ➤**research and development** (R & D) and wider use of technology by the firm. The pace of techno-logical change has had an enormous impact on the activities of firms. New technology developments are just as likely to alter the vision and purpose of the organization as any other area. There are two key areas within a firm that will be most influential in the development of a technology strategy: the R & D function and the ➤**operations function**. These two areas are most directly responsible for developing and using significant amounts of new technology. ➤➤**operations management**.

technology transfer The process of promoting technical ➤**innovation** through the transfer of ideas, knowledge, devices and artefacts from leading-edge companies (➤**research and development**), organizations and academic research to more general and effective application in industry and commerce. The concept of technology transfer is not new. In the thirteenth century, Marco Polo helped introduce to the western world Chinese inventions such as the compass, papermaking, printing and the use of coal for fuel. In more recent years, the concept has generated an enormous amount of debate. Many argue that it was a change in US law that led to the surge of interest in the subject. The passage of the landmark National Co-operative Research Act 1984 officially made co-operation on pre-competitive research legal. This certainly helped to raise the profile of the concept of technology transfer. One of the major problems of research into the area of technology transfer is that over the years the term has been used to describe almost any movement of technology from one place to another, to the ridiculous point at which the purchase of a car could be classified as an example of technology transfer. The technology in question may take a variety of forms, whether it be a product, process, piece of equipment, technical knowledge or expertise, or merely a way of doing things. Further, technology transfer involves the movement of ideas, knowledge and information from one context to another. However, it is in the context of innovation that technology transfer is most appropriate and needs to be considered.

television rating (TVR) ➤audience rating.

tender 1. Generally, to offer a payment, as in a written offer to purchase. **2.** To offer a service in response to advertisement. **3.** To offer to buy ➤**Treasury bill** tender issued by the ➤**Bank of England. 4.** To offer for an issue of securities on the stock exchange. ➤**offer for sale. 5.** To deliver a commodity to the buyer.

term assurance ➤insurance.

term loan A bank advance for a specific period (normally 3–10 years), repaid, with interest, usually by regular periodical payments. Term loans are made by ➤**commercial banks** and other institutions for business finance. For large borrowings, the loan may be syndicated (➤**syndicate**), and it is quite common for loans to large corporations to be unsecured.

terms of trade The ratio of the index of export prices to the index of import prices. An improvement in the terms of trade follows if export prices rise more quickly than import prices (or fall more slowly than import prices). A depreciation of a currency tends to worsen the terms of trade.

term structure of interest rate The relationship between the interest rate paid on a ➤**bond** and the number of years there are until the bond is repaid. Bonds exist for a huge spectrum of different terms, and the rates paid for each term must bear some relationship to each other. If rates for 1-year bonds are low and are expected to remain low, then no one will buy a 10-year bond at a high rate; they would, instead, prefer to buy a series of ten 1-year bonds. The term structure compares the annual yield on each type of bond – it can be graphed in a ➤**yield curve**. It is affected by a number of factors. Most obvious is the expectation of changed interest rates on short-term bonds. If interest rates are expected to rise over time, the 10-year bond will have to offer a higher annual return than the 1-year bond; otherwise, everyone would borrow money on the 10-year loan. ➤**Inflation** expectations also determine the term structure, for if inflation is set to rise, then so will interest rates; and more compensation is required for lenders to offset the devaluing of the money they lend. ➤**Fiscal policy** also affects the term structure. If the government is going to sell many bonds in the future, then the rate it will have to pay to find buyers for them all will have to rise.

It is usually expected that long rates are higher than short ones. But if fiscal policy and ➤**monetary policy** are 'tight', i.e. tending to have a deflationary effect (➤**deflation**), then long-term rates will be lower than usual, relative to short-term rates.

t-group A training group. Unstructured groups of employees brought together freely and openly to exchange ideas, thoughts and concerns about organizational change. T-groups, also called 'encounter groups', are often an integral part of a ➤**change-management programme**, and can be used to help allay people's fears and remove potential obstacles to change.

theory X and theory Y Two contrasting theories of employee ➤**motivation**. Theory X assumes employees dislike work, will attempt to avoid it, dislike responsibility, have a strong desire for security and must be coerced to perform (a negative view of human motivation). Theory Y assumes employees like work, are creative, seek responsibility, and can exercise self-direction and self-control if they are committed to the goals of the organization (a positive view of human motivation).

Despite the popularity of these theories since they were proposed by Douglas ➤McGregor (*The Human Side of Enterprise*, 1960) there is little hard evidence for either – except in a very loose and general sense. Moreover, neither theory addresses the motivation of employees in collectivist societies such as Japan. ➤theory Z.

theory Z A theory of employee ➤motivation, proposed in reaction to ➤theory X **and theory Y**. This offers a positive view of employee motivation, but one that emphasizes social, rather than individual, motives. Employees co-operate, work together in teams, make group decisions, commit to an organization for the long term and value the wisdom that comes from experience. While associated with collectivist societies, this view has become increasingly evident in Western organizations. ➤**work group**.

3 Cs Shorthand for 'consumers, competitors and competencies' – the three major areas of focus for marketers to consider when making plans and decisions. ➤**marketing concept; marketing planning**.

thrifts (US) A general term covering non-bank institutions receiving ➤deposits and making loans. ➤**savings and loan associations**.

throughput time The length of time for the whole operation to be completed, i.e. the total time it takes to obtain the resources, and produce and deliver the product or service.

tie-in A promotional activity designed to coincide with an already scheduled event. For example, a promotion for a fast-food chain to coincide with the cinema release of a new animated movie. There also may be associated merchandise, e.g. toys, apparel, accessories, etc. bearing the logos of the event organizers and the promoter. This has become increasingly common with major sporting events such as the Olympics and soccer World Cup. ➤**promotion**.

time deposit ➤bank deposit.

time management The ability of an individual employee to manage time effectively and efficiently. This is necessary if an employee is to be productive, but is also an important part of ➤stress management. Effective time management usually means removing time-wasters, having clear and feasible goals, setting priorities and keeping to plans unless there are very good reasons not to. Time management is not purely a function of an individual's ability to be organized (although all too often this is how it is discussed). It depends crucially on the resources and technology made available to an employee, the efficiency of organizational structures and systems and the extent to which his performance depends on others. ➤**work group**. For example, an individual might regard committee work as time-wasting, but the organization may insist on employee participation in committee work. Formal appraisal of time management (e.g. using time-and-motion studies and workflow analyses) must take account of these other factors; otherwise, recommendations are likely to be misleading and harmful (perhaps increasing levels of stress).

times covered ➤income gearing.

time series analysis The application of statistical methods to find explanations of movements of variables over time. ➤**econometrics; forecasting**.

time study ➤work measurement study.

time-to-market (TTM) The time it takes to develop a product from concept through to the market-place. There are potentially significant advantages to be gained if a firm is first to the market with its product. There are equally many potential disadvantages, from which firms that enter later can benefit by learning from the mistakes of those who go first. The time from product concept to finished product varies considerably between industries. In the aircraft industry this may take 10–15 years, whereas in the fast-moving consumer goods industries it may be only a few months.

Tokyo Stock Exchange One of the three largest ➤stock exchanges in the world and one of the three central Japanese exchanges; Osaka and Nagoya are the other two, and there are regional stock exchanges in Fukuoka, Hiroshima, Kyoto, Niigata and Sapporo. Tokyo accounts for well over 80 per cent of all the transactions in Japan. Tokyo, Nagoya and Osaka have two main sections – a first section (*ichibu*) which deals in the most actively traded companies and, since 1961, a second section (*nibu*) which has less stringent listing requirements – as well as a third section for foreign stocks. There is also an ➤over-the-counter market.

tombstone ➤lead manager.

top-down ➤investment approach.

total factor productivity A measure of output per unit of inputs to a production process. Typically, when people talk of ➤productivity, they are referring to labour productivity, i.e. the level of output per person employed. Total factor productivity takes account of other inputs, most notably capital. To understand the difference, imagine a factory with a high level of capital equipment employed for each worker. Labour productivity will be high, as the equipment will make each worker productive. But total factor productivity may not be high, as once the high level of equipment is taken into account, output is only what you might have expected.

total quality management (TQM) A collection of concepts and techniques aimed at improving business performance through ensuring quality is defined as meeting a customer's expectations. Quality is therefore measured from the point of view of the customer, and most processes in a firm have several customers, some external (resellers and consumers) and some internal (other departments). Quality is achieved if every customer's expectations are met. This has led to the idea that firms should try to ensure their customer's requirements are met 100 per cent of the time and that it should aim for zero defects. There are several weapons that management may use to direct themselves towards zero defects: the use of statistical process control techniques to provide early warning of any defects, and establishing root causes to quality problems to ensure the problem does not recur. The use of the ➤*kaizen* philosophy is also incorporated in total quality management. ➤Crosby; Deming; Juran.

touch The difference between the highest ➤bid price and the lowest ➤offer price in a market for securities or commodities, i.e. the largest available ➤spread.

tracking study ➤audience measurement.

trade barrier ➤barrier to trade.

trade bill A ➤bill of exchange accepted by a party other than a bank.

trade credit The credit extended by business firms to other businesses, usually arising from the delay of receipts and payments for services performed. ➤➤factoring.

traded option ➤option.

trade investment (UK) A shareholding of one company in another. ➤➤consolidated account.

trade mark Any sign capable of being represented graphically which is capable of distinguishing goods or services of one undertaking from those of other undertakings. Trade marks have particular importance to the world of business. For many businesses, especially in the less technology-intensive industries where the use of ➤patents is limited, trade marks offer one of few methods of differentiating a company's products. The public rely on many trade marks as indicating quality, value for money and origin of goods. Significant changes have been made to trade mark law in the UK. The Trade Marks Act 1994 replaced the Trade Marks Act, 1938, which was widely recognized as being out of touch with business practices today. The UK now complies with the European directive on the approximation of the laws of member states relating to trade marks and ratifies the Madrid Convention for the international registration of trade marks. The law relating to trade marks is complex indeed.

Some of the first trade marks were used by gold- and silversmiths to mark their own work. The first registered trade mark, No 1, was issued to Bass in 1890 for their red triangle mark for pale ale. ➤brand; logo; look-alike.

trade secret Particular knowledge or skills relating to a business activity or process that has been developed over time by an organization. Such ➤know-how is not subject to ➤patent, copyright, or ➤trade mark, and is referred to as a secret of the organization. It could comprise special ways of working, price costings or business strategies. The most famous example is the recipe for Coca-Cola, which is not patented. This is because Coca-Cola did not want to reveal the recipe to their competitors. Unfortunately, the law covering intellectual property is less clear about the term. Indeed, many legal experts argue that there is no satisfactory legal definition of it.

trade union An organization of employees that acts collectively to protect and promote the interests of employees as a counterpoint to the interests of employers (US = *labor union*). Key interests relate to wage and salary levels (➤pay); benefit packages; hours of work and working conditions; occupational health, safety and risk management; equity and diversity issues; employee training and development, and grievance procedures. Trade unions are also sometimes involved in recruitment, hiring, performance appraisal, and promotion (or, at least, they help to specify the criteria and procedures that govern these activities).

In dealing with owners, the interests of trade union members are represented by spokespersons. Through a process of ➤collective bargaining, these spokespersons attempt to represent the interests of all employees. This prevents employers from playing the interests of one employee off against another. It also means employees can use their collective strength to negotiate an attractive deal for members or – if concessions are not forthcoming – to take industrial action. ➤collective action.

This process is inescapably political. ►**politicking**. It concerns the use of influence and the exercise of ►**power** by organized employees in a way that mirrors the use of influence and power by employers.

In some industries, the practice of collective bargaining takes place at a national level, between senior union representatives and senior management representatives. This practice results in a national wage settlement, which all employers in the industry must bear. An alternative is to seek an enterprise agreement. This is agreed at the level of an enterprise (firm, company, factory) and, therefore, it should be better able to take account of specific issues and conditions, e.g. the scope for local productivity packages. Within an enterprise, the role of the 'shop steward' is particularly important, not only because he may be involved in wage negotiations but also as the conduit for making known issues concerning working conditions, occupational health, grievances, etc. Within this structure the interests of ordinary members are channelled through shop stewards (activists) to full-time union officials (bureaucrats).

Historically, since the struggles of fledgling trade unions in early eighteenth-century Britain, they have had a tremendous influence on working conditions and employee–employer relations. From 1824 (when the Combination Acts were repealed in Britain) to about 1980, union membership grew quite steadily. They also became highly organized at a national level – through the Trades Union Congress in the UK, the American Federation of Labor and Congress of Industrial Organizations in the US, and equivalent bodies elsewhere. However, over the past two decades circumstances have changed in a number of significant respects.

(1) Membership levels have waned. This, in part, reflects structural changes in Western economies. The number of manual and blue-collar workers on piece-rates or wages (where, historically, unionization was strong, as in mining, ship-building, transport etc.) has declined. There has been an attendant growth in salaried white-collar workers (where levels of unionization are quite variable).

(2) Confrontational ('them-and-us') style of management has been replaced by more co-operation and collaboration. This is evident in the shift of emphasis from ►**industrial relations** to ►**human resource management** in many organizations. As a consequence, trade unions that have not made matching adjustments appear outdated and have lost their appeal.

(3) The practice of collective bargaining has been criticized for not working in the interests of productive employees. It tends to reward average performance, not exceptional performance. For this reason, more and more employees have been prepared to accept individual contracts. Indeed, because of outsourcing, subcontracting, networking, etc. many workers have moved from an employer–employee relationship (the premise of traditional trade unionism) to a contractual relationship (based on fees or commission for services rendered).

(4) Critics point out that trade unions work in the interests of their own members, rather than employees at large. Steep wage rises can drive away investors and result in higher than expected unemployment levels. On the other hand, it is usual for non-members as well as members to benefit from collective bargaining, e.g. any negotiated improvement in workplace conditions is likely to be shared by all employees. To the extent that unions have not been able to face these issues, they have come under attack.

(5) The political and legislative environment of the past 20 years in many Western

economies has not been favourable to trade unions. Restrictions have been imposed on recruitment (e.g. by restricting or prohibiting 'closed shops' and having employees 'opt in' rather than 'opt out' of membership) and on collective action, e.g. the outlawing of secondary picketing and wildcat strikes.

In response, trade unions have had to reinvent themselves. Militant unionism (with a revolutionary agenda) has tended to give way to reformist and business-oriented unionism. Greater weight is now given to their role as collaborators in human resource management, e.g. through joint-sponsorship of training and development programmes or joint investigation of health and safety issues.

trading floor The area of space in a stock exchange or other trading exchange where members gather to deal face-to-face in securities. Except notably in New York, trading floors have given way to automated screen trading.

transactions cost The cost associated with the process of buying and selling. These are small frictions in markets that can explain why the price system does not operate perfectly. Transactions costs may affect decisions by an organization to make or buy – performing activities in-house may circumvent the transactions costs that would arise if they were bought-in. The study of transactions costs economics, associated notably with Oliver ➤**Williamson**, has implications for a wide range of issues affecting industrial organization and the size of the firm.

transfer pricing The adjustment of prices on sales of material between members of a multicompany group so as to distribute financial burdens between the members in accordance with central financial policy. The term is most common in reference to multinational companies, where transfer pricing is suspected as a method of evading national taxation and customs duties.

transnational company ➤multinational company.

transparency The extent to which transaction prices and volumes in a securities market are visible to all market operators. Transparency is an important condition for full and fair competition. ➤➤**audit trail**.

Treasury bill A ➤**money market** instrument issued by the ➤**central bank**, chiefly in the UK and USA, in principle to supply the government's short-term financial needs but also as a means of influencing ➤**credit** and the ➤**money supply**. Effectively a ➤**bill of exchange** because it carries no interest but is sold at a discount.

Treasury bond A ➤**bond** issued by the US Treasury. Equivalent instruments are issued in France and other countries but not in the UK. ➤**gilt-edged securities**; ➤➤**Treasury bill**.

trend growth The level of ➤**economic growth** of an economy that is sustainable over the long term, without any tendency for the rate of ➤**inflation** to rise or fall. It is sometimes held to be the rate at which the productive capacity of the economy – its potential for production – expands. It could equally be taken as a measure of the growth of the supply side. It is also interpreted as the long-term growth rate, as it is assumed that in the long term the economy must perform according to its potential. The rate is affected by growth in the labour force, and the growth in productivity. Actual growth in any year may exceed, or underperform trend growth, usually because fluctuations in demand affect actual GDP more than they affect the long-term capacity of the economy to produce things. Trend growth is often held as a useful benchmark for whether the economy is growing too quickly or too slowly for long-term stability to prevail. A typical estimate of trend growth in the UK is 2.25 per cent, although debate has raged as to whether the trend growth rate has enjoyed an upswing in recent years as a result of fast progress in the development of information technology. ≫new economy; output gap.

trial purchase ➤buyer behaviour.

trust 1. Goodwill between parties in a relationship. Goodwill in business relationships helps individuals and organizations exchange ideas, information, products and services and therefore enables the parties to work together over time. In concrete terms, it helps to secure repeat business. In this sense, it oils the wheels of business. Management thinkers see it as a critically important element of business relationships, especially where there is interdependence and uncertainty. Thus, a company forging a strategic alliance in a new market might emphasize trust because the parties are interdependent, the situation is uncertain and the consequences of choosing a poor alliance partner could be major. Trusting relationships are characterized by good communications, co-operation between the parties, fewer formal controls, the realistic assessment of what is and isn't possible, and less cheating or deception by individuals in the relationship. These are all aspects of 'social exchange'.

Trust-based relationships are the counterpoint to power-based relationships. The latter rely on fear, guided by the pursuit of self-interest. Communication is one-way, and formal, e.g. using very specific and formal contracts. Power is exercised through coercion and recourse to the legal system. By contrast, the former rely on trust and the pursuit of what is fair. Communication is through dialogue, and quite open contracts. Trust is exercised through expertise and mutual understanding, but if conflict arises, both parties are prepared to accept mediation and arbitration. ≫power.

A more traditional view of trust is to see it in terms of risk, i.e. the confidence between parties in a relationship that neither party will be harmed or put at risk. Confidence increases if parties see each other as honest, dependable and reliable. Confidence is further enhanced when there are tangible guarantees and safeguards to reduce risk – to ensure people are honest and reliable. These are aspects of 'economic exchange'. However, tangible and legalistic mechanisms may smack of mistrust; indeed, it can be argued that where there is true goodwill such mechanisms are unnecessary. In practice, the most robust business relationships blend together social *and* economic exchange. ≫agency theory; conflict; equity theory; transactions cost theory.

2. A legal device under which property, either financial or physical, is placed in the custody of a designated person, or people, named *trustees*, for management on behalf of others; the whole is regulated by a *trust deed* defining the trustee(s), the beneficiaries of the trust and the rights and duties of each. ➤Unit trusts and ➤investment trusts, as the names imply, are regulated by trust arrangements. **3.** A large US ➤conglomerate prevalent in the nineteenth and early twentieth centuries, largely outlawed by anti-trust legislation, the earliest instance of which was the Sherman Act 1890.

trust deed ➤trust.

TSE 300 An index designed to reflect movements in share prices of 300 companies traded on the Toronto Stock Exchange. It was given a base value of 1,000 in 1975.

turnover 1. The total sales revenue of a business, as distinct from ➤**value added.** **2.** The value of transactions carried out on a stock exchange, defined usually as the value of securities changing hands but on the ➤**London Stock Exchange** mainly as the total value of purchases and sales. **3.** The level of staff-churning in an organization. ➤**employee retention.**

24-hour trading The ability to trade in ➤**securities** around the clock. Since some ➤**blue-chip issues** and ➤**bonds** are quoted on several stock exchanges in different time zones, it is now possible, using satellite communications, to buy and sell securities at any time. Even though there are gaps in trading hours, many exchanges allow after-hours trading, i.e. ➤**dealers** are allowed to buy and sell outside the official closing time.

type A and type B personalities ➤personality traits; ➤➤stress.

U

U & A survey Usage and attitude survey ➤**quantitative market research**.

umbrella brand ➤**brand hierarchy**.

unaided recall Questioning in market research in which respondents are not given prompts or cues about the issue of interest. Thus, respondents might be asked to list the commercials they saw the previous night – without any further prompt. This contrasts with ➤**aided recall**, where respondents might be asked whether they saw a commercial for BT or AT & T the previous night – here the company names serve as prompts.

uncertainty ➤risk.

uncertainty-based theories of strategy In environments with substantial turbulence and change, decision-making is based on taking small steps forward and examining the effects and adapting accordingly. In such environments, success is determined by the ability of the organization to survive through innovation and rapidly changing the way it operates. Long-term planning is not possible and only short-term objectives can be set. ➤➤**chaos theory; strategic management**.

undated security (UK) A government security not bearing a ➤**redemption date** or ➤**option**; hence, ➤**irredeemable security**.

undercapitalized A company with insufficient capital to meet its due creditors even though it is making an accounting profit.

underwrite 1. To guarantee to buy or find buyers for all or part of the issue of a security. Normally done in return for a fee by a bank or group (➤**syndicate**) of banks to ensure sale of any part of an issue not bought by the public to which it is directed. **2.** To accept on behalf of an insuring firm or syndicate an insurance risk.

undistributed profit ➤retained earnings.

unemployment The existence of a section of the labour force able and willing to work but unable to find gainful employment. Unemployment is best measured as the percentage of the total labour force out of work. Historically, it was very high in the 1930s; it fell to its lowest level in the 1950s and re-emerged as a worsening phenomenon in Western economies after the oil crisis of 1973, for the first time simultaneously appearing with high inflation. By the late 1990s, unemployment had dipped in many economies again.

Four distinct causes of unemployment can be distinguished:
(1) Frictional unemployment. Caused by people taking time out of work between jobs or looking for a job. This is not a sign of market failure.
(2) Classical unemployment. Caused by workers or unions seeking wages too high to allow viable employment.
(3) Structural unemployment. Refers to a mismatch of job vacancies with the supply of labour available, caused by shifts in the structure of the economy. It is signified by a high level of vacancies, co-existing with a large pool of unemployed workers, either with the wrong skills or in the wrong regions to fill the jobs available.
(4) Keynesian unemployment. This results from a deficiency of demand in the economy; spending or economic activity is simply not great enough to support full employment. In this situation, a fall in wage levels – which should cause an increase in the demand for labour – can merely reduce demand further because it reduces the spending power of the employed and thus fails to clear the excess supply of workers.

In recent years, attention has focused on the particular problem of long-term unemployment (unemployment for a period exceeding 6 months or a year) especially among unskilled men. It is surmised that the market wage of manual workers – especially those in heavy physical occupations – has declined and that work incentives have correspondingly diminished, too.

unemployment, natural rate of The level of unemployment in an economy that is just consistent with a stable rate of ➤**inflation**. It is the unemployment that prevails when all markets in the economy are in equilibrium, and there is no deficiency of overall spending or activity. It can be thought of as the unemployment rate when output in the economy is just at its potential, no more and no less. ➤**output gap**. The natural rate may be non-negligible – in much of Europe it is estimated to have risen to over 8 per cent of the labour force during the 1980s and remained stubbornly high since then.

The point about the natural rate is that it is not easily solvable by ➤**fiscal policy** or ➤**monetary policy**. It is a supply-side feature of the economy (➤**supply-side economics**), a reflection of labour market institutions. The concept of the natural rate was central to the debate in economics of the early 1980s about the effectiveness of economic policies which stimulated spending and activity, given the observation that spending seemed to have to be stoked up to ever higher levels to maintain the same level of unemployment. The economy appeared to exhibit a natural tendency towards some level, and it was not possible to get that level lower by allowing inflation to rise higher. At best, it appeared possible to get it below the natural rate temporarily, or by ever-accelerating rates of inflation. Indeed, on modern accounts, macroeconomic policy cannot even take unemployment below the natural rate at all. To get the natural rate down, it is argued, requires government to consider such factors as the levels of benefits for the out-of-work, the ease with which workers can change jobs and the stigma attached to being out of work.

Because unemployment cannot be held below the natural rate without accelerating inflation, it is often called the non-accelerating inflation rate of unemployment.

unincorporated business A business that has not taken the legal form of a company and may be a ➤**sole proprietorship** or a ➤**partnership**. ➤**incorporation**.

unique selling proposition (USP) Features of a brand that clearly differentiate it from the competition, and which can be heavily promoted to the ➤target audience. Such features usually reflect functional superiority (e.g. most advanced technology) offering a tangible benefit to consumers. However, many directly competing brands are not clearly differentiated. At best, there may be just-noticeable product differences or distinctive brand communications. Over time, even these small points of difference may be eroded and diluted. ➤competitive parity.

unit banking ➤banking.

unit trust (UK) An investment organization (➤trust) that invests funds subscribed by the public in securities and, in return, issues units that it will repurchase at any time. The units, which represent equal shares in the trust's investment portfolio, produce income and fluctuate in value according to the interest and dividends paid and the stock exchange prices of the underlying securities. The subscriber to a unit trust does not, unlike the shareholder in an ➤investment trust, receive any of the ➤profits of the organization managing the trust. Management derives its income from a regular service charge as a percentage of the income of the trust's investments, and the difference (➤spread) between the (bid) price at which it buys in units and the (offer) price at which it sells them, which includes an initial charge. The trust is regulated by a trust deed, the trustees being separate from the management. Some are designed to maximize income, others capital growth. Many unit trusts offer the option of distributed or reinvested income (*accumulation units*). Unit trusts in the UK first appeared in the 1930s and were based upon the principle of ➤mutual funds in the US. (Fr. = *société d'investissement à capital variable*.) ➤➤open-ended fund; open-ended investment company.

universal banking ➤banking.

universal product code (UPC) ➤SKU.

unlisted company A company whose shares are not admitted for trading on a major stock exchange. Unlisted companies, also referred to as *unquoted companies*, may, none the less, have their shares quoted and traded on the ➤unlisted securities market. ➤➤over-the-counter market.

unlisted securities market (USM) **1.** Generally, the markets for shares of public companies (➤incorporation) not included in the official list for the main market (or first tier) of the ➤stock exchange. Most of the larger industrialized countries have organized and regulated lower-tier markets as well as informal *placing markets* in which unlisted shares are traded. These lower stock market segments are less stringently regulated and perform an important function in providing a stepping-stone to the main markets. ➤➤National Association of Securities Dealers Automated Quotation system; over-the-counter market; Paris *Bourse*. **2.** Specifically, a market set up in 1980 by the ➤London Stock Exchange to trade in designated unlisted securities. The market closed at the end of 1996, having been replaced by the ➤Alternative Investment Market.

unprompted recall ➤prompted recall.

unquoted company ➤unlisted company.

unsecured Of a loan, not backed by a ➤security.

UPC ➤universal product code.

Urwick, Lyndall ➤McKinsey, James.

usage and attitude survey (U&A) ➤quantitative market research.

USP ➤unique selling proposition.

V

validity The extent to which a study is free from systematic and random error. If there is error, then we are not measuring what we think we are measuring. This is a statistical and analytical issue, rather than a business one. Nevertheless, many decisions in business are based on the assumption that research studies and the supporting data are valid, when this cannot be assumed without question. For example, from ➤**marketing research** an organization might believe there is an untapped market for boots in Bolton, but the truth of this statement will depend on whether a relevant sample was used, whether appropriate questions were asked and whether the data were analysed with care. From an ➤**attitude survey**, an organization might believe employees are not suffering from ➤**stress**, but this presupposes that stress was properly measured with the attitude survey (in fact, it may have been better to undertake medical examinations rather than rely on a general survey).

Error arises because of the questions asked (a measurement issue) or because of the way the data are collected (a research design issue) or because of how the measures are combined (a construct issue) or because of the analysis techniques used (an analytical issue).

There are four main ways to assess the validity of measures and constructs.

(1) Content validity (also face validity). An expert considers the relevance and appropriateness of the measures. In a study of ➤**consumer loyalty**, for example, an experienced market researcher could say whether repeat-buying is an appropriate measure (it would be for a frequently bought item, but a measure of retention might be of more use in the case of an infrequently bought, but frequently used, item).

(2) Construct validity. Where the relationship between things (constructs) is well established, it is possible to see whether the results from the current study accord with what is known already. If the results do not accord, doubt may be cast on the validity of the measures used. Even where the relationship is not well established, there may be strong theoretical reasons to favour a particular relationship, and, if this is not borne out by analysis, the measures or the constructs might be called into question. For example, there might be theoretical reasons to believe ➤**trust** is related to consumer loyalty. If this proves not to be the case, there could be a question mark over the way trust and loyalty are measured and whether the constructs themselves are well defined. Ideally, each construct should be quite distinct from all other constructs (discriminant validity). Thus, the construct of trust should be distinct from that of loyalty.

(3) Concurrent validity. Two measurements of the same thing are undertaken and compared to see if they agree (correlate). A high correlation suggests concurrent

validity – assuming that the two measures are administered under exactly the same conditions and at the same time. There may be two measures of trust: one requiring many questions to be asked and another with just one question. If there is concurrent validity it would be efficient to use the simpler measure. If two measurements of the same thing are undertaken using different techniques (where conditions cannot be exactly the same), reference is made to convergent validity.

(4) Predictive validity (also criterion-related validity). The ability of a measurement made at one time to predict something else at another time. Consumer intentions might be measured with the aim of predicting subsequent purchasing. Intentions are said to have good predictive validity if the correlation between intentions and purchasing is high (in practice this is by no means always the case, ➤attitudes).

In assessing research designs two additional forms of validity are of central concern.

(5) Internal validity. The extent to which results arise from the variable of interest which are not confounded by variables not of interest. In an experimental study of the effects of advertising on sales, the market researcher wants to be sure that any rise in ➤sales comes from increased ➤advertising, and is not confounded by direct marketing activity. In an ➤experiment the goal is to create a research design where internal validity is not in doubt, i.e. that, if sales rise, this could only have been as a result of advertising. In non-experimental research this assurance cannot be obtained, and therefore the internal validity of the results is often threatened. In the advertising sales example it might mean the relationship is spurious because (unmeasured) direct marketing activity was the main driver of sales.

(6) External validity. The extent to which a specific set of results can be generalized in terms of populations, geographic areas, industries and contexts. Field-based survey research stands a good chance of generating results that can be generalized to a real-world population, region, industry, etc. By contrast, many of the extraneous effects that are controlled-out of an experiment are the very substance of generalization. For example, in the advertising sales example, organizations using direct marketing may have been excluded from the study (this handles a potential confounding effect), thereby restricting the ability to generalize (given that most organizations now use direct marketing); hence, the common criticism that experimental results are artificial.

In making decisions, it is important for managers at least to be aware of the potential threats to the validity of their data, research and analysis.

VALS ➤lifestyle segmentation.

values Convictions. Individuals are seen as having ideas and judgements about their ideas, i.e. judgements about whether the ideas are good or bad, something to strive for or to avoid. Examples include: freedom, wisdom, self-respect and contentedness. Individuals will ascribe importance to these various ideas and therefore a hierarchy of values can be envisaged – this amounts to a value system. For example, freedom might be placed above contentedness. In management, value systems are important at personal and corporate levels. Value systems underlie a person's attitude to work, employment, ➤rewards, conduct at work, expectations of an organization and of people with whom relationships are formed at work and in business. Research shows a number of dominant value systems for various types of employee, depending on age and life stage, role and position, and culture. Contrast the set of values that describes the Protestant work ethic (hard work, conservative, loyal to the organization) with Generation X (flexible, seeking job satisfaction, loyal to personal relationships). Organizations themselves also come to embody certain values, as evident in ➤organizational culture.

value added The amount a firm produces, after subtracting the cost of the things it buys-in from other firms. If a supermarket sells £10 billion of food a year, and spends £9 billion on buying that food from other suppliers, it has a value-added of £1 billion. Clearly, value added will tend to be smaller than ➤turnover. When measuring the total size of the economy, statisticians look at value added, not turnover, because to do otherwise would be to double-count the value of some pieces of output. If a baked beans manufacturer sells beans to a supermarket, which sells them to the public, it would be a mistake to count the value of the same can of beans twice, as output of both the bean company and the supermarket.

value added tax (VAT) A form of sales tax levied on the total sales of firms, minus the amount they have bought in from other firms. The goal of VAT is to tax each piece of output once and only once. Usually, the tax is levied on turnover minus purchased inputs, but as it is necessarily the case that turnover = sales – inputs = labour costs + profits, it can be shown that a VAT is a way of taxing labour income and profits.

Most VAT systems charge VAT on all firms on their total turnover, crediting them with refunded tax on everything they buy-in. Because VAT uses this complex system of tax and credit all the way through the production chain, there is, in principle, no difference between charging VAT of 15 per cent on all firms in this way or charging 15 per cent retail sales tax once only on the final sale of an item as it passes into the hands of a consumer without any credits at all. However, it is generally thought to be easier to enforce the tax by including all firms within its ambit, rather than defining retailers and simply levying all the tax on them.

Most VAT systems exclude exports by charging a zero rate of tax on sales abroad, and cover imports by applying tax as they cross the border into the country.

value at risk (VAR) A measure of the riskiness of a portfolio, based on assessing the maximum amount that would be lost 19 days out of 20, given typical levels of volatility in market prices. If asset prices move by an average of 2 per cent a day, and if that volatility behaves in predictable and neat ways (i.e. if it follows the normal distribution which means big movements in prices are far rarer than small ones) it can be shown that the portfolio will only move by 1.65 × 2 per cent or 3.3 per cent 1 day in 20. A portfolio worth £100 would thus have a VAR of £3.30.

The figure of 1.65 depends crucially on the good behaviour of volatility, however. In practice, markets tend to behave in more complicated ways – when movements occur, they often tend to gather momentum and swing further than simple rules of statistics would predict. So, they may move by more than 3.3 per cent only every 20 days normally but when they move badly, they may move very badly. The VAR is thus not a perfect guide to risk.

value-based pricing ➤pricing policy.

value chain A framework developed by Michael ➤Porter that disaggregates a firm into its strategically relevant activities in order to understand the behaviour of costs and the existing and potential sources of ➤differentiation. Porter argued that a firm gains competitive advantage by performing these strategically important activities more cheaply or better than competitors.

A value chain is embedded in a larger stream of activities called a 'value system'. Gaining and sustaining competitive advantage depends on understanding not only a firm's value chain but how it fits into the overall value system. The activities are divided into primary and support activities.

Key points made by Porter are that technology and development are not restricted to the ➤research and development department but are company-wide responsibilities, as are human resources development, procurement and the infrastructure. Procurement is a key issue concerning whether to buy or build and which alliances to establish. ➤competitive advantage.

value-engineering/analysis A technique for reducing the costs to produce a product by altering the design. The aim is to eliminate any costs that do not contribute to the value and performance of the product. Value-engineering programmes are usually conducted by project teams consisting of designers, purchasing specialists, marketers and operations managers. A variety of methods will be used to scrutinize rigorously the product to identify any components that may be simplified or have their costs reduced.

value investing ➤investment approach.

value system ➤values.

VAR ➤value at risk.

variable A number that may take up different values in different situations. For instance, quantity of a good demanded will vary according to price.

variable-pay programmes ➤performance-related pay.

variable rate security A security for which the rate of interest is not fixed but varies with rates on short-term securities, such as ➤Treasury bills, according to a specified equation that adjusts rates, say, every 6 months. The UK government issued variable rate stock in 1977, but such issues are common in the ➤Eurobond market and in the US, where they are known as *floating rate notes* or, more generally, *floaters*.

variable sum game A game (➤game theory) in which different outcomes yield different overall levels of welfare for the players. A variable sum game contrasts with a ➤zero-sum game where one player's gain is equal to other players' losses, whatever strategy is chosen. A variable sum game is one where the size of the cake the players are competing for varies depending on the strategies the players choose. The ubiquitous ➤prisoners' dilemma game is variable sum, because some outcomes involve better average pay-offs for the players, than others.

variance A measure of the degree of dispersion of a series of numbers around their mean. The larger the variance, the larger the spread of numbers. Variance is calculated by taking the difference between each number and the mean of the group, squaring it, then taking the mean of this series. So, if we have a small group of numbers 4, 5, 6, 7, 8, the mean is 6; the deviations from the mean are -2, -1, 0, 1,

2. The squares of these are 4, 1, 0, 1, 4, and the average of this series is 2. Thus, the variance is 2.

variety seeking A pattern of ➤buyer behaviour in which the consumer deliberately switches brands/lines for the sake of variety. This behaviour is associated mostly with things which are bought and consumed very frequently, e.g. breakfast cereals.

VC ➤venture capital.

VCTS ➤venture capital trust.

vendor placing Where a ➤listed company issues shares to the sellers of another company as full or partial settlement of the acquisition price, the sellers may ask a stockbroker to dispose of the shares by placing them with clients. This is known as 'vendor placing' and may be preferable to selling them on the market, where the offer of a large line of stock might depress the price. ➤➤placing.

venture capital Finance provided by a specialized institution to an entrepreneur, start-up or developing business, where a fairly high degree of risk is involved. The term is also used in a wider sense to include the provision of finance for ➤management buy-outs and refinancings. In this wider sense the correct term is ➤private equity. Strictly, venture capital includes ➤equity capital, and this is often provided in a package including ➤subordinated or other loans. ➤➤development capital; mezzanine; risk capital.

venture capital trust (VCT) A form of tax-sheltered ➤investment trust. Subscribers get 20 per cent income tax relief on investment in new shares. VCT shares are exempt from ➤capital gains tax and income tax on dividends if held for 3 years. Subscribing to a VCT can be used to defer capital gains tax on an existing gain. The maximum annual investment for an individual taxpayer is £100,000. VCTs may invest only in ➤unquoted shares but shares on the ➤alternative investment market and ➤OFEX are eligible. There are some sixty VCTs operated by some twenty professional investment companies.

vertical integration The extent to which a firm extends its operations forward or backward. A manufacturing firm may extend its range of activities backward towards the production of its raw materials. Similarly, it may extend its operations forward towards the customer, or may decide to enter retailing. Vertical integration decisions relate to whether to produce components or other inputs in-house or to buy them in, and whether to use a firm's own resources or third parties to distribute its output. ➤horizontal integration; make-or-buy decision.

The degree to which firms might choose to integrate depends on a number of factors, in particular the costs of doing business with suppliers or customers. ➤transactions costs. Sometimes, having a secure relationship renders it useful to be vertically integrated; film production companies, for example, like to have a stake in film distribution companies, thus ensuring that the arrangement of a distribution contract for each film is not too onerous a negotiation.

It is often popularly supposed that the purpose of vertical integration is somehow to build monopoly power. The suggestion is that integration allows a company to extend a monopoly in one market to other markets (if a company insists that we carry a certain product on its operating systems it can extend the monopoly in operating systems to internet browsers), i.e. allows one competitor in a market to corner the supply of some crucial input or block competitors out of the retail market (film studios might want to own cinemas to prevent competitors from being able to get their films exhibited). There is probably some justification for these suspicions, but it is worth noting that it is harder than is popularly supposed for companies to create value for their shareholders in this way. If a film studio buys-up cinemas, it may enhance the value of its film production by ensuring it has privileged access to cinema screens, but at the same time, the integration detracts from the value of the cinema chain which is now left peddling second-rate films rather than having a choice over exactly what to show.

vertical marketing system A distribution channel where producers, wholesalers and retailers act as one integrated system. Typically, one channel member owns the others or has contracts with them. An 'administered vertical marketing system' exists where control over the whole system is exercised through the size and power of one dominant member.

vertical restraint Any kind of contractual or quasi-contractual restriction placed on the buyer or seller of an item. Vertical restraints can take a variety of forms: (a) ➤**resale price maintenance**; (b) a condition of supply that specifies how the product is to be used, or sold on; (c) the imposition of a territorial limit to the resale of the product; (d) refusal to supply a particular outlet, or (e) a condition that says a product can only be bought in a package with other products (known as *tie-in* sales). The purpose of vertical restraints can be simply to replicate the advantages of full ➤**vertical integration** or to enhance the possibility of ➤**price discrimination** by reducing the scope for trade between different markets with different prices.

Competition authorities have varied in their attitude to vertical restraints, which sometimes are seen simply as a means of limiting competition; at other times they are seen as legitimate tools of business practice. In actual cases, they can involve ingredients of both. For example, the provision of free ice-cream freezers to small vendors by one ice-cream company, on condition that only its ice-cream was stored in them, could be seen as a legitimate way of extending the market for ice-cream by enhancing the number of outlets selling it (and legitimately, it would not want other ice-cream manufacturers to free ride on its strategy by getting their ice-cream into the freezers). Or the same action can be seen as a way of tying-up vendors to keep out competitors. The authorities inevitably end up having to make judgements about the true motivation of such a restraint.

vicarious learning A form of cognitive ➤learning.

VIE theory ➤expectancy theory.

viewdata The provision of selected information, e.g. on ➤share prices, through television screens.

visual equity The value that accrues to a brand because of its physical and aesthetic appearance. This is achieved through the distinctive use of colour, graphics, images, pictures, photographs, designs, logos, shape, 3D effects and structure. Examples include the Kodak yellow, the Nike swoosh, and the shape of Jiff lemon juice. Because these features are distinctive, brand recognition by consumers at the point of purchase is that much easier than for any competing brand. ➤➤**brand communi-**

cation effects. This will help in making purchase of the brand habitual, in much the same way that brand naming helps ➤**brand equity**. However, where the use of visual equity is very successful, it is likely that organizations will copy key elements of the appearance. All brands of film may come to be boxed in yellow cartons (yellow then becomes a 'visual norm' in the product category). ➤➤**look-alike**. Or unrelated organizations adopt a Nike-type swoosh, which devalues the distinctiveness of the symbol for Nike. A measure of legal protection is available to brand owners who invest in visual equity if they can demonstrate that the appearance is theirs and is distinctive ('Kodak yellow' can be protected, but not the colour 'yellow'). ➤**logo**; **trade mark**.

VMS ➤vertical marketing system.

voting share   An equity share entitling the holder to vote in the election of directors of a company. Normally all ➤**ordinary shares** are voting shares, but sometimes a company may create a class of non-voting ordinary shares if the holders of the equity wish to raise more equity capital but exclude the possibility of losing control of the business. ➤**'A' shares**. Bearer shares (➤**bearer security**) are used to raise capital in some countries.

W

WACC ➤weighted average cost of capital.

wage drift The difference between wage rates set by national agreements and the total earnings received by workers, which includes overtime pay, special bonuses and commissions. If wage negotiations take place between union leaders and management bodies at a national level, whatever the outcome of those negotiations in certain areas of the country, the wage agreed may not be high enough to attract all the workers demanded. In this case, local employers will attempt to entice workers with side payments that do not directly infringe national agreements. Such payments are defended as necessary if the labour market is to work freely. If wage drift could lead to cuts in pay as well as increases, it would be a more economically efficient means of introducing pay flexibility. As it happens, though, wage drift has the consequence of making a nationally agreed pay rate the bare minimum anyone receives, with 'top ups' the norm.

Wall Street ➤New York Stock Exchange.

warrant A security giving the holder a right to subscribe to a share or a bond at a given price from a certain date. Warrants, which are commonly issued 'free' alongside the shares of new ➤investment trusts when launched, and carry no income or other rights to ➤equity, immediately trade separately on the stock exchange but at a price lower than the associated security. This provides the investor in warrants with an element of ➤gearing since, if the associated share or bond price ultimately rises above the subscription price, it will have a value corresponding to the difference between the subscription price at which the warrant rights may be exercised and the market price of the share or bond. ➤➤dilution; dividend warrant; option.

Waterman, Robert H ➤Peters, Tom.

wearout Marketing communications (e.g. advertisements) that have ceased to be effective any longer. Members of the ➤target audience may no longer notice the communications, or – if they do notice – may be bored with what they see/hear.

Weber, Max (died 1920) Father of modern sociology. Spent most of his professional life at the University of Heidelberg with a prodigious output in the fields of law, economics, history and much else as well as sociology. He was a critic of Marx's narrowly materialist view of history and foresaw that Marx's predictions about the future of capitalism were unlikely to be fulfilled. His best-known work is *The Protestant Ethic and the Spirit of Capitalism* (1904). Weber was a member of the committee which drafted the constitution of the Weimar Republic in 1918 after the First World

War. He died at the early age of 56 and much of his work, particularly in English translation, did not appear until after his death, notably *Theory of Social and Economic Organization* (1947).

Weber cannot be described as a management guru but his work on management thinking has been very influential right down to the present, particularly his classifications of different types of organization. As distinct from an organization based on power alone, individuals accept authority and regard authority as legitimate in three forms: (a) the *charismatic* organization relies on the authority of a particular individual; (b) the *traditional* organization, as in a family company or even in some very large firms, where things are done the way they have always been done, may follow the charismatic since individuals of that kind can rarely be replaced, and (c) the *bureaucracy*, based upon hierarchy, written rules and records. 'Bureaucracy' is now a pejorative term, but Weber argued that it was the most rational and efficient organizational form. ➤organizational behaviour.

weighted average An average calculated by assigning weights to each item to reflect their relative importance. For example, the weighted average for a share price index calculated in this way could be arrived at by multiplying the prices of securities by their traded volumes (weights), adding them together and dividing by the sum of the weights. This weighted average could then be expressed as a percentage of the weighted average calculated in a similar way for an earlier base year, to give a percentage change in prices. An *unweighted* average or index gives all its constituents an equal value. ➤➤share index; weighted average cost of capital.

weighted average cost of capital (WACC) A measure of the average cost of a firm's capital. It is calculated for each type of capital and combining them weighted in the proportions they account for of total capital. ➤weighted average. The cost of debt (e.g. bank loans) is the interest paid. For ➤equity, it is the current rate of return on government securities plus an allowance for risk. The latter consists of the historical difference between government bond and market equity rates of return, plus or minus an adjustment for company-specific risks as measured by the ➤beta coefficient. ➤alpha coefficient.

weightlessness The term used to describe the decreasing material component in the value of world output. The decline of heavy industry (➤deindustrialization) and the relative growth of the services industries in richer countries accounts for the decline in physical ➤value added. In particular, it is argued, more value derives from 'knowledge-based' industries. The software for a computer game is the more important component of its value, and the resources for writing the software are those which are most scarce, as opposed to those deployed in the manufacture of the console on which the game is played. One important consequence of weightlessness is the potential for activity and value to flow across national boundaries without incurring a burden of transport costs; another is the tendency for workers whose main attribute in the labour market is physical strength, to suffer a relative decline in attainable income. ➤globalization; intellectual assets.

white knight An expression used to describe a company that comes to the rescue of a firm facing a ➤hostile take-over bid from a predator. The term comes from Lewis Carroll's *Through the Looking Glass* (1871) in which Alice is captured by a red knight but then rescued immediately by a white knight; hence, the term.

wholesale banking The making of loans or acceptance of deposits between banks and other ➤**financial institutions**, especially in the ➤**interbank market**. As distinct from *retail banking*, a term for the activities of the ➤**commercial banks** carried out with the general public and business enterprises.

wholesale deposit A deposit, normally of a large amount, obtained by a bank from other banks, or from large companies or institutions, i.e. not a deposit placed directly by an individual client.

wholesale market Of banks, the ➤**money market** that operates between banks, dealing in interbank short-term loans in large amounts. ➤**interbank market**.

Williamson, Oliver E An American economist who, building on foundations laid by 1991 Nobel prizewinner Ronald Coase, has become particularly associated with the economics of ➤**transactions costs**. Transaction costs are costs associated with buying and selling and can affect decisions by companies to contract out the provision of the goods and services they need or make or provide them in-house. In other words, transactions can take place through markets or in hierarchies; which mode is chosen will depend on the amount of information available and the degree of trust between buyer and seller. Transaction cost theory has important implications for industrial organization, competition policy, corporate governance and employment relations, but is heavy going for non-academic economists even though the basic ideas are simple enough.

willingness to pay In pricing studies, the amount of money most consumers (or a defined number of consumers) are prepared to pay for a product. This measure is relevant in situations in which there isn't a free market (e.g. funding of a publicly owned broadcasting service) or where a market has yet to be established, e.g. when launching a really new technological product.

windfall tax A one-off or occasional tax on a company or industry, designed to recoup for the public profits that were considered excessive and undeserved. The UK government has applied such a tax on a handful of occasions, most recently on privatized utilities in 1997. The tax has many desirable properties, most notably if it is well designed and recognizes the deserved profits of firms, it can raise revenue without distorting the incentive of firms to be efficient and make profits. However, windfall profits taxes, if levied too often, would begin to affect incentives, as firms might come to anticipate that any good luck they create for themselves will be creamed-off by the authorities in a new tax. Moreover, as windfall taxes are ultimately borne by the shareholders of the taxed companies, governments can end up taking too much profit from investors who have also held shares in unlucky companies and who have received no windfall subsidy.

winding up ➤liquidation.

window dressing Financial adjustments made solely for the purpose of accounting presentation, normally at the time of auditing of company accounts. For example, a bank may wish to show large holdings of cash at the ➤**balance sheet** date and may in advance of that date sell securities, only to repurchase them immediately afterward.

winner's curse The unfortunate outcome of an auction in which the winning bidder finds he has won simply because he made the most overly optimistic assessment of the value of the item purchased. The curse arises when no one can be sure of the value of the item being sold, e.g. oil exploration rights, a franchise to operate a service, or a government contract. In this event, bidders obviously have to guess the value of the item for which they are bidding. However, even if they make guesses that are correct on average in any single auction, some bidders will guess too high, and some will guess too low. The feature of the auction, however, is that winning bidders will systematically tend to be those who have guessed too high. It is said therefore, that bidders should shave their bids to ensure they do not end up only winning contracts on which they will lose money.

withholding tax Taxation deducted from payments, usually in the form of a standard rate of ➤**income tax** applied to ➤**dividends** or other payments by companies. For non-residents the tax may be reclaimable under double taxation agreements.

without recourse ➤recourse.

with-profits life assurance ➤insurance.

work design The study of who does what, when, where and for how long in an organization. A manager needs to consider these issues to ensure employees know what jobs are expected of them, to plan future workloads and to offer appropriate financial and non-financial ➤**rewards**. A major goal of a review of work design is to reduce effort and improve efficiency, which can be achieved through improved ➤**time management**, and elimination of wasted and duplicated effort by making individuals and ➤**work groups** more accountable. This may entail changing the ➤**roles** of employees, as well as changing aspects of organizational structure (through, for example, business process ➤**re-engineering**). If roles change, employees should be given new ➤**job descriptions**. While the review process can result in an employee being given fewer responsibilities or even losing his job altogether, there are normally opportunities to offer job enhancement and job enrichment.

work group A formal and informal grouping of employees. A project team or task force (in, say, ➤**new product development**) would be an archetypal formal group. Its purpose and composition would be clearly articulated by management, and it would be subject to periodic review and evaluation. Other formal groupings include consultative and advisory bodies such as ➤**quality circles**, ➤**T-groups** and ➤**works councils**. Other groupings are more informal, e.g. those whose members regularly dine, socialize or pursue an extracurricular activity together, as, for example, a works band or sports team.

Work groups are very important parts of any organization. They assist in the process of inducting and socializing new employees. They offer shared experiences which may help to give greater cohesion and focus to activities performed by individuals in an organization. They offer support and advice, which may have very positive effects on levels of ➤**job satisfaction**, ➤**employee retention**, and ➤**stress** management. This is to acknowledge that one of the main reasons for working is social – to meet and interact with other people. In this context, the influence on attitudes and behaviour of social bonds formed within informal groups should not be underestimated. There is also potential for work groups to have a more negative impact on the organization. The process of ➤**group-think** may close-off options that the organization would do well to consider; ➤**collective action** could damage the longer-term interests of the organization.

Because of the potential for gain and harm, more and more attention is being given to the active management of work groups, e.g. their composition, the selection of new members, the allocation of roles within them, team-building efforts, how decisions are made, what resources are available, how individuals and the groups should be evaluated and rewarded. To some extent this more collectivist view of organizations reflects the exposure of Western organizations to Eastern business, especially Japanese business. ➤**theory Z.**

working capital The excess of current ➤**assets** over current ➤**liabilities**; that part of current assets financed from long-term funds. The ratio of current liabilities to the current assets of a business – the current ratio – is sometimes used as a measure of ➤**liquidity**.

work-in-progress (WIP) Work done but not yet invoiced to a customer. Input inventories (e.g. raw materials and components) work their way through the various stages of the production system, and during this period it is known as work-in-progress. (US = *work in process*.)

work measurement study A generic term for those techniques used to study, measure and design methods of working. It is used in the examination of human work to investigate systematically all the factors which affect the efficiency and economy of the situations being reviewed in order to effect improvements. ➤**Method study** is the systematic recording and examination of existing methods of doing work, with the aim of developing easier and more cost-effective methods. Work measurement is the application of techniques developed over time to establish the time for a qualified worker to carry out a specified task. These techniques are part of the wider subject known as *scientific management*.

work sampling The checking of goods against a standard to ensure quality. Once quality standards have been agreed, it is necessary to ensure that the production process produces work that meets this agreed standard. This activity is termed 'quality control', where the quality of the production process is monitored. One key issue is the frequency of checking work against the standard. It is clearly possible to check every item produced, but this would be expensive and probably unnecessary. Taking samples of the items produced (➤**sampling**) is usually the preferred method using ➤**statistical process control.**

works council A group of employee representatives who are consulted about ➤**personnel management**, ➤**human resource management** and ➤**industrial relations** issues. Councils may come to take on a broader remit, being consulted about a wide range of organizational issues, including restructuring and strategic direction. Representatives are elected or nominated from the general body of employees. In unionized organizations, shop stewards perform many of the same functions, and works councils may form part of the ➤**trade union** representation in the organization. However, as a consultative body, works councils are widely found in non-unionized organizations, too.

World Bank ➤International Bank for Reconstruction and Development.

World Trade Organization (WTO) The WTO was set up in 1995 following the conclusion of the long-running Uruguay Round of Trade Negotiations. It extended and replaced the General Agreement on Tariffs and Trade as the organizing framework of rules for trade between most countries of the world. Specifically, the WTO oversees a number of agreements to which member nations have signed-up, e.g. on trade in goods, services, ➤intellectual property, dispute settlement, and trade policy. Of particular importance is the dispute settlement process – countries may complain to the WTO about the behaviour of another member, and a disputes panel will then adjudicate. A country that does not abide by the findings of the panel can be subject to countermeasures. Companies are not allowed to make complaints to the WTO – they must persuade a government to do so. The WTO is also charged with advancing the agenda of free trade with new trade rounds. At the end of 2001, it had over 140 members, representing over 90 per cent of world trade.

written back ➤provisions.

written off ➤provisions.

X

Xd ➤ex-dividend.

X-efficiency The effectiveness of a firm's management in extracting the absolute possible maximum output of the firm, given the resources available. *X-inefficiency* is a measure of waste, or the failure of a firm in a myriad of ways to under-perform, representing the discrepancy between the efficient behaviour as implied by economic theory and the observed behaviour in practice. This is frequently a result of a lack of the competitive pressures assumed. It was labelled with the letter X by H Liebenstein in 1966.

Y

yield The income from a security as a proportion of its current market price. This is the *current yield*. The *dividend yield* is the current dividend as a percentage of the market price of a security. The *earnings yield* is a theoretical figure based on the last dividend paid as a percentage of the current market price. For ➤**fixed interest** securities, the *running yield, interest yield* or *flat yield* is the interest rate as a percentage of the price paid for the stock. For example, a ➤**bond** with a nominal or issued value of £100 but bought for £50, and with an interest rate of 5 per cent, has a running yield of 10 per cent. Where it is a ➤**redeemable security**, the return will also include any capital gain on ➤**redemption**. This is the *redemption yield*, which takes into account the purchase price, interest payments, redemption value and the time remaining to maturity. The initial yield is the estimated income that an investor in a new ➤**unit trust** or other form of managed investment (e.g. an ➤**investment trust**) may expect to receive. It is based upon the present yield of the underlying investment and expressed as a percentage of the ➤**offer price**.

yield curve A graphical representation of interest rates, or yields on bonds, and the terms over which those rates apply. ➤**term structure of interest rates**. The normal tendency of ➤**yields** to rise with the increasing ➤**maturity** of the ➤**security**. When the opposite effect occurs, this is described as a *reverse yield curve*.

yield management The process of controlling customer demand using variable pricing and capacity management to improve profits. The variable pricing component refers to the practice of charging different prices for different times (peak, off-peak, shoulder, etc.) or for different groups of people (business travellers, economy-class travellers, etc.). The capacity management component relates to changes in the use of inventory, e.g. aircraft, flight attendants and ground staff. Consider a flight from London to New York. At peak times the bulk of tickets sold will be for business and full-economy travel, whereas at off-peak times there also will be discounted economy tickets, advance purchase tickets and discounted Internet-purchased tickets. In addition, overbooking, up-front payments and stringent cancellation penalties might be used to protect against 'no shows'. These arrangements maximize revenue potential and minimize the number of unsold tickets – important goals when seating capacity is fixed and where the ratio of fixed costs to variable costs is high (a plane full of business travellers will cost more to operate than one half-full of economy travellers, but not twice as much).

Yield management is used in many service industries, notably airlines, hotels, car rental, trains, sporting venues, convention centres, restaurants, cinemas and theatres. ➤**services marketing**. Mathematical procedures are used to optimize profits, taking into account levels of customer demand, variable pricing options, capacity options and costs. To do this effectively, the needs of different customers must be understood and good information systems must be in place (such as the computerized reservation systems used by airlines).

Z

zero coupon bond/fund A bond issued at a discount (i.e. below ➤**par value**), earning no interest but redeemable at its par value, thus providing a guaranteed capital gain.

zero dividend preference share A ➤preference share that pays no ➤dividend but a fixed sum at a ➤redemption date. ➤investment trust.

zero sum game A game (➤game theory) in which one player's gain is equal to other players' losses, whatever strategy is chosen. In a zero-sum game, the players can only compete for slices of a fixed cake, i.e. there are no opportunities of overall gain through collusion. The sum of gains will always equal the sum of losses, the whole summing to zero. The ubiquitous ➤**prisoners' dilemma** game is not zero sum, because some outcomes involve better average pay-offs for the players than others. There are fewer zero-sum games than one might imagine, simply because even in the most intense conflicts of interest – where every centimetre gain by one party is a centimetre lost by the other – there is usually some shared interest in making the conflict as costless as possible. Even wars can benefit from mutually agreed rules of behaviour.